THE DECLINE AND FALL
OF THE ROMAN EMPIRE

Edward Gibbon
a painting by Joshua Reynolds

THE DECLINE
AND FALL OF THE
ROMAN EMPIRE

Edward Gibbon

*Edited and abridged with an
Introduction and Appreciation
by Hugh Trevor-Roper*

PHOENIX

A PHOENIX PAPERBACK

First published in Great Britain in 1970
by Edito-Service S.A., Geneva and Heron Books
by arrangement with Washington Square Press
Simon & Schuster, Inc.
This paperback edition published in 2005
by Phoenix,
an imprint of Orion Books Ltd,
Orion House, 5 Upper St Martin's Lane,
London WC2H 9EA

An Hachette Livre UK company

3 5 7 9 10 8 6 4 2

A CIP catalogue record for this book
is available from the British Library.

ISBN 978-0-7538-1881-7

Printed and bound in Great Britain by
Clays Ltd, St Ives plc

The Orion Publishing Group's policy is to use papers that
are natural, renewable and recyclable products and
made from wood grown in sustainable forests. The logging
and manufacturing processes are expected to conform to
the environmental regulations of the country of origin.

www.orionbooks.co.uk

CONTENTS

INTRODUCTION

From the publication of its first volume, in 1776, Edward Gibbon's Decline and Fall of the Roman Empire *has kept its position as a classic work not only of literature but of history. This is remarkable because, generally speaking, historical works wear very quickly: new evidence comes to light, new problems usurp the centre of interest. But Gibbon's erudition, scholarship and accuracy have preserved his work while even the most famous of his contemporary historians are now forgotten. Even today, there is no better introduction to the history of the later Roman Empire, and the great problems which he faced—the causes of the decline of Antiquity and the rise of modern European civilisation out of the intervening "Dark Ages"—are as insistent, and as unanswered, in our day, as his.*

Apart from the Decline and Fall, *Gibbon published very little in his own lifetime, and everything that he wrote bears some relation to his great work. His first publication was in French. This was his* Essai sur l'Etude de la Littérature, *the result of his early studies in Lausanne. In this brief work, published in 1761, he expressed his general philosophy of history and his own ambition to be a "philosophic historian." After this, he continued his studies in England, and then, in 1763-65, made his famous journey to Paris, Switzerland and Italy, in the course of which his purpose crystallised. Hitherto he had contemplated various historical subjects, all in modern European history. He actually began a work, in French, on the history of the liberty of the Swiss. But the visit to Rome decided him. There his enthusiasm was fired by the spectacular ruins of the Eternal City, and "as I sat musing amidst the ruins of the Capitol, while the barefooted friars were singing vespers in the temple of Jupiter,*

... the idea of writing the decline and fall of the city first started to my mind."

For the next twenty years, Gibbon worked on his history, first in England, where he combined his study with social and parliamentary life, then in Lausanne, to which he retired in 1783. The last pages were written in the summer-house of his villa in Lausanne on June 27th, 1787. His description of "the hour of my final deliverance" is famous :

After laying down my pen, I took several turns in the berceau, or covered walk of acacias, which commands a prospect of the country, the lake, and the mountains. The air was temperate, the sky was serene, the silver orb of the moon was reflected from the waters, and all nature was silent. I will not dissemble the first emotions of joy on recovery of my freedom and, perhaps, the establishment of my fame. But my pride was soon humbled, and a sober melancholy was spread over my mind, by the idea that I had taken an everlasting leave of an old and agreeable companion, and that whatsoever might be the future fate of my History, the life of the historian must be short and precarious.

On the appearance of the first volume of the Decline and Fall in 1776, a great outcry was caused by the last two chapters —chapters XV and XVI—in which Gibbon described the "human" or "secondary" causes of the rise and establishment of Christianity in the Roman Empire, and several books were written to refute and denounce them. Irritated by these attacks on his honesty as well as on his scholarship, Gibbon finally hit back. In 1779 he published his Vindication and, as Dean Milman afterwards wrote, "with a single discharge from his ponderous artillery of learning and sarcasm, laid prostrate the whole disorderly squadron." After that, there was no further need of justification, and in his last years Gibbon could look back on his life's work with satisfaction. It was then that he drafted his Memoirs of my Life and Writings which were edited and published after his death by his friend and executor Lord Sheffield. The Memoirs are in many ways the most perfect English autobiography, for they are the autobiography of a mind bent—and successfully bent—

towards a single purpose: the production of a vast but unitary work of "philosophic history."

Thus everything that Gibbon wrote emphasises the unity of his life and work; and the centre of that life, the product of that work, is the Decline and Fall. *Nevertheless, what a huge, wide-ranging subject is embraced under that title! The decline of Rome from the great age of the Antonines, which ended in 180 A.D., to the sack of Constantinople by the Turks in 1453, entails the history not only of Rome and Byzantium but that of their neighbours and enemies in Europe and Asia. It involves the rise of new world religions, new social and legal systems. It entangles us in the abstruse heresies of Christianity, takes us to the courts of the Caliphs and the Mamelukes, Ginghiz Khan and Tamerlane, and leads us through the forests and deserts of Northern Europe, the long-ruined cities of Italy, Africa and the East. But all the time, we are made conscious of the unitary philosophy which informs the work: the profound historical questions which cannot be evaded or summarily answered, and which sometimes require comparisons fetched from still farther afield.*

Such a work is not easy to abridge. In order to show something of Gibbon's range with as little violence as possible to his argument, I have thought it best to offer a series of extracts connected by brief summaries which, I hope, will enable the book to be read continuously. Gibbon's footnotes contain so much incidental, and typical, sense and learning, irony and wit, that I have been unwilling to eliminate them altogether. I have excluded all those which refer merely to sources, or which do not seem to me necessary to explain or illustrate the information in the text, but I have printed some which illustrate Gibbon's method, philosophy or idiosyncracies. On rare occasions I have added explanatory notes of my own. These are always distinguished from Gibbon's own notes, being in brackets [ ] and followed by the abbreviation Ed.

HUGH TREVOR-ROPER
Oxford University

THE DECLINE AND FALL
OF THE ROMAN EMPIRE

CHAPTER I

THE EMPIRE OF THE ANTONINES

[Gibbon begins with a general account of the Roman Empire at the height from which he measured its decline: i.e., "the Age of the Antonines," the last phase of the century of peace and prosperity which ran from the death of Domitian (96 A.D.) to that of the second "Antonine," the Stoic Emperor Marcus Aurelius (180 A.D.). In his first chapter he describes the extent and military establishment of the Empire which, at that time, "comprehended the fairest part of the earth and the most civilised portion of mankind"—from the Atlantic to the frontiers of Persia and from the Atlas mountains to the Grampians, the Rhine and the Danube. In Chapter II he deals with its internal prosperity.]

It is not alone by the rapidity, or extent of conquest, that we should estimate the greatness of Rome. The sovereign of the Russian deserts commands a larger portion of the globe. In the seventh summer after his passage of the Hellespont, Alexander erected the Macedonian trophies on the banks of the Hyphasis. Within less than a century, the irresistible Zingis, and the Mogul princes of his race, spread their cruel devastations and transient empire from the sea of China to the confines of Egypt and Germany. But the firm edifice of Roman power was raised and preserved by the wisdom of ages. The obedient provinces of Trajan and the Antonines were united by laws and adorned by arts. They might occasionally suffer from the partial abuse of delegated authority; but the general principle of government was wise, simple, and beneficent. They enjoyed the religion of their ancestors, whilst in civil honours and advantages they were exalted, by just degrees, to an equality with their conquerors.

I.   The policy of the emperors and the senate, as far as it concerned religion, was happily seconded by the reflections of the enlightened, and by the habits of the superstitious, part of their subjects. The various modes of worship, which prevailed in the Roman world, were all considered by the people, as equally true; by the philosopher, as equally false; and by the magistrate, as equally useful. And thus toleration produced not only mutual indulgence, but even religious concord.

The superstition of the people was not embittered by any mixture of theological rancour; nor was it confined by the chains of any speculative system. The devout polytheist, though fondly attached to his national rites, admitted with implicit faith the different religions of the earth.[1] Fear, gratitude, and curiosity, a dream or an omen, a singular disorder, or a distant journey, perpetually disposed him to multiply the articles of his belief, and to enlarge the list of his protectors. The thin texture of the Pagan mythology was interwoven with various but not discordant materials. As soon as it was allowed that sages and heroes, who had lived, or who had died for the benefit of their country, were exalted to a

[1] There is not any writer who describes in so lively a manner as Herodotus, the true genius of Polytheism. The best commentary may be found in Mr. Hume's Natural History of Religion; and the best contrast in Bossuet's Universal History. Some obscure traces of an intolerant spirit appear in the conduct of the Egyptians; and the Christians as well as Jews, who lived under the Roman empire, formed a very important exception: so important, indeed, that the discussion will require a distinct chapter of this work.

state of power and immortality, it was universally confessed that they deserved, if not the adoration, at least the reverence of all mankind. The deities of a thousand groves and a thousand streams possessed, in peace, their local and respective influence; nor could the Roman who deprecated the wrath of the Tiber, deride the Egyptian who presented his offering to the beneficent genius of the Nile. The visible powers of Nature, the planets, and the elements, were the same throughout the universe. The invisible governors of the moral world were inevitably cast in a similar mould of fiction and allegory. Every virtue, and even vice, acquired its divine representative; every art and profession its patron, whose attributes, in the most distant ages and countries, were uniformly derived from the character of their peculiar votaries. A republic of gods of such opposite tempers and interest required, in every system, the moderating hand of a supreme magistrate, who, by the progress of knowledge and flattery, was gradually invested with the sublime perfections of an Eternal Parent, and an Omnipotent Monarch. Such was the mild spirit of antiquity, that the nations were less attentive to the difference than to the resemblance of their religious worship. The Greek, the Roman, and the Barbarian, as they met before their respective altars, easily persuaded themselves, that under various names, and with various ceremonies, they adored the same deities. The elegant mythology of Homer gave a beautiful, and almost a regular form, to the polytheism of the ancient world.

The philosophers of Greece deduced their morals from the nature of man, rather than from that of God. They meditated, however, on the Divine Nature, as a very curious and important speculation; and in the profound inquiry, they displayed the strength and weakness of the human understanding. Of the four most celebrated schools, the Stoics and the Platonists endeavoured to reconcile the jarring interests of reason and piety. They have left us the most sublime proofs of the existence and perfections of the first cause; but, as it was impossible for them to conceive the creation of matter, the workman in the Stoic philosophy was not sufficiently distinguished from the work: whilst, on the contrary, the spiritual God of Plato and his disciples resembled an idea rather than a substance. The opinions of the Academics and Epicureans were of a less religious cast: but whilst the modest science of the former induced them to doubt, the positive ignorance of the latter urged them to deny, the providence of a Supreme Ruler. The spirit of inquiry, prompted by emulation, and supported by freedom, had divided the public teachers of philosophy into a variety of contending sects; but the ingenuous youth who, from every part, resorted to Athens, and the other seats of learning in the Roman empire, were alike instructed in every school to reject and to despise the religion of the multitude. How, indeed, was it possible, that a philosopher should accept, as divine truths, the idle tales of the poets, and the incoherent traditions of antiquity; or, that he should adore, as gods, those imperfect beings whom he must have despised, as men! Against such unworthy adversaries, Cicero condescended to employ the arms of reason and eloquence; but the satire of Lucian was a much more adequate, as well as more efficacious weapon. We may be well assured, that a writer conversant with the world would never have ventured to expose the gods of his country to public ridicule, had they not already been the objects of secret contempt among the polished and enlightened orders of society.

Notwithstanding the fashionable irreligion which prevailed in the age of the Antonines, both the interests of the priests and the credulity of the people were sufficiently respected. In their writings and conversation, the philosophers of antiquity asserted the independent dig-

---

I do not pretend to assert, that, in this irreligious age, the natural terrors of superstition, dreams, omens, apparitions, etc., had lost their efficacy.

nity of reason; but they resigned their actions to the commands of law and of custom. Viewing, with a smile of pity and indulgence, the various errors of the vulgar, they diligently practised the ceremonies of their fathers, devoutly frequented the temples of the gods; and sometimes condescending to act a part on the theatre of superstition, they concealed the sentiments of an Atheist under the sacerdotal robes. Reasoners of such a temper were scarcely inclined to wrangle about their respective modes of faith, or of worship. It was indifferent to them what shape the folly of the multitude might choose to assume; and they approached, with the same inward contempt, and the same external reverence, the altars of the Libyan, the Olympian, or the Capitoline Jupiter.[3]

It is not easy to conceive from what motives a spirit of persecution could introduce itself into the Roman councils. The magistrates could not be actuated by a blind, though honest bigotry, since the magistrates were themselves philosophers; and the schools of Athens had given laws to the senate. They could not be impelled by ambition or avarice, as the temporal and ecclesiastical powers were united in the same hands. The pontiffs were chosen among the most illustrious of the senators; and the office of Supreme Pontiff was constantly exercised by the emperors themselves. They knew and valued the advantages of religion, as it is connected with civil government. They encouraged the public festivals which humanise the manners of the people. They managed the arts of divination, as a convenient instrument of policy; and they respected as the firmest bond of society, the useful persuasion that, either in this or in a future life, the crime of perjury is most assuredly punished by the avenging gods. But whilst they acknowledged the general advantages of religion, they were convinced that the

---

[3] Socrates, Epicurus, Cicero, and Plutarch, always inculcated decent reverence for the religion of their own country, and of mankind. The devotion of Epicurus was assiduous and exemplary.

various modes of worship contributed alike to the same
salutary purposes; and that, in every country, the form
of superstition, which had received the sanction of time
and experience, was the best adapted to the climate and
to its inhabitants. Avarice and taste very frequently
despoiled the vanquished nations of the elegant statues
of their gods, and the rich ornaments of their temples;
but, in the exercise of the religion which they derived
from their ancestors, they uniformly experienced the indulgence, and even protection, of the Roman conquerors.
The province of Gaul seems, and indeed only seems an
exception to this universal toleration. Under the specious
pretext of abolishing human sacrifices, the emperors Tiberius and Claudius suppressed the dangerous power of
the Druids, but the priests themselves, their gods and
their altars, subsisted in peaceful obscurity till the final
destruction of Paganism.

Rome, the capital of a great monarchy, was incessantly
filled with subjects and strangers from every part of the
world, who all introduced and enjoyed the favourite superstitions of their native country. Every city in the empire was justified in maintaining the purity of its ancient
ceremonies; and the Roman senate, using the common
privilege, sometimes interposed, to check this inundation
of foreign rites. The Egyptian superstition, of all the
most contemptible and abject, was frequently prohibited;
the temples of Serapis and Isis demolished and their
worshippers banished from Rome and Italy. But the zeal
of fanaticism prevailed over the cold and feeble efforts
of policy. The exiles returned, the proselytes multiplied,
the temples were restored with increasing splendour, and
Isis and Serapis at length assumed their place among the
Roman deities. Nor was this indulgence a departure from
the old maxims of government. In the purest ages of the
commonwealth, Cybele and Æsculapius had been invited
by solemn embassies; and it was customary to tempt the
protectors of besieged cities, by the promise of more distinguished honours than they possessed in their native

country. Rome gradually became the common temple of her subjects; and the freedom of the city was bestowed on all the gods of mankind.

II. The narrow policy of preserving, without any foreign mixture, the pure blood of the ancient citizens, had checked the fortune, and hastened the ruin, of Athens and Sparta. The aspiring genius of Rome sacrificed vanity to ambition, and deemed it more prudent, as well as honourable, to adopt virtue and merit for her own wheresoever they were found, among slaves or strangers, enemies or barbarians. During the most flourishing era of the Athenian commonwealth, the number of citizens gradually decreased from about thirty to twenty-one thousand. If, on the contrary, we study the growth of the Roman republic, we may discover, that, notwithstanding the incessant demands of wars and colonies, the citizens, who, in the first census of Servius Tullius, amounted to no more than eighty-three thousand, were multiplied, before the commencement of the social war, to the number of four hundred and sixty-three thousand men, able to bear arms in the service of their country. When the allies of Rome claimed an equal share of honours and privileges, the senate indeed preferred the chance of arms to an ignominious concession. The Samnites and the Lucanians paid the severe penalty of their rashness; but the rest of the Italian states, as they successively returned to their duty, were admitted into the bosom of the republic, and soon contributed to the ruin of public freedom. Under a democratical government, the citizens exercise the powers of sovereignty; and those powers will be first abused, and afterwards lost, if they are committed to an unwieldy multitude. But when the popular assemblies had been suppressed by the administration of the emperors, the conquerors were distinguished from the vanquished nations, only as the first and most honourable order of subjects; and their increase, however rapid, was no longer exposed to the same dangers. Yet the wisest princes, who adopted the maxims of Augustus, guarded with the strictest care the dignity of the Roman name, and diffused the freedom of the city with a prudent liberality.

Till the privileges of Romans had been progressively extended to all the inhabitants of the empire, an important distinction was preserved between Italy and the provinces. The former was esteemed the centre of public unity, and the firm basis of the constitution. Italy claimed the birth, or at least the residence, of the emperors and the senate. The estates of the Italians were exempt from taxes, their persons from the arbitrary jurisdiction of governors. Their municipal corporations, formed after the perfect model of the capital, were intrusted, under the immediate eye of the supreme power, with the execution of the laws. From the foot of the Alps to the extremity of Calabria, all the natives of Italy were born citizens of Rome. Their partial distinctions were obliterated, and they insensibly coalesced into one great nation, united by language, manners, and civil institutions, and equal to the weight of a powerful empire. The republic gloried in her generous policy, and was frequently rewarded by the merit and services of her adopted sons. Had she always confined the distinction of Romans to the ancient families within the walls of the city, that immortal name would have been deprived of some of its noblest ornaments. Virgil was a native of Mantua; Horace was inclined to doubt whether he should call himself an Apulian or a Lucanian: it was in Padua that an historian was found worthy to record the majestic series of Roman victories. The patriot family of the Catos emerged from Tusculum; and the little town of Arpinum claimed the double honour of producing Marius and Cicero, the former of whom deserved, after Romulus and Camillus, to be styled the Third Founder of Rome; and the latter, after saving his country from the designs of Catiline, enabled her to contend with Athens for the palm of eloquence.

The provinces of the empire (as they have been described in the preceding chapter) were destitute of any public force, or constitutional freedom. In Etruria, in Greece, and in Gaul, it was the first care of the senate to dissolve those dangerous confederacies, which taught mankind, that as the Roman arts prevailed by division, they might be resisted by union. Those princes, whom the ostentation of gratitude or generosity permitted for a while to hold a precarious sceptre, were dismissed from their thrones as soon as they had performed their appointed task of fashioning to the yoke the vanquished nations. The free states and cities which had embraced the cause of Rome, were rewarded with a nominal alliance, and insensibly sunk into real servitude. The public authority was everywhere exercised by the ministers of the senate and of the emperors, and that authority was absolute, and without control. But the same salutary maxims of government, which had secured the peace and obedience of Italy, were extended to the most distant conquests. A nation of Romans was gradually formed in the provinces, by the double expedient of introducing colonies, and of admitting the most faithful and deserving of the provincials to the freedom of Rome.

"Wheresoever the Roman conquers, he inhabits," is a very just observation of Seneca, confirmed by history and experience. The natives of Italy, allured by pleasure or by interest, hastened to enjoy the advantages of victory; and we may remark, that about forty years after the reduction of Asia, eighty thousand Romans were massacred in one day, by the cruel orders of Mithridates. These voluntary exiles were engaged, for the most part, in the occupations of commerce, agriculture, and the farm of the revenue. But after the legions were rendered permanent by the emperors, the provinces were peopled by a race of soldiers; and the veterans, whether they received the reward of their service in land or in money, usually settled with their families in the country where they had honourably spent their youth. Throughout the empire, but more particularly in the western parts, the most fertile districts, and the most convenient situations, were reserved for the establishment of colonies; some of which were of a civil, and others of a military nature. In their manners and internal policy, the colonies formed a perfect representation of their great parent; and as they were soon endeared to the natives by the ties of friendship and alliance, they effectually diffused a reverence for the Roman name, and a desire, which was seldom disappointed, of sharing, in due time, its honours and advantages. The municipal cities insensibly equalled the rank and splendour of the colonies; and in the reign of Hadrian, it was disputed which was the preferable condition, of those societies which had issued from, or those which had been received into the bosom of Rome. The right of Latium, as it was called, conferred on the cities to which it had been granted a more partial favour. The magistrates only, at the expiration of their office, assumed the quality of Roman citizens; but as those offices were annual, in a few years they circulated round the principal families. Those of the provincials who were permitted to bear arms in the legions; those who exercised any civil employment; all, in a word, who performed any public service, or displayed any personal talents, were rewarded with a present, whose value was continually diminished by the increasing liberality of the emperors. Yet even, in the age of the Antonines, when the freedom of the city had been bestowed on the greater number of their subjects, it was still accompanied with very solid advantages. The bulk of the people acquired, with that title, the benefit of the Roman laws, particularly in the interesting articles of marriage, testaments, and inheritances; and the road of fortune was open to those whose pretensions were seconded by favour or merit. The grandsons of the Gauls, who had besieged Julius Cæsar in Alesia, commanded legions, governed provinces, and were admitted into the senate of Rome. Their ambition, instead of disturbing the tranquillity of the state, was intimately connected with its safety and greatness.

So sensible were the Romans of the influence of language over national manners, that it was their most serious care to extend, with the progress of their arms, the use of the Latin tongue. The ancient dialects of Italy, the Sabine, the Etruscan, and the Venetian, sunk into oblivion; but in the provinces, the east was less docile than the west, to the voice of its victorious preceptors. This obvious difference marked the two portions of the empire with a distinction of colours, which, though it was in some degree concealed during the meridian splendour of prosperity, became gradually more visible as the shades of night descended upon the Roman world. The western countries were civilised by the same hands which subdued them. As soon as the barbarians were reconciled to obedience, their minds were opened to any new impressions of knowledge and politeness. The language of Virgil and Cicero, though with some inevitable mixture of corruption, was so universally adopted in Africa, Spain, Gaul, Britain, and Pannonia, that the faint traces of the Punic or Celtic idioms were preserved only in the mountains, or among the peasants. Education and study insensibly inspired the natives of those countries with the sentiments of Romans; and Italy gave fashions as well as laws to her Latin provincials. They solicited with more ardour, and obtained with more facility, the freedom and honours of the state; supported the national dignity in letters and in arms; and, at length, in the person of Trajan, produced an emperor whom the Scipios would not have disowned for their countryman. . . .

It was by such institutions that the nations of the empire insensibly melted away into the Roman name and people. But there still remained, in the centre of every province and of every family, an unhappy condition of men who endured the weight, without sharing the benefits, of society. In the free states of antiquity the domestic slaves were exposed to the wanton rigour of despotism. The perfect settlement of the Roman empire was preceded by ages of violence and rapine. The slaves consisted, for the most part, of barbarian captives, taken in thousands by the chance of war, purchased at a vile price, accustomed to a life of independence, and impatient to break and to revenge their fetters. Against such internal enemies, whose desperate insurrections had more than once reduced the republic to the brink of destruction, the most severe regulations, and the most cruel treatment, seemed almost justified by the great law of self-preservation. But when the principal nations of Europe, Asia, and Africa, were united under the laws of one sovereign, the source of foreign supplies flowed with much less abundance, and the Romans were reduced to the milder but more tedious method of propagation. In their numerous families, and particularly in their country estates, they encouraged the marriage of their slaves. The sentiments of nature, the habits of education, and the possession of a dependent species of property, contributed to alleviate the hardships of servitude. The existence of a slave became an object of greater value, and though his happiness still depended on the temper and circumstances of the master, the humanity of the latter, instead of being restrained by fear, was encouraged by the sense of his own interest. The progress of manners was accelerated by the virtue or policy of the emperors; and by the edicts of Hadrian and the Antonines, the protection of the laws were extended to the most abject part of mankind. The jurisdiction of life and death over the slaves, a power long exercised and often abused, was taken out of private hands, and reserved to the magistrates alone. The subterraneous prisons were abolished; and, upon a just complaint of intolerable treatment, the injured slave obtained either his deliverance, or a less cruel master.

Hope, the best comfort of our imperfect condition, was not denied to the Roman slave; and if he had any opportunity of rendering himself either useful or agreeable, he might very naturally expect that the diligence and fidelity of a few years would be rewarded with the inestimable gift of freedom. The benevolence of the master was so frequently prompted by the meaner suggestions of vanity and avarice, that the laws found it more necessary to restrain than to encourage a profuse and undistinguishing liberality, which might degenerate into a very dangerous abuse. It was a maxim of ancient jurisprudence, that a slave had not any country of his own; he acquired with his liberty an admission into the political society of which his patron was a member. The consequences of this maxim would have prostituted the privileges of the Roman city to a mean and promiscuous multitude. Some seasonable exceptions were therefore provided; and the honourable distinction was confined to such slaves only, as for just causes, and with the approbation of the magistrate, should receive a solemn and legal manumission. Even these chosen freed-men obtained no more than the private rights of citizens, and were rigorously excluded from civil or military honours. Whatever might be the merit or fortune of their sons, *they* likewise were esteemed unworthy of a seat in the senate; nor were the traces of a servile origin allowed to be completely obliterated till the third or fourth generation. Without destroying the distinction of ranks, a distant prospect of freedom and honours was presented, even to those whom pride and prejudice almost disdained to number among the human species. . . .

The number of subjects who acknowledged the laws of Rome, of citizens, of provincials, and of slaves, cannot now be fixed with such a degree of accuracy, as the importance of the object would deserve. We are informed that when the emperor Claudius exercised the office of censor, he took an account of six millions nine hundred and forty-five thousand Roman citizens, who, with the proportion of women and children, must have amounted to about twenty millions of souls. The multitude of subjects of an inferior rank was uncertain and fluctuating. But, after weighing with attention every circumstance which could influence the balance, it seems probable

13

that there existed, in the time of Claudius, about twice as many provincials as there were citizens, of either sex, and of every age; and that the slaves were at least equal in number to the free inhabitants of the Roman world. The total amount of this imperfect calculation would rise to about one hundred and twenty millions of persons; a degree of population which possibly exceeds that of modern Europe, and forms the most numerous society that has ever been united under the same system of government.

Domestic peace and union were the natural consequences of the moderate and comprehensive policy embraced by the Romans. If we turn our eyes towards the monarchies of Asia, we shall behold despotism in the centre, and weakness in the extremities; the collection of the revenue, or the administration of justice, enforced by the presence of an army; hostile barbarians established in the heart of the country, hereditary satraps usurping the dominion of the provinces, and subjects inclined to rebellion, though incapable of freedom. But the obedience of the Roman world was uniform, voluntary, and permanent. The vanquished nations, blended into one great people, resigned the hope, nay even the wish, of resuming their independence, and scarcely considered their own existence as distinct from the existence of Rome. The established authority of the emperors pervaded without an effort the wide extent of their dominions, and was exercised with the same facility on the banks of the Thames, or of the Nile, as on those of the Tiber. The legions were destined to serve against the public enemy, and the civil magistrate seldom required the aid of a military force. In this state of general security, the leisure as well as opulence both of the prince and people were devoted to improve and to adorn the Roman empire.

Among the innumerable monuments of architecture constructed by the Romans, how many have escaped the notice of history, how few have resisted the ravages of time and barbarism! And yet even the majestic ruins that are still scattered over Italy and the provinces, would be sufficient to prove that those countries were once the seat of a polite and powerful empire. Their greatness alone, or their beauty, might deserve our attention; but they are rendered more interesting by two important circumstances, which connect the agreeable history of the arts with the more useful history of human manners. Many of those works were erected at private expense, and almost all were intended for public benefit.

It is natural to suppose that the greatest number, as well as the most considerable of the Roman edifices, were raised by the emperors, who possessed so unbounded a command both of men and money. Augustus was accustomed to boast that he had found his capital of brick, and that he had left it of marble. The strict economy of Vespasian was the source of his magnificence. The works of Trajan bear the stamp of his genius. The public monuments with which Hadrian adorned every province of the empire, were executed not only by his orders, but under his immediate inspection. He was himself an artist; and he loved the arts, as they conduced to the glory of the monarch. They were encouraged by the Antonines, as they contributed to the happiness of the people. But if the emperors were the first, they were not the only architects of their dominions. Their example was universally imitated by their principal subjects, who were not afraid of declaring to the world that they had spirit to conceive, and wealth to accomplish, the noblest undertakings. Scarcely had the proud structure of the Coliseum been dedicated at Rome, before the edifices of a smaller scale indeed, but of the same design and materials, were erected for the use, and at the expense, of the cities of Capua and Verona. The inscription of the stupendous bridge of Alcantara attests that it was thrown over the Tagus by the contribution of a few Lusitanian communities. When Pliny was intrusted with the government of Bithynia and Pontus, provinces by no means the richest or most considerable of the empire, he found the cities within his jurisdiction striving with each other in every useful and ornamental work, that might deserve the curiosity of strangers, or the gratitude of their citizens. It was the duty of the Proconsul to supply their deficiencies, to direct their taste, and sometimes to moderate their emulation. The opulent senators of Rome and the provinces esteemed it an honour, and almost an obligation, to adorn the splendour of their age and country; and the influence of fashion very frequently supplied the want of taste or generosity. Among a crowd of these private benefactors, we may select Herodes Atticus, an Athenian citizen, who lived in the age of the Antonines. Whatever might be the motive of his conduct, his magnificence would have been worthy of the greatest kings.

The family of Herod, at least after it had been favoured by fortune, was lineally descended from Cimon and Miltiades, Theseus and Cecrops, Æacus and Jupiter. But the posterity of so many gods and heroes was fallen into the most abject state. His grandfather had suffered by the hands of justice, and Julius Atticus, his father, must have ended his life in poverty and contempt, had he not discovered an immense treasure buried under an old house, the last remains of his patrimony. According to the rigour of law, the emperor might have asserted his claim, and the prudent Atticus prevented, by a frank confession, the officiousness of informers. But the equitable Nerva, who then filled the throne, refused to accept any part of it, and commanded him to use, without scruple, the present of fortune. The cautious Athenian still insisted that the treasure was too considerable for a subject, and that he knew not how to *use it. Abuse it, then*, replied the monarch, with a good-natured peevishness; for it is your own. Many will be of opinion that Atticus literally obeyed the emperor's last instructions; since he expended the greatest part of his fortune, which was much increased by an advantageous marriage, in the service of the Public. He had obtained

16

for his son Herod the prefecture of the free cities of Asia; and the young magistrate, observing that the town of Troas was indifferently supplied with water, obtained from the munificence of Hadrian three hundred myriads of drachms (about a hundred thousand pounds) for the construction of a new aqueduct. But in the execution of the work the charge amounted to more than double the estimate, and the officers of the revenue began to murmur, till the generous Atticus silenced their complaints, by requesting that he might be permitted to take upon himself the whole additional expense.

The ablest preceptors of Greece and Asia had been invited by liberal rewards to direct the education of young Herod. Their pupil soon became a celebrated orator according to the useless rhetoric of that age, which, confining itself to the schools, disdained to visit either the Forum or the Senate. He was honoured with the consulship at Rome; but the greatest part of his life was spent in a philosophic retirement at Athens, and his adjacent villas; perpetually surrounded by sophists, who acknowledged, without reluctance, the superiority of a rich and generous rival. The monuments of his genius have perished; some considerable ruins still preserve the fame of his taste and munificence: modern travellers have measured the remains of the stadium which he constructed at Athens. It was six hundred feet in length, built entirely of white marble, capable of admitting the whole body of the people, and finished in four years, whilst Herod was president of the Athenian games. To the memory of his wife Regilla he dedicated a theatre, scarcely to be paralleled in the empire; no wood except cedar, very curiously carved, was employed in any part of the building. The Odeum, designed by Pericles for musical performances, and the rehearsal of new tragedies, had been a trophy of the victory of the arts over Barbaric greatness; as the timbers employed in the construction consisted chiefly of the masts of the Persian vessels. Notwithstanding the repairs bestowed on that ancient edifice by a king of Cappadocia, it was again fallen to decay. Herod restored its ancient beauty and magnificence. Nor was the liberality of that illustrious citizen confined to the walls of Athens. The most splendid ornaments bestowed on the temple of Neptune in the Isthmus, a theatre at Corinth, a stadium at Delphi, a bath at Thermopylæ, and an aqueduct at Canusium in Italy, were insufficient to exhaust his treasures. The people of Epirus, Thessaly, Eubœa, Bœotia, and Peloponnesus, experienced his favours; and many inscriptions of the cities of Greece and Asia gratefully style Herodes Atticus their patron and benefactor.

In the commonwealths of Athens and Rome, the modest simplicity of private houses announced the equal condition of freedom; whilst the sovereignty of the people was represented in the majestic edifices destined to the public use; nor was this republican spirit totally extinguished by the introduction of wealth and monarchy. It was in works of national honour and benefit, that the most virtuous of the emperors affected to display their magnificence. The golden palace of Nero excited a just indignation, but the vast extent of ground which had been usurped by his selfish luxury, was more nobly filled under the succeeding reigns by the Coliseum, the baths of Titus, the Claudian portico, and the temples dedicated to the goddess of Peace, and to the genius of Rome. These monuments of architecture, the property of the Roman people, were adorned with the most beautiful productions of Grecian painting and sculpture; and in the temple of Peace a very curious library was open to the curiosity of the learned. At a small distance from thence was situated the Forum of Trajan. It was surrounded with a lofty portico, in the form of a quadrangle, into which four triumphal arches opened a noble and spacious entrance: in the centre arose a column of marble, whose height, of one hundred and ten feet, denoted the elevation of the hill that had been cut away. This column, which still subsists in its ancient beauty, exhibited an exact representation of the Dacian victories of its founder. The veteran soldier contemplated the story of his own campaigns, and by an easy illusion of national vanity, the peaceful citizen associated himself to the honours of the triumph. All the other quarters of the capital, and all the provinces of the empire, were embellished by the same liberal spirit of public magnificence, and were filled with amphitheatres, theatres, temples, porticos, triumphal arches, baths, and aqueducts, all variously conducive to the health, the devotion, and the pleasures of the meanest citizen. The last mentioned of those edifices deserve our peculiar attention. The boldness of the enterprise, the solidity of the execution, and the uses to which they were subservient, rank the aqueducts among the noblest monuments of Roman genius and power. The aqueducts of the capital claim a just preeminence; but the curious traveller, who, without the light of history, should examine those of Spoleto, of Metz, or of Segovia, would very naturally conclude that those provincial towns had formerly been the residence of some potent monarch. The solitudes of Asia and Africa were once covered with flourishing cities, whose populousness, and even whose existence, was derived from such artificial supplies of a perennial stream of fresh water.

We have computed the inhabitants and contemplated the public works of the Roman empire. The observation of the number and greatness of its cities will serve to confirm the former, and to multiply the latter. It may not be unpleasing to collect a few scattered instances relative to that subject, without forgetting, however, that from the vanity of nations and the poverty of language, the vague appellation of city has been indifferently bestowed on Rome and upon Laurentum. I. *Ancient* Italy is said to have contained eleven hundred and ninety-seven cities; and for whatsoever era of antiquity the expression might be intended, there is not any reason to believe the country less populous in the age of the Antonines than

19

in that of Romulus. The petty states of Latium were contained within the metropolis of the empire, by whose superior influence they had been attracted. Those parts of Italy which have so long languished under the lazy tyranny of priests, and viceroys, had been afflicted only by the more tolerable calamities of war; and the first symptoms of decay which *they* experienced were amply compensated by the rapid improvements of the Cisalpine Gaul. The splendour of Verona may be traced in its remains: yet Verona was less celebrated than Aquileia or Padua, Milan or Ravenna. II. The spirit of improvement had passed the Alps, and been felt even in the woods of Britain, which were gradually cleared away to open a free space for convenient and elegant habitations. York was the seat of government; London was already enriched by commerce; and Bath was celebrated for the salutary effects of its medicinal waters. Gaul could boast of her twelve hundred cities, and though, in the northern parts, many of them, without excepting Paris itself, were little more than the rude and imperfect townships of a rising people, the southern provinces imitated the wealth and elegance of Italy. Many were the cities of Gaul, Marseilles, Arles, Nîmes, Narbonne, Toulouse, Bordeaux, Autun, Vienna, Lyons, Langres, and Treves, whose ancient condition might sustain an equal, and perhaps advantageous comparison with their present state. With regard to Spain, that country flourished as a province, and has declined as a kingdom. Exhausted by the abuse of her strength, by America, and by superstition, her pride might possibly be confounded, if we required such a list of three hundred and sixty cities, as Pliny has exhibited under the reign of Vespasian. III. Three hundred African cities had once acknowledged the authority of Carthage, nor is it likely that their numbers diminished under the administration of the emperors: Carthage itself rose with new splendour from its ashes; and that capital, as well as Capua and Corinth, soon recovered all the advantages which can be separated from in-

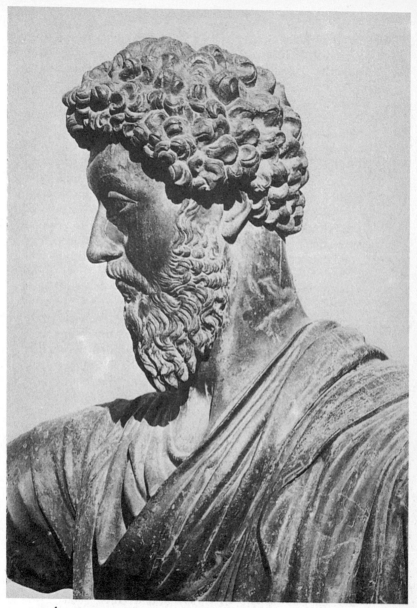

1
Marcus Aurelius, the second "Antonine" emperor.

dependent sovereignty. IV. The provinces of the east present the contrast of Roman magnificence with Turkish barbarism. The ruins of antiquity scattered over uncultivated fields, and ascribed, by ignorance, to the power of magic, scarcely afford a shelter to the oppressed peasant or wandering Arab. Under the reign of the Cæsars, the proper Asia alone contained five hundred populous cities, enriched with all the gifts of nature, and adorned with all the refinements of art. Eleven cities of Asia had once disputed the honour of dedicating a temple to Tiberius, and their respective merits were examined by the senate.[4] Four of them were immediately rejected as unequal to the burden; and among these was Laodicea, whose splendour is still displayed in its ruins. Laodicea collected a very considerable revenue from its flocks of sheep, celebrated for the fineness of their wool, and had received, a little before the contest, a legacy of above four hundred thousand pounds by the testament of a generous citizen. If such was the poverty of Laodicea, what must have been the wealth of those cities, whose claim appeared preferable, and particularly of Pergamus, of Smyrna, and of Ephesus, who so long disputed with each other the titular primacy of Asia. The capitals of Syria and Egypt held a still superior rank in the empire: Antioch and Alexandria looked down with disdain on a crowd of dependent cities, and yielded, with reluctance, to the majesty of Rome itself.

All these cities were connected with each other, and with the capital, by the public highways, which, issuing from the Forum of Rome, traversed Italy, pervaded the

[4] I have taken some pains in consulting and comparing modern travellers, with regard to the fate of those eleven cities of Asia: seven or eight are totally destroyed, Hypæpe, Tralles, Laodicea, Ilium, Halicarnassus, Miletus, Ephesus, and we may add Sardis. Of the remaining three, Pergamus is a straggling village of two or three thousand inhabitants; Magnesia, under the name of Guzel-hissar, a town of some consequence, and Smyrna, a great city, peopled by an hundred thousand souls. But even at Smyrna, while the Franks have maintained commerce, the Turks have ruined the arts.

provinces, and were terminated only by the frontiers of the empire. If we carefully trace the distance from the wall of Antoninus to Rome, and from thence to Jerusalem, it will be found that the great chain of communication, from the north-west to the south-east point of the empire, was drawn out to the length of four thousand and eighty Roman miles. The public roads were accurately divided by mile-stones, and ran in a direct line from one city to another, with very little respect for the obstacles either of nature or private property. Mountains were perforated, and bold arches thrown over the broadest and most rapid streams. The middle part of the road was raised into a terrace which commanded the adjacent country, consisted of several strata of sand, gravel, and cement, and was paved with large stones, or in some places, near the capital, with granite. Such was the solid construction of the Roman highways, whose firmness has not entirely yielded to the effort of fifteen centuries. They united the subjects of the most distant provinces by an easy and familiar intercourse; but their primary object had been to facilitate the marches of the legions; nor was any country considered as completely subdued, till it had been rendered, in all its parts, pervious to the arms and authority of the conqueror. The advantage of receiving the earliest intelligence, and of conveying their orders with celerity, induced the emperors to establish throughout their extensive dominions, the regular institution of posts. Houses were everywhere erected at the distance only of five or six miles; each of them was constantly provided with forty horses, and by the help of these relays it was easy to travel an hundred miles in a day along the Roman roads. The use of the posts was allowed to those who claimed it by an Imperial mandate; but though originally intended for the public service, it was sometimes indulged to the business or conveniency of private citizens. Nor was the communication of the Roman empire less free and open by sea than it was by land. The provinces surrounded and inclosed the Mediterranean; and Italy, in the shape of an immense promontory, advanced into the midst of that great lake. The coasts of Italy are, in general, destitute of safe harbours; but human industry had corrected the deficiencies of nature; and the artificial port of Ostia, in particular, situated at the mouth of the Tiber, and formed by the emperor Claudius, was a useful monument of Roman greatness. From this port, which was only sixteen miles from the capital, a favourable breeze frequently carried vessels in seven days to the columns of Hercules, and in nine or ten, to Alexandria in Egypt.

Whatever evils either reason or declamation have imputed to extensive empire, the power of Rome was attended with some beneficial consequences to mankind; and the same freedom of intercourse which extended the vices, diffused likewise the improvements of social life. In the more remote ages of antiquity, the world was unequally divided. The east was in the immemorial possession of arts and luxury; whilst the west was inhabited by rude and warlike barbarians, who either disdained agriculture, or to whom it was totally unknown. Under the protection of an established government, the productions of happier climates, and the industry of more civilised nations, were gradually introduced into the western countries of Europe; and the natives were encouraged, by an open and profitable commerce, to multiply the former, as well as to improve the latter. It would be almost impossible to enumerate all the articles, either of the animal or the vegetable reign, which were successively imported into Europe, from Asia and Egypt; but it will not be unworthy of the dignity, and much less of the utility, of an historical work, slightly to touch on a few of the principal heads. 1. Almost all the flowers, the herbs, and the fruits, that grow in our European gardens, are of foreign extraction, which, in many cases, is betrayed even by their names: the apple was a native of Italy, and when the Romans had tasted the richer flavour of the apricot, the peach, the pomegranate, the citron, and the orange, they contented themselves with applying to all these new fruits the common denomination of apple, discriminating them from each other by the additional epithet of their country. 2. In the time of Homer, the vine grew wild in the island of Sicily, and most probably in the adjacent continent; but it was not improved by the skill, nor did it afford a liquor grateful to the taste, of the savage inhabitants. A thousand years afterwards, Italy could boast, that of the fourscore most generous and celebrated wines, more than two-thirds were produced from her soil. The blessing was soon communicated to the Narbonnese province of Gaul; but so intense was the cold to the north of the Cevennes, that, in the time of Strabo, it was thought impossible to ripen the grapes in those parts of Gaul. This difficulty, however, was gradually vanquished; and there is some reason to believe, that the vineyards of Burgundy are as old as the age of the Antonines. The olive, in the western world, followed the progress of peace, of which it was considered as the symbol. Two centuries after the foundation of Rome, both Italy and Africa were strangers to that useful plant; it was naturalised in those countries; and at length carried into the heart of Spain and Gaul. The timid errors of the ancients, that it required a certain degree of heat, and could only flourish in the neighbourhood of the sea, were insensibly exploded by industry and experience. The cultivation of flax was transported from Egypt to Gaul, and enriched the whole country, however it might impoverish the particular lands on which it was sown. 5. The use of artificial grasses became familiar to the farmers both of Italy and the provinces, particularly the Lucerne, which derived its name and origin from Media. The assured supply of wholesome and plentiful food for the cattle during winter, multiplied the number of the flocks and herds, which in their turn contributed to the fertility of the soil. To all these improvements may be added an assiduous attention to mines and fisheries, which, by employing a multitude of laborious hands, serve to increase the pleasures of the rich, and the subsistence of the poor. The elegant treatise of Columella describes the advanced state of the Spanish husbandry, under the reign of Tiberius; and it may be observed, that those famines which so frequently afflicted the infant republic, were seldom or never experienced by the extensive empire of Rome. The accidental scarcity, in any single province, was immediately relieved by the plenty of its more fortunate neighbours.

Agriculture is the foundation of manufactures; since the productions of nature are the materials of art. Under the Roman empire, the labour of an industrious and ingenious people was variously, but incessantly employed, in the service of the rich. In their dress, their table, their houses and their furniture, the favourites of fortune united every refinement of conveniency, of elegance, and of splendour, whatever could soothe their pride or gratify their sensuality. Such refinements, under the odious name of luxury, have been severely arraigned by the moralists of every age; and it might perhaps be more conducive to the virtue, as well as happiness, of mankind, if all possessed the necessaries, and none the superfluities, of life. But in the present imperfect condition of society, luxury, though it may proceed from vice or folly, seems to be the only means that can correct the unequal distribution of property. The diligent mechanic, and the skilful artist, who have obtained no share in the division of the earth, receive a voluntary tax from the possessors of land; and the latter are prompted, by a sense of interest, to improve those estates, with whose produce they may purchase additional pleasures. This operation, the particular effects of which are felt in every society, acted with much more diffusive energy in the Roman world. The provinces would soon have been exhausted of their wealth, if the manufactures and commerce of luxury had not insensibly restored to the industrious subjects the sums which were exacted from them by the arms and authority of Rome. As long as the circulation was confined within the bounds of the empire, it impressed the political machine with a new degree of activity, and its consequences, sometimes beneficial, could never become pernicious.

But it is no easy task to confine luxury within the limits of an empire. The most remote countries of the ancient world were ransacked to supply the pomp and delicacy of Rome. The forests of Scythia afforded some valuable furs. Amber was brought over land from the shores of the Baltic to the Danube; and the barbarians were astonished at the price which they received in exchange for so useless a commodity. There was a considerable demand for Babylonian carpets and other manufactures of the East; but the most important and unpopular branch of foreign trade was carried on with Arabia and India. Every year, about the time of the summer solstice, a fleet of an hundred and twenty vessels sailed from Myos-hormos, a port of Egypt, on the Red Sea. By the periodical assistance of the Monsoons, they traversed the ocean in about forty days. The coast of Malabar, or the island of Ceylon, was the usual term of their navigation, and it was in those markets that the merchants from the more remote countries of Asia expected their arrival. The return of the fleet of Egypt was fixed to the months of December or January; and as soon as their rich cargo had been transported on the backs of camels, from the Red Sea to the Nile, and had descended that river as far as Alexandria, it was poured, without delay, into the capital of the empire. The objects of oriental traffic were splendid and trifling: silk, a pound of which was esteemed not inferior in value to a pound of gold; precious stones, among which the pearl claimed the first rank after the diamond; and a variety of aromatics, that were consumed in religious worship and the pomp of funerals. The labour and risk of the voyage was rewarded with almost incredible profit; but the profit was made upon Roman subjects, and a few individuals were enriched at the expense of the Public. As the natives of Arabia and India were contented with the productions and manufactures of their own country, silver, on the side of the Romans, was the principal, if not the only instrument of commerce. It was a complaint worthy of the gravity of the senate, that in the purchase of female ornaments, the wealth of the state was irrecoverably given away to foreign and hostile nations. The annual loss is computed, by a writer of an inquisitive but censorious temper, at upwards of eight hundred thousand pounds sterling. Such was the style of discontent, brooding over the dark prospect of approaching poverty. And yet, if we compare the proportion between gold and silver, as it stood in the time of Pliny, and as it was fixed in the reign of Constantine, we shall discover within that period a very considerable increase. There is not the least reason to suppose that gold was become more scarce; it is therefore evident that silver was grown more common; that whatever might be the amount of the Indian and Arabian exports, they were far from exhausting the wealth of the Roman world; and that the produce of the mines abundantly supplied the demands of commerce.

Notwithstanding the propensity of mankind to exalt the past, and to depreciate the present, the tranquil and prosperous state of the empire was warmly felt, and honestly confessed, by the provincials as well as Romans. "They acknowledged that the true principles of social life, laws, agriculture, and science, which had been first invented by the wisdom of Athens, were now firmly established by the power of Rome, under whose auspicious influence the fiercest barbarians were united by an equal government and common language. They affirm, that with the improvement of arts, the human species was visibly multiplied. They celebrate the increasing splendour of the cities, the beautiful face of the country, cultivated and adorned like an immense garden; and the long festival of peace, which was enjoyed by so many nations, forgetful of their ancient animosities, and delivered from the apprehension of future danger." Whatever suspicions may be suggested by the air of rhetoric and declamation, which seems to prevail in these passages, the substance of them is perfectly agreeable to historic truth.

It was scarcely possible that the eyes of contemporaries should discover in the public felicity the latent causes of decay and corruption. This long peace, and the uniform government of the Romans, introduced a slow and secret poison into the vitals of the empire. The minds of men were gradually reduced to the same level, the fire of genius was extinguished, and even the military spirit evaporated. The natives of Europe were brave and robust, Spain, Gaul, Britain, and Illyricum supplied the legions with excellent soldiers, and constituted the real strength of the monarchy. Their personal valour remained, but they no longer possessed that public courage which is nourished by the love of independence, the sense of national honour, the presence of danger, and the habit of command. They received laws and governors from the will of their sovereign, and trusted for their defence to a mercenary army. The posterity of their boldest leaders was contented with the rank of citizens and subjects. The most aspiring spirits resorted to the court or standard of the emperors; and the deserted provinces, deprived of political strength or union, insensibly sunk into the languid indifference of private life.

The love of letters, almost inseparable from peace and refinement, was fashionable among the subjects of Hadrian and the Antonines, who were themselves men of learning and curiosity. It was diffused over the whole extent of their empire; the most northern tribes of Britons had acquired a taste for rhetoric; Homer as well as Virgil were transcribed and studied on the banks of the Rhine and Danube; and the most liberal rewards sought out the faintest glimmerings of literary merit. The sciences of physic and astronomy were successfully cultivated by the Greeks; the observations of Ptolemy and the writings of Galen are studied by those who have improved their discoveries and corrected their errors; but if we except the inimitable Lucian, this age of indolence passed away without having produced a single writer of original genius, or who excelled in the arts of elegant composition. The authority of Plato and Aristotle, of Zeno and Epicurus, still reigned in the schools; and their systems, transmitted with blind deference from one generation of disciples to another, precluded every generous attempt to exercise the powers, or enlarge the limits, of the human mind. The beauties of the poets and orators, instead of kindling a fire like their own, inspired only cold and servile imitations: or if any ventured to deviate from those models, they deviated at the same time from good sense and propriety. On the revival of letters, the youthful vigour of the imagination, after a long repose, national emulation, a new religion, new languages, and a new world, called forth the genius of Europe. But the provincials of Rome, trained by a uniform artificial foreign education, were engaged in a very unequal competition with those bold ancients, who, by expressing their genuine feelings in their native tongue, had already occupied every place of honour. The name of Poet was almost forgotten; that of Orator was usurped by the sophists. A cloud of critics, of compilers, of commentators, darkened the face of learning, and the decline of genius was soon followed by the corruption of taste.

The sublime Longinus, who in somewhat a later period, and in the court of a Syrian queen, preserved the spirit of ancient Athens, observes and laments this degeneracy of his contemporaries, which debased their sentiments, enervated their courage, and depressed their talents. "In the same manner," says he, "as some children always remain pygmies, whose infant limbs have been too closely confined; thus our tender minds, fettered by the prejudices and habits of a just servitude, are unable to expand themselves, or to attain that well-proportioned greatness which we admire in the ancients; who living under a popular government, wrote with the same freedom as they acted."[5] This diminutive stature of mankind, if we pursue the metaphor, was daily sinking below the old standard, and the Roman world was indeed peopled by a race of pygmies; when the fierce giants of the north broke in, and mended the puny breed. They restored a manly spirit of freedom; and after the revolution of ten centuries, freedom became the happy parent of taste and science.

[*In chapter III Gibbon describes the political constitution of the Empire as established by Augustus and practised by his successors. These emperors no longer feared the senate, which they had deprived of power, but apprehended the power of the army, on which their own authority ultimately rested. They therefore sought to prevent a disputed succession by naming and training their successors. At the end of the chapter, Gibbon describes the planned succession of the golden age of the empire.*]

Nerva had scarcely accepted the purple from the assassins of Domitian before he discovered that his feeble age was unable to stem the torrent of public disorders, which had multiplied under the long tyranny of his predecessor. His mild disposition was respected by the good; but the degenerate Romans required a more vigorous character, whose justice should strike terror into the guilty. Though he had several relations, he fixed his choice on a stranger. He adopted Trajan, then about forty years of age, and who commanded a powerful army in the Lower Germany; and immediately, by a decree of the senate, declared him his colleague and successor in the empire. It is sincerely to be lamented, that whilst we are fatigued with the disgustful relation of Nero's crimes and follies, we are reduced to collect the actions of

[5] [The *Treatise on the Sublime*, traditionally ascribed to Longinus, the minister of Zenobia, queen of Palmyra, is now thought to be by an earlier writer. Gibbon himself, in his Journal, foreshadowed this modern verdict. *Ed.*]

Trajan from the glimmerings of an abridgment, or the doubtful light of a panegyric. There remains, however, one panegyric far removed beyond the suspicion of flattery. Above two hundred and fifty years after the death of Trajan, the senate, in pouring out the customary acclamations on the accession of a new emperor, wished that he might surpass the felicity of Augustus, and the virtue of Trajan.

We may readily believe, that the father of his country hesitated whether he ought to intrust the various and doubtful character of his kinsman Hadrian with sovereign power. In his last moments, the arts of the empress Plotina either fixed the irresolution of Trajan, or boldly supposed a fictitious adoption; the truth of which could not be safely disputed, and Hadrian was peacefully acknowledged as his lawful successor. Under his reign, as has been already mentioned, the empire flourished in peace and prosperity. He encouraged the arts, reformed the laws, asserted military discipline, and visited all his provinces in person. His vast and active genius was equally suited to the most enlarged views, and the minute details of civil policy. But the ruling passions of his soul were curiosity and vanity. As they prevailed, and as they were attracted by different objects, Hadrian was, by turns, an excellent prince, a ridiculous sophist, and a jealous tyrant. The general tenor of his conduct deserved praise for its equity and moderation. Yet in the first days of his reign, he put to death four consular senators, his personal enemies, and men who had been judged worthy of empire; and the tediousness of a painful illness rendered him, at last, peevish and cruel. The senate doubted whether they should pronounce him a god or a tyrant; and the honours decreed to his memory were granted to the prayers of the pious Antoninus.

The caprice of Hadrian influenced his choice of a successor. After revolving in his mind several men of distinguished merit, whom he esteemed and hated, he adopted Ælius Verus, a gay and voluptuous nobleman, recommended by uncommon beauty to the lover of Antinous.[6] But while Hadrian was delighting himself with his own applause, and the acclamations of the soldiers, whose consent had been secured by an immense donative, the new Cæsar was ravished from his embraces by an untimely death. He left only one son. Hadrian commended the boy to the gratitude of the Antonines. He was adopted by Pius; and on the accession of Marcus, was invested with an equal share of sovereign power. Among the many vices of this younger Verus he possessed one virtue; a dutiful reverence for his wiser colleague, to whom he willingly abandoned the ruder cares of empire. The philosophic emperor dissembled his follies, lamented his early death, and cast a decent veil over his memory.

As soon as Hadrian's passion was either gratified or disappointed, he resolved to deserve the thanks of posterity, by placing the most exalted merit on the Roman throne. His discerning eye easily discovered a senator about fifty years of age, blameless in all the offices of life, and a youth of about seventeen, whose riper years opened the fair prospect of every virtue: the elder of these was declared the son and successor of Hadrian, on condition, however, that he himself should immediately adopt the younger. The two Antonines (for it is of them that we are now speaking) governed the Roman world forty-two years, with the same invariable spirit of wisdom and virtue. Although Pius had two sons,[7] he preferred the welfare of Rome to the interest of his family, gave his daughter Faustina in marriage to young Marcus, obtained from the Senate the tribunitian and proconsular powers, and with a noble disdain, or rather

[6] The deification of Antinous, his medals, statues, temples, city, oracles, and constellation, are well known, and still dishonour the memory of Hadrian. Yet we may remark, that of the first fifteen emperors, Claudius was the only one whose taste in love was entirely correct.

[7] Without the help of medals and inscriptions we should be ignorant of this fact, so honourable to the memory of Pius.

ignorance of jealousy, associated him to all the labours of government. Marcus, on the other hand, revered the character of his benefactor, loved him as a parent, obeyed him as his sovereign, and, after he was no more, regulated his own administration by the example and maxims of his predecessor. Their united reigns are possibly the only period of history in which the happiness of a great people was the sole object of government.

Titus Antoninus Pius has been justly denominated a second Numa. The same love of religion, justice, and peace, was the distinguishing characteristic of both princes. But the situation of the latter opened a much larger field for the exercise of those virtues. Numa could only prevent a few neighbouring villages from plundering each other's harvests. Antoninus diffused order and tranquillity over the greatest part of the earth. His reign is marked by the rare advantage of furnishing very few materials for history; which is, indeed, little more thar the register of the crimes, follies, and misfortunes of mankind. In private life, he was an amiable as well as a good man. The native simplicity of his virtue was a stranger to vanity or affectation. He enjoyed with moderation the conveniences of his fortune, and the innocent pleasures of society: and the benevolence of his soul displayed itself in a cheerful serenity of temper.

The virtue of Marcus Aurelius Antoninus was of a severer and more laborious kind. It was the well-earned harvest of many a learned conference, of many a patient lecture, and many a midnight lucubration. At the age of twelve years he embraced the rigid system of the Stoics, which taught him to submit his body to his mind, his passions to his reason; to consider virtue as the only good, vice as the only evil, all things external as things indifferent. His meditations, composed in the tumult of a camp, are still extant; and he even condescended to give lessons of philosophy in a more public manner than was perhaps consistent with the modesty of a sage, or the dignity of an emperor. But his life was the noblest commentary on the precepts of Zeno. He was severe to himself, indulgent to the imperfections of others, just and beneficent to all mankind. He regretted that Avidius Cassius, who excited a rebellion in Syria, had disappointed him, by a voluntary death, of the pleasure of converting an enemy into a friend; and he justified the sincerity of that sentiment, by moderating the zeal of the senate against the adherents of the traitor. War he detested, as the disgrace and calamity of human nature; but when the necessity of a just defence called upon him to take up arms, he readily exposed his person to eight winter campaigns on the frozen banks of the Danube, the severity of which was at last fatal to the weakness of his constitution. His memory was revered by a grateful posterity, and above a century after his death, many persons preserved the image of Marcus Antoninus, among those of their household gods.

If a man were called to fix the period in the history of the world, during which the condition of the human race was most happy and prosperous, he would, without hesitation, name that which elapsed from the death of Domitian to the accession of Commodus. The vast extent of the Roman empire was governed by absolute power, under the guidance of virtue and wisdom. The armies were restrained by the firm but gentle hand of four successive emperors, whose characters and authority commanded involuntary respect. The forms of the civil administration were carefully preserved by Nerva, Trajan, Hadrian, and the Antonines, who delighted in the image of liberty, and were pleased with considering themselves as the accountable ministers of the laws. Such princes deserved the honour of restoring the republic had the Romans of their days been capable of enjoying a rational freedom.

The labours of these monarchs were overpaid by the immense reward that inseparably waited on their success; by the honest pride of virtue, and by the exquisite delight of beholding the general happiness of which they were the authors. A just, but melancholy reflection embittered, however, the noblest of human enjoyments. They must often have recollected the instability of a happiness which depended on the character of a single man. The fatal moment was perhaps approaching, when some licentious youth, or some jealous tyrant, would abuse, to the destruction, that absolute power which they had exerted for the benefit of their people. The ideal restraints of the senate and the laws might serve to display the virtues, but could never correct the vices, of the emperor. The military force was a blind and irresistible instrument of oppression; and the corruption of Roman manners would always supply flatterers eager to applaud, and ministers prepared to serve the fear or the avarice, the lust or the cruelty, of their masters.

These gloomy apprehensions had been already justified by the experience of the Romans. The annals of the emperors exhibit a strong and various picture of human nature, which we should vainly seek among the mixed and doubtful characters of modern history. In the conduct of those monarchs we may trace the utmost lines of vice and virtue; the most exalted perfection, and the meanest degeneracy of our own species. The golden age of Trajan and the Antonines had been preceded by an age of iron. It is almost superfluous to enumerate the unworthy successors of Augustus. Their unparalleled vices, and the splendid theatre on which they were acted, have saved them from oblivion. The dark unrelenting Tiberius, the furious Caligula, the feeble Claudius, the profligate and cruel Nero, the beastly Vitellius,[8] and the timid inhuman Domitian, are condemned to everlasting infamy. During fourscore years (excepting only the short and doubtful respite of Vespasian's reign[9]) Rome groaned

[8]Vitellius consumed in mere eating, at least six millions of our money in about seven months. It is not easy to express his vices with dignity, or even decency. Tacitus fairly calls him a hog; but it is by substituting to a coarse word a very fine image.

[9] The execution of Helvidius Priscus, and the virtuous Eponina, disgraced the reign of Vespasian.

beneath an unremitting tyranny, which exterminated the ancient families of the republic, and was fatal to almost every virtue, and every talent, that arose in that unhappy period.

Under the reign of these monsters the slavery of the Romans was accompanied with two peculiar circum- stances, the one occasioned by their former liberty, the other by their extensive conquests, which rendered their condition more completely wretched than that of the victims of tyranny in any other age or country. From these causes were derived, 1. The exquisite sensibility of the sufferers; and, 2, the impossibility of escaping from the hand of the oppressor.

I. When Persia was governed by the descendants of Sefi, a race of princes whose wanton cruelty often stained their divan, their table, and their bed, with the blood of their favourites, there is a saying recorded of a young nobleman, that he never departed from the sultan's presence without satisfying himself whether his head was still on his shoulders. The experience of every day might almost justify the scepticism of Rustan. Yet the fatal sword, suspended above him by a single thread, seems not to have disturbed the slumbers, or interrupted the tranquillity, of the Persian. The monarch's frown, he well knew, could level him with the dust; but the stroke of lightning or apoplexy might be equally fatal; and it was the part of a wise man to forget the inevitable calamities of human life in the enjoyment of the fleeting hour. He was dignified with the appellation of the king's slave; had, perhaps, been purchased from obscure parents in a country which he had never known; and was trained up from his infancy in the severe discipline of the seraglio. His name, his wealth, his honours, were the gift of a master, who might, without injustice, resume what he had bestowed. Rustan's knowledge, if he possessed any, could only serve to confirm his habits by prejudices. His language afforded not words for any form of government, except absolute monarchy. The history of the East informed him, that such had ever been the condition of mankind. The Koran, and the interpreters of that divine book, inculcated to him, that the sultan was the descendant of the prophet, and the vice-regent of heaven; that patience was the first virtue of a Mussulman, and unlimited obedience the great duty of a subject.

The minds of the Romans were very differently prepared for slavery. Oppressed beneath the weight of their own corruption and of military violence, they for a long while preserved the sentiments, or at least the ideas, of their free-born ancestors. The education of Helvidius and Thrasea, of Tacitus and Pliny, was the same as that of Cato and Cicero. From Grecian philosophy they had imbibed the justest and most liberal notions of the dignity of human nature, and the origin of civil society. The history of their own country had taught them to revere a free, a virtuous, and a victorious commonwealth; to abhor the successful crimes of Cæsar and Augustus; and inwardly to despise those tyrants whom they adored with the most abject flattery. As magistrates and senators, they were admitted into the great council which had once dictated laws to the earth, whose name still gave a sanction to the acts of the monarch, and whose authority was so often prostituted to the vilest purposes of tyranny. Tiberius, and those emperors who adopted his maxims, attempted to disguise their murders by the formalities of justice, and perhaps enjoyed a secret pleasure in rendering the senate their accomplice as well as their victim. By this assembly the last of the Romans were condemned for imaginary crimes and real virtues. Their infamous accusers assumed the language of independent patriots, who arraigned a dangerous citizen before the tribunal of his country; and the public service was rewarded by riches and honours. The servile judges professed to assert the majesty of the commonwealth, violated in the person of its first magistrate; whose clemency they most applauded when they trembled the most at his inexorable and impending cruelty. The tyrant beheld their baseness with just contempt, and encountered their secret sentiments of detestation with sincere and avowed hatred for the whole body of the senate.

II. The division of Europe into a number of independent states, connected, however, with each other, by the general resemblance of religion, language, and manners, is productive of the most beneficial consequences to the liberty of mankind. A modern tyrant, who should find no resistance either in his own breast, or in his people, would soon experience a gentle restraint from the example of his equals, the dread of present censure, the advice of his allies, and the apprehension of his enemies. The object of his displeasure, escaping from the narrow limits of his dominions, would easily obtain, in a happier climate, a secure refuge, a new fortune adequate to his merit, the freedom of complaint, and perhaps the means of revenge. But the empire of the Romans filled the world, and when that empire fell into the hands of a single person, the world became a safe and dreary prison for his enemies. The slave of Imperial despotism, whether he was condemned to drag his gilded chain in Rome and the senate, or to wear out a life of exile on the barren rock of Seriphus, or the frozen banks of the Danube, expected his fate in silent despair![10] To resist was fatal, and it was impossible to fly. On every side he was encompassed with a vast extent of sea and land, which he could never hope to traverse without being discovered, seized, and restored to his irritated master. Beyond the frontiers, his anxious view could discover nothing, except the ocean, inhospitable deserts, hostile tribes of barbarians, of fierce manners and unknown language, or dependent kings, who would gladly purchase the emperor's protec-

---

[10] Seriphus was a small rocky island in the Ægean Sea, the inhabitants of which were despised for their ignorance and obscurity. The place of Ovid's exile is well known, by his just, but unmanly lamentations. It should seem, that he only received an order to leave Rome in so many days, and to transport himself to Tomi. Guards and gaolers were unnecessary.

tion by the sacrifice of an obnoxious fugitive.[11] "Where-ever you are," said Cicero to the exiled Marcellus, "remember that you are equally within the power of the conqueror."

[11] Under Tiberius, a Roman knight attempted to fly to the Parthians. He was stopt in the Straits of Sicily; but so little danger did there appear in the example, that the most jealous of tyrants disdained to punish it.

CHAPTER II

THE HOUSE OF SEVERUS

The death of Marcus Aurelius, in 180 A.D., brought the felicity of the Antonine age to an abrupt end. His son Commodus was a tyrant who degraded the imperial dignity by personally fighting in the amphitheatre both against wild beasts and against professional gladiators. He was murdered after a reign of twelve years. His successor, the senator Pertinax, who sought to return to the methods of Marcus, lasted only twelve weeks. He was murdered by the Praetorian guards who now, resenting the restoration of discipline, "threw their swords into the scale", and, having thus made the throne again vacant, treated it as their property and offered it for sale to the highest bidder. It was bought by a rich senator Didius Julianus. But this claim of the Roman household troops to dispose of the empire aroused the resentment of the legions abroad. By a rapid march on Rome, the commander of the army on the Danube, the African Septimius Severus, deposed Julianus after a reign of 66 days, defeated his rival generals, and inaugurated the rule of a new dynasty: the last imperial dynasty of the pagan Empire.

Septimius Severus reigned from 193 to 211. He was succeeded by his two sons, Bassianus Antoninus (better known as Caracalla) and Geta; of whom the former soon murdered the latter and then reigned alone as "the common enemy of mankind" until 217, when he was assassinated in Syria by discontented Praetorian Guards organised by the prefect Macrinus. Macrinus then prepared to seize the throne for himself. But Caracalla's soldiers resented the disciplinary measures of their new commander, and they were conveniently offered a more attractive emperor by an enterprising old lady in the neighbourhood. This was Julia Maesa, whose sister, Julia Domna, had been the wife of Septimius Severus and the mother of Caracalla, and who now saw the chance of presenting her own Syrian grandson (the son of her daughter Soemias) as the son of Caracalla and heir to his throne. Thus began the extraordinary career of Elagabalus, the Syrian priest of the Sun who became the most dissolute and contemptible of all the emperors of Rome. In 222, Elagabalus in his turn was murdered by the Praetorian Guards, who transferred their support to the last and most reputable of the "Severan" dynasty, Alexander, also a grandson of Julia Maesa, being the son of her other daughter Mamaea.

In the following passage, from chapter VI, Gibbon describes the reigns of Elagabalus and Alexander Severus, and explains, by an account of the imperial finances, Caracalla's most famous legislative act: his extension, in 212, of the rights of Roman citizenship to all subjects of the Empire.

The empress Julia had experienced all the vicissitudes of fortune. From an humble station she had been raised to greatness, only to taste the superior bitterness of an exalted rank. She was doomed to weep over the death of one of her sons, and over the life of the other. The cruel fate of Caracalla, though her own good sense must have long taught her to expect it, awakened the feelings of a mother and of an empress. Notwithstanding the respectful civility expressed by the usurper towards the widow of Severus, she descended with a painful struggle into the condition of a subject, and soon withdrew herself by a voluntary death from the anxious and humiliating dependence. Julia Mæsa, her sister, was ordered to leave the court and Antioch. She retired to Emesa with an immense fortune, the fruit of twenty years' favour, accompanied by her two daughters, Soæmias and Mamæa, each of whom was a widow, and each had an only son. Bassianus, for that was the name of the son of Soæmias, was consecrated to the honourable ministry of high priest of the Sun; and this holy vocation, embraced either from prudence or superstition, contributed to raise the Syrian youth to the empire of Rome. A numerous body of troops was stationed at Emesa; and, as the severe discipline of Macrinus had constrained them to pass the winter encamped, they were eager to revenge the cruelty of such unaccustomed hardships. The soldiers, who resorted in crowds to the temple of the Sun, beheld with veneration and delight the elegant dress and figure of a young Pontiff: they recognised, or they thought that they recognised, the features of Caracalla, whose memory they now adored. The artful Mæsa saw and cherished their rising partiality, and readily sacrificing her daughter's reputation to the fortune of her grandson, she insinuated that Bassianus was the natural son of their murdered sovereign. The sums distributed by her emissaries with a lavish hand silenced every objection, and the profusion sufficiently proved the affinity, or at least the resemblance, of Bassianus with the great original. The young Antoninus (for he had assumed and polluted that respectable name) was (A.D. 218, May 16) declared emperor by the troops of Emesa, asserted his hereditary right, and called aloud on the armies to follow the standard of a young and liberal prince, who had taken up arms to revenge his father's death and the oppression of the military order.

Whilst a conspiracy of women and eunuchs was con-

certed with prudence, and conducted with rapid vigour,
Macrinus, who, by a decisive motion, might have crushed
his infant enemy, floated between the opposite extremes
of terror and security, which alike fixed him inactive at
Antioch. A spirit of rebellion diffused itself through all
the camps and garrisons of Syria, successive detachments murdered their officers, and joined the party of
the rebels; and the tardy restitution of military pay and
privileges was imputed to the acknowledged weakness of
Macrinus. At length he marched out of Antioch, to meet
the increasing and zealous army of the young pretender.
His own troops seemed to take the field with faintness
and reluctance; but (A.D. 218, June 7), in the heat of the
battle, the Prætorian guards, almost by an involuntary
impulse, asserted the superiority of their valour and
discipline. The rebel ranks were broken; when the mother
and grandmother of the Syrian prince, who, according
to their eastern custom, had attended the army, threw
themselves from their covered chariots, and, by exciting
the compassion of the soldiers, endeavoured to animate
their drooping courage. Antoninus himself, who, in the
rest of his life, never acted like a man, in this important
crisis of his fate approved himself a hero, mounted his
horse, and, at the head of his rallied troops, charged
sword in hand among the thickest of the enemy; whilst
the eunuch Gannys, whose occupations had been confined to female cares and the soft luxury of Asia, displayed the talents of an able and experienced general.
The battle still raged with doubtful violence, and
Macrinus might have obtained the victory, had he not
betrayed his own cause by a shameful and precipitate
flight. His cowardice served only to protract his life a
few days, and to stamp deserved ignominy on his misfortunes. It is scarcely necessary to add, that his son
Diadumenianus was involved in the same fate. As soon
as the stubborn Prætorians could be convinced that they
fought for a prince who had basely deserted them, they
surrendered to the conqueror; the contending parties of
the Roman army, mingling tears of joy and tenderness,

united under the banners of the imagined son of Caracalla, and the East acknowledged with pleasure the first
emperor of Asiatic extraction.

The letters of Macrinus had condescended to inform
the senate of the slight disturbance occasioned by an
impostor in Syria, and a decree immediately passed,
declaring the rebel and his family public enemies; with
a promise of pardon, however, to such of his deluded
adherents as should merit it by an immediate return to
their duty. During the twenty days that elapsed from the
declaration to the victory of Antoninus (for in so short
an interval was the fate of the Roman world decided),
the capital and the provinces, more especially those of
the East, were distracted with hopes and fears, agitated
with tumult, and stained with a useless effusion of civil
blood, since whosoever of the rivals prevailed in Syria,
must reign over the empire. The specious letters in which
the young conqueror announced his victory to the obedient senate, were filled with professions of virtue and
moderation; the shining examples of Marcus and Augustus he should ever consider as the great rule of his
administration; and he affected to dwell with pride on
the striking resemblance of his own age and fortunes
with those of Augustus, who in the earliest youth had
revenged by a successful war the murder of his father.
By adopting the style of Marcus Aurelius Antoninus, son
of Antoninus and grandson of Severus, he tacitly asserted
his hereditary claim to the empire; but, by assuming the
tribunitian and proconsular powers before they had been
conferred on him by a decree of the senate, he offended
the delicacy of Roman prejudice. This new and injudicious violation of the constitution was probably dictated
either by the ignorance of his Syrian courtiers, or the
fierce disdain of his military followers.

As the attention of the new emperor was diverted by
the most trifling amusements, he (A.D. 219) wasted
many months in his luxurious progress from Syria to
Italy, passed at Nicomedia his first winter after his victory, and deferred till the ensuing summer his triumphal

entry into the capital. A faithful picture, however, which preceded his arrival, and was placed by his immediate order over the altar of Victory in the senate-house, conveyed to the Romans the just but unworthy resemblance of his person and manners. He was drawn in his sacerdotal robes of silk and gold, after the loose flowing fashion of the Medes and Phœnicians; his head was covered with a lofty tiara, his numerous collars and bracelets were adorned with gems of an inestimable value. His eyebrows were tinged with black, and his cheeks painted with an artificial red and white. The grave senators confessed with a sigh, that, after having long experienced the stern tyranny of their own countrymen, Rome was at length humbled beneath the effeminate luxury of Oriental despotism.

The Sun was worshipped at Emesa, under the name of Elagabalus,[1] and under the form of a black conical stone, which, as it was universally believed, had fallen from heaven on that sacred place. To this protecting deity, Antoninus, not without some reason, ascribed his elevation to the throne. The display of superstitious gratitude was the only serious business of his reign. The triumph of the God of Emesa over all the religions of the earth, was the great object of his zeal and vanity: and the appellation of Elagabalus (for he presumed as pontiff and favourite to adopt that sacred name) was dearer to him than all the titles of Imperial greatness. In a solemn procession through the streets of Rome, the way was strewed with gold dust; the black stone, set in precious gems, was placed on a chariot drawn by six milk-white horses richly caparisoned. The pious emperor held the reins, and, supported by his ministers, moved slowly backwards, that he might perpetually enjoy the felicity of the divine presence. In a magnificent temple raised on the Palatine Mount, the sacrifices of the god of Elagabalus were celebrated with every circumstance of cost

---

[1] This name is derived by the learned from two Syriac words, *Ela* a God and *Gabal*, to form, the forming or plastic God, a proper, and even happy epithet for the Sun.

and solemnity. The richest wines, the most extraordinary victims, and the rarest aromatics, were profusely consumed on his altar. Around the altar a chorus of Syrian damsels performed their lascivious dances to the sound of barbarian music, whilst the gravest personages of the state and army, clothed in long Phœnician tunics, officiated in the meanest functions, with affected zeal and secret indignation.

To this temple, as to the common centre of religious worship, the Imperial fanatic attempted to remove the Ancilia, the Palladium, and all the sacred pledges of the faith of Numa. A crowd of inferior deities attended in various stations the majesty of the god of Emesa; but his court was still imperfect, till a female of distinguished rank was admitted to his bed. Pallas had been first chosen for his comfort; but as it was dreaded lest her warlike terrors might affright the soft delicacy of a Syrian deity, the Moon, adored by the Africans under the name of Astarte, was deemed a more suitable companion for the Sun. Her image, with the rich offerings of her temple as a marriage portion, was transported with solemn pomp from Carthage to Rome, and the day of these mystic nuptials was a general festival in the capital and throughout the empire.

A rational voluptuary adheres with invariable respect to the temperate dictates of nature, and improves the gratifications of sense by social intercourse, endearing connections, and the soft colouring of taste and the imagination. But Elagabalus (I speak of the emperor of that name), corrupted by his youth, his country, and his fortune, abandoned himself to the grossest pleasures with ungoverned fury, and soon found disgust and satiety in the midst of his enjoyments. The inflammatory powers of art were summoned to his aid: the confused multitude of women, of wines, and of dishes, and the studied variety of attitudes and sauces, served to revive his languid appetites. New terms and new inventions in these sciences, the only ones cultivated and patronised by the monarch[2] signalised his reign, and transmitted his infamy to succeeding times. A capricious prodigality supplied the want of taste and elegance; and whilst Elagabalus lavished away the treasures of his people in the wildest extravagance, his own voice and that of his flatterers applauded a spirit and magnificence unknown to the tameness of his predecessors. To confound the order of seasons and climates,[3] to sport with the passions and prejudices of his subjects, and to subvert every law of nature and decency, were in the number of his most delicious amusements. A long train of concubines, and a rapid succession of wives, among whom was a vestal virgin, ravished by force from her sacred asylum, were insufficient to satisfy the impotence of his passions. The master of the Roman world affected to copy the dress and manners of the female sex, preferred the distaff to the sceptre, and dishonoured the principal dignities of the empire by distributing them among his numerous lovers; one of whom was publicly invested with the title and authority of the emperor's, or, as he more properly styled himself, of the empress's husband.[4]

It may seem probable, the vices and follies of Elagabalus have been adorned by fancy, and blackened by prejudice. Yet confining ourselves to the public scenes displayed before the Roman people, and attested by grave and contemporary historians, their inexpressible infamy surpasses that of any other age or country. The licence of an eastern monarch is secluded from the eyes of curiosity by the inaccessible walls of his seraglio. The sentiments of honour and gallantry have introduced a refinement of pleasure, a regard for decency, and a respect for the public opinion, into the modern courts of

[2] The invention of a new sauce was liberally rewarded; but if it was not relished, the inventor was confined to eat of nothing else, till he had discovered another more agreeable to the Imperial palate.

[3] He never would eat sea-fish except at a great distance from the sea; he then would distribute vast quantities of the rarest sorts, brought at an immense expense, to the peasants of the inland country.

[4] Hierocles enjoyed that honour. A dancer was made præfect of the city, a charioteer præfect of the watch, a barber præfect of the provisions.

Europe; but the corrupt and opulent nobles of Rome gratified every vice that could be collected from the mighty conflux of nations and manners. Secure of impunity, careless of censure, they lived without restraint in the patient and humble society of their slaves and parasites. The emperor, in his turn, viewing every rank of his subjects with the same contemptuous indifference, asserted without control his sovereign privilege of lust and luxury.

The most worthless of mankind are not afraid to condemn in others the same disorders which they allow in themselves; and can readily discover some nice difference of age, character, or station to justify the partial distinction. The licentious soldiers, who had raised to the throne the dissolute son of Caracalla, blushed at their ignominious choice, and turned with disgust from that monster, to contemplate with pleasure the opening virtues of his cousin Alexander the son of Mamæa. The crafty Mæsa, sensible that her grandson Elagabalus must inevitably destroy himself by his own vices, had provided another and surer support of her family. Embracing a favourable moment of fondness and devotion, she had persuaded the young emperor to adopt Alexander, and to invest him (A.D. 221) with the title of Cæsar, that his own divine occupations might be no longer interrupted by the care of the earth. In the second rank that amiable prince soon acquired the affections of the public, and excited the tyrant's jealousy, who resolved to terminate the dangerous competition, either by corrupting the manners, or by taking away the life, of his rival. His arts proved unsuccessful; his vain designs were constantly discovered by his own loquacious folly, and disappointed by those virtuous and faithful servants whom the prudence of Mamæa had placed about the person of her son. In a hasty sally of passion, Elagabalus resolved to execute by force what he had been unable to compass by fraud, and by a despotic sentence degraded his cousin from the rank and honours of Cæsar. The message was received in the senate with silence, and in the camp with fury. The Prætorian guards swore to protect Alexander, and to revenge the dishonoured majesty of the throne. The tears and promises of the trembling Elagabalus, who only begged them to spare his life, and to leave him in the possession of his beloved Hierocles, diverted their just indignation; and they contented themselves with empowering their præfects to watch over the safety of Alexander, and the conduct of the emperor.

It was impossible that such a reconciliation should last, or that even the mean soul of Elagabalus could hold an empire on such humiliating terms of dependence. He soon attempted, by a dangerous experiment, to try the temper of the soldiers. The report of the death of Alexander, and the natural suspicion that he had been murdered, inflamed their passions into fury, and the tempest of the camp could only be appeased by the presence and authority of the popular youth. Provoked at this new instance of their affection for his cousin, and their contempt for his person, the emperor ventured to punish some of the leaders of the mutiny. His unseasonable severity proved instantly fatal to his minions, his mother, and himself. Elagabalus was (A.D. 222, 10th March) massacred by the indignant Prætorians, his mutilated corpse dragged through the streets of the city, and thrown into the Tiber. His memory was branded with eternal infamy by the senate; the justice of whose decree has been ratified by posterity.

In the room of Elagabalus, his cousin Alexander was raised to the throne by the Prætorian guards. His relation to the family of Severus, whose name he assumed, was the same as that of his predecessor; his virtue and his danger had already endeared him to the Romans, and the eager liberality of the senate conferred upon him, in one day, the various titles and powers of the Imperial dignity. But as Alexander was a modest and dutiful youth, of only seventeen years of age, the reins of government were in the hands of two women, of his mother

49

Mamæa, and of Mæsa, his grandmother. After the death of the latter, who survived but a short time the elevation of Alexander, Mamæa remained the sole regent of her son and of the empire.

In every age and country, the wiser, or at least the stronger, of the two sexes, has usurped the powers of the state, and confined the other to the cares and pleasures of domestic life. In hereditary monarchies, however, and especially in those of modern Europe, the gallant spirit of chivalry, and the law of succession have accustomed us to allow a singular exception; and a woman is often acknowledged the absolute sovereign of a great kingdom, in which she would be deemed incapable of exercising the smallest employment, civil or military. But as the Roman emperors were still considered as the generals and magistrates of the republic, their wives and mothers, although distinguished by the name of Augusta, were never associated to their personal honours; and a female reign would have appeared an inexpiable prodigy in the eyes of those primitive Romans, who married without love, or loved without delicacy and respect.[5] The haughty Agrippina[6] aspired, indeed, to share the honours of the empire, which she had conferred on her son; but her mad ambition, detested by every citizen who felt for the dignity of Rome, was disappointed by the artful firmness of Seneca and Burrhus. The good sense, or the indifference, of succeeding princes, restrained them from offending the prejudices of their subjects; and it was reserved for the profligate Elagabalus, to discharge the acts of the senate, with the name of his mother Soæmias, who was placed by the side of the consuls, and subscribed, as a regular member, the decrees of the legislative assembly. Her more prudent sister, Mamæa, declined the useless

[5] Metellus Numidicus, the censor, acknowledged to the Roman people in a public oration that had kind Nature allowed us to exist without the help of women, we should be delivered from a very troublesome companion; and he could recommend matrimony, only as the sacrifice of private pleasure to public duty.

[6] [Aqrippina was the mother of Nero. *Ed.*]

and odious prerogative, and a solemn law was enacted, excluding women for ever from the senate, and devoting to the infernal gods, the head of the wretch by whom this sanction should be violated. The substance, not the pageantry, of power was the object of Mamæa's manly ambition. She maintained an absolute and lasting empire over the mind of her son, and in his affection the mother could not brook a rival. Alexander, with her consent, married the daughter of a Patrician; but his respect for his father-in-law, and love for the empress, were inconsistent with the tenderness or interest of Mamæa. The Patrician was executed on the ready accusation of treason, and the wife of Alexander driven with ignominy from the palace, and banished into Africa.

Notwithstanding this act of jealous cruelty, as well as some instances of avarice, with which Mamæa is charged; the general tenor of her administration was equally for the benefit of her son and of the empire. With the approbation of the senate, she chose sixteen of the wisest and most virtuous senators, as a perpetual council of state, before whom every public business of moment was debated and determined. The celebrated Ulpian, equally distinguished by his knowledge of, and his respect for, the laws of Rome, was at their head; and the prudent firmness of this aristocracy restored order and authority to the government. As soon as they had purged the city from foreign superstition and luxury, the remains of the capricious tyranny of Elagabalus, they applied themselves to remove his worthless creatures from every department of public administration, and to supply their places with men of virtue and ability. Learning, and the love of justice, became the only recommendations for civil offices. Valour, and the love of discipline, the only qualifications for military employments.

But the most important care of Mamæa and her wise counsellors, was to form the character of the young emperor, on whose personal qualities the happiness or misery of the Roman world must ultimately depend. The fortunate soil assisted, and even prevented, the hand of cultivation. An excellent understanding soon convinced Alexander of the advantages of virtue, the pleasure of knowledge, and the necessity of labour. A natural mildness and moderation of temper preserved him from the assaults of passion, and the allurements of vice. His unalterable regard for his mother, and his esteem for the wise Ulpian, guarded his inexperienced youth from the poison of flattery.

The simple journal of his ordinary occupations exhibits a pleasing picture of an accomplished emperor, and with some allowance for the difference of manners, might well deserve the imitation of modern princes. Alexander rose early; the first moments of the day were consecrated to private devotion, and his domestic chapel was filled with the images of those heroes, who, by improving or reforming human life, had deserved the grateful reverence of posterity. But, as he deemed the service of mankind the most acceptable worship of the gods, the greatest part of his morning hours was employed in his council, where he discussed public affairs, and determined private causes, with a patience and discretion above his years. The dryness of business was relieved by the charms of literature: and a portion of time was always set apart for his favourite studies of poetry, history, and philosophy. The works of Virgil and Horace, the Republics of Plato and Cicero, formed his taste, enlarged his understanding, and gave him the noblest ideas of man and government. The exercises of the body succeeded to those of the mind; and Alexander, who was tall, active, and robust, surpassed most of his equals in the gymnastic arts. Refreshed by the use of the bath and a slight dinner, he resumed, with new vigour, the business of the day; and, till the hour of supper, the principal meal of the Romans, he was attended by his secretaries, with whom he read and answered the multitude of letters, memorials, and petitions, that must have been addressed to the master of the greatest part of the world. His table was served with the most frugal simpli-

2-3
A detail from Trajan's column showing barbarians storming a Roman fort, and a nineteenth-century painting by Thomas Couture, perhaps inspired by Gibbon's work, illustrating the decadence of the Romans under the Pagan Empire.

city; and whenever he was at liberty to consult his own inclination, the company consisted of a few select friends, men of learning and virtue, amongst whom Ulpian was constantly invited. Their conversation was familiar and instructive; and the pauses were occasionally enlivened by the recital of some pleasing composition, which supplied the place of the dancers, comedians, and even gladiators, so frequently summoned to the tables of the rich and luxurious Romans. The dress of Alexander was plain and modest, his demeanour courteous and affable: at the proper hours his palace was open to all his subjects, but the voice of a crier was heard, as in the Eleusinian mysteries, pronouncing the same salutary admonition; "Let none enter those holy walls, unless he is conscious of a pure and innocent mind."

Such an uniform tenor of life, which left not a moment for vice or folly, is a better proof of the wisdom and justice of Alexander's government, than all the trifling details preserved in the compilation of Lampridius. Since the accession of Commodus, the Roman world had experienced, during a term of forty years, the successive and various vices of four tyrants. From the death of Elagabalus it enjoyed (A.D. 222–235) an auspicious calm of thirteen years. The provinces, relieved from the oppressive taxes invented by Caracalla and his pretended son, flourished in peace and prosperity, under the administration of magistrates, who were convinced by experience, that to deserve the love of the subjects was their best and only method of obtaining the favour of their sovereign. While some gentle restraints were imposed on the innocent luxury of the Roman people, the price of provisions, and the interest of money, were reduced, by the paternal care of Alexander, whose prudent liberality, without distressing the industrious, supplied the wants and amusements of the populace. The dignity, the freedom, the authority of the senate were restored; and every virtuous senator might approach the person of the emperor, without fear, and without a blush.

The name of Antoninus, ennobled by the virtues of Pius and Marcus, had been communicated by adoption to the dissolute Verus, and by descent to the cruel Commodus. It became the honourable appellation of the sons of Severus, was bestowed on young Diadumenianus, and at length prostituted to the infamy of the high priest of Emesa. Alexander, though pressed by the studied, and perhaps sincere, importunity of the senate, nobly refused the borrowed lustre of a name; whilst in his whole conduct he laboured to restore the glories and felicity of the age of the genuine Antonines.

In the civil administration of Alexander, wisdom was enforced by power, and the people, sensible of the public felicity, repaid their benefactor with their love and gratitude. There still remained a greater, a more necessary, but a more difficult enterprise; the reformation of the military order, whose interest and temper, confirmed by long impunity, rendered them impatient of the restraints of discipline, and careless of the blessings of public tranquillity. In the execution of his design the emperor affected to display his love, and to conceal his fear, of the army. The most rigid economy in every other branch of the administration, supplied a fund of gold and silver for the ordinary pay and the extraordinary rewards of the troops. In their marches he relaxed the severe obligation of carrying seventeen days' provision on their shoulders. Ample magazines were formed along the public roads, and as soon as they entered the enemy's country, a numerous train of mules and camels waited on their haughty laziness. As Alexander despaired of correcting the luxury of his soldiers, he attempted, at least, to direct it to objects of martial pomp and ornament, fine horses, splendid armour, and shield enriched with silver and gold. He shared whatever fatigues he was obliged to impose, visited, in person, the sick and wounded, preserved an exact register of their services and his own gratitude, and expressed, on every occasion, the warmest regard for a body of men, whose welfare, as he affected to declare, was so closely connected with that of the state. By the

most gentle arts he laboured to inspire the fierce multitude with a sense of duty, and to restore at least a faint
image of that discipline to which the Romans owed their
empire over so many other nations, as warlike and more
powerful than themselves. But his prudence was vain,
his courage fatal, and the attempt towards a reformation
served only to inflame the ills it was meant to cure.

The Prætorian guards were attached to the youth of
Alexander. They loved him as a tender pupil, whom they
had saved from a tyrant's fury, and placed on the Imperial throne. That amiable prince was sensible of the
obligation; but as his gratitude was restrained within the
limits of reason and justice, they soon were more dissatisfied with the virtues of Alexander, than they had
ever been with the vices of Elagabalus. Their præfect, the
wise Ulpian, was the friend of the laws and of the people;
he was considered as the enemy of the soldiers, and to his
pernicious counsels every scheme of reformation was imputed. Some trifling accident blew up their discontent
into a furious mutiny; and a civil war raged, during three
days, in Rome, whilst the life of that excellent minister
was defended by the grateful people. Terrified, at length,
by the sight of some houses in flames, and by the threats
of a general conflagration, the people yielded with a sigh,
and left the virtuous, but unfortunate, Ulpian to his fate.
He was pursued into the Imperial palace, and massacred
at the feet of his master, who vainly strove to cover him
with the purple, and to obtain his pardon from the inexorable soldiers. Such was the deplorable weakness of
government, that the emperor was unable to revenge his
murdered friend and his insulted dignity, without stoop-
ing to the arts of patience and dissimulation. Epagathus,
the principal leader of the mutiny, was removed from
Rome, by the honourable employment of præfect of
Egypt; from that high rank he was gently degraded to the
government of Crete; and when, at length, his popularity
among the guards was effaced by time and absence,
Alexander ventured to inflict the tardy, but deserved
punishment of his crimes. Under the reign of a just and

virtuous prince, the tyranny of the army threatened with instant death his most faithful ministers, who were suspected of an intention to correct their intolerable disorders. The historian Dion Cassius had commanded the Pannonian legions with the spirit of ancient discipline. Their brethren of Rome, embracing the common cause of military licence, demanded the head of the reformer. Alexander, however, instead of yielding to their seditious clamours, showed a just sense of his merit and services, by appointing him his colleague in the consulship, and defraying from his own treasury the expense of that vain dignity: but as it was justly apprehended, that if the soldiers beheld him with the ensigns of his office, they would revenge the insult in his blood, the nominal first magistrate of the state retired, by the emperor's advice, from the city, and spent the greatest part of his consulship at his villas in Campania.

The lenity of the emperor confirmed the insolence of the troops; the legions imitated the example of the guards, and defended their prerogative of licentiousness with the same furious obstinacy. The administration of Alexander was an unavailing struggle against the corruption of his age. In Illyricum, in Mauritania, in Armenia, in Mesopotamia, in Germany, fresh mutinies perpetually broke out; his officers were murdered, his authority was insulted, and his life at last sacrificed to the fierce discontents of the army. One particular fact well deserves to be recorded, as it illustrates the manners of the troops, and exhibits a singular instance of their return to a sense of duty and obedience. Whilst the emperor lay at Antioch, in his Persian expedition, the particulars of which we shall hereafter relate, the punishment of some soldiers, who had been discovered in the baths of women, excited a sedition in the legion to which they belonged. Alexander ascended his tribunal, and with a modest firmness represented to the armed multitude, the absolute necessity as well as his inflexible resolution of correcting the vices introduced by his impure predecessor, and of maintaining the discipline, which could not be relaxed without the ruin of the Roman name and empire. Their clamours interrupted his mild expostulation. "Reserve your shouts," said the undaunted emperor, "till you take the field against the Persians, the Germans, and the Sarmatians. Be silent in the presence of your sovereign and benefactor, who bestows upon you the corn, the clothing, and the money of the provinces. Be silent, or I shall no longer style you soldiers, but *citizens*,[7] if those indeed who disclaim the laws of Rome deserve to be ranked among the meanest of the people." His menaces inflamed the fury of the legion, and their brandished arms already threatened his person. "Your courage," resumed the intrepid Alexander, "would be more nobly displayed in the field of battle; *me* you may destroy, you cannot intimidate; and the severe justice of the republic would punish your crime, and revenge my death." The legion still persisted in clamorous sedition, when the emperor pronounced with a loud voice, the decisive sentence, "*Citizens!* lay down your arms, and depart in peace to your respective habitations." The tempest was instantly appeased; the soldiers, filled with grief and shame, silently confessed the justice of their punishment and the power of discipline, yielded up their arms and military ensigns, and retired in confusion, not to their camp, but to the several inns of the city. Alexander enjoyed, during thirty days, the edifying spectacle of their repentance; nor did he restore them to their former rank in the army, till he had punished with death those tribunes whose connivance had occasioned the mutiny. The grateful legion served the emperor, whilst living, and revenged him when dead.

The resolutions of the multitude generally depend on a moment; and the caprice of passion might equally determine the seditious legion to lay down their arms at the emperor's feet, or to plunge them into his breast. Perhaps, if the singular transaction had been investigated by the penetration of a philosopher, we should discover the

---

[7] Julius Cæsar had appeased a sedition with the same word *Quirites*; which thus opposed to *Soldiers*, was used in a sense of contempt, and reduced the offenders to the less honourable condition of mere citizens.

secret causes which on that occasion authorised the boldness of the prince, and commanded the obedience of the
troops; and perhaps, if it had been related by a judicious
historian, we should find this action, worthy of Cæsar
himself, reduced nearer to the level of probability and the
common standard of the character of Alexander Severus.
The abilities of that amiable prince seem to have been
inadequate to the difficulties of his situation, the firmness of his conduct inferior to the purity of his intentions.
His virtues, as well as the vices of Elagabalus, contracted
a tincture of weakness and effeminacy from the soft
climate of Syria, of which he was a native; though he
blushed at his foreign origin, and listened with a vain
complacency to the flattering genealogists, who derived
his race from the ancient stock of Roman nobility. The
pride and avarice of his mother cast a shade on the
glories of his reign; and by exacting from his riper years
the same dutiful obedience which she had justly claimed
from his inexperienced youth, Mamæa exposed to public
ridicule, both her son's character and her own. The
fatigues of the Persian war irritated the military discontent; the unsuccessful event degraded the reputation of
the emperor as a general, and even as a soldier. Every
cause prepared, and every circumstance hastened, a revolution, which distracted the Roman empire with a long
series of intestine calamities.

The dissolute tyranny of Commodus, the civil wars
occasioned by his death, and the new maxims of policy
introduced by the house of Severus, had all contributed
to increase the dangerous power of the army, and to
obliterate the faint image of laws and liberty that was
still impressed on the minds of the Romans. This internal
change, which undermined the foundations of the empire, we have endeavoured to explain with some degree of
order and perspicuity. The personal characters of the
emperors, their victories, laws, follies, and fortunes, can
interest us no farther than as they are connected with the
general history of the Decline and Fall of the monarchy.
Our constant attention to that great object will not suffer

us to overlook a most important edict of Antoninus Caracalla, which communicated to all the free inhabitants of the empire the name and privileges of Roman citizens. His unbounded liberality flowed not, however, from the sentiments of a generous mind; it was the sordid result of avarice, and will naturally be illustrated by some observations on the finances of that state, from the victorious ages of the commonwealth to the reign of Alexander Severus.

The siege of Veii in Tuscany, the first considerable enterprise of the Romans, was protracted to the tenth year, much less by the strength of the place than by the unskilfulness of the besiegers. The unaccustomed hardships of so many winter campaigns, at the distance of near twenty miles from home, required more than common encouragements; and the senate wisely prevented the clamours of the people, by the institution of a regular pay for the soldiers, which was levied by a general tribute, assessed according to an equitable proportion on the property of the citizens. During more than two hundred years after the conquest of Veii, the victories of the republic added less to the wealth than to the power of Rome. The states of Italy paid their tribute in military service only, and the vast force both by sea and land, which was exerted in the Punic wars, was maintained at the expense of the Romans themselves. That high-spirited people (such is often the generous enthusiasm of freedom) cheerfully submitted to the most excessive but voluntary burdens, in the just confidence that they should speedily enjoy the rich harvest of their labours. Their expectations were not disappointed. In the course of a few years, the riches of Syracuse, of Carthage, of Macedonia, and of Asia, were brought in triumph to Rome. The treasures of Perseus alone amounted to near two millions sterling, and the Roman people, the sovereign of so many nations, was for ever delivered from the weight of taxes. The increasing revenue of the provinces was found sufficient to defray the ordinary establishment of war and government, and the superfluous mass of gold and silver was deposited in the temple of Saturn, and reserved for any unforeseen emergency of the state.

History has never perhaps suffered a greater or more irreparable injury, than in the loss of the curious register bequeathed by Augustus to the senate, in which that experienced prince so accurately balanced the revenues and expenses of the Roman empire. Deprived of this clear and comprehensive estimate, we are reduced to collect a few imperfect hints from such of the ancients as have accidentally turned aside from the splendid to the more useful parts of history. We are informed that, by the conquests of Pompey, the tributes of Asia were raised from fifty to one hundred and thirty-five millions of drachms; or about four millions and a half sterling. Under the last and most indolent of the Ptolemies, the revenue of Egypt is said to have amounted to twelve thousand five hundred talents; a sum equivalent to more than two millions and a half of our money, but which was afterwards considerably improved by the more exact economy of the Romans, and the increase of the trade of Æthiopia and India. Gaul was enriched by rapine, as Egypt was by commerce, and the tributes of those two great provinces have been compared as nearly equal to each other in value. The ten thousand Euboic or Phœnician talents, about four millions sterling, which vanquished Carthage was condemned to pay within the term of fifty years, were a slight acknowledgment of the superiority of Rome, and cannot bear the least proportion with the taxes afterwards raised both on the lands and on the persons of the inhabitants, when the fertile coast of Africa was reduced into a province.

Spain, by a very singular fatality, was the Peru and Mexico of the old world. The discovery of the rich western continent by the Phœnicians, and the oppression of the simple natives, who were compelled to labour in their own mines for the benefit of strangers, form an exact type of the more recent history of Spanish America. The Phœnicians were acquainted only with the sea-coast of Spain; avarice, as well as ambition, carried the arms of

Rome and Carthage into the heart of the country, and almost every part of the soil was found pregnant with copper, silver, and gold. Mention is made of a mine near Carthagena which yielded every day twenty-five thousand drachms of silver, or about three hundred thousand pounds a year. Twenty thousand pound weight of gold was annually received from the provinces of Asturia, Gallicia, and Lusitania.

We want both leisure and materials to pursue this curious inquiry through the many potent states that were annihilated in the Roman empire. Some notion, however, may be formed of the revenue of the provinces where considerable wealth had been deposited by nature, or collected by man, if we observe the severe attention that was directed to the abodes of solitude and sterility. Augustus once received a petition from the inhabitants of Gyarus, humbly praying that they might be relieved from one-third of their excessive impositions. Their whole tax amounted indeed to no more than one hundred and fifty drachms, or about five pounds; but Gyarus was a little island, or rather a rock, of the Ægean Sea, destitute of fresh water and every necessary of life, and inhabited only by a few wretched fishermen.

From the faint glimmerings of such doubtful and scattered lights we should be inclined to believe, 1st, That (with every fair allowance for the difference of times and circumstances) the general income of the Roman provinces could seldom amount to less than fifteen or twenty millions of our money; and 2ndly, That so ample a revenue must have been fully adequate to all the expenses of the moderate government instituted by Augustus, whose court was the modest family of a private senator, and whose military establishment was calculated for the defence of the frontiers, without any aspiring views of conquest, or any serious apprehension of a foreign invasion.

Notwithstanding the seeming probability of both these conclusions, the latter of them at least is positively disowned by the language and conduct of Augustus. It is not easy to determine whether, on this occasion, he acted as the common father of the Roman world, or as the oppressor of liberty; whether he wished to relieve the provinces, or to impoverish the senate and the equestrian order. But no sooner had he assumed the reins of government than he frequently intimated the insufficiency of the tributes, and the necessity of throwing an equitable proportion of the public burden upon Rome and Italy. In the prosecution of this unpopular design, he advanced, however, by cautious and well-weighed steps. The introduction of customs was followed by the establishment of an excise, and the scheme of taxation was completed by an artful assessment of the real and personal property of the Roman citizens, who had been exempted from any kind of contribution above a century and a half.

I. In a great empire like that of Rome, a natural balance of money must have gradually established itself. It has been already observed, that as the wealth of the provinces was attracted to the capital by the strong hand of conquest and power, so a considerable part of it was restored to the industrious provinces by the gentle influence of commerce and arts. In the reign of Augustus and his successors, duties were imposed on every kind of merchandise, which through a thousand channels flowed to the great centre of opulence and luxury; and in whatsoever manner the law was expressed, it was the Roman purchaser, and not the provincial merchant, who paid the tax. The rate of the customs varied from the eighth to the fortieth part of the value of the commodity; and we have a right to suppose that the variation was directed by the unalterable maxims of policy: that a higher duty was fixed on the articles of luxury than on those of necessity, and that the productions raised or manufactured by the labour of the subjects of the empire, were treated with more indulgence than was shown to the pernicious, or at least the unpopular, commerce of Arabia and India. There is still extant a long but imperfect catalogue of eastern commodities, which about the time of Alexander Severus were subject to the payment of duties; cinnamon, myrrh, pepper, ginger, and the whole tribe of aromatics, a great variety of precious stones, among which the diamond was the most remarkable for its price, and the emerald for its beauty.[8] Parthian and Babylonian leather, cottons, silks, both raw and manufactured, ebony, ivory, and eunuchs. We may observe that the use and value of those effeminate slaves gradually rose with the decline of the empire.

II. The excise, introduced by Augustus after the civil wars, was extremely moderate, but it was general. It seldom exceeded one per cent.; but it comprehended whatever was sold in the markets or by public auction, from the most considerable purchases of lands and houses to those minute objects which can only derive a value from their infinite multitude and daily consumption. Such a tax, as it affects the body of the people, has ever been the occasion of clamour and discontent. An emperor well acquainted with the wants and resources of the state, was obliged to declare by a public edict that the support of the army depended in a great measure on the produce of the excise.

III. When Augustus resolved to establish a permanent military force for the defence of his government against foreign and domestic enemies, he instituted a peculiar treasury for the pay of the soldiers, the rewards of the veterans, and the extraordinary expenses of war. The ample revenue of the excise, though peculiarly appropriated to those uses, was found inadequate. To supply the deficiency, the emperor suggested a new tax of five per cent. on all legacies and inheritances. But the nobles of Rome were more tenacious of property than of freedom. Their indignant murmurs were received by Augustus with his usual temper. He candidly referred the whole business to the senate, and exhorted them to provide for the public service by some other expedient of a less odious nature. They were divided and perplexed. He insinuated

[8] The ancients were unacquainted with the art of cutting diamonds.

to them that their obstinacy would oblige him to *propose* a general land-tax and capitation. They acquiesced in silence. The new imposition on legacies and inheritances was however mitigated by some restrictions. It did not take place unless the object was of a certain value, most probably of fifty or an hundred pieces of gold, nor could it be exacted from the nearest of kin on the father's side. When the rights of nature and poverty were thus secured, it seemed reasonable that a stranger, or a distant relation, who acquired an unexpected accession of fortune, should cheerfully resign a twentieth part of it for the benefit of the state.

Such a tax, plentiful as it must prove in every wealthy community, was most happily suited to the situation of the Romans, who could frame their arbitrary wills, according to the dictates of reason or caprice, without any restraint from the modern fetters of entails and settlements. From various causes the partiality of paternal affection often lost its influence over the stern patriots of the commonwealth and the dissolute nobles of the empire; and if the father bequeathed to his son the fourth part of his estate, he removed all ground of legal complaint. But a rich childless old man was a domestic tyrant, and his power increased with his years and infirmities. A servile crowd, in which he frequently reckoned prætors and consuls, courted his smiles, pampered his avarice, applauded his follies, served his passions, and waited with impatience for his death. The arts of attendance and flattery were formed into a most lucrative science; those who professed it acquired a peculiar appellation; and the whole city, according to the lively descriptions of satire, was divided between two parties, the hunters and their game. Yet, while so many unjust and extravagant wills were every day dictated by cunning, and subscribed by folly, a few were the result of rational esteem and virtuous gratitude. Cicero, who had so often defended the lives and fortunes of his fellow-citizens, was rewarded with legacies to the amount of an hundred and seventy thousand pounds; nor do the friends of the younger Pliny seem to have been less generous to that amiable orator. Whatever was the motive of the testator, the treasury claimed, without distinction, the twentieth part of his estate; and in the course of two or three generations, the whole property of the subject must have gradually passed through the coffers of the state.

In the first and golden years of the reign of Nero, that prince, from a desire of popularity, and perhaps from a blind impulse of benevolence, conceived a wish of abolishing the oppression of the customs and excise. The wisest senators applauded his magnanimity; but they diverted him from the execution of a design, which would have dissolved the strength and resources of the republic. Had it indeed been possible to realise this dream of fancy, such princes as Trajan and the Antonines would surely have embraced with ardour the glorious opportunity of conferring so signal an obligation on mankind. Satisfied, however, with alleviating the public burden, they attempted not to remove it. The mildness and precision of their laws ascertained the rule and measure of taxation, and protected the subject of every rank against arbitrary interpretations, antiquated claims, and the insolent vexation of the farmers of the revenue. For it is somewhat singular that, in every age, the best and wisest of the Roman governors persevered in this pernicious method of collecting the principal branches at least of the excise and customs.

The sentiments, and, indeed, the situation of Caracalla, were very different from those of the Antonines. Inattentive, or rather averse, to the welfare of his people, he found himself under the necessity of gratifying the insatiate avarice, which he had excited in the army. Of the several impositions introduced by Augustus, the twentieth on inheritances and legacies was the most fruitful, as well as the most comprehensive. As its influence was not confined to Rome or Italy, the produce continually increased with the gradual extension of the ROMAN CITY. The new citizens, though charged, on equal terms, with the payment of new taxes, which had not affected them as subjects, derived an ample compensation from the rank they obtained, the privileges they acquired, and the fair prospect of honours and fortune that was thrown open to their ambition. But the favour which implied a distinction, was lost in the prodigality of Caracalla, and the reluctant provincials were compelled to assume the vain title, and the real obligations, of Roman citizens. Nor was the rapacious son of Severus contented with such a measure of taxation, as had appeared sufficient to his moderate predecessors. Instead of a twentieth, he exacted a tenth of all legacies and inheritances; and during his reign (for the ancient proportion was restored after his death) he crushed alike every part of the empire under the weight of his iron sceptre.

When all the provincials became liable to the peculiar impositions of Roman citizens, they seemed to acquire a legal exemption from the tributes which they had paid in their former condition of subjects. Such were not the maxims of government adopted by Caracalla and his pretended son. The old as well as the new taxes were, at the same time, levied in the provinces. It was reserved for the virtue of Alexander to relieve them in a great measure from this intolerable grievance, by reducing the tributes to a thirtieth part of the sum exacted at the time of his accession. It is impossible to conjecture the motive that engaged him to spare so trifling a remnant of the public evil; but the noxious weed, which had not been totally eradicated, again sprang up with the most luxuriant growth, and in the succeeding age darkened the Roman world with its deadly shade. In the course of this history, we shall be too often summoned to explain the land-tax, the capitation, and the heavy contributions of corn, wine, oil, and meat, which were exacted from the provinces for the use of the court, the army, and the capital.

As long as Rome and Italy were respected as the centre of government, a national spirit was preserved by the ancient, and insensibly imbibed by the adopted, citizens.

The principal commands of the army were filled by men who had received a liberal education, were well instructed in the advantages of laws and letters, and who had risen, by equal steps, through the regular succession of civil and military honours. To their influence and example we may partly ascribe the modest obedience of the legions during the two first centuries of the Imperial history.

But when the last enclosure of the Roman constitution was trampled down by Caracalla, the separation of professions gradually succeeded to the distinction of ranks. The more polished citizens of the internal provinces were alone qualified to act as lawyers and magistrates. The rougher trade of arms was abandoned to the peasants and barbarians of the frontiers, who knew no country but their camp, no science but that of war, no civil laws, and scarcely those of military discipline. With bloody hands, savage manners, and desperate resolutions, they sometimes guarded, but much oftener subverted, the throne of the emperors.

CHAPTER III

AURELIAN
AND THE RESTORATION
OF THE EMPIRE

*Alexander Severus was murdered in 235 A.D.
by mutinous soldiers. His death inaugurated the
most anarchical period of the Roman Empire.
Alexander's murderer and supplanter was a barbarian general, Maximin, an uncouth tyrant who
reigned with his army for three years. A revolt in
Africa, supported by the senate in Rome, then
brought to the throne the octogenarian proconsul
of Africa, Gordian, "a last and valuable remains
of the happy age of the Antonines", together with
his son. Though the revolt was defeated in Africa,
and the two Gordians were killed, the senate continued its resistance. It elected new emperors and
declared war on Maximin, who was murdered by
Praetorian guards at Aquileia, as he was invading
Italy. But the Praetorians would not accept the
"emperors of the senate" and murdered them both.
Thereafter one short-lived emperor after another
was raised and destroyed by the soldiers, who
offered to their successive generals "only the
alternative of death or the purple". Meanwhile
the empire was attacked from without by the
Goths in Europe and by the revived Persian empire of the Sassanian dynasty in Asia. The emperor Decius was destroyed by the former (251)
and the emperor Valerian captured and imprisoned by the latter (260). While Valerian's son
Gallienus reigned in Italy, nineteen "tyrants"*

contested his authority and dominated different parts of the Empire. One of these "tyrants" was the senator Tetricus, who reigned as "emperor" in Gaul, Spain and Britain; another was Odenathus, "one of the noblest and most opulent senators of Palmyra", who effectively resisted both the authority of Rome and the power of Persia.

In his tenth chapter, Gibbon describes the "twenty years of shame and misfortune" from 248 to 268 A.D. In his eleventh, which is here printed entire, he describes the beginning of the revival associated with the "Illyrian Emperors", and, in particular, the restoration of the unity of the empire by Aurelian (270–275).

Under the deplorable reigns of Valerian and Gallienus the empire was oppressed and almost destroyed by the soldiers, the tyrants, and the barbarians. It was saved by a series of great princes, who derived their obscure origin from the martial provinces of Illyricum. Within a period of about thirty years, Claudius, Aurelian, Probus, Diocletian and his colleagues, triumphed over the foreign and domestic enemies of the state, re-established, with the military discipline, the strength of the frontiers, and deserved the glorious title of Restorers of the Roman world.

The removal of an effeminate tyrant made way for a succession of heroes. The indignation of the people imputed all their calamities to Gallienus, and the far greater part were, indeed, the consequence of his dissolute manners and careless administration. He was even destitute of a sense of honour, which so frequently supplies the absence of public virtue; and as long as he was permitted to enjoy the possession of Italy, a victory of the barbarians, the loss of a province, or the rebellion of a general, seldom disturbed the tranquil course of his pleasures. At length a considerable army, stationed on the Upper Danube, invested with the Imperial purple their leader Aureolus, who, disdaining a confined and barren reign over the mountains of Rhætia, passed the Alps, occupied Milan, threatened Rome, and challenged Gallienus to dispute in the field the sovereignty of Italy. The emperor, provoked by the insult, and alarmed by the instant danger, suddenly exerted that latent vigour which sometimes broke through the indolence of his temper. Forcing himself from the luxury of the palace, he appeared in arms at the head of his legions, and advanced beyond the Po to encounter his competitor. The corrupted name of Pontirolo still preserves the memory of a bridge over the Adda, which, during the action, must have proved an object of the utmost importance to both armies. The Rhætian usurper, after receiving a total defeat and a dangerous wound, retired into Milan. The siege of that great city was immediately formed; the walls were battered with every engine in use among the ancients; and Aureolus, doubtful of his internal strength and hopeless of foreign succours, already anticipated the fatal consequences of unsuccessful rebellion.

His last resource was an attempt to seduce the loyalty of the besiegers. He scattered libels through their camp, inviting the troops to desert an unworthy master, who sacrificed the public happiness to his luxury, and the lives of his most valuable subjects to the slightest suspicions. The arts of Aureolus diffused fears and discontent among the principal officers of his rival. A conspiracy was formed by Heraclianus, the Prætorian præfect, by Marcian, a general of rank and reputation, and by Cecrops, who commanded a numerous body of Dalmatian guards. The death of Gallienus was resolved, and, notwithstanding their desire of first terminating the siege of Milan, the extreme danger which accompanied every moment's delay obliged them to hasten the execution of their daring purpose. At a late hour of the night, but while the emperor still protracted the pleasures of the table, an alarm was suddenly given that Aureolus, at the head of all his forces, had made a desperate sally from the town; Gallienus, who was never deficient in personal bravery, started from his silken coach, and, without allowing himself time either to put on his armour or to assemble his guards, he mounted on horseback and rode full speed towards the supposed place of the attack. Encompassed by his declared or concealed enemies, he soon, amidst the nocturnal tumult, received a mortal dart from an uncertain hand. Before he expired, a patriotic sentiment rising in the mind of Gallienus induced him to name a deserving successor, and it was his last request that the Imperial ornaments should be delivered to Claudius, who then commanded a detached army in the neighbourhood of Pavia. The report at least was diligently propagated, and the order cheerfully obeyed by the conspirators, who had already agreed to place Claudius on the throne. On the first news of the emperor's death the troops expressed some suspicion and resentment, till the one was removed and the other assuaged by a donative of twenty pieces of gold to each soldier. They then ratified the election and acknowledged the merit of their new sovereign.

The obscurity which covered the origin of Claudius, though it was afterwards embellished by some flattering fictions, sufficiently betrays the meanness of his birth. We can only discover that he was a native of one of the provinces bordering on the Danube, that his youth was spent in arms, and that his modest valour attracted the favour and confidence of Decius. The senate and people already considered him as an excellent officer, equal to the most important trusts, and censured the inattention of Valerian, who suffered him to remain in the subordinate station of a tribune. But it was not long before that emperor distinguished the merit of Claudius, by declaring him general and chief of the Illyrian frontier, with the command of all the troops in Thrace, Mæsia, Dacia, Pannonia, and Dalmatia, the appointments of the præfect of Egypt, the establishment of the proconsul of Africa, and the sure prospect of the consulship. By his victories over the Goths he deserved from the senate the honour of a statue, and excited the jealous apprehensions of Gallienus. It was impossible that a soldier could esteem so dissolute a sovereign, nor is it easy to conceal a just contempt. Some unguarded expressions which dropped from Claudius were officiously transmitted to the royal ear. The emperor's answer to an officer of confidence describes in very lively colours his own character and that of the times. "There is not anything capable of giving me more serious concern than the intelligence contained in your last despatch, that some malicious suggestions have indisposed towards us the mind of our friend and *parent* Claudius. As you regard your allegiance, use every means to appease his resentment, but conduct your negotiation with secrecy; let it not reach the knowledge of the Dacian troops; they are already provoked, and it might inflame their fury. I myself have sent him some presents: be it your care that he accept them with pleasure. Above all, let him not suspect that I am made acquainted with his imprudence. The fear of my anger might urge him to desperate counsels." The presents which accompanied this humble epistle, in which the monarch solicited a reconciliation with his discontented subject, consisted of a considerable sum of money, a splendid wardrobe, and a valuable service of silver and gold plate. By such arts Gallienus softened the indignation and dispelled the fears of his Illyrian general, and during the remainder of that reign the formidable sword of Claudius was always drawn in the cause of a master whom he despised. At last, indeed, he received from the conspirators the bloody purple of Gallienus; but he had been absent from their camp and counsels; and however he might applaud the deed, we may candidly presume that he was innocent of the knowledge of it. When Claudius ascended the throne he was about fifty-four years of age.

The siege of Milan was still continued, and Aureolus soon discovered that the success of his artifices had only raised up a more determined adversary. He attempted to negotiate with Claudius a treaty of alliance and partition. "Tell him," replied the intrepid emperor, "that such proposals should have been made to Gallienus; *he*, perhaps, might have listened to them with patience, and accepted a colleague as despicable as himself." This stern refusal, and a last unsuccessful effort, obliged Aureolus to yield the city and himself to the discretion of the conqueror. The judgment of the army pronounced him worthy of death, and Claudius, after a feeble resistance, consented to the execution of the sentence. Nor was the zeal of the senate less ardent in the cause of their new sovereign. They ratified, perhaps with a sincere transport of zeal, the election of Claudius; and as his predecessor had shown himself the personal enemy of their order, they exercised, under the name of justice, a severe revenge against his friends and family. The senate was permitted to discharge the ungrateful office of punishment, and the emperor reserved for himself the pleasure and merit of obtaining by his intercession a general act of indemnity.

Such ostentatious clemency discovers less of the real character of Claudius than a trifling circumstance in which he seems to have consulted only the dictates of his heart. The frequent rebellions of the provinces had involved almost every person in the guilt of treason, almost every estate in the case of confiscation; and Gallienus often displayed his liberality by distributing among his officers the property of his subjects. On the accession of Claudius, an old woman threw herself at his feet and complained that a general of the late emperor had obtained an arbitrary grant of her patrimony. This general was Claudius himself, who had not entirely escaped the contagion of the times. The emperor blushed at the reproach, but deserved the confidence which she had reposed in his equity. The confession of his fault was accompanied with immediate and ample restitution.

In the arduous task which Claudius had undertaken of restoring the empire to its ancient splendour, it was first necessary to revive among his troops a sense of order and obedience. With the authority of a veteran commander, he represented to them that the relaxation of discipline had introduced a long train of disorders, the effects of which were at length experienced by the soldiers themselves; that a people ruined by oppression, and indolent from despair, could no longer supply a numerous army with the means of luxury, or even of subsistence; that the danger of each individual had increased with the despotism of the military order, since princes who tremble on the throne will guard their safety by the instant sacrifice of every obnoxious subject. The emperor expatiated on the mischiefs of a lawless caprice, which the soldiers could only gratify at the expense of their own blood, as their seditious elections had so frequently been followed by civil wars, which consumed the flower of the legions either in the field of battle or in the cruel abuse of victory. He painted in the most lively colours the exhausted state of the treasury, the desolation of the provinces, the disgrace of the Roman name, and the insolent triumph of rapacious barbarians. It was against those barbarians, he declared, that he intended to point the first effort of their arms. Tetricus might reign for a while over the West, and even Zenobia might preserve the dominion of the East. These usurpers were his personal adversaries, nor could he think of indulging any private resentment till he had saved an empire whose impending ruin would, unless it was timely prevented, crush both the army and the people.

The various nations of Germany and Sarmatia who fought under the Gothic standard had already collected an armament more formidable than any which had yet issued from the Euxine. On the banks of the Dniester, one of the great rivers that discharge themselves into that sea, they constructed a fleet of two thousand, or even of six thousand vessels; numbers which, however incredible they may seem, would have been insufficient to transport their pretended army of three hundred and twenty thousand barbarians. Whatever might be the real strength of the Goths, the vigour and success of the expedition were not adequate to the greatness of the preparations. In their passage through the Bosphorus the unskilful pilots were overpowered by the violence of the current; and while the multitude of their ships were crowded in a narrow channel, many were dashed against each other or against the shore. The barbarians made several descents on the coasts both of Europe and Asia; but the open country was already plundered, and they were repulsed with shame and loss from the fortified cities which they assaulted. A spirit of discouragement and division arose in the fleet, and some of their chiefs sailed away towards the islands of Crete and Cyprus; but the main body, pursuing a more steady course, anchored at length near the foot of Mount Athos, and assaulted the city of Thessalonica, the wealthy capital of all the Macedonian provinces. Their attacks, in which they displayed a fierce but artless bravery, were soon interrupted by the rapid approach of Claudius, hastening to a scene of action that deserved the presence of a warlike prince at the head of the remaining powers of the empire. Impatient for battle, the Goths immediately broke up their camp, relinquished the siege of Thessalonica, left their navy at the foot of Mount Athos, traversed the hills of Macedonia, and pressed forwards to engage the last defence of Italy.

We still possess an original letter addressed by Claudius to the senate and people on this memorable occasion. "Conscript fathers," says the emperor, "know that three hundred and twenty thousand Goths have invaded the Roman territory. If I vanquish them, your gratitude will reward my services. Should I fall, remember that I am the successor of Gallienus. The whole republic is fatigued and exhausted. We shall fight after Valerian, after Ingenuus, Regillianus, Lollianus, Posthumus, Celsus, and a thousand others, whom a just contempt for Gallienus provoked into rebellion. We are in want of darts, of spears, and of shields. The strength of the empire, Gaul, and Spain, are usurped by Tetricus; and we blush to acknowledge that the archers of the East serve under the banners of Zenobia. Whatever we shall perform will be sufficiently great." The melancholy firmness of this epistle announces a hero careless of his fate, conscious of his danger, but still deriving a well-grounded hope from the resources of his own mind.

The event surpassed his own expectations and those

of the world. By the most signal victories he delivered the empire from this host of barbarians, and was distinguished by posterity under the glorious appellation of the Gothic Claudius. The imperfect historians of an irregular war do not enable us to describe the order and circumstances of his exploits; but, if we could be indulged in the allusion, we might distribute into three acts this memorable tragedy. I. The decisive battle was fought near Naissus, a city of Dardania. The legions at first gave way, oppressed by numbers and dismayed by misfortunes. Their ruin was inevitable, had not the abilities of their emperor prepared a seasonable relief. A large detachment, rising out of the secret and difficult passes of the mountains, which by his order they had occupied, suddenly assailed the rear of the victorious Goths. The favourable instant was improved by the activity of Claudius. He revived the courage of his troops, restored their ranks, and pressed the barbarians on every side. Fifty thousand men are reported to have been slain in the battle of Naissus. Several large bodies of barbarians, covering their retreat with a movable fortification of waggons, retired, or rather escaped, from the field of slaughter. II. We may presume that some insurmountable difficulty—the fatigue, perhaps, or the disobedience, of the conquerors—prevented Claudius from completing in one day the destruction of the Goths. The war was diffused over the provinces of Mæsia, Thrace, and Macedonia, and its operations drawn out into a variety of marches, surprises, and tumultuary engagements, as well by sea as by land. When the Romans suffered any loss, it was commonly occasioned by their own cowardice or rashness; but the superior talents of the emperor, his perfect knowledge of the country, and his judicious choice of measures as well as officers, assured on most occasions the success of his arms. The immense booty, the fruit of so many victories, consisted for the greater part of cattle and slaves. A select body of the Gothic youth was received among the Imperial troops; the remainder was sold into servitude; and so considerable was the number of female captives that every soldier obtained as his share two or three women. A circumstance from which we may conclude that the invaders entertained some designs of settlement as well as of plunder; since even in a naval expedition they were accompanied by their families. III. The loss of their fleet, which was either taken or sunk, had intercepted the retreat of the Goths. A vast circle of Roman posts, distributed with skill, supported with firmness, and gradually closing towards a common centre, forced the barbarians into the most inaccessible parts of Mount Hæmus, where they found a safe refuge, but a very scanty subsistence. During the course of a rigorous winter, in which they were besieged by the emperor's troops, famine and pestilence, desertion and the sword, continually diminished the imprisoned multitude. On the return of spring nothing appeared in arms except a hardy and desperate band, the remnant of that mighty host which had embarked at the mouth of the Dniester.

The pestilence which swept away such numbers of the barbarians at length proved fatal to their conqueror. After a short but glorious reign of two years, Claudius expired at Sirmium, amidst the tears and acclamations of his subjects. In his last illness he convened the principal officers of the state and army, and in their presence recommended Aurelian, one of his generals, as the most deserving of the throne, and the best qualified to execute the great design which he himself had been permitted only to undertake. The virtues of Claudius, his valour, affability, justice, and temperance, his love of fame and of his country, place him in that short list of emperors who added lustre to the Roman purple. Those virtues, however, were celebrated with peculiar zeal and complacency by the courtly writers of the age of Constantine, who was the great-grandson of Crispus, the elder brother of Claudius. The voice of flattery was soon taught to repeat that the gods, who so hastily had snatched Claudius from the earth, rewarded his merit and piety by the perpetual establishment of the empire in his family.

Notwithstanding these oracles, the greatness of the Flavian family (a name which it had pleased them to assume) was deferred above twenty years, and the elevation of Claudius occasioned the immediate ruin of his brother Quintilius, who possessed not sufficient moderation or courage to descend into the private station to which the patriotism of the late emperor had condemned him. Without delay or reflection he assumed the purple at Aquileia, where he commanded a considerable force; and though his reign lasted only seventeen days, he had time to obtain the sanction of the senate and to experience a mutiny of the troops. As soon as he was informed that the great army of the Danube had invested the well-known valour of Aurelian with Imperial power, he sunk under the fame and merit of his rival; and, ordering his veins to be opened, prudently withdrew himself from the unequal contest.

The general design of this work will not permit us minutely to relate the actions of every emperor after he ascended the throne, much less to deduce the various fortunes of his private life. We shall only observe that the father of Aurelian was a peasant of the territory of Sirmium, who occupied a small farm, the property of Aurelius, a rich senator. His warlike son enlisted in the troops as a common soldier, successively rose to the rank of a centurion, a tribune, the præfect of a legion, the inspector of the camp, the general, or, as it was then called, the duke of a frontier; and at length, during the Gothic war, exercised the important office of commander-in-chief of the cavalry. In every station he distinguished himself by matchless valour, rigid discipline, and successful conduct. He was invested with the consulship by the emperor Valerian, who styles him, in the pompous language of that age, the deliverer of Illyricum, the restorer of Gaul, and the rival of the Scipios. At the recommendation of Valerian, a senator of the highest rank and merit, Ulpius Crinitus, whose blood was derived from the same source as that of Trajan, adopted the Pannonian peasant, gave him his daughter in marriage, and relieved with his ample fortune the honourable poverty which Aurelian had preserved inviolate.

The reign of Aurelian lasted only four years and about nine months; but every instant of that short period was filled by some memorable achievement. He put an end to the Gothic war, chastised the Germans who invaded Italy, recovered Gaul, Spain, and Britain out of the hands of Tetricus, and destroyed the proud monarchy which Zenobia had erected in the East on the ruins of the afflicted empire.

It was the rigid attention of Aurelian even to the minutest articles of discipline which bestowed such uninterrupted success on his arms. His military regulations are contained in a very concise epistle to one of his inferior officers, who is commanded to enforce them, as he wishes to become a tribune, or as he is desirous to live. Gaming, drinking, and the arts of divination were severely prohibited. Aurelian expected that his soldiers should be modest, frugal, and laborious; that their armour should be constantly kept bright, their weapons sharp, their clothing and horses ready for immediate service; that they should live in their quarters with chastity and sobriety, without damaging the corn-fields, without stealing even a sheep, a fowl, or a bunch of grapes, without exacting from their landlords either salt, or oil, or wood. "The public allowance," continues the emperor, "is sufficient for their support; their wealth should be collected from the spoil of the enemy, not from the tears of the provincials." A single instance will serve to display the rigour, and even cruelty, of Aurelian. One of the soldiers had seduced the wife of his host. The guilty wretch was fastened to two trees forcibly drawn towards each other, and his limbs were torn asunder by their sudden separation. A few such examples impressed a salutary consternation. The punishments of Aurelian were terrible; but he had seldom occasion to punish more than once the same offence. His own conduct gave a sanction to his laws, and the seditious legions dreaded a chief who had learned to obey, and who was worthy to command.

The death of Claudius had revived the fainting spirit of the Goths. The troops which guarded the passes of Mount Hæmus and the banks of the Danube had been drawn away by the apprehension of a civil war; and it seems probable that the remaining body of the Gothic and Vandalic tribes embraced the favourable opportunity, abandoned their settlements of the Ukraine, traversed the rivers, and swelled with new multitudes the destroying host of their countrymen. Their united numbers were at length encountered by Aurelian, and the bloody and doubtful conflict ended only with the approach of night. Exhausted by so many calamities, which they had mutually endured and inflicted during a twenty years' war, the Goths and the Romans consented to a lasting and beneficial treaty. It was earnestly solicited by the barbarians, and cheerfully ratified by the legions, to whose suffrage the prudence of Aurelian referred the decision of that important question. The Gothic nation engaged to supply the armies of Rome with a body of two thousand auxiliaries, consisting entirely of cavalry, and stipulated in return an undisturbed retreat, with a regular market as far as the Danube, provided by the emperor's care, but at their own expense. The treaty was observed with such religious fidelity that, when a party of five hundred men straggled from the camp in quest of plunder, the king or general of the barbarians commanded that the guilty leader should be apprehended and shot to death with darts, as a victim devoted to the sanctity of their engagements. It is, however, not unlikely that the precaution of Aurelian, who had exacted as hostages the sons and daughters of the Gothic chiefs, contributed something to this pacific temper. The youths he trained in the exercise of arms, and near his own person; to the damsels he gave a liberal and Roman education, and, by bestowing them in marriage on some of his principal officers, gradually introduced between

the two nations the closest and most endearing con-
nections.

But the most important condition of peace was understood rather than expressed in the treaty. Aurelian withdrew the Roman forces from Dacia, and tacitly
relinquished that great province to the Goths and
Vandals. His manly judgment convinced him of the solid
advantages, and taught him to despise the seeming disgrace, of thus contracting the frontiers of the monarchy.
The Dacian subjects, removed from those distant possessions which they were unable to cultivate or defend,
added strength and populousness to the southern side of
the Danube. A fertile territory, which the repetition of
barbarous inroads had changed into a desert, was yielded
to their industry, and a new province of Dacia still,
preserved the memory of Trajan's conquests. The old
country of that name detained, however, a considerable
number of its inhabitants, who dreaded exile more than
a Gothic master. These degenerate Romans continued to
serve the empire, whose allegiance they had renounced,
by introducing among their conquerors the first notions
of agriculture, the useful arts, and the conveniences of
civilised life. An intercourse of commerce and language
was gradually established between the opposite banks of
the Danube; and, after Dacia became an independent
state, it often proved the firmest barrier of the empire
against the invasions of the savages of the North. A sense
of interest attached these more settled barbarians to the
alliance of Rome, and a permanent interest very frequently ripens into sincere and useful friendship. This
various colony, which filled the ancient province, and
was insensibly blended into one great people, still acknowledged the superior renown and authority of the
Gothic tribe, and claimed the fancied honour of a Scan-
dinavian origin. At the same time the lucky, though
accidental, resemblance of the name of Getæ infused
among the credulous Goths a vain persuasion that, in a
remote age, their own ancestors, already seated in the
Dacian provinces, had received the instructions of

Zamolxis, and checked the victorious arms of Sesostris and Darius.

While the vigorous and moderate conduct of Aurelian restored the Illyrian frontier, the nation of the Alemanni violated the conditions of peace which either Gallienus had purchased, or Claudius had imposed, and, inflamed by their impatient youth, suddenly flew to arms. Forty thousand horse appeared in the field, and the numbers of the infantry doubled those of the cavalry. The first objects of their avarice were a few cities of the Rhætian frontier; but their hopes soon rising with success, the rapid march of the Alemanni traced a line of devastation from the Danube to the Po.

The emperor was almost at the same time informed of the irruption, and of the retreat of the barbarians. Collecting an active body of troops, he marched with silence and celerity along the skirts of the Hercynian forest; and the Alemanni, laden with the spoils of Italy, arrived at the Danube, without suspecting that on the opposite bank, and in an advantageous post, a Roman army lay concealed and prepared to intercept their return. Aurelian indulged the fatal security of the barbarians, and permitted about half their forces to pass the river without disturbance and without precaution. Their situation and astonishment gave him an easy victory; his skilful conduct improved the advantage. Disposing the legions in a semicircular form, he advanced the two horns of the crescent across the Danube, and, wheeling them on a sudden towards the centre, enclosed the rear of the German host. The dismayed barbarians, on whatsoever side they cast their eyes, beheld with despair a wasted country, a deep and rapid stream, a victorious and implacable enemy.

Reduced to this distressed condition, the Alemanni no longer disdained to sue for peace. Aurelian received their ambassadors at the head of his camp, and with every circumstance of martial pomp that could display the greatness and discipline of Rome. The legions stood to their arms in well-ordered ranks and awful silence. The

principal commanders, distinguished by the ensigns of
their rank, appeared on horseback on either side of the
Imperial throne. Beside the throne the consecrated images of the emperor and his predecessors,[1] the golden
eagles, and the various titles of the legions, engraved in
letters of gold, were exalted in the air on lofty pikes
covered with silver. When Aurelian assumed his seat,
his manly grace and majestic figure taught the barbarians to revere the person as well as the purple of their
conqueror. The ambassadors fell prostrate on the ground
in silence. They were commanded to rise, and permitted
to speak. By the assistance of interpreters they extenu-
ated their perfidy, magnified their exploits, expatiated on
the vicissitudes of fortune and the advantages of peace,
and, with an ill-timed confidence, demanded a large
subsidy as the price of the alliance which they offered to
the Romans. The answer of the emperor was stern and
imperious. He treated their offer with contempt, and
their demand with indignation; reproached the barbarians that they were as ignorant of the arts of war as of the
laws of peace; and finally dismissed them with the choice
only of submitting to his unconditional mercy, or await-
ing the utmost severity of his resentment. Aurelian had
resigned a distant province to the Goths; but it was
dangerous to trust or to pardon these perfidious barbarians, whose formidable power kept Italy itself in
perpetual alarm.

Immediately after this conference it should seem that
some unexpected emergency required the emperor's
presence in Pannonia. He devolved on his lieutenants
the care of finishing the destruction of the Alemanni,
either by the sword, or by the surer operation of famine.
But an active despair has often triumphed over the
indolent assurance of success. The barbarians, finding it
impossible to traverse the Danube and the Roman camp,

---

[1] The emperor Claudius was certainly of the number; but we are
ignorant how far this mark of respect was extended; if to Cæsar and
Augustus, it must have produced a very awful spectacle; a long line
of masters of the world.

broke through the posts in their rear, which were more feebly or less carefully guarded; and with incredible diligence, but by a different road, returned towards the mountains of Italy. Aurelian, who considered the war as totally extinguished, received the mortifying intelligence of the escape of the Alemanni, and of the ravage which they already committed in the territory of Milan. The legions were commanded to follow, with as much expedition as those heavy bodies were capable of exerting, the rapid flight of an enemy, whose infantry and cavalry moved with almost equal swiftness. A few days afterwards the emperor himself marched to the relief of Italy, at the head of a chosen body of auxiliaries (among whom were the hostages and cavalry of the Vandals), and of all the Prætorian guards who had served in the wars on the Danube.

As the light troops of the Alemanni had spread themselves from the Alps to the Apennine, the incessant vigilance of Aurelian and his officers was exercised in the discovery, the attack, and the pursuit of the numerous detachments. Notwithstanding this desultory war, three considerable battles are mentioned, in which the principal force of both armies was obstinately engaged. The success was various. In the first, fought near Placentia, the Romans received so severe a blow that, according to the expression of a writer extremely partial to Aurelian, the immediate dissolution of the empire was apprehended. The crafty barbarians, who had lined the woods, suddenly attacked the legions in the dusk of the evening, and, it is most probable, after the fatigue and disorder of a long march. The fury of their charge was irresistible; but at length, after a dreadful slaughter, the patient firmness of the emperor rallied his troops, and restored, in some degree, the honour of his arms. The second battle was fought near Fano in Umbria; on the spot which, five hundred years before, had been fatal to the brother of Hannibal. Thus far the successful Germans had advanced along the Æmilian and Flaminian way, with a design of sacking the defenceless mistress of

4
Zenobia, the Queen of Palmyra and the East, who was defeated
and brought to Rome by Aurelian.

the world. But Aurelian, who, watchful for the safety of Rome, still hung on their rear, found in this place the decisive moment of giving them a total and irretrievable defeat. The flying remnant of their host was exterminated in a third and last battle near Pavia; and Italy was delivered from the inroads of the Alemanni.

Fear has been the original parent of superstition, and every new calamity urges trembling mortals to deprecate the wrath of their invisible enemies. Though the best hope of the republic was in the valour and conduct of Aurelian, yet such was the public consternation, when the barbarians were hourly expected at the gates of Rome, that, by a decree of the senate, the Sibylline books were consulted. Even the emperor himself, from a motive either of religion or of policy, recommended this salutary measure, chided the tardiness of the senate, and offered to supply whatever expense, whatever animals, whatever captives of any nation, the gods should require. Notwithstanding this liberal offer, it does not appear that any human victims expiated with their blood the sins of the Roman people. The Sibylline books enjoined ceremonies of a more harmless nature—processions of priests in white robes, attended by a chorus of youths and virgins; lustrations of the city and adjacent country; and sacrifices, whose powerful influence disabled the barbarians from passing the mystic ground on which they had been celebrated. However puerile in themselves, these superstitious arts were subservient to the success of the war; and if, in the decisive battle of Fano, the Alemanni fancied they saw an army of spectres combating on the side of Aurelian, he received a real and effectual aid from this imaginary reinforcement.

But whatever confidence might be placed in ideal ramparts, the experience of the past, and the dread of the future, induced the Romans to construct fortifications of a grosser and more substantial kind. The seven hills of Rome had been surrounded, by the successors of Romulus, with an ancient wall of more than thirteen miles. The vast enclosure may seem disproportioned to the strength and numbers of the infant state. But it was necessary to secure an ample extent of pasture and arable land against the frequent and sudden incursions of the tribes of Latium, the perpetual enemies of the republic. With the progress of Roman greatness, the city and its inhabitants gradually increased, filled up the vacant space, pierced through the useless walls, covered the field of Mars, and, on every side, followed the public highways in long and beautiful suburbs. The extent of the new walls, erected by Aurelian, and finished in the reign of Probus, was magnified by popular estimation to near fifty, but is reduced by accurate measurement to about twenty-one miles. It was a great but a melancholy labour, since the defence of the capital betrayed the decline of the monarchy. The Romans of a more prosperous age, who trusted to the arms of the legions the safety of the frontier camps, were very far from entertaining a suspicion that it would ever become necessary to fortify the seat of empire against the inroads of the barbarians.

The victory of Claudius over the Goths, and the success of Aurelian against the Alemanni, had already restored to the arms of Rome their ancient superiority over the barbarous nations of the North. To chastise domestic tyrants, and to reunite the dismembered parts of the empire, was a task reserved for the second of those warlike emperors. Though he was acknowledged by the senate and people, the frontiers of Italy, Africa, Illyricum, and Thrace, confined the limits of his reign. Gaul, Spain, and Britain, Egypt, Syria, and Asia Minor, were still possessed by two rebels, who alone, out of so numerous a list, had hitherto escaped the dangers of their situation; and to complete the ignominy of Rome, these rival thrones had been usurped by women.

A rapid succession of monarchs had arisen and fallen in the provinces of Gaul. The rigid virtues of Posthumus served only to hasten his destruction. After suppressing a competitor who had assumed the purple at Mentz, he refused to gratify his troops with the plunder of the rebellious city; and, in the seventh year of his reign, became the vicitim of their disappointed avarice. The death of Victorinus, his friend and associate, was occasioned by a less worthy cause. The shining accomplishments of that prince were stained by a licentious passion, which he indulged in acts of violence, with too little regard to the laws of society, or even to those of love. He was slain at Cologne, by a conspiracy of jealous husbands, whose revenge would have appeared more justifiable had they spared the innocence of his son. After the murder of so many valiant princes, it is somewhat remarkable that a female for a long time controlled the fierce legions of Gaul, and still more singular that she was the mother of the unfortunate Victorinus. The arts and treasures of Victoria enabled her successively to place Marius and Tetricus on the throne, and to reign with a manly vigour under the name of those dependent emperors. Money of copper, of silver, and of gold, was coined in her name, she assumed the titles of Augusta and Mother of the Camps: her power ended only with her life; but her life was perhaps shortened by the ingratitude of Tetricus.

When, at the instigation of his ambitious patroness, Tetricus assumed the ensigns of royalty, he was governor of the peaceful province of Aquitaine, an employment suited to his character and education. He reigned four or five years over Gaul, Spain, and Britain, the slave and sovereign of a licentious army, whom he dreaded, and by whom he was despised. The valour and fortune of Aurelian at length opened the prospect of a deliverance. He ventured to disclose his melancholy situation, and conjured the emperor to hasten to the relief of his unhappy rival. Had this secret correspondence reached the ears of the soldiers, it would most probably have cost Tetricus his life; nor could he resign the sceptre of the West without committing an act of treason against himself. He affected the appearances of a civil war, led his forces into the field against Aurelian, posted them in the most disadvantageous manner, betrayed his own counsels to the enemy, and with a few chosen friends deserted in the beginning of the action. The rebel legions, though disordered and dismayed by the unexpected treachery of their chief, defended themselves with desperate valour, till they were cut in pieces almost to a man, in this bloody and memorable battle, which was fought near Châlons in Champagne. The retreat of the irregular auxiliaries, Franks and Batavians, whom the conqueror soon compelled or persuaded to repass the Rhine, restored the general tranquillity, and the power of Aurelian was acknowledged from the wall of Antoninus to the Columns of Hercules.

As early as the reign of Claudius, the city of Autun, alone and unassisted, had ventured to declare against the legions of Gaul. After a siege of seven months they stormed and plundered that unfortunate city, already wasted by famine. Lyons, on the contrary, had resisted with obstinate disaffection the arms of Aurelian. We read of the punishment of Lyons, but there is not any mention of the rewards of Autun. Such, indeed, is the policy of civil war: severely to remember injuries, and to forget the most important services. Revenge is profitable, gratitude is expensive.

Aurelian had no sooner secured the person and provinces of Tetricus than he turned his arms against Zenobia, the celebrated queen of Palmyra and the East. Modern Europe has produced several illustrious women who have sustained with glory the weight of empire; nor is our own age destitute of such distinguished characters. But if we except the doubtful achievements of Semiramis, Zenobia is perhaps the only female whose superior genius broke through the servile indolence imposed on her sex by the climate and manners of Asia. She claimed her descent from the Macedonian kings of Egypt, equalled in beauty her ancestor Cleopatra, and far surpassed that princess in chastity[2] and valour. Zenobia was esteemed the most lovely as well as the most heroic of her sex. She was of a dark complexion (for in speaking of a lady these trifles become important). Her teeth were

[2] She never admitted her husband's embraces but for the sake of posterity. If her hopes were baffled, in the ensuing *month* she reiterated the experiment.

of a pearly whiteness, and her large black eyes sparkled with uncommon fire, tempered by the most attractive sweetness. Her voice was strong and harmonious. Her manly understanding was strengthened and adorned by study. She was not ignorant of the Latin tongue, but possessed in equal perfection the Greek, the Syriac, and the Egyptian languages. She had drawn up for her own use an epitome of oriental history, and familiarly compared the beauties of Homer and Plato under the tuition of the sublime Longinus.[3]

This accomplished woman gave her hand to Odenathus, who, from a private station, raised himself to the dominion of the East. She soon became the friend and companion of a hero. In the intervals of war Odenathus passionately delighted in the exercise of hunting; he pursued with ardour the wild beasts of the desert, lions, panthers, and bears; and the ardour of Zenobia in that dangerous amusement was not inferior to his own. She had inured her constitution to fatigue, disdained the use of a covered carriage, generally appeared on horseback in a military habit, and sometimes marched several miles on foot at the head of the troops. The success of Odenathus was in a great measure ascribed to her incomparable prudence and fortitude. Their splendid victories over the Great King, whom they twice pursued as far as the gates of Ctesiphon, laid the foundations of their united fame and power. The armies which they commanded, and the provinces which they had saved, acknowledged not any other sovereigns than their invincible chiefs. The senate and people of Rome revered a stranger who had avenged their captive emperor, and even the insensible son of Valerian accepted Odenathus for his legitimate colleague.

After a successful expedition against the Gothic plunderers of Asia, the Palmyrenian prince returned to the city of Emesa in Syria. Invincible in war, he was there

---

[3]|Longinus, the minister of Zenobia, was generally believed, in Gibbon's time, to be the author of a famous Greek work of literary criticism, *On the Sublime*. The work is now believed to be by another, and earlier hand. *Ed.*]

cut off by domestic treason, and his favourite amusement of hunting was the cause, or at least the occasion,
of his death. His nephew, Mæonius, presumed to dart his
javelin before that of his uncle; and though admonished
of his error, repeated the same insolence. As a monarch,
and as a sportsman, Odenathus was provoked, took away
his horse, a mark of ignominy among the barbarians, and
chastised the rash youth by a short confinement. The
offence was soon forgot, but the punishment was remembered; and Mæonius, with a few daring associates, assassinated his uncle in the midst of a great entertainment.
Herod, the son of Odenathus, though not of Zenobia, a
young man of a soft and effeminate temper, was killed
with his father. But Mæonius obtained only the pleasure
of revenge by this bloody deed. He had scarcely time to
assume the title of Augustus before he was sacrificed by
Zenobia to the memory of her husband.

With the assistance of his most faithful friends, she
immediately filled the vacant throne, and governed with
manly counsels Palmyra, Syria, and the East, above five
years. By the death of Odenathus, that authority was at
an end which the senate had granted him only as a personal distinction; but his martial widow, disdaining both
the senate and Gallienus, obliged one of the Roman
generals who was sent against her to retreat into Europe,
with the loss of his army and his reputation. Instead of
the little passions which so frequently perplex a female
reign, the steady administration of Zenobia was guided
by the most judicious maxims of policy. If it was expedient to pardon, she could calm her resentment; if it
was necessary to punish, she could impose silence on the
voice of pity. Her strict economy was accused of avarice;
yet on every proper occasion she appeared magnificent
and liberal. The neighbouring states of Arabia, Armenia,
and Persia, dreaded her enmity, and solicited her
alliance. To the dominions of Odenathus, which extended
from the Euphrates to the frontiers of Bithynia, his
widow added the inheritance of her ancestors, the popu-

lous and fertile kingdom of Egypt. The emperor Claudius acknowledged her merit, and was content that, while *he* pursued the Gothic war, *she* should assert the dignity of the empire in the East. The conduct, however, of Zenobia was attended with some ambiguity; nor is it unlikely that she had conceived the design of erecting an independent and hostile monarchy. She blended with the popular manners of Roman princes the stately pomp of the courts of Asia, and exacted from her subjects the same adoration that was paid to the successors of Cyrus. She bestowed on her three sons a Latin education, and often showed them to the troops adorned with the Imperial purple. For herself she reserved the diadem, with the splendid but doubtful title of Queen of the East.

When Aurelian passed over into Asia, against an adversary whose sex alone could render her an object of contempt, his presence restored obedience to the province of Bithynia, already shaken by the arms and intrigues of Zenobia. Advancing at the head of his legions, he accepted the submission of Ancyra, and was admitted into Tyana, after an obstinate siege, by the help of a perfidious citizen. The generous though fierce temper of Aurelian abandoned the traitor to the rage of the soldiers: a superstitious reverence induced him to treat with lenity the countrymen of Apollonius the philosopher.[4] Antioch was deserted on his approach, till the emperor, by his salutary edicts, recalled the fugitives, and granted a general pardon to all who, from necessity rather than choice, had been engaged in the service of the Palmyrenian queen. The unexpected mildness of such a conduct reconciled the minds of the Syrians, and, as far as the gates of Emesa, the wishes of the people seconded the terror of his arms.

Zenobia would have ill deserved her reputation had she indolently permitted the emperor of the West to

---

[4]Apollonius of Tyana was born about the same time as Jesus Christ. His life (that of the former) is related in so fabulous a manner by his disciples, that we are at a loss to discover whether he was a sage, an imposter, or a fanatic.

approach within an hundred miles of her capital. The fate of the East was decided in two great battles; so similar in almost every circmustance, that we can scarcely distinguish them from each other, except by observing that the first was fought near Antioch, and the second near Emesa. In both the queen of Palmyra animated the armies by her presence, and devolved the execution of her orders on Zabdas, who had already signalised his military talents by the conquest of Egypt. The numerous forces of Zenobia consisted for the most part of light archers, and of heavy cavalry clothed in complete steel. The Moorish and Illyrian horse of Aurelian were unable to sustain the ponderous charge of their antagonists. They fled in real or affected disorder, engaged the Palmyrenians in a laborious pursuit, harassed them by a desultory combat, and at length discomfited this impenetrable but unwieldy body of cavalry. The light infantry, in the meantime, when they had exhausted their quivers, remaining without protection against a closer onset, exposed their naked sides to the swords of the legions. Aurelian had chosen these veteran troops who were usually stationed on the Upper Danube, and whose valour had been severely tried in the Alemannic war. After the defeat of Emesa, Zenobia found it impossible to collect a third army. As far as the frontier of Egypt, the nations subject to her empire had joined the standard of the conqueror, who detached Probus, the bravest of his generals, to possess himself of the Egyptian provinces. Palmyra was the last resource of the widow of Odenathus. She retired within the walls of her capital, made every preparation for a vigorous resistance, and declared, with the intrepidity of a heroine, that the last moment of her reign and of her life should be the same.

Amid the barren deserts of Arabia a few cultivated spots rise like islands out of the sandy ocean. Even the name of Tadmor, or Palmyra, by its signification in the Syriac as well as in the Latin language, denoted the multitude of palm-trees which afforded shade and verdure to that temperate region. The air was pure, and the soil, watered by some invaluable springs, was capable of producing fruits as well as corn. A place possessed of such singular advantages, and situated at a convenient distance between the Gulf of Persia and the Mediterranean, was soon frequented by the caravans which conveyed to the nations of Europe a considerable part of the rich commodites of India. Palmyra insensibly increased into an opulent and independent city, and, connecting the Roman and the Parthian monarchies by the mutual benefits of commerce, was suffered to observe an humble neutrality, till at length, after the victories of Trajan, the little republic sunk into the bosom of Rome, and flourished more than one hundred and fifty years in the subordinate though honourable rank of a colony. It was during that peaceful period, if we may judge from a few remaining inscriptions, that the wealthy Palmyrians constructed those temples, palaces, and porticos of Grecian architecture, whose ruins, scattered over an extent of several miles, have deserved the curiosity of our travellers. The elevation of Odenathus and Zenobia appeared to reflect new splendour on their country, and Palmyra, for a while, stood forth the rival of Rome; but the competition was fatal, and ages of prosperity were sacrificed to a moment of glory.

In his march over the sandy desert between Emesa and Palmyra, the emperor Aurelian was perpetually harassed by the Arabs; nor could he always defend his army, and especially his baggage, from those flying troops of active and daring robbers, who watched the moment of surprise, and eluded the slow pursuit of the legions. The siege of Palmyra was an object far more difficult and important, and the emperor, who, with incessant vigour, pressed the attacks in person, was himself wounded with a dart. "The Roman people," says Aurelian, in an original letter, "speak with contempt of the war which I am waging against a woman. They are ignorant both of the character and of the power of Zenobia. It is impossible to enumerate her warlike preparations, of stones, of arrows, and of every species of missile weapons. Every part of the walls is provided with two or three *balistæ*, and artificial fires are thrown from her military engines. The fear of punishment has armed her with a desperate courage. Yet still I trust in the protecting deities of Rome, who have hitherto been favourable to all my undertakings." Doubtful, however, of the protection of the gods, and of the event of the siege, Aurelian judged it more prudent to offer terms of an advantageous capitulation; to the queen, a splendid retreat; to the citizens, their ancient privileges. His proposals were obstinately rejected, and the refusal was accompanied with insult.

The firmness of Zenobia was supported by the hope that in a very short time famine would compel the Roman army to repass the desert; and by the reasonable expectation that the kings of the East, and particularly the Persian monarch, would arm in the defence of the most natural ally. But fortune and the perseverance of Aurelian overcame every obstacle. The death of Sapor, which happened about this time, distracted the councils of Persia, and the inconsiderable succours that attempted to relieve Palmyra were easily intercepted either by the arms or the liberality of the emperor. From every part of Syria a regular succession of convoys safely arrived in the camp, which was increased by the return of Probus with his victorious troops from the conquest of Egypt. It was then that Zenobia resolved to fly. She mounted the fleetest of her dromedaries, and had already reached the banks of the Euphrates, about sixty miles from Palmyra, when she was overtaken by the pursuit of Aurelian's light horse, seized and brought back a captive to the feet of the emperor. Her capital soon afterwards surrendered, and was treated with unexpected lenity. The arms, horses, and camels, with an immense treasure of gold, silver, silk, and precious stones, were all delivered to the conqueror, who, leaving only a garrison of six hundred archers, returned to Emesa, and employed some time in the distribution of rewards and punishments at the end of so memorable a war, which restored to the obedience of

Rome those provinces that had renounced their allegiance since the captivity of Valerian.

When the Syrian queen was brought into the presence of Aurelian, he sternly asked her, How she had presumed to rise in arms against the emperors of Rome? The answer of Zenobia was a prudent mixture of respect and firmness. "Because I disdained to consider as Roman emperors an Aureolus or a Gallienus. You alone I acknowledge as my conqueror and my sovereign." But as female fortitude is commonly artificial, so it is seldom steady or consistent. The courage of Zenobia deserted her in the hour of trial; she trembled at the angry clamours of the soldiers, who called aloud for her immediate execution, forgot the generous despair of Cleopatra, which she had proposed as her model, and ignominiously purchased life by the sacrifice of her fame and her friends. It was to their counsels, which governed the weakness of her sex, that she imputed the guilt of her obstinate resistance; it was on their heads that she directed the vengeance of the cruel Aurelian. The fame of Longinus, who was included among the numerous and perhaps innocent victims of her fear, will survive that of the queen who betrayed, or the tyrant who condemned him. Genius and learning were incapable of moving a fierce unlettered soldier, but they had served to elevate and harmonise the soul of Longinus. Without uttering a complaint, he calmly followed the executioner, pitying his unhappy mistress, and bestowing comfort on his afflicted friends.

Returning from the conquest of the East, Aurelian had already crossed the Straits which divide Europe from Asia, when he was provoked by the intelligence that the Palmyrenians had massacred the governor and garrison which he had left among them, and again erected the standard of revolt. Without a moment's deliberation, he once more turned his face towards Syria. Antioch was alarmed by his rapid approach, and the helpless city of Palmyra felt the irresistible weight of his resentment. We have a letter of Aurelian himself, in which he acknowledges that old men, women, children, and peasants, had been involved in that dreadful execution, which should have been confined to armed rebellion; and although his principal concern seems directed to the re-establishment of a temple of the Sun, he discovers some pity for the remnant of the Palmyrenians, to whom he grants the permission of rebuilding and inhabiting their city. But it is easier to destroy than to restore. The seat of commerce, of arts, and of Zenobia, gradually sunk into an obscure town, a trifling fortress, and at length a miserable village. The present citizens of Palmyra, consisting of thirty or forty families, have erected their mud-cottages within the spacious court of a magnificent temple.

Another and a last labour still awaited the indefatig-able Aurelian; to suppress a dangerous though obscure rebel, who, during the revolt of Palmyra, had arisen on the banks of the Nile. Firmus, the friend and ally, as he proudly styled himself, of Odenathus and Zenobia, was no more than a wealthy merchant of Egypt. In the course of his trade to India he had formed very intimate con-nections with the Saracens and the Blemmyes, whose situation, on either coast of the Red Sea, gave them an easy introduction into the Upper Egypt. The Egyptians he inflamed with the hope of freedom, and, at the head of their furious multitude, broken into the city of Alexan-dria, where he assumed the Imperial purple, coined money, published edicts, and raised an army, which, as he vainly boasted, he was capable of maintaining from the sole profits of his paper trade. Such troops were a feeble defence against the approach of Aurelian; and it seems almost unnecessary to relate that Firmus was routed, taken, tortured, and put to death. Aurelian might now congratulate the senate, the people, and himself, that, in little more than three years, he had restored universal peace and order to the Roman world.

Since the foundation of Rome no general had more nobly deserved a triumph than Aurelian; nor was a triumph ever celebrated with superior pride and magnifi-cence. The pomp was opened by twenty elephants, four royal tigers, and above two hundred of the most curious animals from every climate of the North, the East, and the South. They were followed by sixteen hundred gladiators, devoted to the cruel amusement of the amphitheatre. The wealth of Asia, the arms and ensigns of so many conquered nations, and the magnificent plate and wardrobe of the Syrian queen, were disposed in exact symmetry or artful disorder. The ambassadors of the most remote parts of the earth, of Æthiopia, Arabia, Persia, Bactriana, India, and China, all remarkable by their rich or singular dresses, displayed the fame and power of the Roman emperor, who exposed likewise to the public view the presents that he had received, and particularly a great number of crowns of gold, the offerings of grateful cities. The victories of Aurelian were attested by the long train of captives who reluctantly attended his triumph—Goths, Vandals, Sarmatians, Alemanni, Franks, Gauls, Syrians, and Egyptians. Each people was distinguished by its peculiar inscription, and the title of Amazons was bestowed on ten martial heroines of the Gothic nation who had been taken in arms.[5] But every eye, disregarding the crowd of captives, was fixed on the emperor Tetricus and the queen of the East. The former, as well as his son, whom he had created Augustus, was dressed in Gallic trousers,[6] a saffron tunic, and a robe of purple. The beauteous figure of Zenobia was confined by fetters of gold; a slave supported the gold chain which encircled her neck, and she almost fainted under the intolerable weight of jewels. She preceded on foot the magnificent chariot in which she once hoped to enter the gates of Rome. It was followed by two other chariots, still more sumptuous, of Odenathus and

[5] Among barbarous nations women have often combated by the side of their husbands. But it is *almost* impossible that a society of Amazons should ever have existed either in the old or new world.

[6] The use of *braccæ*, breeches, or trousers, was still considered in Italy as a Gallic and barbarian fashion. The Romans, however, had made great advances towards it. To encircle the legs and thighs with *fasciæ*, or bands, was understood, in the time of Pompey and Horace, to be a proof of ill health or effeminacy. In the age of Trajan the custom was confined to the rich and luxurious. It gradually was adopted by the meanest of the people.

of the Persian monarch. The triumphal car of Aurelian (it had formerly been used by a Gothic king) was drawn, on this memorable occasion, either by four stags or by four elephants. The most illustrious of the senate, the people, and the army closed the solemn procession. Unfeigned joy, wonder, and gratitude swelled the acclamations of the multitude; but the satisfaction of the senate was clouded by the appearance of Tetricus; nor could they suppress a rising murmur that the haughty emperor should thus expose to public ignominy the person of a Roman and a magistrate.

But, however, in the treatment of his unfortunate rivals Aurelian might indulge his pride, he behaved towards them with a generous clemency which was seldom exercised by the ancient conquerors. Princes who, without success, had defended their throne or freedom, were frequently strangled in prison as soon as the triumphal pomp ascended the Capitol. These usurpers, whom their defeat had convicted of the crime of treason, were permitted to spend their lives in affluence and honourable repose. The emperor presented Zenobia with an elegant villa at Tibur or Tivoli, about twenty miles from the capital; the Syrian queen insensibly sunk into a Roman matron, her daughters married into noble families, and her race was not yet extinct in the fifth century. Tetricus and his son were reinstated in their rank and fortunes. They erected on the Cælian hill a magnificent palace, and, as soon as it was finished invited Aurelian to supper. On his entrance he was agreeably surprised with a picture which represented their singular history. They were delineated offering to the emperor a civic crown and the sceptre of Gaul, and again receiving at his hands the ornaments of the senatorial dignity. The father was afterwards invested with the government of Lucania, and Aurelian, who soon admitted the abdicated monarch to his friendship and conversation, familiarly asked him, Whether it were not more desirable to administer a province of Italy than to reign beyond the Alps? The son long continued a respectable member of the senate; nor was there any one of the Roman nobility more esteemed by Aurelian, as well as by his successors.

So long and so various was the pomp of Aurelian's triumph, that, although it opened with the dawn of day, the slow majesty of the procession ascended not the Capitol before the ninth hour; and it was already dark when the emperor returned to the palace. The festival was protracted by theatrical representations, the games of the circus, the hunting of wild beasts, combats of gladiators, and naval engagements. Liberal donatives were distributed to the army and people, and several institutions, agreeable or beneficial to the city, contributed to perpetuate the glory of Aurelian. A considerable portion of his oriental spoils was consecrated to the gods of Rome; the Capitol, and every other temple, glittered with the offerings of his ostentatious piety; and the temple of the Sun alone received above fifteen thousand pounds of gold. This last was a magnificent structure, erected by the emperor on the side of the Quirinal hill, and dedicated, soon after the triumph, to that deity whom Aurelian adored as the parent of his life and fortunes. His mother had been an inferior priestess in a chapel of the Sun; a peculiar devotion to the god of Light was a sentiment which the fortunate peasant imbibed in his infancy; and every step of his elevation, every victory of his reign, fortified superstition by gratitude.

The arms of Aurelian had vanquished the foreign and domestic foes of the republic. We are assured that, by his salutary rigour, crimes and factions, mischievous arts and pernicious connivance, the luxuriant growth of a feeble and oppressive government, were eradicated throughout the Roman world. But if we attentively reflect how much swifter is the progress of corruption than its cure, and if we remember that the years abandoned to public disorders exceeded the months allotted to the martial reign of Aurelian, we must confess that a few short intervals of peace were insufficient for the arduous work of reformation. Even his attempt to restore the integrity of the coin was opposed by a formidable insurrection. The emperor's vexation breaks out in one of his private letters: "Surely," says he, "the gods have decreed that my life should be a perpetual warfare. A sedition within the walls has just now given birth to a very serious civil war. The workmen of the mint, at the instigation of Felicissimus, a slave to whom I had intrusted an employment in the finances, have risen in rebellion. They are at length suppressed; but seven thousand of my soldiers have been slain in the contest, of those troops whose ordinary station is in Dacia and the camps along the Danube." Other writers, who confirm the same fact, add likewise, that it happened soon after Aurelian's triumph; that the decisive engagement was fought on the Cælian hill; that the workmen of the mint had adulterated the coin; and that the emperor restored the public credit, by delivering out good money in exchange for the bad, which the people were commanded to bring into the treasury.

We might content ourselves with relating this extraordinary transaction, but we cannot dissemble how much, in its present form, it appears to us inconsistent and incredible. The debasement of the coin is indeed well suited to the administration of Gallienus; nor is it unlikely that the instruments of the corruption might dread the inflexible justice of Aurelian. But the guilt, as well as the profit, must have been confined to a few; nor is it easy to conceive by what arts they could arm a people whom they had injured against a monarch whom they had betrayed. We might naturally expect that such miscreants should have shared the public detestation with the informers and the other ministers of oppression; and that the reformation of the coin should have been an action equally popular with the destruction of those obsolete accounts which, by the emperor's order, were burnt in the forum of Trajan. In an age when the principles of commerce were so imperfectly understood, the most desirable end might perhaps be effected by harsh and injudicious means; but a temporary grievance of such a nature can scarcely excite and support a serious civil war. The repetition of intolerable taxes, imposed either on the land or on the necessaries of life, may at last provoke those who will not, or who cannot, relinquish their country. But the case is far otherwise in every operation which, by whatsoever expedients, restores the just value of money. The transient evil is soon obliterated by the permanent benefit, the loss is divided among multitudes; and if a few wealthy individuals experience a sensible diminution of treasure, with their riches they at the same time lose the degree of weight and importance which they derived from the possession of them. However Aurelian might choose to disguise the real cause of the insurrection, his reformation of the coin could furnish only a faint pretence to a party already powerful and discontented. Rome, though deprived of freedom, was distracted by faction. The people, towards whom the emperor, himself a plebeian, always expressed a peculiar fondness, lived in perpetual dissension with the senate, the equestrian order, and the Prætorian guards. Nothing less than the firm though secret conspiracy of those orders, of the authority of the first, the wealth of the second, and the arms of the third, could have displayed a strength capable of contending in battle with the veteran legions of the Danube, which, under the conduct of a martial sovereign, had achieved the conquest of the West and of the East.

Whatever was the cause or the object of this rebellion, imputed with so little probability to the workmen of the mint, Aurelian used his victory with unrelenting rigour. He was naturally of a severe disposition. A peasant and a soldier, his nerves yielded not easily to the impressions of sympathy, and he could sustain without emotion the sight of tortures and death. Trained from his earliest youth in the exercise of arms, he set too small a value on the life of a citizen, chastised by military execution the slightest offences, and transferred the stern discipline of the camp into the civil administration of the laws. His love of justice often became a blind and furious passion; and, whenever he deemed his own or the public safety endangered, he disregarded the rules of evidence and the proportion of punishments. The unprovoked rebellion with which the Romans rewarded his services exasperated his haughty spirit. The noblest families of the capital were involved in the guilt or suspicion of this dark conspiracy. A hasty spirit of revenge urged the bloody prosecution, and it proved fatal to one of the nephews of the emperor. The executioners (if we may use the expression of a contemporary poet) were fatigued, the prisons were crowded, and the unhappy senate lamented the death or absence of its most illustrious members. Nor was the pride of Aurelian less offensive to that assembly than his cruelty. Ignorant or impatient of the restraints of civil institutions, he disdained to hold his power by any other title than that of the sword, and governed by right of conquest an empire which he had saved and subdued.

It was observed by one of the most sagacious of the Roman princes, that the talents of his predecessor Aurelian were better suited to the command of an army than to the government of an empire.[7] Conscious of the character in which nature and experience had enabled him to excel, he again took the field a few months after his triumph. It was expedient to exercise the restless temper of the legions in some foreign war, and the Persian monarch, exulting in the shame of Valerian, still braved with impunity the offended majesty of Rome. At the head of an army, less formidable by its numbers than by its discipline and valour, the emperor advanced as far as the Straits which divide Europe from Asia. He there experienced that the most absolute power is a weak defence against the effects of despair. He had threatened one of his secretaries who was accused of extortion, and it was known that he seldom threatened in vain. The last hope which remained for the criminal was to involve some of the principal officers of the army in his danger, or at least in his fears. Artfully counterfeiting his mas-

[7] It was the observation of Diocletian.

ter's hand, he showed them, in a long and bloody list, their own names devoted to death. Without suspecting or examining the fraud, they resolved to secure their lives by the murder of the emperor. On his march, between Byzantium and Heraclea, Aurelian was suddenly attacked by the conspirators, whose stations gave them a right to surround his person, and, after a short resistance, fell by the hand of Mucapor, a general whom he had always loved and trusted. He died regretted by the army, detested by the senate, but universally acknowledged as a warlike and fortunate prince, the useful though severe reformer of a degenerate state.

CHAPTER IV

DIOCLETIAN

Aurelian was succeeded by a series of short-lived rulers. The ablest of them was another "Illyrian" peasant, Probus, who "in a short reign of about six years, equalled the fame of ancient heroes and restored peace and order to every province of the Roman world". But the greatest of the "Illyrian" emperors was Diocletian, who, in a long reign (284–305 A.D.), so transformed the whole system of government that he could be described by Gibbon as a second Augustus, "the founder of a new empire". Modern historians agree with Gibbon, and distinguish the "Principate", created by Augustus, which had foundered in the anarchy of the third century, from the "Lower Empire", created by Diocletian and christianised by Constantine.

Diocletian was born a Dalmatian slave. He rose in the army, and was elected emperor by the army, at Chalcedon, to succeed the emperor Numerian, who had died there on his return from a Persian campaign. Once in power Diocletian recognised that a single, centralised government could no longer defend an empire threatened on all its frontiers, and he divided his authority between two "Augusti" or senior emperors, himself and Maximian, and two junior emperors, or "Cæsars", Galerius and Constantius. This combination successfully defended the frontiers on all

sides, recovered Britain from a usurper, sup-
pressed revolt in Gaul and Africa, vindicated the
Rome protectorate over Armenia, and imposed a
victorious and lasting settlement on the king of
Persia, extending the Roman frontier beyond the
Tigris.

Having reigned for twenty years, triumphed
over all his enemies, reorganised the government
of the empire, transferred its capital from Rome
to Nicomedia in Asia, and discarded the old re-
publican forms for the declared absolutism of the
Persian monarchy, Diocletian condescended to
visit Rome for a ceremonial triumph; after which
he astonished the world by abdicating his throne
and retiring to his native city of Spalato in Dal-
matia. The following passage, from chapter XIII,
describes Diocletian's triumph and abdication,
and summarises his achievement.

The arduous work of rescuing the distressed empire
from tyrants and barbarians had now been completely
achieved by a succession of Illyrian peasants. As soon as
Diocletian entered into the twentieth year of his reign,
he celebrated that memorable era, as well as the success
of his arms, by the pomp of a Roman triumph. Maximian,
the equal partner of his power, was his only companion
in the glory of that day. The two Cæsars had fought and
conquered, but the merit of their exploits was ascribed,
according to the rigour of ancient maxims, to the auspicious influence of their fathers and emperors. The
triumph of Diocletian and Maximian was less magnificent, perhaps, than those of Aurelian and Probus, but it
was dignified by several circumstances of superior fame
and good fortune. Africa and Britain, the Rhine, the
Danube, and the Nile, furnished their respective trophies;
but the most distinguished ornament was of a more
singular nature, a Persian victory followed by an important conquest. The representations of rivers, mountains,
and provinces were carried before the Imperial car. The

images of the captive wives, the sisters, and the children of the Great King afforded a new and grateful spectacle to the vanity of the people. In the eyes of posterity this triumph is remarkable by a distinction of a less honourable kind. It was the last that Rome ever beheld. Soon after this period the emperors ceased to vanquish, and Rome ceased to be the capital of the empire.

The spot on which Rome was founded had been consecrated by ancient ceremonies and imaginary miracles. The presence of some god, or the memory of some hero, seemed to animate every part of the city, and the empire of the world had been promised to the Capitol. The native Romans felt and confessed the power of this agreeable illusion. It was derived from their ancestors, had grown up with their earliest habits of life, and was protected, in some measure, by the opinion of political utility. The form and the seat of government were intimately blended together, nor was it esteemed possible to transport the one without destroying the other. But the sovereignty of the capital was gradually annihilated in the extent of conquest; the provinces rose to the same level, and the vanquished nations acquired the name and privileges, without imbibing the partial affections, of Romans. During a long period, however, the remains of the ancient constitution and the influence of custom preserved the dignity of Rome. The emperors, though perhaps of African or Illyrian extraction, respected their adopted country as the seat of their power and the centre of their extensive dominions. The emergencies of war very frequently required their presence on the frontiers; but Diocletian and Maximian were the first Roman princes who fixed, in time of peace, their ordinary residence in the provinces; and their conduct, however it might be suggested by private motives, was justified by very specious considerations of policy. The court of the emperor of the West was, for the most part, established at Milan, whose situation, at the foot of the Alps, appeared far more convenient than that of Rome, for the important purpose of watching the motions of the barbarians of Germany.

Milan soon assumed the splendour of an Imperial city. The houses are described as numerous and well built; the manners of the people as polished and liberal. A circus, a theatre, a mint, a palace, baths, which bore the name of their founder Maximian; porticoes adorned with statues, and a double circumference of walls, contributed to the beauty of the new capital; nor did it seem oppressed even by the proximity of Rome. To rival the majesty of Rome was the ambition likewise of Diocletian, who employed his leisure and the wealth of the East in the embellishment of Nicomedia, a city placed on the verge of Europe and Asia, almost at an equal distance between the Danube and the Euphrates. By the taste of the monarch, and at the expense of the people, Nicomedia acquired, in the space of a few years, a degree of magnificence which might appear to have required the labour of ages, and became inferior only to Rome, Alexandria, and Antioch in extent or populousness. The life of Diocletian and Maximian was a life of action, and a considerable portion of it was spent in camps, or in their long and frequent marches; but whenever the public business allowed them any relaxation, they seem to have retired with pleasure to their favourite residences of Nicomedia and Milan. Till Diocletian, in the twentieth year of his reign, celebrated his Roman triumph, it is extremely doubtful whether he ever visited the ancient capital of the empire. Even on that memorable occasion his stay did not exceed two months. Disgusted with the licentious familiarity of the people, he quitted Rome with precipitation thirteen days before it was expected that he should have appeared in the senate invested with the ensigns of the consular dignity.

The dislike expressed by Diocletian towards Rome and Roman freedom was not the effect of momentary caprice, but the result of the most artful policy. That crafty prince had framed a new system of Imperial government, which was afterwards completed by the family of Constantine; and as the image of the old constitution was religiously preserved in the senate, he resolved to deprive that order of its small remains of power and consideration. We may recollect, about eight years before the elevation of Diocletian, the transient greatness and the ambitious hopes of the Roman senate. As long as that enthusiasm prevailed, many of the nobles imprudently displayed their zeal in the cause of freedom; and after the successors of Probus had withdrawn their countenance from the republican party, the senators were unable to disguise their impotent resentment. As the sovereign of Italy, Maximian was intrusted with the care of extinguishing this troublesome rather than dangerous spirit, and the task was perfectly suited to his cruel temper. The most illustrious members of the senate, whom Diocletian always affected to esteem, were involved, by his colleague, in the accusation of imaginary plots; and the possession of an elegant villa, or a well-cultivated estate, was interpreted as a convincing evidence of guilt. The camp of the Prætorians, which had so long oppressed, began to protect, the majesty of Rome; and as those haughty troops were conscious of the decline of their power, they were naturally disposed to unite their strength with the authority of the senate. By the prudent measures of Diocletian, the numbers of the Prætorians were insensibly reduced, their privileges abolished, and their place supplied by two faithful legions of Illyricum, who, under the new titles of Jovians and Herculians, were appointed to perform the service of the Imperial guards. But the most fatal though secret wound which the senate received from the hands of Diocletian and Maximian was inflicted by the inevitable operation of their absence. As long as the emperors resided at Rome, that assembly might be oppressed, but it could scarcely be neglected. The successors of Augustus exercised the power of dictating whatever laws their wisdom or caprice might suggest; but those laws were ratified by the sanction of the senate. The model of ancient freedom was preserved in its deliberations and decrees; and wise princes, who respected the prejudices of the Roman people, were in some measure obliged to assume the language and behaviour suitable to the general and first magistrate of the republic. In the armies and in the provinces they displayed the dignity of monarchs; and when they fixed their residence at a distance from the capital, they for ever laid aside the dissimulation which Augustus had recommended to his successors. In the exercise of the legislative as well as the executive power, the sovereign advised with his ministers, instead of consulting the great council of the nation. The name of the senate was mentioned with honour till the last period of the empire; the vanity of its members were still flattered with honorary distinctions; but the assembly which had so long been the source, and so long the instrument of power, was respectfully suffered to sink into oblivion. The senate of Rome, losing all connection with the Imperial court and the actual constitution, was left a venerable but useless monument of antiquity on the Capitoline hill.

When the Roman princes had lost sight of the senate and of their ancient capital, they easily forgot the origin and nature of their legal power. The civil offices of consul, of proconsul, of censor, and of tribune, by the union of which it had been formed, betrayed to the people its republican extraction. These modest titles were laid aside; and if they still distinguished their high station by the appellation of Emperor, or IMPERATOR, that word was understood in a new and more dignified sense, and no longer denoted the general of the Roman armies, but the sovereign of the Roman world. The name of Emperor, which was at first of a military nature, was associated with another of a more servile kind. The epithet of DOMINUS, or Lord, in its primitive signification, was expressive not of the authority of a prince over his subjects, or of a commander over his soldiers, but of the despotic power of a master over his domestic slaves. Viewing it in that odious light, it had been rejected with abhorrence by the first Cæsars. Their resistance insensibly became more feeble, and the name less odious; till at length the style of *our Lord and Emperor* was not only bestowed by flattery, but was regularly admitted into the laws and public monuments. Such lofty epithets were sufficient to elate and satisfy the most excessive vanity; and if the successors of Diocletian still declined the title of King, it seems to have been the effect not so much of their moderation as of their delicacy. Wherever the Latin tongue was in use (and it was the language of government throughout the empire), the Imperial title, as it was peculiar to themselves, conveyed a more respectable idea than the name of king, which they must have shared with an hundred barbarian chieftains; or which at the best, they could derive only from Romulus, or from Tarquin. But the sentiments of the East were very different from those of the West. From the earliest period of history, the sovereigns of Asia had been celebrated in the Greek language by the title of BASILEUS, or King; and since it was considered as the first distinction among men, it was soon employed by the servile provincials of the East in their humble addresses to the Roman throne. Even the attributes, or at least the titles, of the DIVINITY were usurped by Diocletian and Maximian, who transmitted them to a succession of Christian emperors. Such extravagant compliments, however, soon lose their impiety by losing their meaning; and when the ear is once accustomed to the sound, they are heard with indifference as vague though excessive professions of respect.

From the time of Augustus to that of Diocletian, the Roman princes, conversing in a familiar manner among their fellow-citizens, were saluted only with the same respect that was usually paid to senators and magistrates. Their principal distinction was the Imperial or military robe of purple; whilst the senatorial garment was marked by a broad, and the equestrian by a narrow, band or stripe of the same honourable colour. The pride, or rather the policy, of Diocletian, engaged that artful prince to introduce the stately magnificence of the court of Persia. He ventured to assume the diadem, an ornament detested by the Romans as the odious ensign of royalty, and the use of which had been considered as the most desperate

5
Diocletian, the great "Illyrian" emperor who transformed the
system of government of the empire, and who later harshly
persecuted the Christians.

act of the madness of Caligula. It was no more than a broad white fillet set with pearls, which encircled the emperor's head. The sumptuous robes of Diocletian and his successors were of silk and gold; and it is remarked with indignation that even their shoes were studded with the most precious gems. The access to their sacred person was every day rendered more difficult by the institution of new forms and ceremonies. The avenues of the palace were strictly guarded by the various *schools*, as they began to be called, of domestic officers. The interior apartments were intrusted to the jealous vigilance of the eunuchs; the increase of whose numbers and influence was the most infallible symptom of the progress of despotism. When a subject was at length admitted to the Imperial presence, he was obliged, whatever might be his rank, to fall prostrate on the ground, and to adore, according to the eastern fashion, the divinity of his lord and master. Diocletian was a man of sense, who, in the course of private as well as public life, had formed a just estimate both of himself and of mankind: nor is it easy to conceive that in substituting the manners of Persia to those of Rome he was seriously actuated by so mean a principle as that of vanity. He flattered himself that an ostentation of splendour and luxury would subdue the imagination of the multitude; that the monarch would be less exposed to the rude licence of the people and the soldiers, as his person was secluded from the public view; and that habits of submission would insensibly be productive of sentiments of veneration. Like the modesty affected by Augustus, the state maintained by Diocletian was a theatrical representation; but it must be confessed that, of the two comedies, the former was of a much more liberal and manly character than the latter. It was the aim of the one to disguise, and the object of the other to display, the unbounded power which the emperors possessed over the Roman world.

Ostentation was the first principle of the new system instituted by Diocletian. The second was division. He divided the empire, the provinces, and every branch of the civil as well as military administration. He multiplied the wheels of the machine of government, and rendered its operations less rapid but more secure. Whatever advantages and whatever defects might attend these innovations, they must be ascribed in a very great degree to the first inventor; but as the new frame of policy was gradually improved and completed by succeeding princes, it will be more satisfactory to delay the consideration of it till the season of its full maturity and perfection. Reserving, therefore, for the reign of Constantine a more exact picture of the new empire, we shall content ourselves with describing the principal and decisive outline, as it was traced by the hand of Diocletian. He had associated three colleagues in the exercise of the supreme power; and as he was convinced that the abilities of a single man were inadequate to the public defence, he considered the joint administration of four princes not as a temporary expedient, but as a fundamental law of the constitution. It was his intention that the two elder princes should be distinguished by the use of the diadem and the title of *Augusti;* that, as affection or esteem might direct their choice, they should regularly call to their assistance two subordinate colleagues; and that the *Cæsars,* rising in their turn to the first rank, should supply an uninterrupted succession of emperors. The empire was divided into four parts. The East and Italy were the most honourable, the Danube and the Rhine the most laborious stations. The former claimed the presence of the *Augusti,* the latter were intrusted to the administration of the *Cæsars.* The strength of the legions was in the hands of the four partners of sovereignty, and the despair of successively vanquishing four formidable rivals might intimidate the ambition of an aspiring general. In their civil government the emperors were supposed to exercise the undivided power of the monarch, and their edicts, inscribed with their joint names, were received in all the provinces as promulgated by their mutual councils and authority. Notwithstanding these precautions, the political union of the Roman world was gradually dissolved, and a principle of division was introduced, which, in the course of a few years, occasioned the perpetual separation of the eastern and western empires.

The system of Diocletian was accompanied with another very material disadvantage, which cannot even at present be totally overlooked; a more expensive establishment, and consequently an increase of taxes, and the oppression of the people. Instead of a modest family of slaves and freedmen, such as had contented the simple greatness of Augustus and Trajan, three or four magnificent courts were established in the various parts of the empire, and as many Roman *kings* contended with each other and with the Persian monarch for the vain superiority of pomp and luxury. The number of ministers, of magistrates, of officers, and of servants, who filled the different departments of the state, was multiplied beyond the example of former times; and (if we may borrow the warm expression of a contemporary), "when the proportion of those who received exceeded the proportion of those who contributed, the provinces were oppressed by the weight of tribute." From this period to the extinction of the empire, it would be easy to deduce an uninterrupted series of clamours and complaints. According to his religion and situation, each writer chooses either Diocletian, or Constantine, or Valens, or Theodosius, for the object of his invectives; but they unanimously agree in representing the burden of the public impositions, and particularly the land-tax and capitation, as the intolerable and increasing grievance of their own times. From such a concurrence, an impartial historian, who is obliged to extract truth from satire, as well as from panegyric, will be inclined to divide the blame among the princes whom they accuse, and to ascribe their exactions much less to their personal vices than to the uniform system of their administration. The emperor Diocletian was indeed the author of that system; but during his reign the growing evil was confined within the bounds of modesty and discretion, and he deserves the reproach

113

of establishing pernicious precedents, rather than of exercising actual oppression. It may be added, that his revenues were managed with prudent economy; and that, after all the current expenses were discharged, there still remained in the Imperial treasury an ample provision either for judicious liberality or for any emergency of the state.

It was in the twenty-first year of his reign that Diocletian executed his memorable resolution of abdicating the empire; an action more naturally to have been expected from the elder or the younger Antoninus than from a prince who had never practised the lessons of philosophy either in the attainment or in the use of supreme power. Diocletian acquired the glory of giving to the world the first example of a resignation which has not been very frequently imitated by succeeding monarchs. The parallel of Charles the Fifth, however, will naturally offer itself to our mind, not only since the eloquence of a modern historian[1] has rendered that name so familiar to an English reader, but from the very striking resemblance between the characters of the two emperors, whose political abilities were superior to their military genius, and whose specious virtues were much less the effect of nature than of art. The abdication of Charles appears to have been hastened by the vicissitude of fortune; and the disappointment of his favourite schemes urged him to relinquish a power which he found inadequate to his ambition. But the reign of Diocletian had flowed with a tide of uninterrupted success; nor was it till after he had vanquished all his enemies, and accomplished all his designs, that he seems to have entertained any serious thoughts of resigning the empire. Neither Charles nor Diocletian were arrived at a very advanced period of life; since the one was only fifty-five, and the other was no more than fifty-nine years of age; but the active life of those princes, their wars and journeys, the cares of royalty, and their application to

---

[1] [The reference is to William Robertson's *History of the Reign of the Emperor Charles V*, 1769. *Ed.*]

business, had already impaired their constitution, and brought on the infirmities of a premature old age.

Notwithstanding the severity of a very cold and rainy winter, Diocletian left Italy soon after the ceremony of his triumph, and began his progress towards the East round the circuit of the Illyrian provinces. From the inclemency of the weather and the fatigue of the journey, he soon contracted a slow illness; and though he made easy marches, and was generally carried in a close litter, his disorder, before he arrived at Nicomedia, about the end of the summer, was become very serious and alarming. During the whole winter he was confined to his palace; his danger inspired a general and unaffected concern; but the people could only judge of the various alterations of his health from the joy or consternation which they discovered in the countenances and behaviour of his attendants. The rumour of his death was for some time universally believed, and it was supposed to be concealed with a view to prevent the troubles that might have happened during the absence of the Cæsar Galerius. At length, however, on the first of March, Diocletian once more appeared in public, but so pale and emaciated that he could scarcely have been recognised by those to whom his person was the most familiar. It was time to put an end to the painful struggle, which he had sustained during more than a year, between the care of his health and that of his dignity. The former required indulgence and relaxation, the latter compelled him to direct, from the bed of sickness, the administration of a great empire. He resolved to pass the remainder of his days in honourable repose, to place his glory beyond the reach of fortune, and to relinquish the theatre of the world to his younger and more active associates.

The ceremony of his abdication was performed in a spacious plain, about three miles from Nicomedia. The emperor ascended a lofty throne, and, in a speech full of reason and dignity, declared his intention, both to the people and to the soldiers who were assembled on this extraordinary occasion. As soon as he had divested him-

self of the purple, he withdrew from the gazing multitude, and, traversing the city in a covered chariot,
proceeded without delay to the favourite retirement
which he had chosen in his native country of Dalmatia.
On the same day, which was the first of May, Maximian,
as it had been previously concerted, made his resignation
of the Imperial dignity at Milan. Even in the splendour
of the Roman triumph, Diocletian had meditated his
design of abdicating the government. As he wished to
secure the obedience of Maximian, he exacted from him
either a general assurance that he would submit his
actions to the authority of his benefactor, or a particular
promise that he would descend from the throne whenever
he should receive the advice and the example. This
engagement, though it was confirmed by the solemnity
of an oath before the altar of the Capitoline Jupiter,
would have proved a feeble restraint on the fierce temper
of Maximian, whose passion was the love of power, and
who neither desired present tranquillity nor future
reputation. But he yielded, however reluctantly, to the
ascendant which his wiser colleague had acquired over
him, and retired immediately after his abdication to a
villa in Lucania, where it was almost impossible that
such an impatient spirit could find any lasting tranquillity.

Diocletian, who, from a servile origin, had raised himself to the throne, passed the nine last years of his life in
a private condition. Reason had dictated, and content
seems to have accompanied, his retreat, in which he
enjoyed for a long time the respect of those princes to
whom he had resigned the possession of the world. It is
seldom that minds long exercised in business have
formed any habits of conversing with themselves, and in
the loss of power they principally regret the want of
occupation. The amusements of letters and of devotion,
which afford so many resources in solitude, were incapable of fixing the attention of Diocletian; but he had
preserved, or at least he soon recovered, a taste for the
most innocent as well as natural pleasures, and his

leisure hours were sufficiently employed in building, planting, and gardening. His answer to Maximian is deservedly celebrated. He was solicited by that restless old man to reassume the reins of government and the Imperial purple. He rejected the temptation with a smile of pity, calmly observing that, if he could show Maximian the cabbages which he had planted with his own hands at Salona, he should no longer be urged to relinquish the enjoyment of happiness for the pursuit of power. In his conversations with his friends he frequently acknowledged that of all arts the most difficult was the art of reigning; and he expressed himself on that favourite topic with a degree of warmth which could be the result only of experience. "How often," was he accustomed to say, "is it the interest of four or five ministers to combine together to deceive their sovereign! Secluded from mankind by his exalted dignity, the truth is concealed from his knowledge; he can see only with their eyes, he hears nothing but their misrepresentations. He confers the most important offices upon vice and weakness, and disgraces the most virtuous and deserving among his subjects. By such infamous arts," added Diocletian, "the best and wisest princes are sold to the venal corruption of their courtiers." A just estimate of greatness, and the assurance of immortal fame, improve our relish for the pleasures of retirement; but the Roman emperor had filled too important a character in the world to enjoy without alloy the comforts and security of a private condition. It was impossible that he could remain ignorant of the troubles which afflicted the empire after his abdication. It was important that he could be indifferent to their consequences. Fear, sorrow, and discontent sometimes pursued him into the solitude of Salona. His tenderness, or at least his pride, was deeply wounded by the misfortunes of his wife and daughter; and the last moments of Diocletian were embittered by some affronts, which Licinius and Constantine might have spared the father of so many emperors, and the first author of their own fortune. A report, though of a very doubtful nature, has reached our times that he prudently withdrew himself from their power by a voluntary death.

Before we dismiss the consideration of the life and character of Diocletian, we may for a moment direct our view to the place of his retirement. Salona, a principal city of his native province of Dalmatia, was near two hundred Roman miles (according to the measurement of the public highways) from Aquileia and the confines of Italy, and about two hundred and seventy from Sirmium, the usual residence of the emperors whenever they visited the Illyrian frontier. A miserable village still preserves the name of Salona; but so late as the sixteenth century the remains of a theatre, and a confused prospect of broken arches and marble columns, continued to attest its ancient splendour. About six or seven miles from the city Diocletian constructed a magnificent palace, and we may infer, from the greatness of the work, how long he had meditated his design of abdicating the empire. The choice of a spot which united all that could contribute either to health or to luxury did not require the partiality of a native. "The soil was dry and fertile, the air is pure and wholesome, and, though extremely hot during the summer months, this country seldom feels those sultry and noxious winds to which the coasts of Istria and some parts of Italy are exposed. The views from the palace are no less beautiful than the soil and climate were inviting. Towards the west lies the fertile shore that stretches along the Adriatic, in which a number of small islands are scattered in such a manner as to give this part of the sea the appearance of a great lake. On the north side lies the bay, which led to the ancient city of Salona; and the country beyond it, appearing in sight, forms a proper contrast to that more extensive prospect of water which the Adriatic presents both to the south and to the east. Towards the north the view is terminated by high and irregular mountains, situated at a proper distance, and in many places covered with villages, woods, and vineyards."

Though Constantine, from a very obvious prejudice, affects to mention the palace of Diocletian with contempt, yet one of their successors, who could only see it in a neglected and mutilated state, celebrates its magnificence in terms of the highest admiration. It covered an extent of ground consisting of between nine and ten English acres. The form was quadrangular, flanked with sixteen towers. Two of the sides were near six hundred, and the other two near seven hundred, feet in length. The whole was constructed of a beautiful free-stone, excavated from the neighbouring quarries of Trau, or Tragutium, and very little inferior to marble itself. Four streets, intersecting each other at right angles, divided the several parts of this great edifice, and the approach to the principal apartment was from a very stately entrance, which is still denominated the Golden Gate. The approach was terminated by a *peristylium* of granite columns, on one side of which we discover the square temple of Æsculapius, on the other the octagon temple of Jupiter. The latter of those deities Diocletian revered as the patron of his fortunes, the former as the protector of his health. By comparing the present remains with the precepts of Vitruvius, the several parts of the building, the baths, bedchamber, the *atrium*, the *basilica*, and the Cyzicene, Corinthian, and Egyptian halls have been described with some degree of precision, or at least of probability. Their forms were various, their proportions just, but they were all attended with two imperfections, very repugnant to our modern notions of taste and conveniency. These stately rooms had neither windows nor chimneys. They were lighted from the top (for the building seems to have consisted of no more than one story), and they received their heat by the help of pipes that were conveyed along the walls. The range of principal apartments was protected towards the south-west by a portico five hundred and seventeen feet long, which must have formed a very noble and delightful walk, when the beauties of painting and sculpture were added to those of the prospect.

119

Had this magnificent edifice remained in a solitary country, it would have been exposed to the ravages of time; but it might, perhaps, have escaped the rapacious industry of man. The village of Aspalathus, and, long afterwards, the provincial town of Spalatro, have grown out of its ruins. The Golden Gate now opens into the market-place. St. John the Baptist has usurped the honours of Æsculapius; and the temple of Jupiter, under the protection of the Virgin, is converted into the cathedral church. For this account of Diocletian's palace we are principally indebted to an ingenious artist of our own time and country, whom a very liberal curiosity carried into the heart of Dalmatia.[2] But there is room to suspect that the elegance of his designs and engraving has somewhat flattered the objects which it was their purpose to represent. We are informed by a more recent and very judicious traveller that the awful ruins of Spalatro are not less expressive of the decline of the arts than of the greatness of the Roman empire in the time of Diocletian. If such was indeed the state of architecture, we must naturally believe that painting and sculpture had experienced a still more sensible decay. The practice of architecture is directed by a few general and even mechanical rules. But sculpture, and, above all, painting, propose to themselves the imitation not only of the forms of nature, but of the characters and passions of the human soul. In those sublime arts the dexterity of the hand is of little avail unless it is animated by fancy and guided by the most correct taste and observation.

It is almost unnecessary to remark that the civil distractions of the empire, the licence of the soldiers, the inroads of the barbarians, and the progress of despotism, had proved very unfavourable to genius, and even to learning. The succession of Illyrian princes restored the empire without restoring the sciences. Their military

[2] Messieurs Adam and Clerisseau, attended by two draughtsmen, visited Spalatro in the month of July, 1757. The magnificent work which their journey produced was published in London seven years afterwards.

education was not calculated to inspire them with the love of letters; and even the mind of Diocletian, however active and capacious in business, was totally uninformed by study or speculation. The professions of law and physic are of such common use and certain profit that they will always secure a sufficient number of practitioners endowed with a reasonable degree of abilities and knowledge; but it does not appear that the students in those two faculties appeal to any celebrated masters who have flourished within that period. The voice of poetry was silent. History was reduced to dry and confused abridgments, alike destitute of amusement and instruction. A languid and affected eloquence was still retained in the pay and service of the emperors, who encouraged not any arts except those which contributed to the gratification of their pride or the defence of their power.

The declining age of learning and of mankind is marked, however, by the rise and rapid progress of the new Platonists. The school of Alexandria silenced those of Athens; and the ancient sects enrolled themselves under the banners of the more fashionable teachers, who recommended their system by the novelty of their method and the austerity of their manners. Several of these masters—Ammonius, Plotinus, Amelius, and Porphyry[3] —were men of profound thought and intense application; but, by mistaking the true object of philosophy, their labours contributed much less to improve than to corrupt the human understanding. The knowledge that is suited to our situation and powers, the whole compass of moral, natural, and mathematical science, was neglected by the new Platonists; whilst they exhausted their strength in the verbal disputes of metaphysics, attempted to explore the secrets of the invisible world, and studied to reconcile Aristotle with Plato, on subjects of which both these philosophers were as ignorant as the rest of mankind. Consuming their reason in these deep but

[3] Porphyry died about the time of Diocletian's abdication. The life of his master Plotinus, which he composed, will give us the most complete idea of the genius of the sect and the manners of its professors.

unsubstantial meditations, their minds were exposed to illusions of fancy. They flattered themselves that they possessed the secret of disengaging the soul from its corporeal prison; claimed a familiar intercourse with dæmons and spirits; and by a very singular revolution, converted the study of philosophy into that of magic. The ancient sages had derided the popular superstition; after disguising its extravagance by the thin pretence of allegory, the disciples of Plotinus and Porphyry became its most zealous defenders. As they agreed with the Christians in a few mysterious points of faith, they attacked the remainder of their theological system with all the fury of civil war. The new Platonists would scarcely deserve a place in the history of science, but in that of the church the mention of them will very frequently occur.

CHAPTER V

THE PROGRESS OF CHRISTIANITY IN THE PAGAN EMPIRE

Diocletian had reorganised the administration and provided for the defence of the Empire; but he had not solved the problem of the succession. After the abdication of himself and his colleague Maximian, the two "Caesars", or junior emperors, Galerius and Constantius, replaced them as "Augusti", and two new Caesars were nominated to replace them. But this delicate balance of power did not last. On the death of Constantius, at York, his son Constantine was declared emperor by his soldiers; Maximian's son Maxentius put himself at the head of a revolt in Rome and became the emperor of the senate; and on the death of Galerius, his client Licinius gradually became the master of the East. Between these three the monarchy of the Empire was disputed as it had once been between the triumvirate of Octavian, Antony and Lepidus. After "eighteen years of discord and confusion" and five civil wars, Constantine emerged as universal victor, defeating Maxentius outside Rome, at the battle of the Milvian Bridge (312), and Licinius at Chrysopolis in Bithynia (324).

Constantine marked his victory over Maxentius by first disarming, and then abandoning the city of Rome. He abolished the Praetorian Guards who, in the past century, had made and unmade so many emperors. But his two most important

*innovations—the two which make him the in-
augurator of a new era in history—are his acceptance of Christianity as the religion of state for
the whole empire, and his foundation of a new
capital at Constantinople.*

*In his fourteenth chapter Gibbon describes the
years of disorder between the abdication of Diocletian and the final victory of Constantine. So
far, he has traced the history of the pagan empire,
on which Christianity had made but little public
impact. Now, before narrating the reign of Constantine, he turns back and, in his next two
chapters—the famous chapters XV and XVI with
which he closed his first volume and which
caused him to be accused of "infidelity"—he
describes the history of Christianity in the Roman
Empire from the time of the apostles till the
accession of Constantine. In chapter XV, which
is here printed almost entire, he describes the
progress of Christianity "and the sentiments,
manners, numbers and condition of the primitive
Christians".*

A candid but rational inquiry into the progress and establishment of Christianity may be considered as a very
essential part of the history of the Roman empire. While
that great body was invaded by open violence, or undermined by slow decay, a pure and humble religion gently
insinuated itself into the minds of men, grew up in
silence and obscurity, derived new vigour from opposition, and finally erected the triumphant banner of the
Cross on the ruins of the Capitol. Nor was the influence
of Christianity confined to the period or to the limits of
the Roman empire. After a revolution of thirteen or fourteen centuries, that religion is still professed by the nations of Europe, the most distinguished portion of human
kind in arts and learning as well as in arms. By the industry and zeal of the Europeans it has been widely dif-

fused to the most distant shores of Asia and Africa; and by the means of their colonies has been firmly established from Canada to Chile, in a world unknown to the ancients.

But this inquiry, however useful or entertaining, is attended with two peculiar difficulties. The scanty and suspicious materials of ecclesiastical history seldom enable us to dispel the dark cloud that hangs over the first age of the church. The great law of impartiality too often obliges us to reveal the imperfections of the uninspired teachers and believers of the Gospel; and, to a careless observer, *their* faults may seem to cast a shade on the faith which they professed. But the scandal of the pious Christian, and the fallacious triumph of the Infidel, should cease as soon as they recollect not only *by whom*, but likewise *to whom*, the Divine Revelation was given. The theologian may indulge the pleasing task of describing Religion as she descended from Heaven, arrayed in her native purity. A more melancholy duty is imposed on the historian. He must discover the inevitable mixture of error and corruption which she contracted in a long residence upon earth, among a weak and degenerate race of beings.

Our curiosity is naturally prompted to inquire by what means the Christian faith obtained so remarkable a victory over the established religions of the earth. To this inquiry an obvious but satisfactory answer may be returned; that it was owing to the convincing evidence of the doctrine itself, and to the ruling providence of its great Author. But as truth and reason seldom find so favourable a reception in the world, and as the wisdom of Providence frequently condescends to use the passions of the human heart, and the general circumstances of mankind, as instruments to execute its purpose, we may still be permitted, though with becoming submission, to ask, not indeed what were the first, but what were the secondary causes of the rapid growth of the Christian church? It will, perhaps, appear that it was most effectu-

ally favoured and assisted by the five following causes:—
I. The inflexible, and, if we may use the expression,
the intolerant zeal of the Christians, derived, it is true,
from the Jewish religion, but purified from the narrow
and unsocial spirit which, instead of inviting, had deterred the Gentiles from embracing the law of Moses.
II. The doctrine of a future life, improved by every additional circumstance which could give weight and effi
cacy to that important truth. III. The miraculous powers
ascribed to the primitive church. IV. The pure and austere morals of the Christians. V. The union and discipline of the Christian republic, which gradually formed
an independent and increasing state in the heart of the
Roman empire.

I. We have already described the religious harmony
of the ancient world, and the facility with which the
most different and even hostile nations embraced, or at
least respected, each other's superstitions. A single people refused to join in the common intercourse of mankind. The Jews, who, under the Assyrian and Persian
monarchies, had languished for many ages the most
despised portion of their slaves, emerged from obscurity
under the successors of Alexander; and as they multiplied to a surprising degree in the East, and afterwards
in the West, they soon excited the curiosity and wonder
of other nations. The sullen obstinacy with which they
maintained their peculiar rites and unsocial manners
seemed to mark them out a distinct species of men, who
boldly professed, or who faintly disguised, their implacable hatred to the rest of human kind. Neither the violence of Antiochus, nor the arts of Herod, nor the example of the circumjacent nations, could ever persuade the
Jews to associate with the institutions of Moses the elegant mythology of the Greeks. According to the maxims
of universal toleration, the Romans protected a superstition which they despised. The polite Augustus condescended to give orders that sacrifices should be offered
for his prosperity in the temple of Jerusalem; while the

meanest of the posterity of Abraham, who should have paid the same homage to the Jupiter of the Capitol, would have been an object of abhorrence to himself and to his brethren. But the moderation of the conquerors was insufficient to appease the jealous prejudices of their subjects, who were alarmed and scandalised at the ensigns of paganism, which necessarily introduced themselves into a Roman province. The mad attempt of Caligula to place his own statue in the temple of Jerusalem was defeated by the unanimous resolution of a people who dreaded death much less than such an idolatrous profanation. Their attachment to the law of Moses was equal to their detestation of foreign religions. The current of zeal and devotion, as it was contracted into a narrow channel, ran with the strength, and sometimes with the fury, of a torrent.

This inflexible perseverance, which appeared so odious or so ridiculous to the ancient world, assumes a more awful character, since Providence has deigned to reveal to us the mysterious history of the chosen people. But the devout and even scrupulous attachment to the Mosaic religion, so conspicuous among the Jews who lived under the second temple, becomes still more surprising if it is compared with the stubborn incredulity of their forefathers. When the law was given in thunder from Mount Sinai; when the tides of the ocean and the course of the planets were suspended for the convenience of the Israelites; and when temporal rewards and punishments were the immediate consequences of their piety or disobedience, they perpetually relapsed into rebellion against the visible majesty of their Divine King, placed the idols of the nations in the sanctuary of Jehovah, and imitated every fantastic ceremony that was practised in the tents of the Arabs, or in the cities of Phœnicia. As the protection of Heaven was deservedly withdrawn from the ungrateful race, their faith acquired a proportionable degree of vigour and purity. The contemporaries of Moses and Joshua had beheld with careless indifference the most amazing miracles. Under the pressure of every calamity, the belief of those miracles has preserved the Jews of a later period from the universal contagion of idolatry; and in contradiction to every known principle of the human mind, that singular people seems to have yielded a stronger and more ready assent to the traditions of their remote ancestors than to the evidence of their own senses.

The Jewish religion was admirably fitted for defence, but it was never designed for conquest; and it seems probable that the number of proselytes was never much superior to that of apostates. The divine promises were originally made, and the distinguishing rite of circumcision was enjoined, to a single family. When the posterity of Abraham had multiplied like the sands of the sea, the Deity, from whose mouth they received a system of laws and ceremonies, declared himself the proper and as it were the national God of Israel; and with the most jealous care separated his favourite people from the rest of mankind. The conquest of the land of Canaan was accompanied with so many wonderful and with so many bloody circumstances, that the victorious Jews were left in a state of irreconcilable hostility with all their neighbours. They had been commanded to extirpate some of the most idolatrous tribes, and the execution of the Divine will had seldom been retarded by the weakness of humanity. With the other nations they were forbidden to contract any marriages or alliances; and the prohibition of receiving them into the congregation, which in some cases was perpetual, almost always extended to the third, to the seventh, or even to the tenth generation. The obligation of preaching to the Gentiles the faith of Moses had never been inculcated as a precept of the law, nor were the Jews inclined to impose it on themselves as a voluntary duty.

In the admission of new citizens that unsocial people was actuated by the selfish vanity of the Greeks rather than by the generous policy of Rome. The descendants of Abraham were flattered by the opinion that they alone were the heirs of the covenant, and they were apprehensive of diminishing the value of their inheritance by sharing it too easily with the strangers of the earth. A larger acquaintance with mankind extended their knowledge without correcting their prejudices; and whenever the God of Israel acquired any new votaries, he was much more indebted to the inconstant humour of polytheism than to the active zeal of his own missionaries. The religion of Moses seems to be instituted for a particular country as well as for a single nation; and if a strict obedience had been paid to the order that every male, three times in the year, should present himself before the Lord Jehovah, it would have been impossible that the Jews could ever have spread themselves beyond the narrow limits of the promised land. That obstacle was indeed removed by the destruction of the temple of Jerusalem; but the most considerable part of the Jewish religion was involved in its destruction; and the Pagans, who had long wondered at the strange report of an empty sanctuary, were at a loss to discover what could be the object, or what could be the instruments, of a worship which was destitute of temples and of altars, of priests and of sacrifices. Yet even in their fallen state, the Jews, still asserting their lofty and exclusive privileges, shunned, instead of courting, the society of strangers. They still insisted with inflexible rigour on those parts of the law which it was in their power to practise. Their peculiar distinctions of days, of meats, and a variety of trivial though burdensome observances, were so many objects of disgust and aversion for the other nations, to whose habits and prejudices they were diametrically opposite. The painful and even dangerous rite of circumcision was alone capable of repelling a willing proselyte from the door of the synagogue.

Under these circumstances, Christianity offered itself to the world, armed with the strength of the Mosaic law, and delivered from the weight of its fetters. An exclusive zeal for the truth of religion and the unity of God was as carefully inculcated in the new as in the ancient system: and whatever was now revealed to mankind concerning the nature and designs of the Supreme Being was fitted to increase their reverence for that mysterious doctrine. The divine authority of Moses and the prophets was admitted, and even established, as the firmest basis of Christianity. From the beginning of the world an uninterrupted series of predictions had announced and prepared the long-expected coming of the Messiah, who, in compliance with the gross apprehensions of the Jews, had been more frequently represented under the character of a King and Conqueror, than under that of a Prophet, a Martyr, and the Son of God. By his expiatory sacrifice the imperfect sacrifices of the temple were at once consummated and abolished. The ceremonial law, which consisted only of types and figures, was succeeded by a pure and spiritual worship, equally adapted to all climates, as well as to every condition of mankind; and to the initiation of blood, was substituted a more harmless initiation of water. The promise of divine favour, instead of being partially confined to the posterity of Abraham, was universally proposed to the freeman and the slave, to the Greek and to the barbarian, to the Jew and to the Gentile. Every privilege that could raise the proselyte from earth to heaven, that could exalt his devotion, secure his happiness, or even gratify that secret pride which, under the semblance of devotion, insinuates itself into the human heart, was still reserved for the members of the Christian church; but at the same time all mankind was permitted, and even solicited, to accept the glorious distinction, which was not only proffered as a favour, but imposed as an obligation. It became the most sacred duty of a new convert to diffuse among his friends and relations the inestimable blessing which he had received, and to warn them against a refusal that would be severely punished as a criminal disobedience to the will of a benevolent but all-powerful Deity.

The enfranchisement of the church from the bonds of the synagogue was a work, however, of some time and of some difficulty. The Jewish converts, who acknowledged Jesus in the character of the Messiah foretold by their ancient oracles, respected him as a prophetic teacher of virtue and religion; but they obstinately adhered to the ceremonies of their ancestors, and were desirous of imposing them on the Gentiles, who continually augmented the number of believers. These Judaising Christians seem to have argued with some degree of plausibility from the Divine origin of the Mosaic law, and from the immutable perfections of its great Author. They affirmed, *that,* if the Being who is the same through all eternity had designed to abolish those sacred rites which had served to distinguish his chosen people, the repeal of them would have been no less clear and solemn than their first promulgation: *that,* instead of those frequent declarations which either suppose or assert the perpetuity of the Mosaic religion, it would have been represented as a provisionary scheme intended to last only till the coming of the Messiah, who should instruct mankind in a more perfect mode of faith and of worship: *that* the Messiah himself, and his disciples who conversed with him on earth, instead of authorising by their example the most minute observances of the Mosaic law, would have published to the world the abolition of those useless and obsolete ceremonies, without suffering Christianity to remain during so many years obscurely confounded among the sects of the Jewish church. Arguments like these appear to have been used in the defence of the expiring cause of the Mosaic law; but the industry of our learned divines has abundantly explained the ambiguous language of the Old Testament, and the ambiguous conduct of the apostolic teachers. It was proper gradually to unfold the system of the Gospel, and to pronounce with the utmost caution and tenderness a sentence of condemnation so repugnant to the inclination and prejudices of the believing Jews. . . .

[*After describing, as evidence of "the necessity of these
precautions," the conflict within the Church of Jerusalem
between the Nazarenes, (and their extremists, the Ebionites) who clung to the Mosaic law, and their rivals,
who rejected it, and incidentally thereby enjoyed Roman
protection, Gibbon proceeds.*]

While the orthodox church preserved a just medium
between excessive veneration and improper contempt for
the law of Moses, the various heretics deviated into equal
but opposite extremes of error and extravagance. From
the acknowledged truth of the Jewish religion, the Ebionites had concluded that it could never be abolished.
From its supposed imperfections, the Gnostics as hastily
inferred that it never was instituted by the wisdom of the
Deity. There are some objections against the authority of
Moses and the prophets which too readily present themselves to the sceptical mind; though they can only be derived from our ignorance of remote antiquity, and from
our incapacity to form an adequate judgment of the
Divine economy. These objections were eagerly embraced
and as petulantly urged by the vain science of the Gnostics. As those heretics were, for the most part, averse to
the pleasures of sense, they morosely arraigned the polygamy of the patriarchs, the gallantries of David, and
the seraglio of Solomon. The conquest of the land of
Canaan, and the extirpation of the unsuspecting natives,
they were at a loss how to reconcile with the common notions of humanity and justice. But when they recollected
the sanguinary list of murders, of executions, and of
massacres, which stain almost every page of the Jewish
annals, they acknowledged that the barbarians of Palestine had exercised as much compassion towards their idolatrous enemies as they had ever shown to their friends or
countrymen. Passing from the sectaries of the law to the
law itself, they asserted that it was impossible that a
religion which consisted only of bloody sacrifices and
trifling ceremonies, and whose rewards as well as punish-

ments were all of a carnal and temporal nature, could inspire the love of virtue, or restrain the impetuosity of passion. The Mosaic account of the creation and fall of man was treated with profane derision by the Gnostics, who would not listen with patience to the repose of the Deity after six days' labour, to the rib of Adam, the garden of Eden, the trees of life and of knowledge, the speaking serpent, the forbidden fruit, and the condemnation pronounced against human kind for the venial offence of their first progenitors. The God of Israel was impiously represented by the Gnostics as a being liable to passion and to error, capricious in his favour, implacable in his resentment, meanly jealous of his superstitious worship, and confining his partial providence to a single people, and to this transitory life. In such a character they could discover none of the features of the wise and omnipotent Father of the universe. They allowed that the religion of the Jews was somewhat less criminal than the idolatry of the Gentiles: but it was their fundamental doctrine that the Christ whom they adored as the first and brightest emanation of the Deity appeared upon earth to rescue mankind from their various errors, and to reveal a *new* system of truth and perfection. The most learned of the fathers, by a very singular condescension, have imprudently admitted the sophistry of the Gnostics. Acknowledging that the literal sense is repugnant to every principle of faith as well as reason, they deem themselves secure and invulnerable behind the ample veil of allegory, which they carefully spread over every tender part of the Mosaic dispensation.

It has been remarked with more ingenuity than truth that the virgin purity of the church was never violated by schism or heresy before the reign of Trajan or Hadrian, about one hundred years after the death of Christ. We may observe with much more propriety that, during that period, the disciples of the Messiah were indulged in a freer latitude both of faith and practice than has ever been allowed in succeeding ages. As the terms of communion were insensibly narrowed, and the spiritual authority of the prevailing party was exercised with increasing severity, many of its most respectable adherents, who were called upon to renounce, were provoked to assert their private opinions, to pursue the consequences of their mistaken principles, and openly to erect the standard of rebellion against the unity of the church. The Gnostics were distinguished as the most polite, the most learned, and the most wealthy of the Christian name; and that general appellation, which expressed a superiority of knowledge, was either assumed by their own pride, or ironically bestowed by the envy of their adversaries. They were almost without exception of the race of the Gentiles, and their principal founders seem to have been natives of Syria or Egypt, where the warmth of the climate disposes both the mind and the body to indolent and contemplative devotion. The Gnostics blended with the faith of Christ many sublime but obscure tenets, which they derived from oriental philosophy, and even from the religion of Zoroaster, concerning the eternity of matter, the existence of two principles, and the mysterious hierarchy of the invisible world. As soon as they launched out into that vast abyss, they delivered themselves to the guidance of a disordered imagination; and as the paths of error are various and infinite, the Gnostics were imperceptibly divided into more than fifty particular sects, of whom the most celebrated appear to have been the Basilidians, the Valentinians, the Marcionites, and, in a still later period, the Manichæans. Each of these sects could boast of its bishops and congregations, of its doctors and martyrs; and, instead of the Four Gospels adopted by the church, the heretics produced a multitude of histories, in which the actions and discourses of Christ and of his apostles were adapted to their respective tenets. The success of the Gnostics was rapid and extensive. They covered Asia and Egypt, established themselves in Rome, and sometimes penetrated into the provinces of the West. For the most part they arose in the second century, flourished during the third, and were suppressed in the fourth or fifth, by the prevalence of more fashionable controversies, and by the superior ascendant of the reigning power. Though they constantly disturbed the peace, and frequently disgraced the name of religion, they contributed to assist rather than to retard the progress of Christianity. The Gentile converts, whose strongest objections and prejudices were directed against the law of Moses, could find admission into many Christian societies, which required not from their untutored mind any belief of an antecedent revelation. Their faith was insensibly fortified and enlarged, and the church was ultimately benefited by the conquests of its most inveterate enemies.

But whatever difference of opinion might subsist between the Orthodox, the Ebionites, and the Gnostics, concerning the divinity or the obligation of the Mosaic law, they were all equally animated by the same exclusive zeal, and by the same abhorrence for idolatry, which had distinguished the Jews from the other nations of the ancient world. The philosopher, who considered the system of polytheism as a composition of human fraud and error, could disguise a smile of contempt under the mask of devotion, without apprehending that either the mockery or the compliance would expose him to the resentment of any invisible, or, as he conceived them, imaginary powers. But the established religions of Paganism were seen by the primitive Christians in a much more odious and formidable light. It was the universal sentiment both of the church and of heretics, that the dæmons were the authors, the patrons, and the objects of idolatry. Those rebellious spirits who had been degraded from the rank of angels, and cast down into the infernal pit, were still permitted to roam upon earth, to torment the bodies and to seduce the minds of sinful men. The dæmons soon discovered and abused the natural propensity of the human heart towards devotion, and, artfully withdrawing the adoration of mankind from their Creator, they usurped the place and honours of the Supreme Deity. By the success of their malicious contrivances, they at once gratified their own vanity and revenge, and obtained the only comfort of which they were yet susceptible, the hope of involving the human species in the participation of their guilt and misery. It was confessed, or at least it was imagined, that they had distributed among themselves the most important characters of polytheism, one dæmon assuming the name and attributes of Jupiter, another of Æsculapius, a third of Venus, and a fourth perhaps of Apollo, and that, by the advantage of their long experience and aërial nature, they were enabled to execute, with sufficient skill and dignity, the parts which they had undertaken. They lurked in the temples, instituted festivals and sacrifices, invented fables, pronounced oracles, and were frequently allowed to perform miracles. The Christians, who, by the interposition of evil spirits, could so readily explain every præternatural appearance, were disposed and even desirous to admit the most extravagant fictions of the Pagan mythology. But the belief of the Christian was accompanied with horror. The most trifling mark of respect to the national worship he considered as a direct homage yielded to the dæmon, and as an act of rebellion against the majesty of God.

In consequence of this opinion, it was the first but arduous duty of a Christian to preserve himself pure and undefiled by the practice of idolatry. The religion of the nations was not merely a speculative doctrine professed in the schools or preached in the temples. The innumerable deities and rites of polytheism were closely interwoven with every circumstance of business or pleasure, of public or of private life; and it seemed impossible to escape the observance of them, without, at the same time, renouncing the commerce of mankind, and all the offices and amusements of society. The important transactions of peace and war were prepared or concluded by solemn sacrifices, in which the magistrate, the senator, and the soldier were obliged to preside or to participate. The public spectacles were an essential part of the cheerful devotion of the Pagans, and the gods were supposed to accept, as the most grateful offering, the games that the prince and people celebrated in honour of their peculiar festivals.[1] The Christian, who with pious horror avoided the abomination of the circus or the theatre, found himself encompassed with infernal snares in every convivial entertainment, as often as his friends, invoking the hospitable deities, poured out libations to each other's happiness. When the bride, struggling with well-affected reluctance, was forced in hymenæal pomp over the threshold of her new habitation, or when the sad procession of the dead slowly moved towards the funeral pile, the Christian, on these interesting occasions, was compelled to desert the persons who were the dearest to him, rather than contract the guilt inherent to those impious ceremonies. Every art and every trade that was in the least concerned in the framing or adorning of idols was polluted by the stain of idolatry; a severe sentence, since it devoted to eternal misery the far greater part of the community which is employed in the exercise of liberal or mechanic professions. If we cast our eyes over the numerous remains of antiquity, we shall perceive that, besides the immediate representations of the gods and the holy instruments of their worship, the elegant forms and agreeable fictions consecrated by the imagination of the Greeks were introduced as the richest ornaments of the houses, the dress, and the furniture of the Pagans. Even the arts of music and painting, of eloquence and poetry, flowed from the same impure origin. In the style of the fathers, Apollo and the Muses were the organs of the infernal spirit; Homer and Virgil were the most eminent of his servants; and the beautiful mythology

---

[1] See Tertullian, *De Spectaculis*. This severe reformer shows no more indulgence to a tragedy of Euripides than to a combat of gladiators. The dress of the actors particularly offends him. By the use of the lofty buskin they impiously strive to add a cubit to their stature: c. 23.

which pervades and animates the compositions of their genius is destined to celebrate the glory of the dæmons. Even the common language of Greece and Rome abounded with familiar but impious expressions, which the imprudent Christian might too carelessly utter, or too patiently hear.

The dangerous temptations which on every side lurked in ambush to surprise the unguarded believer assailed him with redoubled violence on the days of solemn festivals. So artfully were they framed and disposed throughout the year, that superstition always wore the appearance of pleasure, and often of virtue. Some of the most sacred festivals in the Roman ritual were destined to salute the new calends of January with vows of public and private felicity; to indulge the pious remembrance of the dead and living; to ascertain the inviolable bounds of property; to hail, on the return of spring, the genial powers of fecundity; to perpetuate the two memorable eras of Rome, the foundation of the city, and that of the republic; and to restore, during the humane licence of the Saturnalia, the primitive equality of mankind. Some idea may be conceived of the abhorrence of the Christians for such impious ceremonies, by the scrupulous delicacy which they displayed on a much less alarming occasion. On days of general festivity it was the custom of the ancients to adorn their doors with lamps and with branches of laurel, and to crown their heads with a garland of flowers. This innocent and elegant practice might perhaps have been tolerated as a mere civil institution. But it most unluckily happened that the doors were under the protection of the household gods, that the laurel was sacred to the lover of Daphne, and that garlands of flowers, though frequently worn as a symbol either of joy or mourning, had been dedicated in their first origin to the service of superstition. The trembling Christians, who were persuaded in this instance to comply with the fashion of their country and the commands of the magistrate, laboured under the most gloomy apprehensions, from the reproaches of their own conscience, the censures of the church, and the denunciations of divine vengeance.

Such was the anxious diligence which was required to guard the chastity of the Gospel from the infectious breath of idolatry. The superstitious observances of public or private rites were carelessly practised, from education and habit, by the followers of the established religion. But as often as they occurred, they afforded the Christians an opportunity of declaring and confirming their zealous opposition. By these frequent protestations their attachment to the faith was continually fortified; and in proportion to the increase of zeal, they combated with the more ardour and success in the holy war which they had undertaken against the empire of the dæmons.

II. The writings of Cicero represent in the most lively colours the ignorance, the errors, and the uncertainty of the ancient philosophers with regard to the immortality of the soul. When they are desirous of arming their disciples against the fear of death, they inculcate, as an obvious though melancholy position, that the fatal stroke of our dissolution releases us from the calamities of life; and that those can no longer suffer who no longer exist. Yet there were a few sages of Greece and Rome who had conceived a more exalted, and, in some respects, a juster idea of human nature, though it must be confessed that, in the sublime inquiry, their reason had been often guided by their imagination, and that their imagination had been prompted by their vanity. When they viewed with complacency the extent of their own mental powers, when they exercised the various faculties of memory, of fancy, and of judgement, in the most profound speculations or the most important labours, and when they reflected on the desire of fame, which transported them into future ages, far beyond the bounds of death and of the grave, they were unwilling to confound themselves with the beasts of the field, or to suppose that a being, for whose dignity they en-

tertained the most sincere admiration, could be limited
to a spot of earth, and to a few years of duration. With
this favourable prepossession they summoned to their
aid the science, or rather the language, of Metaphysics.
They soon discovered that, as none of the properties of
matter will apply to the operations of the mind, the human soul must consequently be a substance distinct from
the body, pure, simple, and spiritual, incapable of dissolution, and susceptible of a much higher degree of
virtue and happiness after the release from its corporeal
prison. From these specious and noble principles the
philosophers who trod in the footsteps of Plato deduced
a very unjustifiable conclusion, since they asserted, not
only the future immortality, but the past eternity of the
human soul, which they were too apt to consider as a
portion of the infinite and self-existing spirit which pervades and sustains the universe. A doctrine thus removed
beyond the senses and the experience of mankind might
serve to amuse the leisure of a philosophic mind; or, in
the silence of solitude, it might sometimes impart a ray
of comfort to desponding virtue; but the faint impression
which had been received in the schools was soon obliterated by the commerce and business of active life. We
are sufficiently acquainted with the eminent persons who
flourished in the age of Cicero and of the first Cæsars,
with their actions, their characters, and their motives,
to be assured that their conduct in this life was never
regulated by any serious conviction of the rewards or
punishments of a future state. At the bar and in the
senate of Rome the ablest orators were not apprehensive
of giving offence to their hearers by exposing that doctrine as an idle and extravagant opinion, which was rejected with contempt by every man of a liberal education
and understanding.

Since therefore the most sublime efforts of philosophy
can extend no farther than feebly to point out the desire,
the hope, or, at most, the probability of a future state,
there is nothing, except a divine revelation that can as-

certain the existence and describe the condition of the invisible country which is destined to receive the souls of men after their separation from the body. But we may perceive several defects inherent to the popular religions of Greece and Rome which rendered them very unequal to so arduous a task. 1. The general system of their mythology was unsupported by any solid proofs; and the wisest among the Pagans had already disclaimed its usurped authority. 2. The description of the infernal regions had been abandoned to the fancy of painters and of poets, who peopled them with so many phantoms and monsters who dispensed their rewards and punishments with so little equity, that a solemn truth, the most congenial to the human heart, was oppressed and disgraced by the absurd mixture of the wildest fictions. 3. The doctrine of a future state was scarcely considered among the devout polytheists of Greece and Rome as a fundamental article of faith. The providence of the gods, as it related to public communities rather than to private individuals, was principally displayed on the visible theatre of the present world. The petitions which were offered on the altars of Jupiter or Apollo expressed the anxiety of their worshippers for temporal happiness, and their ignorance or indifference concerning a future life. The important truth of the immortality of the soul was inculcated with more diligence as well as success in India, in Assyria, in Egypt, and in Gaul; and since we cannot attribute such a difference to the superior knowledge of the barbarians, we must ascribe it to the influence of an established priesthood, which employed the motives of virtue as the instrument of ambition.

We might naturally expect that a principle so essential to religion would have been revealed in the clearest terms to the chosen people of Palestine, and that it might safely have been intrusted to the hereditary priesthood of Aaron. It is incumbent on us to adore the mysterious dispensations of Providence, when we discover that the doctrine of the immortality of the soul is omitted in the law of Moses;

it is darkly insinuated by the prophets; and during the long period which elapsed between the Egyptian and the Babylonian servitudes, the hopes as well as fears of the Jews appear to have been confined within the narrow compass of the present life. After Cyrus had permitted the exiled nation to return into the promised land, and after Ezra had restored the ancient records of their religion, two celebrated sects, the Sadducees and the Pharisees, insensibly arose at Jerusalem. The former, selected from the more opulent and distinguished ranks of society, were strictly attached to the literal sense of the Mosaic law, and they piously rejected the immortality of the soul as an opinion that received no countenance from the divine book, which they revered as the only rule of their faith. To the authority of Scripture the Pharisees added that of tradition, and they accepted, under the name of traditions, several speculative tenets from the philosophy or religion of the eastern nations. The doctrines of fate or predestination, of angels and spirits, and of a future state of rewards and punishments, were in the number of these new articles of belief; and as the Pharisees, by the austerity of their manners, had drawn into their party the body of the Jewish people, the immortality of the soul became the prevailing sentiment of the synagogue under the reign of the Asmonæan princes and pontiffs. The temper of the Jews was incapable of contenting itself with such a cold and languid assent as might satisfy the mind of a Polytheist; and as soon as they admitted the idea of a future state, they embraced it with the zeal which has always formed the characteristic of the nation. Their zeal, however, added nothing to its evidence, or even probability; and it was still necessary that the doctrine of life and immortality, which had been dictated by nature, approved by reason, and received by superstition, should obtain the sanction of divine truth from the authority and example of Christ.

When the promise of eternal happiness was proposed to mankind on condition of adopting the faith, and of observing the precepts, of the Gospel, it is no wonder that so advantageous an offer should have been accepted by great numbers of every religion, of every rank, and of every province in the Roman empire. The ancient Christians were animated by a contempt for their present existence, and by a just confidence of immortality, of which the doubtful and imperfect faith of modern ages cannot give us any adequate notion. In the primitive church the influence of truth was very powerfully strengthened by an opinion which, however it may deserve respect for its usefulness and antiquity, has not been found agreeable to experience. It was universally believed that the end of the world, and the kingdom of heaven, were at hand. The near approach of this wonderful event had been predicted by the apostles; the tradition of it was preserved by their earliest disciples, and those who understood in their literal sense the discourses of Christ himself were obliged to expect the second and glorious coming of the Son of Man in the clouds, before that generation was totally extinguished which had beheld his humble condition upon earth, and which might still be witness of the calamities of the Jews under Vespasian or Hadrian. The revolution of seventeen centuries has instructed us not to press too closely the mysterious language of prophecy and revelation; but as long as, for wise purposes, this error was permitted to subsist in the church, it was productive of the most salutary effects on the faith and practice of Christians, who lived in the awful expectation of that moment when the globe itself, and all the various race of mankind, should tremble at the appearance of their divine Judge.[2]

The ancient and popular doctrine of the Millennium

[2] This expectation was countenanced by the twenty-fourth chapter of St. Matthew, and by the first epistle of St. Paul to the Thessalonians. Erasmus removes the difficulty by the help of allegory and metaphor; and the learned Grotius ventures to insinuate, that, for wise purposes, the pious deception was permitted to take place.

143

was intimately connected with the second coming of
Christ. As the works of the creation had been finished in
six days, their duration in their present state, according
to a tradition which was attributed to the prophet Elijah,
was fixed to six thousand years. By the same analogy
it was inferred that this long period of labour and contention, which was now almost elapsed, would be succeeded by a joyful Sabbath of a thousand years; and that
Christ, with the triumphant band of the saints and the
elect who had escaped death, or who had been miraculously revived, would reign upon earth till the time appointed for the last and general resurrection. So pleasing
was this hope to the mind of believers, that the *New
Jerusalem*, the seat of this blissful kingdom, was quickly
adorned with all the gayest colours of the imagination. A
felicity consisting only of pure and spiritual pleasure
would have appeared too refined for its inhabitants, who
were still supposed to possess their human nature and
senses. A garden of Eden, with the amusements of the
pastoral life, was no longer suited to the advanced state
of society which prevailed under the Roman empire. A
city was therefore erected of gold and precious stones,
and a supernatural plenty of corn and wine was bestowed
on the adjacent territory; in the free enjoyment of whose
spontaneous productions the happy and benevolent people was never to be restrained by any jealous laws of
exclusive property. The assurance of such a Millennium
was carefully inculcated by a succession of fathers from
Justin Martyr and Irenæus, who conversed with the immediate disciples of the apostles, down to Lactantius, who
was preceptor to the son of Constantine. Though it might
not be universally received, it appears to have been the
reigning sentiment of the orthodox believers; and it seems
so well adapted to the desires and apprehensions of mankind, that it must have contributed in a very considerable degree to the progress of the Christian faith. But
when the edifice of the church was almost completed,

the temporary support was laid aside. The doctrine of Christ's reign upon earth was at first treated as a profound allegory, was considered by degrees as a doubtful and useless opinion, and was at length rejected as the absurd invention of heresy and fanaticism. A mysterious prophecy, which still forms a part of the sacred canon, but which was thought to favour the exploded sentiment, has very narrowly escaped the proscription of the church.[3]

Whilst the happiness and glory of a temporal reign were promised to the disciples of Christ, the most dreadful calamities were denounced against an unbelieving world. The edification of the new Jerusalem was to advance by equal steps with the destruction of the mystic Babylon; and as long as the emperors who reigned before Constantine persisted in the profession of idolatry, the epithet of Babylon was applied to the city and to the empire of Rome. A regular series was prepared of all the moral and physical evils which can afflict a flourishing nation; intestine discord, and the invasion of the fiercest barbarians from the unknown regions of the North; pestilence and famine, comets and eclipses, earth-

---

[3]In the council of Laodicea (about the year 360) the Apocalypse was tacitly excluded from the sacred canon by the same churches of Asia to which it is addressed; and we may learn from the complaint of Sulpicius Severus that their sentence had been ratified by the greater number of Christians of his time. From what causes then is the Apocalypse at present so generally received by the Greek, the Roman, and the Protestant churches? The following ones may be assigned:—1. The Greeks were subdued by the authority of an impostor, who, in the sixth century, assumed the character of Dionysius the Areopagite. 2. A just apprehension that the grammarians might become more important than the theologians engaged the council of Trent to fix the seal of their infallibility on all the books of Scripture contained in the Latin Vulgate, in the number of which the Apocalypse was fortunately included. 3. The advantage of turning those mysterious prophecies against the See of Rome inspired the Protestants with uncommon veneration for so useful an ally. See the ingenious and elegant discourses of the present bishop of Lichfield on that unpromising subject.

quakes and inundations. All these were only so many preparatory and alarming signs of the great catastrophe of Rome, when the country of the Scipios and Cæsars should be consumed by a flame from Heaven, and the city of the seven hills, with her palaces, her temples, and her triumphal arches, should be buried in a vast lake of fire and brimstone. It might, however, afford some consolation to Roman vanity, that the period of their empire would be that of the world itself; which, as it had once perished by the element of water, was destined to experience a second and a speedy destruction from the element of fire. In the opinion of a general conflagration the faith of the Christian very happily coincided with the tradition of the East, the philosophy of the Stoics, and the analogy of Nature; and even the country which, from religious motives, had been chosen for the origin and principal scene of the conflagration, was the best adapted for that purpose by natural and physical causes—by its deep caverns, beds of sulphur, and numerous volcanoes, of which those of Ætna, of Vesuvius, and of Lipari exhibit a very imperfect representation. The calmest and most intrepid sceptic could not refuse to acknowledge that the destruction of the present system of the world by fire was in itself extremely probable. The Christian, who founded his belief much less on the fallacious arguments of reason than on the authority of tradition and the interpretation of Scripture, expected it with terror and confidence as a certain and approaching event; and as his mind was perpetually filled with the solemn idea, he considered every disaster that happened to the empire as an infallible symptom of an expiring world.

The condemnation of the wisest and most virtuous of the Pagans, on account of their ignorance or disbelief of the divine truth, seems to offend the reason and the humanity of the present age. But the primitive church, whose faith was of a much firmer consistence, delivered over, without hesitation, to eternal torture the far greater

part of the human species. A charitable hope might perhaps be indulged in favour of Socrates, or some other
sages of antiquity, who had consulted the light of reason
before that of the Gospel had arisen. But it was unanimously affirmed that those who, since the birth or the
death of Christ, had obstinately persisted in the worship
of the dæmons, neither deserved nor could expect a pardon from the irritated justice of the Deity. These rigid
sentiments, which had been unknown to the ancient
world, appear to have infused a spirit of bitterness into
a system of love and harmony. The ties of blood and
friendship were frequently torn asunder by the difference of religious faith; and the Christians, who, in this
world, found themselves oppressed by the power of the
Pagans, were sometimes seduced by resentment and spiritual pride to delight in the prospect of their future
triumph. "You are fond of spectacles," exclaims the stern
Tertullian, "expect the greatest of all spectacles, the last
and eternal judgment of the universe. How shall I admire, how laugh, how rejoice, how exult, when I behold
so many proud monarchs, and fancied gods, groaning
in the lowest abyss of darkness; so many magistrates,
who persecuted the name of the Lord, liquefying in
fiercer fires than they ever kindled against the Christians;
so many sage philosophers blushing in red-hot flames
with their deluded scholars; so many celebrated poets
trembling before the tribunal, not of Minos, but of Christ;
so many tragedians, more tuneful in the expression of
their own sufferings; so many dancers—" But the humanity of the reader will permit me to draw a veil over the
rest of this infernal description, which the zealous African pursues in a long variety of affected and unfeeling
witticisms.

Doubtless there were many among the primitive Christians of a temper more suitable to the meekness and
charity of their profession. There were many who felt
a sincere compassion for the danger of their friends and
countrymen, and who exerted the most benevolent zeal

to save them from the impending destruction. The careless Polytheist, assailed by new and unexpected terrors, against which neither his priests nor his philosophers could afford him any certain protection, was very frequently terrified and subdued by the menace of eternal tortures. His fears might assist the progress of his faith and reason; and if he could once persuade himself to suspect that the Christian religion might possibly be true, it became an easy task to convince him that it was the safest and most prudent party that he could possibly embrace.

III. The supernatural gifts, which even in this life were ascribed to the Christians above the rest of mankind, must have conduced to their own comfort, and very frequently to the conviction of infidels. Besides the occasional prodigies, which might sometimes be effected by the immediate interposition of the Deity when he suspended the laws of Nature for the service of religion, the Christian church, from the time of the apostles and their first disciples, has claimed an uninterrupted succession of miraculous powers, the gift of tongues, of vision, and of prophecy, the power of expelling dæmons, of healing the sick, and of raising the dead. The knowledge of foreign languages was frequently communicated to the contemporaries of Irenæus, though Irenæus himself was left to struggle with the difficulties of a barbarous dialect whilst he preached the Gospel to the natives of Gaul. The divine inspiration, whether it was conveyed in the form of a waking or of a sleeping vision, is described as a favour very liberally bestowed on all ranks of the faithful, on women as on elders, on boys as well as upon bishops. When their devout minds were sufficiently prepared by a course of prayer, of fasting, and of vigils, to receive the extraordinary impulse, they were transported out of their senses, and delivered in ecstasy what was inspired, being mere organs of the Holy Spirit, just as a pipe or flute is of him who blows into it.

148

We may add that the design of these visions was, for the most part, either to disclose the future history, or to guide the present administration, of the church. The expulsion of the dæmons from the bodies of those unhappy persons whom they had been permitted to torment was considered as a signal though ordinary triumph of religion, and is repeatedly alleged by the ancient apologists as the most convincing evidence of the truth of Christianity. The awful ceremony was usually performed in a public manner, and in the presence of a great number of spectators; the patient was relieved by the power or skill of the exorcist, and the vanquished dæmon was heard to confess that he was one of the fabled gods of antiquity, who had impiously usurped the adoration of mankind. But the miraculous cure of diseases of the most inveterate or even præternatural kind can no longer occasion any surprise, when we recollect that in the days of Irenæus, about the end of the second century, the resurrection of the dead was very far from being esteemed an uncommon event; that the miracle was frequently performed on necessary occasions, by great fasting and the joint supplication of the church of the place, and that the persons thus restored to their prayers had lived afterwards among them many years. At such a period, when faith could boast of so many wonderful victories over death, it seems difficult to account for the scepticism of those philosophers who still rejected and derided the doctrine of the resurrection. A noble Grecian had rested on this important ground the whole controversy, and promised Theophilus, bishop of Antioch, that, if he could be gratified with the sight of a single person who had been actually raised from the dead, he would immediately embrace the Christian religion. It is somewhat remarkable that the prelate of the first eastern church, however anxious for the conversion of his friend, thought proper to decline this fair and reasonable challenge.

The miracles of the primitive church, after obtaining

the sanction of ages, have been lately attacked in a very free and ingenious inquiry;[4] which, though it has met with the most favourable reception from the public, appears to have excited a general scandal among the divines of our own as well as of the other Protestant churches of Europe.[5] Our different sentiments on this subject will be much less influenced by any particular arguments than by our habits of study and reflection, and, above all, by the degree of the evidence which we have accustomed ourselves to require for the proof of a miraculous event. The duty of an historian does not call upon him to interpose his private judgment in this nice and important controversy; but he ought not to dissemble the difficulty of adopting such a theory as may reconcile the interest of religion with that of reason, of making a proper application of that theory, and of defining with precision the limits of that happy period, exempt from error and from deceit, to which we might be disposed to extend the gift of supernatural powers. From the first of the fathers to the last of the popes, a succession of bishops, of saints, of martyrs, and of miracles, is continued without interruption; and the progress of superstition was so gradual and almost imperceptible, that we know not in what particular link we should break the chain of tradition. Every age bears testimony to the wonderful events by which it was distinguished, and its testimony appears no less weighty and respectable than that of the preceding generation, till we are insensibly led on to accuse our own inconsistency if, in the eighth or in the twelfth century, we deny to the venerable Bede,

[4] Dr. Middleton sent out his Introduction in the year 1747, published his Free Inquiry in 1749, and before his death, which happened in 1750, he had prepared a vindication of it against his numerous adversaries.

[5] The university of Oxford conferred degrees on his opponents. From the indignation of Mosheim we may discover the sentiments of the Lutheran divines.

or to the holy Bernard, the same degree of confidence which, in the second century, we had so liberally granted to Justin or to Irenæus.[6] If the truth of any of those miracles is appreciated by their apparent use and propriety, every age had unbelievers to convince, heretics to confute, and idolatrous nations to convert; and sufficient motives might always be produced to justify the interposition of Heaven. And yet, since every friend to revelation is persuaded of the reality, and every reasonable man is convinced of the cessation, of miraculous powers, it is evident that there must have been *some period* in which they were either suddenly or gradually withdrawn from the Christian church. Whatever era is chosen for that purpose, the death of the apostles, the conversion of the Roman empire, or the extinction of the Arian heresy, the insensibility of the Christians who lived at that time will equally afford a just matter of surprise. They still supported their pretensions after they had lost their power. Credulity performed the office of faith; fanaticism was permitted to assume the language of inspiration, and the effects of accident or contrivance were ascribed to supernatural causes. The recent experience of genuine miracles should have instructed the Christian world in the ways of Providence, and habituated their eye (if we may use a very inadequate expression) to the style of the Divine artist. Should the most skilful painter of modern Italy presume to decorate his feeble imitations with the name of Raphael or of Correggio, the insolent fraud would be soon discovered and indignantly rejected.

Whatever opinion may be entertained of the miracles of the primitive church since the time of the apostles, this unresisting softness of temper, so conspicuous

---

[6] It may seem somewhat remarkable that Bernard of Clairvaux, who records so many miracles of his friend St. Malachi, never takes any notice of his own, which, in their turn, however, are carefully related by his companions and disciples. In the long series of ecclesiastical history, does there exist a single instance of a saint asserting that he himself possessed the gift of miracles?

among the believers of the second and third centuries, proved of some accidental benefit to the cause of truth and religion. In modern times, a latent and even involuntary scepticism adheres to the most pious dispositions. Their admission of supernatural truths is much less an active consent than a cold and passive acquiescence. Accustomed long since to observe and to respect the invariable order of Nature, our reason, or at least our imagination, is not sufficiently prepared to sustain the visible action of the Deity. But in the first ages of Christianity the situation of mankind was extremely different. The most curious, or the most credulous, among the Pagans were often persuaded to enter into a society which asserted an actual claim of miraculous powers. The primitive Christians perpetually trod on mystic ground, and their minds were exercised by the habits of believing the most extraordinary events. They felt, or they fancied, that on every side they were incessantly assaulted by dæmons, comforted by visions, instructed by prophecy, and surprisingly delivered from danger, sickness, and from death itself, by the supplications of the church. The real or imaginary prodigies, of which they so frequently conceived themselves to be the objects, the instruments, or the spectators, very happily disposed them to adopt with the same ease, but with far greater justice, the authentic wonders of the evangelic history; and thus miracles that exceeded not the measure of their own experience inspired them with the most lively assurance of mysteries which were acknowledged to surpass the limits of their understanding. It is this deep impression of supernatural truths which has been so much celebrated under the name of faith; a state of mind described as the surest pledge of the Divine favour and of future felicity, and recommended as the first or perhaps the only merit of a Christian. According to the more rigid doctors, the moral virtues, which may be equally practised by infidels, are destitute of any value or efficacy in the work of our justification.

IV. But the primitive Christian demonstrated his faith by his virtues; and it was very justly supposed that the Divine persuasion, which enlightened or subdued the understanding, must at the same time purify the heart and direct the actions of the believer. The first apologists of Christianity who justify the innocence of their brethren, and the writers of a later period who celebrate the sanctity of their ancestors, display, in the most lively colours, the reformation of manners which was introduced into the world by the preaching of the Gospel. As it is my intention to remark only such human causes as were permitted to second the influence of revelation, I shall slightly mention two motives which might naturally render the lives of the primitive Christians much purer and more austere than those of their Pagan contemporaries or their degenerate successors—repentance for their past sins, and the laudable desire of supporting the reputation of the society in which they were engaged.

It is a very ancient reproach, suggested by the ignorance or the malice of infidelity, that the Christians allured into their party the most atrocious criminals, who, as soon as they were touched by a sense of remorse, were easily persuaded to wash away, in the water of baptism, the guilt of their past conduct, for which the temples of the gods refused to grant them any expiation. But this reproach, when it is cleared from misrepresentation, contributes as much to the honour as it did to the increase of the church. The friends of Christianity may acknowledge without a blush that many of the most eminent saints had been before their baptism the most abandoned sinners. Those persons who in the world had followed, though in an imperfect manner, the dictates of benevolence and propriety, derived such a calm satisfaction from the opinion of their own rectitude as rendered them much less susceptible of the sudden emotions of shame, of grief, and of terror, which have given birth to so many wonderful conversions. After the example of their Divine Master, the missionaries of the Gospel disdained not the society of men, and especially of women, oppressed by the consciousness, and very often by the effects, of their vices. As they emerged from sin and superstition to the glorious hope of immortality, they resolved to devote themselves to a life, not only of virtue, but of penitence. The desire of perfection became the ruling passion of their soul; and it is well known that, while reason embraces a cold mediocrity, our passions hurry us with rapid violence over the space which lies between the most opposite extremes.

When the new converts had been enrolled in the number of the faithful, and were admitted to the sacraments of the church, they found themselves restrained from relapsing into their past disorders by another consideration of a less spiritual but of a very innocent and respectable nature. Any particular society that has departed from the great body of the nation, or the religion to which it belonged, immediately becomes the object of universal as well as invidious observation. In proportion to the smallness of its numbers, the character of the society may be affected by the virtue and vices of the persons who compose it; and every member is engaged to watch with the most vigilant attention over his own behaviour, and over that of his brethren, since, as he must expect to incur a part of the common disgrace, he may hope to enjoy a share of the common reputation. When the Christians of Bithynia were brought before the tribunal of the younger Pliny, they assured the proconsul that, far from being engaged in any unlawful conspiracy, they were bound by a solemn obligation to abstain from the commission of those crimes which disturb the private or public peace of society, from theft, robbery, adultery, perjury, and fraud. Near a century afterwards, Tertullian with an honest pride could boast that very few Christians had suffered by the hand of the executioner, except on account of their religion. Their serious and sequestered life, averse to the gay luxury of the age, inured them to chastity, temperance, economy, and all the sober and

6
A gigantic head of Constantine, the emperor who christianized the empire and founded a new capital in Constantinople.

domestic virtues. As the greater number were of some trade or profession, it was incumbent on them, by the strictest integrity and the fairest dealing, to remove the suspicions which the profane are too apt to conceive against the appearances of sanctity. The contempt of the world exercised them in the habits of humility, meekness, and patience. The more they were persecuted, the more closely they adhered to each other. Their mutual charity and unsuspecting confidence has been remarked by infidels, and was too often abused by perfidious friends.

It is a very honourable circumstance for the morals of the primitive Christians, that even their faults, or rather errors, were derived from an excess of virtue. The bishops and doctors of the church, whose evidence attests, and whose authority might influence, the professions, the principles, and even the practice of their contemporaries, had studied the Scriptures with less skill than devotion; and they often received in the most literal sense those rigid precepts of Christ and the apostles to which the prudence of succeeding commentators has applied a looser and more figurative mode of interpretation. Ambitious to exalt the perfection of the Gospel above the wisdom of philosophy, the zealous fathers have carried the duties of self-mortification, of purity, and of patience, to a height which it is scarcely possible to attain, and much less to preserve, in our present state of weakness and corruption. A doctrine so extraordinary and so sublime must inevitably command the veneration of the people; but it was ill calculated to obtain the suffrage of those worldly philosophers who, in the conduct of this transitory life, consult only the feelings of nature and the interest of society.

There are two very natural propensities which we may distinguish in the most virtuous and liberal dispositions, the love of pleasure and the love of action. If the former is refined by art and learning, improved by the charms of social intercourse, and corrected by a just regard to economy, to health, and to reputation, it is productive of the greatest part of the happiness of private life. The love of action is a principle of a much stronger and more doubtful nature. It often leads to anger, to ambition, and to revenge; but when it is guided by the sense of propriety and benevolence, it becomes the parent of every virtue, and, if those virtues are accompanied with equal abilities, a family, a state, or an empire may be indebted for their safety and prosperity to the undaunted courage of a single man. To the love of pleasure we may therefore ascribe most of the agreeable, to the love of action we may attribute most of the useful and respectable, qualifications. The character in which both the one and the other should be united and harmonised would seem to constitute the most perfect idea of human nature. The insensible and inactive disposition, which should be supposed alike destitute of both, would be rejected, by the common consent of mankind, as utterly incapable of procuring anv happiness to the individual, or any public benefit to the world. But it was not in *this* world that the primitive Christians were desirous of making themselves either agreeable or useful.

The acquisition of knowledge, the exercise of our reason or fancy, and the cheerful flow of unguarded conversation, may employ the leisure of a liberal mind. Such amusements, however, were rejected with abhorrence, or admitted with the utmost caution, by the severity of the fathers, who despised all knowledge that was not useful to salvation, and who considered all levity of discourse as a criminal abuse of the gift of speech. In our present state of existence the body is so inseparably connected with the soul, that it seems to be our interest to taste, with innocence and moderation, the enjoyments of which that faithful companion is susceptible. Very different was the reasoning of our devout predecessors; vainly aspiring to imitate the perfection of angels, they disdained, or they affected to disdain, every earthly and corporeal delight. Some of our senses indeed are necessary for our preservation, others for our subsistence, and others again for our information; and thus far it was impossible to reject the use of them. The first sensation of pleasure was marked as the first moment of their abuse. The unfeeling candidate for heaven was instructed, not only to resist the grosser allurements of the taste or smell, but even to shut his ears against the profane harmony of sounds, and to view with indifference the most finished productions of human art. Gay apparel, magnificent houses, and elegant furniture were supposed to unite the double guilt of pride and of sensuality: a simple and mortified appearance was more suitable to the Christian who was certain of his sins and doubtful of his salvation. In their censures of luxury the fathers are extremely minute and circumstantial; and among the various articles which excite their pious indignation, we may enumerate false hair, garments of any colour except white, instruments of music, vases of gold or silver, downy pillows (as Jacob reposed his head on a stone), white bread, foreign wines, public salutations, the use of warm baths, and the practice of shaving the beard, which, according to the expression of Tertullian, is a lie against our own faces, and an impious attempt to improve the works of the Creator. When Christianity was introduced among the rich and the polite, the observation of these singular laws was left, as it would be at present, to the few who were ambitious of superior sanctity. But it is always easy, as well as agreeable, for the inferior ranks of mankind to claim a merit from the contempt of that pomp and pleasure which fortune has placed beyond their reach. The virtue of the primitive Christians, like that of the first Romans, was very frequently guarded by poverty and ignorance.

The chaste severity of the fathers in whatever related to the commerce of the two sexes flowed from the same principle—their abhorrence of every enjoyment which might gratify the sensual and degrade the spiritual nature of man. It was their favourite opinion, that if Adam had preserved his obedience to the Creator, he would have lived for ever in a state of virgin purity, and that some harmless mode of vegetation might have peopled paradise with a race of innocent and immortal beings. The use of marriage was permitted only to his fallen posterity, as a necessary expedient to continue the human species, and as a restraint, however imperfect, on the natural licentiousness of desire. The hesitation of the orthodox casuists on this interesting subject betrays the perplexity of men unwilling to approve an institution which they were compelled to tolerate. The enumeration of the very whimsical laws which they most circumstantially imposed on the marriage-bed would force a smile from the young and a blush from the fair. It was their unanimous sentiment that a first marriage was adequate to all the purposes of nature and of society. The sensual connection was refined into a resemblance of the mystic union of Christ with his church, and was pronounced to be indissoluble either by divorce or by death. The practice of second nuptials was branded with the name of a legal adultery; and the persons who were guilty of so scandalous an offence against Christian purity were soon excluded from the honours, and even from the arms, of the church. Since desire was imputed as a crime, and marriage was tolerated as a defect, it was consistent with the same principles to consider a state of celibacy as the nearest approach to the Divine perfection. It was with the utmost difficulty that ancient Rome could support the institution of six vestals; but the primitive church was filled with a great number of persons of either sex who had devoted themselves to the profession of perpetual chastity. A few of these, among whom we may reckon the learned Origen, judged it the most prudent to disarm the tempter.[7] Some were in-

---

[7] Before the fame of Origen had excited envy and persecution, this extraordinary action was rather admired than censured. As it was his general practice to allegorise Scripture, it seems unfortunate that, in this instance only, he should have adopted the literal sense. [Origen castrated himself, taking too literally the Pauline text, "Some have made themselves eunuchs for the sake of Christ." *Ed.*]

sensible and some were invincible against the assaults of the flesh. Disdaining an ignominious flight, the virgins of the warm climate of Africa encountered the enemy in the closest engagement; they permitted priests and deacons to share their bed, and gloried amidst the flames in their unsullied purity. But insulted Nature sometimes vindicated her rights, and this new species of martyrdom served only to introduce a new scandal into the church.[8] Among the Christian ascetics, however (a name which they soon acquired from their painful exercise), many, as they were less presumptuous, were probably more successful. The loss of sensual pleasure was supplied and compensated by spiritual pride. Even the multitude of Pagans were inclined to estimate the merit of the sacrifice by its apparent difficulty; and it was in the praise of these chaste spouses of Christ that the fathers have poured forth the troubled stream of their eloquence. Such are the early traces of monastic principles and institutions, which, in a subsequent age, have counterbalanced all the temporal advantages of Christianity.

The Christians were not less averse to the business than to the pleasures of this world. The defence of our persons and property they knew not how to reconcile with the patient doctrine which enjoined an unlimited forgiveness of past injuries, and commanded them to invite the repetition of fresh insults. Their simplicity was offended by the use of oaths, by the pomp of magistracy, and by the active contention of public life; nor could their humane ignorance be convinced that it was lawful on any occasion to shed the blood of our fellow-creatures, either by the sword of justice or by that of war, even though their criminal or hostile attempts should threaten the peace and safety of the whole community. It was acknowledged that, under a less perfect law, the powers

---

[8] Something like this rash attempt was long afterwards imputed to the founder of the order of Fontevrault. Bayle has amused himself and his readers on that very delicate subject.

of the Jewish constitution had been exercised, with the approbation of Heaven, by inspired prophets and by anointed kings. The Christians felt and confessed that such institutions might be necessary for the present system of the world, and they cheerfully submitted to the authority of their Pagan governors. But while they inculcated the maxims of passive obedience, they refused to take any active part in the civil administration or the military defence of the empire. Some indulgence might perhaps be allowed to those persons who, before their conversion, were already engaged in such violent and sanguinary occupations; but it was impossible that the Christians, without renouncing a more sacred duty, could assume the character of soldiers, of magistrates, or of princes. This indolent, or even criminal disregard to the public welfare, exposed them to the contempt and reproaches of the Pagans, who very frequently asked, what must be the fate of the empire, attacked on every side by the barbarians, if all mankind should adopt the pusillanimous sentiments of the new sect? To this insulting question the Christian apologists returned obscure and ambiguous answers, as they were unwilling to reveal the secret cause of their security: the expectation that, before the conversion of mankind was accomplished, war, government, the Roman empire, and the world itself, would be no more. It may be observed that, in this instance likewise, the situation of the first Christians coincided very happily with their religious scruples, and that their aversion to an active life contributed rather to excuse them from the service than to exclude them from the honours of the state and army.

V. But the human character, however it may be exalted or depressed by a temporary enthusiasm, will return by degrees to its proper and natural level, and will resume those passions that seem the most adapted to its present condition. The primitive Christians were dead to the business and pleasures of the world; but their love of action, which could never be entirely extinguished, soon revived, and found a new occupation in the government of the church. A separate society, which attacked the established religion of the empire, was obliged to adopt some form of internal policy, and to appoint a sufficient number of ministers, intrusted not only with the spiritual functions, but even with the temporal direction of the Christian commonwealth. The safety of the society, its honour, its aggrandisement, were productive, even in the most pious minds, of a spirit of patriotism, such as the first of the Romans had felt for the republic, and sometimes of a similar indifference in the use of whatever means might probably conduce to so desirable an end. The ambition of raising themselves or their friends to the honours and offices of the church was disguised by the laudable intention of devoting to the public benefit the power and consideration which, for that purpose only, it became their duty to solicit. In the exercise of their functions they were frequently called upon to detect the errors of heresy or the arts of faction, to oppose the designs of perfidious brethren, to stigmatise their characters with deserved infamy, and to expel them from the bosom of a society whose peace and happiness they had attempted to disturb. The ecclesiastical governors of the Christians were taught to unite the wisdom of the serpent with the innocence of the dove; but as the former was refined, so the latter was insensibly corrupted, by the habits of government. In the church as well as in the world, the persons who were placed in any public station rendered themselves considerable by their eloquence and firmness, by their knowledge of mankind, and by their dexterity in business; and while they concealed from others, and perhaps from themselves, the secret motives of their conduct, they too frequently relapsed into all the turbulent passions of active life, which were tinctured with an additional degree of bitterness and obstinacy from the infusion of spiritual zeal.

The government of the church has often been the subject, as well as the prize, of religious contention. The hostile disputants of Rome, of Paris, of Oxford, and of Geneva, have alike struggled to reduce the primitive and apostolic model to the respective standards of their own policy. The few who have pursued this inquiry with more candour and impartiality are of opinion that the apostles declined the office of legislation, and rather chose to endure some partial scandals and divisions, than to exclude the Christians of a future age from the liberty of varying their forms of ecclesiastical government according to the changes of times and circumstances. The scheme of policy which, under their approbation, was adopted for the use of the first century, may be discovered from the practice of Jerusalem, of Ephesus, or of Corinth. The societies which were instituted in the cities of the Roman empire were united only by the ties of faith and charity. Independence and equality formed the basis of their internal constitution. The want of discipline and human learning was supplied by the occasional assistance of the *prophets,* who were called to that function without distinction of age, of sex, or of natural abilities, and who, as often as they felt the divine impulse, poured forth the effusions of the Spirit in the assembly of the faithful. But these extraordinary gifts were frequently abused or misapplied by the prophetic teachers. They displayed them at an improper season, presumptuously disturbed the service of the assembly, and by their pride or mistaken zeal they introduced, particularly into the apostolic church of Corinth, a long and melancholy train of disorders. As the institution of prophets became useless, and even pernicious, their powers were withdrawn, and their office abolished.

The public functions of religion were solely intrusted to the established ministers of the church, the *bishops* and the *presbyters;* two appellations which, in their first origin, appear to have distinguished the same office and the same order of persons. The name of Presbyter was expressive of their age, or rather of their gravity and wisdom. The title of Bishop denoted their inspection over the faith and manners of the Christians who were committed to their pastoral care. In proportion to the respective numbers of the faithful, a larger or smaller number of these *episcopal presbyters* guided each infant congregation with equal authority and with united counsels.

But the most perfect equality of freedom requires the directing hand of a superior magistrate: and the order of public deliberations soon introduces the office of a president, invested at least with the authority of collecting the sentiments, and of executing the resolutions, of the assembly. A regard for the public tranquillity, which would so frequently have been interrupted by annual or by occasional elections, induced the primitive Christians to constitute an honorable and perpetual magistracy, and to choose one of the wisest and most holy among their presbyters to execute, during his life, the duties of their ecclesiastical governor. It was under these circumstances that the lofty title of Bishop began to raise itself above the humble appellation of Presbyter; and while the latter remained the most natural distinction for the members of every Christian senate, the former was appropriated to the dignity of its new president. The advantages of this episcopal form of government, which appears to have been introduced before the end of the first century, were so obvious, and so important for the future greatness, as well as the present peace, of Christianity, that it was adopted without delay by all the societies which were already scattered over the empire, had acquired in a very early period the sanction of antiquity, and is still revered by the most powerful churches, both of the East and of the West, as a primitive and even as a divine establishment. It is needless to observe that the pious and humble presbyters who were first dignified with the episcopal title could not possess, and would probably have rejected, the power and pomp which now encircles the tiara of the Roman pontiff, or the mitre of a German prelate. But we may define in a few words the narrow limits of their original jurisdiction, which was chiefly of a spiritual, though in some instances of a temporal nature. It consisted in the administration of the sacraments and discipline of the church, the superintendency of religious ceremonies, which imperceptibly increased in number and variety, the consecration of ecclesiastical ministers, to whom the bishop assigned their respective functions, the management of the public fund, and the determination of all such differences as the faithful were unwilling to expose before the tribunal of an idolatrous judge. These powers, during a short period, were exercised according to the advice of the presbyteral college, and with the consent and approbation of the assembly of Christians. The primitive bishops were considered only as the first of their equals, and the honourable servants of a free people. Whenever the episcopal chair became vacant by death, a new president was chosen among the presbyters by the suffrage of the whole congregation, every member of which supposed himself invested with a sacred and sacerdotal character.

Such was the mild and equal constitution by which the Christians were governed more than an hundred years after the death of the apostles. Every society formed within itself a separate and independent republic; and although the most distant of these little states maintained a mutual as well as friendly intercourse of letters and deputations, the Christian world was not yet connected by any supreme authority or legislative assembly. As the numbers of the faithful were gradually multiplied, they discovered the advantages that might result from a closer union of their interest and designs. Towards the end of the second century, the churches of Greece and Asia adopted the useful institutions of provincial synods, and they may justly be supposed to have borrowed the model of a representative council from the celebrated examples of their own country, the Amphictyons, the

Achæan league, or the assemblies of the Ionian cities. It was soon established as a custom and as a law, that the bishops of the independent churches should meet in the capital of the province at the stated periods of spring and autumn. Their deliberations were assisted by the advice of a few distinguished presbyters, and moderated by the presence of a listening multitude. Their decrees, which were styled Canons, regulated every important controversy of faith and discipline; and it was natural to believe that a liberal effusion of the Holy Spirit would be poured on the united assembly of the delegates of the Christian people. The institution of synods was so well suited to private ambition and to public interest, that in the space of a few years it was received throughout the whole empire. A regular correspondence was established between the provincial councils, which mutually communicated and approved their respective proceedings; and the catholic church soon assumed the form, and acquired the strength, of a great federative republic.

As the legislative authority of the particular churches was insensibly superseded by the use of councils, the bishops obtained by their alliance a much larger share of executive and arbitrary power; and as soon as they were connected by a sense of their common interest, they were enabled to attack, with united vigour, the original rights of their clergy and people. The prelates of the third century imperceptibly changed the language of exhortation into that of command, scattered the seeds of future usurpations, and supplied, by Scripture allegories and declamatory rhetoric, their deficiency of force and of reason. They exalted the unity and power of the church, as it was represented in the EPISCOPAL OFFICE, of which every bishop enjoyed an equal and undivided portion. Princes and magistrates, it was often repeated, might boast an earthly claim to a transitory dominion: it was the episcopal authority alone which was derived from the Deity, and extended itself over this and over another world. The bishops were the viceregents of Christ, the successors of the apostles, and the mystic substitutes of the high priest of the Mosaic law. Their exclusive privilege of conferring the sacerdotal character invaded the freedom both of clerical and of popular elections: and if, in the administration of the church, they still consulted the judgment of the presbyters or the inclination of the people, they most carefully inculcated the merit of such a voluntary condescension. The bishops acknowledged the supreme authority which resided in the assembly of their brethren; but in the government of his peculiar diocese each of them exacted from his *flock* the same implicit obedience as if that favourite metaphor had been literally just, and as if the shepherd had been of a more exalted nature than that of his sheep. This obedience, however, was not imposed without some efforts on one side, and some resistance on the other. The democratical part of the constitution was, in many places, very warmly supported by the zealous or interested opposition of the inferior clergy. But their patriotism received the ignominious epithets of faction and schism, and the episcopal cause was indebted for its rapid progress to the labours of many active prelates, who, like Cyprian of Carthage, could reconcile the arts of the most ambitious statesman with the Christian virtues which seem adapted to the character of a saint and martyr.

The same causes which at first had destroyed the equality of the presbyters introduced among the bishops a pre-eminence of rank, and from thence a superiority of jurisdiction. As often as in the spring and autumn they met in provincial synod, the difference of personal merit and reputation was very sensibly felt among the members of the assembly, and the multitude was governed by the wisdom and eloquence of the few. But the order of public proceedings required a more regular and less invidious distinction; the office of perpetual presidents in the councils of each province was conferred on the bishops of the principal city; and these aspiring prelates, who soon acquired the lofty titles of Metropolitans and Primates, secretly prepared themselves to usurp over their episcopal brethren the same authority which the bishops had so lately assumed above the college of presbyters. Nor was it long before an emulation of pre-eminence and power prevailed among the Metropolitans themselves, each of them affecting to display, in the most pompous terms, the temporal honours and advantages of the city over which he presided; the numbers and opulence of the Christians who were subject to their pastoral care; the saints and martyrs who had arisen among them; and the purity with which they preserved the tradition of the faith as it had been transmitted through a series of orthodox bishops from the apostle or the apostolic disciple to whom the foundation of their church was ascribed. From every cause, either of a civil or of an ecclesiastical nature, it was easy to foresee that Rome must enjoy the respect, and would soon claim the obedience, of the provinces. The society of the faithful bore a just proportion to the capital of the empire; and the Roman church was the greatest, the most numerous, and, in regard to the West, the most ancient of all the Christian establishments, many of which had received their religion from the pious labours of her missionaries. Instead of *one* apostolic founder, the utmost boast of Antioch, of Ephesus, or of Corinth, the banks of the Tiber were supposed to have been honoured with the preaching and martyrdom of the *two* most eminent among the apostles; and the bishops of Rome very prudently claimed the inheritance of whatsoever prerogatives were attributed either to the person or to the office of St. Peter. The bishops of Italy and of the provinces were disposed to allow them a primacy of order and association (such was their very accurate expression) in the Christian aristocracy. But the power of a monarch was rejected with abhorrence, and the aspiring genius of Rome experienced from the nations of Asia and Africa a more vigorous resistance to her spiritual than she had formerly done to her temporal dominion. The patriotic Cyprian, who ruled with the most absolute sway the church of Carthage and the provincial synods, opposed with resolution and success the ambition of the Roman pontiff, artfully connected his own cause with that of the eastern bishops, and, like Hannibal, sought out new allies in the heart of Asia. If this Punic war was carried on without any effusion of blood, it was owing much less to the moderation than to the weakness of the contending prelates. Invectives and excommunications were *their* only weapons; and these, during the progress of the whole controversy, they hurled against each other with equal fury and devotion. The hard necessity of censuring either a pope or a saint and martyr distresses the modern Catholics whenever they are obliged to relate the particulars of a dispute in which the champions of religion indulged such passions as seem much more adapted to the senate or to the camp.

The progress of the ecclesiastical authority gave birth to the memorable distinction of the laity and of the clergy, which had been unknown to the Greeks and Romans. The former of these appellations comprehended the body of the Christian people; the latter, according to the signification of the word, was appropriated to the chosen portion that had been set apart for the service of religion; a celebrated order of men which has furnished the most important, though not always the most edifying, subjects for modern history. Their mutual hostilities sometimes disturbed the peace of the infant church, but their zeal and activity were united in the common cause, and the love of power, which (under the most artful disguises) could insinuate itself into the breasts of bishops and martyrs, animated them to increase the number of their subjects, and to enlarge the limits of the Christian empire. They were destitute of any temporal force, and they were for a long time discouraged and oppressed, rather than assisted, by the civil magistrate;

but they had acquired, and they employed within their own society, the two most efficacious instruments of government, rewards and punishments; the former derived from the pious liberality, the latter from the devout apprehensions, of the faithful. . . .

[*After describing the gradual acquisition of wealth by the church, at the disposal of its bishops, and the development of ecclesiastical penalties, especially excommunication, Gibbon goes on.*]

The well-tempered mixture of liberality and rigour, the judicious dispensation of rewards and punishments, according to the maxims of policy as well as justice, constituted the *human* strength of the church. The bishops, whose paternal care extended itself to the government of both worlds, were sensible of the importance of these prerogatives; and, covering their ambition with the fair pretence of the love of order, they were jealous of any rival in the exercise of a discipline so necessary to prevent the desertion of those troops which had enlisted themselves under the banner of the Cross, and whose numbers every day became more considerable. From the imperious declamations of Cyprian we should naturally conclude that the doctrines of excommunication and penance formed the most essential part of religion; and that it was much less dangerous for the disciples of Christ to neglect the observance of the moral duties than to despise the censures and authority of their bishops. Sometimes we might imagine that we were listening to the voice of Moses, when he commanded the earth to open, and to swallow up, in consuming flames, the rebellious race which refused obedience to the priesthood of Aaron; and we should sometimes suppose that we heard a Roman consul asserting the majesty of the republic, and declaring his inflexible resolution to enforce the rigour of the laws. "If such irregularities are suffered with impunity" (it is thus that the bishop of Carthage chides the lenity of his colleague), "if such irregularities are suffered, there is an end of EPISCOPAL VIGOUR; an end of the sublime and divine power of governing the Church; an end of Christianity itself." Cyprian had renounced those temporal honours which it is probable he would never have obtained; but the acquisition of such absolute command over the consciences and understanding of a congregation, however obscure or despised by the world, is more truly grateful to the pride of the human heart than the possession of the most despotic power imposed by arms and conquest on a reluctant people.

In the course of this important, though perhaps tedious, inquiry, I have attempted to display the secondary causes which so efficaciously assisted the truth of the Christian religion. If among these causes we have discovered any artificial ornaments, any accidental circumstances, or any mixture of error and passion, it cannot appear surprising that mankind should be the most sensibly affected by such motives as were suited to their imperfect nature. It was by the aid of these causes—exclusive zeal, the immediate expectation of another world, the claim of miracles, the practice of rigid virtue, and the constitution of the primitive church—that Christianity spread itself with so much success in the Roman empire. To the first of these the Christians were indebted for their invincible valour, which disdained to capitulate with the enemy whom they were resolved to vanquish. The three succeeding causes supplied their valour with the most formidable arms. The last of these causes united their courage, directed their arms, and gave their efforts that irresistible weight which even a small band of well-trained and intrepid volunteers has so often possessed over an undisciplined multitude, ignorant of the subject and careless of the event of the war. In the various religions of Polytheism, some wandering fanatics of Egypt and Syria, who addressed themselves to the credulous superstition of the populace, were perhaps the only order of priests that derived their whole support and credit from their sacerdotal profession, and were very deeply affected by a personal concern for the safety or prosperity of their tutelar deities. The ministers of Polytheism, both in Rome and in the provinces, were, for the most part, men of a noble birth and of an affluent fortune, who received, as an honourable distinction, the care of a celebrated temple or of a public sacrifice, exhibited, very frequently at their own expense, the sacred games, and with cold indifference performed the ancient rites, according to the laws and fashion of their country. As they were engaged in the ordinary occupations of life, their zeal and devotion were seldom animated by a sense of interest, or by the habits of an ecclesiastical character. Confined to their respective temples and cities, they remained without any connection of discipline or government; and whilst they acknowledged the supreme jurisdiction of the senate, of the college of pontiffs, and of the emperor, those civil magistrates contented themselves with the easy task of maintaining in peace and dignity the general worship of mankind. We have already seen how various, how loose, and how uncertain were the religious sentiments of Polytheists. They were abandoned, almost without control, to the natural workings of a superstitious fancy. The accidental circumstances of their life and situation determined the object as well as the degree of their devotion; and as long as their adoration was successively prostituted to a thousand deities, it was scarcely possible that their hearts could be susceptible of a very sincere or lively passion for any of them.

When Christianity appeared in the world, even these faint and imperfect impressions had lost much of their original power. Human reason, which by its unassisted strength is incapable of perceiving the mysteries of faith, had already obtained an easy triumph over the folly of Paganism; and when Tertullian or Lactantius employ their labours in exposing its falsehood and extravagance, they are obliged to transcribe the eloquence of Cicero or the wit of Lucian. The contagion of these sceptical writings had been diffused far beyond the number of their readers. The fashion of incredulity was communicated from the philosopher to the man of pleasure or business, from the noble to the plebeian, and from the master to the menial slave who waited at his table, and who eagerly listened to the freedom of his conversation. On public occasions the philosophic part of mankind affected to treat with respect and decency the religious institutions of their country, but their secret contempt penetrated through the thin and awkward disguise; and even the people, when they discovered that their deities were rejected and derided by those whose rank or understanding they were accustomed to reverence, were filled with doubts and apprehensions concerning the truth of those doctrines to which they had yielded the most implicit belief. The decline of ancient prejudice exposed a very numerous portion of human kind to the danger of a painful and comfortless situation. A state of scepticism and suspense may amuse a few inquisitive minds. But the practice of superstition is so congenial to the multitude that, if they are forcibly awakened, they still regret the loss of their pleasing vision. Their love of the marvellous and supernatural, their curiosity with regard to future events, and their strong propensity to extend their hopes and fears beyond the limits of the visible world, were the principal causes which favoured the establishment of Polytheism. So urgent on the vulgar is the necessity of believing, that the fall of any system of mythology will most probably be succeeded by the introduction of some other mode of superstition. Some deities of a more recent and fashionable cast might soon have occupied the deserted temples of Jupiter and Apollo, if, in the decisive moment, the wisdom of Providence had not interposed a genuine revelation fitted to inspire the most rational esteem and conviction, whilst, at the same time, it was adorned with all that could attract the curiosity, the wonder, and the veneration of the people. In their actual disposition, as many were almost disengaged from their artificial prejudices, but equally susceptible and desirous of a devout attachment, an object much less deserving would have been sufficient to fill the vacant place in their hearts, and to gratify the uncertain eagerness of their passions. Those who are inclined to pursue this reflection, instead of viewing with astonishment the rapid progress of Christianity, will perhaps be surprised that its success was not still more rapid and still more universal.

It has been observed, with truth as well as propriety, that the conquests of Rome prepared and facilitated those of Christianity. In the second chapter of this work we have attempted to explain in what manner the most civilised provinces of Europe, Asia, and Africa were united under the dominion of one sovereign, and gradually connected by the most intimate ties of laws, of manners, and of language. The Jews of Palestine, who had fondly expected a temporal deliverer, gave so cold a reception to the miracles of the divine prophet, that it was found unnecessary to publish, or at least to preserve, any Hebrew gospel.[9] The authentic histories of the actions of Christ were composed in the Greek language, at a considerable distance from Jerusalem, and after the Gentile converts were grown extremely numerous. As soon as those histories were translated into the Latin tongue they were perfectly intelligible to all the subjects of Rome, excepting only to the peasants of Syria and Egypt, for whose benefit particular versions were afterwards made. The public highways, which had been constructed for the use of the legions, opened an easy passage for the Christian missionaries from Damascus to Corinth, and from Italy to the extremity of Spain or

[9] The modern critics are not disposed to believe what the fathers almost unanimously assert, that St. Matthew composed a Hebrew gospel, of which only the Greek translation is extant. It seems, however, dangerous to reject their testimony.

Britain; nor did those spiritual conquerors encounter any of the obstacles which usually retard or prevent the introduction of a foreign religion into a distant country. There is the strongest reason to believe that before the reigns of Diocletian and Constantine the faith of Christ had been preached in every province, and in all the great cities of the empire; but the foundation of the several congregations, the numbers of the faithful who composed them, and their proportion to the unbelieving multitude, are now buried in obscurity or disguised by fiction and declamation. Such imperfect circumstances, however, as have reached our knowledge concerning the increase of the Christian name in Asia and Greece, in Egypt, in Italy, and in the West, we shall now proceed to relate, without neglecting the real or imaginary acquisitions which lay beyond the frontiers of the Roman empire.

The rich provinces that extend from the Euphrates to the Ionian sea were the principal theatre on which the apostle of the Gentiles displayed his zeal and piety. The seeds of the Gospel, which he had scattered in a fertile soil, were diligently cultivated by his disciples; and it should seem that, during the two first centuries, the most considerable body of Christians was contained within those limits. Among the societies which were instituted in Syria, none were more ancient or more illustrious than those of Damascus, of Berœa or Aleppo, and of Antioch. The prophetic introduction of the Apocalypse has described and immortalised the seven churches of Asia—Ephesus, Smyrna, Pergamus, Thyatira, Sardes, Laodicea, and Philadelphia; and their colonies were soon diffused over that populous country. In a very early period, the islands of Cyprus and Crete, the provinces of Thrace and Macedonia, gave a favourable reception to the new religion; and Christian republics were soon founded in the cities of Corinth, of Sparta, and of Athens. The antiquity of the Greek and Asiatic churches allowed a sufficient space of time for their increase and multiplication; and even the swarms of Gnostics and other heretics serve to display the flourishing condition of the orthodox church, since the appellation of heretics has always been applied to the less numerous party. To these domestic testimonies we may add the confession, the complaints, and the apprehensions of the Gentiles themselves. From the writings of Lucian, a philosopher who had studied mankind, and who describes their manners in the most lively colours, we may learn that, under the reign of Commodus, his native country of Pontus was filled with Epicureans and *Christians*. Within fourscore years after the death of Christ, the humane Pliny laments the magnitude of the evil which he vainly attempted to eradicate. In his very curious epistle to the emperor Trajan he affirms that the temples were almost deserted, that the sacred victims scarcely found any purchasers, and that the superstition had not only infected the cities, but had even spread itself into the villages and the open country of Pontus and Bithynia.

Without descending into a minute scrutiny of the expressions or of the motives of those writers who either celebrate or lament the progress of Christianity in the East, it may in general be observed that none of them have left us any grounds from whence a just estimate might be formed of the real numbers of the faithful in those provinces. One circumstance, however, has been fortunately preserved, which seems to cast a more distinct light on this obscure but interesting subject. Under the reign of Theodosius, after Christianity had enjoyed, during more than sixty years, the sunshine of Imperial favour, the ancient and illustrious church of Antioch consisted of one hundred thousand persons, three thousand of whom were supported out of the public oblations. The splendour and dignity of the queen of the East, the acknowledged populousness of Cæsarea, Seleucia, and Alexandria, and the destruction of two hundred and fifty thousand souls in the earthquake which afflicted Antioch under the elder Justin, are so many convincing proofs that the whole number of its inhabitants was not less than half a million, and that the Christians, however multiplied by zeal and power, did not exceed a fifth part of that great city. How different a proportion must we adopt when we compare the persecuted with the triumphant church, the West with the East, remote villages with populous towns, and countries recently converted to the faith with the place where the believers first received the appellation of Christians! It must not, however, be dissembled that, in another passage, Chrysostom, to whom we are indebted for this useful information, computes the multitude of the faithful as even superior to that of the Jews and Pagans. But the solution of this apparent difficulty is easy and obvious. The eloquent preacher draws a parallel between the civil and the ecclesiastical constitution of Antioch; between the list of Christians who had acquired heaven by baptism, and the list of citizens who had a right to share the public liberality. Slaves, strangers, and infants were comprised in the former; they were excluded from the latter.

The extensive commerce of Alexandria, and its proximity to Palestine, gave an easy entrance to the new religion. It was at first embraced by great numbers of the Therapeutæ, or Essenians, of the lake Mareotis, a Jewish sect which had abated much of its reverence for the Mosaic ceremonies. The austere life of the Essenians, their fasts and excommunications, the community of goods, the love of celibacy, their zeal for martyrdom, and the warmth though not the purity of their faith, already offered a very lively image of the primitive discipline. It was in the school of Alexandria that the Christian theology appears to have assumed a regular and scientifical form; and when Hadrian visited Egypt, he found a church composed of Jews and of Greeks, sufficiently important to attract the notice of that inquisitive prince. But the progress of Christianity was for a long time confined within the limits of a single city, which was itself a foreign colony, and till the close of the second century the predecessors of Demetrius were the only prelates of the Egyptian church. Three bishops were consecrated by the hands of Demetrius, and the number was increased to twenty by his successor Heraclas. The body of the natives, a people distinguished by a sullen inflexibility of temper, entertained the new doctrine with coldness and reluctance; and even in the time of Origen it was rare to meet with an Egyptian who had surmounted his early prejudices in favour of the sacred animals of his country. As soon, indeed, as Christianity ascended the throne, the zeal of those barbarians obeyed the prevailing impulsion; the cities of Egypt were filled with bishops, and the deserts of Thebais swarmed with hermits.

A perpetual stream of strangers and provincials flowed into the capacious bosom of Rome. Whatever was strange or odious, whoever was guilty or suspected, might hope, in the obscurity of that immense capital, to elude the vigilance of the law. In such a various conflux of nations, every teacher, either of truth or of falsehood, every founder, whether of a virtuous or a criminal association, might easily multiply his disciples or accomplices. The Christians of Rome, at the time of the accidental persecution of Nero, are represented by Tacitus as already amounting to a very great multitude, and the language of that great historian is almost similar to the style employed by Livy, when he relates the introduction and the suppression of the rites of Bacchus. After the Bacchanals had awakened the severity of the senate, it was likewise apprehended that a very great multitude, as it were *another people*, had been initiated into those abhorred mysteries. A more careful inquiry soon demonstrated that the offenders did not exceed seven thousand; a number indeed sufficiently alarming when considered as the object of public justice. It is with the same candid allowance that we should interpret the vague expressions of Tacitus, and in a former instance of Pliny, when they exaggerate the crowds of deluded fanatics who had forsaken the established worship of the gods. The church of Rome was undoubtedly the first and most populous of the empire; and we are possessed of an authentic record which attests the state of religion in that city about the middle of the third century, and after a peace of thirty-eight years. The clergy, at that time, consisted of a bishop, forty-six presbyters, seven deacons, as many sub-deacons, forty-two acolytes, and fifty readers, exorcists, and porters. The number of widows, of the infirm, and of the poor, who were maintained by the oblations of the faithful, amounted to fifteen hundred. From reason, as well as from the analogy of Antioch, we may venture to estimate the Christians of Rome at about fifty thousand. The populousness of that great capital cannot perhaps be exactly ascertained; but the most modest calculation will not surely reduce it lower than a million of inhabitants, of whom the Christians might constitute at the most a twentieth part.

The western provincials appeared to have derived the knowledge of Christianity from the same source which had diffused among them the language, the sentiments, and the manners of Rome. In this more important circumstance, Africa, as well as Gaul, was gradually fashioned to the imitation of the capital. Yet notwithstanding the many favourable occasions which might invite the Roman missionaries to visit their Latin provinces, it was late before they passed either the sea or the Alps; nor can we discover in those great countries any assured traces either of faith or of persecution that ascend higher than the reign of the Antonines. The slow progress of the Gospel in the cold climate of Gaul was extremely different from the eagerness with which it seems to have been received on the burning sands of Africa. The African Christians soon formed one of the principal members of the primitive church. The practice introduced into that province of appointing bishops to the most inconsiderable towns, and very frequently to the most obscure villages, contributed to multiply the splendour and importance of their religious societies, which during the course of the third century were animated by the zeal of Tertullian, directed by the abilities of Cyprian, and adorned by the eloquence of Lactantius. But if, on the contrary, we turn our eyes towards Gaul, we must content ourselves with discovering, in the time of Marcus Antoninus, the feeble and united congregations of Lyons and Vienne; and even as late as the reign of Decius we are assured that in a few cities only—Arles, Narbonne, Toulouse, Limoges, Clermont, Tours, and Paris—some scattered churches were supported by the devotion of a small number of Christians. Silence is indeed very consistent with devotion; but as it is seldom compatible with zeal we may perceive and lament the languid state of Christianity in those provinces which had exchanged the Celtic for the Latin tongue, since they did not, during the three first centuries, give birth to a single ecclesiastical writer. From Gaul, which claimed a just pre-eminence of learning and authority over all the countries on this side of the Alps, the light of the Gospel was more faintly reflected on the remote provinces of Spain and Britain; and if we may credit the vehement assertions of Tertullian, they had already received the first rays of the faith when he addressed his Apology to the magistrates of the emperor Severus. But the obscure and imperfect origin of the western churches of Europe has been so negligently recorded, that, if we would relate the time and manner of their foundation, we must supply the silence of antiquity by those legends which avarice or superstition long afterwards dictated to the monks in the lazy gloom of their convents.[10] Of these

[10]In the fifteenth century there were few who had either inclination or courage to question whether Joseph of Arimathea founded the monastery of Glastonbury, and whether Dionysius the Areopagite preferred the residence of Paris to that of Athens.

holy romances, that of the apostle St. James can alone, by its singular extravagance, deserve to be mentioned. From a peaceful fisherman of the lake of Gennesareth, he was transformed into a valorous knight, who charged at the head of the Spanish chivalry in their battles against the Moors. The gravest historians have celebrated his exploits; the miraculous shrine of Compostella displayed his power; and the sword of a military order, assisted by the terrors of the Inquisition, was sufficient to remove every objection of profane criticism.

The progress of Christianity was not confined to the Roman empire; and, according to the primitive fathers, who interpret facts by prophecy, the new religion, within a century after the death of its Divine Author, had already visited every part of the globe. "There exists not," says Justin Martyr, "a people, whether Greek or barbarian, or any other race of men, by whatsoever appellation or manners they may be distinguished, however ignorant of arts or agriculture, whether they dwell under tents, or wander about in covered waggons, among whom prayers are not offered up in the name of a crucified Jesus to the Father and Creator of all things." But this splendid exaggeration, which even at present it would be extremely difficult to reconcile with the real state of mankind, can be considered only as the rash sally of a devout but careless writer, the measure of whose belief was regulated by that of his wishes. But neither the belief nor the wishes of the fathers can alter the truth of history. It will still remain an undoubted fact that the barbarians of Scythia and Germany, who afterwards subverted the Roman monarchy, were involved in the darkness of paganism; and that even the conversion of Iberia, of Armenia, or of Æthiopia, was not attempted with any degree of success till the sceptre was in the hands of an orthodox emperor. Before that time the various accidents of war and commerce might indeed diffuse an imperfect knowledge of the Gospel among the tribes of Caledonia, and among the borders of the Rhine, the Danube, and the Euphrates. Beyond the last-mentioned river, Edessa was distinguished by a firm and early adherence to the faith. From Edessa the principles of Christianity were easily introduced into the Greek and Syrian cities which obeyed the successors of Artaxerxes; but they do not appear to have made any deep impression on the minds of the Persians, whose religious system, by the labours of a well-disciplined order of priests, had been constructed with much more art and solidity than the uncertain mythology of Greece and Rome.

From this impartial though imperfect survey of the progress of Christianity, it may perhaps seem probable that the number of its proselytes has been excessively magnified by fear on the one side, and by devotion on the other. According to the irreproachable testimony of Origen, the proportion of the faithful was very inconsiderable, when compared with the multitude of an unbelieving world; but, as we are left without any distinct information, it is impossible to determine, and it is difficult even to conjecture, the real numbers of the primitive Christians. The most favourable calculation, however, that can be deduced from the examples of Antioch and of Rome will not permit us to imagine that more than a twentieth part of the subjects of the empire had enlisted themselves under the banner of the Cross before the important conversion of Constantine. But their habits of faith, of zeal, and of union, seemed to multiply their numbers; and the same causes which contributed to their future increase served to render their actual strength more apparent and more formidable.

Such is the constitution of civil society, that, whilst a few persons are distinguished by riches, by honours, and by knowledge, the body of the people is condemned to obscurity, ignorance, and poverty. The Christian religion, which addressed itself to the whole human race, must consequently collect a far greater number of proselytes from the lower than from the superior ranks of life. This innocent and natural circumstance has been improved into a very odious imputation, which seems to be less strenuously denied by the apologists than it is urged by the adversaries of the faith; that the new sect of Christians was almost entirely composed of the dregs of the populace, of peasants and mechanics, of boys and women, of beggars and slaves, the last of whom might sometimes introduce the missionaries into the rich and noble families to which they belonged. These obscure teachers (such was the charge of malice and infidelity) are as mute in public as they are loquacious and dog-matical in private. Whilst they cautiously avoid the dangerous encounter of philosophers, they mingle with the rude and illiterate crowd, and insinuate themselves into those minds whom their age, their sex, or their education has the best disposed to receive the impression of superstitious terrors.

This unfavourable picture, though not devoid of a faint resemblance, betrays, by its dark colouring and distorted features, the pencil of an enemy. As the humble faith of Christ diffused itself through the world, it was embraced by several persons who derived some consequence from the advantages of nature or fortune. Aristides, who presented an eloquent apology to the emperor Hadrian, was an Athenian philosopher. Justin Martyr had sought divine knowledge in the schools of Zeno, of Aristotle, of Pythagoras, and of Plato, before he fortunately was accosted by the old man, or rather the angel, who turned his attention to the study of the Jewish prophets. Clemens of Alexandria had acquired much various reading in the Greek, and Tertullian in the Latin, language. Julius Africanus and Origen possessed a very considerable share of the learning of their times; and although the style of Cyprian is very different from that of Lactantius, we might almost discover that both those writers had been public teachers of rhetoric. Even the study of philosophy was at length introduced among the Christians, but it was not always productive of the most salutary effects; knowledge was as often the parent of heresy as of devotion, and the description which was designed for the followers of Artemon may, with equal propriety, be applied to the various sects that resisted the successors of the apostles. "They presume to alter the holy Scriptures, to abandon the ancient rule of faith, and to form their opinions according to the subtile precepts of logic. The science of the church is neglected for the study of geometry, and they lose sight of heaven while they are employed in measuring the earth. Euclid is perpetually in their hands. Aristotle and Theophrastus are the objects of their admiration; and they express an uncommon reverence for the works of Galen. Their errors are derived from the abuse of the arts and sciences of the infidels, and they corrupt the simplicity of the Gospel by the refinements of human reason." Nor can it be affirmed with truth that the advantages of birth and fortune were always separated from the profession of Christianity. Several Roman citizens were brought before the tribunal of Pliny, and he soon discovered that a great number of persons of *every order* of men in Bithynia had deserted the religion of their ancestors. His unsuspected testimony may, in this instance, obtain more credit than the bold challenge of Tertullian, when he addresses himself to the fears as well as to the humanity of the proconsul of Africa, by assuring him that if he persists in his cruel intentions he must decimate Carthage, and that he will find among the guilty many persons of his own rank, senators and matrons of noblest extraction, and the friends or relations of his most intimate friends. It appears, however, that about forty years afterwards the emperor Valerian was persuaded of the truth of this assertion, since in one of his rescripts he evidently supposes that senators, Roman knights, and ladies of quality, were engaged in the Christian

183

sect. The church still continued to increase its outward splendour as it lost its internal purity; and, in the reign of Diocletian, the palace, the courts of justice, and even the army, concealed a multitude of Christians, who endeavoured to reconcile the interests of the present with those of a future life.

And yet these exceptions are either too few in number, or too recent in time, entirely to remove the imputation of ignorance and obscurity which has been so arrogantly cast on the first proselytes of Christianity. Instead of employing in our defence the fictions of later ages, it will be more prudent to convert the occasion of scandal into a subject of edification. Our serious thoughts will suggest to us that the apostles themselves were chosen by Providence among the fishermen of Galilee, and that, the lower we depress the temporal condition of the first Christians, the more reason we shall find to admire their merit and success. It is incumbent on us diligently to remember that the kingdom of heaven was promised to the poor in spirit, and that minds afflicted by calamity and the contempt of mankind cheerfully listen to the divine promise of future happiness; while, on the contrary, the fortunate are satisfied with the possession of this world; and the wise abuse in doubt and dispute their vain superiority of reason and knowledge.

We stand in need of such reflections to comfort us for the loss of some illustrious characters, which in our eyes might have seemed the most worthy of the heavenly present. The names of Seneca, of the elder and the younger Pliny, of Tacitus, of Plutarch, of Galen, of the slave Epictetus, and of the emperor Marcus Antoninus, adorn the age in which they flourished, and exalt the dignity of human nature. They filled with glory their respective stations, either in active or contemplative life; their excellent understandings were improved by study; philosophy had purified their minds from the prejudices of the popular superstition; and their days were spent

184

in the pursuit of truth and the practice of virtue. Yet all these sages (it is no less an object of surprise than of concern) overlooked or rejected the perfection of the Christian system. Their language or their silence equally discover their contempt for the growing sect which in their time had diffused itself over the Roman empire. Those among them who condescend to mention the Christians consider them only as obstinate and perverse enthusiasts, who exacted an implicit submission to their mysterious doctrines, without being able to produce a single argument that could engage the attention of men of sense and learning.

It is at least doubtful whether any of these philosophers perused the apologies which the primitive Christians repeatedly published in behalf of themselves and of their religion; but it is much to be lamented that such a cause was not defended by abler advocates. They expose with superfluous wit and eloquence the extravagance of Polytheism. They interest our compassion by displaying the innocence and sufferings of their injured brethren. But when they would demonstrate the divine origin of Christianity, they insist much more strongly on the predictions which announced, than on the miracles which accompanied, the appearance of the Messiah. Their favourite argument might serve to edify a Christian or to convert a Jew, since both the one and the other acknowledge the authority of those prophecies, and both are obliged, with devout reverence, to search for their sense and their accomplishment. But this mode of persuasion loses much of its weight and influence when it is addressed to those who neither understand nor respect the Mosaic dispensation and the prophetic style. In the unskilful hands of Justin and of the succeeding apologists, the sublime meaning of the Hebrew oracles evaporates in distant types, affected conceits, and cold allegories; and even their authenticity was rendered suspicious to an unenlightened Gentile, by the mixture of pious forgeries which, under the names of Orpheus,

Hermes, and the Sibyls, were obtruded on him as of equal value with the genuine inspirations of Heaven. The adoption of fraud and sophistry in the defence of revelation too often reminds us of the injudicious conduct of those poets who load their *invulnerable* heroes with a useless weight of cumbersome and brittle armour.

But how shall we excuse the supine inattention of the Pagan and philosophic world to those evidences which were presented by the hand of Omnipotence, not to their reason, but to their senses? During the age of Christ, of his apostles, and of their first disciples, the doctrine which they preached was confirmed by innumerable prodigies. The lame walked, the blind saw, the sick were healed, the dead were raised, dæmons were expelled, and the laws of Nature were frequently suspended for the benefit of the church. But the sages of Greece and Rome turned aside from the awful spectacle, and, pursuing the ordinary occupations of life and study, appeared unconscious of any alterations in the moral or physical government of the world. Under the reign of Tiberius, the whole earth, or at least a celebrated province of the Roman empire, was involved in a preternatural darkness of three hours. Even this miraculous event, which ought to have excited the wonder, the curiosity, and the devotion of mankind, passed without notice in an age of science and history. It happened during the lifetime of Seneca and the elder Pliny, who must have experienced the immediate effects, or received the earliest intelligence, of the prodigy. Each of these philosophers, in a laborious work, has recorded all the great phenomena of Nature, earthquakes, meteors, comets, and eclipses, which his indefatigable curiosity could collect. Both the one and the other have omitted to mention the greatest phenomenon to which the mortal eye has been witness since the creation of the globe. A distinct chapter of Pliny is designed for eclipses of an extraordinary nature and unusual duration; but he contents himself with describing the singular defect of light which followed the murder of Cæsar, when, during the greatest part of a year, the orb of the sun appeared pale and without splendour. This season of obscurity, which cannot surely be compared with the preternatural darkness of the Passion, had been already celebrated by most of the poets and historians of that memorable age.

CHAPTER VI

CHURCH AND STATE
IN THE ROMAN EMPIRE:
THE PERSECUTION
OF DIOCLETIAN

For the first two centuries after Christ, the Roman State had generally tolerated the Christian Church as one religion among many. But in the convulsions of the third century, the claims of the Church seemed to threaten society, and under Diocletian a direct collision occurred. Diocletian finally ranged himself against the Church, which suffered, under his edicts, its last great persecution by the Roman state. In his chapter XVI, Gibbon describes the situation of the Church in the years before its final triumph under Constantine.

Amidst the frequent revolutions of the empire the Christians still flourished in peace and prosperity; and notwithstanding a celebrated era of martyrs has been deduced from the accession of Diocletian, the new system of policy, introduced and maintained by the wisdom of that prince, continued, during more than eighteen years, to breathe the mildest and most liberal spirit of religious toleration. The mind of Diocletian himself was less adapted indeed to speculative inquiries than to the active labours of war and government. His prudence rendered him averse to any great innovation, and, though his temper was not very susceptible of zeal or enthusiasm, he always maintained an habitual regard for the ancient deities of the empire. But the leisure of the two empresses, of his wife Prisca, and of Valeria his daughter, permitted them to listen with more attention and respect to the truths of Christianity, which in every age has acknowledged its important obligations to female devotion. The principal eunuchs, Lucian and Dorotheus, Gorgonius and Andrew, who attended the person, possessed the favour, and governed the household of Diocletian, protected by their powerful influence the faith which they had embraced. Their example was imitated by many of the most considerable officers of the palace, who, in their respective stations, had the care of the Imperial ornaments, of the robes, of the furniture, of the jewels, and even of the private treasury; and, though it might sometimes be incumbent on them to accompany the emperor when he sacrificed in the temple, they enjoyed, with their wives, their children, and their slaves, the free exercise of the Christian religion. Diocletian and his colleagues frequently conferred the most important offices on those persons who avowed their abhorrence for the worship of the gods, but who had displayed abilities proper for the service of the state. The bishops held an honourable rank in their respective provinces, and were treated with distinction and respect, not only by the people, but by the magistrates themselves. Almost in every city the ancient churches were found insufficient to contain the increasing multitude of proselytes; and in their place more stately and capacious edifices were erected for the public worship of the faithful. The corruption of manners and principles, so forcibly lamented by Eusebius, may be considered, not only as a consequence, but as a proof, of the liberty which the Christians enjoyed and abused under the reign of Diocletian. Prosperity had relaxed the nerves of discipline. Fraud, envy, and malice prevailed in every congregation. The presbyters aspired to the episcopal office, which every day became an object more worthy of their ambition. The bishops, who contended with each other for ecclesiastical pre-eminence, appeared by their conduct to claim a secular and tyrannical power in the church; and the lively faith which still distinguished the Christians from the Gentiles was shown much less in their lives than in their controversial writings.

Notwithstanding this seeming security, an attentive observer might discern some symptoms that threatened the church with a more violent persecution than any which she had yet endured. The zeal and rapid progress of the Christians awakened the Polytheists from their supine indifference in the cause of those deities whom custom and education had taught them to revere. The mutual provocations of a religious war, which had already continued above two hundred years, exasperated the animosity of the contending parties. The Pagans were incensed at the rashness of a recent and obscure sect, which presumed to accuse their countrymen of error, and to devote their ancestors to eternal misery. The habits of justifying the popular mythology against the invectives of an implacable enemy, produced in their minds some sentiments of faith and reverence for a system which they had been accustomed to consider with the most careless levity. The supernatural powers assumed by the church inspired at the same time terror and emulation. The followers of the established religion intrenched themselves behind a similar fortification of prodigies; invented new modes of sacrifice, of expiation, and of initiation;[1] attempted to revive the credit of their expiring oracles; and listened with eager credulity to every impostor who flattered their prejudices by a tale of wonders. Both parties seemed to acknowledge the truth of those miracles which were claimed by their adversaries; and while they were contented with ascribing them to the arts of magic, and to the power of dæmons, they mutually concurred in restoring and establishing the reign of superstition.

---

[1]We might quote, among a great number of instances, the mysterious worship of Mithras and the Taurobolia; the latter of which became fashionable in the time of the Antonines. The romance of Apuleius is as full of devotion as of satire.

Philosophy, her most dangerous enemy, was now converted into her most useful ally. The groves of the Academy, the gardens of Epicurus, and even the portico of the Stoics, were almost deserted, as so many different schools of scepticism or impiety; and many among the Romans were desirous that the writings of Cicero should be condemned and suppressed by the authority of the senate. The prevailing sect of the new Platonicians judged it prudent to connect themselves with the priest, whom perhaps they despised, against the Christians, whom they had reason to fear. These fashionable philosophers prosecuted the design of extracting allegorical wisdom from the fictions of the Greek poets; instituted mysterious rites of devotion for the use of their chosen disciples; recommended the worship of the ancient gods as the emblems or ministers of the Supreme Deity, and composed against the faith of the Gospel many elaborate treatises, which have since been committed to the flames by the prudence of orthodox emperors.

Although the policy of Diocletian and the humanity of Constantius inclined them to preserve inviolate the maxims of toleration, it was soon discovered that their two associates, Maximian and Galerius, entertained the most implacable aversion for the name and religion of the Christians. The minds of those princes had never been enlightened by science; education had never softened their temper. They owed their greatness to their swords, and in their most elevated fortune they still retained their superstitious prejudices of soldiers and peasants. In the general administration of the provinces they obeyed the laws which their benefactor had established; but they frequently found occasions of exercising within their camp and palaces a secret persecution,[2] for which

[2]Eusebius, limits the number of military martyrs, by a remarkable expression (σπανίως τούτων είς που καὶ δεύτερος), of which neither his Latin nor French translator have rendered the energy. Notwithstanding the authority of Eusebius, and the silence of Lactantius, Ambrose, Sulpicius, Orosius, etc., it has been long

the imprudent zeal of the Christians sometimes offered the most specious pretences. A sentence of death was executed upon Maximilianus, an African youth, who had been produced by his own father before the magistrate as a sufficient and legal recruit, but who obstinately persisted in declaring that his conscience would not permit him to embrace the profession of a soldier. It could scarcely be expected that any government should suffer the action of Marcellus the centurion to pass with impunity. On the day of a public festival, that officer threw away his belt, his arms, and the ensigns of his office, and exclaimed with a loud voice that he would obey none but Jesus Christ the eternal King, and that he renounced for ever the use of carnal weapons, and the service of an idolatrous master. The soldiers, as soon as they recovered from their astonishment, secured the person of Marcellus. He was examined in the city of Tingi by the president of that part of Mauritania; and as he was convicted by his own confession, he was condemned and beheaded for the crime of desertion. Examples of such a nature savour much less of religious persecution than of martial or even civil law: but they served to alienate the mind of the emperors; to justify the severity of Galerius, who dismissed a great number of Christian officers from their employments; and to authorise the opinion that a sect of enthusiasts, which avowed principles so repugnant to the public safety, must either remain useless, or would soon become dangerous subjects of the empire.

After the success of the Persian war had raised the hopes and the reputation of Galerius, he passed a winter

believed that the Thebæan legion, consisting of 6000 Christians, suffered martyrdom by the order of Maximian, in the valley of the Pennine Alps. The story was first published about the middle of the fifth century, by Eucherius bishop of Lyons, who received it from certain persons, who received it from Isaac bishop of Geneva, who is said to have received it from Theodore bishop of Octodurum. The abbey of St. Maurice still subsists, a rich monument of the credulity of Sigismund, king of Burgundy.

with Diocletian in the palace of Nicomedia; and the fate of Christianity became the object of their secret consultations. The experienced emperor was still inclined to pursue measures of lenity; and though he readily consented to exclude the Christians from holding any employments in the household or the army, he urged in the strongest terms the danger as well as cruelty of shedding the blood of those deluded fanatics. Galerius at length extorted from him the permission of summoning a council, composed of a few persons the most distinguished in the civil and military departments of the state. The important question was agitated in their presence, and those ambitious courtiers easily discerned that it was incumbent on them to second, by their eloquence, the importunate violence of the Cæsar. It may be presumed that they insisted on every topic which might interest the pride, the piety, or the fears, of their sovereign in the destruction of Christianity. Perhaps they represented that the glorious work of the deliverance of the empire was left imperfect, as long as an independent people was permitted to subsist and multiply in the heart of the provinces. The Christians (it might speciously be alleged), renouncing the gods and the institutions of Rome, had constituted a distinct republic, which might yet be suppressed before it had acquired any military force; but which was already governed by its own laws and magistrates, was possessed of a public treasure, and was intimately connected in all its parts by the frequent assemblies of the bishops, to whose decrees their numerous and opulent congregations yielded an implicit obedience. Arguments like these may seem to have determined the reluctant mind of Diocletian to embrace a new system of persecution: but though we may suspect, it is not in our power to relate, the secret intrigues of the palace, the private views and resentments, the jealousy of women or eunuchs, and all those trifling but decisive causes which so often influence the fate of empires and the councils of the wisest monarchs.

193

The pleasure of the emperors was at length signified to the Christians, who, during the course of this melancholy winter, had expected, with anxiety, the result of so many secret consultations. The twenty-third of February, which coincided with the Roman festival of the Terminalia, was appointed (whether from accident or design) to set bounds to the progress of Christianity. At the earliest dawn of day the Prætorian præfect, accompanied by several generals, tribunes, and officers of the revenue, repaired to the principal church of Nicomedia, which was situated on an eminence in the most populous and beautiful part of the city. The doors were instantly broke open; they rushed into the sanctuary; and as they searched in vain for some visible object of worship, they were obliged to content themselves with committing to the flames the volumes of Holy Scripture. The ministers of Diocletian were followed by a numerous body of guards and pioneers, who marched in order of battle, and were provided with all the instruments used in the destruction of fortified cities. By their incessant labour, a sacred edifice, which towered above the Imperial palace, and had long excited the indignation and envy of the Gentiles, was in a few hours levelled with the ground.

The next day the general edict of persecution was published; and though Diocletian, still averse to the effusion of blood, had moderated the fury of Galerius, who proposed that every one refusing to offer sacrifice should immediately be burnt alive, the penalties inflicted on the obstinacy of the Christians might be deemed sufficiently rigorous and effectual. It was enacted that their churches, in all the provinces of the empire, should be demolished to their foundations; and the punishment of death was denounced against all who should presume to hold any secret assemblies for the purpose of religious worship. The philosophers, who now assumed the unworthy office of directing the blind zeal of persecution, had diligently studied the nature and genius of the Christian religion;

and as they were not ignorant that the speculative doctrines of the faith were supposed to be contained in the writings of the prophets, of the evangelists, and of the apostles, they most probably suggested the order that the bishops and presbyters should deliver all their sacred books into the hands of the magistrates; who were commanded, under the severest penalties, to burn them in a public and solemn manner. By the same edict, the property of the church was at once confiscated; and the several parts of which it might consist were either sold to the highest bidder, united to the Imperial domain, bestowed on the cities and corporations, or granted to the solicitations of rapacious courtiers. After taking such effectual measures to abolish the worship and to dissolve the government of the Christians, it was thought necessary to subject to the most intolerable hardships the condition of those perverse individuals who should still reject the religion of nature, of Rome, and of their ancestors. Persons of a liberal birth were declared incapable of holding any honours or employments; slaves were for ever deprived of the hopes of freedom; and the whole body of the people were put out of the protection of the law. The judges were authorised to hear and to determine every action that was brought against a Christian. But the Christians were not permitted to complain of any injury which they themselves had suffered; and thus those unfortunate sectaries were exposed to the severity, while they were excluded from the benefits, of public justice. This new species of martyrdom, so painful and lingering, so obscure and ignominious, was, perhaps, the most proper to weary the constancy of the faithful: nor can it be doubted that the passions and interest of mankind were disposed on this occasion to second the designs of the emperors. But the policy of a well-ordered government must sometimes have interposed in behalf of the oppressed Christians; nor was it possible for the Roman princes entirely to remove the apprehension of punishment, or to connive at every act of fraud and violence, without exposing their own authority and the rest of their subjects to the most alarming dangers.

This edict was scarcely exhibited to the public view, in the most conspicuous place of Nicomedia, before it was torn down by the hands of a Christian, who expressed at the same time, by the bitterest invectives, his contempt as well as abhorrence for such impious and tyrannical governors. His offence, according to the mildest laws, amounted to treason, and deserved death. And if it be true that he was a person of rank and education, those circumstances could serve only to aggravate his guilt. He was burnt, or rather roasted, by a slow fire; and his executioners, zealous to revenge the personal insult which had been offered to the emperors, exhausted every refinement of cruelty, without being able to subdue his patience, or to alter the steady and insulting smile which, in his dying agonies, he still preserved in his countenance. The Christians, though they confessed that his conduct had not been strictly conformable to the laws of prudence, admired the divine fervour of his zeal; and the excessive commendations which they lavished on the memory of their hero and martyr contributed to fix a deep impression of terror and hatred in the mind of Diocletian.

His fears were soon alarmed by the view of a danger from which he very narrowly escaped. Within fifteen days the palace of Nicomedia, and even the bedchamber of Diocletian, were twice in flames; and though both times they were extinguished without any material damage, the singular repetition of the fire was justly considered as an evident proof that it had not been the effect of chance or negligence. The suspicion naturally fell on the Christians; and it was suggested, with some degree of probability, that those desperate fanatics, provoked by their present sufferings, and apprehensive of impending calamities, had entered into a conspiracy with their faithful brethren, the eunuchs of the palace, against the lives of two emperors whom they detested as the irreconcilable enemies of the church of God. Jealousy and resentment prevailed in every breast, but especially in that of Diocletian. A great number of persons, distinguished either by the offices which they had filled or by the favour which they had enjoyed, were thrown into prison. Every mode of torture was put in practice, and the court, as well as city, was polluted with many bloody executions. But as it was found impossible to extort any discovery of this mysterious transaction, it seems incumbent on us either to presume the innocence, or to admire the resolution, of the sufferers. A few days afterwards Galerius hastily withdrew himself from Nicomedia, declaring that, if he delayed his departure from that devoted palace, he should fall a sacrifice to the rage of the Christians. The ecclesiastical historians, from whom alone we derive a partial and imperfect knowledge of this persecution, are at a loss how to account for the fears and danger of the emperors. Two of these writers, a prince and a rhetorician, were eye-witnesses of the fire of Nicomedia. The one ascribes it to lightning and the divine wrath, the other affirms that it was kindled by the malice of Galerius himself.

As the edict against the Christians was designed for a general law of the whole empire, and as Diocletian and Galerius, though they might not wait for the consent, were assured of the concurrence, of the Western princes, it would appear more consonant to our ideas of policy that the governors of all the provinces should have received secret instructions to publish, on one and the same day, this declaration of war within their respective departments. It was at least to be expected that the convenience of the public highways and established posts would have enabled the emperors to transmit their orders with the utmost despatch from the palace of Nicomedia to the extremities of the Roman world; and that they would not have suffered fifty days to elapse before the edict was published in Syria, and near four months before it was signified to the cities of Africa. This delay may perhaps be imputed to the cautious temper of Diocletian, who had yielded a reluctant consent to the measures of persecution, and who was desirous of trying the experiment under his more immediate eye before he gave way to the disorders and discontent which it must inevitably occasion in the distant provinces. At first, indeed, the magistrates were restrained from the effusion of blood; but the use of every other severity was permitted, and even recommended to their zeal; nor could the Christians, though they cheerfully resigned the ornaments of their churches, resolve to interrupt their religious assemblies, or to deliver their sacred books to the flames. The pious obstinacy of Felix, an African bishop, appears to have embarrassed the subordinate ministers of the government. The curator of his city sent him in chains to the proconsul. The proconsul transmitted him to the Prætorian præfect of Italy; and Felix, who disdained even to give an evasive answer, was at length beheaded at Venusia, in Lucania, a place on which the birth of Horace has conferred fame. This precedent, and perhaps some Imperial rescript, which was issued in consequence of it, appeared to authorise the governors of provinces in punishing with death the refusal of the Christians to deliver up their sacred books. There were undoubtedly many persons who embraced this opportunity of obtaining the crown of martyrdom; but there were likewise too many who purchased an ignominious life by discovering and betraying the Holy Scripture into the hands of infidels. A great number even of bishops and presbyters acquired, by this criminal compliance, the opprobrious epithet of *Traditors;* and their offence was productive of much present scandal and of much future discord in the African church.

The copies as well as the versions of Scripture were already so multiplied in the empire, that the most severe inquisition could no longer be attended with any fatal consequences; and even the sacrifice of those volumes which, in every congregation, were preserved for public use, required the consent of some treacherous and unworthy Christians. But the ruin of the churches was easily effected by the authority of the government and by the labour of the Pagans. In some provinces, however, the magistrates contented themselves with shutting up the places of religious worship. In others they more literally complied with the terms of the edict; and, after taking away the doors, the benches, and the pulpit, which they burnt as it were in a funeral pile, they completely demolished the remainder of the edifice. It is perhaps to this melancholy occasion that we should apply a very remarkable story, which is related with so many circumstances of variety and improbability that it serves rather to excite than to satisfy our curiosity. In a small town in Phrygia, of whose name as well as situation we are left ignorant, it should seem that the magistrates and the body of the people had embraced the Christian faith; and as some resistance might be apprehended to the execution of the edict, the governor of the province was supported by a numerous detachment of legionaries. On their approach the citizens threw themselves into the church, with the resolution either of defending by arms that sacred edifice or of perishing in its ruins. They indignantly rejected the notice and permission which was given them to retire, till the soldiers, provoked by their obstinate refusal, set fire to the building on all sides, and consumed, by this extraordinary kind of martyrdom, a great number of Phrygians, with their wives and children.

Some slight disturbances, though they were suppressed almost as soon as excited, in Syria and the frontiers of Armenia, afforded the enemies of the church a very plausible occasion to insinuate that those troubles had been secretly fomented by the intrigues of the bishops, who had already forgotten their ostentatious professions of passive and unlimited obedience. The resentment, or the fears, of Diocletian at length transported him beyond the bounds of moderation which he had hitherto preserved, and he declared, in a series of cruel edicts, his intention of abolishing the Christian name. By the first of these edicts the governors of the provinces were directed to apprehend all persons of the ecclesiastical order; and the prisons destined for the vilest criminals were soon filled with a multitude of bishops, presbyters, deacons, readers, and exorcists. By a second edict the magistrates were commanded to employ every method of severity which might reclaim them from their odious superstition, and oblige them to return to the established worship of the gods. This rigorous order was extended, by a subsequent edict, to the whole body of Christians, who were exposed to a violent and general persecution. Instead of those salutary restraints which had required the direct and solemn testimony of an accuser, it became the duty as well as the interest of the Imperial officers to discover, to pursue, and to torment the most obnoxious among the faithful. Heavy penalties were denounced against all who should presume to save a proscribed sectary from the just indignation of the gods and of the emperors. Yet, notwithstanding the severity of this law, the virtuous courage of many of the Pagans, in concealing their friends or relations, affords an honourable proof that the rage of superstition had not extinguished in their minds the sentiments of nature and humanity.

Diocletian had no sooner published his edicts against the Christians than, as if he had been desirous of committing to other hands the work of persecution, he divested himself of the Imperial purple. The character and situation of his colleagues and successors sometimes urged them to enforce, and sometimes inclined them to suspend, the execution of these rigorous laws; nor can we acquire a just and distinct idea of this important period of ecclesiastical history unless we separately consider the state of Christianity, in the different parts of the empire, during the space of ten years which elapsed between the first edicts of Diocletian and the final peace of the church.

PVRPVREVS ENTINVS ~ BACCIBVS

ASTIVVS

7-8
Two fourth-century mosaics showing gladiators in the amphitheatre, and dancing girls of the "decadent," pre-Christian period of the empire.

The mild and humane temper of Constantius was averse to the oppression of any part of his subjects. The principal offices of his palace were exercised by Christians. He loved their persons, esteemed their fidelity, and entertained not any dislike to their religious principles. But as long as Constantius remained in the subordinate station of Cæsar, it was not in his power openly to reject the edicts of Diocletian, or to disobey the commands of Maximian. His authority contributed, however, to alleviate the sufferings which he pitied and abhorred. He consented with reluctance to the ruin of the churches, but he ventured to protect the Christians themselves from the fury of the populace and from the rigour of the laws. The provinces of Gaul (under which we may probably include those of Britain) were indebted for the singular tranquillity which they enjoyed to the gentle interposition of their sovereign. But Datianus, the president or governor of Spain, actuated either by zeal or policy, chose rather to execute the public edicts of the emperors than to understand the secret intentions of Constantius; and it can scarcely be doubted that his provincial administration was stained with the blood of a few martyrs. The elevation of Constantius to the supreme and independent dignity of Augustus gave a free scope to the exercise of his virtues, and the shortness of his reign did not prevent him from establishing a system of toleration of which he left the precept and the example to his son Constantine. His fortunate son, from the first moment of his accession declaring himself the protector of the church, at length deserved the appellation of the first emperor who publicly professed and established the Christian religion. The motives of his conversion, as they may variously be deduced from benevolence, from policy, from conviction, or from remorse, and the progress of the revolution, which, under his powerful influence and that of his sons, rendered Christianity the reigning religion of the Roman empire, will form a very interesting and important chapter in the second volume of this history. At present it may be sufficient to observe that every victory of Constantine was productive of some relief or benefit to the church.

The provinces of Italy and Africa experienced a short but violent persecution. The rigorous edicts of Diocletian were strictly and cheerfully executed by his associate Maximian, who had long hated the Christians, and who delighted in acts of blood and violence. In the autumn of the first year of the persecution the two emperors met at Rome to celebrate their triumph; several oppressive laws appear to have issued from their secret consultations, and the diligence of the magistrates was animated by the presence of their sovereigns. After Diocletian had divested himself of the purple, Italy and Africa were administered under the name of Severus, and were exposed, without defence, to the implacable resentment of his master Galerius. Among the martyrs of Rome, Adauctus deserves the notice of posterity. He was of a noble family in Italy, and had raised himself, through the successive honours of the palace, to the important office of treasurer of the private demesnes. Adauctus is the more remarkable for being the only person of rank and distinction who appears to have suffered death during the whole course of this general persecution.

The revolt of Maxentius immediately restored peace to the churches of Italy and Africa, and the same tyrant who oppressed every other class of his subjects showed himself just, humane, and even partial, towards the afflicted Christians. He depended on their gratitude and affection, and very naturally presumed that the injuries which they had suffered, and the dangers which they still apprehended, from his most inveterate enemy, would secure the fidelity of a party already considerable by their numbers and opulence. Even the conduct of Maxentius towards the bishops of Rome and Carthage may be considered as the proof of his toleration, since it is probable that the most orthodox princes would adopt the same measures with regard to their established clergy. Mar-

cellus, the former of those prelates, had thrown the
capital into confusion by the severe penance which he
imposed on a great number of Christians who, during
the late persecution, had renounced or dissembled their
religion. The rage of faction broke out in frequent and
violent seditions; the blood of the faithful was shed by
each other's hands; and the exile of Marcellus, whose
prudence seems to have been less eminent than his zeal,
was found to be the only measure capable of restoring
peace to the distracted church of Rome. The behaviour
of Mensurius, bishop of Carthage, appears to have been
still more reprehensible. A deacon of that city had published a libel against the emperor. The offender took
refuge in the episcopal palace, and, though it was somewhat early to advance any claims of ecclesiastical immunities, the bishop refused to deliver him up to the
officers of justice. For this treasonable resistance Mensurius was summoned to court, and, instead of receiving
a legal sentence of death or banishment, he was permitted, after a short examination, to return to his diocese. Such was the happy condition of the Christian subjects of Maxentius, that, whenever they were desirous of
procuring for their own use any bodies of martyrs, they
were obliged to purchase them from the most distant
provinces of the East. A story is related of Algæ, a Roman lady, descended from a consular family, and possessed of so ample an estate that it required the management of seventy-three stewards. Among these Boniface
was the favourite of his mistress, and, as Algæ mixed
love with devotion, it is reported that he was admitted to
share her bed. Her fortune enabled her to gratify the
pious desire of obtaining some sacred relics from the
East. She intrusted Boniface with a considerable sum
of gold and a large quantity of aromatics, and her lover,
attended by twelve horsemen and three covered chariots,
undertook a remote pilgrimage as far as Tarsus in Cilicia.

The sanguinary temper of Galerius, the first and principal author of the persecution, was formidable to those

Christians whom their misfortunes had placed within the limits of his dominions; and it may fairly be presumed that many persons of a middle rank, who were not confined by the chains either of wealth or of poverty, very frequently deserted their native country, and sought a refuge in the milder climate of the West. As long as he commanded only the armies and provinces of Illyricum, he could with difficulty either find or make a considerable number of martyrs in a warlike country which had entertained the missionaries of the Gospel with more coldness and reluctance than any other part of the empire. But when Galerius had obtained the supreme power and the government of the East, he indulged in their fullest extent his zeal and cruelty, not only in the provinces of Thrace and Asia, which acknowledged his immediate jurisdiction, but in those of Syria, Palestine, and Egypt, where Maximian gratified his own inclination by yielding a rigorous obedience to the stern commands of his benefactor.

The frequent disappointments of his ambitious views, the experience of six years of persecution, and the salutary reflections which a lingering and painful distemper suggested to the mind of Galerius, at length convinced him that the most violent efforts of despotism are insufficient to extirpate a whole people, or to subdue their religious prejudices. Desirous of repairing the mischief that he had occasioned, he published in his own name, and in those of Licinius and Constantine, a general edict, which, after a pompous recital of the Imperial titles, proceeded in the following manner:

"Among the important cares which have occupied our mind for the utility and preservation of the empire, it was our intention to correct and re-establish all things according to the ancient laws and public discipline of the Romans. We were particularly desirous of reclaiming into the way of reason and nature the deluded Christians who had renounced the religion and ceremonies instituted by their fathers, and, presumptuously despising the practice of antiquity, had invented extravagant laws and opinions according to the dictates of their fancy, and had collected a various society from the different provinces of our empire. The edicts which we have published to enforce the worship of the gods having exposed many of the Christians to danger and distress, many having suffered death, and many more, who still persist in their impious folly, being left destitute of *any* public exercise of religion, we are disposed to extend to those unhappy men the effects of our wonted clemency. We permit them, therefore, freely to profess their private opinions, and to assemble in their conventicles without fear or molestation, provided always that they preserve a due respect to the established laws and government. By another rescript we shall signify our intentions to the judges and magistrates, and we -hope that our indulgence will engage the Christians to offer up their prayers to the Deity whom they adore for our safety and prosperity, for their own, and for that of the republic." It is not usually in the language of edicts and manifestos that we should search for the real character of the secret motives of princes; but as these were the words of a dying emperor, his situation, perhaps, may be admitted as a pledge of his sincerity.

When Galerius subscribed this edict of toleration, he was well assured that Licinius would readily comply with the inclinations of his friend and benefactor, and that any measures in favour of the Christians would obtain the approbation of Constantine. But the emperor would not venture to insert in the preamble the name of Maximian, whose consent was of the greatest importance, and who succeeded a few days afterwards to the provinces of Asia. In the first six months, however, of his new reign, Maximian affected to adopt the prudent counsels of his predecessor; and though he never condescended to secure the tranquillity of the church by a public edict, Sabinus, his Prætorian præfect, addressed a circular letter to all the governors and magistrates of the provinces, expatiating on the Imperial clemency, acknowledging the invincible obstinacy of the Christians, and directing the officers of justice to cease their ineffectual prosecutions, and to connive at the secret assemblies of those enthusiasts. In consequence of these orders, great numbers of Christians were released from prison, or delivered from the mines. The confessors, singing hymns of triumph, returned into their own countries, and those who had yielded to the violence of the tempest, solicited with tears of repentance their re-admission into the bosom of the church.

But this treacherous calm was of short duration; nor could the Christians of the East place any confidence in the character of their sovereign. Cruelty and superstition were the ruling passions of the soul of Maximian. The former suggested the means, the latter pointed out the objects, of persecution. The emperor was devoted to the worship of the gods, to the study of magic, and to the belief of oracles. The prophets or philosophers, whom he revered as the favourites of Heaven, were frequently raised to the government of provinces, and admitted into his most secret councils. They easily convinced him that the Christians had been indebted for their victories to their regular discipline, and that the weakness of polytheism had principally flowed from a want of union and subordination among the ministers of religion. A system of government was therefore instituted, which was evidently copied from the policy of the church. In all the great cities of the empire, the temples were repaired and beautified by the order of Maximian, and the officiating priests of the various deities were subjected to the authority of a superior pontiff destined to oppose the bishop, and to promote the cause of paganism. These pontiffs acknowledged, in their turn, the supreme jurisdiction of the metropolitans or high priests of the province, who acted as the immediate viceregents of the emperor himself. A white robe was the ensign of their dignity; and these new prelates were carefully selected from the most noble and opulent families. By the influence of the magistrates, and of the sacerdotal order, a great number of dutiful addresses were obtained, particularly from the cities of Nicomedia, Antioch, and Tyre, which artfully represented the well-known intentions of the court as the general sense of the people; solicited the emperor to consult the laws of justice rather than the dictates of his clemency; expressed their abhorrence of the Christians, and humbly prayed that those impious sectaries might at least be excluded from the limits of their respective territories. The answer of Maximian to the address which he obtained from the citizens of Tyre is still extant. He praises their zeal and devotion in terms of the highest satisfaction, descants on the obstinate impiety of the Christians, and betrays, by the readiness with which he consents to their banishment, that he considered himself as receiving, rather than as conferring, an obligation. The priests as well as the magistrates were empowered to enforce the execution of his edicts, which were engraved on tables of brass; and though it was recommended to them to avoid the effusion of blood, the most cruel and ignominious punishments were inflicted on the refractory Christians.

The Asiatic Christians had everything to dread from the severity of a bigoted monarch who prepared his measures of violence with such deliberate policy. But a few months had scarcely elapsed before the edicts published by the two Western emperors obliged Maximian to suspend the prosecution of his designs: the civil war which he so rashly undertook against Licinius employed all his attention; and the defeat and death of Maximian soon delivered the church from the last and most implacable of her enemies.

In this general view of the persecution which was first authorised by the edicts of Diocletian, I have purposely refrained from describing the particular sufferings and deaths of the Christian martyrs. It would have been an easy task, from the history of Eusebius, from the declamations of Lactantius, and from the most ancient acts, to collect a long series of horrid and disgusting pictures, and to fill many pages with racks and scourges, with iron hooks and red-hot beds, and with all the variety of tortures which fire and steel, savage beasts, and more savage executioners, could inflict on the human body. These melancholy scenes might be enlivened by a crowd of visions and miracles destined either to delay the death, to celebrate the triumph, or to discover the relics of those canonised saints who suffered for the name of Christ. But I cannot determine what I ought to transcribe, till I am satisfied how much I ought to believe. The gravest of the ecclesiastical historians, Eusebius himself, indirectly confesses that he has related whatever might redound to the glory, and that he has suppressed all that could tend to the disgrace, of religion. Such an acknowledgment will naturally excite a suspicion that a writer who has so openly violated one of the fundamental laws of history has not paid a very strict regard to the observance of the other; and the suspicion will derive additional credit from the character of Eusebius, which was less tinctured with credulity, and more practised in the arts of courts, than that of almost any of his contemporaries. On some particular occasions, when the magistrates were exasperated by some personal motives of interest or resentment, when the zeal of the martyrs urged them to forget the rules of prudence, and perhaps of decency, to overturn the altars, to pour out imprecations against the emperors, or to strike the judge as he sat on his tribunal, it may be presumed that every mode of torture which cruelty could invent, or constancy could endure, was exhausted on those devoted victims. Two circumstances, however, have been unwarily mentioned, which insinuate that the general treatment of the Christians who had been apprehended by the officers of justice was less intolerable than it is usually imagined to have been. 1. The confessors who were condemned to work in the mines were permitted by the humanity or the negligence of their keepers to build chapels, and freely to profess their religion in the midst of those dreary habitations. 2. The bishops were obliged to check and to censure the forward zeal of the Christians, who voluntarily threw themselves into the hands of the magistrates. Some of these were persons oppressed by poverty and debts, who blindly sought to terminate a miserable existence by a glorious death. Others were allured by the hope that a short confinement would expiate the sins of a whole life; and others again were actuated by the less honourable motive of deriving a plentiful subsistence, and perhaps a considerable profit, from the alms which the charity of the faithful bestowed on the prisoners. After the church had triumphed over all her enemies, the interest as well as vanity of the captives prompted them to magnify the merit of their respective suffering. A convenient distance of time or place gave an ample scope to the progress of fiction; and the frequent instances which might be alleged of holy martyrs whose wounds had been instantly healed, whose strength had been renewed, and whose lost members had miraculously been restored, were extremely convenient for the purpose of removing every difficulty, and of silencing every objection. The most extravagant legends, as they conduced to the honour of the church, were applauded by the credulous multitude, countenanced by the power of the clergy, and attested by the suspicious evidence of ecclesiastical history.

The vague descriptions of exile and imprisonment, of pain and torture, are so easily exaggerated or softened by the pencil of an artful orator, that we are naturally induced to inquire into a fact of a more distinct and stubborn kind; the number of persons who suffered death in consequence of the edicts published by Diocletian, his associates, and his successors. The recent legendaries record whole armies and cities which were at once swept away by the undistinguishing rage of persecution. The more ancient writers content themselves with pouring out a liberal effusion of loose and tragical invectives, without condescending to ascertain the precise number of those persons who were permitted to seal with their blood their belief of the Gospel. From the history of Eusebius it may however be collected that only nine bishops were punished with death; and we are assured, by his particular enumeration of the martyrs of Palestine, that no more than ninety-two Christians were entitled to that honourable appellation. As we are unacquainted with the degree of episcopal zeal and courage which prevailed at that time, it is not in our power to draw any useful inferences from the former of these facts: but the latter may serve to justify a very important and probable conclusion. According to the distribution of Roman provinces, Palestine may be considered as the sixteenth part of the Eastern empire: and since there were some governors who, from a real or affected clemency, had preserved their hands unstained with the blood of the faithful, it is reasonable to believe that the country which had given birth to Christianity produced at least the sixteenth part of the martyrs who suffered death within the dominions of Galerius and Maximian; the whole might consequently amount to about fifteen hundred, a number which, if it is equally divided between the ten years of the persecution, will allow an annual consumption of one hundred and fifty martyrs. Allotting the same proportion to the provinces of Italy, Africa, and perhaps Spain, where, at the end of two or three years, the rigour of the penal laws was either suspended or abolished, the multitude of Christians in the Roman empire, on whom a capital punishment was inflicted by a judicial sentence, will be reduced to somewhat less than two thousand persons. Since it cannot be doubted that the Christians were more numerous, and their enemies more exasperated, in the time of Diocletian than they had ever been in any former persecution, this probable and moderate computation may teach us to estimate the number of primitive saints and martyrs who sacrificed their lives for the important purpose of introducing Christianity into the world.

We shall conclude this chapter by a melancholy truth which obtrudes itself on the reluctant mind; that, even admitting, without hesitation or inquiry, all that history has recorded, or devotion has feigned, on the subject of martyrdoms, it must still be acknowledged that the Christians, in the course of their intestine dissensions, have inflicted far greater severities on each other than they had experienced from the zeal of infidels. During the ages of ignorance which followed the subversion of the Roman empire in the West, the bishops of the Imperial city extended their dominion over the laity as well as clergy of the Latin church. The fabric of superstition which they had erected, and which might long have defied the feeble efforts of reason, was at length assaulted by a crowd of daring fanatics, who, from the twelfth to the sixteenth century, assumed the popular character of reformers. The church of Rome defended by violence the empire which she had acquired by fraud; a system of peace and benevolence was soon disgraced by the proscriptions, wars, massacres, and the institution of the holy office. And as the reformers were animated by the love of civil as well as of religious freedom, the Catholic princes connected their own interest with that of the clergy, and enforced by fire and the sword the terrors of spiritual censures. In the Netherlands alone more than one hundred thousand of the subjects of Charles V are said to have suffered by the hand of the executioner; and this extraordinary number is attested by Grotius, a man of genius and learning, who preserved his moderation amidst the fury of contending sects, and who composed the annals of his own age and country at a time when the invention of printing had facilitated the means of intelligence and increased the danger of detection. If we are obliged to submit our belief to the authority of Grotius, it must be allowed that the number of Protestants who were executed in a single province and a single reign far exceeded that of the primitive martyrs in the space of three centuries and of the Roman empire. But if the improbability of the fact itself should prevail over the weight of evidence; if Grotius should be convicted of exaggerating the merit and sufferings of the reformers; we shall be naturally led to inquire what confidence can be placed in the doubtful and imperfect monuments of ancient credulity; what degree of credit can be assigned to a courtly bishop and a passionate declaimer, who, under the protection of Constantine, enjoyed the exclusive privilege of recording the persecutions inflicted on the Christians by the vanquished rivals or disregarded predecessors of their gracious sovereign.

CHAPTER VII

THE RISE OF MONASTICISM

[In chapter XXXVI Gibbon describes "the origins, progress, and effects of the monastic life." He admits that it is there "delayed"; for convenience of arrangement I have here brought it forward.]

Prosperity and peace introduced the distinction of the *vulgar* and the *Ascetic Christians*. The loose and imperfect practice of religion satisfied the conscience of the multitude. The prince or magistrate, the soldier or merchant, reconciled their fervent zeal and implicit faith with the exercise of their profession, the pursuit of their interest, and the indulgence of their passions: but the Ascetics, who obeyed and abused the rigid precepts of the Gospel, were inspired by the savage enthusiasm which represents man as a criminal, and God as a tyrant. They seriously renounced the business and the pleasures of the age; abjured the use of wine, of flesh, and of marriage; chastised their body, mortified their affections, and embraced a life of misery, as the price of eternal happiness. In the reign of Constantine the Ascetics fled from a profane and degenerate world to perpetual solitude or religious society. Like the first Christians of Jerusalem, they resigned the use or the property of their temporal possessions; established regular communities of the same sex and a similar disposition; and assumed the names of *Hermits, Monks,* and *Anachorets,* expressive of their lonely retreat in a natural or artificial desert. They soon acquired the respect of the world, which they despised; and the loudest applause was bestowed on this DIVINE PHILOSOPHY, which surpassed, without the aid of science or reason, the laborious virtues of the Grecian schools. The monks might indeed contend with the Stoics in the contempt of fortune, of pain, and of death: the Pythagorean silence and submission were revived in their servile discipline; and they disdained as firmly as the Cynics themselves all the forms and decencies of civil society. But the votaries of this Divine Philosophy aspired to imitate a purer and more perfect model. They trod in the footsteps of the prophets, who had retired to the desert; and they restored the devout and contemplative life, which had been instituted by the Essenians in Palestine and Egypt. The philosophic eye of Pliny had surveyed with astonishment a solitary people, who dwelt among the palm-trees near the Dead Sea; who subsisted without money; who were propagated without women; and who derived from the disgust and repentance of mankind a perpetual supply of voluntary associates.

Egypt, the fruitful parent of superstition, afforded the first example of the monastic life. Antony, an illiterate youth of the lower parts of Thebais, distributed his patrimony, deserted his family and native home, and executed his *monastic* penance with original and intrepid fanaticism. After a long and painful novitiate among the tombs and in a ruined tower, he boldly advanced into the desert three days' journey to the eastward of the Nile; discovered a lonely spot, which possessed the advantages of shade and water; and fixed his last residence on Mount Colzim, near the Red Sea, where an ancient monastery still preserves the name and memory of the saint. The curious devotion of the Christians pursued him to the desert; and when he was obliged to appear at Alexandria, in the face of mankind, he supported his fame with discretion and dignity. He enjoyed the friendship of Athanasius, whose doctrine he approved; and the Egyptian peasant respectfully declined a respectful invitation from the emperor Constantine. The venerable patriarch (for Antony attained the age of one hundred and five years) beheld the numerous progeny which had been formed by his example and his lessons. The prolific colonies of monks multiplied with rapid increase on the sands of Libya, upon the rocks of Thebais, and in the cities of the Nile. To the south of Alexandria, the mountain, and adjacent desert, of Nitria was peopled by five thousand anachorets; and the traveller may still investigate the ruins of fifty monasteries, which were planted in that barren soil by the disciples of Antony. In the Upper Thebais, the vacant island of Tabenne was occupied by Pachomius and fourteen hundred of his brethren. That holy abbot successively founded nine monasteries of men, and one of women; and the festival of Easter sometimes collected fifty thousand religious persons, who followed his *angelic* rule of discipline. The stately and populous city of Oxyrinchus, the seat of Christian orthodoxy, had devoted the temples, the public edifices, and even the ramparts, to pious and charitable uses; and the bishop, who might preach in twelve churches, computed ten thousand females, and twenty thousand males, of the monastic profession. The Egyptians, who gloried in this marvellous revolution, were disposed to hope, and to believe, that the number of the monks was equal to the remainder of the people; and posterity might repeat the saying which had formerly been applied to the sacred animals of the same country, that in Egypt it was less difficult to find a god than a man.

Athanasius introduced into Rome the knowledge and practice of the monastic life; and a school of this new philosophy was opened by the disciples of Antony, who accompanied their primate to the holy threshold of the Vatican. The strange and savage appearance of these Egyptians excited, at first, horror and contempt, and, at length, applause and zealous imitation. The senators, and more especially the matrons, transformed their palaces and villas into religious houses; and the narrow institution of *six* Vestals was eclipsed by the frequent monasteries, which were seated on the ruins of ancient temples and in the midst of the Roman forum. Inflamed by the example of Antony, a Syrian youth, whose name was Hilarion,[1] fixed his dreary abode on a sandy beach between the sea and a morass, about seven miles from Gaza. The austere penance, in which he persisted forty-eight years, diffused a similar enthusiasm; and the holy man was followed by a train of two or three thousand anachorets, whenever he visited the innumerable monasteries of Palestine. The fame of Basil is immortal in the monastic history of the East. With a mind that had tasted the learning and eloquence of Athens; with an ambition scarcely to be satisfied by the archbishopric of Cæsarea, Basil retired to a savage solitude in Pontus; and deigned, for a while, to give laws to the spiritual colonies which he profusely scattered along the coast of the Black Sea. In the West, Martin of Tours, a soldier, a hermit, a bishop, and a saint, established the monasteries of Gaul, two thousand of his disciples followed him to the grave; and his eloquent historian challenges the deserts of Thebais to produce, in a more favourable climate, a champion of equal virtue. The progress of the monks was not less rapid or universal than that of Christianity itself. Every province, and, at last, every city, of the empire was filled with their increasing multitudes; and the bleak and barren isles, from Lerins to Lipari, that arise out of the Tuscan Sea, were chosen by the anachorets for the place of their voluntary exile. An easy and perpetual intercourse by sea and land connected the provinces of the Roman world; and the life of Hilarion displays the facility with which an indigent

---

[1]See the Life of Hilarion, by St. Jerom. The stories of Paul, Hilarion, and Malchus, by the same author, are admirably told; and the only defect of these pleasing compositions is the want of truth and common sense.

hermit of Palestine might traverse Egypt, embark for Sicily, escape to Epirus, and finally settle in the island of Cyprus. The Latin Christians embraced the religious institutions of Rome. The pilgrims who visited Jerusalem eagerly copied, in the most distant climates of the earth, the faithful model of the monastic life. The disciples of Antony spread themselves beyond the tropic, over the Christian empire of Æthiopia. The monastery of Banchor, in Flintshire, which contained above two thousand brethren, dispersed a numerous colony among the barbarians of Ireland; and Iona, one of the Hebrides, which was planted by the Irish monks, diffused over the northern regions a doubtful ray of science and superstition.[2]

These unhappy exiles from social life were impelled by the dark and implacable genius of superstition. Their mutual resolution was supported by the example of millions, of either sex, of every age, and of every rank; and each proselyte who entered the gates of a monastery was persuaded that he trod the steep and thorny path of eternal happiness. But the operation of these religious motives was variously determined by the temper and situation of mankind. Reason might subdue, or passion might suspend, their influence; but they acted most forcibly on the infirm minds of children and females; they were strengthened by secret remorse or accidental misfortune; and they might derive some aid from the temporal considerations of vanity or interest. It was naturally supposed that the pious and humble monks, who had renounced the world to accomplish the work of their salvation, were the best qualified for the spiritual government of the Christians. The reluctant hermit was torn from his cell, and seated, amidst the acclamations of the

[2] This small though not barren spot, Iona, Hy, or Columbkill, only two miles in length and one mile in breadth, has been distinguished—1. By the monastery of St. Columba, founded A.D. 566, whose abbot exercised an extraordinary jurisdiction over the bishops of Caledonia; 2. By a *classic* library, which afforded some hopes of an entire Livy; and, 3. By the tombs of sixty kings, Scots, Irish, and Norwegians, who reposed in holy ground.

people, on the episcopal throne: the monasteries of Egypt, of Gaul, and of the East, supplied a regular succession of saints and bishops; and ambition soon discovered the secret road which led to the possession of wealth and honours. The popular monks, whose reputation was connected with the fame and success of the order, assiduously laboured to multiply the number of their fellow-captives. They insinuated themselves into noble and opulent families; and the specious arts of flattery and seduction were employed to secure those proselytes who might bestow wealth or dignity on the monastic profession. The indignant father bewailed the loss, perhaps, of an only son; the credulous maid was betrayed by vanity to violate the laws of nature; and the matron aspired to imaginary perfection by renouncing the virtues of domestic life. Paula yielded to the persuasive eloquence of Jerom; and the profane title of mother-in-law of God tempted that illustrious widow to consecrate the virginity of her daughter Eustochium. By the advice, and in the company, of her spiritual guide, Paula abandoned Rome and her infant son; retired to the holy village of Bethlem; founded an hospital and four monasteries; and acquired, by her alms and penance, an eminent and conspicuous station in the catholic church. Such rare and illustrious penitents were celebrated as the glory and example of their age; but the monasteries were filled by a crowd of obscure and abject plebeians, who gained in the cloister much more than they had sacrificed in the world. Peasants, slaves, and mechanics might escape from poverty and contempt to a safe and honourable profession, whose apparent hardships were mitigated by custom, by popular applause, and by the secret relaxation of discipline. The subjects of Rome, whose persons and fortunes were made responsible for unequal and exorbitant tributes, retired from the oppression of the Imperial government; and the pusillanimous youth preferred the penance of a monastic, to the dangers of a military, life. The affrighted provincials of every rank, who fled before the barbarians, found shelter and subsistence; whole legions were buried in these religious sanctuaries; and the same cause which relieved the distress of individuals impaired the strength and fortitude of the empire.

The monastic profession of the ancients was an act of voluntary devotion. The inconstant fanatic was threatened with eternal vengeance of the God whom he deserted; but the doors of the monastery were still open for repentance. Those monks whose conscience was fortified by reason or passion were at liberty to resume the character of men and citizens; and even the spouses of Christ might accept the legal embraces of an earthly lover. The examples of scandal, and the progress of superstition, suggested the propriety of more forcible restraints. After a sufficient trial, the fidelity of the novice was secured by a solemn and perpetual vow; and his irrevocable engagement was ratified by the laws of the church and state. A guilty fugitive was pursued, arrested, and restored to his perpetual prison; and the interposition of the magistrate oppressed the freedom and merit which had alleviated, in some degree, the abject slavery of the monastic discipline. The actions of a monk, his words, and even his thoughts, were determined by an inflexible rule or a capricious superior: the slightest offences were corrected by disgrace or confinement, extraordinary fasts, or bloody flagellation; and disobedience, murmur, or delay were ranked in the catalogue of the most heinous sins.[3] A blind submission to the commands of the abbot, however absurd, or even criminal, they might seem, was the ruling principle, the first virtue of

[3] The rule of Columbanus, so prevalent in the West, inflicts one hundred lashes for very slight offences. Before the time of Charlemagne the abbots indulged themselves in mutilating their monks, or putting out their eyes—a punishment much less cruel than the tremendous *vade in pace* (the subterraneous dungeon, or sepulchre), which was afterwards invented. See an admirable discourse of the learned Mabillon, who, on this occasion, seems to be inspired by the genius of humanity. For such an effort, I can forgive his defence of the holy tear of Vendome.

the Egyptian monks; and their patience was frequently exercised by the most extravagant trials. They were directed to remove an enormous rock; assiduously to water a barren staff that was planted in the ground, till, at the end of three years, it should vegetate and blossom like a tree; to walk into a fiery furnace; or to cast their infant into a deep pond: and several saints, or madmen, have been immortalised in monastic story by their thoughtless and fearless obedience. The freedom of the mind, the source of every generous and rational sentiment, was destroyed by the habits of credulity and submission; and the monk, contracting the vices of a slave, devoutly followed the faith and passions of his ecclesiastical tyrant. The peace of the Eastern church was invaded by a swarm of fanatics, incapable of fear, or reason, or humanity; and the Imperial troops acknowledged, without shame, that they were much less apprehensive of an encounter with the fiercest barbarians.

Superstition has often framed and consecrated the fantastic garments of the monks: but their apparent singularity sometimes proceeds from their uniform attachment to a simple and primitive model, which the revolutions of fashion have made ridiculous in the eyes of mankind. The father of the Benedictines expressly disclaims all idea of choice or merit; and soberly exhorts his disciples to adopt the coarse and convenient dress of the countries which they may inhabit. The monastic habits of the ancients varied with the climate and their mode of life; and they assumed, with the same indifference, the sheepskin of the Egyptian peasants or the cloak of the Grecian philosophers. They allowed themselves the use of linen in Egypt, where it was a cheap and domestic manufacture; but in the West they rejected such an expensive article of foreign luxury. It was the practice of the monks either to cut or shave their hair; they wrapped their heads in a cowl, to escape the sight of profane objects; their legs and feet were naked, except in the extreme cold of winter; and their slow and feeble

9
A late fifteenth-century painting by Bosch depicting the temptation of St. Antony, known as the first Christian monk.

steps were supported by a long staff. The aspect of a genuine anachoret was horrid and disgusting: every sensation that is offensive to man was thought acceptable to God; and the angelic rule of Tabenne condemned the salutary custom of bathing the limbs in water and of anointing them with oil. The austere monks slept on the ground, on a hard mat or a rough blanket; and the same bundle of palm-leaves served them as a seat in the day and a pillow in the night. Their original cells were low narrow huts, built of the slightest materials; which formed, by the regular distribution of the streets, a large and populous village, enclosing, within the common wall, a church, a hospital, perhaps a library, some necessary offices, a garden, and a fountain or reservoir of fresh water. Thirty or forty brethren composed a family of separate discipline and diet; and the great monasteries of Egypt consisted of thirty or forty families.

Pleasure and guilt are synonymous terms in the language of the monks, and they had discovered, by experience, that rigid fasts and abstemious diet are the most effectual preservatives against the impure desires of the flesh. The rules of abstinence which they imposed, or practised, were not uniform or perpetual: the cheerful festival of the Pentecost was balanced by the extraordinary mortification of Lent; the fervour of new monasteries was insensibly relaxed; and the voracious appetite of the Gauls could not imitate the patient and temperate virtue of the Egyptians. The disciples of Antony and Pachomius were satisfied with their daily pittance[4] of twelve ounces of bread, or rather biscuit, which they divided into two frugal repasts, of the afternoon and of the evening. It was esteemed a merit, and almost a duty, to abstain from the boiled vegetables which were provided for the refectory; but the extraordinary bounty of the abbot sometimes indulged them with the luxury of

[4] "Those who drink only water, and have no nutritious liquor, ought at least to have a pound and a half (*twenty-four ounces*) of bread every day." State of Prisons, p. 40, by Mr. Howard.

cheese, fruit, salad, and the small dried fish of the Nile. A more ample latitude of sea and river fish was gradually allowed or assumed; but the use of flesh was long confined to the sick or travellers: and when it gradually prevailed in the less rigid monasteries of Europe, a singular distinction was introduced; as if birds, whether wild or domestic, had been less profane than the grosser animals of the field. Water was the pure and innocent beverage of the primitive monks; and the founder of the Benedictines regrets the daily portion of half a pint of wine which had been extorted from him by the intemperance of the age. Such an allowance might be easily supplied by the vineyards of Italy; and his victorious disciples, who passed the Alps, the Rhine, and the Baltic, required, in the place of wine, an adequate compensation of strong beer or cider.

The candidate who aspired to the virtue of evangelical poverty, abjured, at his first entrance into a regular community, the idea, and even the name, of all separate or exclusive possession. The brethren were supported by their manual labour; and the duty of labour was strenuously recommended as a penance, as an exercise, and as the most laudable means of securing their daily subsistence. The garden and fields, which the industry of the monks had often rescued from the forest or the morass, were diligently cultivated by their hands. They performed, without reluctance, the menial offices of slaves and domestics; and the several trades that were necessary to provide their habits, their utensils, and their lodging, were exercised within the precincts of the great monasteries. The monastic studies have tended, for the most part, to darken, rather than to dispel, the cloud of superstition. Yet the curiosity or zeal of some learned solitaries has cultivated the ecclesiastical and even the profane sciences: and posterity must gratefully acknowledge that the monuments of Greek and Roman literature have been preserved and multiplied by their indefatigable pens. But the more humble industry of the monks, especially in Egypt, was contented with the silent, sedentary occupation of making wooden sandals, or of twisting the leaves of the palm-tree into mats and baskets. The superfluous stock, which was not consumed in domestic use, supplied, by trade, the wants of the community: the boats of Tabenne, and the other monasteries of Thebais, descended the Nile as far as Alexandria; and, in a Christian market, the sanctity of the workmen might enhance the intrinsic value of the work.

But the necessity of manual labour was insensibly superseded. The novice was tempted to bestow his fortune on the saints in whose society he was resolved to spend the remainder of his life; and the pernicious indulgence of the laws permitted him to receive, for their use, any future accessions of legacy or inheritance. Melania contributed her plate, three hundred pounds' weight of silver, and Paula contracted an immense debt for the relief of their favourite monks, who kindly imparted the merits of their prayers and penance to a rich and liberal sinner. Time continually increased, and accidents could seldom diminish, the estates of the popular monasteries, which spread over the adjacent country and cities: and, in the first century of their institution, the infidel Zosimus has maliciously observed, that, for the benefit of the poor, the Christian monks had reduced a great part of mankind to a state of beggary. As long as they maintained their original fervour, they approved themselves, however, the faithful and benevolent stewards of the charity which was intrusted to their care. But their discipline was corrupted by prosperity: they gradually assumed the pride of wealth, and at last indulged the luxury of expense. Their public luxury might be excused by the magnificence of religious worship, and the decent motive of erecting durable habitations for an immortal society. But every age of the church has accused the licentiousness of the degenerate monks; who no longer remembered the object of their institution, embraced the vain and sensual pleasures of the world which they had renounced, and scandalously abused the riches which had been acquired by the austere virtues of their founders.[5] Their natural descent, from such painful and dangerous virtue, to the common vices of humanity, will not, perhaps, excite much grief or indignation in the mind of a philosopher.

The lives of the primitive monks were consumed in penance and solitude, undisturbed by the various occupations which fill the time, and exercise the faculties, of reasonable, active, and social beings. Whenever they were permitted to step beyond the precincts of the monastery, two jealous companions were the mutual guards and spies of each other's actions; and, after their return, they were condemned to forget, or, at least, to suppress, whatever they had seen or heard in the world. Strangers, who professed the orthodox faith, were hospitably entertained in a separate apartment; but their dangerous conversation was restricted to some chosen elders of approved discretion and fidelity. Except in their presence, the monastic slave might not receive the visits of his friends or kindred; and it was deemed highly meritorious, if he afflicted a tender sister, or an aged parent, by the obstinate refusal of a word or look.[6] The monks themselves passed their lives, without personal attachments, among a crowd which had been formed by accident, and was detained, in the same prison, by force or prejudice. Recluse fanatics have few ideas or sentiments to communicate: a special licence of the abbot regulated the time and duration of their familiar visits; and, at their silent meals, they were enveloped in their cowls, inac-

[5] I have somewhere heard or read the frank confession of a Benedictine abbot: "My vow of poverty has given me an hundred thousand crowns a year; my vow of obedience has raised me to the rank of a sovereign prince." I forget the consequences of his vow of chastity.

[6] Pior, an Egyptian monk, allowed his sister to see him; but he shut his eyes during the whole visit. Many such examples might be added.

cessible, and almost invisible, to each other. Study is the resource of solitude; but education had not prepared and qualified for any liberal studies the mechanics and peasants who filled the monastic communities. They might work; but the vanity of spiritual perfection was tempted to disdain the exercise of manual labour; and the industry must be faint and languid which is not excited by the sense of personal interest.

According to their faith and zeal, they might employ the day, which they passed in their cells, either in vocal or mental prayer: they assembled in the evening, and they were awakened in the night, for the public worship of the monastery. The precise moment was determined by the stars, which are seldom clouded in the serene sky of Egypt; and a rustic horn, or trumpet, the signal of devotion, twice interrupted the vast silence of the desert. Even sleep, the last refuge of the unhappy, was rigorously measured: the vacant hours of the monk heavily rolled along, without business or pleasure; and, before the close of each day, he had repeatedly accused the tedious progress of the sun. In this comfortless state, superstition still pursued and tormented her wretched votaries. The repose which they had sought in the cloister was disturbed by tardy repentance, profane doubts, and guilty desires; and, while they considered each natural impulse as an unpardonable sin, they perpetually trembled on the edge of a flaming and bottomless abyss. From the painful struggles of disease and despair, these unhappy victims were sometimes relieved by madness or death; and, in the sixth century, a hospital was founded at Jerusalem for a small portion of the austere penitents who were deprived of their senses. Their visions, before they attained this extreme and acknowledged term of frenzy, have afforded ample materials of supernatural history. It was their firm persuasion that the air which they breathed was peopled with invisible enemies; with innumerable dæmons, who watched every occasion, and assumed every form, to terrify, and above all to tempt, their unguarded virtue. The imagination, and even the senses, were deceived by the illusions of distempered fanaticism; and the hermit, whose midnight prayer was oppressed by involuntary slumber, might easily confound the phantoms of horror or delight which had occupied his sleeping and his waking dreams.

The monks were divided into two classes: the *Cœnobites,* who lived under a common and regular discipline; and the *Anachorets,* who indulged their unsocial, independent fanaticism. The most devout, or the most ambitious, of the spiritual brethren renounced the convent, as they had renounced the world. The fervent monasteries of Egypt, Palestine, and Syria were surrounded by a *Laura,* a distant circle of solitary cells; and the extravagant penance of the Hermits was stimulated by applause and emulation. They sunk under the painful weight of crosses and chains; and their emaciated limbs were confined by collars, bracelets, gauntlets, and greaves of massy and rigid iron. All superfluous incumbrance of dress they contemptuously cast away; and some savage saints of both sexes have been admired, whose naked bodies were only covered by their long hair. They aspired to reduce themselves to the rude and miserable state in which the human brute is scarcely distinguished above his kindred animals; and the numerous sect of Anachorets derived their name from their humble practice of grazing in the fields of Mesopotamia with the common herd. They often usurped the den of some wild beast whom they affected to resemble; they buried themselves in some gloomy cavern, which art or nature had scooped out of the rock; and the marble quarries of Thebais are still inscribed with the monuments of their penance. The most perfect Hermits are supposed to have passed many days without food, many nights without sleep, and many years without speaking; and glorious was the *man* (I abuse that name) who contrived any cell, or seat, of a peculiar construction, which might expose him, in the most inconvenient posture, to the inclemency of the seasons.

Among these heroes of the monastic life, the name and genius of Simeon Stylites have been immortalised by the singular invention of an aërial penance. At the age of thirteen the young Syrian deserted the profession of a shepherd, and threw himself into an austere monastery. After a long and painful novitiate, in which Simeon was repeatedly saved from pious suicide, he established his residence on a mountain, about thirty or forty miles to the east of Antioch. Within the space of a *mandra,* or circle of stones, to which he had attached himself by a ponderous chain, he ascended a column, which was successively raised from the height of nine, to that of sixty, feet from the ground. In this last and lofty station, the Syrian Anachoret resisted the heat of thirty summers, and the cold of as many winters. Habit and exercise instructed him to maintain his dangerous situation without fear or giddiness, and successively to assume the different postures of devotion. He sometimes prayed in an erect attitude, with his outstretched arms in the figure of a cross; but his most familiar practice was that of bending his meagre skeleton from the forehead to the feet; and a curious spectator, after numbering twelve hundred and forty-four repetitions, at length desisted from the endless account. The progress of an ulcer in his thigh[7] might shorten, but it could not disturb, this *celestial* life; and the patient Hermit expired without descending from his column. A prince, who should capriciously inflict such tortures, would be deemed a tyrant; but it would surpass the power of a tyrant to impose a long and miserable existence on the reluctant victims of his cruelty. This voluntary martyrdom must have

[7] I must not conceal a piece of ancient scandal concerning the origin of this ulcer. It has been reported that the Devil, assuming an angelic form, invited him to ascend, like Elijah, into a fiery chariot. The saint too hastily raised his foot, and Satan seized the moment of inflicting this chastisement on his vanity.

gradually destroyed the sensibility both of the mind and body; nor can it be presumed that the fanatics who torment themselves are susceptible of any lively affection for the rest of mankind. A cruel, unfeeling temper has distinguished the monks of every age and country: their stern indifference, which is seldom mollified by personal friendship, is inflamed by religious hatred; and their merciless zeal has strenuously administered the holy office of the Inquisition.

The monastic saints, who excite only the contempt and pity of a philosopher, were respected and almost adored by the prince and people. Successive crowds of pilgrims from Gaul and India saluted the divine pillar of Simeon; the tribes of Saracens disputed in arms the honour of his benediction; the queens of Arabia and Persia gratefully confessed his supernatural virtue; and the angelic Hermit was consulted by the younger Theodosius in the most important concerns of the church and state. His remains were transported from the mountain of Telenissa, by a solemn procession of the patriarch, the master-general of the East, six bishops, twenty-one counts or tribunes, and six thousand soldiers; and Antioch revered his bones as her glorious ornament and impregnable defence. The fame of the apostles and martyrs was gradually eclipsed by these recent and popular Anachorets; the Christian world fell prostrate before their shrines; and the miracles ascribed to their relics exceeded, at least in number and duration, the spiritual exploits of their lives. But the golden legend of their lives was embellished by the artful credulity of their interested brethren; and a believing age was easily persuaded that the slightest caprice of an Egyptian or a Syrian monk had been sufficient to interrupt the eternal laws of the universe. The favourites of Heaven were accustomed to cure inveterate diseases with a touch, a word, or a distant message; and to expel the most obstinate dæmons from the souls or bodies which they possessed. They familiarly accosted, or imperiously commanded, the lions and serpents of the desert; infused vegetation into a sapless trunk; suspended iron on the surface of the water; passed the Nile on the back of a crocodile; and refreshed themselves in a fiery furnace. These extravagant tales, which display the fiction, without the genius, of poetry, have seriously affected the reason, the faith, and the morals of the Christians. Their credulity debased and vitiated the faculties of the mind: they corrupted the evidence of history; and superstition gradually extinguished the hostile light of philosophy and science. Every mode of religious worship which had been practised by the saints, every mysterious doctrine which they believed, was fortified by the sanction of divine revelation, and all the manly virtues were oppressed by the servile and pusillanimous reign of the monks. If it be possible to measure the interval between the philosophic writings of Cicero and the sacred legend of Theodoret, between the character of Cato and that of Simeon, we may appreciate the memorable revolution which was accomplished in the Roman empire within a period of five hundred years.

CHAPTER VIII

THE FOUNDATION
OF CONSTANTINOPLE

[*Diocletian had reorganised the Empire; Constantine, who ultimately succeeded to his power and policy, drew two important conclusions from the work of his predecessor. He came to terms with Christianity, which Diocletian had persecuted; and he completed Diocletian's administrative redistribution by founding a new capital, Constantinople. In chapter XVII Gibbon describes the foundation of this "new Rome" which was to continue the name of the Roman Empire, and part of its substance, for a thousand years after the collapse of the old Rome, itself now a thousand years old.*]

After the defeat and abdication of Licinius his victorious rival proceeded to lay the foundations of a city destined to reign in future times the mistress of the East, and to survive the empire and religion of Constantine. The motives, whether of pride or of policy, which first induced Diocletian to withdraw himself from the ancient seat of government, had acquired additional weight by the example of his successors and the habits of forty years. Rome was insensibly confounded with the dependent kingdoms which had once acknowledged her supremacy; and the country of the Cæsars was viewed with cold indifference by a martial prince, born in the neighbourhood of the Danube, educated in the courts and armies of Asia, and invested with the purple by the legions of Britain. The Italians, who had received Constantine as their deliverer, submissively obeyed the edicts which he sometimes condescended to address to the senate and people of Rome; but they were seldom honoured with the presence of their new sovereign. During the vigour of his age Constantine, according to the various exigencies of peace and war, moved with slow dignity or with active diligence along the frontiers of his extensive dominions; and was always prepared to take the field either against a foreign or a domestic enemy. But as he gradually reached the summit of prosperity and the decline of life, he began to meditate the design of fixing in a more permanent station the strength as well as majesty of the throne. In the choice of an advantageous situation he preferred the confines of Europe and Asia; to curb with a powerful arm the barbarians who dwelt between the Danube and the Tanais; to watch with an eye of jealousy the conduct of the Persian monarch, who indignantly supported the yoke of an ignominious treaty. With these views Diocletian had selected and embellished the residence of Nicomedia: but the memory of Diocletian was justly abhorred by the protector of the church; and Constantine was not insensible to ambition of founding a city which might perpetuate the glory of his own name. During the late operations of the war against Licinius he had sufficient opportunity to contemplate, both as a soldier and as a statesman, the incomparable position of Byzantium; and to observe how strongly it was guarded by nature against an hostile attack, whilst it was accessible on every side to the benefits of commercial intercourse. Many ages before Constantine, one of the most judicious historians of antiquity had described the advantages of a situation from whence a feeble colony of Greeks derived the command of the sea, and the honours of a flourishing and independent republic.

If we survey Byzantium in the extent which it acquired

with the august name of Constantinople, the figure of the Imperial city may be represented under that of an unequal triangle. The obtuse point, which advances towards the east and the shores of Asia, meets and repels the waves of the Thracian Bosphorus. The northern side of the city is bounded by the harbour, and the southern is washed by the Propontis or Sea of Marmora. The basis of the triangle is opposed to the west, and terminates the continent of Europe. But the admirable form and division of the circumjacent land and water cannot, without a more ample explanation, be clearly or sufficiently understood.

The winding channel through which the waters of the Euxine flow with a rapid and incessant course towards the Mediterranean received the appellation of Bosphorus, a name not less celebrated in the history than in the fables of antiquity. A crowd of temples and of votive altars, profusely scattered along its steep and woody banks, attested the unskilfulness, the terrors, and the devotion of the Grecian navigators who, after the example of the Argonauts, explored the dangers of the inhospitable Euxine. On these banks tradition long preserved the memory of the palace of Phineus, infested by the obscene harpies;[1] and of the sylvan reign of Amycus, who defied the son of Leda to the combat of the Cestus.[2] The straits of the Bosphorus are terminated by the Cyanean rocks, which, according to the description of the poets, had once floated on the face of the waters, and were destined by the gods to protect the entrance of the Euxine against the eye of profane curiosity. From the Cyanean rocks to the point and harbour of Byzantium the winding length of the Bosphorus extends about sixteen miles, and its most ordi-

[1]There are very few conjectures so happy as that of Le Clerc who supposes that the harpies were only locusts. The Syriac or Phœnician name of those insects, their noisy flight, the stench and devastation which they occasion, and the north wind which drives them into the sea, all contribute to form the striking resemblance.

[2][Cestus—the ancient boxing glove. Ed.]

nary breadth may be computed at about one mile and a half. The *new* castles of Europe and Asia are constructed, on either continent, upon the foundations of two celebrated temples, of Serapis and of Jupiter Urius. The *old* castles, a work of the Greek emperors, command the narrowest part of the channel, in a place where the opposite banks advance within five hundred paces of each other. These fortresses were restored and strengthened by Mahomet the Second when he meditated the siege of Constantinople: but the Turkish conqueror was most probably ignorant that, near two thousand years before his reign, Darius had chosen the same situation to connect the two continents by a bridge of boats. At a small distance from the old castles we discover the little town of Chrysopolis, or Scutari, which may almost be considered as the Asiatic suburb of Constantinople. The Bosphorus, as it begins to open into the Propontis, passes between Byzantium and Chalcedon. The latter of those cities was built by the Greeks a few years before the former; and the blindness of its founders, who overlooked the superior advantages of the opposite coast, has been stigmatised by a proverbial expression of contempt.

The harbour of Constantinople, which may be considered as an arm of the Bosphorus, obtained, in a very remote period, the denomination of the *Golden Horn*. The curve which it describes might be compared to the horn of a stag, or as it should seem, with more propriety, to that of an ox. The epithet of *golden* was expressive of the riches which every wind wafted from the most distant countries into the secure and capacious port of Constantinople. The river Lycus, formed by the conflux of two little streams, pours into the harbour a perpetual supply of fresh water, which serves to cleanse the bottom and to invite the periodical shoals of fish to seek their retreat in that convenient recess. As the vicissitudes of tides are scarcely felt in those seas, the constant depth of the harbour allows goods to be landed on the quays without the assistance of boats; and it has been observed that, in many places, the largest vessels may rest their prows against the houses while their sterns are floating in the water. From the mouth of the Lycus to that of the harbour this arm of the Bosphorus is more than seven miles in length. The entrance is about five hundred yards broad, and a strong chain could be occasionally drawn across it to guard the port and city from the attack of an hostile navy.

Between the Bosphorus and the Hellespont, the shores of Europe and Asia receding on either side inclose the Sea of Marmora, which was known to the ancients by the denomination of Propontis. The navigation from the issue of the Bosphorus to the entrance of the Hellespont is about one hundred and twenty miles. Those who steer their westward course through the middle of the Propontis may at once descry the high lands of Thrace and Bithynia, and never lose sight of the lofty summit of Mount Olympus, covered with eternal snows. They leave on the left a deep gulf, at the bottom of which Nicomedia was seated, the imperial residence of Diocletian; and they pass the small islands of Cyzicus and Proconnesus before they cast anchor at Gallipoli, where the sea, which separates Asia from Europe, is again contracted into a narrow channel.

The geographers who, with the most skilful accuracy, have surveyed the form and extent of the Hellespont, assign about sixty miles for the winding course, and about three miles for the ordinary breadth, of those celebrated straits. But the narrowest part of the channel is found to the northward of the old Turkish castles, between the cities of Sestus and Abydus. It was here that the adventurous Leander braved the passage of the flood for the possession of his mistress. It was here likewise, in a place where the distance between the opposite banks cannot exceed five hundred paces, that Xerxes imposed a stupendous bridge of boats, for the purpose of transporting into Europe a hundred and seventy myriads of barbarians. A sea contracted within such narrow limits may seem but ill to deserve the singular epithet of *broad,* which Homer, as well as Orpheus, has frequently bestowed on the Hellespont. But our ideas of greatness are of a relative nature: the traveller, and especially the poet, who sailed along the Hellespont, who pursued the windings of the stream, and contemplated the rural scenery, which appeared on every side to terminate the prospect, insensibly lost the remembrance of the sea; and his fancy painted those celebrated straits with all the attributes of a mighty river, flowing with a swift current, in the midst of a woody and inland country, and at length, through a wide mouth, discharging itself into the Ægean or Archipelago. Ancient Troy, seated on an eminence at the foot of Mount Ida, overlooked the mouth of the Hellespont, which scarcely received an accession of waters from the tribute of those immortal rivulets the Simois and Scamander. The Grecian camp had stretched twelve miles along the shore, from the Sigean to the Rhœtean promontory; and the flanks of the army were guarded by the bravest chiefs who fought under the banners of Agamemnon. The first of those promontories was occupied by Achilles with his invincible myrmidons, and the dauntless Ajax pitched his tents on the other. After Ajax had fallen a sacrifice to his disappointed pride and to the ingratitude of the Greeks, his sepulchre was erected on the ground where he had defended the navy against the rage of Jove and of Hector; and the citizens of the rising town of Rhœteum celebrated his memory with divine honours. Before Constantine gave a just preference to the situation of Byzantium, he had conceived the design of erecting the seat of empire on this celebrated spot, from whence the Romans derived their fabulous origin. The extensive plain which lies below ancient Troy, towards the Rhœtean promontory and the tomb of Ajax, was first chosen for his new capital; and, though the undertaking was soon relinquished, the stately remains of unfinished walls and towers attracted the notice of all who sailed through the straits of the Hellespont.

We are at present qualified to view the advantageous position of Constantinople, which appears to have been formed by nature for the centre and capital of a great monarchy. Situated in the forty-first degree of latitude, the Imperial city commanded, from her seven hills, the opposite shores of Europe and Asia; the climate was healthy and temperate, the soil fertile, the harbour secure and capacious, and the approach on the side of the continent was of small extent and easy defence. The Bosphorus and the Hellespont may be considered as the two gates of Constantinople, and the prince who possessed those important passages could always shut them against a naval enemy and open them to the fleets of commerce. The preservation of the eastern provinces may, in some degree, be ascribed to the policy of Constantine, as the barbarians of the Euxine, who in the preceding age had poured their armaments into the heart of the Mediterranean, soon desisted from the exercise of piracy, and despaired of forcing this insurmountable barrier. When the gates of the Hellespont and Bosphorus were shut, the capital still enjoyed within their spacious enclosure every production which could supply the wants or gratify the luxury of its numerous inhabitants. The sea-coasts of Thrace and Bithynia, which languish under the weight of Turkish oppression, still exhibit a rich prospect of vineyards, of gardens, and of plentiful harvests; and the Propontis has ever been renowned for an inexhaustible store of the most exquisite fish, that are taken in their stated seasons, without skill, and almost without labour. But when the passages of the straits were thrown open for trade, they alternately admitted the natural and artificial riches of the north and south, of the Euxine and of the Mediterranean. Whatever rude commodities were collected in the forests of Germany and Scythia, as far as the sources of the Tanais and the Borysthenes; whatsoever was manufactured by the skill of Europe or Asia; the corn of Egypt, and the gems and spices of the farthest India, were brought by the varying winds into the port of Constantinople, which, for many ages, attracted the commerce of the ancient world.

The prospect of beauty, of safety, and of wealth, united in a single spot, was sufficient to justify the choice of Constantine. But as some decent mixture of prodigy and fable has, in every age, been supposed to reflect a becoming majesty on the origin of great cities, the emperor was desirous of ascribing his resolution not so much to the uncertain counsels of human policy as to the infallible and eternal decrees of divine wisdom. In one of his laws he has been careful to instruct posterity that, in obedience to the commands of God, he laid the everlasting foundations of Constantinople; and though he has not condescended to relate in what manner the celestial inspiration was communicated to his mind, the defect of his modest silence has been liberally supplied by the ingenuity of succeeding writers, who describe the nocturnal vision which appeared to the fancy of Constantine as he slept within the walls of Byzantium. The tutelar genius of the city, a venerable matron sinking under the weight of years and infirmities, was suddenly transformed into a blooming maid, whom his own hands adorned with all the symbols of Imperial greatness. The monarch awoke, interpreted the auspicious omen, and obeyed, without hesitation, the will of Heaven. The day which gave birth to a city or colony was celebrated by the Romans with such ceremonies as had been ordained by a generous superstition; and though Constantine might omit some rites which savoured too strongly of their Pagan origin, yet he was anxious to leave a deep impression of hope and respect on the minds of the spectators. On foot, with a lance in his hand, the emperor himself led the solemn procession, and directed the line which was traced as the boundary of the destined capital, till the growing circumference was observed with astonishment by the assistants, who, at length, ventured to

observe that he had already exceeded the most ample
measure of the great city. "I shall still advance," replied
Constantine, "till HE, the invisible guide who marches before me, thinks proper to stop." Without presuming to
investigate the nature or motives of this extraordinary
conductor, we shall content ourselves with the more humble task of describing the extent and limits of Constantinople.

In the actual state of the city, the palace and gardens
of the Seraglio occupy the eastern promontory, the first
of the seven hills, and cover about one hundred and
fifty acres of our own measure. The seat of Turkish
jealousy and despotism is erected on the foundations of
a Grecian republic; but it may be supposed that the
Byzantines were tempted by the conveniency of the harbour to extend their habitations on that side beyond the
modern limits of the Seraglio. The new walls of Constantine stretched from the port to the Propontis across
the enlarged breadth of the triangle, at the distance of
fifteen stadia from the ancient fortification, and with the
city of Byzantium they enclosed five of the seven hills
which, to the eyes of those who approach Constantinople,
appear to rise above each other in beautiful order. About
a century after the death of the founder, the new buildings, extending on one side up the harbour, and on the
other along the Propontis, already covered the narrow
ridge of the sixth and the broad summit of the seventh
hill. The necessity of protecting those suburbs from the
incessant inroads of the barbarians engaged the younger
Theodosius to surround his capital with an adequate and
permanent enclosure of walls. From the eastern promontory to the golden gate, the extreme length of Constantinople was about three Roman miles, the circumference
measured between ten and eleven, and the surface might
be computed as equal to about two thousand English
acres. It is impossible to justify the vain and credulous
exaggerations of modern travellers, who have sometimes
stretched the limits of Constantinople over the adjacent

villages of the European and even of the Asiatic coast. But the suburbs of Pera and Galata, though situated beyond the harbour, may deserve to be considered as a part of the city; and this addition may perhaps authorise the measure of a Byzantine historian, who assigns sixteen Greek (about fourteen Roman) miles for the circumference of his native city. Such an extent may seem not unworthy of an Imperial residence. Yet Constantinople must yield to Babylon and Thebes, to ancient Rome, to London, and even to Paris.

The master of the Roman world, who aspired to erect an eternal monument of the glories of his reign, could employ in the prosecution of that great work the wealth, the labour, and all that yet remained of the genius, of obedient millions. Some estimate may be formed of the expense bestowed with Imperial liberality on the foundation of Constantinople by the allowance of about two millions five hundred thousand pounds for the construction of the walls, the porticoes, and the aqueducts. The forests that overshadowed the shores of the Euxine, and the celebrated quarries of white marble in the little island of Proconnesus, supplied an inexhaustible stock of materials, ready to be conveyed, by the convenience of a short water-carriage, to the harbour of Byzantium. A multitude of labourers and artificers urged the conclusion of the work with incessant toil; but the impatience of Constantine soon discovered that, in the decline of the arts, the skill as well as numbers of his architects bore a very unequal proportion to the greatness of his designs. The magistrates of the most distant provinces were therefore directed to institute schools, to appoint professors, and, by the hopes of rewards and privileges, to engage in the study and practice of architecture a sufficient number of ingenious youths who had received a liberal education. The buildings of the new city were executed by such artificers as the reign of Constantine could afford; but they were decorated by the hands of the most celebrated masters of the age of Pericles and Alexander. To revive the genius of Phidias and Lysippus surpassed indeed the power of a Roman emperor; but the immortal productions which they had bequeathed to posterity were exposed without defence to the rapacious vanity of a despot. By his commands the cities of Greece and Asia were despoiled of their most valuable ornaments. The trophies of memorable wars, the objects of religious veneration, the most finished statues of the gods and heroes, of the sages and poets of ancient times, contributed to the splendid triumph of Constantinople; and gave occasion to the remark of the historian Cedrenus, who observes, with some enthusiasm, that nothing seemed wanting except the souls of the illustrious men whom these admirable monuments were intended to represent. But it is not in the city of Constantine, nor in the declining period of an empire, when the human mind was depressed by civil and religious slavery, that we should seek for the souls of Homer and of Demosthenes.

During the siege of Byzantium the conqueror had pitched his tent on the commanding eminence of the second hill. To perpetuate the memory of his success, he chose the same advantageous position for the principal Forum, which appears to have been of a circular or rather elliptical form. The two opposite entrances formed triumphal arches; the porticoes, which enclosed it on every side, were filled with statues, and the centre of the Forum was occupied by a lofty column, of which a mutilated fragment is now degraded by the appellation of the *burnt pillar*. This column was erected on a pedestal of white marble twenty feet high, and was composed of ten pieces of porphyry, each of which measured about ten feet in height, and about thirty-three in circumference. On the summit of the pillar, above one hundred and twenty feet from the ground, stood the colossal statue of Apollo. It was of bronze, had been transported either from Athens or from a town of Phrygia, and was supposed to be the work of Phidias. The artist had repre-

sented the god of day, or, as it was afterwards interpreted, the emperor Constantine himself, with a sceptre
in his right hand, the globe of the world in his left, and
a crown of rays glittering on his head. The Circus, or
Hippodrome, was a stately building about four hundred
paces in length, and one hundred in breadth. The space
between the two *metœ* or goals was filled with statues
and obelisks; and we may still remark a very singular
fragment of antiquity, the bodies of three serpents
twisted into one pillar of brass. Their triple heads had
once supported the golden tripod which, after the defeat of Xerxes, was consecrated in the temple of Delphi
by the victorious Greeks. The beauty of the Hippodrome
has been long since defaced by the rude hands of the
Turkish conquerors, but, under the similar appellation of
Atmeidan, it still serves as a place of exercise for their
horses. From the throne, whence the emperor viewed the
Circensian games, a winding staircase descended to the
palace; a magnificent edifice, which scarcely yielded to
the residence of Rome itself, and which, together with
the dependent courts, gardens, and porticoes, covered a
considerable extent of ground upon the banks of the
Propontis, between the Hippodrome and the church of
St. Sophia. We might likewise celebrate the baths, which
still retained the name of Zeuxippus, after they had been
enriched by the munificence of Constantine, with lofty
columns, various marbles, and above threescore statues
of bronze. But we should deviate from the design of this
history if we attempted minutely to describe the different buildings or quarters of the city. It may be sufficient
to observe that whatever could adorn the dignity of a
great capital, or contribute to the benefit or pleasure of
its numerous inhabitants, was contained within the walls
of Constantinople. A particular description, composed
about a century after its foundation, enumerates a capitol or school of learning, a circus, two theatres, eight
public and one hundred and fifty-three private baths,
fifty-two porticoes, five granaries, eight aqueducts or

reservoirs of water, four spacious halls for the meetings of the senate or courts of justice, fourteen churches, fourteen palaces, and four thousand three hundred and eighty-eight houses which, for their size or beauty, deserved to be distinguished from the multitude of plebeian habitations.

The populousness of his favoured city was the next and most serious object of the attention of its founder. In the dark ages which succeeded the translation of the empire, the remote and the immediate consequences of that memorable event were strangely confounded by the vanity of the Greeks and the credulity of the Latins. It was asserted and believed that all the noble families of Rome, the senate, and the equestrian order, with their innumerable attendants, had followed their emperor to the banks of the Propontis; that a spurious race of strangers and plebeians was left to possess the solitude of the ancient capital; and that the lands of Italy, long since converted into gardens, were at once deprived of cultivation and inhabitants. In the course of this history such exaggerations will be reduced to their just value; yet, since the growth of Constantinople cannot be ascribed to the general increase of mankind and of industry, it must be admitted that this artificial colony was raised at the expense of the ancient cities of the empire. Many opulent senators of Rome and of the eastern provinces were probably invited by Constantine to adopt for their country the fortunate spot which he had chosen for his own residence. The invitations of a master are scarcely to be distinguished from commands, and the liberality of the emperor obtained a ready and cheerful obedience. He bestowed on his favourites the palaces which he had built in the several quarters of the city, assigned them lands and pensions for the support of their dignity, and alienated the demesnes of Pontus and Asia to grant hereditary estates by the easy tenure of maintaining a house in the capital. But these encouragements and obligations soon became superfluous, and were gradually abolished. Wherever the seat of government is fixed, a considerable part of the public revenue will be expended by the prince himself, by his ministers, by the officers of justice, and by the domestics of the palace. The most wealthy of the provincials will be attracted by the powerful motives of interest and duty, of amusement and curiosity. A third and more numerous class of inhabitants will insensibly be formed, of servants, of artificers, and of merchants, who derive their subsistence from their own labour, and from the wants or luxury of the superior ranks. In less than a century Constantinople disputed with Rome itself the pre-eminence of riches and numbers. New piles of buildings, crowded together with too little regard to health or convenience, scarcely allowed the intervals of narrow streets for the perpetual throng of men, of horses, and of carriages. The allotted space of ground was insufficient to contain the increasing people, and the additional foundations, which on either side were advanced into the sea, might alone have composed a very considerable city.

The frequent and regular distributions of wine and oil, of corn or bread, of money or provisions, had almost exempted the poorer citizens of Rome from the necessity of labour. The magnificence of the first Cæsars was in some measure imitated by the founder of Constantinople: but his liberality, however it might excite the applause of the people, has incurred the censure of posterity. A nation of legislators and conquerors might assert their claim to the harvests of Africa, which had been purchased with their blood; and it was artfully contrived by Augustus, that, in the enjoyment of plenty, the Romans should lose the memory of freedom. But the prodigality of Constantine could not be excused by any consideration either of public or private interest; and the annual tribute of corn imposed upon Egypt for the benefit of his new capital was applied to feed a lazy and insolent populace, at the expense of the husbandmen of an industrious province. Some other regulations of this emperor are less liable to blame, but they are less deserving of notice. He divided Constantinople into fourteen regions or quarters, dignified the public council with the appellation of senate, communicated to the citizens the privileges of Italy, and bestowed on the rising city the title of Colony, the first and most favoured daughter of ancient Rome. The venerable parent still maintained the legal and acknowledged supremacy, which was due to her age, to her dignity, and to the remembrance of her former greatness.

As Constantine urged the progress of the work with the impatience of a lover, the walls, the porticoes, and the principal edifices were completed in a few years, or, according to another account, in a few months: but this extraordinary diligence should excite the less admiration, since many of the buildings were finished in so hasty and imperfect a manner, that, under the succeeding reign, they were preserved with difficulty from impending ruin. But while they displayed the vigour and freshness of youth, the founder prepared to celebrate the dedication of his city. The games and largesses which crowned the pomp of this memorable festival may easily be supposed; but there is one circumstance of a more singular and permanent nature, which ought not entirely to be overlooked. As often as the birthday of the city returned, the statue of Constantine, framed by his order, of gilt wood, and bearing in its right hand a small image of the genius of the place, was erected on a triumphal car. The guards, carrying white tapers, and clothed in their richest apparel, accompanied the solemn procession as it moved through the Hippodrome. When it was opposite to the throne of the reigning emperor, he rose from his seat, and with grateful reverence adored the memory of his predecessor. At the festival of the dedication, an edict, engraved on a column of marble, bestowed the title of SECOND or NEW ROME on the city of Constantine. But the name of Constantinople has prevailed over that honourable epithet, and after the revolution of fourteen centuries still perpetuates the fame of its author.

The foundation of a new capital is naturally connected with the establishment of a new form of civil and military administration. The distinct view of the complicated system of policy introduced by Diocletian, improved by Constantine, and completed by his immediate successors, may not only amuse the fancy by the singular picture of a great empire, but will tend to illustrate the secret and internal causes of its rapid decay. In the pursuit of any remarkable institution, we may be frequently led into the more early or the more recent times of the Roman history; but the proper limits of this inquiry will be included within a period of about one hundred and thirty years, from the accession of Constantine to the publication of the Theodosian code; from which, as well as from the *Notitia* of the East and West, we derive the most copious and authentic information of the state of the empire. This variety of objects will suspend, for some time, the course of the narrative; but the interruption will be censured only by those readers who are insensible to the importance of laws and manners, while they peruse, with eager curiosity, the transient intrigues of a court, or the accidental event of a battle.

The manly pride of the Romans, content with substantial power, had left to the vanity of the East the forms and ceremonies of ostentatious greatness. But when they lost even the semblance of those virtues which were derived from their ancient freedom, the simplicity of Roman manners was insensibly corrupted by the stately affectation of the courts of Asia. The distinctions of personal merit and influence, so conspicuous in a republic, so feeble and obscure under a monarchy, were abolished by the despotism of the emperors; who substituted in their room a severe subordination of rank and office, from the titled slaves who were seated on the steps of the throne, to the meanest instruments of arbitrary power. This multitude of abject dependents was interested in the support of the actual government, from the dread of a revolution which might at once confound their hopes and intercept the reward of their services. In this divine hierarchy (for such it is frequently styled) every rank was marked with the most scrupulous exactness, and its dignity was displayed in a variety of trifling and solemn ceremonies, which it was a study to learn, and a sacrilege to neglect. The purity of the Latin language was debased, by adopting, in the intercourse of pride and flattery, a profusion of epithets which Tully would scarcely have understood, and which Augustus would have rejected with indignation. The principal officers of the empire were saluted, even by the sovereign himself, with the deceitful titles of your *Sincerity,* your *Gravity,* your *Excellency,* your *Eminence,* your *sublime and wonderful Magnitude,* your *illustrious and magnificent Highness.* The codicils or patents of their office were curiously emblazoned with such emblems as were best adapted to explain its nature and high dignity—the image or portrait of the reigning emperors; a triumphal car; the book of mandates placed on a table, covered with a rich carpet, and illuminated by four tapers; the allegorical figures of the provinces which they governed; or the appellations and standards of the troops whom they commanded. Some of these official ensigns were really exhibited in their hall of audience; others preceded their pompous march whenever they appeared in public; and every circumstance of their demeanour, their dress, their ornaments, and their train, was calculated to inspire a deep reverence for the representatives of supreme majesty. By a philosophic observer the system of the Roman government might have been mistaken for a splendid theatre, filled with players of every character and degree, who repeated the language, and imitated the passions, of their original model.

CHAPTER IX

JULIAN THE APOSTATE
AND THE PAGAN REACTION

[*For three-quarters of a century, the heirs and successors of Constantine struggled to maintain the reorganised, Christianised empire against the onslaughts of barbarians, Persians, heretics, and usurpers. Only one of them, Constantine's nephew Julian, educated in the old philosophy, sought to reject both the new religion and the new despotism and to return to the paganism and stoic virtue of the Antonines. In chapters XXXII and XXXIII Gibbon describes, first, the political reforms of Julian, then his attempt to restore paganism in the Empire.*]

Julian was not insensible of the advantages of freedom. From his studies he had imbibed the spirit of ancient sages and heroes; his life and fortunes had depended on the caprice of a tyrant; and, when he ascended the throne, his pride was sometimes mortified by the reflection that the slaves who would not dare to censure his defects were not worthy to applaud his virtues. He sincerely abhorred the system of oriental despotism which Diocletian, Constantine, and the patient habits of fourscore years, had established in the empire. A motive of superstition prevented the execution of the design which Julian had frequently meditated, of relieving his head from the weight of a costly diadem; but he absolutely refused the title of *Dominus* or *Lord,* a word which was grown so familiar to the ears of the Romans, that they no longer remembered its servile and humiliating origin. The office, or rather the name, of consul was cherished by a prince who contemplated with reverence the ruins of the republic; and the same behaviour which had been assumed by the prudence of Augustus was adopted by Julian from choice and inclination. On the calends of January, at break of day, the new consuls, Mamertinus and Nevitta, hastened to the palace to salute the emperor. As soon as he was informed of their approach, he leaped from his throne, eagerly advanced to meet them, and compelled the blushing magistrates to receive the demonstrations of his affected humility. From the palace they proceeded to the senate. The emperor, on foot, marched before their litters, and the gazing multitude admired the image of ancient times, or secretly blamed a conduct which, in their eyes, degraded the majesty of the purple. But the behaviour of Julian was uniformly supported. During the games of the Circus, he had, imprudently or designedly, performed the manumission of a slave in the presence of the consul. The moment he was reminded that he had trespassed on the jurisdiction of *another* magistrate, he condemned himself to pay a fine of ten pounds of gold, and embraced this public occasion of declaring to the world that he was subject, like the rest of his fellow-citizens, to the laws, and even to the forms, of the republic. The spirit of his administration, and his regard for the place of his nativity, induced Julian to confer on the senate of Constantinople the same honours, privileges, and authority which were still enjoyed by the senate of ancient Rome. A legal fiction was introduced and gradually established, that one half of the national council had migrated into the East, and the despotic successors of Julian, accepting the title of Senators, acknowledged themselves the members of a respectable body which was permitted to represent the majesty of the Roman name. From Constantinople the attention of the monarch was extended to the municipal senates of the provinces. He abolished, by repeated edicts, the unjust and pernicious exemptions which had withdrawn so many idle citizens from the service of their country; and by imposing an equal distribution of public duties, he restored the strength, the splendour, or, according to the glowing expression of Libanius, the soul of the expiring cities of his empire. The venerable age of Greece excited the most tender compassion in the mind of Julian, which kindled into rapture when he recollected the gods, the heroes, and the men superior to heroes and to gods, who had bequeathed to the latest posterity the monuments of their genius or the example of their virtues. He relieved the distress and restored the beauty of the cities of Epirus and Peloponnesus. Athens acknowledged him for her benefactor, Argos for her deliverer. The pride of Corinth, again rising from her ruins with the honours of a Roman colony, exacted a tribute from the adjacent republics for the purpose of defraying the games of the Isthmus, which were celebrated in the amphitheatre with the hunting of bears and panthers. From this tribute the cities of Elis, of Delphi, and of Argos, which had inherited from their remote ancestors the sacred office of perpetuating the Olympic, the Pythian, and the Nemean games, claimed a just exemption. The immunity of Elis and Delphi was respected by the Corinthians, but the poverty of Argos tempted the insolence of oppression, and the feeble complaints of its deputies were silenced by the decree of a provincial magistrate, who seems to have consulted only the interest of the capital in which he resided. Seven years after the sentence Julian allowed the cause to be referred to a superior tribunal, and his eloquence was interposed, most probably with success, in the defence of a city which had been the royal seat of Agamemnon, and had given to Macedonia a race of kings and conquerors.

The laborious administration of military and civil affairs, which were multiplied in proportion to the extent of the empire, exercised the abilities of Julian; but he frequently assumed the two characters of Orator and of Judge, which are almost unknown to the modern sovereigns of Europe. The arts of persuasion, so diligently cultivated by the first Cæsars, were neglected by the military ignorance and Asiatic pride of their successors, and, if they condescended to harangue the soldiers, whom they feared, they treated with silent disdain the senators, whom they despised The assemblies of the senate, which Constantius had avoided, were considered by Julian as the place where he could exhibit with the most propriety the maxims of a republican and the talents of a rhetorician. He alternately practised, as in a school of declamation, the several modes of praise, of censure, of exhortation; and his friend Libanius has remarked that the study of Homer taught him to imitate the simple, concise style of Menelaus, the copiousness of Nestor, whose words descended like the flakes of a winter's snow, or the pathetic and forcible eloquence of Ulysses. The functions of a judge, which are sometimes incompatible with those of a prince, were exercised by Julian not only as a duty, but as an amusement; and although he might have trusted the integrity and discernment of his Prætorian præfects, he often placed himself by their side on the seat of judgment. The acute penetration of his mind was agreeably occupied in detecting and defeating the chicanery of the advocates, who laboured to disguise the truth of facts and to pervert the sense of the laws. He sometimes forgot the gravity of his station, asked indiscreet or unseasonable questions, and betrayed, by the loudness of his voice and the agitation of his body, the earnest vehemence with which he maintained his opinion against the judges, the advocates, and their clients. But his knowledge of his own temper prompted him to encourage, and even to solicit, the reproof of his friends and ministers: and whenever they ventured to oppose the irregular sallies of his passions, the spectators could observe the shame as well as the gratitude of their monarch. The decrees of Julian were almost always founded on the principles of justice, and he had the firmness to resist the two most dangerous temptations which assault the tribunal of a sovereign under the specious forms of compassion and equity. He decided the merits of the cause without weighing the circumstances of the parties; and the poor, whom he wished to relieve, were condemned to satisfy the just demands of a noble and wealthy adversary. He carefully distinguished the judge from the legislator; and though he meditated a necessary reformation of the Roman jurisprudence, he pronounced sentence according to the strict and literal interpretation of those laws which the magistrates were bound to execute and the subjects to obey.

The generality of princes, if they were stripped of their purple and cast naked into the world, would immediately sink to the lowest rank of society, without a hope of emerging from their obscurity. But the personal merit of Julian was, in some measure, independent of his fortune. Whatever had been his choice of life, by the force of intrepid courage, lively wit, and intense application, he would have obtained, or at least he would have deserved, the highest honours of his profession, and Julian might have raised himself to the rank of minister or general of the state in which he was born a private citizen. If the jealous caprice of power had disappointed his expectations; if he had prudently declined the paths of greatness, the employment of the same talents in studious solitude would have placed beyond the reach of kings his present happiness and his immortal fame. When we inspect with minute, or perhaps malevolent, attention the portrait of Julian, something seems wanting to the grace and perfection of the whole figure. His genius was less powerful and sublime than that of Cæsar, nor did he possess the consummate prudence of Augustus. The virtues of Trajan appear more steady and natural, and the philosophy of Marcus is more simple and consistent. Yet Julian sustained adversity with firmness, and prosperity with moderation. After an interval of one hundred and twenty years from the death of Alexander Severus, the Romans beheld an emperor who made no distinction between his duties and his pleasures, who laboured to relieve the distress and to revive the spirit of his subjects, and who endeavoured always to connect authority with merit, and happiness with virtue. Even faction, and religious faction, was constrained to acknowledge the superiority of his genius in peace as well as in war, and to confess, with a sigh, that the apostate Julian was a lover of his country, and that he deserved the empire of the world.

The character of Apostate has injured the reputation of Julian; and the enthusiasm which clouded his virtues has exaggerated the real and apparent magnitude of his faults. Our partial ignorance may represent him as a philosophic monarch, who studied to protect, with an equal hand, the religious factions of the empire, and to allay the theological fever which had inflamed the minds of the people from the edicts of Diocletian to the exile of Athanasius. A more accurate view of the character and conduct of Julian will remove this favourable prepossession for a prince who did not escape the general contagion of the times. We enjoy the singular advantage of comparing the pictures which have been delineated by his fondest admirers and his implacable enemies. The actions of Julian are faithfully related by a judicious and candid historian, the impartial spectator of his life and death. The unanimous evidence of his contemporaries is confirmed by the public and private declarations of the emperor himself; and his various writings express the uniform tenor of his religious sentiments, which policy would have prompted him to dissemble rather than to affect. A devout and sincere attachment for the gods of Athens and Rome constituted the ruling passion of Julian; the powers of an enlightened understanding were betrayed and corrupted by the influence of superstitious prejudice; and the phantoms which existed only in the mind of the emperor had a real and pernicious effect on the government of the empire. The vehement zeal of the Christians, who despised the worship, and overturned the altars, of those fabulous deities, engaged their votary in a state of irreconcilable hostility with a very numerous party of his subjects; and he was sometimes tempted, by the desire of victory or the shame of a repulse, to violate the laws of prudence, and even of justice. The triumph of the party which he deserted and opposed has fixed a stain of infamy on the name of Julian; and the unsuccessful apostate has been overwhelmed with a torrent of pious invectives, of which the signal was given by the sonorous trumpet of Gregory Nazianzen. The interesting nature of the events which were crowded into the short reign of this active emperor deserves a just and circumstantial narrative. His motive, his counsels, and his actions, as far as they are connected with the history of religion, will be the subject of the present chapter.

The cause of his strange and fatal apostasy may be derived from the early period of his life when he was left an orphan in the hands of the murderers of his family.[1] The names of Christ and of Constantius, the ideas of slavery and of religion, were soon associated in a youthful imagination, which was susceptible of the most lively impressions. The care of his infancy was intrusted to Eusebius, bishop of Nicomedia, who was related to him on the side of his mother; and till Julian reached the twentieth year of his age, he received from his Christian preceptors the education not of a hero but of a saint. The emperor, less jealous of a heavenly than of an earthly crown, contented himself with the imperfect character of a catechumen, while he bestowed the advantages of baptism on the nephews of Constantine.

[1] [On the death of Constantine, his son Constantius II secured his power by a general massacre of his collateral kinsmen, of whom only Julian and his brother Gallus survived. Ed.]

They were even admitted to the inferior offices of the ecclesiastical order; and Julian publicly read the Holy Scriptures in the church of Nicomedia. The study of religion, which they assiduously cultivated, appeared to produce the fairest fruits of faith and devotion.[2] They prayed, they fasted, they distributed alms to the poor, gifts to the clergy, and oblations to the tombs of the martyrs; and the splendid monument of St. Mamas, at Cæsarea, was erected, or at least was undertaken, by the joint labour of Gallus and Julian. They respectfully conversed with the bishops who were eminent for superior sanctity, and solicited the benediction of the monks and hermits who had introduced into Cappadocia the voluntary hardships of the ascetic life. As the two princes advanced towards the years of manhood, they discovered, in their religious sentiments, the difference of their characters. The dull and obstinate understanding of Gallus embraced, with implicit zeal, the doctrines of Christianity, which never influenced his conduct, or moderated his passions. The mild disposition of the younger brother was less repugnant to the precepts of the Gospel; and his active curiosity might have been gratified by a theological system which explains the mysterious essence of the Deity, and opens the boundless prospect of invisible and future worlds. But the independent spirit of Julian refused to yield the passive and unresisting obedience which was required, in the name of religion, by the haughty ministers of the church. Their speculative opinions were imposed as positive laws, and guarded by the terrors of eternal punishments; but while they prescribed the rigid formulary of the thoughts, the words, and the actions of the young prince, whilst they silenced his objections, and severely checked the freedom of his inquiries, secretly provoked his impatient genius to

---

[2] See his Christian, and even ecclesiastical education, in Gregory, Socrates, and Sozomen. He escaped very narrowly from being a bishop, and perhaps a saint.

disclaim the authority of his ecclesiastical guides. He was educated in the Lesser Asia, amidst the scandals of the Arian controversy. The fierce contests of the Eastern bishops, the incessant alterations of their creeds, and the profane motives which appeared to actuate their conduct, insensibly strengthened the prejudice of Julian that they neither understood nor believed the religion for which they so fiercely contended. Instead of listening to the proofs of Christianity with that favourable attention which adds weight to the most respectable evidence, he heard with suspicion, and disputed with obstinacy and acuteness, the doctrines for which he already entertained an invincible aversion. Whenever the young princes were directed to compose declamations on the subject of the prevailing controversies, Julian always declared himself the advocate of Paganism, under the specious excuse that, in the defence of the weaker cause, his learning and ingenuity might be more advantageously exercised and displayed. . . .

[*From scepticism Julian proceeded to anti-Christian faith. At the age of twenty he was initiated into the Eleusinian mysteries in a cave at Ephesus. But he prudently concealed his views during the reign of his cousin Constantius.*]

The dissimulation of Julian lasted above ten years, from his secret initiation of Ephesus at the beginning of the civil war; when he declared himself at once the implacable enemy of Christ and of Constantius. This state of constraint might contribute to strengthen his devotion; and as soon as he had satisfied the obligation of assisting, on solemn festivals, at the assemblies of the Christians, Julian returned, with the impatience of a lover, to burn his free and voluntary incense in the domestic chapels of Jupiter and Mercury. But as every act of dissimulation must be painful to an ingenuous spirit, the profession of Christianity increased the aversion of

Julian for a religion which oppressed the freedom of his mind, and compelled him to hold a conduct repugnant to the noblest attributes of human nature—sincerity and courage.

The inclination of Julian might prefer the gods of Homer and of the Scipios to the new faith which his uncle had established in the Roman empire, and in which he himself had been sanctified by the sacrament of baptism. But, as a philosopher, it was incumbent on him to justify his dissent from Christianity, which was supported by the number of its converts, by the chain of prophecy, the splendour of miracles, and the weight of evidence. The elaborate work which he composed amidst the preparations of the Persian war contained the substance of those arguments which he had long revolved in his mind. Some fragments have been transcribed and preserved by his adversary, the vehement Cyril of Alexandria; and they exhibit a very singular mixture of wit and learning, of sophistry and fanaticism. The elegance of the style and the rank of the author recommended his writings to the public attention; and in the impious list of the enemies of Christianity the celebrated name of Porphyry was effaced by the superior merit or reputation of Julian. The minds of the faithful were either seduced, or scandalised, or alarmed; and the Pagans, who sometimes presumed to engage in the unequal dispute, derived, from the popular work of their Imperial missionary, an inexhaustible supply of fallacious objections. But in the assiduous prosecution of these theological studies the emperor of the Romans imbibed the illiberal prejudices and passions of a polemic divine. He contracted an irrevocable obligation to maintain and propagate his religious opinions; and whilst he secretly applauded the strength and dexterity with which he wielded the weapons of controversy, he was tempted to distrust the sincerity, or to despise the understandings, of his antagonists, who could obstinately resist the force of reason and eloquence.

The Christians, who beheld with horror and indignation the apostasy of Julian, had much more to fear from his power than from his arguments. The Pagans, who were conscious of his fervent zeal, expected, perhaps with impatience, that the flames of persecution should be immediately kindled against the enemies of the gods; and that the ingenious malice of Julian would invent some cruel refinements of death and torture which had been unknown to the rude and inexperienced fury of his predecessors. But the hopes, as well as the fears, of the religious factions were apparently disappointed by the prudent humanity of a prince who was careful of his own fame, of the public peace, and of the rights of mankind. Instructed by history and reflection, Julian was persuaded that, if the diseases of the body may sometimes be cured by salutary violence, neither steel nor fire can eradicate the erroneous opinions of the mind. The reluctant victim may be dragged to the foot of the altar; but the heart still abhors and disclaims the sacrilegious act of the hand. Religious obstinacy is hardened and exasperated by oppression; and, as soon as the persecution subsides, those who have yielded are restored as penitents, and those who have resisted are honoured as saints and martyrs. If Julian adopted the unsuccessful cruelty of Diocletian and his colleagues, he was sensible that he should stain his memory with the name of tyrant, and add new glories to the catholic church, which had derived strength and increase from the severity of the Pagan magistrates. Actuated by these motives, and apprehensive of disturbing the repose of an unsettled reign, Julian surprised the world by an edict which was not unworthy of a statesman or a philosopher. He extended to all the inhabitants of the Roman world the benefits of a free and equal toleration; and the only hardship which he inflicted on the Christians was to deprive them of the power of tormenting their fellow-subjects, whom they stigmatised with the odious titles of idolaters and heretics. The Pagans received a gracious permission, or rather

257

an express order, to open ALL their temples; and they were at once delivered from the oppressive laws and arbitrary vexations which they had sustained under the reign of Constantine and of his sons. At the same time, the bishops and clergy who had been banished by the Arian monarch were recalled from exile, and restored to their respective churches; the Donatists, the Novatians, the Macedonians, the Eunomians, and those who, with a more prosperous fortune, adhered to the doctrine of the council of Nice. Julian, who understood and derided their theological disputes, invited to the palace the leaders of the hostile sects, that he might enjoy the agreeable spectacle of their furious encounters. The clamour of controversy sometimes provoked the emperor to exclaim, "Hear me! the Franks have heard me, and the Alemanni;" but he soon discovered that he was now engaged with more obstinate and implacable enemies; and though he exerted the powers of oratory to persuade them to live in concord, or at least in peace, he was perfectly satisfied, before he dismissed them from his presence, that he had nothing to dread from the union of the Christians. The impartial Ammianus has ascribed this affected clemency to the desire of fomenting the intestine divisions of the church; and the insidious design of undermining the foundations of Christianity was inseparably connected with the zeal which Julian professed to restore the ancient religion of the empire.

As soon as he ascended the throne, he assumed, according to the custom of his predecessors, the character of supreme pontiff; not only as the most honourable title of Imperial greatness, but as a sacred and important office, the duties of which he was resolved to execute with pious diligence. As the business of the state prevented the emperor from joining every day in the public devotion of his subjects, he dedicated a domestic chapel to his tutelar deity the Sun; his gardens were filled with statues and altars of the gods; and each apartment of the palace displayed the appearance of a magnificent temple. Every morning he saluted the parent of light with a sacrifice; the blood of another victim was shed at the moment when the Sun sunk below the horizon; and the Moon, the Stars, and the Genii of the night received their respective and seasonable honours from the indefatigable devotion of Julian. On solemn festivals he regularly visited the temple of the god or goddess to whom the day was peculiarly consecrated, and endeavoured to excite the religion of the magistrates and people by the example of his own zeal. Instead of maintaining the lofty state of a monarch, distinguished by the splendour of his purple, and encompassed by the golden shields of his guards, Julian solicited, with respectful eagerness, the meanest offices which contributed to the worship of the gods. Amidst the sacred but licentious crowd of priests, of inferior ministers, and of female dancers, who were dedicated to the service of the temple, it was the business of the emperor to bring the wood, to blow the fire, to handle the knife, to slaughter the victim, and, thrusting his bloody hands into the bowels of the expiring animal, to draw forth the heart or liver, and to read, with the consummate skill of an haruspex, the imaginary signs of future events. The wisest of the Pagans censured this extravagant superstition, which affected to despise the restraints of prudence and decency. Under the reign of a prince who practised the rigid maxims of economy, the expense of religious worship consumed a very large portion of the revenue; a constant supply of the scarcest and most beautiful birds was transported from distant climates, to bleed on the altars of the gods; an hundred oxen were frequently sacrificed by Julian on one and the same day; and it soon became a popular jest, that, if he should return with conquest from the Persian war, the breed of horned cattle must infallibly be extinguished. Yet this expense may appear inconsiderable, when it is compared with the splendid presents which were offered, either by the hand or by order of the emperor, to all the celebrated places of de-

votion in the Roman world; and with the sums allotted
to repair and decorate the ancient temples, which had
suffered the silent decay of time, or the recent injuries of
Christian rapine. Encouraged by the example, the ex-
hortations, the liberality of their pious sovereign, the
cities and families resumed the practice of their neglected ceremonies. "Every part of the world," exclaims
Libanius, with devout transport, "displayed the triumph
of religion, and the grateful prospect of flaming altars,
bleeding victims, the smoke of incense, and a solemn
train of priests and prophets, without fear and without
danger. The sound of prayer and of music was heard on
the tops of the highest mountains; and the same ox
afforded a sacrifice for the gods, and a supper for their
joyous votaries."

But the genius and power of Julian were unequal to
the enterprise of restoring a religion which was destitute
of theological principles, of moral precepts, and of ecclesiastical discipline; which rapidly hastened to decay
and dissolution, and was not susceptible of any solid or
consistent reformation. The jurisdiction of the supreme
pontiff, more especially after that office had been united
with the Imperial dignity, comprehended the whole extent of the Roman empire. Julian named for his vicars,
in the several provinces, the priests and philosophers,
whom he esteemed the best qualified to co-operate in the
execution of his great design; and his pastoral letters, if
we may use that name, still represent a very curious
sketch of his wishes and intentions. He directs that in
every city the sacerdotal order should be composed, without any distinction of birth or fortune, of those persons
who were the most conspicuous for their love of the gods
and of men. "If they are guilty," continues he, "'of any
scandalous offence, they should be censured or degraded
by the superior pontiff; but as long as they retain their
rank, they are entitled to the respect of the magistrates
and people. Their humility may be shown in the plain-
ness of their domestic garb; their dignity, in the pomp

of holy vestments. When they are summoned in their turn to officiate before the altar, they ought not, during the appointed number of days, to depart from the precincts of the temple; nor should a single day be suffered to elapse without the prayers and the sacrifice which they are obliged to offer for the prosperity of the state and of individuals. The exercise of their sacred functions requires an immaculate purity both of mind and body; and even when they are dismissed from the temple to the occupations of common life, it is incumbent on them to excel in decency and virtue the rest of their fellow-citizens. The priest of the gods should never be seen in theatres or taverns. His conversation should be chaste, his diet temperate, his friends of honourable reputation; and if he sometimes visits the Forum or the Palace, he should appear only as the advocate of those who have vainly solicited either justice or mercy. His studies should be suited to the sanctity of his profession. Licentious tales, or comedies, or satires, must be banished from his library, which ought solely to consist of historical and philosophical writings; of history, which is founded in truth, and of philosophy, which is connected with religion. The impious opinions of the Epicureans and sceptics deserve his abhorrence and contempt;[3] but he should diligently study the systems of Pythagoras, of Plato, and of the Stoics, which unanimously teach that there *are* gods; that the world is governed by their providence; that their goodness is the source of every temporal blessing; and that they have prepared for the human soul a future state of reward or punishment." The Imperial pontiff inculcates, in the most persuasive language, the duties of benevolence and hospitality; exhorts his inferior clergy to recommend the universal practice of

[3] The exultation of Julian that these impious sects, and even their writings, are extinguished, may be consistent enough with the sacerdotal character; but it is unworthy of a philosopher to wish that any opinions and arguments the most repugant to his own should be concealed from the knowledge of mankind.

those virtues; promises to assist their indigence from the
public treasury; and declares his resolution of establishing hospitals in every city, where the poor should be
received without any invidious distinction of country or
of religion. Julian beheld with envy the wise and humane
regulations of the church; and he very frankly confesses
his intention to deprive the Christians of the applause,
as well as advantage, which they had acquired by the
exclusive practice of charity and beneficence. The same
spirit of imitation might dispose the emperor to adopt
several ecclesiastical institutions, the use and importance
of which were approved by the success of his enemies.
But if these imaginary plans of reformation had been
realised, the forced and imperfect copy would have been
less beneficial to Paganism than honourable to Christianity. The Gentiles, who peaceably followed the customs of their ancestors, were rather surprised than
pleased with the introduction of foreign manners; and,
in the short period of his reign, Julian had frequent occasions to complain of the want of fervour of his own
party. . . .

[*Gibbon gives various instances of the violence caused by
Julian's acts of restitution, which included an attempt
to restore the Temple of Jerusalem, and concludes with
the spectacular episode of George of Cappadocia, archbishop of Alexandria, who is presumed (though, as Gibbon admits, not with certainty) to be the original St.
George.*]

George, from his parents or his education, surnamed
the Cappadocian, was born at Epiphania in Cilicia, in
a fuller's shop. From this obscure and servile origin he
raised himself by the talents of a parasite; and the patrons whom he assiduously flattered procured for their
worthless dependent a lucrative commission, or contract,
to supply the army with bacon. His employment was
mean; he rendered it infamous. He accumulated wealth

by the basest arts of fraud and corruption; but his mal-
versations were so notorious, that George was compelled
to escape from the pursuits of justice. After this disgrace,
in which he appears to have saved his fortune at the expense of his honour, he embraced, with real or affected
zeal, the profession of Arianism. From the love, or the
ostentation, of learning, he collected a valuable library
of history, rhetoric, philosophy, and theology; and the
choice of the prevailing faction promoted George of Cappadocia to the throne of Athanasius. The entrance of the
new archbishop was that of a barbarian conqueror; and
each moment of his reign was polluted by cruelty and
avarice. The catholics of Alexandria and Egypt were
abandoned to a tyrant, qualified by nature and education to exercise the office of persecution; but he oppressed with an impartial hand the various inhabitants
of his extensive diocese. The primate of Egypt assumed
the pomp and insolence of his lofty station; but he still
betrayed the vices of his base and servile extraction. The
merchants of Alexandria were impoverished by the unjust and almost universal monopoly, which he acquired,
of nitre, salt, paper, funerals, etc.: and the spiritual
father of a great people condescended to practise the vile
and pernicious arts of an informer. The Alexandrians
could never forget, nor forgive, the tax which he suggested on all the houses of the city, under an obsolete
claim that the royal founder had conveyed to his successors, the Ptolemies and the Cæsars, the perpetual
property of the soil. The Pagans, who had been flattered
with the hopes of freedom and toleration, excited his
devout avarice; and the rich temples of Alexandria were
either pillaged or insulted by the haughty prelate, who
exclaimed in a loud and threatening tone, "How long will
these sepulchres be permitted to stand?" Under the reign
of Constantius he was expelled by the fury, or rather
by the justice, of the people; and it was not without a
violent struggle that the civil and military powers of the
state could restore his authority, and gratify his revenge.

The messenger who proclaimed at Alexandria the accession of Julian announced the downfall of the archbishop. George, with two of his obsequious ministers, Count Diodorus, and Dracontius, master of the mint, were ignominiously dragged in chains to the public prison. At the end of twenty-four days the prison was forced open by the rage of a superstitious multitude, impatient of the tedious forms of judicial proceedings. The enemies of gods and men expired under their cruel insults; the lifeless bodies of the archbishop and his associates were carried in triumph through the streets on the back of a camel; and the inactivity of the Athanasian party was esteemed a shining example of evangelical patience. The remains of these guilty wretches were thrown into the sea; and the popular leaders of the tumult declared their resolution to disappoint the devotion of the Christians, and to intercept the future honours of these *martyrs,* who had been punished, like their predecessors, by the enemies of their religion. The fears of the Pagans were just, and their precautions ineffectual. The meritorious death of the archbishop obliterated the memory of his life. The rival of Athanasius was dear and sacred to the Arians, and the seeming conversion of those sectaries introduced his worship into the bosom of the catholic church. The odious stranger, disguising every circumstance of time and place, assumed the mask of a martyr, a saint, and a Christian hero; and the infamous George of Cappadocia has been transformed into the renowned St. George of England, the patron of arms, of chivalry, and of the garter.

[*The murder of the Arian archbishop George opened the way for the return to Alexandria of his rival Athanasius, who quickly established himself as "ecclesiastical dictator"; but Julian interposed and issued an edict exiling Athanasius from Egypt.*]

The execution of the sentence was still delayed by the

caution or negligencĕ of Ecdicius, præfect of Egypt, who was at length awakened from his lethargy by a severe reprimand. "Though you neglect," says Julian, "to write to me on any other subject, at least it is your duty to inform me of your conduct towards Athanasius, the enemy of the gods. My intentions have been long since communicated to you. I swear by the great Serapis, that unless, on the calends of December, Athanasius has departed from Alexandria, nay, from Egypt, the officers of your government shall pay a fine of one hundred pounds of gold. You know my temper: I am slow to condemn, but I am still slower to forgive." This epistle was enforced by a short postscript written with the emperor's own hand. "The contempt that is shown for all the gods fills me with grief and indignation. There is nothing that I should see, nothing that I should hear, with more pleasure, than the expulsion of Athanasius from all Egypt. The abominable wretch! Under my reign, the baptism of several Grecian ladies of the highest rank has been the effect of his persecutions." The death of Athanasius was not *expressly* commanded; but the præfect of Egypt understood that it was safer for him to exceed than to neglect the orders of an irritated master. The archbishop prudently retired to the monasteries of the Desert; eluded, with his usual dexterity, the snares of the enemy; and lived to triumph over the ashes of a prince who, in words of formidable import, had declared his wish that the whole venom of the Galilæan school were contained in the single person of Athanasius.

I have endeavoured faithfully to represent the artful system by which Julian proposed to obtain the effects, without incurring the guilt or reproach, of persecution. But if the deadly spirit of fanaticism perverted the heart and understanding of a virtuous prince, it must, at the same time, be confessed, that the *real* sufferings of the Christians were inflamed and magnified by human passions and religious enthusiasm. The meekness and resignation which had distinguished the primitive disciples of the Gospel was the object of the applause, rather than of the imitation, of their successors. The Christians, who had now possessed above forty years the civil and ecclesiastical government of the empire, had contracted the insolent vices of prosperity, and the habit of believing that the saints alone were entitled to reign over the earth. As soon as the enmity of Julian deprived the clergy of the privileges which had been conferred by the favour of Constantine, they complained of the most cruel oppression; and the free toleration of idolaters and heretics was a subject of grief and scandal to the orthodox party. The acts of violence, which were no longer countenanced by the magistrates, were still committed by the zeal of the people. At Pessinus the altar of Cybele was overturned almost in the presence of the emperor; and in the city of Cæsarea, in Cappadocia, the temple of Fortune, the sole place of worship which had been left to the Pagans, was destroyed by the rage of a popular tumult. On these occasions, a prince who felt for the honour of the gods was not disposed to interrupt the course of justice; and his mind was still more deeply exasperated when he found that the fanatics, who had deserved and suffered the punishment of incendiaries, were rewarded with the honours of martyrdom. The Christian subjects of Julian were assured of the hostile designs of their sovereign; and, to their jealous apprehension, every circumstance of his government might afford some grounds of discontent and suspicion. In the ordinary administration of the laws, the Christians, who formed so large a part of the people, must frequently be condemned; but their indulgent brethren, without examining the merits of the cause, presumed their innocence, allowed their claims, and imputed the severity of their judge to the partial malice of religious persecution. These present hardships, intolerable as they might appear, were represented as a slight prelude of the impending calamities. The Christians considered Julian as a cruel and crafty tyrant, who suspended the execution of his revenge till he should return victorious from the Persian war. They expected that, as soon as he had triumphed over the foreign enemies of Rome, he would lay aside the irksome mask of dissimulation; that the amphitheatres would stream with the blood of hermits and bishops; and that the Christians who still persevered in the profession of the faith would be deprived of the common benefits of nature and society. Every calumny that could wound the reputation of the Apostate was credulously embraced by the fears and hatred of his adversaries; and their indiscreet clamours provoked the temper of a sovereign whom it was their duty to respect, and their interest to flatter. They still protested that prayers and tears were their only weapons against the impious tyrant, whose head they devoted to the justice of offended Heaven. But they insinuated, with sullen resolution, that their submission was no longer the effect of weakness; and that, in the imperfect state of human virtue, the patience which is founded on principle may be exhausted by persecution. It is impossible to determine how far the zeal of Julian would have prevailed over his good sense and humanity; but, if we seriously reflect on the strength and spirit of the church, we shall be convinced that, before the emperor could have extinguished the religion of Christ, he must have involved his country in the horrors of a civil war.

CHAPTER X

THEODOSIUS THE GREAT
AND THE FINAL DESTRUCTION
OF PAGANISM

[*The hope of a successful return to paganism was dashed by the death of Julian in the Persian War (363 A.D.) after a reign of only two years. Thereafter, the emperors were Christian; but Arians (who exalted God above Christ) and Athanasians (whose doctrine of an equal Trinity had been promulgated at the Council of Nice or Nicæa in 325) still contended for supremacy, and Arianism was particularly strong in the East. The decisive change came in 378, when the Arian emperor Valens, who administered the Eastern provinces, was defeated and killed by the Goths at Adrianople, and his Western colleague Gratian adopted, in his place, the Spanish-born General Theodosius, "the first of the Emperors baptised in the true faith of the Trinity." The reign of Theodosius, who became sole emperor after his defeat of the usurper Maximus in 388, is as important as that of Constantine himself. By his own military genius he secured, for a time, the safety of the whole empire; and thanks to the support, not to say domination, of St. Ambrose, bishop of Milan, he achieved the final triumph of Athanasian Christianity over both Arianism and paganism. In Chapter XXVII Gibbon describes Theodosius' intervention in the ecclesiastical politics of Constantinople and the ruin of the Arian party at*

*the Council of Constantinople (381); in chapter
XXVIII (from which the following passage is
taken) he describes his final destruction of paganism and the introduction of the worship of saints
and relics among Christians.*]

The ruin of Paganism, in the age of Theodosius, is perhaps the only example of the total extirpation of any
ancient and popular superstition, and may therefore deserve to be considered as a singular event in the history
of the human mind. The Christians, more especially the
clergy, had impatiently supported the prudent delays of
Constantine and the equal toleration of the elder Valentinian; nor could they deem their conquest perfect or
secure as long as their adversaries were permitted to
exist. The influence which Ambrose and his brethren
had acquired over the youth of Gratian and the piety of
Theodosius was employed to infuse the maxims of persecution into the breasts of their Imperial proselytes. Two
specious principles of religious jurisprudence were established, from whence they deduced a direct and rigorous conclusion against the subjects of the empire who
still adhered to the ceremonies of their ancestors: *that*
the magistrate is, in some measure, guilty of the crimes
which he neglects to prohibit or to punish; and *that* the
idolatrous worship of fabulous deities and real dæmons
is the most abominable crime against the supreme majesty of the Creator. The laws of Moses and the examples
of Jewish history were hastily, perhaps erroneously, applied by the clergy to the mild and universal reign of
Christianity. The zeal of the emperors was excited to
vindicate their own honour and that of the Deity; and
the temples of the Roman world were subverted about
sixty years after the conversion of Constantine.

From the age of Numa to the reign of Gratian, the
Romans preserved the regular succession of the several
colleges of the sacerdotal order. Fifteen PONTIFFS exercised their supreme jurisdiction over all things and per-

sons that were consecrated to the service of the gods; and the various questions which perpetually arose in a loose and traditionary system were submitted to the judgment of their holy tribunal. Fifteen grave and learned AUGURS observed the face of the heavens, and prescribed the actions of heroes according to the flight of birds. Fifteen keepers of the Sibylline books (their name of QUINDECEMVIRS was derived from their number) occasionally consulted the history of future, and, as it should seem, of contingent events. Six VESTALS devoted their virginity to the guard of the sacred fire and of the unknown pledges of the duration of Rome, which no mortal had been suffered to behold with impunity. Seven EPULOS prepared the table of the gods, conducted the solemn procession, and regulated the ceremonies of the annual festival. The three FLAMENS of Jupiter, of Mars, and of Quirinus, were considered as the peculiar ministers of the three most powerful deities, who watched over the fate of Rome and of the universe. The KING of the SACRIFICES represented the person of Numa and of his successors in the religious functions, which could be performed only by royal hands. The confraternities of the SALIANS, the LUPERCALS, etc., practised such rites as might extort a smile of contempt from every reasonable man, with a lively confidence of recommending themselves to the favour of the immortal gods. The authority which the Roman priests had formerly obtained in the counsels of the republic was gradually abolished by the establishment of monarchy and the removal of the seat of empire. But the dignity of their sacred character was still protected by the laws and manners of their country; and they still continued, more especially the college of pontiffs, to exercise in the capital, and sometimes in the provinces, the rights of their ecclesiastical and civil jurisdiction. Their robes of purple, chariots of state, and sumptuous entertainments attracted the admiration of the people; and they received, from the consecrated lands and the public revenue, an ample stipend, which liberally supported the splendour of the priesthood and all the expenses of the religious worship of the state. As the service of the altar was not incompatible with the command of armies, the Romans, after their consulships and triumphs, aspired to the place of pontiff or of augur; the seats of Cicero[1] and Pompey were filled, in the fourth century, by the most illustrious members of the senate; and the dignity of their birth reflected additional splendour on their sacerdotal character. The fifteen priests who composed the college of pontiffs enjoyed a more distinguished rank as the companions of their sovereign; and the Christian emperors condescended to accept the robe and ensigns which were appropriated to the office of supreme pontiff. But when Gratian ascended the throne, more scrupulous or more enlightened, he sternly rejected those profane symbols; applied to the service of the state or of the church the revenues of the priests and vestals; abolished their honours and immunities; and dissolved the ancient fabric of Roman superstition, which was supported by the opinions and habits of eleven hundred years. Paganism was still the constitutional religion of the senate. The hall or temple in which they assembled was adorned by the statue and altar of Victory: a majestic female standing on a globe, with flowing garments, expanded wings, and a crown of laurel in her outstretched hand. The senators were sworn on the altar of the goddess to observe the laws of the emperor and of the empire; and a solemn offering of wine and incense was the ordinary prelude of their public deliberations. The removal of this ancient monument was the only injury which Constantius had offered to the superstition of the Romans. The altar of Victory was again restored by Julian, tolerated by Valentinian, and once more banished

---

[1] Cicero frankly or indirectly confesses that the *Augurate* is the supreme object of his wishes. Pliny is proud to tread in the footsteps of Cicero, and the chain of tradition might be continued from history and marbles.

from the senate by the zeal of Gratian. But the emperor yet spared the statues of the gods which were exposed to the public veneration: four hundred and twenty-four temples, or chapels, still remained to satisfy the devotion of the people, and in every quarter of Rome the delicacy of the Christians was offended by the fumes of idolatrous sacrifice.

But the Christians formed the least numerous party in the senate of Rome; and it was only by their absence that they could express their dissent from the legal, though profane, acts of a Pagan majority. In that assembly the dying embers of freedom were, for a moment, revived and inflamed by the breath of fanaticism. Four respectable deputations were successively voted to the Imperial court, to represent the grievances of the priesthood and the senate, and to solicit the restoration of the altar of Victory. The conduct of this important business was intrusted to the eloquent Symmachus, a wealthy and noble senator, who united the sacred characters of pontiff and augur with the civil dignities of proconsul of Africa and præfect of the city. The breast of Symmachus was animated by the warmest zeal for the cause of expiring Paganism; and his religious antagonists lamented the abuse of his genius and the inefficacy of his moral virtues. The orator, whose petition is extant to the emperor Valentinian, was conscious of the difficulty and danger of the office which he had assumed. He cautiously avoids every topic which might appear to reflect on the religion of his sovereign; humbly declares that prayers and entreaties are his only arms; and artfully draws his arguments from the schools of rhetoric rather than from those of philosophy. Symmachus endeavours to seduce the imagination of a young prince, by displaying the attributes of the goddess of Victory; he insinuates that the confiscation of the revenues which were consecrated to the service of the gods was a measure unworthy of his liberal and disinterested character; and he maintains that the Roman sacrifices would be deprived of their force and energy, if they were no longer celebrated at the expense as well as in the name of the republic. Even scepticism is made to supply an apology for superstition. The great and incomprehensible *secret* of the universe eludes the inquiry of man. Where reason cannot instruct, custom may be permitted to guide; and every nation seems to consult the dictates of prudence, by a faithful attachment to those rites and opinions which have received the sanction of ages. If those ages have been crowned with glory and prosperity—if the devout people has frequently obtained the blessings which they have solicited at the altars of the gods—it must appear still more advisable to persist in the same salutary practice, and not to risk the unknown perils that may attend any rash innovations. The test of antiquity and success was applied with singular advantage to the religion of Numa; and ROME herself, the celestial genius that presided over the fates of the city, is introduced by the orator to plead her own cause before the tribunal of the emperors. "Most excellent princes," says the venerable matron, "fathers of your country! pity and respect my age, which has hitherto flowed in an uninterrupted course of piety. Since I do not repent, permit me to continue in the practice of my ancient rites. Since I am born free, allow me to enjoy my domestic institutions. This religion has reduced the world under my laws. These rites have repelled Hannibal from the city, and the Gauls from the Capitol. Were my grey hairs reserved for such intolerable disgrace? I am ignorant of the new system that I am required to adopt; but I am well assured that the correction of old age is always an ungrateful and ignominious office." The fears of the people supplied what the discretion of the orator had suppressed; and the calamities which afflicted or threatened the declining empire were unanimously imputed by the Pagans to the new religion of Christ and of Constantine.

But the hopes of Symmachus were repeatedly baffled by the firm and dextrous opposition of the archbishop of

273

Milan, who fortified the emperors against the fallacious
eloquence of the advocate of Rome. In this controversy
Ambrose condescends to speak the language of a philosopher, and to ask, with some contempt, why it should
be thought necessary to introduce an imaginary and invisible power as the cause of those victories, which were
sufficiently explained by the valour and discipline of the
legions. He justly derides the absurd reverence for antiquity, which could only tend to discourage the improvements of art and to replunge the human race into their
original barbarism. From thence gradually rising to a
more lofty and theological tone, he pronounces that
Christianity alone is the doctrine of truth and salvation,
and that every mode of Polytheism conducts its deluded
votaries through the paths of error to the abyss of eternal
perdition. Arguments like these, when they were suggested by a favourite bishop, had power to prevent the
restoration of the altar of Victory; but the same arguments fell with much more energy and effect from the
mouth of a conqueror, and the gods of antiquity were
dragged in triumph at the chariot-wheels of Theodosius.
In a full meeting of the senate the emperor proposed,
according to the forms of the republic, the important
question, whether the worship of Jupiter or that of Christ
should be the religion of the Romans. The liberty of
suffrages, which he affected to allow, was destroyed by
the hopes and fears that his presence inspired; and the
arbitrary exile of Symmachus was a recent admonition
that it might be dangerous to oppose the wishes of the
monarch. On a regular division of the senate, Jupiter was
condemned and degraded by the sense of a very large
majority; and it is rather surprising that any members
should be found bold enough to declare, by their speeches
and votes, that they were still attached to the interest of
an abdicated deity. The hasty conversion of the senate
must be attributed either to supernatural or to sordid
motives; and many of these reluctant proselytes betrayed, on every favourable occasion, their secret dis-

position to throw aside the mask of odious dissimulation. But they were gradually fixed in the new religion, as the cause of the ancient became more hopeless; they yielded to the authority of the emperor, to the fashion of the times, and to the entreaties of their wives and children,[2] who were instigated and governed by the clergy of Rome and the monks of the East. The edifying example of the Anician family was soon imitated by the rest of the nobility: the Bassi, the Paullini, the Gracchi, embraced the Christian religion; and "the luminaries of the world, the venerable assembly of Catos (such are the high-flown expressions of Prudentius), were impatient to strip themselves of their pontifical garment—to cast the skin of the old serpent—to assume the snowy robes of baptismal innocence—and to humble the pride of the consular fasces before the tombs of the martyrs." The citizens, who subsisted by their own industry, and the populace, who were supported by the public liberality, filled the churches of the Lateran and Vatican with an incessant throng of devout proselytes. The decrees of the senate, which proscribed the worship of idols, were ratified by the general consent of the Romans; the splendour of the Capitol was defaced, and the solitary temples were abandoned to ruin and contempt. Rome submitted to the yoke of the Gospel; and the vanquished provinces had not yet lost their reverence for the name and authority of Rome.

The filial piety of the emperors themselves engaged them to proceed with some caution and tenderness in the reformation of the eternal city. Those absolute monarchs acted with less regard to the prejudices of the provincials. The pious labour, which had been suspended near twenty years since the death of Constantius, was vigorously resumed, and finally accomplished, by the zeal

[2] Jerome specifies the pontiff Albinus, who was surrounded with such a believing family of children and grandchildren as would have been sufficient to convert even Jupiter himself—an extraordinary proselyte!

of Theodosius. Whilst that warlike prince yet struggled with the Goths, not for the glory, but for the safety of the republic, he ventured to offend a considerable party of his subjects, by some acts which might perhaps secure the protection of Heaven, but which must seem rash and unseasonable in the eye of human prudence. The success of his first experiments against the Pagans encouraged the pious emperor to reiterate and enforce his edicts of proscription: the same laws which had been originally published in the provinces of the East, were applied, after the defeat of Maximus, to the whole extent of the Western empire; and every victory of the orthodox Theodosius contributed to the triumph of the Christian and catholic faith. He attacked superstition in her most vital part, by prohibiting the use of sacrifices, which he declared to be criminal as well as infamous; and if the terms of his edicts more strictly condemned the impious curiosity which examined the entrails of the victims, every subsequent explanation tended to involve in the same guilt the general practice of *immolation,* which essentially constituted the religion of the Pagans. As the temples had been erected for the purpose of sacrifice, it was the duty of a benevolent prince to remove from his subjects the dangerous temptation of offending against the laws which he had enacted. A special commission was granted to Cynegius, the Prætorian præfect of the East, and afterwards to the Counts Jovius and Gaudentius, two officers of distinguished rank in the West, by which they were directed to shut the temples, to seize or destroy the instruments of idolatry, to abolish the privileges of the priests, and to confiscate the consecrated property for the benefit of the emperor, of the church, or of the army. Here the desolation might have stopped: and the naked edifices, which were no longer employed in the service of idolatry, might have been protected from the destructive rage of fanaticism. Many of those temples were the most splendid and beautiful monuments of Grecian architecture: and the emperor himself was interested not to deface the splendour of his own cities, or to diminish the value of his own possessions. Those stately edifices might be suffered to remain, as so many lasting trophies of the victory of Christ. In the decline of the arts, they might be usefully converted into magazines, manufactures, or places of public assembly: and perhaps, when the walls of the temple had been sufficiently purified by holy rites, the worship of the true Deity might be allowed to expiate the ancient guilt of idolatry. But as long as they subsisted, the Pagans fondly cherished the secret hope that an auspicious revolution, a second Julian, might again restore the altars of the gods: and the earnestness with which they addressed their unavailing prayers to the throne increased the zeal of the Christian reformers to extirpate, without mercy, the root of superstition. The laws of the emperors exhibit some symptoms of a milder disposition: but their cold and languid efforts were insufficient to stem the torrent of enthusiasm and rapine, which was conducted, or rather impelled, by the spiritual rulers of the church. In Gaul, the holy Martin, bishop of Tours, marched at the head of his faithful monks to destroy the idols, the temples, and the consecrated trees of his extensive diocese; and, in the execution of this arduous task, the prudent reader will judge whether Martin was supported by the aid of miraculous powers or of carnal weapons. In Syria, the divine and excellent Marcellus, as he is styled by Theodoret, a bishop animated with apostolic fervour, resolved to level with the ground the stately temples within the diocese of Apamea. His attack was resisted by the skill and solidity with which the temple of Jupiter had been constructed. The building was seated on an eminence: on each of the four sides the lofty roof was supported by fifteen massy columns, sixteen feet in circumference; and the large stones of which they were composed were firmly cemented with lead and iron. The force of the strongest and sharpest tools had been tried without effect. It was found necessary to undermine the foundations of the columns, which fell down as soon as the temporary wooden props had been consumed with fire; and the difficulties of the enterprise are described under the allegory of a black dæmon, who retarded, though he could not defeat, the operations of the Christian engineers. Elated with victory, Marcellus took the field in person against the powers of darkness; a numerous troop of soldiers and gladiators marched under the episcopal banner, and he successively attacked the villages and country temples of the diocese of Apamea. Whenever any resistance or danger was apprehended, the champion of the faith, whose lameness would not allow him either to fight or fly, placed himself at a convenient distance, beyond the reach of darts. But this prudence was the occasion of his death; he was surprised and slain by a body of exasperated rustics; and the synod of the province pronounced, without hesitation, that the holy Marcellus had sacrificed his life in the cause of God. In the support of this cause, the monks, who rushed with tumultuous fury from the desert, distinguished themselves by their zeal and diligence. They deserved the enmity of the Pagans; and some of them might deserve the reproaches of avarice and intemperance—of avarice, which they gratified with holy plunder; and of intemperance, which they indulged at the expense of the people, who foolishly admired their tattered garments, loud psalmody, and artificial paleness. A small number of temples was protected by the fears, the venality, the taste, or the prudence of the civil and ecclesiastical governors. The temple of the Celestial Venus at Carthage, whose sacred precincts formed a circumference of two miles, was judiciously converted into a Christian church; and a similar consecration has preserved inviolate the majestic dome of the Pantheon at Rome. But in almost every province of the Roman world, an army of fanatics, without authority and without discipline, invaded the peaceful inhabitants; and the ruin of the fairest structures of antiquity still displays the ravages of *those* barbarians who alone had time and inclination to execute such laborious destruction.

In this wide and various prospect of devastation, the spectator may distinguish the ruins of the temple of Serapis, at Alexandria. Serapis does not appear to have been one of the native gods, or monsters, who sprung from the fruitful soil of superstitious Egypt. The first of the Ptolemies had been commanded, by a dream, to import the mysterious stranger from the coast of Pontus, where he had been long adored by the inhabitants of Sinope; but his attributes and his reign were so imperfectly understood, that it became a subject of dispute whether he represented the bright orb of day, or the gloomy monarch of the subterraneous regions. The Egyptians, who were obstinately devoted to the religion of their fathers, refused to admit this foreign deity within the walls of their cities. But the obsequious priests, who were seduced by the liberality of the Ptolemies, submitted, without resistance, to the power of the god of Pontus: an honourable and domestic genealogy was provided; and this fortunate usurper was introduced into the throne and bed of Osiris, the husband of Isis, and the celestial monarch of Egypt. Alexandria, which claimed his peculiar protection, gloried in the name of the city of Serapis. His temple, which rivalled the pride and magnificence of the Capitol, was erected on the spacious summit of an artificial mount, raised one hundred steps above the level of the adjacent parts of the city; and the interior cavity was strongly supported by arches, and distributed into vaults and subterraneous apartments. The consecrated buildings were surrounded by a quadrangular portico; the stately halls and exquisite statues displayed the triumph of the arts; and the treasures of ancient learning were preserved in the famous Alexandrian library, which had arisen with new splendour from its ashes. After the edicts of Theodosius had severely prohibited the sacrifices of the Pagans, they were still tolerated in the city and temple of Serapis; and this singular indulgence was imprudently ascribed to the superstitious terrors of the Christians themselves: as if they had feared to abolish those ancient rites which could alone secure the inundations of the Nile, the harvests of Egypt, and the subsistence of Constantinople.

At that time the archiepiscopal throne of Alexandria was filled by Theophilus, the perpetual enemy of peace and virtue; a bold, bad man, whose hands were alternately polluted with gold and with blood. His pious indignation was excited by the honours of Serapis; and the insults which he offered to an ancient chapel of Bacchus convinced the Pagans that he meditated a more important and dangerous enterprise. In the tumultuous capital of Egypt, the slightest provocation was sufficient to inflame a civil war. The votaries of Serapis, whose strength and numbers were much inferior to those of their antagonists, rose in arms at the instigation of the philosopher Olympius, who exhorted them to die in the defence of the altars of the gods. These Pagan fanatics fortified themselves in the temple, or rather fortress, of Serapis; repelled the besiegers by daring sallies and a resolute defence; and, by the inhuman cruelties which they exercised on their Christian prisoners, obtained the last consolation of despair. The efforts of the prudent magistrate were usefully exerted for the establishment of a truce till the answer of Theodosius should determine the fate of Serapis. The two parties assembled, without arms, in the principal square; and the Imperial rescript was publicly read. But when a sentence of destruction against the idols of Alexandria was pronounced, the Christians sent up a shout of joy and exultation, whilst the unfortunate Pagans, whose fury had given way to consternation, retired with hasty and silent steps, and eluded, by their flight or obscurity, the resentment of their enemies. Theophilus proceeded to demolish the temple of Serapis, without any other difficulties than those which he found in the weight and solidity of the materials; but these obstacles proved so insuperable that he was obliged to leave the foundations, and to content himself with reducing the edifice itself to a heap of rubbish, a part of which was soon afterwards cleared away, to make room for a church erected in honour of the Christian martyrs. The valuable library of Alexandria was pillaged or destroyed; and near twenty years afterwards, the appearance of the empty shelves excited the regret and indignation of every spectator whose mind was not totally darkened by religious prejudice. The compositions of ancient genius, so many of which have irretrievably perished, might surely have been excepted from the wreck of idolatry, for the amusement and instruction of succeeding ages; and either the zeal or the avarice of the archbishop might have been satiated with the rich spoils which were the reward of his victory. While the images and vases of gold and silver were carefully melted, and those of a less valuable metal were contemptuously broken and cast into the streets, Theophilus laboured to expose the frauds and vices of the ministers of the idols: their dexterity in the management of the loadstone; their secret methods of introducing an human actor into a hollow statue; and their scandalous abuse of the confidence of devout husbands and unsuspecting females. Charges like these may seem to deserve some degree of credit, as they are not repugnant to the crafty and interested spirit of superstition. But the same spirit is equally prone to the base practice of insulting and calumniating a fallen enemy; and our belief is naturally checked by the reflection that it is much less difficult to invent a fictitious story than to support a practical fraud. The colossal statue of Serapis was involved in the ruin of his temple and religion. A great number of plates of different metals, artificially joined together, composed the majestic figure of the deity, who touched on either side the walls of the sanctuary. The aspect of Serapis, his sitting posture, and the sceptre which he bore in his left hand, were extremely similar to the ordinary representations of Jupiter. He was distinguished

from Jupiter by the basket, or bushel, which was placed
on his head; and by the emblematic monster which he
held in his right hand; the head and body of a serpent
branching into three tails, which were again terminated
by the triple heads of a dog, a lion, and a wolf. It was
confidently affirmed that, if any impious hand should
dare to violate the majesty of the god, the heavens and
the earth would instantly return to their original chaos.
An intrepid soldier, animated by zeal, and armed with a
weighty battle-axe, ascended the ladder; and even the
Christian multitude expected with some anxiety the event
of the combat. He aimed a vigorous stroke against the
cheek of Serapis; the cheek fell to the ground; the thunder was still silent, and both the heavens and the earth
continued to preserve their accustomed order and tranquillity. The victorious soldier repeated his blows: the
huge idol was overthrown and broken in pieces; and the
limbs of Serapis were ignominiously dragged through the
streets of Alexandria. His mangled carcase was burnt in
the amphitheatre, amidst the shouts of the populace;
and many persons attributed their conversion to this discovery of the impotence of their tutelar deity. The popular modes of religion, that propose any visible and
material objects of worship, have the advantage of adapting and familiarising themselves to the senses of mankind; but this advantage is counterbalanced by the
various and inevitable accidents to which the faith of the
idolater is exposed. It is scarcely possible that, in every
disposition of mind, he should preserve his implicit reverence for the idols, or the relics, which the naked eye
and the profane hand are unable to distinguish from the
most common productions of art or nature; and if, in
the hour of danger, their secret and miraculous virtue
does not operate for their own preservation, he scorns the
vain apologies of his priests, and justly derides the
object and the folly of his superstitious attachment. After
the fall of Serapis, some hopes were still entertained by

the Pagans that the Nile would refuse his annual supply to the impious masters of Egypt; and the extraordinary delay of the inundation seemed to announce the displeasure of the river-god. But this delay was soon compensated by the rapid swell of the waters. They suddenly rose to such an unusual height as to comfort the discontented party with the pleasing expectation of a deluge; till the peaceful river again subsided to the well-known and fertilising level of sixteen cubits, or about thirty English feet.

The temples of the Roman empire were deserted or destroyed; but the ingenious superstition of the Pagans still attempted to elude the laws of Theodosius, by which all sacrifices had been severely prohibited. The inhabitants of the country, whose conduct was less exposed to the eye of malicious curiosity, disguised their *religious* under the appearance of *convivial* meetings. On the days of solemn festivals they assembled in great numbers under the spreading shade of some consecrated trees; sheep and oxen were slaughtered and roasted; and this rural entertainment was sanctified by the use of incense and by the hymns which were sung in honour of the gods. But it was alleged that, as no part of the animal was made a burnt-offering, as no altar was provided to receive the blood, and as the previous oblation of salt cakes and the concluding ceremony of libations were carefully omitted, these festal meetings did not involve the guests in the guilt or penalty of an illegal sacrifice. Whatever might be the truth of the facts' or the merit of the distinction, these vain pretences were swept away by the last edict of Theodosius, which inflicted a deadly wound on the superstition of the Pagans. This prohibitory law is expressed in the most absolute and comprehensive terms. "It is our will and pleasure," says the emperor, "that none of our subjects, whether magistrates or private citizens, however exalted or however humble may be their rank and condition, shall presume in any city or in any place to worship an inanimate idol by the sacrifice of a guiltless victim." The act of sacrificing and the practice of divination by the entrails of the victim are declared (without any regard to the object of the inquiry) a crime of high treason against the state, which can be expiated only by the death of the guilty. The rites of Pagan superstition which might seem less bloody and atrocious are abolished as highly injurious to the truth and honour of religion; luminaries, garlands, frankincense, and libations of wine are specially enumerated and condemned; and the harmless claims of the domestic genius, of the household gods, are included in this rigorous proscription. The use of any of these profane and illegal ceremonies subjects the offender to the forfeiture of the house or estate where they have been performed; and if he has artfully chosen the property of another for the scene of his impiety, he is compelled to discharge, without delay, a heavy fine of twenty-five pounds of gold, or more than one thousand pounds sterling. A fine not less considerable is imposed on the connivance of the secret enemies of religion who shall neglect the duty of their respective stations, either to reveal or to punish the guilt of idolatry. Such was the persecuting spirit of the laws of Theodosius, which were repeatedly enforced by his sons and grandsons, with the loud and unanimous applause of the Christian world. . . .

The ruin of the Pagan religion is described by the sophists as a dreadful and amazing prodigy, which covered the earth with darkness and restored the ancient dominion of chaos and of night. They relate in solemn and pathetic strains that the temples were converted into sepulchres, and that the holy places, which had been adorned by the statues of the gods, were basely polluted by the relics of Christian martyrs. "The monks" (a race of filthy animals, to whom Eunapius is tempted to refuse the name of men) "are the authors of the new worship, which, in the place of those deities who are conceived by the understanding, has substituted the meanest and most contemptible slaves. The heads, salted and pickled, of those infamous malefactors, who for the multitude of their crimes have suffered a just and ignominious death; their bodies, still marked by the impression of the lash and the scars of those tortures which were inflicted by the sentence of the magistrate; such" (continues Eunapius) "are the gods which the earth produces in our days; such are the martyrs, the supreme arbitrators of our prayers and petitions to the Deity, whose tombs are now consecrated as the objects of the veneration of the people." Without approving the malice, it is natural enough to share the surprise of the sophist, the spectator of a revolution which raised those obscure victims of the laws of Rome to the rank of celestial and invisible protectors of the Roman empire. The grateful respect of the Christians for the martyrs of the faith was exalted, by time and victory, into religious adoration; and the most illustrious of the saints and prophets were deservedly associated to the honours of the martyrs. One hundred and fifty years after the glorious deaths of St. Peter and St. Paul, the Vatican and the Ostian road were distinguished by the tombs, or rather by the trophies, of those spiritual heroes. In the age which followed the conversion of Constantine, the emperors, the consuls, and the generals of armies devoutly visited the sepulchres of a tentmaker and a fisherman; and their venerable bones were deposited under the altars of Christ, on which the bishops of the royal city continually offered the unbloody sacrifice. The new capital of the Eastern world, unable to produce any ancient and domestic trophies, was enriched by the spoils of dependent provinces. The bodies of St. Andrew, St. Luke, and St. Timothy had reposed near three hundred years in the obscure graves from whence they were transported, in solemn pomp, to the church of the apostles, which the magnificence of Constantine had founded on the banks of the Thracian Bosphorus. About fifty years afterwards the same banks were honoured by the presence of Samuel, the judge and prophet of the people of Israel. His ashes, deposited in a golden vase, and covered with a silken veil, were delivered by the bishops into each other's hands. The relics of Samuel were received by the people with the same joy and reverence which they would have shown to the living prophet; the highways, from Palestine to the gates of Constantinople, were filled with an uninterrupted procession; and the emperor Arcadius himself, at the head of the most illustrious members of the clergy and senate, advanced to meet his extraordinary guest, who had always deserved and claimed the homage of kings. The example of Rome and Constantinople confirmed the faith and discipline of the catholic world. The honours of the saints and martyrs, after a feeble and ineffectual murmur of profane reason,[3] were universally established; and in the age of Ambrose and Jerom something was still deemed wanting to the sanctity of a Christian church, till it had been consecrated by some portion of holy relics, which fixed and inflamed the devotion of the faithful.

In the long period of twelve hundred years, which elapsed between the reign of Constantine and the reformation of Luther, the worship of saints and relics corrupted the pure and perfect simplicity of the Christian model; and some symptoms of degeneracy may be observed even in the first generations which adopted and cherished this pernicious innovation.

I. The satisfactory experience that the relics of saints were more valuable than gold or precious stones stimulated the clergy to multiply the treasures of the church. Without much regard for truth or probability, they in-

---

[3] The presbyter Vigilantius, the protestant of his age, firmly, though ineffectually, withstood the superstition of monks, relics, saints, fasts, etc., for which Jerom compares him to the Hydra, Cerberus, the Centaurs, etc., and considers him only as the organ of the Dæmon. Whoever will peruse the controversy of St. Jerom and Vigilantius, and St. Augustin's account of the miracles of St. Stephen, may speedily gain some idea of the spirit of the Fathers.

vented names for skeletons, and actions for names. The fame of the apostles, and of the holy men who had imitated their virtues, was darkened by religious fiction. To the invincible band of genuine and primitive martyrs they added myriads of imaginary heroes, who had never existed, except in the fancy of crafty or credulous legendaries; and there is reason to suspect that Tours might not be the only diocese in which the bones of a malefactor were adored instead of those of a saint. A superstitious practice, which tended to increase the temptations of fraud and credulity, insensibly extinguished the light of history and of reason in the Christian world.

II. But the progress of superstition would have been much less rapid and victorious if the faith of the people had not been assisted by the seasonable aid of visions and miracles to ascertain the authenticity and virtue of the most suspicious relics. In the reign of the younger Theodosius, Lucian, a presbyter of Jerusalem, and the ecclesiastical minister of the village of Caphargamala, about twenty miles from the city, related a very singular dream, which, to remove his doubts, had been repeated on three successive Saturdays. A venerable figure stood before him, in the silence of the night, with a long beard, a white robe, and a gold rod; announced himself by the name of Gamaliel; and revealed to the astonished presbyter, that his own corpse, with the bodies of his son Abibas, his friend Nicodemus, and the illustrious Stephen, the first martyr of the Christian faith, were secretly buried in the adjacent field. He added, with some impatience, that it was time to release himself and his companions from their obscure prison; that their appearance would be salutary to a distressed world; and that they had made choice of Lucian to inform the bishop of Jerusalem of their situation and their wishes. The doubts and difficulties which still retarded this important discovery were successively removed by new visions; and the ground was opened by the bishop, in the presence of an innumerable multitude. The coffins of Gamaliel, of

his son, and of his friend, were found in regular order;
but when the fourth coffin, which contained the remains
of Stephen, was shown to the light, the earth trembled,
and an odour such as that of Paradise was smelt, which
instantly cured the various diseases of seventy-three of
the assistants. The companions of Stephen were left
in their peaceful residence of Caphargamala; but the
relics of the first martyr were transported, in solemn
procession, to a church constructed in their honour on
Mount Sion; and the minute particles of those relics, a
drop of blood, or the scrapings of a bone, were acknowledged, in almost every province of the Roman world, to
possess a divine and miraculous virtue. The grave and
learned Augustin, whose understanding scarcely admits
the excuse of credulity, has attested the innumerable
prodigies which were performed in Africa by the relics
of St. Stephen; and this marvellous narrative is inserted
in the elaborate work of the City of God, which the bishop of Hippo designed as a solid and immortal proof of
the truth of Christianity. Augustin solemnly declares
that he has selected those miracles only which were
publicly certified by the persons who were either the
objects, or the spectators, of the power of the martyr.
Many prodigies were omitted or forgotten; and Hippo had
been less favourably treated than the other cities of the
province. And yet the bishop enumerates above seventy
miracles, of which three were resurrections from the
dead, in the space of two years, and within the limits
of his own diocese. If we enlarge our view to all the
dioceses, and all the saints, of the Christian world, it
will not be easy to calculate the fables, and the errors,
which issued from this inexhaustible source. But we
may surely be allowed to observe that a miracle, in that
age of superstition and credulity, lost its name and its
merit, since it could scarcely be considered as a deviation
from the ordinary and established laws of nature.

III. The innumerable miracles, of which the tombs of
the martyrs were the perpetual theatre, revealed to the

pious believer the actual state and constitution of the invisible world; and his religious speculations appeared to be founded on the firm basis of fact and experience. Whatever might be the condition of vulgar souls in the long interval between the dissolution and the resurrection of their bodies, it was evident that the superior spirits of the saints and martyrs did not consume that portion of their existence in silent and inglorious sleep. It was evident (without presuming to determine the place of their habitation, or the nature of their felicity) that they enjoyed the lively and active consciousness of their happiness, their virtue, and their powers; and that they had already secured the possession of their eternal reward. The enlargement of their intellectual faculties surpassed the measure of the human imagination; since it was proved by *experience* that they were capable of hearing and understanding the various petitions of their numerous votaries, who, in the same moment of time, but in the most distant parts of the world, invoked the name and assistance of Stephen or of Martin. The confidence of their petitioners was founded on the persuasion that the saints, who reigned with Christ, cast an eye of pity upon earth; that they were warmly interested in the prosperity of the catholic church; and that the individuals who imitated the example of their faith and piety were the peculiar and favourite objects of their most tender regard. Sometimes, indeed, their friendship might be influenced by considerations of a less exalted kind: they viewed with partial affection the places which had been consecrated by their birth, their residence, their death, their burial, or the possession of their relics. The meaner passions of pride, avarice, and revenge, may be deemed unworthy of a celestial breast; yet the saints themselves condescended to testify their grateful approbation of the liberality of their votaries; and the sharpest bolts of punishment were hurled against those impious wretches who violated their magnificent shrines, or disbelieved their supernatural power. Atrocious, indeed, must have been the guilt, and strange would have been the scepticism, of those men, if they had obstinately resisted the proofs of a divine agency, which the elements, the whole range of the animal creation, and even the subtle and invisible operations of the human mind, were compelled to obey.[4] The immediate, and almost instantaneous, effects, that were supposed to follow the prayer, or the offence, satisfied the Christians of the ample measure of favour and authority which the saints enjoyed in the presence of the Supreme God; and it seemed almost superfluous to inquire whether they were continually obliged to intercede before the throne of grace, or whether they might not be permitted to exercise, according to the dictates of their benevolence and justice, the delegated powers of their subordinate ministry. The imagination, which had been raised by a painful effort to the contemplation and worship of the Universal Cause, eagerly embraced such inferior objects of adoration as were more proportioned to its gross conceptions and imperfect faculties. The sublime and simple theology of the primitive Christians was gradually corrupted: and the MONARCHY of heaven, already clouded by metaphysical subtleties, was degraded by the introduction of a popular mythology which tended to restore the reign of polytheism.

IV. As the objects of religion were gradually reduced to the standard of the imagination, the rites and ceremonies were introduced that seemed most powerfully to affect the senses of the vulgar. If, in the beginning of the fifth century, Tertullian, or Lactantius, had been suddenly raised from the dead, to assist at the festival of some popular saint or martyr, they would have gazed with astonishment and indignation on the profane spectacle which had succeeded to the pure and spiritual

---

[4]At Minorca, the relics of St. Stephen converted in eight days 540 Jews; with the help, indeed, of some wholesome severities, such as burning the synagogue, driving the obstinate infidels to starve among the rocks, etc.

worship of a Christian congregation. As soon as the doors of the church were thrown open, they must have been offended by the smoke of incense, the perfume of flowers, and the glare of lamps and tapers, which diffused, at noon-day, a gaudy, superfluous, and, in their opinion, a sacrilegious light. If they approached the balustrade of the altar, they made their way through the prostrate crowd, consisting, for the most part, of strangers and pilgrims, who resorted to the city on the vigil of the feast; and who already felt the strong intoxication of fanaticism, and, perhaps, of wine. Their devout kisses were imprinted on the walls and pavement of the sacred edifice; and their fervent prayers were directed, whatever might be the language of their church, to the bones, the blood, or the ashes of the saint, which were usually concealed, by a linen or silken veil, from the eyes of the vulgar. The Christians frequented the tombs of the martyrs, in the hope of obtaining, from their powerful intercession, every sort of spiritual, but more especially of temporal, blessings. They implored the preservation of their health, or the cure of their infirmities; the fruitfulness of their barren wives, or the safety and happiness of their children. Whenever they undertook any distant or dangerous journey, they requested that the holy martyrs would be their guides and protectors on the road; and if they returned without having experienced any misfortune, they again hastened to the tombs of the martyrs, to celebrate, with grateful thanksgivings, their obligations to the memory and relics of those heavenly patrons. The walls were hung round with symbols of the favours which they had received; eyes, and hands, and feet, of gold and silver: and edifying pictures, which could not long escape the abuse of indiscreet or idolatrous devotion, represented the image, the attributes, and the miracles of the tutelar saint. The same uniform original spirit of superstition might suggest, in the most distant ages and countries, the same methods of deceiving the credulity, and of affecting the senses of mankind: but it must ingenuously be confessed that the ministers of the Catholic Church thereby imitated the profane model which they were impatient to destroy. The most respectable bishops had persuaded themselves that the ignorant rustics would more cheerfully renounce the superstitions of Paganism, if they found some resemblance, some compensation, in the bosom of Christianity. The religion of Constantine achieved, in less than a century, the final conquest of the Roman empire: but the victors themselves were insensibly subdued by the arts of their vanquished rivals.

CHAPTER XI

THEOLOGY AND FACTION
IN THE EASTERN EMPIRE

[*"The genius of Rome,"* says Gibbon, *"expired
with Theodosius, the last of the successors of
Augustus and Constantine who appeared in the
field at the head of their armies and whose
authority was recognised throughout the whole
extent of the empire." After his death (395 A.D.),
Rome and Constantinople became the separate
capitals of his sons, Arcadius and Honorius, and
were never effectively reunited. Their courses also
diverged. While Rome, united in religious uniformity, crumbled beneath barbarian attacks, Constantinople survived the attacks but was convulsed by theological controversy. Whatever its
intellectual significance, this controversy was
sharpened by the rivalry between the patriarchs
of the two greatest cities of the East, Alexandria
and Constantinople. In chapter XXXII Gibbon
describes the fate of St. John Chrysostom, archbishop of Constantinople, in the court of Arcadius,
which was managed by "the mild and absolute
dominion of his wife, the fair and artful Eudoxia"
and by the "deformed and decrepit eunuch"
Eutropius.]*

After the death of the indolent Nectarius, the successor
of Gregory Nazianzen, the church of Constantinople
was distracted by the ambition of rival candidates, who

were not ashamed to solicit, with gold or flattery, the suffrage of the people or of the favourite. On this occasion Eutropius seems to have deviated from his ordinary maxims; and his uncorrupted judgement was determined only by the superior merit of a stranger. In a late journey into the East he had admired the sermons of John, a native and presbyter of Antioch, whose name has been distinguished by the epithet of Chrysostom, or the Golden Mouth. A private order was despatched to the governor of Syria; and as the people might be unwilling to resign their favourite preacher, he was transported, with speed and secrecy, in a post-chariot, from Antioch to Constantinople. The unanimous and unsolicited consent of the court, the clergy, and the people ratified the choice of the minister; and, both as a saint and as an orator, the new archbishop surpassed the sanguine expectations of the public. Born of a noble and opulent family in the capital of Syria, Chrysostom had been educated, by the care of a tender mother, under the tuition of the most skilful masters. He studied the art of rhetoric in the school of Libanius; and that celebrated sophist, who soon discovered the talents of his disciple, ingenuously confessed that John would have deserved to succeed him had he not been stolen away by the Christians. His piety soon disposed him to receive the sacrament of baptism; to renounce the lucrative and honourable profession of the law; and to bury himself in the adjacent desert, where he subdued the lusts of the flesh by an austere penance of six years. His infirmities compelled him to return to the society of mankind; and the authority of Meletius devoted his talents to the service of the church: but in the midst of his family, and afterwards on the archiepiscopal throne, Chrysostom still persevered in the practice of the monastic virtues. The ample revenues, which his predecessors had consumed in pomp and luxury, he diligently applied to the establishment of hospitals; and the multitudes who were supported by his charity preferred the eloquent and edifying discourses of their archbishop to the amusements of the theatre or the circus. The monuments of that eloquence, which was admired near twenty years at Antioch and Constantinople, have been carefully preserved; and the possession of near one thousand sermons or homilies has authorised the critics of succeeding times to appreciate the genuine merit of Chrysostom. They unanimously attribute to the Christian orator the free command of an elegant and copious language; the judgment to conceal the advantages which he derived from the knowledge of rhetoric and philosophy; an inexhaustible fund of metaphors and similitudes, of ideas and images, to vary and illustrate the most familiar topics; the happy art of engaging the passions in the service of virtue, and of exposing the folly as well as the turpitude of vice almost with the truth and spirit of a dramatic representation.

The pastoral labours of the archbishop of Constantinople provoked and gradually united against him two sorts of enemies; the aspiring clergy, who envied his success, and the obstinate sinners, who were offended by his reproofs. When Chrysostom thundered from the pulpit of St. Sophia against the degeneracy of the Christians, his shafts were spent among the crowd, without wounding or even marking the character of any individual. When he declaimed against the peculiar vices of the rich, poverty might obtain a transient consolation from his invectives: but the guilty were still sheltered by their numbers; and the reproach itself was dignified by some ideas of superiority and enjoyment. But as the pyramid rose towards the summit, it insensibly diminished to a point; and the magistrates, the ministers, the favourite eunuchs, the ladies of the court, the empress Eudoxia herself, had a much larger share of guilt to divide among a smaller proportion of criminals. The personal applications of the audience were anticipated or confirmed by the testimony of their own conscience; and the intrepid preacher assumed the dangerous right

295

of exposing both the offence and the offender to the public abhorrence. The secret resentment of the court encouraged the discontent of the clergy and monks of Constantinople, who were too hastily reformed by the fervent zeal of their archbishop. He had condemned from the pulpit the domestic females of the clergy of Constantinople, who, under the name of servants or sisters, afforded a perpetual occasion either of sin or of scandal. The silent and solitary ascetics, who had secluded themselves from the world, were entitled to the warmest approbation of Chrysostom; but he despised and stigmatised, as the disgrace of their holy profession, the crowd of degenerate monks, who, from some unworthy motives of pleasure or profit, so frequently infested the streets of the capital. To the voice of persuasion the archbishop was obliged to add the terrors of authority; and his ardour in the exercise of ecclesiastical jurisdiction was not always exempt from passion; nor was it always guided by prudence. Chrysostom was naturally of a choleric disposition. Although he struggled, according to the precepts of the Gospel, to love his private enemies, he indulged himself in the privilege of hating the enemies of God and of the church; and his sentiments were sometimes delivered with too much energy of countenance and expression. He still maintained, from some considerations of health or abstinence, his former habits of taking his repasts alone; and this inhospitable custom, which his enemies imputed to pride, contributed at least to nourish the infirmity of a morose and unsocial humour. Separated from that familiar intercourse which facilitates the knowledge and the despatch of business, he reposed an unsuspecting confidence in his deacon Serapion; and seldom applied his speculative knowledge of human nature to the particular characters either of his dependents or of his equals. Conscious of the purity of his intentions, and perhaps of the superiority of his genius, the archbishop of Constantinople extended the jurisdiction of the Imperial city, that he might enlarge the sphere of his pastoral labours; and the conduct which the profane imputed to an ambitious motive, appeared to Chrysostom himself in the light of a sacred and indispensable duty. In his visitation through the Asiatic provinces he deposed thirteen bishops of Lydia and Phrygia; and indiscreetly declared that a deep corruption of simony and licentiousness had infected the whole episcopal order. If those bishops were innocent, such a rash and unjust condemnation must excite a well-grounded discontent. If they were guilty, the numerous associates of their guilt would soon discover that their own safety depended on the ruin of the archbishop, whom they studied to represent as the tyrant of the Eastern church.

This ecclesiastical conspiracy was managed by Theophilus, archbishop of Alexandria, an active and ambitious prelate, who displayed the fruits of rapine in monuments of ostentation. His national dislike to the rising greatness of a city which degraded him from the second to the third rank in the Christian world was exasperated by some personal disputes with Chrysostom himself. By the private invitation of the empress, Theophilus landed at Constantinople, with a stout body of Egyptian mariners, to encounter the populace; and a train of dependent bishops, to secure by their voices the majority of a synod. The synod was convened in the suburb of Chalcedon, surnamed the *Oak*, where Rufinus had erected a stately church and monastery; and their proceedings were continued during fourteen days or sessions. A bishop and a deacon accused the archbishop of Constantinople; but the frivolous or improbable nature of the forty-seven articles which they presented against him may justly be considered as a fair and unexceptionable panegyric. Four successive summons were signified to Chrysostom; but he still refused to trust either his person or his reputation in the hands of his implacable enemies, who, prudently declining the examination of any particular charges, condemned his contumacious disobedience, and hastily pronounced a sentence of deposition. The synod of the *Oak* immediately addressed the emperor to ratify and execute their judgement, and charitably insinuated that the penalties of treason might be inflicted on the audacious preacher, who had reviled, under the name of Jezebel, the empress Eudoxia herself. The archbishop was rudely arrested, and conducted through the city, by one of the Imperial messengers, who landed him, after a short navigation, near the entrance of the Euxine; from whence, before the expiration of two days, he was gloriously recalled.

The first astonishment of his faithful people had been mute and passive: they suddenly rose with unanimous and irresistible fury. Theophilus escaped, but the promiscuous crowd of monks and Egyptian mariners was slaughtered without pity in the streets of Constantinople. A seasonable earthquake justified the interposition of Heaven; the torrent of sedition rolled forwards to the gates of the palace; and the empress, agitated by fear or remorse, threw herself at the feet of Arcadius, and confessed that the public safety could be purchased only by the restoration of Chrysostom. The Bosphorus was covered with innumerable vessels; the shores of Europe and Asia were profusely illuminated; and the acclamations of a victorious people accompanied, from the port to the cathedral, the triumph of the archbishop, who too easily consented to resume the exercise of his functions, before his sentence had been legally reversed by the authority of an ecclesiastical synod. Ignorant, or careless, of the impending danger, Chrysostom indulged his zeal, or perhaps his resentment; declaimed with peculiar asperity against *female* vices; and condemned the profane honours which were addressed, almost in the precincts of St. Sophia, to the statue of the empress. His imprudence tempted his enemies to inflame the haughty spirit of Eudoxia, by reporting, or perhaps inventing, the famous exordium of a sermon, "Herodias is again furious; Herodias again dances; she once more requires the head of John": an insolent allusion, which, as a woman and a sovereign, it was impossible for her to forgive. The short interval of a perfidious truce was employed to concert more effectual measures for the disgrace and ruin of the archbishop. A numerous council of the Eastern prelates, who were guided from a distance by the advice of Theophilus, confirmed the validity, without examining the justice, of the former sentence; and a detachment of barbarian troops was introduced into the city, to suppress the emotions of the people. On the vigil of Easter the solemn administration of baptism was rudely interrupted by the soldiers, who alarmed the modesty of the naked catechumens, and violated, by their presence, the awful mysteries of the Christian worship. Arsacius occupied the church of St. Sophia and the archiepiscopal throne. The catholics retreated to the baths of Constantine, and afterwards to the fields, where they were still pursued and insulted by the guards, the bishops, and the magistrates. The fatal day of the second and final exile of Chrysostom was marked by the conflagration of the cathedral, of the senate-house, and of the adjacent buildings; and this calamity was imputed, without proof, but not without probability, to the despair of a persecuted faction.

Cicero might claim some merit if his voluntary banishment preserved the peace of the republic; but the submission of Chrysostom was the indispensable duty of a Christian and a subject. Instead of listening to his humble prayer that he might be permitted to reside at Cyzicus or Nicomedia, the inflexible empress assigned for his exile the remote and desolate town of Cucusus, among the ridges of Mount Taurus, in the Lesser Armenia. A secret hope was entertained that the archbishop might perish in a difficult and dangerous march of seventy days in the heat of summer, through the provinces of Asia Minor, where he was continually threatened by the hostile attacks of the Isaurians, and the more implacable fury of the monks. Yet Chrysostom arrived in safety at the place of his confinement; and the three years which he spent at Cucusus, and the neighbouring town of Arabissus, were the last and most glorious of his life. His character was consecrated by absence and persecution; the faults of his administration were no longer remembered; but every tongue repeated the praises of his genius and virtue: and the respectful attention of the Christian world was fixed on a desert spot among the mountains of Taurus. From that solitude the archbishop, whose active mind was invigorated by misfortunes, maintained a strict and frequent correspondence with the most distant provinces; exhorted the separate congregation of his faithful adherents to persevere in their allegiance; urged the destruction of the temples of Phœnicia, and the extirpation of heresy in the isle of Cyprus; extended his pastoral care to the missions of Persia and Scythia; negotiated, by his ambassadors, with the Roman pontiff and the emperor Honorius; and boldly appealed, from a partial synod, to the supreme tribunal of a free and general council. The mind of the illustrious exile was still independent; but his captive body was exposed to the revenge of the oppressors, who continued to abuse the name and authority of Arcadius.[1] An order was despatched for the instant removal of Chrysostom to the extreme desert of Pityus: and his guards so faithfully obeyed their cruel instructions, that, before he reached the sea-coast of the Euxine, he expired at Comana, in Pontus, in the sixtieth year of his age. The succeeding generation acknowledged his innocence and merit. The archbishops of the

[1] After the exile of Chrysostom, Theophilus published an *enormous* and *horrible* volume against him, in which he perpetually repeats the polite expressions of *hosten humanitatis, sacrilegorum principem immundum dæmonem;* he affirms that John Chrysostom had delivered his soul to be adulterated by the devil; and wishes that some farther punishment, adequate (if possible) to the magnitude of his crimes, may be inflicted on him. St. Jerom, at the request of his friend Theophilus, translated this edifying performance from Greek into Latin.

East, who might blush that their predecessors had been the enemies of Chrysostom, were gradually disposed, by the firmness of the Roman pontiff, to restore the honours of that venerable name. At the pious solicitation of the clergy and people of Constantinople, his relics, thirty years after his death, were transported from their obscure sepu.chre to the royal city. The emperor Theodosius[2] advanced to receive them as far as Chalcedon; and, falling prostrate on the coffin, implored, in the name of his guilty parents, Arcadius and Eudoxia, the forgiveness of the injured saint.

[*The rivalry of Chrysostom and Theophilus was consecrated by rival theories about the incarnation of Christ. In chapter XLVII Gibbon goes more closely into these theories, which, in the succeeding reign of Theodosius II, provided the fuel for yet greater controversies, first between Cyril (the nephew and successor of Theophilus) in Alexandria and Nestorius in Constantinople, then between their successors in the same sees, Dioscorus and Flavian.*]

All those who believe the immateriality of the soul, a specious and noble tenet, must confess, from their present experience, the incomprehensible union of mind and matter. A similar union is not inconsistent with a much higher, or even with the highest, degree of mental faculties; and the incarnation of an æon or archangel, the most perfect of created spirits, does not involve any positive contradiction or absurdity. In the age of religious freedom, which was determined by the council of Nice, the dignity of Christ was measured by private judgment according to the indefinite rule of Scripture, or reason, or tradition. But when his pure and proper divinity had been established on the ruins of Arianism, the faith of the Catholics trembled on the edge of a precipice where it was impossible to recede, dangerous to stand, dreadful to fall; and the manifold

[2] [i.e., Theodosius II, the son of Arcadius, who reigned 408-450. *Ed.*]

301

inconveniences of their creed were aggravated by the sublime character of their theology. They hesitated to pronounce—*that* God himself, the second person of an equal and consubstantial trinity, was manifested in the flesh; *that* a being who pervades the universe had been confined in the womb of Mary; *that* his eternal duration had been marked by the days, and months, and years of human existence; *that* the Almighty had been scourged and crucified; *that* his impassible essence had felt pain and anguish; *that* his omniscience was not exempt from ignorance; and *that* the source of life and immortality expired on Mount Calvary. These alarming consequences were affirmed with unblushing simplicity by Apollinaris, bishop of Laodicea, and one of the luminaries of the church. The son of a learned grammarian, he was skilled in all the sciences of Greece; eloquence, erudition, and philosophy, conspicuous in the volumes of Apollinaris, were humbly devoted to the service of religion. The worthy friend of Athanasius, the worthy antagonist of Julian, he bravely wrestled with the Arians and Polytheists, and, though he affected the rigour of geometrical demonstration, his commentaries revealed the literal and allegorical sense of the Scriptures. A mystery which had long floated in the looseness of popular belief was defined by his perverse diligence in a technical form; and he first proclaimed the memorable words, "One incarnate nature of Christ," which are still re-echoed with hostile clamours in the churches of Asia, Egypt, and Æthiopia. He taught that the Godhead was united or mingled with the body of a man; and that the *Logos,* the eternal wisdom, supplied in the flesh the place and office of a human soul. Yet, as the profound doctor had been terrified at his own rashness, Apollinaris was heard to mutter some faint accents of excuse and explanation. He acquiesced in the old distinction of the Greek philosophers between the rational and sensitive soul of man; that he might reserve the *Logos* for intellectual functions, and employ the subordinate human principle in the meaner actions

302

of animal life. With the moderate Docetes he revered
Mary as the spiritual, rather than as the carnal, mother
of Christ, whose body either came from heaven, impassible and incorruptible, or was absorbed, and as it
were transformed, into the essence of the Deity. The
system of Apollinaris was strenuously encountered by
the Asiatic and Syrian divines, whose schools are
honoured by the names of Basil, Gregory, and Chrysostom, and tainted by those of Diodorus, Theodore, and
Nestorius. But the person of the aged bishop of Laodicea,
his character and dignity, remained inviolate; and his
rivals, since we may not suspect them of the weakness
of toleration, were astonished, perhaps, by the novelty
of the argument, and diffident of the final sentence of
the Catholic church. Her judgment at length inclined in
their favour; the heresy of Apollinaris was condemned,
and the separate congregations of his disciples were
proscribed by the Imperial laws. But his principles were
secretly entertained in the monasteries of Egypt, and
his enemies felt the hatred of Theophilus and Cyril, the
successive patriarchs of Alexandria.

The grovelling Ebionite and the fantastic Docetes were
rejected and forgotten: the recent zeal against the errors
of Apollinaris reduced the Catholics to a seeming agreement with the double nature of Cerinthus.[3] But instead
of a temporary and occasional alliance, *they* established,
and *we* still embrace, the substantial, indissoluble, and
everlasting union of a perfect God with a perfect man,
of the second person of the trinity with a reasonable soul
and human flesh. In the beginning of the fifth century
the *unity* of the *two natures* was the prevailing doctrine
of the church. On all sides it was confessed that the mode
of their co-existence could neither be represented by our
ideas nor expressed by our language. Yet a secret and
incurable discord was cherished between those who were

[3] Cerinthus of Asia was the original theorist of the complete
separation of the divine and human nature of Christ. *Ed.*]

most apprehensive of confounding, and those who were most fearful of separating, the divinity and the humanity of Christ. Impelled by religious frenzy, they fled with adverse haste from the error which they mutually deemed most destructive of truth and salvation. On either hand they were anxious to guard, they were jealous to defend, the union and the distinction of the two natures, and to invent such forms of speech, such symbols of doctrine, as were least susceptible of doubt or ambiguity. The poverty of ideas and language tempted them to ransack art and nature for every possible comparison, and each comparison misled their fancy in the explanation of an incomparable mystery. In the polemic microscope an atom is enlarged to a monster, and each party was skilful to exaggerate the absurd or impious conclusions that might be extorted from the principles of their adversaries. To escape from each other they wandered through many a dark and devious thicket, till they were astonished by the horrid phantoms of Cerinthus and Apollinaris, who guarded the opposite issues of the theological labyrinth. As soon as they beheld the twilight of sense and heresy, they started, measured back their steps, and were again involved in the gloom of impenetrable orthodoxy. To purge themselves from the guilt or reproach of damnable error, they disavowed their consequences, explained their principles, excused their indiscretions, and unanimously pronounced the sounds of concord and faith. Yet a latent and almost invisible spark still lurked among the embers of controversy: by the breath of prejudice and passion it was quickly kindled to a mighty flame, and the verbal disputes of the Oriental sects have shaken the pillars of the church and state.

The name of CYRIL of Alexandria is famous in controversial story, and the title of *saint* is a mark that his opinions and his party have finally prevailed. In the house of his uncle, the archbishop Theophilus, he imbibed the orthodox lessons of zeal and dominion, and five years

10
A fine example of a mosaic of the early Byzantine Empire, from
Daphni.

of his youth were profitably spent in the adjacent monasteries of Nitria. Under the tuition of the abbot Serapion, he applied himself to ecclesiastical studies with such indefatigable ardour, that in the course of *one* sleepless night he has perused the four gospels, the catholic epistles, and the epistle to the Romans. Origen he detested; but the writings of Clemens and Dionysius, of Athanasius and Basil, were continually in his hands: by the theory and practice of dispute, his faith was confirmed and his wit was sharpened; he extended round his cell the cobwebs of scholastic theology, and meditated the works of allegory and metaphysics, whose remains, in seven verbose folios, now peaceably slumber by the side of their rivals. Cyril prayed and fasted in the desert, but his thoughts (it is the reproach of a friend) were still fixed on the world; and the call of Theophilus, who summoned him to the tumult of cities and synods, was too readily obeyed by the aspiring hermit. With the approbation of his uncle he assumed the office and acquired the fame of a popular preacher. His comely person adorned the pulpit; the harmony of his voice resounded in the cathedral; his friends were stationed to lead or second the applause of the congregation; and the hasty notes of the scribes preserved his discourses, which, in their effect, though not in their composition, might be compared with those of the Athenian orators. The death of Theophilus expanded and realised the hopes of his nephew. The clergy of Alexandria was divided; the soldiers and their general supported the claims of the archdeacon; but a resistless multitude, with voices and with hands, asserted the cause of their favourite; and after a period of thirty-nine years Cyril was seated on the throne of Athanasius.

The prize was not unworthy of his ambition. At a distance from the court, and at the head of an immense capital, the patriarch, as he was now styled, of Alexandria had gradually usurped the state and authority of a civil magistrate. The public and private charities of the city were managed by his discretion; his voice inflamed or appeased the passions of the multitude; his commands were blindly obeyed by his numerous and fanatic *parabolani*,[4] familiarised in their daily office with scenes of death; and the præfects of Egypt were awed or provoked by the temporal power of these Christian pontiffs. Ardent in the prosecution of heresy, Cyril auspiciously opened his reign by oppressing the Novatians, the most innocent and harmless of the sectaries. The interdiction of their religious worship appeared in his eyes a just and meritorious act; and he confiscated their holy vessels, without apprehending the guilt of sacrilege. The toleration, and even the privileges of the Jews, who had multiplied to the number of forty thousand, were secured by the laws of the Cæsars and Ptolemies, and a long prescription of seven hundred years since the foundation of Alexandria. Without any legal sentence, without any royal mandate, the patriarch, at the dawn of day, led a seditious multitude to the attack of the synagogues. Unarmed and unprepared, the Jews were incapable of resistance; their houses of prayer were levelled with the ground, and the episcopal warrior, after rewarding his troops with the plunder of their goods, expelled from the city the remnant of the unbelieving nation. Perhaps he might plead the insolence of their prosperity, and their deadly hatred of the Christians, whose blood they had recently shed in a malicious or accidental tumult. Such crimes would have deserved the animadversion of the magistrate; but in this promiscuous outrage the innocent were confounded with the guilty, and Alexandria was impoverished by the loss

---

[4] The *Parabolani* of Alexandria were a charitable corporation, instituted during the plague of Gallienus, to visit the sick and to bury the dead. They gradually enlarged, abused, and sold the privileges of their order. Their outrageous conduct during the reign of Cyril provoked the emperor to deprive the patriarch of their nomination, and to restrain their number to five or six hundred. But these restraints were transient and ineffectual.

of a wealthy and industrious colony. The zeal of Cyril exposed him to the penalties of the Julian law; but in a feeble government and a superstitious age he was secure of impunity, and even of praise. Orestes complained; but his just complaints were too quickly forgotten by the ministers of Theodosius, and too deeply remembered by a priest who affected to pardon, and continued to hate, the præfect of Egypt. As he passed through the streets his chariot was assaulted by a band of five hundred of the Nitrian monks; his guards fled from the wild beasts of the desert; his protestations that he was a Christian and a Catholic were answered by a volley of stones, and the face of Orestes was covered with blood. The loyal citizens of Alexandria hastened to his rescue; he instantly satisfied his justice and revenge against the monk by whose hand he had been wounded, and Ammonius expired under the rod of the lictor. At the command of Cyril his body was raised from the ground, and transported in solemn procession to the cathedral; the name of Ammonius was changed to that of Thaumasius, the *wonderful;* his tomb was decorated with the trophies of martyrdom; and the patriarch ascended the pulpit to celebrate the magnanimity of an assassin and a rebel. Such honours might incite the faithful to combat and die under the banners of the saint; and he soon prompted, or accepted, the sacrifice of a virgin, who professed the religion of the Greeks, and cultivated the friendship of Orestes. Hypatia, the daughter of Theon the mathematician, was initiated in her father's studies; her learned comments have elucidated the geometry of Apollonius and Diophantus; and she publicly taught, both at Athens and Alexandria, the philosophy of Plato and Aristotle. In the bloom of beauty, and in the maturity of wisdom, the modest maid refused her lovers and instructed her disciples; the persons most illustrious for their rank or merit were impatient to visit the female philosopher; and Cyril beheld with a jealous eye the gorgeous train of horses and slaves who crowded the door of her academy. A rumour was spread among the Christians that the daughter of Theon was the only obstacle to the reconciliation of the præfect and the archbishop; and that obstacle was speedily removed. On a fatal day, in the holy season of Lent, Hypatia was torn from her chariot, stripped naked, dragged to the church, and inhumanly butchered by the hands of Peter the reader and a troop of savage and merciless fanatics: her flesh was scraped from her bones with sharp oyster-shells, and her quivering limbs were delivered to the flames. The just progress of inquiry and punishment was stopped by seasonable gifts; but the murder of Hypatia has imprinted an indelible stain on the character and religion of Cyril of Alexandria.[5]

Superstition, perhaps, would more gently expiate the blood of a virgin than the banishment of a saint; and Cyril had accompanied his uncle to the iniquitous synod of the Oak.[6] When the memory of Chrysostom was restored and consecrated, the nephew of Theophilus, at the head of a dying faction, still maintained the justice of his sentence; nor was it till after a tedious delay and an obstinate resistance that he yielded to the consent of the Catholic world. His enmity to the Byzantine pontiffs was a sense of interest, not a sally of passion: he envied their fortunate station in the sunshine of the Imperial court; and he dreaded their upstart ambition, which oppressed the metropolitans of Europe and Asia, invaded the provinces of Antioch and Alexandria, and measured

---

[5] These exploits of St. Cyril are recorded by Socrates (1. vii. c. 13, 14, 15); and the most reluctant bigotry is compelled to copy an historian who coolly styles the murders of Hypatia ἄνδρες τὸ φρόνημα ἔνθερμοι [men of warm zeal. *Ed.*] At the mention of that injured name, I am pleased to observe a blush even on the cheek of Baronius.

[6] He was deaf to the entreaties of Atticus of Constantinople, and of Isidore of Pelusium, and yielded only (if we may believe Nicephorus) to the personal intercession of the Virgin. Yet in his last years he still muttered that John Chrysostom had been justly condemned.

their diocese by the limits of the empire. The long moderation of Atticus, the mild usurper of the throne of Chrysostom, suspended the animosities of the Eastern patriarchs; but Cyril was at length awakened by the exaltation of a rival more worthy of his esteem and hatred. After the short and troubled reign of Sisinnius, bishop of Constantinople, the factions of the clergy and people were appeased by the choice of the emperor, who, on this occasion, consulted the voice of fame, and invited the merit of a stranger. Nestorius, a native of Germanicia and a monk of Antioch, was recommended by the austerity of his life and the eloquence of his sermons; but the first homily which he preached before the devout Theodosius betrayed the acrimony and impatience of his zeal. "Give me, O Cæsar!" he exclaimed, "give me the earth purged of heretics, and I will give you in exchange the kingdom of heaven. Exterminate with me the heretics, and with you I will exterminate the Persians." On the fifth day, as if the treaty had been already signed, the patriarch of Constantinople discovered, surprised, and attacked a secret conventicle of the Arians; they preferred death to submission; the flames that were kindled by their despair soon spread to the neighbouring houses, and the triumph of Nestorius was clouded by the name of *incendiary*. On either side of the Hellespont his episcopal vigour imposed a rigid formulary of faith and discipline—a chronological error concerning the festival of Easter was punished as an offence against the church and state. Lydia and Caria, Sardes and Miletus, were purified with the blood of the obstinate Quartodecimans; and the edict of the emperor, or rather of the patriarch, enumerates three-and-twenty degrees and denominations in the guilt and punishment of heresy. But the sword of persecution which Nestorius so furiously wielded was soon turned against his own breast. Religion was the pretence; but, in the judgement of a contemporary saint, ambition was the genuine motive of episcopal warfare.

In the Syrian school Nestorius had been taught to abhor the confusion of the two natures, and nicely to discriminate the humanity of his *master* Christ from the divinity of the *Lord* Jesus. The Blessed Virgin he revered as the mother of Christ, but his ears were offended with the rash and recent title of mother of God, which had been insensibly adopted since the origin of the Arian controversy. From the pulpit of Constantinople, a friend of the patriarch, and afterwards the patriarch himself, repeatedly preached against the use, or the abuse, of a word unknown to the apostles, unauthorised by the church, and which could only tend to alarm the timorous, to mislead the simple, to amuse the profane, and to justify, by a seeming resemblance, the old genealogy of Olympus. In his calmer moments Nestorius confessed that it might be tolerated or excused by the union of the two natures, and the communication of their *idioms:* but he was exasperated by contradiction to disclaim the worship of a new-born, an infant Deity, to draw his inadequate similes from the conjugal or civil partnerships of life, and to describe the manhood of Christ as the robe, the instrument, the tabernacle of his Godhead. At these blasphemous sounds the pillars of the sanctuary were shaken. The unsuccessful competitors of Nestorius indulged their pious or personal resentment, the Byzantine clergy was secretly displeased with the intrusion of a stranger: whatever is superstitious or absurd might claim the protection of the monks; and the people was interested in the glory of their virgin patroness. The sermons of the archbishop, and the service of the altar, were disturbed by seditious clamour; his authority and doctrine were renounced by separate congregations; every wind scattered round the empire the leaves of controversy; and the voice of the combatants on a sonorous theatre re-echoed in the cells of Palestine and Egypt. It was the duty of Cyril to enlighten the zeal and ignorance of his innumerable monks: in the school of Alexandria he had imbibed and professed the incarnation of one nature; and the successor of Athanasius consulted his pride and ambition when he rose in arms against another Arius, more formidable and more guilty, on the second throne of the hierarchy. After a short correspondence, in which the rival prelates disguised their hatred in the hollow language of respect and charity, the patriarch of Alexandria denounced to the prince and people, to the East and to the West, the damnable errors of the Byzantine pontiff. From the East, more especially from Antioch, he obtained the ambiguous counsels of toleration and silence, which were addressed to both parties while they favoured the cause of Nestorius. But the Vatican received with open arms the messengers of Egypt. The vanity of Celestine was flattered by the appeal; and the partial version of a monk decided the faith of the pope, who, with his Latin clergy, was ignorant of the language, the arts, and the theology of the Greeks. At the head of an Italian synod, Celestine weighed the merits of the cause, approved the creed of Cyril, condemned the sentiments and person of Nestorius, degraded the heretic from his episcopal dignity, allowed a respite of ten days for recantation and penance, and delegated to his enemy the execution of this rash and illegal sentence. But the patriarch of Alexandria, whilst he darted the thunders of a god, exposed the errors and passions of a mortal; and his twelve anathemas still torture the orthodox slaves who adore the memory of a saint without forfeiting their allegiance to the synod of Chalcedon. These bold assertions are indelibly tinged with the colours of the Apollinarian heresy; but the serious, and perhaps the sincere, professions of Nestorius have satisfied the wiser and less partial theologians of the present times.

Yet neither the emperor nor the primate of the East were disposed to obey the mandate of an Italian priest; and a synod of the Catholic, or rather of the Greek, church was unanimously demanded as the sole remedy that could appease or decide this ecclesiastical quarrel.

Ephesus, on all sides accessible by sea and land, was chosen for the place, the festival of Pentecost for the day, of the meeting; a writ of summons was despatched to each metropolitan, and a guard was stationed to protect and confine the fathers till they should settle the mysteries of heaven and the faith of the earth. Nestorius appeared not as a criminal, but as a judge; he depended on the weight rather than the number of his prelates, and his sturdy slaves from the baths of Zeuxippus were armed for every service of injury or defence. But his adversary Cyril was more powerful in the weapons both of the flesh and of the spirit. Disobedient to the letter, or at least to the meaning, of the royal summons, he was attended by fifty Egyptian bishops, who expected from their patriarch's nod the inspiration of the Holy Ghost. He had contracted an intimate alliance with Memnon bishop of Ephesus. The despotic primate of Asia disposed of the ready succours of thirty or forty episcopal votes: a crowd of peasants, the slaves of the church, was poured into the city to support with blows and clamours a metaphysical argument; and the people zealously asserted the honour of the Virgin, whose body reposed within the walls of Ephesus.[7] The fleet which had transported Cyril from Alexandria was laden with the riches of Egypt; and he disembarked a numerous body of mariners, slaves, and fanatics, enlisted with blind obedience under the banner of St. Mark and the mother of God. The fathers, and even the guards, of the council were awed by this martial array; the adversaries of Cyril and Mary were insulted in the streets or threatened in their houses; his eloquence and liberality made a daily increase in the number of his adherents;

[7] The Christians of the four first centuries were ignorant of the death and burial of Mary. The tradition of Ephesus is affirmed by the synod; yet it has been superseded by the claim of Jerusalem; and her *empty* sepulchre, as it was shown to the pilgrims, produced the fable of her resurrection and assumption, in which the Greek and Latin churches have piously acquiesced.

and the Egyptian soon computed that he might command the attendance and the voices of two hundred bishops. But the author of the twelve anathemas foresaw and dreaded the opposition of John of Antioch, who, with a small though respectable train of metropolitans and divines, was advancing by slow journeys from the distant capital of the East. Impatient of a delay which he stigmatised as voluntary and culpable, Cyril announced the opening of the synod sixteen days after the festival of Pentecost. Nestorius, who depended on the near approach of his Eastern friends, persisted, like his predecessor Chrysostom, to disclaim the jurisdiction, and to disobey the summons, of his enemies: they hastened his trial and his accuser presided in the seat of judgment. Sixty-eight bishops, twenty-two of metropolitan rank, defended his cause by a modest and temperate protest: they were excluded from the councils of their brethren. Candidian, in the emperor's name, requested a delay of four days; the profane magistrate was driven with outrage and insult from the assembly of the saints. The whole of this momentous transaction was crowded into the compass of a summer's day: the bishops delivered their separate opinions; but the uniformity of style reveals the influence or the hand of a master, who has been accused of corrupting the public evidence of their acts and subscriptions. Without a dissenting voice they recognised in the epistles of Cyril the Nicene creed and the doctrine of the fathers: but the partial extracts from the letters and homilies of Nestorius were interrupted by curses and anathemas; and the heretic was degraded from his episcopal and ecclesiastical dignity. The sentence, maliciously inscribed to the new Judas, was affixed and proclaimed in the streets of Ephesus: the weary prelates, as they issued from the church of the mother of God, were saluted as her champions; and her victory was celebrated by the illuminations, the songs, and the tumult of the night.

On the fifth day the triumph was clouded by the arrival and indignation of the Eastern bishops. In a chamber of the inn, before he had wiped the dust from his shoes, John of Antioch gave audience to Candidian the Imperial minister, who related his ineffectual efforts to prevent or to annul the hasty violence of the Egyptian. With equal haste and violence the Oriental synod of fifty bishops degraded Cyril and Memnon from their episcopal honours; condemned, in the twelve anathemas, the purest venom of the Apollinarian heresy; and described the Alexandrian primate as a monster, born and educated for the destruction of the church. *His* throne was distant and inaccessible; but they instantly resolved to bestow on the flock of Ephesus the blessing of a faithful shepherd. By the vigilance of Memnon the churches were shut against them, and a strong garrison was thrown into the cathedral. The troops, under the command of Candidian, advanced to the assault; the outguards were routed and put to the sword, but the place was impregnable: the besiegers retired; their retreat was pursued by a vigorous sally; they lost their horses, and many of the soldiers were dangerously wounded with clubs and stones. Ephesus, the city of the Virgin, was defiled with rage and clamour, with sedition and blood; the rival synods darted anathemas and excommunications from their spiritual engines; and the court of Theodosius was perplexed by the adverse and contradictory narratives of the Syrian and Egyptian factions. During a busy period of three months the emperor tried every method, except the most effectual means of indifference and contempt, to reconcile this theological quarrel. He attempted to remove or intimidate the leaders by a common sentence of acquittal or condemnation; he invested his representatives at Ephesus with ample power and military force; he summoned from either party eight chosen deputies to a free and candid conference in the neighbourhood of the capital, far from the contagion of popular frenzy. But the Orientals refused to yield, and the Catholics, proud of their num-

314

bers and of their Latin allies, rejected all terms of union or toleration. The patience of the meek Theodosius was provoked, and he dissolved in anger this episcopal tumult, which at the distance of thirteen centuries assumes the venerable aspect of the third œcumenical council. "God is my witness," said the pious prince, "that I am not the author of this confusion. His providence will discern and punish the guilty. Return to your provinces, and may your private virtues repair the mischief and scandal of your meeting." They returned to their provinces; but the same passions which had distracted the synod of Ephesus were diffused over the Eastern world. After three obstinate and equal campaigns, John of Antioch and Cyril of Alexandria condescended to explain and embrace: but their seeming re-union must be imputed rather to prudence than to reason, to the mutual lassitude rather than to the Christian charity of the patriarchs.

The Byzantine pontiff had instilled into the royal ear a baleful prejudice against the character and conduct of his Egyptian rival. An epistle of menace and invective, which accompanied the summons, accused him as a busy, insolent, and envious priest, who perplexed the simplicity of the faith, violated the peace of the church and state, and, by his artful and separate addresses to the wife and sister of Theodosius, presumed to suppose, or to scatter, the seeds of discord in the Imperial family. At the stern command of his sovereign, Cyril had repaired to Ephesus, where he was resisted, threatened, and confined, by the magistrates in the interest of Nestorius and the Orientals, who assembled the troops of Lydia and Ionia to suppress the fanatic and disorderly train of the patriarch. Without expecting the royal licence, he escaped from his guards, precipitately embarked, deserted the imperfect synod, and retired to his episcopal fortress of safety and independence. But his artful emissaries, both in the court and city, successfully laboured to appease the resentment, and to conciliate the favour, of the emperor. The feeble son of Arcadius was alternately swayed by his wife and sister, by the eunuchs and women of the palace: superstition and avarice were their ruling passions; and the orthodox chiefs were assiduous in their endeavours to alarm the former and to gratify the latter. Constantinople and the suburbs were sanctified with frequent monasteries, and the holy abbots, Dalmatius and Eutyches, had devoted their zeal and fidelity to the cause of Cyril, the worship of Mary, and the unity of Christ. From the first moment of their monastic life they had never mingled with the world, or trod the profane ground of the city. But in this awful moment of the danger of the church, their vow was superseded by a more sublime and indispensable duty. At the head of a long order of monks and hermits, who carried burning tapers in their hands, and chanted litanies to the mother of God, they proceeded from their monasteries to the palace. The people was edified and inflamed by this extraordinary spectacle, and the trembling monarch listened to the prayers and adjurations of the saints, who boldly pronounced that none could hope for salvation unless they embraced the person and the creed of the orthodox successor of Athanasius. At the same time every avenue of the throne was assaulted with gold. Under the decent names of *eulogies* and *benedictions*, the courtiers of both sexes were bribed according to the measure of their power and rapaciousness. But their incessant demands despoiled the sanctuaries of Constantinople and Alexandria; and the authority of the patriarch was unable to silence the just murmur of his clergy, that a debt of sixty thousand pounds had already been contracted to support the expense of this scandalous corruption. Pulcheria, who relieved her brother from the weight of an empire, was the firmest pillar of orthodoxy; and so intimate was the alliance between the thunders of the synod and the whispers of the court, that Cyril was assured of success if he could displace one eunuch, and substitute another in the favour of

Theodosius. Yet the Egyptian could not boast of a glorious or decisive victory. The emperor, with unaccustomed firmness, adhered to his promise of protecting the innocence of the Oriental bishops; and Cyril softened his anathemas, and confessed, with ambiguity and reluctance, a twofold nature of Christ, before he was permitted to satiate his revenge against the unfortunate Nestorius.

The rash and obstinate Nestorius, before the end of the synod, was oppressed by Cyril, betrayed by the court, and faintly supported by his Eastern friends. A sentiment of fear or indignation prompted him, while it was yet time, to affect the glory of a voluntary abdication: his wish, or at least his request, was readily granted; he was conducted with honour from Ephesus to his old monastery of Antioch; and, after a short pause, his successors, Maximian and Proclus, were acknowledged as the lawful bishops of Constantinople. But in the silence of his cell the degraded patriarch could no longer resume the innocence and security of a private monk. The past he regretted, he was discontented with the present, and the future he had reason to dread: the Oriental bishops successively disengaged their cause from his unpopular name, and each day decreased the number of the schismatics who revered Nestorius as the confessor of the faith. After a residence at Antioch of four years, the hand of Theodosius subscribed an edict which ranked him with Simon the magician, proscribed his opinions and followers, condemned his writings to the flames, and banished his person first to Petra in Arabia, and at length to Oasis, one of the *islands* of the Libyan desert. Secluded from the church and from the world, the exile was still pursued by the rage of bigotry and war. A wandering tribe of the Blemmyes or Nubians invaded his solitary prison: in their retreat they dismissed a crowd of useless captives; but no sooner had Nestorius reached the banks of the Nile, than he would gladly have escaped from a Roman and orthodox city to the

317

milder servitude of the savages. His flight was punished as a new crime: the soul of the patriarch inspired the civil and ecclesiastical powers of Egypt; the magistrates, the soldiers, the monks, devoutly tortured the enemy of Christ and St. Cyril; and, as far as the confines of Æthiopia, the heretic was alternately dragged and recalled, till his aged body was broken by the hardships and accidents of these reiterated journeys. Yet his mind was still independent and erect; the president of Thebais was awed by his pastoral letters; he survived the Catholic tyrant of Alexandria, and, after sixteen years' banishment, the synod of Chalcedon would perhaps have restored him to the honours, or at least to the communion, of the church. The death of Nestorius prevented his obedience to their welcome summons; and his disease might afford some colour to the scandalous report, that his tongue, the organ of blasphemy, had been eaten by the worms. He was buried in a city of Upper Egypt, known by the names of Chemnis, or Panopolis, or Akmim; but the immortal malice of the Jacobites has persevered for ages to cast stones against his sepulchre, and to propagate the foolish tradition that it was never watered by the rain of heaven, which equally descends on the righteous and the ungodly. Humanity may drop a tear on the fate of Nestorius; yet justice must observe that he suffered the persecution which he had approved and inflicted.

The death of the Alexandrian primate, after a reign of thirty-two years, abandoned the Catholics to the intemperance of zeal and the abuse of victory. The *monophysite* doctrine (one incarnate nature) was rigorously preached in the churches of Egypt and the monasteries of the East; the primitive creed of Apollinaris was protected by the sanctity of Cyril; and the name of EUTYCHES, his venerable friend, has been applied to the sect most adverse to the Syrian heresy of Nestorius. His rival Eutyches was the abbot, or archimandrite, or superior of three hundred monks; but the opinions of a simple and illiterate recluse might have expired in the cell where he had slept above seventy years if the resentment or indiscretion of Flavian, the Byzantine pontiff, had not exposed the scandal to the eyes of the Christian world. His domestic synod was instantly convened, their proceedings were sullied with clamour and artifice, and the aged heretic was surprised into a seeming confession that Christ had not derived his body from the substance of the Virgin Mary. From their partial decree Eutyches appealed to a general council; and his cause was vigorously asserted by his godson Chrysaphius, the reigning eunuch of the palace, and his accomplice Dioscorus, who had succeeded to the throne, the creed, the talents, and the vices of the nephew of Theophilus. By the special summons of Theodosius, the second synod of Ephesus was judiciously composed of ten metropolitans and ten bishops from each of the six dioceses of the Eastern empire: some exceptions of favour or merit enlarged the number to one hundred and thirty-five; and the Syrian Barsumas, as the chief and representative of the monks, was invited to sit and vote with the successors of the apostles. But the despotism of the Alexandrian patriarch again oppressed the freedom of debate: the same spiritual and carnal weapons were again drawn from the arsenals of Egypt; the Asiatic veterans, a band of archers, served under the orders of Dioscorus; and the more formidable monks, whose minds were inaccessible to reason or mercy, besieged the doors of the cathedral. The general and, as it should seem, the unconstrained voice of the fathers accepted the faith and even the anathemas of Cyril; and the heresy of the two natures was formally condemned in the persons and writings of the most learned Orientals. "May those who divide Christ be divided with the sword, may they be hewn in pieces, may they be burned alive!" were the charitable wishes of a Christian synod. The innocence and sanctity of

319

Eutyches were acknowledged without hesitation; but the prelates, more especially those of Thrace and Asia, were unwilling to depose their patriarch for the use or even the abuse of his lawful jurisdiction. They embraced the knees of Dioscorus, as he stood with a threatening aspect on the footstool of his throne, and conjured him to forgive the offences and to respect the dignity of his brother. "Do you mean to raise a sedition?" exclaimed the relentless tyrant. "Where are the officers?" At these words a furious multitude of monks and soldiers, with stakes, and swords, and chains, burst into the church: the trembling bishops hid themselves behind the altar or under the benches; and as they were not inspired with the zeal of martyrdom, they successively subscribed a blank paper, which was afterwards filled with the condemnation of the Byzantine pontiff. Flavian was instantly delivered to the wild beasts of this spiritual amphitheatre: the monks were stimulated by the voice and example of Barsumas to avenge the injuries of Christ: it is said that the patriarch of Alexandria reviled, and buffeted, and kicked, and trampled his brother of Constantinople: it is certain that the victim, before he could reach the place of his exile, expired on the third day of the wounds and bruises which he had received at Ephesus. This second synod has been justly branded as a gang of robbers and assassins; yet the accusers of Dioscorus would magnify his violence, to alleviate the cowardice and inconstancy of their own behaviour.

The faith of Egypt had prevailed: but the vanquished party was supported by the same pope who encountered without fear the hostile rage of Attila and Genseric. The theology of Leo, his famous *tome* or epistle on the mystery of the incarnation, had been disregarded by the synod of Ephesus: his authority, and that of the Latin church, was insulted in his legates, who escaped from slavery and death to relate the melancholy tale of the tyranny of Dioscorus and the martyrdom of Flavian. His provincial synod annulled the irregular proceedings of Ephesus; but as this step was itself irregular, he solicited the convocation of a general council in the free and orthodox provinces of Italy. From his independent throne the Roman bishop spoke and acted without danger as the head of the Christians, and his dictates were obsequiously transcribed by Placidia and her son Valentinian,[8] who addressed their Eastern colleague to restore the peace and unity of the church. But the pageant of Oriental royalty was moved with equal dexterity by the hand of the eunuch; and Theodosius could pronounce, without hesitation, that the church was already peaceful and triumphant, and that the recent flame had been extinguished by the just punishment of the Nestorians. Perhaps the Greeks would be still involved in the heresy of the Monophysites, if the emperor's horse had not fortunately stumbled; Theodosius expired; his orthodox sister, Pulcheria, with a nominal husband, succeeded to the throne; Chrysaphius was burnt, Dioscorus was disgraced, the exiles were recalled, and the *tome* of Leo was subscribed by the Oriental bishops. Yet the pope was disappointed in his favourite project of a Latin council: he disdained to preside in the Greek synod which was speedily assembled at Nice in Bithynia; his legates required in a peremptory tone the presence of the emperor; and the weary fathers were transported to Chalcedon under the immediate eye of Marcian and the senate of Constantinople. A quarter of a mile from the Thracian Bosphorus the church of St. Euphemia was built on the summit of a gentle though lofty ascent: the triple structure was celebrated as a prodigy of art, and the boundless prospect of the land and sea might have raised the mind of a sectary to the contemplation of the God of the universe. Six hundred and thirty bishops were ranged in order in the nave of the church; but the patriarchs of the East were

[8] [Placidia, daughter of Theodosius the Great, ruled the Western Empire in the name of her son Valentinian III from 425 till her death in 450. *Ed.*]

preceded by the legates, of whom the third was a simple priest; and the place of honour was reserved for twenty laymen of consular or senatorian rank. The gospel was ostentatiously displayed in the centre, but the rule of faith was defined by the papal and imperial ministers, who moderated the thirteen sessions of the council of Chalcedon. Their partial interposition silenced the intemperate shouts and execrations which degraded the episcopal gravity; but on the formal accusation of the legates, Dioscorus was compelled to descend from his throne to the rank of a criminal, already condemned in the opinion of his judges. The Orientals, less adverse to Nestorius than to Cyril, accepted the Romans as their deliverers: Thrace, and Pontus, and Asia, were exasperated against the murderer of Flavian, and the new patriarchs of Constantinople and Antioch secured their places by the sacrifice of their benefactor. The bishops of Palestine, Macedonia, and Greece were attached to the faith of Cyril; but in the face of the synod, in the heat of the battle, the leaders, with their obsequious train, passed from the right to the left wing, and decided the victory by this seasonable desertion. Of the seventeen suffragans who sailed from Alexandria, four were tempted from their allegiance, and the thirteen, falling prostrate on the ground, implored the mercy of the council, with sighs and tears, and a pathetic declaration, that, if they yielded, they should be massacred, on their return to Egypt, by the indignant people. A tardy repentance was allowed to expiate the guilt or error of the accomplices of Dioscorus: but their sins were accumulated on his head; he neither asked nor hoped for pardon, and the moderation of those who pleaded for a general amnesty was drowned in the prevailing cry of victory and revenge. To save the reputation of his late adherents, some *personal* offences were skilfully detected; his rash and illegal excommunication of the pope, and his contumacious refusal (while he was detained a prisoner) to attend the summons of the synod. Witnesses were introduced to prove the special facts of his pride, avarice, and cruelty; and the fathers heard with abhorrence that the alms of the church were lavished on the female dancers, that his palace, and even his bath, was open to the prostitutes of Alexandria, and that the infamous Pansophia, or Irene, was publicly entertained as the concubine of the patriarch.

For these scandalous offences Dioscorus was deposed by the synod and banished by the emperor; but the purity of his faith was declared in the presence, and with the tacit approbation, of the fathers. Their prudence supposed rather than pronounced the heresy of Eutyches, who was never summoned before their tribunal; and they sat silent and abashed when a bold Monophysite, casting at their feet a volume of Cyril, challenged them to anathematise in his person the doctrine of the saint. If we fairly peruse the acts of Chalcedon as they are recorded by the orthodox party, we shall find that a great majority of the bishops embraced the simple unity of Christ; and the ambiguous concession that he was formed OF or FROM two natures might imply either their previous existence, or their subsequent confusion, or some dangerous interval between the conception of the man and the assumption of the God. The Roman theology, more positive and precise, 'adopted the term most offensive to the ears of the Egyptians, that Christ existed IN two natures; and this momentous particle (which the memory, rather than the understanding, must retain) had almost produced a schism among the Catholic bishops. The *tome* of Leo had been respectfully, perhaps sincerely, subscribed; but they protested, in two successive debates, that it was neither expedient nor lawful to transgress the sacred landmarks which had been fixed at Nice, Constantinople, and Ephesus, according to the rule of Scripture and tradition. At length they yielded to the importunities of their masters, but their infallible decree, after it had been ratified with deliberate votes and vehement acclamations, was overturned in the next session by the opposition of the legates and their Oriental friends. It was in vain that a multitude of episcopal voices repeated in chorus, "The definition of the fathers is orthodox and immutable! The heretics are now discovered! Anathema to the Nestorians! Let them depart from the synod! Let them repair to Rome." The legates threatened, the emperor was absolute, and a committee of eighteen bishops prepared a new decree, which was imposed on the reluctant assembly. In the name of the fourth general council, the Christ in one person, but *in* two natures, was announced to the Catholic world: an invisible line was drawn between the heresy of Apollinaris and the faith of St. Cyril; and the road to paradise, a bridge as sharp as a razor, was suspended over the abyss by the master-hand of the theological artist. During ten centuries of blindness and servitude Europe received her religious opinions from the oracle of the Vatican; and the same doctrine, already varnished with the rust of antiquity, was admitted without dispute into the creed of the reformers, who disclaimed the supremacy of the Roman pontiff. The synod of Chalcedon still triumphs in the Protestant churches: but the ferment of controversy has subsided, and the most pious Christians of the present day are ignorant, or careless, of their own belief concerning the mystery of the incarnation.

CHAPTER XII

THE END
OF THE WESTERN EMPIRE

[*Meanwhile the Western Empire was slowly crumbling under the blows of the barbarians. By the middle of the fifth century the Goths were partly romanised and Christianised (through Arian); but the Vandals, who conquered Africa, were barbarians and the Saxons, who invaded England, and the Huns, who overran Gaul, were heathen as well. In its last days, the Western Empire was a barbarian protectorate, and in 476 its protector, Odoacer, "resolved to abolish the useless and expensive office" of Emperor. Having forced the abdication of its last holder, Romulus Augustulus, he made himself King of Italy. At this point (chapter XXXVIII) Gibbon inserted his "General Observations on the Fall of the Roman Empire in the West."*]

The Greeks, after their country had been reduced into a province, imputed the triumphs of Rome, not to the merit, but to the FORTUNE, of the republic. The inconstant goddess, who so blindly distributes and resumes her favours, had *now* consented (such was the language of envious flattery) to resign her wings, to descend from her globe, and to fix her firm and immutable throne on the banks of the Tiber. A wiser Greek, who has composed, with a philosophic spirit, the memorable history of his own times, deprived his countrymen of this vain and delusive comfort, by opening to their view the deep foundations of the greatness of Rome. The fidelity of the citizens to each other and to the state was confirmed by the habits of education and the prejudices of religion. Honour, as well as virtue, was the principle of the republic; the ambitious citizens laboured to deserve the solemn glories of a triumph; and the ardour of the Roman youth was kindled into active emulation as often as they beheld the domestic images of their ancestors. The temperate struggles of the patricians and plebeians had finally established the firm and equal balance of the constitution, which united the freedom of popular assemblies with the authority and wisdom of a senate and the executive powers of a regal magistrate. When the consul displayed the standard of the republic, each citizen bound himself, by the obligation of an oath, to draw his sword in the cause of his country till he had discharged the sacred duty by a military service of ten years. This wise institution continually poured into the field the rising generations of freemen and soldiers; and their numbers were reinforced by the warlike and populous states of Italy, who, after a brave resistance, had yielded to the valour and embraced the alliance of the Romans. The sage historian, who excited the virtue of the younger Scipio and beheld the ruin of Carthage, has accurately described their military system; their levies, arms, exercises, subordination, marches, encampments; and the invincible legion, superior in active strength to the Macedonian phalanx of Philip and Alexander. From these institutions of peace and war Polybius has deduced the spirit and success of a people incapable of fear and impatient of repose. The ambitious design of conquest, which might have been defeated by the seasonable conspiracy of mankind, was attempted and achieved; and the perpetual violation of justice was maintained by the political virtues of prudence and courage. The arms of the republic, sometimes vanquished in battle, always victorious in war, advanced with rapid steps to the Euphrates, the Danube, the Rhine, and the Ocean; and the images of gold, or silver, or brass, that might serve to represent the nations and their kings, were successively broken by the *iron* monarchy of Rome.

The rise of a city, which swelled into an empire, may deserve, as a singular prodigy, the reflection of a philosophic mind. But the decline of Rome was the natural and inevitable effect of immoderate greatness. Prosperity ripened the principle of decay; the causes of destruction multiplied with the extent of conquest; and as soon as time or accident had removed the artificial supports, the stupendous fabric yielded to the pressure of its own weight. The story of its ruin is simple and obvious; and instead of inquiring *why* the Roman empire was destroyed, we should rather be surprised that it had subsisted so long. The victorious legions, who, in distant wars, acquired the vices of strangers and mercenaries, first oppressed the freedom of the republic, and afterwards violated the majesty of the purple. The emperors, anxious for their personal safety and the public peace, were reduced to the base expedient of corrupting the discipline which rendered them alike formidable to their sovereign and to the enemy; the vigour of the military government was relaxed and finally dissolved by the partial institutions of Constantine; and the Roman world was overwhelmed by a deluge of barbarians.

The decay of Rome has been frequently ascribed to the translation of the seat of empire; but this history has already shown that the powers of government were *divided* rather than *removed*. The throne of Constantinople was erected in the East; while the West was still possessed by a series of emperors who held their residence in Italy, and claimed their equal inheritance of the legions and provinces. This dangerous novelty impaired the strength and fomented the vices of a double reign: the instruments of an oppressive and arbitrary system were multiplied; and a vain emulation of luxury, not of merit, was introduced and supported between the degenerate successors of Theodosius. Extreme distress, which unites the virtue of a free people, embitters the factions of a declining monarchy. The hostile favourites of Arcadius and Honorius betrayed the republic to its common enemies; and the Byzantine court beheld with indifference, perhaps with pleasure, the disgrace of Rome, the misfortunes of Italy, and the loss of the West. Under the succeeding reigns the alliance of the two empires was restored; but the aid of the Oriental Romans was tardy, doubtful, and ineffectual; and the national schism of the Greeks and Latins was enlarged by the perpetual difference of language and manners, of interests, and even of religion. Yet the salutary event approved in some measure the judgement of Constantine. During a long period of decay his impregnable city repelled the victorious armies of barbarians, protected the wealth of Asia, and commanded, both in peace and war, the important straits which connect the Euxine and Mediterranean seas. The foundation of Constantinople more essentially contributed to the preservation of the East than to the ruin of the West.

As the happiness of a *future* life is the great object of religion, we may hear without surprise or scandal that the introduction, or at least the abuse of Christianity, had some influence on the decline and fall of the Roman empire. The clergy successfully preached the doctrines of patience and pusillanimity; the active virtues of society were discouraged; and the last remains of military spirit were buried in the cloister: a large portion of public and private wealth was consecrated to the specious demands of charity and devotion; and the soldiers' pay was lavished on the useless multitudes of both sexes who could only plead the merits of abstinence and chastity. Faith, zeal, curiosity, and the more earthly passions of malice and ambition, kindled the flame of theological discord; the church, and even the state, were distracted by religious factions, whose conflicts were sometimes bloody and always implacable; the attention of the emperors was diverted from camps to synods; the Roman world was oppressed by a new species of tyranny; and the persecuted sects became the secret enemies of their country. Yet party-spirit, however pernicious or absurd, is a principle of union as well as of dissension. The bishops, from eighteen hundred pulpits, inculcated the duty of passive obedience to a lawful and orthodox sovereign; their frequent assemblies and perpetual correspondence maintained the communion of distant churches; and the benevolent temper of the Gospel was strengthened, though confined, by the spiritual alliance of the catholics. The sacred indolence of the monks was devoutly embraced by a servile and effeminate age; but if superstition had not afforded a decent retreat, the same vices would have tempted the unworthy Romans to desert, from baser motives, the standard of the republic. Religious precepts are easily obeyed which indulge and sanctify the natural inclinations of their votaries; but the pure and genuine influence of Christianity may be traced in its beneficial, though imperfect, effects on the barbarian proselytes of the North. If the decline of the Roman empire was hastened by the conversion of Constantine, his victorious religion broke the violence of the fall, and mollified the ferocious temper of the conquerors.

This awful revolution may be usefully applied to the instruction of the present age. It is the duty of a patriot to prefer and promote the exclusive interest and glory of his native country: but a philosopher may be permitted to enlarge his views, and to consider Europe as one great republic, whose various inhabitants have attained almost the same level of politeness and cultivation. The balance of power will continue to fluctuate, and the prosperity of our own or the neighbouring kingdoms may be alternately exalted or depressed; but these partial events cannot essentially injure our general state of happiness, the system of arts, and laws, and manners, which so advantageously distinguish, above the rest of mankind, the Europeans and their colonies. The savage nations of the globe are the common enemies of civilised society; and we may inquire, with anxious curiosity, whether Europe is still threatened with a repetition of those calamities which formerly oppressed the arms and institutions of Rome. Perhaps the same reflections will illustrate the fall of that mighty empire, and explain the probable causes of our actual security.

I. The Romans were ignorant of the extent of their danger and the number of their enemies. Beyond the Rhine and Danube the northern countries of Europe and Asia were filled with innumerable tribes of hunters and shepherds, poor, voracious, and turbulent; bold in arms, and impatient to ravish the fruits of industry. The barbarian world was agitated by the rapid impulse of war; and the peace of Gaul or Italy was shaken by the distant revolutions of China. The Huns, who fled before a victorious enemy, directed their march towards the West; and the torrent was swelled by the gradual accession of captives and allies. The flying tribes who yielded to the Huns assumed in *their* turn the spirit of conquest; the endless column of barbarians pressed on the Roman empire with accumulated weight; and, if the foremost were destroyed, the vacant space was instantly replenished by new assailants. Such formidable emigrations no longer issue from the North; and the long repose, which has been imputed to the decrease of population, is the happy consequence of the progress of arts and agriculture. Instead of some rude villages thinly scattered among its woods and morasses, Germany now produces a list of two thousand three hundred walled towns: the Christian kingdoms of Denmark, Sweden, and Poland have been successively established; and the Hanse merchants, with the Teutonic knights, have extended their colonies along the coast of the Baltic as far as the Gulf of Finland. From the Gulf of Finland to the Eastern Ocean, Russia now assumes the form of a powerful and civilised empire. The plough, the loom, and the forge are introduced on the banks of the Volga, the Oby, and the

Lena; and the fiercest of the Tartar hordes have been taught to tremble and obey. The reign of independent barbarism is now contracted to a narrow span; and the remnant of Calmucks or Uzbecks, whose forces may be almost numbered, cannot seriously excite the apprehensions of the great republic of Europe. Yet this apparent security should not tempt us to forget that new enemies and unknown dangers may *possibly* arise from some obscure people, scarcely visible in the map of the world. The Arabs or Saracens, who spread their conquests from India to Spain, had languished in poverty and contempt till Mahomet breathed into those savage bodies the soul of enthusiasm.

II. The empire of Rome was firmly established by the singular and perfect coalition of its members. The subject nations, resigning the hope and even the wish of independence, embraced the character of Roman citizens; and the provinces of the West were reluctantly torn by the barbarians from the bosom of their mother country. But this union was purchased by the loss of national freedom and military spirit; and the servile provinces, destitute of life and motion, expected their safety from the mercenary troops and governors who were directed by the orders of a distant court. The happiness of an hundred millions depended on the personal merit of one or two men, perhaps children, whose minds were corrupted by education, luxury, and despotic power. The deepest wounds were inflicted on the empire during the minorities of the sons and grandsons of Theodosius; and, after those incapable princes seemed to attain the age of manhood, they abandoned the church to the bishops, the state to the eunuchs, and the provinces to the barbarians. Europe is now divided into twelve powerful, though unequal kingdoms, three respectable commonwealths, and a variety of smaller, though independent states: the chances of royal and ministerial talents are multiplied, at least, with the number of its rulers; and a Julian, or Semiramis, may reign in the North, while Arcadius and Honorius again slumber on the thrones of the South. The abuses of tyranny are restrained by the mutual influence of fear and shame; republics have acquired order and stability; monarchies have imbibed the principles of freedom, or, at least, of moderation; and some sense of honour and justice is introduced into the most defective constitutions by the general manners of the times. In peace, the progress of knowledge and industry is accelerated by the emulation of so many active rivals: in war, the European forces are exercised by temperate and undecisive contests. If a savage conqueror should issue from the deserts of Tartary, he must repeatedly vanquish the robust peasants of Russia, the numerous armies of Germany, the gallant nobles of France, and the intrepid freemen of Britain; who, perhaps, might confederate for their common defence. Should the victorious barbarians carry slavery and desolation as far as the Atlantic Ocean, ten thousand vessels would transport beyond their pursuit the remains of civilised society; and Europe would revive and flourish in the American world, which is already filled with her colonies and institutions.

III. Cold, poverty, and a life of danger and fatigue fortify the strength and courage of barbarians. In every age they have oppressed the polite and peaceful nations of China, India, and Persia, who neglected, and still neglect, to counterbalance these natural powers by the resources of military art. The warlike states of antiquity, Greece, Macedonia, and Rome, educated a race of soldiers; exercised their bodies, disciplined their courage, multiplied their forces by regular evolutions, and converted the iron which they possessed into strong and serviceable weapons. But this superiority insensibly declined with their laws and manners: and the feeble policy of Constantine and his successors armed and instructed, for the ruin of the empire, the rude valour of the barbarian mercenaries. The military art has been changed by the invention of gunpowder; which enables man to command the two most powerful agents of nature, air and fire. Mathematics, chemistry, mechanics, architecture, have been applied to the service of war; and the adverse parties oppose to each other the most elaborate modes of attack and of defence. Historians may indignantly observe that the preparations of a siege would found and maintain a flourishing colony; yet we cannot be displeased that the subversion of a city should be a work of cost and difficulty; or that an industrious people should be protected by those arts which survive and supply the decay of military virtue. Cannon and fortifications now form an impregnable barrier against the Tartar horse; and Europe is secure from any future eruption of barbarians; since, before they can conquer, they must cease to be barbarous. Their gradual advances in the science of war would always be accompanied, as we may learn from the example of Russia, with a proportionable improvement in the arts of peace and civil policy; and they themselves must deserve a place among the polished nations whom they subdue.

Should these speculations be found doubtful or fallacious, there still remains a more humble source of comfort and hope. The discoveries of ancient and modern navigators, and the domestic history or tradition of the most enlightened nations, represent the *human savage* naked both in mind and body, and destitute of laws, of arts, of ideas, and almost of language. From this abject condition, perhaps the primitive and universal state of man, he has gradually arisen to command the animals, to fertilise the earth, to traverse the ocean, and to measure the heavens. His progress in the improvement and exercise of his mental and corporeal faculties has been irregular and various; infinitely slow in the beginning, and increasing by degrees with redoubled velocity: ages of laborious ascent have been followed by a moment of rapid downfall; and the several climates of the globe have felt the vicissitudes of light and darkness. Yet the experience of four thousand years should enlarge our hopes and diminish our apprehensions: we cannot determine to what height the human species may aspire in their advances towards perfection; but it may safely be presumed that no people, unless the face of nature is changed, will relapse into their original barbarism. The improvements of society may be viewed under a threefold aspect. 1. The poet or philosopher illustrates his age and country by the efforts of a *single* mind; but these superior powers of reason or fancy are rare and spontaneous productions; and the genius of Homer, or Cicero, or Newton, would excite less admiration if they could be created by the will of a prince or the lessons of a preceptor. 2. The benefits of law and policy, of trade and manufactures, of arts and sciences, are more solid and permanent; and *many* individuals may be qualified, by education and discipline, to promote, in their respective stations, the interest of the community. But this general order is the effect of skill and labour; and the complex machinery may be decayed by time, or injured by violence. 3. Fortunately for mankind, the more useful, or, at least, more necessary arts, can be performed without superior talents or national subordination; without the powers of *one*, or the union of *many*. Each village, each family, each individual, must always possess both ability and inclination to perpetuate the use of fire and of metals; the propagation and service of domestic animals; the methods of hunting and fishing; the rudiments of navigation; the imperfect cultivation of corn or other nutritive grain; and the simple practice of the mechanic trades. Private genius and public industry may be extirpated; but these hardy plants survive the tempest, and strike an everlasting root into the most unfavourable soil. The splendid days of Augustus and Trajan were eclipsed by a cloud of ignorance; and the barbarians subverted the laws and palaces of Rome. But the scythe, the invention or emblem of Saturn, still continued annually to mow the harvests of Italy; and the human feasts of the Læstrigons have never been renewed on the coast of Campania.

334

Since the first discovery of the arts, war, commerce, and religious zeal have diffused among the savages of the Old and New World these inestimable gifts: they have been successively propagated; they can never be lost. We may therefore acquiesce in the pleasing conclusion that every age of the world has increased and still increases the real wealth, the happiness, the knowledge, and perhaps the virtue, of the human race.[1]

[1] The merit of discovery has too often been stained with avarice, cruelty, and fanaticism; and the intercourse of nations has produced the communication of disease and prejudice. A singular exception is due to the virtue of our own times and country. The five great voyages, successively undertaken by the command of his present Majesty, were inspired by the pure and generous love of science and of mankind. The same prince, adapting his benefactions to the different stages of society, has founded a school of painting in his capital, and has introduced into the islands of the South Sea the vegetables and animals most useful to human life.

CHAPTER XIII

THE GOTHIC KINGDOM OF ITALY

[*The Western Empire might have collapsed, but the Dark Age had not yet begun; for the barbarian successor-states retained and cherished much of the old structure. In Italy, Theodoric the Ostrogoth, having destroyed Odoacer, established himself in the old imperial capital of Ravenna and reigned for 26 years (493-526 A.D.), under the nominal sovereignty of Constantinople. This stable Gothic kingdom of Italy, which Gibbon describes in chapter XXXIX, continued Roman institutions after the end of the Western Empire. Theodoric himself is described by Gibbon as a "rare and meritorious example of a barbarian who sheathed his sword in the pride of victory and the vigour of his age," "a Gothic king who might have deserved a statue among the best and bravest of the ancient Romans." The most famous of his ministers was the senator Boethius, whose* Consolation of Philosophy *was afterwards translated into Anglo-Saxon by King Alfred, and became a favourite book of the Middle Ages.*]

The union of the Goths and Romans might have fixed for ages the transient happiness of Italy; and the first of nations, a new people of free subjects and enlightened soldiers, might have gradually arisen from the mutual emulation of their respective virtues. But the sublime merit of guiding or seconding such a revolution was not reserved for the reign of Theodoric: he wanted either the genius or the opportunities of a legislator; and while he indulged the Goths in the enjoyment of rude liberty, he servilely copied the institutions, and even the abuses, of the political system which had been framed by Constantine and his successors. From a tender regard to the expiring prejudices of Rome, the barbarian declined the name, the purple, and the diadem of the emperors; but he assumed, under the hereditary title of king, the whole substance and plenitude of Imperial prerogative. His addresses to the Eastern throne were respectful and ambiguous: he celebrated in pompous style the harmony of the two republics, applauded his own government as the perfect similitude of a sole and undivided empire, and claimed above the kings of the earth the same preeminence which he modestly allowed to the person or rank of Anastasius. The alliance of the East and West was annually declared by the unanimous choice of two consuls; but it should seem that the Italian candidate, who was named by Theodoric, accepted a formal confirmation from the sovereign of Constantinople. The Gothic palace of Ravenna reflected the image of the court of Theodosius or Valentinian. The Prætorian præfect, the præfect of Rome, the quæstor, the master of the offices, with the public and patrimonial treasurers, whose functions are painted in gaudy colours by the rhetoric of Cassiodorus, still continued to act as the ministers of state. And the subordinate care of justice and the revenue was delegated to seven consulars, three correctors, and five presidents, who governed the fifteen *regions* of Italy according to the principles, and even the forms, of Roman jurisprudence. The violence of the conquerors was abated or eluded by the slow artifice of judicial proceedings; the civil administration, with its honours and emoluments, was confined to the Italians; and the people still preserved their dress and language, their laws and customs, their personal freedom, and two-thirds of their landed property. It had been the object of Augustus to conceal the introduction of monarchy; it was the policy of Theodoric to disguise the reign of a barbarian. If his subjects were sometimes awakened from this pleasing vision of a Roman government, they derived more substantial comfort from the character of a Gothic prince who had penetration to discern, and firmness to pursue, his own and the public interest. Theodoric loved the virtues which he possessed, and the talents of which he was destitute. Liberius was promoted to the office of Prætorian præfect for his unshaken fidelity to the unfortunate cause of Odoacer. The ministers of Theodoric, Cassiodorus, and Boethius, have reflected on his reign the lustre of their genius and learning. More prudent or more fortunate than his colleague, Cassiodorus preserved his own esteem without forfeiting the royal favour; and after passing thirty years in the honours of the world, he was blessed with an equal term of repose in the devout and studious solitude of Squillace.

As the patron of the republic, it was the interest and duty of the Gothic king to cultivate the affections of the senate and people. The nobles of Rome were flattered by sonorous epithets and formal professions of respect, which had been more justly applied to the merit and authority of their ancestors. The people enjoyed, without fear or danger, the three blessings of a capital, order, plenty, and public amusements. A visible diminution of their numbers may be found even in the measure of liberality; yet Apulia, Calabria, and Sicily poured their tribute of corn into the granaries of Rome; an allowance of bread and meat was distributed to the indigent citizens; and every office was deemed honourable which was consecrated to the care of their health and happiness. The public games, such as a Greek ambassador might politely applaud, exhibited a faint and feeble copy of the magnificence of the Cæsars: yet the musical, the gymnastic, and the pantomime arts, had not totally sunk in oblivion; the wild beasts of Africa still exercised

in the amphitheatre the courage and dexterity of the
hunters; and the indulgent Goth either patiently tolerated or gently restrained the blue and green factions,
whose contests so often filled the circus with clamour,
and even with blood. In the seventh year of his peaceful
reign, Theodoric visited the old capital of the world;
the senate and people advanced in solemn procession
to salute a second Trajan, a new Valentinian; and he
nobly supported that character, by the assurance of a
just and legal government, in a discourse which he was
not afraid to pronounce in public and to inscribe on a
tablet of brass. Rome, in this august ceremony, shot a
last ray of declining glory; and a saint, the spectator of
this pompous scene, could only hope, in his pious fancy,
that it was excelled by the celestial splendour of the
New Jerusalem. During a residence of six months, the
fame, the person, and the courteous demeanour of the
Gothic king excited the admiration of the Romans, and
he contemplated, with equal curiosity and surprise, the
monuments that remained of their ancient greatness.
He imprinted the footsteps of a conqueror on the Capitoline hill, and frankly confessed that each day he
viewed with fresh wonder the forum of Trajan and
his lofty column. The theatre of Pompey appeared, even
in its decay, as a huge mountain, artificially hollowed
and polished, and adorned by human industry; and he
vaguely computed that a river of gold must have been
drained to erect the colossal amphitheatre of Titus. From
the mouths of fourteen aqueducts a pure and copious
stream was diffused into every part of the city; among
these the Claudian water, which arose at the distance
of thirty-eight miles in the Sabine mountains, was conveyed along a gentle though constant declivity of solid
arches, till it descended on the summit of the Aventine
hill. The long and spacious vaults which had been constructed for the purpose of common sewers subsisted
after twelve centuries in their pristine strength; and
these subterraneous channels have been preferred to all

the visible wonders of Rome. The Gothic kings, so injuriously accused of the ruin of antiquity, were anxious to preserve the monuments of the nation whom they had subdued. The royal edicts were framed to prevent the abuses, the neglect, or the depredations of the citizens themselves; and a professed architect, the annual sum of two hundred pounds of gold, twenty-five thousand tiles, and the receipt of customs from the Lucrine port, were assigned for the ordinary repairs of the walls and public edifices. A similar care was extended to the statues of metal or marble of men or animals. The spirit of the horses which have given a modern name to the Quirinal was applauded by the barbarians; the brazen elephants of the *Via sacra* were diligently restored; the famous heifer of Myron deceived the cattle, as they were driven through the forum of peace; and an officer was created to protect those works of art, which Theodoric considered as the noblest ornament of his kingdom.

After the example of the last emperors, Theodoric preferred the residence of Ravenna, where he cultivated an orchard with his own hands. As often as the peace of his kingdom was threatened (for it was never invaded) by the barbarians, he removed his court to Verona on the northern frontier, and the image of his palace, still extant on a coin, represents the oldest and most authentic model of Gothic architecture. These two capitals, as well as Pavia, Spoleto, Naples, and the rest of the Italian cities, acquired under his reign the useful or splendid decorations of churches, aqueducts, baths, porticoes, and palaces. But the happiness of the subject was more truly conspicuous in the busy scene of labour and luxury, in the rapid increase and bold enjoyment of national wealth. From the shades of Tibur and Præneste, the Roman senators still retired in the winter season to the warm sun and salubrious springs of Baiæ; and their villas, which advanced on solid moles into the bay of Naples, commanded the various prospect of the sky, the earth, and the water. On the eastern side of the Hadri-

atic a new Campania was formed in the fair and fruitful province of Istria, which communicated with the
palace of Ravenna by an easy navigation of one hundred
miles. The rich productions of Lucania and the adjacent
provinces were exchanged at the Marcilian fountain, in
a populous fair annually dedicated to trade, intemperance, and superstition. In the solitude of Comum, which
had once been animated by the mild genius of Pliny, a
transparent basin above sixty miles in length still reflected the rural seats which encompassed the margin of
the Larian lake; and the gradual ascent of the hills was
covered by a triple plantation of olives, of vines, and of
chestnut-trees. Agriculture revived under the shadow of
peace, and the number of husbandmen was multiplied
by the redemption of captives. The iron-mines of Dalmatia, a gold-mine in Bruttium, were carefully explored,
and the Pomptine marshes, as well as those of Spoleto,
were drained and cultivated by private undertakers,
whose distant reward must depend on the continuance
of the public prosperity. Whenever the seasons were less
propitious, the doubtful precautions of forming magazines of corn, fixing the price, and prohibiting the exportation, attested at least the benevolence of the state;
but such was the extraordinary plenty which an industrious people produced from a grateful soil, that a gal-
lon of wine was sometimes sold in Italy for less than
three farthings, and a quarter of wheat at about five
shillings and sixpence. A country possessed of so many
valuable objects of exchange soon attracted the merchants of the world, whose beneficial traffic was encouraged and protected by the liberal spirit of Theodoric.
The free intercourse of the provinces by land and water
was restored and extended; the city gates were never
shut either by day or by night; and the common saying,
that a purse of gold might be safely left in the fields,
was expressive of the conscious security of the inhabitants.

A difference of religion is always pernicious and often

fatal to the harmony of the prince and people: the Gothic conqueror had been educated in the profession of Arianism, and Italy was devoutly attached to the Nicene faith. But the persuasion of Theodoric was not infected by zeal: and he piously adhered to the heresy of his fathers, without condescending to balance the subtile arguments of theological metaphysics. Satisfied with the private toleration of his Arian sectaries, he justly conceived himself to be the guardian of the public worship, and his external reverence for a superstition which he despised may have nourished in his mind the salutary indifference of a statesman or philosopher. The catholics of his dominions acknowledged, perhaps with reluctance, the peace of the church; their clergy, according to the degrees of rank or merit, were honourably entertained in the palace of Theodoric; he esteemed the living sanctity of Cæsarius and Epiphanius, the orthodox bishops of Arles and Pavia; and presented a decent offering on the tomb of St. Peter, without any scrupulous inquiry into the creed of the apostle. His favourite Goths, and even his mother, were permitted to retain or embrace the Athanasian faith, and his long reign could not afford the example of an Italian catholic who, either from choice or compulsion, had deviated into the religion of the conqueror. The people, and the barbarians themselves, were edified by the pomp and order of religious worship; the magistrates were instructed to defend the just immunities of ecclesiastical persons and possessions; the bishops held their synods, the metropolitans exercised their jurisdiction, and the privileges of sanctuary were maintained or moderated according to the spirit of the Roman jurisprudence. With the protection, Theodoric assumed the legal supremacy, of the church; and his firm administration restored or extended some useful prerogatives which had been neglected by the feeble emperors of the West. He was not ignorant of the dignity and importance of the Roman pontiff, to whom the venerable name of POPE was now appropriated. The peace or the revolt of Italy might depend on the character of a wealthy and popular bishop, who claimed such ample dominion both in heaven and earth; who had been declared in a numerous synod to be pure from all sin, and exempt from all judgment. When the chair of St. Peter was disputed by Symmachus and Laurence, they appeared at his summons before the tribunal of an Arian monarch, and he confirmed the election of the most worthy or the most obsequious candidate. At the end of his life, in a moment of jealousy and resentment, he prevented the choice of the Romans, by nominating a pope in the palace of Ravenna. The danger and furious contests of a schism were mildly restrained, and the last decree of the senate was enacted to extinguish, if it were possible, the scandalous venality of the papal elections.

I have descanted with pleasure on the fortunate condition of Italy, but our fancy must not hastily conceive that the golden age of the poets, a race of men without vice or misery, was realised under the Gothic conquest. The fair prospect was sometimes overcast with clouds; the wisdom of Theodoric might be deceived, his power might be resisted, and the declining age of the monarch was sullied with popular hatred and patrician blood. In the first insolence of victory he had been tempted to deprive the whole party of Odoacer of the civil and even the natural rights of society; a tax, unseasonably imposed after the calamities of war, would have crushed the rising agriculture of Liguria; a rigid pre-emption of corn, which was intended for the public relief, must have aggravated the distress of Campania. These dangerous projects were defeated by the virtue and eloquence of Epiphanius and Boethius, who, in the presence of Theodoric himself, successfully pleaded the cause of the people: but, if the royal ear was open to the voice of truth, a saint and a philosopher are not always to be found at the ear of kings. The privileges of rank, or office, or favour were too frequently abused by Italian fraud and Gothic violence, and the avarice of the king's nephew was publicly exposed, at first by the usurpation, and afterwards by the restitution, of the estates which he had unjustly extorted from his Tuscan neighbours. Two hundred thousand barbarians, formidable even to their master, were seated in the heart of Italy; they indignantly supported the restraints of peace and discipline; the disorders of their march were always felt and sometimes compensated; and where it was dangerous to punish, it might be prudent to dissemble, the sallies of their native fierceness. When the indulgence of Theodoric had remitted two-thirds of the Ligurian tribute, he condescended to explain the difficulties of his situation, and to lament the heavy though inevitable burdens which he imposed on his subjects for their own defence. These ungrateful subjects could never be cordially reconciled to the origin, the religion, or even the virtues of the Gothic conqueror; past calamities were forgotten, and the sense or suspicion of injuries was rendered still more exquisite by the present felicity of the times.

Even the religious toleration which Theodoric had the glory of introducing into the Christian world was painful and offensive to the orthodox zeal of the Italians. They respected the armed heresy of the Goths; but their pious rage was safely pointed against the rich and defenceless Jews, who had formed their establishments at Naples, Rome, Ravenna, Milan, and Genoa, for the benefit of trade and under the sanction of the laws. Their persons were insulted, their effects were pillaged, and their synagogues were burnt by the mad populace of Ravenna and Rome, inflamed, as it should seem, by the most frivolous or extravagant pretences. The government which could neglect, would have deserved such an outrage. A legal inquiry was instantly directed; and, as the authors of the tumult had escaped in the crowd, the whole community was condemned to repair the damage, and the obstinate bigots, who refused their contributions, were whipped through the streets by the hand of the executioner. This simple act of justice exasperated the discontent of the catholics, who applauded the merit and patience of these holy confessors. Three hundred pulpits deplored the persecution of the church; and if the chapel of St. Stephen at Verona was demolished by the command of Theodoric, it is probable that some miracle hostile to his name and dignity had been performed on that sacred theatre. At the close of a glorious life, the king of Italy discovered that he had excited the hatred of a people whose happiness he had so assiduously laboured to promote; and his mind was soured by indignation, jealousy, and the bitterness of unrequited love. The Gothic conqueror condescended to disarm the unwarlike natives of Italy, interdicting all weapons of offence, and excepting only a small knife for domestic use. The deliverer of Rome was accused of conspiring with the vilest informers against the lives of senators whom he suspected of a secret and treasonable correspondence with the Byzantine court. After the death of Anastasius, the diadem had been placed on the head of a feeble old man, but the powers of government were assumed by his nephew Justinian, who already meditated the extirpation of heresy and the conquest of Italy and Africa. A rigorous law, which was published at Constantinople, to reduce the Arians, by the dread of punishment, within the pale of the church, awakened the just resentment of Theodoric, who claimed for his distressed brethren of the East the same indulgence which he had so long granted to the catholics of his dominions. At his stern command the Roman pontiff, with four *illustrious* senators, embarked on an embassy of which he must have alike dreaded the failure or the success. The singular veneration shown to the first pope who had visited Constantinople was punished as a crime by this jealous monarch; the artful or peremptory refusal of the Byzantine court might excuse an equal, and would provoke a larger, measure of retaliation; and a mandate was prepared in Italy to prohibit, after a stated day, the exercise of the catholic worship. By the bigotry of his subjects and enemies the most tolerant of princes was driven to the brink of persecution, and the life of Theodoric was too long, since he lived to condemn the virtue of Boethius and Symmachus.

The senator Boethius is the last of the Romans whom Cato or Tully could have acknowledged for their countryman. As a wealthy orphan, he inherited the patrimony and honours of the Anician family, a name ambitiously assumed by the kings and emperors of the age, and the appellation of Manlius asserted his genuine or fabulous descent from a race of consuls and dictators who had repulsed the Gauls from the Capitol, and sacrificed their sons to the discipline of the republic. In the youth of Boethius the studies of Rome were not totally abandoned; a Virgil is now extant corrected by the hand of a consul; and the professors of grammar, rhetoric, and jurisprudence were maintained in their privileges and pensions by the liberality of the Goths. But the erudition of the Latin language was insufficient to satiate his ardent curiosity; and Boethius is said to have employed eighteen laborious years in the schools of Athens, which were supported by the zeal, the learning, and the diligence of Proclus and his disciples. The reason and piety of their Roman pupil were fortunately saved from the contagion of mystery and magic which polluted the groves of the Academy; but he imbibed the spirit, and imitated the method, of his dead and living masters, who attempted to reconcile the strong and subtle sense of Aristotle with the devout contemplation and sublime fancy of Plato. After his return to Rome, and his marriage with the daughter of his friend the patrician Symmachus, Boethius still continued, in a palace of ivory and marble, to prosecute the same studies. The church was edified by his profound defence of the orthodox creed against the Arian, the Eutychian, and the Nestorian heresies; and the catholic unity was explained or exposed in a formal treatise by the *indifference* of three distinct though consubstantial persons. For the benefit of his Latin readers, his genius submitted to teach the first elements of the arts and sciences of Greece. The geometry of Euclid, the music of Pythagoras, the arithmetic of Nicomachus, the mechanics of Archimedes, the astronomy of Ptolemy, the theology of Plato, and the logic of Aristotle, with the commentary of Porphyry, were translated and illustrated by the indefatigable pen of the Roman senator. And he alone was esteemed capable of describing the wonders of art, a sundial, a water-clock, or a sphere which represented the motions of the planets. From these abstruse speculations Boethius stooped—or, to speak more truly, he rose—to the social duties of public and private life; the indigent were relieved by his liberality, and his eloquence, which flattery might compare to the voice of Demosthenes or Cicero, was uniformly exerted in the cause of innocence and humanity. Such conspicuous merit was felt and rewarded by a discerning prince: the dignity of Boethius was adorned with the titles of consul and patrician, and his talents were usefully employed in the important station of master of the offices. Notwithstanding the equal claims of the East and West, his two sons were created, in their tender youth, the consuls of the same year. On the memorable day of their inauguration they proceeded in solemn pomp from their palace to the forum amidst the applause of the senate and people; and their joyful father, the true consul of Rome, after pronouncing an oration in the praise of his royal benefactor, distributed a triumphal largess in the games of the circus. Prosperous in his fame and fortunes, in his public honours and private alliances, in the cultivation of science and the consciousness of virtue, Boethius might have been styled happy, if that precarious epithet could be safely applied before the last term of the life of man.

A philosopher, liberal of his wealth and parsimonious of his time, might be insensible to the common allurements of ambition, the thirst of gold and employment. And some credit may be due to the asseveration of Boethius, that he had reluctantly obeyed the divine Plato, who enjoins every virtuous citizen to rescue the state from the usurpation of vice and ignorance. For the integrity of his public conduct he appeals to the memory of his country. His authority had restrained the pride and oppression of the royal officers, and his eloquence had delivered Paulianus from the dogs of the palace. He had always pitied, and often relieved, the distress of the provincials, whose fortunes were exhausted by public and private rapine; and Boethius alone had courage to oppose the tyranny of the barbarians, elated by conquest, excited by avarice, and, as he complains, encouraged by impunity. In these honourable contests his spirit soared above the consideration of danger, and perhaps of prudence; and we may learn from the example of Cato that a character of pure and inflexible virtue is the most apt to be misled by prejudice, to be heated by enthusiasm, and to confound private enmities with public justice. The disciple of Plato might exaggerate the infirmities of nature and the imperfections of society; and the mildest form of a Gothic kingdom, even the weight of allegiance and gratitude, must be insupportable to the free spirit of a Roman patriot. But the favour and fidelity of Boethius declined in just proportion with the public happiness, and an unworthy colleague was imposed to divide and control the power of the master of the offices. In the last gloomy season of Theodoric he indignantly felt that he was a slave; but as his master had only power over his life, he stood, without arms and without fear, against the face of an angry barbarian, who had been provoked to believe that the safety of the senate was incompatible with his own. The senator Albinus was accused and already convicted on the presumption of *hoping*, as it was said, the liberty of Rome. "If Albinus be criminal," exclaimed the orator, "the senate and myself are all guilty of the same crime. If we are innocent, Albinus is equally entitled to the protection of the laws." These laws might not have punished the simple and barren wish of an unattainable blessing; but they would have shown less indulgence to the rash confession of Boethius, that, had he known of a conspiracy, the tyrant never should. The advocate of Albinus was soon involved in the danger and perhaps the guilt of his client; their signature (which they denied as a forgery) was affixed to the original address inviting the emperor to deliver Italy from the Goths; and three witnesses of honourable rank, perhaps of infamous reputation, attested the treasonable designs of the Roman patrician. Yet his innocence must be presumed, since he was deprived by Theodoric of the means of justification, and rigorously confined in the tower of Pavia, while the senate, at the distance of five hundred miles, pronounced a sentence of confiscation and death against the most illustrious of its members. At the command of the barbarians, the occult science of a philosopher was stigmatised with the names of sacrilege and magic. A devout and dutiful attachment to the senate was condemned as criminal by the trembling voices of the senators themselves; and their ingratitude deserved the wish or prediction of Boethius, that, after him, none should be found guilty of the same offence.

While Boethius, oppressed with fetters, expected each moment the sentence of the stroke of death, he composed in the tower of Pavia the *Consolation of Philosophy;* a golden volume not unworthy of the leisure of Plato or Tully, but which claims incomparable merit from the barbarism of the times and the situation of the author. The celestial guide whom he had so long invoked at Rome and Athens now condescended to illumine his dungeon, to revive his courage, and to pour into his wounds her salutary balm. She taught him to compare his long prosperity and his recent distress, and to conceive new hopes from the inconstancy of fortune. Reason had informed him of the precarious condition of her gifts; experience had satisfied him of their real value; he had enjoyed them without guilt, he might resign them without a sigh, and calmly disdain the impotent malice of his enemies, who had left him happiness, since they had left him virtue. From the earth Boethius ascended to heaven in search of the SUPREME GOOD; explored the metaphysical labyrinth of chance and destiny, of prescience and free-will, of time and eternity; and generously attempted to reconcile the perfect attributes of the Deity with the apparent disorders of his moral and physical government. Such topics of consolation, so obvious, so vague, or so abstruse, are ineffectual to subdue the feelings of human nature. Yet the sense of misfortune may be diverted by the labour of thought; and the sage who could artfully combine in the same work the various riches of philosophy, poetry, and eloquence, must already have possessed the intrepid calmness which he affected to seek. Suspense, the worst of evils, was at length determined by the ministers of death, who executed, and perhaps exceeded, the inhuman mandate of Theodoric. A strong cord was fastened round the head of Boethius, and forcibly tightened till his eyes almost started from their sockets; and some mercy may be discovered in the milder torture of beating him with clubs till he expired. But his genius survived to diffuse a ray of knowledge over the darkest ages of the Latin world; the writings of the philosopher were translated by the most glorious of the English kings, and the third emperor of the name of Otho removed to a more honourable tomb the bones of a catholic saint who, from his Arian persecutors, had acquired the honours of martyrdom and the fame of miracles. In the last hours of Boethius he derived some comfort from the safety of his two sons, of his wife, and of his father-in-law, the venerable Symmachus. But the grief of Symmachus was indiscreet, and perhaps disrespectful: he had presumed to lament, he might dare to revenge, the death of an injured friend. He was dragged in chains from Rome to the palace of Ravenna, and the suspicions of Theodoric could only be appeased by the blood of an innocent and aged senator.

Humanity will be disposed to encourage any report which testifies the jurisdiction of conscience and the remorse of kings; and philosophy is not ignorant that the most horrid spectres are sometimes created by the powers of a disordered fancy, and the weakness of a distempered body. After a life of virtue and glory, Theodoric was now descending with shame and guilt into the grave: his mind was humbled by the contrast of the past, and justly alarmed by the invisible terrors of futurity. One evening, as it is related, when the head of a large fish was served on the royal table, he suddenly exclaimed that he beheld the angry countenance of Symmachus, his eyes glaring fury and revenge, and his mouth armed with long sharp teeth, which threatened to devour him. The monarch instantly retired to his chamber, and, as he lay trembling with aguish cold under a weight of bed-clothes, he expressed in broken murmurs to his physician Elpidius his deep repentance for the murders of Boethius and Symmachus. His malady increased, and, after a dysentery which continued three days, he expired in the palace of Ravenna, in the thirty-third, or, if we compute from the invasion of Italy, in the thirty-seventh year of his reign. Conscious of his approaching end, he divided his treasures and provinces between his two grandsons, and fixed the Rhône as their common boundary. Amalaric was restored to the throne of Spain. Italy, with all the conquests of the Ostrogoths, was bequeathed to Athalaric, whose age did not exceed ten years, but who was cherished as the last male offspring of the line of Amali, by the short-lived marriage of his mother Amalasuntha with a royal fugitive of the same blood. In the presence of the dying monarch the Gothic chiefs and Italian magistrates mutually engaged their faith and loyalty to the young prince and to his guardian mother; and received, in the same awful moment, his last salutary advice to maintain the laws, to love the senate and people of Rome, and to cultivate with decent reverence the friendship of the emperor. The monument of Theodoric was erected by his daughter Amalasuntha in a conspicuous situation, which commanded the city of Ravenna, the harbour, and the adjacent coast. A chapel of a circular form, thirty feet in diameter, is crowned by a dome of one entire piece of granite: from the centre of the dome four columns arose, which supported in a vase of porphyry the remains of the Gothic king, surrounded by the brazen statues of the twelve apostles. His spirit, after some previous expiation, might have been permitted to mingle with the benefactors of mankind, if an Italian hermit had not been witness in a vision to the damnation of Theodoric, whose soul was plunged by the ministers of divine vengeance into the volcano of Lipari, one of the flaming mouths of the infernal world.

CHAPTER XIV

JUSTINIAN

[*The Gothic kingdom of Italy was the twilight after the end of the Western Empire. It barely survived the death of Theodoric. Already, in his last years, Constantinople was in the power of its most famous ruler, Justinian. Justinian ruled in effect under his uncle, the self-made usurper Justin, from 518; on Justin's death, in 527, he became legal emperor; in his long reign (he died in 565), thanks to his generals Belisarius and Narses, he conquered the Vandals in Africa, the Visigoths in Spain and the Ostrogoths in Italy, and so restored, to some extent, the old unity of the Empire. It was a brief and costly restoration; the Dark Age of Italy begins with the Byzantine-Gothic war. Meanwhile Justinian, aided by his less orthodox empress Theodora, was refashioning the institutions and the aspect of Constantinople. He codified the law, built or rebuilt numerous churches (including Santa Sophia), and studded the restored empire with fortresses. In chapter XL Gibbon describes some of the events and achievements of this long, magnificent, expensive reign.*]

From his elevation to his death, Justinian governed the Roman empire thirty-eight years, seven months, and thirteen days. The events of his reign, which excite our curious attention by their number, variety, and importance, are diligently related by the secretary of Belisarius, a rhetorician, whom eloquence had promoted to the rank of senator and præfect of Constantinople. According to the vicissitudes of courage or servitude, of favour or disgrace, Procopius successively composed the *history*, the *panegyric*, and the *satire* of his own times. . . . From these various materials I shall now proceed to describe the reign of Justinian, which will deserve and occupy an ample space. The present chapter will explain the elevation and character of Theodora, the factions of the circus, and the peaceful administration of the sovereign of the East. In the three succeeding chapters I shall relate the wars of Justinian, which achieved the conquest of Africa and Italy; and I shall follow the victories of Belisarius and Narses, without disguising the vanity of their triumphs, or the hostile virtue of the Persian and Gothic heroes. The series of this volume will embrace the jurisprudence and theology of the emperor; the controversies and sects which still divide the Oriental church; the reformation of the Roman law which is obeyed or respected by the nations of modern Europe.

In the exercise of supreme power, the first act of Justinian was to divide it with the woman whom he loved, the famous Theodora, whose strange elevation cannot be applauded as the triumph of female virtue. Under the reign of Anastasius, the care of the wild beasts maintained by the green faction at Constantinople was intrusted to Acacius, a native of the isle of Cyprus, who, from his employment, was surnamed the master of the bears. This honourable office was given after his death to another candidate, notwithstanding the diligence of his widow, who had already provided a husband and a successor. Acacius had left three daughters, Comito, THEODORA, and Anastasia, the eldest of whom did not then exceed the age of seven years. On a solemn festival, these helpless orphans were sent by their distressed and indignant mother, in the garb of suppliants, into the midst of the theatre: the green faction received them with contempt, the blues with compassion; and this difference, which sunk deep into the mind of Theodora, was felt long afterwards in the administration of the empire. As they improved in age and beauty, the three sisters were successively devoted to the public and private pleasures of the Byzantine people; and Theodora, after following Comito on the stage, in the dress of a slave, with a stool on her head, was at length permitted to exercise her independent talents. She neither danced, nor sung, nor played on the flute; her skill was confined to the pantomime arts; she excelled in buffoon characters; and as often as the comedian swelled her cheeks, and complained with a ridiculous tone and gesture of the blows that were inflicted, the whole theatre of Constantinople resounded with laughter and applause. The beauty of Theodora was the subject of more flattering praise, and the source of more exquisite delight. Her features were delicate and regular; her complexion, though somewhat pale, was tinged with a natural colour; every sensation was instantly expressed by the vivacity of her eyes; her easy motions displayed the graces of a small but elegant figure; and either love or adulation might proclaim that painting and poetry were incapable of delineating the matchless excellence of her form. But this form was degraded by the facility with which it was exposed to the public eye, and prostituted to licentious desire. Her venal charms were abandoned to a promiscuous crowd of citizens and strangers, of every rank and of every profession: the fortunate lover who had been promised a night of enjoyment was often driven from her bed by a stronger or more wealthy favourite; and when she passed through the streets, her presence was avoided by all who wished to escape 'either the scandal or the temptation. The satirical historian has not blushed to describe the naked scenes which Theodora was not ashamed to exhibit in the theatre. After exhausting the arts of sensual pleasure, she most ungratefully mur-

mured against the parsimony of Nature;[1] but her murmurs, her pleasures, and her arts, must be veiled in the obscurity of a learned language. After reigning for some time the delight and contempt of the capital, she condescended to accompany Ecebolus, a native of Tyre, who had obtained the government of the African Pentapolis. But this union was frail and transient: Ecebolus soon rejected an expensive or faithless concubine; she was reduced at Alexandria to extreme distress; and in her laborious return to Constantinople, every city of the East admired and enjoyed the fair Cyprian, whose merit appeared to justify her descent from the peculiar island of Venus. The vague commerce of Theodora, and the most detestable precautions, preserved her from the danger which she feared; yet once, and once only, she became a mother. The infant was saved and educated in Arabia by his father, who imparted to him on his death-bed that he was the son of an empress. Filled with ambitious hopes, the unsuspecting youth immediately hastened to the palace of Constantinople, and was admitted to the presence of his mother. As he was never more seen, even after the decease of Theodora, she deserves the foul imputation of extinguishing with his life a secret so offensive to her imperial virtue.

In the most abject state of her fortune and reputation, some vision, either of sleep or of fancy, had whispered to Theodora the pleasing assurance that she was destined to become the spouse of a potent monarch. Conscious of her approaching greatness, she returned from Paphlagonia to Constantinople; assumed, like a skilful actress, a more decent character; relieved her poverty by the laudable industry of spinning wool; and affected a life of chastity and solitude in a small house, which she afterwards changed into a magnificent temple. Her beauty, assisted by art or accident, soon attracted,

---

[1] She wished for a *fourth* altar on which she might pour libations to the god of love.

captivated, and fixed, the patrician Justinian, who already reigned with absolute sway under the name of his uncle. Perhaps she contrived to enhance the value of a gift which she had so often lavished on the meanest of mankind; perhaps she inflamed, at first by modest delays, and at last by sensual allurements, the desires of a lover who, from nature or devotion, was addicted to long vigils and abstemious diet. When his first transports had subsided, she still maintained the same ascendant over his mind by the more solid merit of temper and understanding. Justinian delighted to ennoble and enrich the object of his affection: the treasures of the East were poured at her feet, and the nephew of Justin was determined, perhaps by religious scruples, to bestow on his concubine the sacred and legal character of a wife. But the laws of Rome expressly prohibited the marriage of a senator with any female who had been dishonoured by a servile origin or theatrical profession: the empress Lupicina or Euphemia, a barbarian of rustic manners, but of irreproachable virtue, refused to accept a prostitute for her niece; and even Vigilantia, the superstitious mother of Justinian, though she acknowledged the wit and beauty of Theodora, was seriously apprehensive lest the levity and arrogance of that artful paramour might corrupt the piety and happiness of her son. These obstacles were removed by the inflexible constancy of Justinian. He patiently expected the death of the empress; he despised the tears of his mother, who soon sunk under the weight of her affliction; and a law was promulgated, in the name of the emperor Justin, which abolished the rigid jurisprudence of antiquity. A glorious repentance (the words of the edict) was left open for the unhappy females who had prostituted their persons on the theatre, and they were permitted to contract a legal union with the most illustrious of the Romans. This indulgence was speedily followed by the solemn nuptials of Justinian and Theodora; her dignity was gradually exalted with that of her lover; and, as soon as Justin had invested his nephew with the purple, the patriarch of Constantinople placed the diadem on the heads of the emperor and empress of the East. But the usual honours which the severity of Roman manners had allowed to the wives of princes could not satisfy either the ambition of Theodora or the fondness of Justinian. He seated her on the throne as an equal and independent colleague in the sovereignty of the empire, and an oath of allegiance was imposed on the governors of the provinces in the joint names of Justinian and Theodora. The Eastern world fell prostrate before the genius and fortune of the daughter of Acacius. The prostitute who, in the presence of innumerable spectators, had polluted the theatre of Constantinople, was adored as a queen in the same city, by grave magistrates, orthodox bishops, victorious generals, and captive monarchs.

Those who believe that the female mind is totally depraved by the loss of chastity will eagerly listen to all the invectives of private envy or popular resentment, which have dissembled the virtues of Theodora, exaggerated her vices, and condemned with rigour the venal or voluntary sins of the youthful harlot. From a motive of shame or contempt, she often declined the servile homage of the multitude, escaped from the odious light of the capital, and passed the greatest part of the year in the palaces and gardens which were pleasantly seated on the seacoast of the Propontis and the Bosphorus. Her private hours were devoted to the prudent as well as grateful care of her beauty, the luxury of the bath and table, and the long slumber of the evening and the morning. Her secret apartments were occupied by the favourite women and eunuchs, whose interests and passions she indulged at the expense of justice: the most illustrious personages of the state were crowded into a dark and sultry antechamber; and when at last, after tedious attendance, they were admitted to kiss the feet of Theodora, they experienced, as her humour might suggest, the silent arrogance of an empress or the capricious levity of a comedian. Her rapacious avarice to accumulate an immense treasure may be excused by the apprehension of her husband's death, which could leave no alternative between ruin and the throne; and fear as well as ambition might exasperate Theodora against two generals who, during a malady of the emperor, had rashly declared that they were not disposed to acquiesce in the choice of the capital. But the reproach of cruelty, so repugnant even to her softer vices, has left an indelible stain on the memory of Theodora. Her numerous spies observed and zealously reported every action, or word, or look, injurious to their royal mistress. Whomsoever they accused were cast into her peculiar prisons, inaccessible to the inquiries of justice; and it was rumoured that the torture of the rack or scourge had been inflicted in the presence of a female tyrant, insensible to the voice of prayer or of pity. Some of these unhappy victims perished in deep unwholesome dungeons, while others were permitted, after the loss of their limbs, their reason, or their fortune, to appear in the world, the living monuments of her vengeance, which was commonly extended to the children of those whom she had suspected or injured. The senator or bishop whose death or exile Theodora had pronounced, was delivered to a trusty messenger, and his diligence was quickened by a menace from her own mouth. "If you fail in the execution of my commands, I swear by him who liveth for ever that your skin shall be flayed from your body."

If the creed of Theodora had not been tainted with heresy, her exemplary devotion might have atoned, in the opinion of her contemporaries, for pride, avarice, and cruelty; but if she employed her influence to assuage the intolerant fury of the emperor, the present age will allow some merit to her religion, and much indulgence to her speculative errors. The name of Theodora was introduced, with equal honour, in all the pious and charitable foundations of Justinian; and the most benevolent institution of his reign may be ascribed to the sympathy of the empress for her less fortunate sisters, who had been seduced or compelled to embrace the trade of prostitution. A palace, on the Asiatic side of the Bosphorus, was converted into a stately and spacious monastery, and a liberal maintenance was assigned to five hundred women who had been collected from the streets and brothels of Constantinople. In this safe and holy retreat they were devoted to perpetual confinement; and the despair of some, who threw themselves headlong into the sea, was lost in the gratitude of the penitents who had been delivered from sin and misery by their generous benefactress. The prudence of Theodora is celebrated by Justinian himself; and his laws are attributed to the sage counsels of his most reverend wife, whom he had received as the gift of the Deity. Her courage was displayed amidst the tumult of the people and the terrors of the court. Her chastity, from the moment of her union with Justinian, is founded on the silence of her implacable enemies; and although the daughter of Acacius might be satiated with love, yet some applause is due to the firmness of a mind which could sacrifice pleasure and habit to the stronger sense either of duty or interest. The wishes and prayers of Theodora could never obtain the blessing of a lawful son, and she buried an infant daughter, the sole offspring of her marriage. Notwithstanding this disappointment, her dominion was permanent and absolute; she preserved, by art or merit, the affections of Justinian; and their seeming dissensions were always fatal to the courtiers who believed them to be sincere. Perhaps her health had been impaired by the licentiousness of her youth; but it was always delicate, and she was directed by her physicians to use the Pythian warmbaths. In this journey the empress was followed by the Prætorian præfect, the great treasurer, several counts and patricians, and a splendid train of four thousand attendants: the highways were repaired at her approach; a palace was erected for her reception; and as she passed through Bithynia she distributed liberal alms to the churches, the monasteries, and the hospitals, that they might implore Heaven for the restoration of her health. At length, in the twenty-fourth year of her marriage, and the twenty-second of her reign, she was consumed by a cancer; and the irreparable loss was deplored by her husband, who, in the room of a theatrical prostitute, might have selected the purest and most noble virgin of the East.

A material difference may be observed in the games of antiquity: the most eminent of the Greeks were actors, the Romans were merely spectators. The Olympic stadium was open to wealth, merit, and ambition; and if the candidates could depend on their personal skill and activity, they might pursue the footsteps of Diomede and Menelaus, and conduct their own horses in the rapid career. Ten, twenty, forty chariots, were allowed to start at the same instant; a crown of leaves was the reward of the victor, and his fame, with that of his family and country, was chanted in lyric strains more durable than monuments of brass and marble. But a senator, or even a citizen, conscious of his dignity, would have blushed to expose his person or his horses in the circus of Rome. The games were exhibited at the expense of the republic, the magistrates, or the emperors; but the reins were abandoned to servile hands; and if the profits of a favourite charioteer sometimes exceeded those of an advocate, they must be considered as the effects of popular extravagance, and the high wages of a disgraceful profession. The race, in its first institution, was a simple contest of two chariots, whose drivers were distinguished by *white* and *red* liveries: two additional colours, a light *green* and a cærulean *blue*, were afterwards introduced; and, as the races were repeated twenty-five times, one hundred chariots contributed in the same day to the pomp of the circus. The four *factions* soon acquired a legal establishment and a mysterious origin, and their fanciful colours were derived from the various appearances of nature in the four seasons of the year; the red dog-star of summer, the snows of winter, the deep shades of autumn, and the cheerful verdure of the spring. Another interpretation preferred the elements to the seasons, and the struggle of the green and blue was supposed to represent the conflict of the earth and sea. Their respective victories announced either a plentiful harvest or a prosperous navigation, and the hostility of the husbandmen and mariners was somewhat less absurd than the blind ardour of the Roman people, who devoted their lives and fortunes to the colour which they had espoused. Such folly was disdained and indulged by the wisest princes; but the names of Caligula, Nero, Vitellius, Verus, Commodus, Caracalla, and Elagabalus, were enrolled in the blue or green factions of the circus: they frequented their stables, applauded their favourites, chastised their antagonists, and deserved the esteem of the populace by the natural or affected imitation of their manners. The bloody and tumultuous contest continued to disturb the public festivity till the last age of the spectacles of Rome; and Theodoric, from a motive of justice or affection, interposed his authority to protect the greens against the violence of a consul and a patrician who were passionately addicted to the blue faction of the circus.

Constantinople adopted the follies, though not the virtues, of ancient Rome; and the same factions which had agitated the circus raged with redoubled fury in the hippodrome. Under the reign of Anastasius, this popular frenzy was inflamed by religious zeal; and the greens, who had treacherously concealed stones and daggers under baskets of fruit, massacred at a solemn festival three thousand of their blue adversaries. From the capital this pestilence was diffused into the provinces and cities of the East, and the sportive distinction of two colours produced two strong and irreconcilable factions, which shook the foundations of a feeble government. The popular dissensions, founded on the most serious interest or holy pretence, have scarcely equalled the obstinacy of this wanton discord, which invaded the peace of families, divided friends and brothers, and tempted the female sex, though seldom seen in the circus, to espouse the inclinations of their lovers, or to contradict the wishes of their husbands. Every law, either human or divine, was trampled under foot; and as long as the party was successful, its deluded followers appeared careless of private distress or public calamity. The licence, without the freedom, of democracy, was revived at Antioch and Constantinople, and the support of a faction became necessary to every candidate for civil or ecclesiastical honours. A secret attachment to the family or sect of Anastasius was imputed to the greens; the blues were zealously devoted to the cause of orthodoxy and Justinian, and their grateful patron protected, above five years, the disorders of a faction whose seasonable tumults overawed the palace, the senate, and the capitals of the East. Insolent with royal favour, the blues affected to strike terror by a peculiar and barbaric dress—the long hair of the Huns, their close sleeves and ample garments, a lofty step, and a sonorous voice. In the day they concealed their two-edged poniards, but in the night they boldly assembled in arms and in numerous bands, prepared for every act of violence and rapine. Their adversaries of the green faction, or even inoffensive citizens, were stripped and often murdered by these nocturnal robbers, and it became dangerous to wear any gold buttons or girdles, or to appear at a late hour in the streets of a peaceful capital. . . . The despair of the greens, who were persecuted by their enemies and deserted by the magistrate, assumed the privilege of defence, perhaps of retaliation; but those who survived the combat were dragged to execution, and the unhappy fugitives, escaping to woods and caverns, preyed without mercy on the society from whence they were expelled. Those ministers of justice who had courage to punish the crimes and to brave the resentment of the blues became the victims of their indiscreet zeal: a præfect of Constantinople fled for refuge to the holy sepulchre, a count of the East was ignominiously whipped, and a governor of Cilicia was hanged, by the order of Theodora, on the tomb of two assassins whom he had condemned for the murder of his groom, and a daring attack upon his own life. An aspiring candidate may be tempted to build his greatness on the public confusion, but it is the interest as well as duty of a sovereign to maintain the authority of the laws. The first edict of Justinian, which was often repeated and sometimes executed, announced his firm resolution to support the innocent, and to chastise the guilty, of every denomination and *colour*. Yet the balance of justice was still inclined in favour of the blue faction, by the secret affection, the habits, and the fears of the emperor; his equity, after an apparent struggle, submitted without reluctance to the implacable passions of Theodora, and the empress never forgot or forgave the injuries of the comedian. At the accession of the younger Justin, the proclamation of equal and rigorous justice indirectly condemned the partiality of the former reign. "Ye blues, Justinian is no more! ye greens, he is still alive."

A sedition, which almost laid Constantinople in ashes, was excited by the mutual hatred and momentary reconciliation of the two factions. In the fifth year of his reign Justinian celebrated the festival of the ides of January: the games were incessantly disturbed by the clamorous discontent of the greens; till the twenty-second race the emperor maintained his silent gravity; at length, yielding to his impatience, he condescended to hold, in abrupt sentences, and by the voice of a crier, the most singular dialogue that ever passed between a prince and his subjects. Their first complaints were respectful and modest; they accused the subordinate ministers of oppression, and proclaimed their wishes for the long life and victory of the emperor. "Be patient and attentive, ye insolent railers!" exclaimed Justinian; "be mute, ye Jews, Samaritans, and Manichæans!" The greens still attempted to awaken his compassion. "We are poor, we are innocent, we are injured, we dare not pass through the streets: a general persecution is exercised against our name and colour. Let us die, O emperor! but let us die by your command, and for your service!" But the repetition of partial and passionate invectives degraded, in their eyes, the majesty of the purple; they renounced allegiance to the prince who refused justice to his people, lamented that the father of Justinian had been born, and branded his son with the opprobrious names of a homicide, an ass, and a perjured tyrant. "Do you despise your lives?" cried the indignant monarch. The blues rose with fury from their seats, their hostile clamours thundered in the hippodrome, and their adversaries, deserting the unequal contest, spread terror and despair through the streets of Constantinople. At this dangerous moment, seven notorious assassins of both factions, who had been condemned by the præfect, were carried round the city, and afterwards transported to the place of execution in the suburb of Pera. Four were immediately beheaded; a fifth was hanged; but, when the same punishment was inflicted on the remaining two, the rope broke, they fell alive to the ground, the populace applauded their escape, and the monks of St. Conon, issuing from the neighbouring convent, conveyed them in a boat to the sanctuary of the church. As one of these criminals was of the blue, and the other of the green, livery, the two factions were equally provoked by the cruelty of their oppressor or the ingratitude of their patron, and a short truce was concluded till they had delivered their prisoners and satisfied their revenge. The palace of the præfect, who withstood the seditious torrent, was instantly burnt, his officers and guards were massacred, the prisons were forced open, and freedom was restored to those who could only use it for the public destruction. A military force which had been despatched to the aid of the civil magistrate was fiercely encountered by an armed multitude, whose numbers and boldness continually increased: and the Heruli, the wildest barbarians in the service of empire, overturned the priests and their relics, which, from a pious motive, had been rashly interposed to separate the bloody conflict. The tumult was exasperated by this sacrilege; the people fought with enthusiasm in the cause of God; the women, from the roofs and windows, showered stones on the heads of the soldiers, who darted firebrands against the houses; and the various flames, which had been kindled by the hands of citizens and strangers, spread without control over the face of the city. The conflagration involved the cathedral of St. Sophia, the baths of Zeuxippus, a part of the palace from the first entrance to the altar of Mars, and the long portico from the palace to the forum of Constantine: a large hospital, with the sick patients, was consumed; many churches and stately edifices were destroyed; and an immense treasure of gold and silver was either melted or lost. From such scenes of horror and distress the wise and wealthy citizens escaped over the Bosphorus to the Asiatic side, and during five days Constantinople was abandoned to the factions, whose watchword, NIKA, *vanquish!* has given a name to this memorable sedition.

As long as the factions were divided, the triumphant blues and desponding greens appeared to behold with the same indifference the disorders of the state. They agreed to censure the corrupt management of justice and the finance; and the two responsible ministers, the artful Tribonian and the rapacious John of Cappadocia, were loudly arraigned as the authors of the public misery. The peaceful murmurs of the people would have been disregarded: they were heard with respect when the city was in flames; the quæstor and the præfect were instantly removed, and their offices were filled by two senators of blameless integrity. After this popular concession Justinian proceeded to the hippodrome to confess his own errors, and to accept the repentance of his grateful subjects; but they distrusted his assurances, though solemnly pronounced in the presence of the holy gospels; and the emperor, alarmed by their distrust, retreated with precipitation to the strong fortress of the palace. The obstinacy of the tumult was now imputed to a secret and ambitious conspiracy, and a suspicion was entertained that the insurgents, more especially the green faction, had been supplied with arms and money by Hypatius and Pompey, two patricians who could neither forget with honour, nor remember with safety, that they were the nephews of the emperor Anastasius. Capriciously trusted, disgraced, and pardoned by the jealous levity of the monarch, they had appeared as loyal servants before the throne, and, during five days of the tumult, they were detained as important hostages; till at length, the fears of Justinian prevailing over his prudence, he viewed the two brothers in the light of spies, perhaps of assassins, and sternly commanded them to depart from the palace. After a fruitless representation that obedience might lead to involuntary treason, they retired to their houses, and in the morning of the sixth day Hypatius was surrounded and seized by the people, who, regardless of his virtuous resistance and the tears of his wife, transported their favourite to the forum of Constantine, and, instead of a diadem, placed a rich collar on his head. If the usurper, who afterwards pleaded the merit of his delay, had complied with the advice of his senate, and urged the fury of the multitude, their first irresistible effort might have oppressed or expelled his trembling competitor. The Byzantine palace enjoyed a free communication with the sea, vessels lay ready at the garden-stairs, and a secret resolution was already formed to convey the emperor with his family and treasures to a safe retreat at some distance from the capital.

Justinian was lost, if the prostitute whom he raised from the theatre had not renounced the timidity as well as the virtues of her sex. In the midst of a council where Belisarius was present, Theodora alone displayed the spirit of a hero, and she alone, without apprehending his future hatred, could save the emperor from the imminent danger and his unworthy fears. "If flight," said the consort of Justinian, "were the only means of safety, yet I should disdain to fly. Death is the condition of our birth, but they who have reigned should never survive the loss of dignity and dominion. I implore Heaven that I may never be seen, not a day, without my diadem and purple; that I may no longer behold the light when I cease to be saluted with the name of queen. If you resolve, O Cæsar! to fly, you have treasures; I behold the sea, you have ships; but tremble lest the desire of life should expose you to wretched exile and ignominious death. For my own part, I adhere to the maxim of antiquity, that the throne is a glorious sepulchre." The firmness of a woman restored the courage to deliberate and act, and courage soon discovers the resources of the most desperate situation. It was an easy and a decisive measure to revive the animosity of the factions; the blues were astonished at their own guilt and folly, that a trifling injury should provoke them to conspire with their implacable enemies against a gracious and liberal benefactor; they again proclaimed the majesty of Justinian; and the greens, with their upstart emperor, were left alone in the hippodrome. The fidelity of the guards was doubtful; but the military force of Justinian consisted in three thousand veterans, who had been trained to valour and discipline in the Persian and Illyrian wars. Under the command of Belisarius and Mundus, they silently marched in two divisions from the palace, forced their obscure way through narrow passages, expiring flames, and falling edifices, and burst open at the same moment the two opposite gates of the hippodrome. In this narrow space the disorderly and affrighted crowd was incapable of resisting on either side a firm and regular attack; the blues signalised the fury of their repentance, and it is computed that above thirty thousand persons were slain in the merciless and promiscuous carnage of the day. Hypatius was dragged from his throne, and conducted with his brother Pompey to the feet of the emperor; they implored his clemency, but their crime was manifest, their innocence uncertain, and Justinian had

11-12
Sixth-century mosaics depicting the emperor Justinian with his ministers, and his empress Theodora with her court.

been too much terrified to forgive. The next morning the two nephews of Anastasius, with eighteen *illustrious* accomplices, of patrician or consular rank, were privately executed by the soldiers, their bodies were thrown into the sea, their palaces razed, and their fortunes confiscated. The hippodrome itself was condemned, during several years, to a mournful silence; with the restoration of the games the same disorders revived, and the blue and green factions continued to afflict the reign of Justinian, and to disturb the tranquillity of the Eastern empire.

That empire, after Rome was barbarous, still embraced the nations whom she had conquered beyond the Hadriatic, and as far as the frontiers of Ethiopia and Persia. Justinian reigned over sixty-four provinces and nine hundred and thirty-five cities; his dominions were blessed by nature with the advantages of soil, situation, and climate, and the improvements of human art had been perpetually diffused along the coast of the Mediterranean and the banks of the Nile from ancient Troy to the Egyptian Thebes. Abraham had been relieved by the well-known plenty of Egypt; the same country, a small and populous tract, was still capable of exporting each year two hundred and sixty thousand quarters of wheat for the use of Constantinople; and the capital of Justinian was supplied with the manufactures of Sidon fifteen centuries after they had been celebrated in the poems of Homer. The annual powers of vegetation, instead of being exhausted by two thousand harvests, were renewed and invigorated by skilful husbandry, rich manure, and seasonable repose. The breed of domestic animals was infinitely multiplied. Plantations, buildings, and the instruments of labour and luxury, which are more durable than the term of human life, were accumulated by the care of successive generations. Tradition preserved, and experience simplified, the humble practice of the arts; society was enriched by the division of labour and the facility of exchange; and every Roman was lodged, clothed, and subsisted by the industry of a thousand hands. The invention of the loom and distaff has been piously ascribed to the gods. In every age a variety of animal and vegetable productions, hair, skins, wool, flax, cotton, and at length *silk*, have been skilfully manufactured to hide or adorn the human body; they were stained with an infusion of permanent colours, and the pencil was successfully employed to improve the labours of the loom. In the choice of those colours which imitate the beauties of nature, the freedom of taste and fashion was indulged; but the deep purple which the Phœnicians extracted from a shell-fish was restrained to the sacred person and palace of the emperor, and the penalties of treason were denounced against the ambitious subjects who dared to usurp the prerogative of the throne.

I need not explain that *silk* is originally spun from the bowels of a caterpillar, and that it composes the golden tomb from whence a worm emerges in the form of a butterfly. Till the reign of Justinian, the silkworms who feed on the leaves of the white mulberry-tree were confined to China; those of the pine, the oak, and the ash were common in the forests both of Asia and Europe; but as their education is more difficult, and their produce more uncertain, they were generally neglected. . . . Whatever suspicions may be raised by the garments of the Medes and Assyrians, Virgil is the most ancient writer who expressly mentions the soft wool which was combed from the trees of the Seres or Chinese; and this natural error, less marvellous than the truth, was slowly corrected by the knowledge of a valuable insect, the first artificer of the luxury of nations. That rare and elegant luxury was censured, in the reign of Tiberius, by the gravest of the Romans; and Pliny, in affected though forcible language, has condemned the thirst of gain, which explored the last confines of the earth for the pernicious purpose of exposing to the public eye naked draperies and transparent matrons. A dress which showed the turn of the limbs and colour of the skin might gratify vanity or provoke desire;

the silks which had been closely woven in China were sometimes unravelled by the Phœnician women, and the precious materials were multiplied by a looser texture, and the intermixture of linen threads. Two hundred years after the age of Pliny the use of pure or even of mixed silks was confined to the female sex, till the opulent citizens of Rome and the provinces were insensibly familiarised with the example of Elagabalus, the first who, by this effeminate habit, had sullied the dignity of an emperor and a man. Aurelian complained that a pound of silk was sold at Rome for twelve ounces of gold; but the supply increased with the demand, and the price diminished with the supply. If accident or monopoly sometimes raised the value even above the standard of Aurelian, the manufacturers of Tyre and Berytus were sometimes compelled, by the operation of the same causes, to content themselves with a ninth part of that extravagant rate. A law was thought necessary to discriminate the dress of comedians from that of senators, and of the silk exported from its native country the far greater part was consumed by the subjects of Justinian. They were still more intimately acquainted with a shellfish of the Mediterranean, surnamed the silkworm of the sea: the fine wool or hair by which the mother-of-pearl affixes itself to the rock is now manufactured for curiosity rather than use; and a robe obtained from the same singular materials was the gift of the Roman emperor to the satraps of Armenia.[2]

A valuable merchandise of small bulk is capable of defraying the expense of land-carriage, and the caravans traversed the whole latitude of Asia in two hundred and forty-three days from the Chinese ocean to the sea-coast of Syria. Silk was immediately delivered to the Romans by the Persian merchants, who frequented the fairs of Armenia and Nisibis; but this trade, which in the inter-

[2] These *pinnes de mer* are found near Smyrna, Sicily, Corsica, and Minorca; and a pair of gloves of their silk was presented to Pope Benedict XIV.

vals of truce was oppressed by avarice and jealousy, was totally interrupted by the long wars of the rival monarchies. The Great King might proudly number Sogdiana, and even *Serica,* among the provinces of his empire, but his real dominion was bounded by the Oxus, and his useful intercourse with the Sogdoites, beyond the river, depended on the pleasure of their conquerors, the white Huns and the Turks, who successively reigned over that industrious people. Yet the most savage dominion has not extirpated the seeds of agriculture and commerce in a region which is celebrated as one of the four gardens of Asia; the cities of Samarcand and Bochara are advantageously seated for the exchange of its various productions, and their merchants purchased from the Chinese the raw or manufactured silk which they transported into Persia for the use of the Roman empire. In the vain capital of China the Sogdian caravans were entertained as the suppliant embassies of tributary kingdoms, and, if they returned in safety, the bold adventure was rewarded with exorbitant gain. But the difficult and perilous march from Samarcand to the first town of Shensi could not be performed in less than sixty, eighty, or one hundred days; as soon as they had passed the Jaxartes they entered the desert, and the wandering hordes, unless they are restrained by armies and garrisons, have always considered the citizen and the traveller as the objects of lawful rapine. To escape the Tartar robbers and the tyrants of Persia, the silk-caravans explored a more southern road: they traversed the mountains of Thibet, descended the streams of the Ganges or the Indus, and patiently expected, in the ports of Guzerat and Malabar, the annual fleets of the West. But the dangers of the desert were found less intolerable than toil, hunger, and the loss of time; the attempt was seldom renewed, and the only European who has passed that unfrequented way applauds his own diligence that, in nine months after his departure from Pekin, he reached the mouth of the Indus. The ocean, however, was open to the

free communication of mankind. From the great river to
the tropic of Cancer the provinces of China were subdued and civilised by the emperors of the North; they
were filled about the time of the Christian era with cities
and men, mulberry-trees and their precious inhabitants;
and if the Chinese, with the knowledge of the compass,
had possessed the genius of the Greeks or Phœnicians,
they might have spread their discoveries over the southern hemisphere. I am not qualified to examine, and I
am not disposed to believe, their distant voyages to the
Persian Gulf or the Cape of Good Hope; but their ancestors might equal the labours and success of the present
race, and the sphere of their navigation might extend
from the isles of Japan to the straits of Malacca, the
Pillars, if we may apply that name, of an Oriental Hercules. Without losing sight of land, they might sail along
the coast to the extreme promontory of Achin, which
is annually visited by ten or twelve ships laden with the
productions, the manufactures, and even the artificers of
China; the island of Sumatra and the opposite peninsula
are faintly delineated as the regions of gold and silver,
and the trading cities named in the geography of Ptolemy
may indicate that this wealth was not solely derived from
the mines. The direct interval between Sumatra and Ceylon is about three hundred leagues; the Chinese and Indian navigators were conducted by the flight of birds and
periodical winds, and the ocean might be securely traversed in square-built ships, which, instead of iron, were
sewed together with the strong thread of the cocoanut.
Ceylon, Serendib, or Taprobana was divided between two
hostile princes, one of whom possessed the mountains, the
elephants, and the luminous carbuncle, and the other
enjoyed the more solid riches of domestic industry, foreign trade, and the capacious harbour of Trinquemale,
which received and dismissed the fleets of the East and
West. In this hospitable isle, at an equal distance (as it
was computed) from their respective countries, the silk-
merchants of China, who had collected in their voyages

aloes, cloves, nutmeg, and sandal-wood, maintained a free and beneficial commerce with the inhabitants of the Persian Gulf. The subjects of the Great King exalted, without a rival, his power and magnificence; and the Roman, who confounded their vanity by comparing his paltry coin with a gold medal of the emperor Anastasius, had sailed to Ceylon, in an Æthiopian ship, as a simple passenger.

As silk became of indispensable use, the emperor Justinian saw with concern that the Persians had occupied by land and sea the monopoly of this important supply, and that the wealth of his subjects was continually drained by a nation of enemies and idolators. An active government would have restored the trade of Egypt and the navigation of the Red Sea, which had decayed with the prosperity of the empire; and the Roman vessels might have sailed for the purchase of silk to the ports of Ceylon, of Malacca, or even of China. Justinian embraced a more humble expedient, and solicited the aid of his Christian allies, the Æthiopians of Abyssinia, who had recently acquired the arts of navigation, the spirit of trade, and the seaport of Adulis, still decorated with the trophies of a Grecian conqueror. Along the African coast they penetrated to the equator in search of gold, emeralds, and aromatics; but they wisely declined an unequal competition, in which they must be always prevented by the vicinity of the Persians to the markets of India: and the emperor submitted to the disappointment till his wishes were gratified by an unexpected event. The Gospel had been preached to the Indians: a bishop already governed the Christians of St. Thomas on the pepper-coast of Malabar; a church was planted in Ceylon, and the missionaries pursued the footsteps of commerce to the extremities of Asia. Two Persian monks had long resided in China, perhaps in the royal city of Nankin, the seat of a monarch addicted to foreign superstitions, and who actually received an embassy from the isle of Ceylon. Amidst their pious occupations they viewed with a

curious eye the common dress of the Chinese, the manufactures of silk, and the myriads of silkworms, whose
education (either on trees or in houses) had once been
considered as the labour of queens. They soon discovered
that it was impracticable to transport the short-lived insect, but that in the eggs a numerous progeny might be
preserved and multiplied in a distant climate. Religion
or interest had more power over the Persian monks than
the love of their country: after a long journey they arrived at Constantinople, imparted their project to the
emperor, and were liberally encouraged by the gifts and
promises of Justinian. To the historians of that prince
a campaign at the foot of Mount Caucasus has seemed
more deserving of a minute relation than the labours of
these missionaries of commerce, who again entered
China, deceived a jealous people by concealing the eggs
of the silkworm in a hollow cane, and returned in triumph with the spoils of the East. Under their direction
the eggs were hatched at the proper season by the artificial heat of dung; the worms were fed with mulberry-
leaves; they lived and laboured in a foreign climate; a
sufficient number of butterflies was saved to propagate
the race, and trees were planted to supply the nourishment of the rising generations. Experience and reflection corrected the errors of a new attempt, and the Sog-
doite ambassadors acknowledged in the succeeding reign
that the Romans were not inferior to the natives of China
in the education of the insects and the manufactures of
silk, in which both China and Constantinople have been
surpassed by the industry of modern Europe. I am not
insensible of the benefits of elegant luxury; yet I reflect
with some pain that if the importers of silk had introduced the art of printing, already practised by the Chinese, the comedies of Menander and the entire decads
of Livy would have been perpetuated in the editions of
the sixth century. A larger view of the globe might at
least have promoted the improvement of speculative science; but the Christian geography was forcibly extracted

from texts of Scripture, and the study of nature was the surest symptom of an unbelieving mind. The orthodox faith confined the habitable world to *one* temperate zone, and represented the earth as an oblong surface, four hundred days' journey in length, two hundred in breadth, encompassed by the ocean and covered by the solid crystal of the firmament.

The subjects of Justinian were dissatisfied with the times and with the government. Europe was overrun by the barbarians and Asia by the monks: the poverty of the West discouraged the trade and manufactures of the East: the produce of labour was consumed by the unprofitable servants of the church, the state, and the army; and a rapid decrease was felt in the fixed and circulating capitals which constitute the national wealth. The public distress had been alleviated by the economy of Anastasius, and that prudent emperor accumulated an immense treasure while he delivered his people from the most odious or oppressive taxes. . . . His example was neglected, and his treasure was abused, by the nephew of Justin. The riches of Justinian were speedily exhausted by alms and buildings, by ambitious wars and ignominious treaties. His revenues were found inadequate to his expenses. Every art was tried to extort from the people the gold and silver which he scattered with a lavish hand from Persia to France: his reign was marked by the vicissitudes, or rather by the combat, of rapaciousness and avarice, of splendour and poverty; he lived with the reputation of hidden treasures, and bequeathed to his successor the payment of his debts.

[*After describing the heavy cost, in taxes, of Justinian's rule, Gibbon goes on to describe his equally costly buildings.*]

The *edifices* of Justinian were cemented with the blood and treasure of his people; but those stately structures appeared to announce the prosperity of the empire, and actually displayed the skill of their architects. Both the theory and practice of the arts which depend on mathematical science and mechanical power were cultivated under the patronage of the emperors; the fame of Archimedes was rivalled by Proclus and Anthemius; and if their *miracles* had been related by intelligent spectators, they might now enlarge the speculations, instead of exciting the distrust, of philosophers. A tradition has prevailed that the Roman fleet was reduced to ashes in the port of Syracuse by the burning-glasses of Archimedes; and it is asserted that a similar expedient was employed by Proclus to destroy the Gothic vessels in the harbour of Constantinople, and to protect his benefactor Anastasius against the bold enterprise of Vitalian. A machine was fixed on the walls of the city, consisting of a hexagon mirror of polished brass, with many smaller and movable polygons to receive and reflect the rays of the meridian sun; and a consuming flame was darted to the distance, perhaps, of two hundred feet. The truth of these two extraordinary facts is invalidated by the silence of the most authentic historians; and the use of burning-glasses was never adopted in the attack or defence of places. Yet the admirable experiments of a French philosopher have demonstrated the possibility of such a mirror; and, since it is possible, I am more disposed to attribute the art to the greatest mathematicians of antiquity, than to give the merit of the fiction to the idle fancy of a monk or a sophist. According to another story, Proclus applied sulphur to the destruction of the Gothic fleet; in a modern imagination, the name of sulphur is instantly connected with the suspicion of gunpowder, and that suspicion is propagated by the secret arts of his disciple Anthemius. A citizen of Tralles in Asia had five sons, who were all distinguished in their respective professions by merit and success. Olympius excelled in the knowledge and practice of the Roman jurisprudence. Dioscorus and Alexander became learned physicians; but the skill of the former was exercised for the benefit of his fellow-citizens, while his more ambitious brother acquired wealth and reputation at Rome. The fame of Metrodorus the grammarian, and of Anthemius the mathematician and architect, reached the ears of the emperor Justinian, who invited them to Constantinople; and while the one instructed the rising generation in the schools of eloquence, the other filled the capital and provinces with more lasting monuments of his art. . . . The genius of Anthemius, and his colleague Isidore the Milesian, was excited and employed by a prince whose taste for architecture had degenerated into a mischievous and costly passion. His favourite architects submitted their designs and difficulties to Justinian, and discreetly confessed how much their laborious meditations were surpassed by the intuitive knowledge or celestial inspiration of an emperor whose views were always directed to the benefit of his people, the glory of his reign, and the salvation of his soul.

The principal church, which was dedicated by the founder of Constantinople to Saint Sophia, or the eternal wisdom, had been twice destroyed by fire; after the exile of John Chrysostom and during the *Nika* of the blue and green factions. No sooner did the tumult subside than the Christian populace deplored their sacrilegious rashness; but they might have rejoiced in the calamity, had they foreseen the glory of the new temple, which at the end of forty days was strenuously undertaken by the piety of Justinian. The ruins were cleared away, a more spacious plan was described, and, as it required the consent of some proprietors of ground, they obtained the most exorbitant terms from the eager desires and timorous conscience of the monarch. Anthemius formed the design, and his genius directed the hands of ten thousand workmen, whose payment in pieces of fine silver was never delayed beyond the evening. The emperor himself, clad in a linen tunic, surveyed each day their rapid progress, and encouraged their diligence by his familiarity, his zeal, and his rewards. The new cathedral of St. Sophia was consecrated by the patriarch, five years, eleven months, and ten days from the first foundation; and in the midst of the solemn festival Justinian exclaimed with devout vanity, "Glory be to God, who hath thought me worthy to accomplish so great a work; I have vanquished thee, O Solomon!" But the pride of the Roman Solomon, before twenty years had elapsed, was humbled by an earthquake, which overthrew the eastern part of the dome. Its splendour was again restored by the perseverance of the same prince; and in the thirty-sixth year of his reign Justinian celebrated the second dedication of a temple which remains, after twelve centuries, a stately monument of his fame. The architecture of St. Sophia, which is now converted into the principal mosque, has been imitated by the Turkish sultans, and that venerable pile continues to excite the fond admiration of the Greeks, and the more rational curiosity of European travellers. The eye of the spectator is disappointed by an irregular prospect of half-domes and shelving roofs: the western front, the principal approach, is destitute of simplicity and magnificence; and the scale of dimensions has been much surpassed by several of the Latin cathedrals. But the architect who first erected an *aërial* cupola is entitled to the praise of bold design and skilful execution. The dome of St. Sophia, illuminated by four-and-twenty windows, is formed with so small a curve, that the depth is equal only to one-sixth of its diameter; the measure of that diameter is one hundred and fifteen feet, and the lofty centre, where a crescent has supplanted the cross, rises to the perpendicular height of one hundred and eighty feet above the pavement. The circle which encompasses the dome lightly reposes on four strong arches, and their weight is firmly supported by four massy piles, whose strength is assisted on the northern and southern sides by four columns of Egyptian granite. A Greek cross, inscribed in a quadrangle, represents the form of the edifice; the exact breadth is two hundred and forty-three feet, and two hundred and sixty-nine may be assigned for the extreme length, from the sanctuary in the east to the nine western doors which open into the vestibule, and from thence into the *narthex* or exterior portico. That portico was the humble station of the penitents. The nave or body of the church was filled by the congregation of the faithful; but the two sexes were prudently distinguished, and the upper and lower galleries were allotted for the more private devotion of the women. Beyond the northern and southern piles, a balustrade, terminated on either side by the thrones of the emperor and the patriarch, divided the nave from the choir; and the space, as far as the steps of the altar, was occupied by the clergy and singers. The altar itself, a name which insensibly became familiar to Christian ears, was placed in the eastern recess, artificially built in the form of a demicylinder; and this sanctuary communicated by several doors with the sacristy, the vestry, the baptistery, and the contiguous buildings, subservient either to the pomp of worship, or the private use of the ecclesiastical ministers. The memory of past calamities inspired Justinian with a wise resolution that no wood, except for the doors, should be admitted into the new edifice; and the choice of the materials was applied to the strength, the lightness, or the splendour of the respective parts. The solid piles which sustained the cupola were composed of huge blocks of freestone, hewn into squares and triangles, fortified by circles of iron, and firmly cemented by the infusion of lead and quicklime; but the weight of the cupola was diminished by the levity of its substance, which consists either of pumice-stone that floats in the water, or of bricks, from the isle of Rhodes, five times less ponderous than the ordinary sort. The whole frame of the edifice was constructed of brick; but those base materials were concealed by a crust of marble; and the inside of St. Sophia, the cupola, the two larger and the six smaller semidomes, the walls, the hundred columns, and the pavement, delight even the eyes of barbarians with a rich and variegated picture.

A poet, who beheld the primitive lustre of St. Sophia, enumerates the colours, the shades, and the spots of ten or twelve marbles, jaspers, and porphyries, which nature had profusely diversified, and which were blended and contrasted as it were by a skilful painter. The triumph of Christ was adorned with the last spoils of Paganism, but the greater part of these costly stones was extracted from the quarries of Asia Minor, the isles and continent of Greece, Egypt, Africa, and Gaul. Eight columns of porphyry, which Aurelian had placed in the Temple of the Sun, were offered by the piety of a Roman matron; eight others of green marble were presented by the ambitious zeal of the magistrates of Ephesus: both are admirable by their size and beauty, but every order of architecture disclaims their fantastic capitals. A variety of ornaments and figures was curiously expressed in mosaic; and the images of Christ, of the Virgin, of saints, and of angels, which have been defaced by Turkish fanaticism, were dangerously exposed to the superstition of the Greeks. According to the sanctity of each object, the precious metals were distributed in thin leaves or in solid masses. The balustrade of the choir, the capitals of the pillars, the ornaments of the doors and galleries, were of gilt bronze. The spectator was dazzled by the glittering aspect of the cupola. The sanctuary contained forty thousand pound weight of silver, and the holy vases and vestments of the altar were of the purest gold, enriched with inestimable gems. Before the structure of the church had arisen two cubits above the ground, forty-five thousand two hundred pounds were already consumed, and the whole expense amounted to three hundred and twenty thousand. Each reader, according to the measure of his belief, may estimate their value either in gold or silver; but the sum of one million sterling is the result of the lowest computation. A magnificent temple is a laudable monument of national taste and religion, and the enthusiast who entered the dome of St. Sophia might be tempted to suppose that it was the residence, or even the workmanship, of the Deity. Yet how dull is the artifice, how insignificant is the labour, if it be compared with the formation of the vilest insect that crawls upon the surface of the temple!

So minute a description of an edifice which time has respected may attest the truth and excuse the relation of the innumerable works, both in the capital and provinces, which Justinian constructed on a smaller scale and less durable foundations. In Constantinople alone, and the adjacent suburbs, he dedicated twenty-five churches to the honour of Christ, the Virgin, and the saints. Most of these churches were decorated with marble and gold; and their various situation was skilfully chosen in a populous square or a pleasant grove, on the margin of the seashore or on some lofty eminence which overlooked the continents of Europe and Asia. The church of the Holy Apostles at Constantinople, and that of St. John at Ephesus, appear to have been framed on the same model: their domes aspired to imitate the cupolas of St. Sophia, but the altar was more judiciously placed under the centre of the dome, at the junction of four stately porticoes, which more accurately expressed the figure of the Greek cross. The Virgin of Jerusalem might exult in the temple erected by her imperial votary on a most ungrateful spot, which afforded neither ground nor materials to the architect. A level was formed by raising part of a deep valley to the height of the mountain. The stones of a neighbouring quarry were hewn into regular forms; each block was fixed on a peculiar carriage drawn by forty of the strongest oxen, and the roads were widened for the passage of such enormous weights. Lebanon furnished her loftiest cedars for the timbers of the church; and the seasonable discovery of a vein of red marble supplied its beautiful columns, two of which, the supporters of the exterior portico, were esteemed the largest in the world. The pious munificence of the emperor was diffused over the Holy Land; and if reason should condemn the monasteries of both sexes which were built or restored by Justinian, yet charity must applaud the wells which he sunk, and the hospitals which he founded, for the relief of the weary pilgrims. The schismatical temper of Egypt was ill entitled to the royal bounty; but in Syria and Africa some remedies were applied to the disasters of wars and earthquakes, and both Carthage and Antioch, emerging from their ruins, might revere the name of their gracious benefactor. Almost every saint in the calendar acquired the honours of a temple—almost every city of the empire obtained the solid advantages of bridges, hospitals, and aqueducts; but the severe liberality of the monarch disdained to indulge his subjects in the popular luxury of baths and theatres. While Justinian laboured for the public service, he was not unmindful of his own dignity and ease. The Byzantine palace, which had been damaged by the conflagration, was restored with new magnificence; and some notion may be conceived of the whole edifice by the vestibule or hall, which, from the doors perhaps, or the roof, was surnamed *chalce,* or the brazen. The dome of a spacious quadrangle was supported by massy pillars; the pavement and walls were incrusted with many-coloured marbles—the emerald green of Laconia, the fiery red, and the white Phrygian stone, intersected with veins of a sea-green hue. The mosaic paintings of the dome and sides represented the glories of the African and Italian triumphs. On the Asiatic shore of the Propontis, at a small distance to the east of Chalcedon, the costly palace and gardens of Heræum were prepared for the summer residence of Justinian, and more especially of Theodora. The poets of the age have celebrated the rare alliance of nature and art, the harmony of the nymphs of the groves, the fountains and the waves; yet the crowd of attendants who followed the court complained of their inconvenient lodgings, and the nymphs were too often alarmed by the famous Porphyrio, a whale of ten cubits in breadth and thirty in length, who was stranded at the mouth of the river Sangaris after he had infested more than half a century the seas of Constantinople.

The fortifications of Europe and Asia were multiplied by Justinian; but the repetition of those timid and fruitless precautions exposes, to a philosophic eye, the debility of the empire.[3] From Belgrade to the Euxine, from the conflux of the Save to the mouth of the Danube, a chain of above fourscore fortified places was extended along the banks of the great river. Single watch-towers were changed into spacious citadels; vacant walls, which the engineers contracted or enlarged according to the nature of the ground, were filled with colonies or garrisons; a strong fortress defended the ruins of Trajan's bridge; and several military stations affected to spread beyond the Danube the pride of the Roman name. But that name was divested of its terrors; the barbarians, in their annual inroads, passed and contemptuously repassed before these useless bulwarks; and the inhabitants of the frontier, instead of reposing under the shadow of the general defence, were compelled to guard with incessant vigilance their separate habitations. The solitude of ancient cities was replenished; the new foundations of Justinian acquired, perhaps too hastily, the epithets of impregnable and populous; and the auspicious place of his own nativity attracted the grateful reverence of the vainest of princes. Under the name of *Justiniana prima*, the obscure village of Tauresium became the seat of an archbishop and a præfect, whose jurisdiction extended over seven warlike provinces of Illyricum; and the corrupt appellation of *Giustendil* still indicates, about twenty miles to the south of Sophia, the residence of a Turkish sanjak. For the use of the emperor's countrymen, a cathedral, a palace, and an aqueduct were speedily con-

---

[3] Montesquieu observes that Justinian's empire was like France in the time of the Norman inroads—never so weak as when every village was fortified.

structed; the public and private edifices were adapted to
the greatness of a royal city; and the strength of the
walls resisted, during the lifetime of Justinian, the unskilful assaults of the Huns and Sclavonians. Their progress was sometimes retarded, and their hopes of rapine
were disappointed, by the innumerable castles which, in
the provinces of Dacia, Epirus, Thessaly, Macedonia, and
Thrace, appeared to cover the whole face of the country.
Six hundred of these forts were built or repaired by the
emperor; but it seems reasonable to believe that the far
greater part consisted only of a stone or brick tower in
the midst of a square or circular area, which was surrounded by a wall and ditch, and afforded in a moment
of danger some protection to the peasants and cattle of
the neighbouring villages. Yet these military works, which
exhausted the public treasure, could not remove the just
apprehensions of Justinian and his European subjects.
The warm-baths of Anchialus, in Thrace, were rendered
as safe as they were salutary; but the rich pastures of
Thessalonica were foraged by the Scythian cavalry; the
delicious vale of Tempe, three hundred miles from the
Danube, was continually alarmed by the sound of war;
and no unfortified spot, however distant or solitary, could
securely enjoy the blessings of peace. The straits of Thermopylæ, which seemed to protect, but which had so often
betrayed, the safety of Greece, were diligently strengthened by the labours of Justinian. From the edge of the
sea-shore, through the forests and valleys, and as far as
the summit of the Thessalian mountains, a strong wall
was continued which occupied every practicable entrance.
Instead of a hasty crowd of peasants, a garrison of two
thousand soldiers was stationed along the rampart,
granaries of corn and reservoirs of water were provided
for their use, and, by a precaution that inspired the cowardice which it foresaw, convenient fortresses were
erected for their retreat. The walls of Corinth, overthrown
by an earthquake, and the mouldering bulwarks of
Athens and Platæa, were carefully restored; the bar-

barians were discouraged by the prospect of successive and painful sieges, and the naked cities of Peloponnesus were covered by the fortifications of the isthmus of Corinth. At the extremity of Europe, another peninsula, the Thracian Chersonesus, runs three days' journey into the sea, to form, with the adjacent shores of Asia, the straits of the Hellespont. The intervals between eleven populous towns were filled by lofty woods, fair pastures, and arable lands; and the isthmus, of thirty-seven stadia or furlongs, had been fortified by a Spartan general nine hundred years before the reign of Justinian. In an age of freedom and valour the slightest rampart may prevent a surprise; and Procopius appears insensible of the superiority of ancient times, while he praises the solid construction and double parapet of a wall whose long arms stretched on either side into the sea, but whose strength was deemed insufficient to guard the Chersonesus, if each city, and particularly Gallipoli and Sestus, had not been secured by their peculiar fortifications. . . .

[*After describing the fortifications with which Justinian sought to protect the eastern frontier, from the Crimea to the borders of Abyssinia, Gibbon concludes the chapter with the destruction of two ancient institutions, the most distinctive institutions of independent Greece and republican Rome.*]

Justinian suppressed the schools of Athens and the consulship of Rome, which had given so many sages and heroes to mankind. Both these institutions had long since degenerated from their primitive glory, yet some reproach may be justly inflicted on the avarice and jealousy of a prince by whose hand such venerable ruins were destroyed.

Athens, after her Persian triumphs, adopted the philosophy of Ionia and the rhetoric of Sicily; and these studies became the patrimony of a city whose inhabitants, about thirty thousand males, condensed, within the period of a single life, the genius of ages and millions. Our sense of the dignity of human nature is exalted by the simple recollection that Isocrates was the companion of Plato and Xenophon; that he assisted, perhaps with the historian Thucydides, at the first representations of the Œdipus of Sophocles and the Iphigenia of Euripides; and that his pupils Æschines and Demosthenes contended for the crown of patriotism in the presence of Aristotle, the master of Theophrastus, who taught at Athens with the founders of the Stoic and Epicurean sects. The ingenuous youth of Attica enjoyed the benefits of their domestic education, which was communicated without envy to the rival cities. Two thousand disciples heard the lessons of Theophrastus; the schools of rhetoric must have been still more populous than those of philosophy; and a rapid succession of students diffused the fame of their teachers as far as the utmost limits of the Grecian language and name. Those limits were enlarged by the victories of Alexander; the arts of Athens survived her freedom and dominion; and the Greek colonies which the Macedonians planted in Egypt, and scattered over Asia, undertook long and frequent pilgrimages to worship the Muses in their favourite temple on the banks of the Ilissus. The Latin conquerors respectfully listened to the instructions of their subjects and captives; the names of Cicero and Horace were enrolled in the schools of Athens; and after the perfect settlement of the Roman empire, the natives of Italy, of Africa, and of Britain, conversed in the groves of the Academy with their fellow-students of the East. The studies of philosophy and eloquence are congenial to a popular state, which encourages the freedom of inquiry, and submits only to the force of persuasion. In the republics of Greece and Rome the art of speaking was the powerful engine of patriotism or ambition; and the schools of rhetoric poured forth a colony of statesmen and legislators. When the liberty of public debate was suppressed, the orator, in the honourable profession of an advocate, might plead the cause of innocence and justice; he might abuse his talents in the more profitable trade of panegyric; and the same precepts continued to dictate the fanciful declamations of the sophist, and the chaster beauties of historical composition. The systems which professed to unfold the nature of God, of man, and of the universe, entertained the curiosity of the philosophic student; and according to the temper of his mind, he might doubt with the Sceptics, or decide with the Stoics, sublimely speculate with Plato, or severely argue with Aristotle. The pride of the adverse sects had fixed an unattainable term of moral happiness and perfection: but the race was glorious and salutary; the disciples of Zeno, and even those of Epicurus, were taught both to act and to suffer; and the death of Petronius was not less effectual than that of Seneca to humble a tyrant by the discovery of his impotence. The light of science could not indeed be confined within the walls of Athens. Her incomparable writers address themselves to the human race; the living masters emigrated to Italy and Asia; Berytus, in later times, was devoted to the study of the law; astronomy and physic were cultivated in the museum of Alexandria; but the Attic schools of rhetoric and philosophy maintained their superior reputation from the Peloponnesian war to the reign of Justinian. Athens, though situate in a barren soil, possessed a pure air, a free navigation, and the monuments of ancient art. That sacred retirement was seldom disturbed by the business of trade or government; and the last of the Athenians were distinguished by their lively wit, the purity of their taste and language, their social manners, and some traces, at least in discourse, of the magnanimity of their fathers. In the suburbs of the city, the *Academy* of the Platonists, the *Lyceum* of the Peripatetics, the *Portico* of the Stoics, and the *Garden* of the Epicureans, were planted with trees and decorated with statues; and the philosophers, instead of being immured in a cloister, delivered their instructions in spacious and pleasant walks, which at different hours were consecrated to the exercises of the mind and body. The genius of the founders still lived in those venerable seats; the ambition of succeeding to the masters of human reason excited a generous emulation; and the merit of the candidates was determined, on each vacancy, by the free voices of an enlightened people. The Athenian professors were paid by their disciples: according to their mutual wants and abilities, the price appears to have varied from a mina to a talent; and Isocrates himself, who derides the avarice of the sophists, required, in his school of rhetoric, about thirty pounds from each of his hundred pupils. The wages of industry are just and honourable, yet the same Isocrates shed tears at the first receipt of a stipend: the Stoic might blush when he was hired to preach the contempt of money; and I should be sorry to discover that Aristotle or Plato so far degenerated from the example of Socrates as to exchange knowledge for gold. But some property of lands and houses was settled, by the permission of the laws, and the legacies of deceased friends, on the philosophic chairs of Athens. Epicurus bequeathed to his disciples the gardens which he had purchased for eighty minæ or two hundred and fifty pounds, with a fund sufficient for their frugal subsistence and monthly festivals; and the patrimony of Plato afforded an annual rent, which, in eight centuries, was gradually increased from three to one thousand pieces of gold. The schools of Athens were protected by the wisest and most virtuous of the Roman princes. The library, which Hadrian founded, was placed in a portico adorned with pictures, statues, and a roof of alabaster, and supported by one hundred columns of Phrygian marble. The public salaries were assigned by the generous spirit of the Antonines; and each professor, of politics, of rhetoric, of the Platonic, the Peripatetic, the Stoic, and the Epicurean philosophy, received an annual stipend of ten thousand drachmæ, or more than three hundred pounds sterling. After the death of Marcus, these liberal donations, and the privileges attached to the *thrones* of science, were abolished and revived, diminished and enlarged; but some vestige of royal bounty may be found under the successors of Constantine; and their arbitrary choice of an unworthy candidate might tempt the philosophers of Athens to regret the days of independence and poverty. It is remarkable that the impartial favour of the Antonines was bestowed on the four adverse sects of philosophy, which they considered as equally useful, or at least as equally innocent. Socrates had formerly been the glory and the reproach of his country; and the first lessons of Epicurus so strangely scandalised the pious ears of the Athenians, that by his exile, and that of his antagonists, they silenced all vain disputes concerning the nature of the gods. But in the ensuing year they recalled the hasty decree, restored the liberty of the schools, and were convinced by the experience of ages that the moral character of philosophers is not affected by the diversity of their theological speculations.

The Gothic arms were less fatal to the schools of Athens than the establishment of a new religion, whose ministers superseded the exercise of reason, resolved every question by an article of faith, and condemned the infidel or sceptic to eternal flames. In many a volume of laborious controversy they exposed the weakness of the understanding and the corruption of the heart, insulted human nature in the sages of antiquity, and proscribed the spirit of philosophical inquiry, so repugnant to the doctrine, or at least to the temper, of a humble believer. The surviving sect of the Platonists, whom Plato would have blushed to acknowledge, extravagantly mingled a sublime theory with the practice of superstition and magic; and as they remained alone in the midst of a Christian world, they indulged a secret rancour against the government of the church and state, whose severity was still suspended over their heads. About a century after the reign of Julian, Proclus was permitted to teach in the philosophic chair of the Academy; and such was his industry, that he frequently, in the same day, pronounced five lessons, and composed seven hundred lines. His sagacious mind explored the deepest questions of morals and metaphysics, and he ventured to urge eighteen arguments against the Christian doctrine of the creation of the world. But in the intervals of study he *personally* conversed with Pan, Æsculapius, and Minerva, in whose mysteries he was secretly initiated, and whose prostrate statues he adored; in the devout persuasion that the philosopher, who is a citizen of the universe, should be the priest of its various deities. An eclipse of the sun announced his approaching end; and his Life, with that of his scholar Isidore, compiled by two of their most learned disciples, exhibits a deplorable picture of the second childhood of human reason. Yet the golden chain, as it was fondly styled, of the Platonic succession, continued forty-four years from the death of Proclus to the edict of Justinian, which imposed a perpetual silence on the schools of Athens, and excited the grief and indignation of the few remaining votaries of Grecian science and superstition. Seven friends and philosophers, Diogenes and Hermias, Eulalius and Priscian, Damascius, Isidore, and Simplicius, who dissented from the religion of their sovereign, embraced the resolution of seeking in a foreign land the freedom which was denied in their native country. They had heard, and they credulously believed, that the republic of Plato was realised in the despotic government of Persia, and that a patriot king reigned over the happiest and most virtuous of nations. They were soon astonished by the natural discovery that Persia resembled the other countries of the globe; that Chosroes, who affected the name of a philosopher, was vain, cruel, and ambitious; that bigotry, and a spirit of intolerance, prevailed among the Magi; that the nobles were haughty, the courtiers servile, and the magistrates unjust; that the guilty sometimes escaped, and that the innocent were often oppressed. The disappointment of the philosophers provoked them to overlook the real virtues of the Persians; and they were scandalised, more deeply perhaps than became their profession, with the plurality of wives and concubines, the incestuous marriages, and the custom of exposing dead bodies to the dogs and vultures, instead of hiding them in the earth, or consuming them with fire. Their repentance was expressed by a precipitate return, and they loudly declared that they had rather die on the borders of the empire than enjoy the wealth and favour of the barbarian. From this journey, however, they derived a benefit which reflects the purest lustre on the character of Chosroes. He required that the seven sages who had visited the court of Persia should be exempted from the penal laws which Justinian enacted against his Pagan subjects; and this privilege, expressly stipulated in a treaty of peace, was guarded by the vigilance of a powerful mediator. Simplicius and his companions ended their lives in peace and obscurity; and as they left no disciples, they terminate the long list of Grecian philosophers, who may be justly praised, notwithstanding their defects, as the wisest and most virtuous of their contemporaries. The writings of Simplicius are now extant. His physical and metaphysical commentaries on Aristotle have passed away with the fashion of the times; but his moral interpretation of Epictetus is preserved in the library of nations, as a classic book, most excellently adapted to direct the will, to purify the heart, and to confirm the understanding, by a just confidence in the nature both of God and man.

About the same time that Pythagoras first invented the appellation of philosopher, liberty and the consulship were founded at Rome by the elder Brutus. The revolutions of the consular office, which may be viewed in the successive lights of a substance, a shadow, and a name, have been occasionally mentioned in the present history. The first magistrates of the republic had been chosen by the people, to exercise, in the senate and in the camp, the powers of peace and war, which were afterwards translated to the emperors. But the tradition of ancient dignity was long revered by the Romans and barbarians. A Gothic historian applauds the consulship of Theodoric as the height of all temporal glory and greatness; the king of Italy himself congratulates those annual favourites of fortune who, without the cares, enjoyed the splendour of the throne; and at the end of a thousand years two consuls were created by the sovereigns of Rome and Constantinople for the sole purpose of giving a date to the year and a festival to the people. But the expenses of this festival, in which the wealthy and the vain aspired to surpass their predecessors, insensibly arose to the enormous sum of fourscore thousand pounds; the wisest senators declined a useless honour which involved the certain ruin of their families, and to this reluctance I should impute the frequent chasms in the last age of the consular *Fasti*. The predecessors of Justinian had assisted from the public treasures the dignity of the less opulent candidates; the avarice of that prince preferred the cheaper and more convenient method of advice and regulation. Seven *processions* or spectacles were the number to which his edict confined the horse and chariot races, the athletic sports, the music and pantomimes of the theatre, and the hunting of wild beasts; and small pieces of silver were discreetly substituted to the gold medals, which had always excited tumult and drunkenness when they were scattered with a profuse hand among the populace. Notwithstanding these precautions and his own example, the succession of consuls finally ceased in the thirteenth year of Justinian, whose despotic temper might be gratified by the silent extinction of a title which admonished the Romans of their ancient freedom. Yet the annual consulship still lived in the minds of the people; they fondly expected its speedy restoration; they applauded the gracious condescension of successive princes, by which it was assumed in the first year of their reign; and three centuries elapsed, after the death of Justinian, before that obsolete dignity, which had been suppressed by custom, could be abolished by law. The imperfect mode of distinguishing each year by the name of a magistrate was usefully supplied by the date of a permanent era: the creation of the world, according to the Septuagint version, was adopted by the Greeks; and the Latins, since the age of Charlemagne, have computed their time from the birth of Christ.

CHAPTER XV

THE LOMBARD INVASIONS AND POPE GREGORY THE GREAT

The restored empire of Justinian did not last long. He died in 565 A.D. Three years later the Lombards, from their position on the Danube, invaded Italy. They conquered the valley of the Po, since known as Lombardy, and from their capital in Pavia terrorised the whole peninsula. They threatened the Byzantine citadel of Ravenna, besieged Rome, and destroyed the monastery of Monte Cassino. In his chapter XLV Gibbon describes their conquests and pays tribute to Pope Gregory I, who, in the universal calamity of the times, unsupported by the Byzantine emperor or his exarch in Ravenna, sustained the city of Rome and, from it, evangelised the barbarians.

During a period of two hundred years Italy was unequally divided between the kingdom of the Lombards and the exarchate of Ravenna. The offices and professions which the jealousy of Constantine had separated were united by the indulgence of Justinian; and eighteen successive exarchs were invested, in the decline of the empire, with the full remains of civil, of military, and even of ecclesiastical power. Their immediate jurisdiction, which was afterwards consecrated as the patrimony of St. Peter, extended over the modern Romagna, the marshes or valleys of Ferrara and Commachio, five maritime cities from Rimini to Ancona, and a second inland Pentapolis, between the Hadriatic coast and the hills of the Apennine. Three subordinate provinces of Rome, of Venice, and of Naples, which were divided by hostile lands from the palace of Ravenna, acknowledged, both in peace and war, the supremacy of the exarch. The duchy of Rome appears to have included the Tuscan, Sabine, and Latin conquests of the first four hundred years of the city, and the limits may be distinctly traced along the coast, from Civita Vecchia to Terracina, and with the course of the Tiber from Ameria and Narni to the port of Ostia. The numerous islands from Grado to Chiozza composed the infant dominion of Venice; but the more accessible towns on the continent were overthrown by the Lombards, who beheld with impotent fury a new capital rising from the waves. The power of the dukes of Naples was circumscribed by the bay and the adjacent isles, by the hostile territory of Capua, and by the Roman colony of Amalphi, whose industrious citizens, by the invention of the mariner's compass, have unveiled the face of the globe. The three islands of Sardinia, Corsica, and Sicily still adhered to the empire; and the acquisition of the farther Calabria removed the landmark of Autharis from the shore of Rhegium to the isthmus of Consentia. In Sardinia the savage mountaineers preserved the liberty and religion of their ancestors; but the husbandmen of Sicily were chained to their rich and cultivated soil. Rome was oppressed by the iron sceptre of the exarchs, and a Greek, perhaps a eunuch, insulted with impunity the ruins of the Capitol. But Naples soon acquired the privilege of electing her own dukes: the independence of Amalphi was the fruit of commerce; and the voluntary attachment of Venice was finally ennobled by an equal alliance with the Eastern empire. On the map of Italy the measure of the exarchate occupies a very inadequate space, but it included an ample proportion of wealth, industry, and population. The most faithful and valuable subjects escaped from the barbarian yoke; and the banners of Pavia and Verona, of Milan and Padua, were displayed in their respective quarters by the new inhabitants of Ravenna. The remainder of Italy was possessed by the Lombards; and from Pavia, the royal seat, their kingdom was extended to the east, the north, and the west, as far as the confines of the Avars, the Bavarians, and the Franks of Austrasia and Burgundy. In the language of modern geography, it is now represented by the Terra Firma of the Venetian republic, Tyrol, the Milanese, Piedmont, the coast of Genoa, Mantua, Parma, and Modena, the grand duchy of Tuscany, and a large portion of the ecclesiastical state from Perugia to the Hadriatic. The dukes, and at length the princes, of Beneventum, survived the monarchy, and propagated the name of the Lombards. From Capua to Tarentum, they reigned near five hundred years over the greatest part of the present kingdom of Naples.

In comparing the proportion of the victorious and the vanquished people, the change of language will afford the most probable interference. According to this standard it will appear that the Lombards of Italy, and the Visigoths of Spain, were less numerous than the Franks or Burgundians; and the conquerors of Gaul must yield, in their turn, to the multitude of Saxons and Angles who almost eradicated the idioms of Britain. The modern Italian has been insensibly formed by the mixture of nations: the awkwardness of the barbarians in the nice management of declensions and conjugations reduced them to the use of articles and auxiliary verbs; and many new ideas have been expressed by Teutonic appellations. Yet the principal stock of technical and familiar words is found to be of Latin derivation; and, if we were sufficiently conversant with the obsolete, the rustic, and the muncipal dialects of ancient Italy, we should trace the origin of many terms which might, perhaps, be rejected by the classic purity of Rome. A numerous army constitutes but a small nation, and the powers of the Lombards were soon diminished by the retreat of twenty thousand Saxons, who scorned a dependent situation, and returned, after many bold and perilous adventures, to their native country. The camp of Alboin was of formidable extent, but the extent of a camp would be easily circumscribed within the limits of a city; and its martial inhabitants must be thinly scattered over the face of a large country. When Alboin descended from the Alps, he invested his nephew, the first duke of Friuli, with the command of the province and the people: but the prudent Gisulf would have declined the dangerous office, unless he had been permitted to choose among the nobles of the Lombards, a sufficient number of families to form a perpetual colony of soldiers and subjects. In the progress of conquest, the same option could not be granted to the dukes of Brescia or Bergamo, of Pavia or Turin, of Spoleto or Beneventum; but each of these, and each of their colleagues, settled in his appointed district with a band of followers who resorted to his standard in war and his tribunal in peace. Their attachment was free and honourable: resigning the gifts and benefits which they had accepted, they might emigrate with their families into the jurisdiction of another duke; but their absence from the kingdom was punished with death, as a crime of military desertion. The posterity of the first conquerors struck a deeper root into the soil, which, by every motive of interest and honour, they were bound to defend. A Lombard was born the soldier of his king and his duke; and the civil assemblies of the nation displayed the banners, and assumed the appellation, of a regular army. Of this army the pay and the rewards were drawn from the conquered provinces; and the distribution, which was not effected till after the death of Alboin, is disgraced by the foul marks of injustice and rapine. Many of the most wealthy Italians were slain or banished; the remainder were divided among the strangers, and a tributary obligation was imposed (under the name of hospitality) of paying to the Lombards a third part of the fruits of the earth. Within less than seventy years this artificial system was abolished by a more simple and solid tenure. Either the Roman landlord was expelled by his strong and insolent guest, or the annual payment, a third of the produce, was exchanged by a more equitable transaction for an adequate proportion of landed property. Under these foreign masters, the business of agriculture, in the cultivation of corn, vines, and olives, was exercised with degenerate skill and industry by the labour of the slaves and natives. But the occupations of a pastoral life were more pleasing to the idleness of the barbarians. In the rich meadows of Venetia they restored and improved the breed of horses, for which that province had once been illustrious[1] ; and the Italians beheld with astonishment a foreign race of oxen or buffaloes.[2] The depopulation of Lombardy, and the increase of forests, afforded an ample range for the pleasures of the chase. That marvellous art which teaches the birds of the air to acknowledge the voice, and execute the commands, of their master had been unknown to the ingenuity of the Greeks and Romans.[3] Scandinavia and Scythia produce the boldest and most tractable falcons: they were tamed and educated by the roving inhabitants, always on horseback and in the field. This favourite amusement of our ancestors was introduced by the barbarians into the Roman provinces: and the laws of Italy esteem the sword and the hawk as of equal dignity and importance in the hands of a noble Lombard.

So rapid was the influence of climate and example, that the Lombards of the fourth generation surveyed with curiosity and affright the portraits of their savage fore-

---

[1] The studs of Dionysius of Syracuse, and his frequent victories in the Olympic games, had diffused among the Greeks the fame of the Venetian horses; but the breed was extinct in the time of Strabo. Gisulf obtained from his uncle generosarum equarum greges. The Lombards afterwards introduced caballi silvatici—wild horses.

[2] The buffaloes, whose native climate appears to be Africa and India, are unknown to Europe, except in Italy, where they are numerous and useful. The ancients were ignorant of these animals, unless Aristotle has described them as the wild oxen of Arachosia. Yet I must not conceal the suspicion that Paul, by a vulgar error, may have applied the name of bubalus to the aurochs, or wild bull, of ancient Germany.

[3] Their ignorance is proved by the silence even of those who professedly treat of the arts of hunting and the history of animals. Aristotle, Pliny, Ælian and perhaps Homer, describe with astonishment a tacit league and common chase between the hawks and the Thracian fowlers.

fathers. Their heads were shaven behind, but the shaggy locks hung over their eyes and mouth, and a long beard represented the name and character of the nation. Their dress consisted of loose linen garments, after the fashion of the Anglo-Saxons, which were decorated, in their opinion, with broad stripes of variegated colours. The legs and feet were clothed in long hose and open sandals, and even in the security of peace a trusty sword was constantly girt to their side. Yet this strange apparel and horrid aspect often concealed a gentle and generous disposition; and as soon as the rage of battle had subsided, the captives and subjects were sometimes surprised by the humanity of the victor. The vices of the Lombards were the effect of passion, of ignorance, of intoxication; their virtues are the more laudable, as they were not affected by the hypocrisy of social manners, nor imposed by the rigid constraint of laws and education. I should not be apprehensive of deviating from my subject, if it were in my power to delineate the private life of the conquerors of Italy; and I shall relate with pleasure the adventurous gallantry of Autharis, which breathes the true spirit of chivalry and romance. After the loss of his promised bride, a Merovingian princess, he sought in marriage the daughter of the king of Bavaria, and Garibald acepted the alliance of the Italian monarch. Impatient of the slow progress of negotiation, the ardent lover escaped from his palace and visited the court of Bavaria in the train of his own embassy. At the public audience the unknown stranger advanced to the throne, and informed Garibald that the ambassador was indeed the minister of state, but that he alone was the friend of Autharis, who had trusted him with the delicate commission of making a faithful report of the charms of his spouse. Theudelinda was summoned to undergo this important examination, and, after a pause of silent rapture, he hailed her as the queen of Italy, and humbly requested that, according to the custom of the nation, she would present a cup of wine to the first of her new subjects. By the command of her father she obeyed: Autharis received the cup in his turn, and, in restoring it to the princess, he secretly touched her hand, and drew his own finger over his face and lips. In the evening Theudelinda imparted to her nurse the indiscreet familiarity of the stranger, and was comforted by the assurance that such boldness could proceed only from the king her husband, who, by his beauty and courage, appeared worthy of her love. The ambassadors were dismissed: no sooner did they reach the confines of Italy than Autharis, raising himself on his horse, darted his battle-axe against a tree with incomparable strength and dexterity: "Such," said he to the astonished Bavarians, "such are the strokes of the king of the Lombards." On the approach of a French army, Garibald and his daughter took refuge in the dominions of their ally, and the marriage was consummated in the palace of Verona. At the end of one year it was dissolved by the death of Autharis; but the virtues of Theudelinda had endeared her to the nation, and she was permitted to bestow, with her hand, the sceptre of the Italian kingdom.

From this fact, as well as from similar events, it is certain that the Lombards possessed freedom to elect their sovereign, and sense to decline the frequent use of that dangerous privilege. The public revenue arose from the produce of land and the profits of justice. When the independent dukes agreed that Autharis should ascend the throne of his father, they endowed the regal office with a fair moiety of their respective domains. The proudest nobles aspired to the honours of servitude near the person of their prince; he rewarded the fidelity of his vassals by the precarious gift of pensions and *benefices*, and atoned for the injuries of war by the rich foundation of monasteries and churches. In peace a judge, a leader in war, he never usurped the powers of a sole and absolute legislator. The king of Italy convened the national assemblies in the palace, or more probably in the fields, of Pavia; his great council was composed of the persons most eminent by their birth and dignities; but the validity, as well as the execution, of their decrees depended on the approbation of the *faithful* people, the *fortunate* army of the Lombards. About fourscore years after the conquest of Italy their traditional customs were transcribed in Teutonic Latin, and ratified by the consent of the prince and people; some new regulations were introduced, more suitable to their present condition; the example of Rotharis was imitated by the wisest of his successors: and the laws of the Lombards have been esteemed the least imperfect of the barbaric codes. Secure by their courage in the possession of liberty, these rude and hasty legislators were incapable of balancing the powers of the constitution, or of discussing the nice theory of political government. Such crimes as threatened the life of the sovereign or the safety of the state were adjudged worthy of death; but their attention was principally confined to the defence of the person and property of the subject. According to the strange jurisprudence of the times, the guilt of blood might be redeemed by a fine; yet the high price of nine hundred pieces of gold declares a just sense of the value of a simple citizen. Less atrocious injuries, a wound, a fracture, a blow, an opprobrious word, were measured with scrupulous and almost ridiculous diligence; and the prudence of the legislator encouraged the ignoble practice of bartering honour and revenge for a pecuniary compensation. The ignorance of the Lombards in the state of Paganism or Christianity gave implicit credit to the malice and mischief of witchcraft: but the judges of the seventeenth century might have been instructed and confounded by the wisdom of Rotharis, who derides the absurd superstition, and protects the wretched victims of popular or judicial cruelty. The same spirit of a legislator superior to his age and country may be ascribed to Liutprand, who condemns while he tolerates the impious and inveterate abuse of duels, observing, from his own experience, that the juster cause had often been oppressed by successful violence. Whatever merit may be discovered in the laws of the Lombards, they are the genuine fruit of the reason of the barbarians, who never admitted the bishops of

Italy to a seat in their legislative councils. But the succession of their kings is marked with virtue and ability; the troubled series of their annals is adorned with fair intervals of peace, order, and domestic happiness; and the Italians enjoyed a milder and more equitable government than any of the other kingdoms which had been founded on the ruins of the Western empire.

Amidst the arms of the Lombards, and under the despotism of the Greeks, we again inquire into the fate of Rome, which had reached, about the close of the sixth century, the lowest period of her depression. By the removal of the seat of empire and the successive loss of the provinces, the sources of public and private opulence were exhausted: the lofty tree, under whose shade the nations of the earth had reposed, was deprived of its leaves and branches, and the sapless trunk was left to wither on the ground. The ministers of command and the messengers of victory no longer met on the Appian or Flaminian way, and the hostile approach of the Lombards was often felt and continually feared. The inhabitants of a potent and peaceful capital, who visit without an anxious thought the garden of the adjacent country, will faintly picture in their fancy the distress of the Romans: they shut or opened their gates with a trembling hand, beheld from the walls the flames of their houses, and heard the lamentations of their brethren, who were coupled together like dogs, and dragged away into distant slavery beyond the sea and the mountains. Such incessant alarms must annihilate the pleasures and interrupt the labours of a rural life; and the Campagna of Rome was speedily reduced to the state of a dreary wilderness, in which the land is barren, the waters are impure, and the air is infectious. Curiosity and ambition no longer attracted the nations to the capital of the world; but, if chance or necessity directed the steps of a wandering stranger, he contemplated with horror the vacancy and solitude of the city, and might be tempted to ask, where is the senate, and where are the people? In a season of excessive rains the Tiber swelled above its banks, and rushed with irresistible violence into the valleys of the seven hills. A pestilential disease arose from the stagnation of the deluge, and so rapid was the contagion that fourscore persons expired in an hour in the midst of a solemn procession which implored the mercy of Heaven. A society in which marriage is encouraged and industry prevails soon repairs the accidental losses of pestilence and war; but, as the far greater part of the Romans was condemned to hopeless indigence and celibacy, the depopulation was constant and visible, and the gloomy enthusiasts might expect the approaching failure of the human race. Yet the number of citizens still exceeded the measure of subsistence: their precarious food was supplied from the harvests of Sicily or Egypt, and the frequent repetition of famine betrays the inattention of the emperor to a distant province. The edifices of Rome were exposed to the same ruin and decay; the mouldering fabrics were easily overthrown by inundations, tempests, and earthquakes; and the monks, who had occupied the most advantageous stations, exulted in their base triumph over the ruins of antiquity. It is commonly believed that pope Gregory the First attacked the temples and mutilated the statues of the city; that, by the command of the barbarian, the Palatine library was reduced to ashes, and that the history of Livy was the peculiar mark of his absurd and mischievous fanaticism. The writings of Gregory himself reveal his implacable aversion to the monuments of classic genius, and he points his severest censure against the profane learning of a bishop who taught the art of grammar, studied the Latin poets, and pronounced with the same voice the praises of Jupiter and those of Christ. But the evidence of his destructive rage is doubtful and recent: the Temple of Peace or the Theatre of Marcellus have been demolished by the slow operation of ages, and a formal proscription would have multiplied the copies of Virgil and Livy in the countries which were not subject to the ecclesiastical dictator.

Like Thebes, or Babylon, or Carthage, the name of

Rome might have been erased from the earth, if the city had not been animated by a vital principle, which again restored her to honour and dominion. A vague tradition was embraced, that two Jewish teachers, a tent-maker and a fisherman, had formerly been executed in the circus of Nero, and at the end of five hundred years their genuine or fictitious relics were adored as the Palladium of Christian Rome. The pilgrims of the East and West resorted to the holy threshold; but the shrines of the apostles were guarded by miracles and invisible terrors, and it was not without fear that the pious catholic approached the object of his worship. It was fatal to touch, it was dangerous to behold, the bodies of the saints; and those who, from the purest motives, presumed to disturb the repose of the sanctuary were affrighted by visions or punished with sudden death. The unreasonable request of an empress, who wished to deprive the Romans of their sacred treasure, the head of St. Paul, was rejected with the deepest abhorrence; and the pope asserted, most probably with truth, that a linen which had been sanctified in the neighbourhood of his body, or the filings of his chain, which it was sometimes easy and sometimes impossible to obtain, possessed an equal degree of miraculous virtue. But the power as well as virtue of the apostles resided with living energy in the breast of their successors: and the chair of St. Peter was filled under the reign of Maurice by the first and greatest of the name of Gregory. His grandfather Felix had himself been pope, and, as the bishops were already bound by the law of celibacy, his consecration must have been preceded by the death of his wife. The parents of Gregory, Sylvia and Gordian, were the noblest of the senate and the most pious of the church of Rome; his female relations were numbered among the saints and virgins, and his own figure, with those of his father and mother, were represented near three hundred years in a family portrait which he offered to the monastery of St. Andrew. The design and colouring of this picture afford an honourable testimony that the art of painting was cultivated by the Italians of the sixth century; but the most abject ideas must be entertained of their taste and learning, since the epistles of Gregory, his sermons, and his dialogues, are the work of a man who was second in erudition to none of his contemporaries: his birth and abilities had raised him to the office of præfect of the city, and he enjoyed the merit of renouncing the pomp and vanities of this world. His ample patrimony was dedicated to the foundation of seven monasteries, one in Rome and six in Sicily; and it was the wish of Gregory that he might be unknown in this life and glorious only in the next. Yet his devotion, and it might be sincere, pursued the path which would have been chosen by a crafty and ambitious statesman. The talents of Gregory, and the splendour which accompanied his retreat, rendered him dear and useful to the church, and implicit obedience has been always inculcated as the first duty of a monk. As soon as he had received the character of deacon, Gregory was sent to reside at the Byzantine court, the nuncio or minister of the apostolic see; and he boldly assumed, in the name of St. Peter, a tone of independent dignity which would have been criminal and dangerous in the most illustrious layman of the empire. He returned to Rome with a just increase of reputation, and, after a short exercise of the monastic virtues, he was dragged from the cloister to the papal throne by the unanimous voice of the clergy, the senate, and the people. He alone resisted, or seemed to resist, his own elevation; and his humble petition that Maurice would be pleased to reject the choice of the Romans could only serve to exalt his character in the eyes of the emperor and the public. When the fatal mandate was proclaimed, Gregory solicited the aid of some friendly merchants to convey him in a basket beyond the gates of Rome, and modestly concealed himself some days among the woods and mountains, till his retreat was discovered, as it is said, by a celestial light.

The pontificate of Gregory the *Great*, which lasted thirteen years, six months, and ten days, is one of the most edifying periods of the history of the church. His virtues, and even his faults, a singular mixture of simplicity and cunning, of pride and humility, of sense and superstition, were happily suited to his station and to the temper of the times. In his rival, the patriarch of Constantinople, he condemned the antichristian title of universal bishop, which the succcessor of St. Peter was too haughty to concede and too feeble to assume; and the ecclesiastical jurisdiction of Gregory was confined to the triple character of Bishop of Rome, Primate of Italy, and Apostle of the West. He frequently ascended the pulpit, and kindled, by his rude though pathetic eloquence, the congenial passions of his audience: the language of the Jewish prophets was interpreted and applied; and the minds of a people depressed by their present calamities were directed to the hopes and fears of the invisible world. His precepts and example defined the model of the Roman liturgy; the distribution of the parishes, the calendar of festivals, the order of processions, the service of the priests and deacons, the variety and change of sacerdotal garments. Till the last days of his life he officiated in the canon of the mass, which continued about three hours: the Gregorian chant has preserved the vocal and instrumental music of the theatre, and the rough voices of the barbarians attempted to imitate the melody of the Roman school. Experience had shown him the efficacy of these solemn and pompous rites to soothe the distress, to confirm the faith, to mitigate the fierceness, and to dispel the dark enthusiasm of the vulgar, and he readily forgave their tendency to promote the reign of priesthood and superstition. The bishops of Italy and the adjacent islands acknowledged the Roman pontiff as their special metropolitan. Even the existence, the union, or the translation of episcopal seats was decided by his absolute discretion: and his successful inroads into the provinces of Greece, of Spain, and of Gaul, might countenance the more lofty pretensions of succeeding popes. He interposed to prevent the abuses of popular elections; his jealous care maintained the purity of faith and discipline; and the apostolic shepherd assiduously watched over the faith and discipline of the subordinate pastors. Under his reign the Arians of Italy and Spain were reconciled to the catholic church, and the conquest of Britain reflects less glory on the name of Cæsar than on that of Gregory the First. Instead of six legions, forty monks were embarked for that distant island, and the pontiff lamented the austere duties which forbade him to partake the perils of their spiritual warfare. In less than two years he could announce to the archbishop of Alexandria that they had baptised the king of Kent with ten thousand of his Anglo-Saxons; and that the Roman missionaries, like those of the primitive church, were armed only with spiritual and supernatural powers. The credulity or the prudence of Gregory was always disposed to confirm the truths of religion by the evidence of ghosts, miracles, and resurrections; and posterity has paid to *his* memory the same tribute which he freely granted to the virtue of his own or the preceding generation. The celestial honours have been liberally bestowed by the authority of the popes, but Gregory is the last of their own order whom they have presumed to inscribe in the calendar of saints.

Their temporal power insensibly arose from the calamities of the times; and the Roman bishops, who have deluged Europe and Asia with blood, were compelled to reign as the ministers of charity and peace. I. The church of Rome, as it has been formerly observed, was endowed with ample possessions in Italy, Sicily, and the more distant provinces; and her agents, who were commonly subdeacons, had acquired a civil and even criminal jurisdiction over their tenants and husbandmen. The successor of St. Peter administered his patrimony with the temper of a vigilant and moderate landlord; and the epistles of Gregory are filled with salutary instructions to abstain from doubtful or vexatious lawsuits, to preserve the integrity of weights and measures, to grant every reasonable delay, and to reduce the capitation of the slaves of the glebe, who purchased the right of marriage by the payment of an arbitrary fine. The rent or the produce of these estates was transported to the mouth of the Tiber, at the risk and expense of the pope: in the use of wealth he acted like a faithful steward of the church and the poor, and liberally applied to their wants the inexhaustible resources of abstinence and order. The voluminous account of his receipts and disbursements was kept above three hundred years in the Lateran, as the model of Christian economy. On the four great festivals he divided their quarterly allowance to the clergy, to his domestics, to the monasteries, the churches, the places of burial, the almshouses, and the hospitals of Rome, and the rest of the diocese. On the first day of every month he distributed to the poor, according to the season, their stated portion of corn, wine, cheese, vegetables, oil, fish, fresh provisions, clothes, and money; and his treasurers were continually summoned to satisfy, in his name, the extraordinary demands of indigence and merit. The instant distress of the sick and helpless, of strangers and pilgrims, was relieved by the bounty of each day and of every hour; nor would the pontiff indulge himself in a frugal repast till he had sent the dishes from his own table to some objects deserving of his compassion. The misery of the times had reduced the nobles and matrons of Rome to accept, without a blush, the benevolence of the church: three thousand virgins received their food and raiment from the hand of their benefactor; and many bishops of Italy escaped from the barbarians to the hospitable threshold of the Vatican. Gregory might justly be styled the Father of his country; and such was the extreme sensibility of his conscience, that, for the death of a beggar who had perished in the streets, he interdicted himself during several days from the exercise of sacerdotal functions. II. The misfortunes of Rome involved the apostolical pastor in the business of peace and war; and it might be doubtful to himself whether piety or ambition prompted him to supply the place of his absent sovereign. Gregory awakened the emperor from a long slumber; exposed the guilt or incapacity of the exarch and his inferior ministers; complained that the veterans were withdrawn from Rome for the defence of Spoleto; encouraged the Italians to guard their cities and altars; and condescended, in the crisis of danger, to name the tribunes and to direct the operations of the provincial troops. But the martial spirit of the pope was checked by the scruples of humanity and religion: the imposition of tribute, though it was employed in the Italian war, he freely condemned as odious and oppressive; whilst he protected, against the Imperial edicts, the pious cowardice of the soldiers who deserted a military for a monastic life. If we may credit his own declarations, it would have been easy for Gregory to exterminate the Lombards by their domestic factions, without leaving a king, a duke, or a count, to save that unfortunate nation from the vengeance of their foes. As a Christian bishop, he preferred the salutary offices of peace; his mediation appeased the tumult of arms; but he was too conscious of the arts of the Greeks and the passions of the Lombards to engage his sacred promise for the observance of the truce. Disappointed in the hope of a general and lasting treaty, he presumed to save his country without the consent of the emperor or the exarch. The sword of the enemy was suspended over Rome; it was averted by the mild eloquence and seasonable gifts of the pontiff, who commanded the respect of heretics and barbarians. The merits of Gregory were treated by the Byzantine court with reproach and insult; but in the attachment of a grateful people he found the purest reward of a citizen, and the best right of a sovereign.

CHAPTER XVI

HERACLIUS

The Lombard invasion of Italy was only the beginning of trouble for the emperors in Byzantium, who soon found themselves menaced more directly both in the West and in the East. In the West the threat came from the Avars, a tribe who had replaced the Lombards in their former position on the Danube. Having besieged and captured Sirmium (Belgrade) in 581, the Avars regularly invaded the Balkan provinces and, in Gibbon's phrase, alternately bathed their horses in the Euxine and the Adriatic. In the East, pressure was renewed by the old enemy, Persia. Here, at first, the successors of Justinian had been at peace, for after the death of Nushirvan (Chosroes I) in 579, the Persian monarchy had been distracted by civil war, and Nushirvan's grandson, Chosroes II, recovered his lost throne thanks to the support of the emperor Maurice. But once established in power, Chosroes soon asserted his independence. The attacks of the Avars in Europe gave him the opportunity, and the murder of his benefactor Maurice and the usurpation of his throne by Phocas (602) supplied the pretext, for renewal of the war with "Rome". In 610, when Phocas in his turn had been deposed and murdered, Constantinople was threatened both by the "chagan" or ruler of the Avars, pressing down the Danube, and by the "Great King" of Persia, already in possession of most of Syria.

411

The new emperor, who faced this double threat, was Heraclius, the son of the exarch of Africa, who had led his forces from Carthage to over- throw the tyrannical Phocas. By his reorganisa- tion of the army, and his victories over both Persians and Avars, Heraclius saved the city of Constantinople and founded an imperial dynasty which would last for a century.

In chapter XLVI Gibbon describes the military achievement of Heraclius.

The first intelligence from the East which Heraclius received was that of the loss of Antioch; but the aged metropolis, so often overturned by earthquakes and pil- laged by the enemy, could supply but a small and languid stream of treasure and blood. The Persians were equally successful and more fortunate in the sack of Cæsarea, the capital of Cappadocia; and as they advanced beyond the ramparts of the frontier, the boundary of ancient war, they found a less obstinate resistance and a more plenti- ful harvest. The pleasant vale of Damascus has been adorned in every age with a royal city: her obscure feli- city has hitherto escaped the historian of the Roman empire: but Chosroes reposed his troops in the paradise of Damascus before he ascended the hills of Libanus or invaded the cities of the Phœnician coast. The conquest of Jerusalem, which had been meditated by Nushirvan, was achieved by the zeal and avarice of his grandson; the ruin of the proudest monument of Christianity was vehemently urged by the intolerant spirit of the Magi; and he could enlist for this holy warfare an army of six- and twenty thousand Jews, whose furious bigotry might compensate in some degree for the want of valour and discipline. After the reduction of Galilee and the region beyond the Jordan, whose resistance appears to have delayed the fate of the capital, Jerusalem itself was taken by assault. The sepulchre of Christ and the stately churches of Helena and Constantine were consumed, or at least damaged, by the flames; the devout offerings of

three hundred years were rifled in one sacrilegious day;
the patriarch Zachariah and the *true cross* were transplanted into Persia; and the massacre of ninety thousand
Christians is imputed to the Jews and Arabs, who swelled
the disorder of the Persian march. The fugitives of Palestine were entertained at Alexandria by the charity of
John the archbishop, who is distinguished among a crowd
of saints by the epithet of *almsgiver:* and the revenues of
the church, with a treasure of three hundred thousand
pounds, were restored to the true proprietors, the poor of
every country and every denomination. But Egypt itself,
the only province which had been exempt since the time
of Diocletian from foreign and domestic war, was again
subdued by the successors of Cyrus. Pelusium, the key of
that impervious country, was surprised by the cavalry of
the Persians: they passed with impunity the innumerable
channels of the Delta, and explored the long valley of the
Nile from the pyramids of Memphis to the confines of
Æthiopia. Alexandria might have been relieved by a
naval force, but the archbishop and the præfect embarked for Cyprus; and Chosroes entered the second city
of the empire, which still preserved a wealthy remnant of
industry and commerce. His western trophy was erected,
not on the walls of Carthage,[1] but in the neighbourhood
of Tripoli: the Greek colonies of Cyrene were finally extirpated; and the conqueror, treading in the footsteps of
Alexander, returned in triumph through the sands of the
Libyan desert. In the same campaign another army advanced from the Euphrates to the Thracian Bosphorus;
Chalcedon surrendered after a long siege, and a Persian
camp was maintained above ten years in the presence of
Constantinople. The sea-coast of Pontus, the city of
Ancyra, and the isle of Rhodes are enumerated among
the last conquests of the Great King; and if Chosroes had
possessed any maritime power, his boundless ambition

[1] [As had been stated in error by several of Gibbon's predecessors,
who had confused the Greek words Χαλχήδων (Chalcedon) and Καρχήδων
(Carthage) *Ed.*]

would have spread slavery and desolation over the provinces of Europe.

From the long-disputed banks of the Tigris and Euphrates, the reign of the grandson of Nushirvan was suddenly extended to the Hellespont and the Nile, the ancient limits of the Persian monarchy. But the provinces, which had been fashioned by the habits of six hundred years to the virtues and vices of the Roman government, supported with reluctance the yoke of the barbarians. The idea of a republic was kept alive by the institutions, or at least by the writings, of the Greeks and Romans, and the subjects of Heraclius had been educated to pronounce the words of liberty and law. But it has always been the pride and policy of Oriental princes to display the titles and attributes of their omnipotence; to upbraid a nation of slaves with their true name and abject condition; and to enforce, by cruel and insolent threats, the rigour of their absolute commands. The Christians of the East were scandalised by the worship of fire and the impious doctrine of the two principles: the Magi were not less intolerant than the bishops; and the martyrdom of some native Persians who had deserted the religion of Zoroaster was conceived to be the prelude of a fierce and general persecution. By the oppressive laws of Justinian the adversaries of the church were made the enemies of the state; the alliance of the Jews, Nestorians, and Jacobites had contributed to the success of Chosroes, and his partial favour to the sectaries provoked the hatred and fears of the catholic clergy. Conscious of their fear and hatred, the Persian conqueror governed his new subjects with an iron sceptre; and, as if he suspected the stability of his dominion, he exhausted their wealth by exorbitant tributes and licentious rapine; despoiled or demolished the temples of the East; and transported to his hereditary realms the gold, the silver, the precious marbles, the arts, and the artists of the Asiatic cities. In the obscure picture of the calamities of the empire it is not easy to discern the figure of Chosroes himself, to separate his actions from those of his lieutenants, or to ascertain his personal merit in the general blaze of glory and magnificence. He enjoyed with ostentation the fruits of victory, and frequently retired from the hardships of war to the luxury of the palace. But, in the space of twenty-four years, he was deterred by superstition or resentment from approaching the gates of Ctesiphon: and his favourite residence of Artemita, or Dastagerd, was situate beyond the Tigris, about sixty miles to the north of the capital. The adjacent pastures were covered with flocks and herds: the paradise or park [2] was replenished with pheasants, peacocks, ostriches, roebucks, and wild boars; and the noble game of lions and tigers was sometimes turned loose for the bolder pleasures of the chase. Nine hundred and sixty elephants were maintained for the use or splendour of the Great King; his tents and baggage were carried into the field by twelve thousand great camels and eight thousand of a smaller size; and the royal stables were filled with six thousand mules and horses, among whom the names of Shebdiz and Barid are renowned for their speed or beauty. Six thousand guards successively mounted before the palace gate; the service of the interior apartments was performed by twelve thousand slaves; and in the number of three thousand virgins, the fairest of Asia, some happy concubine might console her master for the age or the indifference of Sira. The various treasures of gold, silver, gems, silk, and aromatics were deposited in a hundred subterraneous vaults; and the chamber *Badaverd* denoted the accidental gift of the winds which wafted the spoils of Heraclius into one of the Syrian harbours of his rival. The voice of flattery, and perhaps of fiction, is not ashamed to compute the thirty thousand rich hangings that adorned the walls; the forty thousand columns of silver, or more probably of marble, and plated wood, that supported the roof; and the thousand globes of gold suspended in the dome, to imitate the motions of the planets and the constellations of the zodiac. While the Persian

[2] ['Paradise', the Greek work for Park, is of Persian origin. *Ed.*]

monarch contemplated the wonders of his art and power, he received an epistle from an obscure citizen of Mecca, inviting him to acknowledge Mohammed as the apostle of God. He rejected the invitation, and tore the epistle. "It is thus," exclaimed the Arabian prophet, "that God will tear the kingdom and reject the supplications of Chosroes." Placed on the verge of the two great empires of the East, Mohammed observed with secret joy the progress of their mutual destruction; and in the midst of the Persian triumphs he ventured to foretell that, before many years should elapse, victory would again return to the banners of the Romans.

At the time when this prediction is said to have been delivered, no prophecy could be more distant from its accomplishment, since the first twelve years of Heraclius announced the approaching dissolution of the empire. If the motives of Chosroes had been pure and honourable, he must have ended the quarrel with the death of Phocas, and he would have embraced, as his best ally, the fortunate African who had so generously avenged the injuries of his benefactor Maurice. The prosecution of the war revealed the true character of the barbarian; and the suppliant embassies of Heraclius to beseech his clemency, that he would spare the innocent, accept a tribute, and give peace to the world, were rejected with contemptuous silence or insolent menace. Syria, Egypt, and the provinces of Asia were subdued by the Persian arms; while Europe, from the confines of Istria to the long wall of Thrace, was oppressed by the Avars, unsatiated with the blood and rapine of the Italian war. They had coolly massacred their male captives in the sacred field of Pannonia; the women and children were reduced to servitude, and the noblest virgins were abandoned to the promiscuous lust of the barbarians. The amorous matron who opened the gates of Friuli passed a short night in the arms of her royal lover; the next evening Romilda was condemned to the embraces of twelve Avars; and, the third day, the Lombard princess was impaled in the sight of the camp, while the chagan observed, with a cruel

smile, that such a husband was the fit recompense of
her lewdness and perfidy. By these implacable enemies
Heraclius, on either side, was insulted and besieged: and
the Roman empire was reduced to the walls of Constantinople, with the remnant of Greece, Italy, and Africa,
and some maritime cities, from Tyre to Trebizond, of the
Asiatic coast. After the loss of Egypt the capital was
afflicted by famine and pestilence; and the emperor, incapable of resistance and hopeless of relief, had resolved
to transfer his person and government to the more secure
residence of Carthage. His ships were already laden with
the treasures of the palace; but his flight was arrested by
the patriarch, who armed the powers of religion in the
defence of his country, led Heraclius to the altar of St.
Sophia, and extorted a solemn oath that he would live
and die with the people whom God had intrusted to his
care. The chagan was encamped in the plains of Thrace;
but he dissembled his perfidious designs, and solicited an
interview with the emperor near the town of Heraclea.
Their reconciliation was celebrated with equestrian
games; the senate and people, in their gayest apparel,
resorted to the festival of peace; and the Avars beheld,
with envy and desire, the spectacle of Roman luxury. On
a sudden the hippodrome was encompassed by the
Scythian cavalry, who had pressed their secret and nocturnal march: the tremendous sound of the chagan's
whip gave the signal of the assault; and Heraclius, wrap-
ping his diadem round his arm, was saved, with extreme
hazard, by the fleetness of his horse. So rapid was the
pursuit, that the Avars almost entered the golden gate of
Constantinople with the flying crowds: but the plunder
of the suburbs rewarded their treason, and they transported beyond the Danube two hundred and seventy
thousand captives. On the shore of Chalcedon the emperor held a safer conference with a more honourable foe,
who, before Heraclius descended from his galley, saluted
with reverence and pity the majesty of the purple. The
friendly offer of Sain, the Persian general, to conduct an
embassy to the presence of the Great King was accepted

with the warmest gratitude; and the prayer for pardon and peace was humbly presented by the prætorian præfect, the præfect of the city, and one of the first ecclesiastics of the patriarchal church. But the lieutenant of Chosroes had fatally mistaken the intentions of his master. "It was not an embassy," said the tyrant of Asia, "it was the person of Heraclius, bound in chains, that he should have brought to the foot of my throne. I will never give peace to the emperor of Rome till he has abjured his crucified God and embraced the worship of the sun." Sain was flayed alive, according to the inhuman practice of his country; and the separate and rigorous confinement of the ambassadors violated the law of nations and the faith of an express stipulation. Yet the experience of six years at length persuaded the Persian monarch to renounce the conquest of Constantinople, and to specify the annual tribute or ransom of the Roman empire: a thousand talents of gold, a thousand talents of silver, a thousand silk robes, a thousand horses, and a thousand virgins. Heraclius subscribed these ignominious terms; but the time and space which he obtained to collect such treasures from the poverty of the East was industriously employed in the preparations of a bold and desperate attack.

Of the characters conspicuous in history, that of Heraclius is one of the most extraordinary and inconsistent. In the first and the last years of a long reign the emperor appears to be the slave of sloth, of pleasure, or of superstition; the careless and impotent spectator of the public calamities. But the languid mists of the morning and evening are separated by the brightness of the meridian sun: the Arcadius of the palace arose the Cæsar of the camp; and the honour of Rome and Heraclius was gloriously retrieved by the exploits and trophies of six adventurous campaigns. It was the duty of the Byzantine historians to have revealed the causes of his slumber and vigilance. At this distance we can only conjecture that he was endowed with more personal courage than political resolution; that he was detained by the charms, and per-

haps the arts, of his niece Martina, with whom, after the
death of Eudocia, he contracted an incestuous marriage;[3]
and that he yielded to the base advice of the counsellors
who urged, as a fundamental law, that the life of the
emperor should never be exposed in the field. Perhaps he
was awakened by the last insolent demand of the Persian
conqueror; but at the moment when Heraclius assumed
the spirit of a hero, the only hopes of the Romans were
drawn from the vicissitudes of fortune, which might
threaten the proud prosperity of Chosroes, and must be
favourable to those who had attained the lowest period of
depression. To provide for the expenses of war was the
first care of the emperor; and for the purpose of collecting the tribute he was allowed to solicit the benevolence
of the Eastern provinces. But the revenue no longer
flowed in the usual channels; the credit of an arbitrary
prince is annihilated by his power; and the courage of
Heraclius was first displayed in daring to borrow the
consecrated wealth of churches, under the solemn vow of
restoring, with usury, whatever he had been compelled
to employ in the service of religion and of the empire.
The clergy themselves appear to have sympathised with
the public distress; and the discreet patriarch of Alexandria, without admitting the precedent of sacrilege,
assisted his sovereign by the miraculous or seasonable
revelation of a secret treasure. Of the soldiers who had
conspired with Phocas, only two were found to have survived the stroke of time and of the barbarians; the loss
even of these seditious veterans was imperfectly supplied
by the new levies of Heraclius; and the gold of the sanctuary united, in the same camp, the names, and arms,
and languages of the East and West. He would have been
content with the neutrality of the Avars; and his friendly
entreaty that the chagan would act not as the enemy, but
as the guardian of the empire, was accompanied with a

---

[3] Nicephorus (p. 10, 11), who brands this marriage with the names
of ἀθεσμου and ἀθέμιτου, is happy to observe, that of two sons, its
incestuous fruit, the elder was marked by Providence with a stiff neck,
the younger with the loss of hearing.

more persuasive donative of two hundred thousand pieces of gold. Two days after the festival of Easter, the emperor, exchanging his purple for the simple garb of a penitent and warrior, gave the signal of his departure. To the faith of the people Heraclius recommended his children; the civil and military powers were vested in the most deserving hands; and the discretion of the patriarch and senate was authorised to save or surrender the city, if they should be oppressed in his absence by the superior forces of the enemy.

The neighbouring heights of Chalcedon were covered with tents and arms; but if the new levies of Heraclius had been rashly led to the attack, the victory of the Persians in the sight of Constantinople might have been the last day of the Roman empire. As imprudent would it have been to advance into the provinces of Asia, leaving their innumerable cavalry to intercept his convoys, and continually to hang on the lassitude and disorder of his rear. But the Greeks were still masters of the sea; a fleet of galleys, transports, and store-ships was assembled in the harbour; the barbarians consented to embark; a steady wind carried them through the Hellespont; the western and southern coast of Asia Minor lay on their left hand; the spirit of their chief was first displayed in a storm; and even the eunuchs of his train were excited to suffer and to work by the example of their master. He landed his troops on the confines of Syria and Cilicia, in the gulf of Scanderoon, where the coast suddenly turns to the south; and his discernment was expressed in the choice of this important post. From all sides the scattered garrisons of the maritime cities and the mountains might repair with speed and safety to his Imperial standard. The natural fortifications of Cilicia protected and even concealed the camp of Heraclius, which was pitched near Issus, on the same ground where Alexander had vanquished the host of Darius. The angle which the emperor occupied was deeply indented into a vast semicircle of the Asiatic, Armenian, and Syrian provinces; and to whatsoever point of the circumference he should direct his attack, it was easy for him to dissemble his own motions, and to prevent those of the enemy. In the camp of Issus the Roman general reformed the sloth and disorder of the veterans, and educated the new recruits in the knowledge and practice of military virtue. Unfolding the miraculous image of Christ, he urged them to *revenge* the holy altars which had been profaned by the worshippers of fire; addressing them by the endearing appellations of sons and brethren, he deplored the public and private wrongs of the republic. The subjects of a monarch were persuaded that they fought in the cause of freedom, and a similar enthusiasm was communicated to the foreign mercenaries, who must have viewed with equal indifference the interest of Rome and of Persia. Heraclius himself, with the skill and patience of a centurion, inculcated the lessons of the school of tactics, and the soldiers were assiduously trained in the use of their weapons and the exercises and evolutions of the field. The cavalry and infantry, in light or heavy armour, were divided into two parties; the trumpets were fixed in the centre, and their signals directed the march, the charge, the retreat or pursuit, the direct or oblique order, the deep or extended phalanx, to represent in fictitious combat the operations of genuine war. Whatever hardship the emperor imposed on the troops, he inflicted with equal severity on himself; their labour, their diet, their sleep, were measured by the inflexible rules of discipline; and, without despising the enemy, they were taught to repose an implicit confidence in their own valour and the wisdom of their leader. Cilicia was soon encompassed with the Persian arms, but their cavalry hesitated to enter the defiles of Mount Taurus till they were circumvented by the evolutions of Heraclius, who insensibly gained their rear, whilst he appeared to present his front in order of battle. By a false motion, which seemed to threaten Armenia, he drew them against their wishes to a general action. They were tempted by the artful disorder of his camp; but when they advanced to combat, the ground, the sun, and the expectation of both armies, were unpropitious to the barbarians: the Romans successfully repeated their tactics in a field of battle, and the event of the day declared to the world that the Persians were not invincible, and that a hero was invested with the purple. Strong in victory and fame, Heraclius boldly ascended the heights of Mount Taurus, directed his march through the plains of Cappadocia, and established his troops for the winter season in safe and plentiful quarters on the banks of the river Halys. His soul was superior to the vanity of entertaining Constantinople with an imperfect triumph; but the presence of the emperor was indispensably required to soothe the restless and rapacious spirit of the Avars.

Since the days of Scipio and Hannibal, no bolder enterprise has been attempted than that which Heraclius achieved for the deliverance of the empire. He permitted the Persians to oppress for awhile the provinces, and to insult with impunity the capital of the East, while the Roman emperor explored his perilous way through the Black Sea and the mountains of Armenia, penetrated into the heart of Persia, and recalled the armies of the Great King to the defence of their bleeding country.

With a select band of five thousand soldiers, Heraclius sailed from Constantinople to Trebizond; assembled his forces which had wintered in the Pontic regions; and from the mouth of the Phasis to the Caspian Sea, encouraged his subjects and allies to march with the successor of Constantine under the faithful and victorious banner of the cross. When the legions of Lucullus and Pompey first passed the Euphrates, they blushed at their easy victory over the natives of Armenia. But the long experience of war had hardened the minds and bodies of that effeminate people; their zeal and bravery were approved in the service of a declining empire; they abhorred and feared the usurpation of the house of Sassan, and the memory of persecution envenomed their pious hatred of the enemies of Christ. The limits of Armenia, as it had been ceded to the emperor Maurice, extended as far as the Araxes: the river submitted to the indignity of a bridge, and Heraclius, in the footsteps of Mark Antony,

13-14
Pope Gregory the Great, who enabled Rome to withstand the
Lombard invasions; and the Angel Gabriel appearing before
Mohammed, founder of Islam. The two were near contempo-
raries.

advanced towards the city of Tauris or Gandzaca, the ancient and modern capital of one of the provinces of Media. At the head of forty thousand men, Chosroes himself had returned from some distant expedition to oppose the progress of the Roman arms; but he retreated on the approach of Heraclius, declining the generous alternative of peace or of battle. Instead of half a million of inhabitants, which have been ascribed to Tauris under the reign of the Sophys, the city contained no more than three thousand houses; but the value of the royal treasures was enhanced by a tradition that they were the spoils of Crœsus, which had been transported by Cyrus from the citadel of Sardes. The rapid conquests of Heraclius were suspended only by the winter season; a motive of prudence or superstition determined his retreat into the province of Albania, along the shores of the Caspian; and his tents were most probably pitched in the plains of Mogan, the favourite encampment of Oriental princes. In the course of this successful inroad he signalised the zeal and revenge of a Christian emperor: at his command the soldiers extinguished the fire, and destroyed the temples, of the Magi; the statues of Chosroes, who aspired to divine honours, were abandoned to the flames; and the ruin of Thebarma or Ormia, which had given birth to Zoroaster himself, made some atonement for the injuries of the holy sepulchre. A purer spirit of religion was shown in the relief and deliverance of fifty thousand captives. Heraclius was rewarded by their tears and grateful acclamations; but this wise measure, which spread the fame of his benevolence, diffused the murmurs of the Persians against the pride and obstinacy of their own sovereign.

Amidst the glories of the succeeding campaign, Heraclius is almost lost to our eyes, and to those of the Byzantine historians. From the spacious and fruitful plains of Albania, the emperor appears to follow the chain of Hyrcanian mountains, to descend into the province of Media or Irak, and to carry his victorious arms as far as the royal cities of Casbin and Ispahan, which had never been approached by a Roman conqueror. Alarmed by the danger of his kingdom, the powers of Chosroes were already recalled from the Nile and the Bosphorus, and three formidable armies surrounded, in a distant and hostile land, the camp of the emperor. The Colchian allies prepared to desert his standard; and the fears of the bravest veterans were expressed, rather than concealed, by their desponding silence. "Be not terrified," said the intrepid Heraclius, "by the multitude of your foes. With the aid of Heaven, one Roman may triumph over a thousand barbarians. But if we devote our lives for the salvation of our brethren, we shall obtain the crown of martyrdom, and our immortal reward will be liberally paid by God and posterity." These magnanimous sentiments were supported by the vigour of his actions. He repelled the threefold attack of the Persians, improved the divisions of their chiefs, and, by a well-concerted train of marches, retreats, and successful actions, finally chased them from the field into the fortified cities of Media and Assyria. In the severity of the winter season, Sarbaraza deemed himself secure in the walls of Salban: he was surprised by the activity of Heraclius, who divided his troops, and performed a laborious march in the silence of the night. The flat roofs of the houses were defended with useless valour against the darts and torches of the Romans: the satraps and nobles of Persia, with their wives and children, and the flower of their martial youth, were either slain or made prisoners. The general escaped by a precipitate flight, but his golden armour was the prize of the conqueror; and the soldiers of Heraclius enjoyed the wealth and repose which they had so nobly deserved. On the return of spring, the emperor traversed in seven days the mountains of Curdistan, and passed without resistance the rapid stream of the Tigris. Oppressed by the weight of their spoils and captives, the Roman army halted under the walls of Amida; and Heraclius informed the senate of Constantinople of his safety and success, which they had already felt by the retreat of the besiegers. The bridges of the

Euphrates were destroyed by the Persians; but as soon as the emperor had discovered a ford, they hastily retired to defend the banks of the Sarus, in Cilicia. That river, an impetuous torrent, was about three hundred feet broad; the bridge was fortified with strong turrets; and the banks were lined with barbarian archers. After a bloody conflict, which continued till the evening, the Romans prevailed in the assault; and a Persian of gigantic size was slain and thrown into the Sarus by the hand of the emperor himself. The enemies were dispersed and dismayed; Heraclius pursued his march to Sebaste in Cappadocia; and at the expiration of three years, the same coast of the Euxine applauded his return from a long and victorious expedition.

Instead of skirmishing on the frontier, the two monarchs who disputed the empire of the East aimed their desperate strokes at the heart of their rival. The military force of Persia was wasted by the marches and combats of twenty years, and many of the veterans, who had survived the perils of the sword and the climate, were still detained in the fortresses of Egypt and Syria. But the revenge and ambition of Chosroes exhausted his kingdom; and the new levies of subjects, strangers and slaves, were divided into three formidable bodies. The first army of fifty thousand men, illustrious by the ornament and title of the *golden spears*, was destined to march against Heraclius; the second was stationed to prevent his junction with the troops of his brother Theodorus; and the third was commanded to besiege Constantinople, and to second the operations of the chagan, with whom the Persian king had ratified a treaty of alliance and partition. Sarbar, the general of the third army, penetrated through the provinces of Asia to the well-known camp of Chalcedon, and amused himself with the destruction of the sacred and profane buildings of the Asiatic suburbs, while he impatiently waited the arrival of his Scythian friends on the opposite side of the Bosphorus. On the twenty-ninth of June, thirty thousand barbarians, the vanguard of the Avars, forced the long wall, and drove into the capital a promiscuous crowd of peasants, citizens, and soldiers. Fourscore thousand of his native subjects, and of the vassal tribes of Gepidæ, Russians, Bulgarians, and Sclavonians, advanced under the standard of the chagan; a month was spent in marches and negotiations, but the whole city was invested on the thirty-first of July, from the suburbs of Pera and Galata to the Blachernæ and seven towers; and the inhabitants descried with terror the flaming signals of the European and Asiatic shores. In the meanwhile the magistrates of Constantinople repeatedly strove to purchase the retreat of the chagan; but their deputies were rejected and insulted; and he suffered the patricians to stand before his throne, while the Persian envoys, in silk robes, were seated by his side. "You see," said the haughty barbarian, "the proofs of my perfect union with the Great King; and his lieutenant is ready to send into my camp a select band of three thousand warriors. Presume no longer to tempt your master with a partial and inadequate ransom: your wealth and your city are the only presents worthy of my acceptance. For yourselves, I shall permit you to depart, each with an undergarment and a shirt; and, at my entreaty, my friend Sarbar will not refuse a passage through his lines. Your absent prince, even now a captive or a fugitive, has left Constantinople to its fate; nor can you escape the arms of the Avars and Persians, unless you could soar into air like birds, unless like fishes you could dive into the waves." During ten successive days the capital was assaulted by the Avars, who had made some progress in the science of attack; they advanced to sap or batter the wall, under the cover of the impenetrable tortoise; their engines discharged a perpetual volley of stones and darts; and twelve lofty towers of wood exalted the combatants to the height of the neighbouring ramparts. But the senate and people were animated by the spirit of Heraclius, who had detached to their relief a body of twelve thousand cuirassiers; the powers of fire and mechanics were used with superior art and success in the defence of Constantinople; and the galleys, with two and three ranks of oars, commanded the Bosphorus, and rendered the Persians the idle spectators of the defeat of their allies. The Avars were repulsed; a fleet of Sclavonian canoes was destroyed in the harbour; the vassals of the chagan threatened to desert, his provisions were exhausted, and, after burning his engines, he gave the signal of a slow and formidable retreat. The devotion of the Romans ascribed this signal deliverance to the Virgin Mary; but the mother of Christ would surely have condemned their inhuman murder of the Persian envoys, who were entitled to the rights of humanity, if they were not protected by the laws of nations.

After the division of his army, Heraclius prudently retired to the banks of the Phasis, from whence he maintained a defensive war against the fifty thousand gold spears of Persia. His anxiety was relieved by the deliverance of Constantinople; his hopes were confirmed by a victory of his brother Theodorus; and to the hostile league of Chosroes with the Avars, the Roman emperor opposed the useful and honourable alliance of the Turks. At his liberal invitation, the horde of Chozars transported their tents from the plains of the Volga to the mountains of Georgia; Heraclius received them in the neighbourhood of Teflis, and the khan with his nobles dismounted from their horses, if we may credit the Greeks, and fell prostrate on the ground to adore the purple of the Cæsar. Such voluntary homage and important aid were entitled to the warmest acknowledgments, and the emperor, taking off his own diadem, placed it on the head of the Turkish prince, whom he saluted with a tender embrace and the appellation of son. After a sumptuous banquet he presented Ziebel with the plate and ornaments, the gold, the gems, and the silk which had been used at the Imperial table, and, with his own hand, distributed rich jewels and earrings to his new allies. In a secret interview he produced the portrait of his daughter Eudocia, condescended to flatter the barbarian with the promise of a fair and *august* bride, obtained an immediate succour of forty thousand horse, and negotiated a strong diversion of the Turkish arms on the side of the Oxus. The Persians, in their turn, retreated with precipitation; in the camp of Edessa Heraclius reviewed an army of seventy thousand Romans and strangers; and some months were successfully employed in the recovery of the cities of Syria, Mesopotamia, and Armenia, whose fortifications had been imperfectly restored. Sarbar still maintained the important station of Chalcedon, but the jealousy of Chosroes, or the artifice of Heraclius, soon alienated the mind of that powerful satrap from the service of his king and country. A messenger was intercepted with a real or fictitious mandate to the cadarigan, or second in command, directing him to send, without delay, to the throne the head of a guilty or unfortunate general. The despatches were transmitted to Sarbar himself, and, as soon as he read the sentence of his own death, he dexterously inserted the names of four hundred officers, assembled a military council, and asked the *cadarigan* whether he was prepared to execute the commands of their tyrant? The Persians unanimously declared that Chosroes had forfeited the sceptre; a separate treaty was concluded with the government of Constantinople; and if some considerations of honour or policy restrained Sarbar from joining the standard of Heraclius, the emperor was assured that he might prosecute without interruption his designs of victory and peace.

Deprived of his firmest support, and doubtful of the fidelity of his subjects, the greatness of Chosroes was still conspicuous in its ruins. The number of five hundred thousand may be interpreted as an Oriental metaphor to describe the men and arms, the horses and elephants, that covered Media and Assyria against the invasion of Heraclius. Yet the Romans boldly advanced from the Araxes to the Tigris, and the timid prudence of Rhazates was content to follow them by forced marches through a desolate country, till he received a peremptory mandate to risk the fate of Persia in a decisive battle. Eastward of the Tigris, at the end of the bridge of Mosul, the great

Nineveh had formerly been erected: the city, and even the ruins of the city, had long since disappeared; the vacant space afforded a spacious field for the operations of the two armies. But these operations are neglected by the Byzantine historians, and, like the authors of epic poetry and romance, they ascribe the victory, not to the military conduct, but to the personal valour of their favourite hero. On this memorable day Heraclius, on his horse Phallas, surpassed the bravest of his warriors; his lip was pierced with a spear, the steed was wounded in the thigh, but he carried his master safe and victorious through the triple phalanx of the barbarians. In the heat of the action three valiant chiefs were successively slain by the sword and lance of the emperor: among these was Rhazates himself; he fell like a soldier, but the sight of his head scattered grief and despair through the fainting ranks of the Persians. His armour of pure and massy gold, the shield of one hundred and twenty plates, the sword and belt, the saddle and cuirass, adorned the triumph of Heraclius; and if he had not been faithful to Christ and his mother, the champion of Rome might have offered the fourth *opime*[4] spoils to the Jupiter of the Capitol. In the battle of Nineveh, which was fiercely fought from daybreak to the eleventh hour, twenty-eight standards besides those which might be broken or torn, were taken from the Persians; the greatest part of their army was cut to pieces; and the victors, concealing their own loss, passed the night on the field. They acknowledged that, on this occasion, it was less difficult to kill than to discomfit the soldiers of Chosroes; amidst the bodies of their friends, no more than two bow-shot from the enemy, the remnant of the Persian cavalry stood firm till the seventh hour of the night; about the eighth hour they retired to their unrifled camp, collected their baggage, and dispersed on all sides from the want of orders rather than of resolution. The diligence of Herac-

[4] [*spolia opima*, or spoils of honour, were the spoils taken from a victorious Roman general, in personal combat, from the general of the enemy and solemnly dedicated to Jupiter Capitolinus. *Ed.*]

lius was not less admirable in the use of victory; by a march of forty-eight miles in four-and-twenty hours his vanguard occupied the bridges of the great and the lesser Zab, and the cities and palaces of Assyria were open for the first time to the Romans. By a just gradation of magnificent scenes they penetrated to the royal seat of Dastagerd, and, though much of the treasure had been removed and much had been expended, the remaining wealth appears to have exceeded their hopes, and even to have satiated their avarice. Whatever could not be easily transported they consumed with fire, that Chosroes might feel the anguish of those wounds which he had so often inflicted on the provinces of the empire; and justice might allow the excuse, if the desolation had been confined to the works of regal luxury—if national hatred, military licence, and religious zeal had not wasted with equal rage the habitations and the temples of the guiltless subject. The recovery of three hundred Roman standards and the deliverance of the numerous captives of Edessa and Alexandria reflect a purer glory on the arms of Heraclius. From the palace of Dastagerd he pursued his march within a few miles of Modain or Ctesiphon, till he was stopped, on the banks of the Arba, by the difficulty of the passage, the rigour of the season, and perhaps the fame of an impregnable capital. The return of the emperor is marked by the modern name of the city of Sherhzour: he fortunately passed Mount Zara before the snow, which fell incessantly thirty-four days; and the citizens of Gandzaca, or Tauris, were compelled to entertain his soldiers and their horses with an hospitable reception.

When the ambition of Chosroes was reduced to the defence of his hereditary kingdom, the love of glory, or even the sense of shame, should have urged him to meet his rival in the field. In the battle of Nineveh his courage might have taught the Persians to vanquish, or he might have fallen with honour by the lance of a Roman emperor. The successor of Cyrus chose rather, at a secure distance, to expect the event, to assemble the relics of the defeat, and to retire by measured steps before the march of Heraclius, till he beheld with a sigh the once loved mansions of Dastagerd. Both his friends and enemies were persuaded that it was the intention of Chosroes to bury himself under the ruins of the city and palace: and as both might have been equally adverse to his flight, the monarch of Asia, with Sira and three concubines, escaped through a hole in the wall nine days before the arrival of the Romans. The slow and stately procession in which he showed himself to the prostrate crowd was changed to a rapid and secret journey; the first evening he lodged in the cottage of a peasant, whose humble door would scarcely give admittance to the Great King. His superstition was subdued by fear: on the third day he entered with joy the fortifications of Ctesiphon; yet he still doubted of his safety till he had opposed the river Tigris to the pursuit of the Romans. The discovery of his flight agitated with terror and tumult the palace, the city, and the camp of Dastagerd: the satraps hesitated whether they had most to fear from their sovereign or the enemy; and the females of the harem were astonished and pleased by the sight of mankind, till the jealous husband of three thousand wives again confined them to a more distant castle. At his command the army of Dastagerd retreated to a new camp: the front was covered by the Arba and a line of two hundred elephants; the troops of the more distant provinces successively arrived; and the vilest domestics of the king and satraps were enrolled for the last defence of the throne. It was still in the power of Chosroes to obtain a reasonable peace; and he was repeatedly pressed by the messengers of Heraclius to spare the blood of his subjects, and to relieve a humane conqueror from the painful duty of carrying fire and sword through the fairest countries of Asia. But the pride of the Persian had not yet sunk to the level of his fortune; he derived a momentary confidence from the retreat of the emperor; he wept with impotent rage over the ruins of his Assyrian palaces; and disregarded too long the rising murmurs of the nation, who complained that their

lives and fortunes were sacrificed to the obstinacy of an
old man. That unhappy old man was himself tortured
with the sharpest pains both of mind and body; and, in
the consciousness of his approaching end, he resolved to
fix the tiara on the head of Merdaza, the most favoured
of his sons. But the will of Chosroes was no longer
revered, and Siroes, who gloried in the rank and merit
of his mother Sira, had conspired with the malcontents
to assert and anticipate the rights of primogeniture.
Twenty-two satraps, they styled themselves patriots, were
tempted by the wealth and honours of a new reign: to
the soldiers the heir of Chosroes promised an increase of
pay; to the Christians, the free exercise of their religion;
to the captives, liberty and rewards; and to the nation,
instant peace and the reduction of taxes. It was determined by the conspirators that Siroes, with the ensigns
of royalty, should appear in the camp; and if the enterprise should fail, his escape was contrived to the Imperial
court. But the new monarch was saluted with unanimous
acclamations; the flight of Chosroes (yet where could he
have fled?) was rudely arrested, eighteen sons were massacred before his face, and he was thrown into a dungeon,
where he expired on the fifth day. The Greeks and
modern Persians minutely describe how Chosroes was
insulted, and famished, and tortured, by the command of
an inhuman son, who so far surpassed the example of his
father; but at the time of his death what tongue would
relate the story of the parricide? what eye could penetrate
into the *tower of darkness*? According to the faith and
mercy of his Christian enemies, he sunk without hope
into a still deeper abyss, and it will not be denied that
tyrants of every age and sect are the best entitled to such
infernal abodes. The glory of the house of Sassan ended
with the life of Chosroes; his unnatural son enjoyed only
eight months the fruit of his crimes; and in the space of
four years the regal title was assumed by nine candidates, who disputed, with the sword or dagger, the fragments of an exhausted monarchy. Every province and
each city of Persia was the scene of independence, of

discord, and of blood; and the state of anarchy prevailed about eight years longer, till the factions were silenced and united under the common yoke of the Arabian caliphs.

As soon as the mountains became passable the emperor received the welcome news of the success of the conspiracy, the death of Chosroes, and the elevation of his eldest son to the throne of Persia. The authors of the revolution, eager to display their merits in the court or camp of Tauris, preceded the ambassadors of Siroes, who delivered the letters of their master to his *brother* the emperor of the Romans. In the language of the usurpers of every age, he imputes his own crimes to the Deity, and, without degrading his equal majesty, he offers to reconcile the long discord of the two nations by a treaty of peace and alliance more durable than brass or iron. The conditions of the treaty were easily defined and faithfully executed. In the recovery of the standards and prisoners which had fallen into the hands of the Persians, the emperor imitated the example of Augustus; their care of the national dignity was celebrated by the poets of the times, but the decay of genius may be measured by the distance between Horace and George of Pisidia; the subjects and brethren of Heraclius were redeemed from persecution, slavery, and exile; but, instead of the Roman eagles, the true wood of the holy cross was restored to the importunate demands of the successor of Constantine. The victor was not ambitious of enlarging the weakness of the empire; the son of Chosroes abandoned without regret the conquests of his father; the Persians who evacuated the cities of Syria and Egypt were honourably conducted to the frontier; and a war which had wounded the vitals of the two monarchies produced no change in their external and relative situation. The return of Heraclius from Tauris to Constantinople was a perpetual triumph, and after the exploits of six glorious campaigns he peaceably enjoyed the sabbath of his toils. After a long impatience, the senate, the clergy, and the people went forth to meet their hero with tears and acclamations, with olive-branches and innumerable lamps; he entered the capital in a chariot drawn by four elephants, and, as soon as the emperor could disengage himself from the tumult of public joy, he tasted more genuine satisfaction in the embraces of his mother and his son.

The succeeding year was illustrated by a triumph of a very different kind, the restitution of the true cross to the holy sepulchre. Heraclius performed in person the pilgrimage of Jerusalem: the identity of the relic was verified by the discreet patriarch, and this august ceremony has been commemorated by the annual festival of the exaltation of the cross. Before the emperor presumed to tread the consecrated ground he was instructed to strip himself of the diadem and purple, the pomp and vanity of the world; but in the judgment of his clergy, the persecution of the Jews was more easily reconciled with the precepts of the Gospel. He again ascended his throne to receive the congratulations of the ambassadors of France and India; and the fame of Moses, Alexander, and Hercules was eclipsed, in the popular estimation, by the superior merit and glory of the great Heraclius. Yet the deliverer of the East was indigent and feeble. Of the Persian spoils the most valuable portion had been expended in the war, distributed to the soldiers, or buried, by an unlucky tempest, in the waves of the Euxine. The conscience of the emperor was oppressed by the obligation of restoring the wealth of the clergy, which he had borrowed for their own defence: a perpetual fund was required to satisfy these inexorable creditors; the provinces, already wasted by the arms and avarice of the Persians, were compelled to a second payment of the same taxes; and the arrears of a simple citizen, the treasurer of Damascus, were commuted to a fine of one hundred thousand pieces of gold. The loss of two hundred thousand soldiers, who had fallen by the sword, was of less fatal importance than the decay of arts, agriculture, and population in this long and destructive war; and although a victorious army had been formed under the standard of Heraclius, the unnatural effort appears to have exhausted rather than exercised their strength. While the emperor triumphed at Constantinople or Jerusalem, an obscure town on the confines of Syria was pillaged by the Saracens, and they cut in pieces some troops who advanced to its relief; an ordinary and trifling occurrence, had it not been the prelude of a mighty revolution. These robbers were the apostles of Mohammed; their fanatic valour had emerged from the desert; and in the last eight years of his reign Heraclius lost to the Arabs the same provinces which he had rescued from the Persians.

CHAPTER XVII

THE NEW BYZANTINE EMPIRE

Gibbon ended his fourth volume with the reign of Heraclius (610–641). He might have been content to stop there: the best modern historians regard the reign of Heraclius as the real end of the Roman empire; for it was then that the Mohammedan revolution, rolling out from Arabia, destroyed the known landmarks of Antiquity. With the ruin of the Persian Empire and the destruction of Mediterranean unity, the old Roman empire lost its balance and its base; the triumphs of Justinian seemed, in retrospect, a belated anachronism; and from now on the Eastern Empire was not Roman but Greco-Asiatic, looking east. Nevertheless, this "Byzantine" empire, diminished in extent, but reorganised in form, lasted, through many vicissitudes, for another 800 years, and Gibbon, captivated by his story, decided to cover these 800 years, even if it meant quickening his pace. In chapter XLVIII, the first chapter of his fifth volume, he explained the plan of the last two volumes.]

I have now deduced from Trajan to Constantine, from Constantine to Heraclius, the regular series of the Roman emperors; and faithfully exposed the prosperous and adverse fortunes of their reigns. Five centuries of the decline and fall of the empire have already elapsed; but a period of more than eight hundred years still separates me from the term of my labours, the taking of Constantinople by the Turks. Should I persevere in the same course, should I observe the same measure, a prolix and slender thread would be spun through many a volume, nor would the patient reader find an adequate reward of instruction or amusement. At every step, as we sink deeper in the decline and fall of the Eastern empire, the annals of each succeeding reign would impose a more ungrateful and melancholy task. These annals must continue to repeat a tedious and uniform tale of weakness and misery; the natural connection of causes and events would be broken by frequent and hasty transitions, and a minute accumulation of circumstances must destroy the light and effect of those general pictures which compose the use and ornament of a remote history. From the time of Heraclius the Byzantine theatre is contracted and darkened: the line of empire, which had been defined by the laws of Justinian and the arms of Belisarius, recedes on all sides from our view; the Roman name, the proper subject of our inquiries, is reduced to a narrow corner of Europe, to the lonely suburbs of Constantinople; and the fate of the Greek empire has been compared to that of the Rhine, which loses itself in the sands before its waters can mingle with the ocean. The scale of dominion is diminished to our view by the distance of time and place; nor is the loss of external splendour compensated by the nobler gifts of virtue and genius. In the last moments of her decay Constantinople was doubtless more opulent and populous than Athens at her most flourishing era, when a scanty sum of six thousand talents, or twelve hundred thousand pounds sterling, was possessed by twenty-one thousand male citizens of an adult age. But each of these citizens was a freeman who dared to assert the liberty of his thoughts, words, and actions; whose person and property were guarded by equal law; and who exercised his independent vote in the government of the republic. Their numbers seem to be multiplied by the strong and various discriminations of character; under the shield of freedom, on the wings of emulation and vanity, each Athenian aspired to the level of the national dignity; from this commanding eminence some chosen spirits soared beyond the reach of a vulgar eye; and the chances of superior merit in a great and populous kingdom, as they are proved by experience, would excuse the computation of imaginary millions. The territories of Athens, Sparta, and their allies, do not exceed a moderate province of France or England; but after the trophies of Salamis and Platæa, they expand in our fancy to the gigantic size of Asia, which had been trampled under the feet of the victorious Greeks. But the subjects of the Byzantine empire, who assume and dishonour the names both of Greeks and Romans, present a dead uniformity of abject vices, which are neither softened by the weakness of humanity nor animated by the vigour of memorable crimes. The freemen of antiquity might repeat with generous enthusiasm the sentence of Homer, "that on the first day of his servitude the captive is deprived of one half of his manly virtue." But the poet had only seen the effects of civil or domestic slavery, nor could he foretell that the second moiety of manhood must be annihilated by the spiritual despotism, which shackles not only the actions but even the thoughts of the prostrate votary. By this double yoke the Greeks were oppressed under the successors of Heraclius; the tyrant, a law of eternal justice, was degraded by the vices of his subjects; and on the throne, in the camp, in the schools, we search, perhaps with fruitless diligence, the names and characters that may deserve to be rescued from oblivion. Nor are the defects of the subject compensated by the skill and variety of the painters. Of a space of eight hundred years, the four first centuries are overspread with a cloud interrupted by some faint and broken rays of historic light: in the lives of the emperors, from Maurice to Alexius, Basil the Macedonian has alone been the theme of a separate work; and the absence, or loss, or imperfection of contemporary evidence, must be poorly supplied by the doubtful authority of more recent compilers. The four last centuries are exempt from the reproach of penury; and with the Comnenian family the historic muse of Constantinople again revives, but her apparel is gaudy, her motions are without elegance or grace. A succession of priests, or courtiers, treads in each other's footsteps in the same path of servitude and superstition: their views are narrow, their judgment is feeble or corrupt: and we close the volume of copious barrenness, still ignorant of the causes of events, the characters of the actors, and the manners of the times, which they celebrate or deplore. The observation which has been applied to a man may be extended to a whole people, that the energy of the sword is communicated to the pen; and it will be found by experience that the tone of history will rise or fall with the spirit of the age.

From these considerations I should have abandoned without regret the Greek slaves and their servile historians, had I not reflected the fate of the Byzantine monarchy is *passively* connected with the most splendid and important revolutions which have changed the state of the world. The space of the lost provinces was immediately replenished with new colonies and rising kingdoms: the active virtues of peace and war deserted from the vanquished to the victorious nations; and it is in their origin and conquests, in their religion and government, that we must explore the causes and effects of the decline and fall of the Eastern empire. Nor will this scope of narrative, the riches and variety of these materials, be incompatible with the unity of design and composition. As, in his daily prayers, the Musulman of Fez or Delhi still turns his face towards the temple of Mecca, the historian's eye shall be always fixed on the city of Constantinople. The excursive line may embrace the wilds of Arabia and Tartary, but the circle will be ultimately reduced to the decreasing limit of the Roman monarchy.

On this principle I shall now establish the plan of the

last two volumes of the present work. The first chapter
will contain, in a regular series, the emperors who reigned
at Constantinople during a period of six hundred years,
from the days of Heraclius to the Latin conquest: a rapid
abstract, which may be supported by a *general* appeal
to the order and text of the original historians. In this
introduction I shall confine myself to the revolutions of
the throne, the succession of families, the personal characters of the Greek princes, the mode of their life and
death, the maxims and influence of their domestic government, and the tendency of their reign to accelerate or
suspend the downfall of the Eastern empire. Such a
chronological review will serve to illustrate the various
argument of the subsequent chapters; and each circumstance of the eventful story of the barbarians will adapt
itself in a proper place to the Byzantine annals. The
internal state of the empire, and the dangerous heresy
of the Paulicians, which shook the East and enlightened
the West, will be the subject of two separate chapters;
but these inquiries must be postponed till our farther
progress shall have opened the view of the world in the
ninth and tenth centuries of the Christian era. After this
foundation of Byzantine history, the following nations
will pass before our eyes, and each will occupy the space
to which it may be entitled by greatness or merit, or the
degree of connection with the Roman world and the
present age. I. The FRANKS; a general appellation which
includes all the barbarians of France, Italy, and Germany,
who were united by the sword and sceptre of Charlemagne. The persecution of images and their votaries
separated Rome and Italy from the Byzantine throne, and
prepared the restoration of the Roman empire in the
West. II. The ARABS or SARACENS. Three ample chapters
will be devoted to this curious and interesting object. In
the first, after a picture of the country and its inhabitants, I shall investigate the character of Mohammed; the
character, religion, and success of the prophet. In the
second I shall lead the Arabs to the conquest of Syria,

Egypt, and Africa, the provinces of the Roman empire; nor can I check their victorious career till they have overthrown the monarchies of Persia and Spain. In the third I shall inquire how Constantinople and Europe were saved by the luxury and arts, the division and decay, of the empire of the caliphs. A single chapter will include, III. The BULGARIANS, IV. HUNGARIANS, and V. RUSSIANS, who assaulted by sea or by land the provinces and the capital; but the last of these, so important in their present greatness, will excite some curiosity in their origin and infancy. VI. The NORMANS; or rather the private adventurers of that warlike people, who founded a powerful kingdom in Apulia and Sicily, shook the throne of Constantinople, displayed the trophies of chivalry, and almost realised the wonders of romance. VII. The LATINS; the subjects of the pope, the nations of the West, who enlisted under the banner of the cross for the recovery or relief of the holy sepulchre. The Greek emperors were terrified and preserved by the myriads of pilgrims who marched to Jerusalem with Godfrey of Bouillon and the peers of Christendom. The second and third crusades trod in the footsteps of the first: Asia and Europe were mingled in a sacred war of two hundred years; and the Christian powers were bravely resisted and finally expelled by Saladin and the Mamalukes of Egypt. In these memorable crusades a fleet and army of French and Venetians were diverted from Syria to the Thracian Bosphorus: they assaulted the capital, they subverted the Greek monarchy: and a dynasty of Latin princes was seated near threescore years on the throne of Constantine. VIII. The GREEKS themselves, during this period of captivity and exile, must be considered as a foreign nation; the enemies, and again the sovereigns of Constantinople. Misfortune had rekindled a spark of national virtue; and the Imperial series may be continued with some dignity from their restoration to the Turkish conquest. IX. The MOGULS and TARTARS. By the arms of Zingis and his descendants the globe was shaken from China to Poland and Greece: the sultans were overthrown: the caliphs fell, and the Cæsars trembled on their throne. The victories of Timour suspended above fifty years the final ruin of the Byzantine empire. X. I have already noticed the first appearance of the TURKS; and the names of the fathers, of *Seljuk* and *Othman*, discriminate the two successive dynasties of the nation which emerged in the eleventh century from the Scythian wilderness. The former established a potent and splendid kingdom from the banks of the Oxus to Antioch and Nice; and the first crusade was provoked by the violation of Jerusalem and the danger of Constantinople. From a humble origin the *Ottomans* arose the scourge and terror of Christendom. Constantinople was besieged and taken by Mohammed II., and his triumph annihilates the remnant, the image, the title, of the Roman empire in the East. The schism of the Greeks will be connected with their last calamities and the restoration of learning in the Western world. I shall return from the captivity of the new to the ruins of ancient ROME; and the venerable name, the interesting theme, will shed a ray of glory on the conclusion of my labours.

CHAPTER XVIII

MOHAMMED

Gibbon's "three ample chapters" on the Arab conquests are his chapters L-LII. In chapter L he describes the career of Mohammed (569–632) and the establishment of the Moslem power in Arabia.

AFTER pursuing above six hundred years the fleeting Cæsars of Constantinople and Germany, I now descend, in the reign of Heraclius, on the eastern borders of the Greek monarchy. While the state was exhausted by the Persian war, and the church was distracted by the Nestorian and Monophysite sects, Mohammed, with the sword in one hand and the Koran in the other, erected his throne on the ruins of Christianity and of Rome. The genius of the Arabian prophet, the manners of his nation, and the spirit of his religion, involve the causes of the decline and fall of the Eastern empire; and our eyes are curiously intent on one of the most memorable revolutions which have impressed a new and lasting character on the nations of the globe.[1]

In the vacant space between Persia, Syria, Egypt, and Æthopia, the Arabian peninsular may be conceived as a triangle of spacious but irregular dimensions. From the northern point of Beles, on the Euphrates, a line of fifteen hundred miles is terminated by the Straits of Babelman-

[1]As in this and the following chapter I shall display much Arabic learning, I must profess my total ignorance of the Oriental tongues, and my gratitude to the learned interpreters, who have transfused their science into the Latin, French, and English languages.

deb and the land of frankincense. About half this length
may be allowed for the middle breadth, from east to west,
from Bassora to Suez, from the Persian Gulf to the Red
Sea. The sides of the triangle are gradually enlarged, and
the southern basis presents a front of a thousand miles
to the Indian Ocean. The entire surface of the peninsula
exceeds in a fourfold proportion that of Germany or
France; but the far greater part has been justly stigmatised with the epithets of the *stony* and the *sandy*.
Even the wilds of Tartary are decked, by the hand of
nature, with lofty trees and luxuriant herbage; and the
lonesome traveller derives a sort of comfort and society
from the presence of vegetable life. But in the dreary
waste of Arabia a boundless level of sand is intersected
by sharp and naked mountains; and the face of the
desert, without shade or shelter, is scorched by the direct
and intense rays of a tropical sun. Instead of refreshing
breezes, the winds, particularly from the south-west,
diffuse a noxious and even deadly vapour; the hillocks
of sand which they alternately raise and scatter are
compared to the billows of the ocean, and whole caravans,
whole armies, have been lost and buried in the whirlwind.
The common benefits of water are an object of desire and
contest; and such is the scarcity of wood, that some art is
requisite to preserve and propagate the element of fire.
Arabia is destitute of navigable rivers, which fertilise the
soil, and convey its produce to the adjacent regions: the
torrents that fall from the hills are imbibed by the thirsty
earth: the rare and hardy plants, the tamarind or the
acacia, that strike their roots into the clefts of the rocks,
are nourished by the dews of the night: a scanty supply
of rain is collected in cisterns and aqueducts: the wells
and springs are the secret treasure of the desert; and the
pilgrim of Mecca, after many a dry and sultry march, is
disgusted by the taste of the waters which have rolled
over a bed of sulphur or salt. Such is the general and
genuine picture of the climate of Arabia. The experience
of evil enhances the value of any local or partial enjoyments. A shady grove, a green pasture, a stream of fresh

water, are sufficient to attract a colony of sedentary Arabs to the fortunate spots which can afford food and refreshment to themselves and their cattle, and which encourages their industry in the cultivation of the palm-tree and the vine. The high lands that border on the Indian Ocean are distinguished by their superior plenty of wood and water: the air is more temperate, the fruits are more delicious, the animals and the human race more numerous: the fertility of the soil invites and rewards the toil of the husbandman; and the peculiar gifts of frankincense and coffee have attracted in different ages the merchants of the world. If it be compared with the rest of the peninsula, this sequestered region may truly deserve the appellation of the *happy;* and the splendid colouring of fancy and fiction has been suggested by contrast and countenanced by distance. It was for this earthly paradise that nature had reserved her choicest favours and her most curious workmanship: the incompatible blessings of luxury and innocence were ascribed to the natives: the soil was impregnated with gold and gems, and both the land and sea were taught to exhale the odours of aromatic sweets. This division of the *sandy*, the *stony*, and the *happy*, so familiar to the Greeks and Latins, is unknown to the Arabians themselves; and it is singular enough, that a country whose language and inhabitants have ever been the same should scarcely retain a vestige of its ancient geography. The maritime districts of *Bahrein* and *Oman* are opposite to the realm of Persia. The kingdom of *Yemen* displays the limits, or at least the situation, of Arabia Felix: the name of *Neged* is extended over the inland space; and the birth of Mohammed has illustrated the province of *Hejaz* along the coast of the Red Sea.

The measure of population is regulated by the means of subsistence; and the inhabitants of this vast peninsula might be out-numbered by the subjects of a fertile and industrious province. Along the shores of the Persian Gulf, of the ocean, and even of the Red Sea, the *Ichthyophagi*, or fish-eaters, continued to wander in quest of their precarious food. In this primitive and abject state, which ill deserves the name of society, the human brute, without arts or laws, almost without sense or language, is poorly distinguished from the rest of the animal creation. Generations and ages might roll away in silent oblivion, and the helpless savage was restrained from multiplying his race by the wants and pursuits which confined his existence to the narrow margin of the sea-coast. But in an early period of antiquity the great body of the Arabs had emerged from this scene of misery; and as the naked wilderness could not maintain a people of hunters, they rose at once to the more secure and plentiful condition of the pastoral life. The same life is uniformly pursued by the roving tribes of the desert; and in the portrait of the modern *Bedoweens* we may trace the features of their ancestors, who, in the age of Moses or Mohammed, dwelt under similar tents, and conducted their horses, and camels, and sheep to the same springs and the same pastures. Our toil is lessened, and our wealth is increased, by our dominion over the useful animals; and the Arabian shepherd had acquired the absolute possession of a faithful friend and a laborious slave.[2] Arabia, in the opinion of the naturalist, is the genuine and original country of the *horse;* the climate most propitious, not indeed to the size, but to the spirit and swiftness, of that generous animal. The merit of the Barb, the Spanish, and the English breed is derived from a mixture of Arabian blood:[3] the Bedoweens preserve, with superstitious care, the honours and the memory of the purest race: the males are sold at a high price, but the females are seldom alienated; and the birth of a noble foal was esteemed among the tribes as a subject of joy

[2] Read (it is no unpleasing task) the incomparable articles on the *Horse* and the *Camel*, in the Natural History of M. de Buffon.

[3] For the Arabian horses, see D'Arvieux (p. 159–173) and Niebuhr (p. 142–144). At the end of the thirteenth century the horses of Neged were esteemed sure-footed, those of Yemen strong and serviceable, those of Hejaz most noble. The horses of Europe, the tenth and last class, were generally despised as having too much body and too little spirit (D'Herbelot, Biblioth. Orient. p. 339): their strength was requisite to bear the weight of the knight and his armour.

and mutual congratulation. These horses are educated in
the tents, among the children of the Arabs, with a tender
familiarity, which trains them in the habits of gentleness
and attachment. They are accustomed only to walk and
to gallop: their sensations are not blunted by the incessant abuse of the spur and the whip: their powers are
reserved for the moments of flight and pursuit: but no
sooner do they feel the touch of the hand or the stirrup,
than they dart away with the swiftness of the wind; and
if their friend be dismounted in the rapid career, they
instantly stop till he has recovered his seat. In the sands
of Africa and Arabia the *camel* is a sacred and precious
gift. That strong and patient beast of burden can perform, without eating or drinking, a journey of several
days; and a reservoir of fresh water is preserved in a
large bag, a fifth stomach of the animal, whose body is
imprinted with the marks of servitude: the larger breed
is capable of transporting a weight of a thousand pounds;
and the dromedary, of a lighter and more active frame,
outstrips the fleetest courser in the race. Alive or dead,
almost every part of the camel is serviceable to man:
her milk is plentiful and nutritious: the young and tender
flesh has the taste of veal: a valuable salt is extracted
from the urine: the dung supplies the deficiency of fuel;
and the long hair, which falls each year and is renewed,
is coarsely manufactured into the garments, the furniture, and the tents of the Bedoweens. In the rainy seasons
they consume the rare and insufficient herbage of the
desert: during the heats of summer and the scarcity of
winter they remove their encampments to the sea-coast,
the hills of Yemen, or the neighbourhood of the Euphrates, and have often extorted the dangerous licence of
visiting the banks of the Nile and the villages of Syria
and Palestine. The life of a wandering Arab is a life of
danger and distress; and though sometimes, by rapine
or exchange, he may appropriate the fruits of industry,
a private citizen in Europe is in the possession of more
solid and pleasing luxury than the proudest emir who
marches in the field at the head of ten thousand horse.

Yet an essential difference may be found between the hordes of Scythia and the Arabian tribes; since many of the latter were collected into towns, and employed in the labours of trade and agriculture. A part of their time and industry was still devoted to the management of their cattle: they mingled, in peace and war, with their brethren of the desert; and the Bedoweens derived from their useful intercourse some supply of their wants, and some rudiments of art and knowledge. Among the forty-two cities of Arabia, enumerated by Abulfeda, the most ancient and populous were situate in the *happy* Yemen: the towers of Saana, and the marvellous reservoir of Merab, were constructed by the kings of the Homerites; but their profane lustre was eclipsed by the prophetic glories of MEDINA and MECCA, near the Red Sea, and at the distance from each other of two hundred and seventy miles. The last of these holy places was known to the Greeks under the name of Macoraba; and the termination of the word is expressive of its greatness, which has not indeed, in the most flourishing period, exceeded the size and populousness of Marseilles. Some latent motive, perhaps of superstition, must have impelled the founders in the choice of a most unpromising situation. They erected their habitations of mud or stone in a plain about two miles long and one mile broad, at the foot of three barren mountains: the soil is a rock; the water even of the holy well of Zemzem is bitter or brackish; the pastures are remote from the city; and grapes are transported above seventy miles from the gardens of Tayef. The fame and spirit of the Koreishites, who reigned in Mecca, were conspicuous among the Arabian tribes; but their ungrateful soil refused the labours of agriculture, and their position was favourable to the enterprises of trade. By the seaport of Gedda, at the distance only of forty miles, they maintained an easy correspondence with Abyssinia; and that Christian kingdom afforded the first refuge to the disciples of Mohammed. The treasures of Africa were conveyed over the peninsula to Gerrha or Katif, in the province of Bahrein, a city built, as it is said, of rock-salt, by the Chaldæan exiles; and from thence, with the native pearls of the Persian Gulf, they were floated on rafts to the mouth of the Euphrates. Mecca is placed almost at an equal distance, a month's journey, between Yemen on the right and Syria on the left hand. The former was the winter, the latter the summer, station of her caravans; and their seasonable arrival relieved the ships of India from the tedious and troublesome navigation of the Red Sea. In the markets of Saana and Merab, in the harbours of Oman and Aden, the camels of the Koreishites were laden with a precious cargo of aromatics; a supply of corn and manufactures was purchased in the fairs of Bostra and Damascus; the lucrative exchange diffused plenty and riches in the streets of Mecca; and the noblest of her sons united the love of arms with the profession of merchandise.

The perpetual independence of the Arabs has been the theme of praise among strangers and natives; and the arts of controversy transform this singular event into a prophecy and a miracle in favour of the posterity of Ismael. Some exceptions, that can neither be dissembled nor eluded, render this mode of reasoning as indiscreet as it is superfluous; the kingdom of Yemen has been successively subdued by the Abyssinians, the Persians, the sultans of Egypt, and the Turks: the holy cities of Mecca and Medina have repeatedly bowed under a Scythian tyrant; and the Roman province of Arabia embraced the peculiar wilderness in which Ismael and his sons must have pitched their tents in the face of their brethren. Yet these exceptions are temporary or local; the body of the nation has escaped the yoke of the most powerful monarchies: the arms of Sesostris and Cyrus, of Pompey and Trajan, could never achieve the conquest of Arabia; the present sovereign of the Turks may exercise a shadow of jurisdiction, but his pride is reduced to solicit the friendship of a people whom it is dangerous to provoke and fruitless to attack. The obvious causes of their freedom are inscribed on the character and country of the Arabs. Many ages before Mohammed, their intrepid valour had been severely felt by their neighbours in offensive and defensive war. The patient and active virtues of a soldier are insensibly nursed in the habits and discipline of a pastoral life. The care of the sheep and camels is abandoned to the women of the tribe; but the martial youth, under the banner of the emir, is ever on horseback, and in the field, to practise the exercise of the bow, the javelin, and the scymetar. The long memory of their independence is the firmest pledge of its perpetuity, and succeeding generations are animated to prove their descent and to maintain their inheritance. Their domestic feuds are suspended on the approach of a common enemy; and in their last hostilities against the Turks, the caravan of Mecca was attacked and pillaged by fourscore thousand of the confederates. When they advance to battle, the hope of victory is in the front; in the rear, the assurance of a retreat. Their horses and camels, who in eight or ten days can perform a march of four or five hundred miles, disappear before the conqueror; the secret waters of the desert elude his search; and his victorious troops are consumed with thirst, hunger, and fatigue in the pursuit of an invisible foe, who scorns his efforts, and safely reposes in the heart of the burning solitude. The arms and deserts of the Bedoweens are not only the safeguards of their own freedom, but the barriers also of the happy Arabia, whose inhabitants, remote from war, are enervated by the luxury of the soil and climate. The legions of Augustus melted away in disease and lassitude; and it is only by a naval power that the reduction of Yemen has been successfully attempted. When Mohammed erected his holy standard, that kingdom was a province of the Persian empire; yet seven princes of the Homerites still reigned in the mountains; and the viceregent of Chosroes was tempted to forget his distant country and his unfortunate master. The historians of the age of Justinian represent the state of the independent Arabs, who were divided by interest or affection in the long quarrel of the East: the tribe of *Gassan* was allowed to encamp on the Syrian territory:

the princes of *Hira* were permitted to form a city about
forty miles to the southward of the ruins of Babylon.
Their service in the field was speedy and vigorous; but
their friendship was venal, their faith inconstant, their
enmity capricious: it was an easier task to excite than to
disarm these roving barbarians; and, in the familiar
intercourse of war, they learned to see and despise the
splendid weakness both of Rome and of Persia. From
Mecca to the Euphrates, the Arabian tribes were confounded by the Greeks and Latins under the general
appellation of SARACENS, a name which every Christian
mouth has been taught to pronounce with terror and
abhorrence.

The slaves of domestic tyranny may vainly exult in
their national independence: but the Arab is personally
free; and he enjoys, in some degree, the benefits of
society, without forfeiting the prerogatives of nature. In
every tribe, superstition, or gratitude, or fortune has
exalted a particular family above the heads of their
equals. The dignities of sheick and emir invariably
descend in this chosen race; but the order of succession
is loose and precarious; and the most worthy or aged of
the noble kinsmen are preferred to the simple though
important office of composing disputes by their advice,
and guiding valour by their example. Even a female of
sense and spirit has been permitted to command the
countrymen of Zenobia. The momentary junction of
several tribes produces an army: their more lasting union
constitutes a nation: and the supreme chief, the emir of
emirs, whose banner is displayed at their head, may
deserve, in the eyes of strangers, the honours of the
kingly name. If the Arabian princes abuse their power,
they are quickly punished by the desertion of their subjects, who had been accustomed to a mild and parental
jurisdiction. Their spirit is free, their steps are uncon-
fined, the desert is open, and the tribes and families are
held together by a mutual and voluntary compact. The
softer natives of Yemen supported the pomp and majesty

of a monarch; but if he could not leave his palace without endangering his life, the active powers of government must have been devolved on his nobles and magistrates. The cities of Mecca and Medina present, in the heart of Asia, the form, or rather the substance, of a commonwealth. The grandfather of Mohammed, and his lineal ancestors, appear in foreign and domestic transactions as the princes of their country; but they reigned, like Pericles at Athens, or the Medici at Florence, by the opinion of their wisdom and integrity; their influence was divided with their patrimony; and the sceptre was transferred from the uncles of the prophet to a younger branch of the tribe of Koreish. On solemn occasions they convened the assembly of the people; and, since mankind must be either compelled or persuaded to obey, the use and reputation of oratory among the ancient Arabs is the clearest evidence of public freedom. But their simple freedom was of a very different cast from the nice and artificial machinery of the Greek and Roman republics, in which each member possessed an undivided share of the civil and political rights of the community. In the more simple state of the Arabs, the nation is free, because each of her sons disdains a base submission to the will of a master. His breast is fortified with the austere virtues of courage, patience, and sobriety; the love of independence prompts him to exercise the habits of self-command; and the fear of dishonour guards him from the meaner apprehension of pain, of danger, and of death. The gravity and firmness of the mind is conspicuous in his outward demeanour: his speech is slow, weighty, and concise; he is seldom provoked to laughter; his only gesture is that of stroking his beard, the venerable symbol of manhood; and the sense of his own importance teaches him to accost his equals without levity, and his superiors without awe. The liberty of the Saracens survived their conquests: the first caliphs indulged the gold and familiar language of their subjects: they ascended the pulpit to persuade and edify the congregation; nor was it before the seat of empire was removed to the Tigris that the Abbassides adopted the proud and pompous ceremonial of the Persian and Byzantine courts.

Before the time of Mohammed, the religion of the Arabs was a worship of the sun, moon and stars, varied by local cults, deformed by human sacrifice, and centralised in Mecca, where the temple and sanctuary of the Caaba was controlled by the tribe of Koreish and served by Mohammed's own family, the Hashemites. But other forms of religion had also penetrated Arabia and were to provide important elements in the amalgam of Mohammedanism.

Arabia was free: the adjacent kingdoms were shaken by the storms of conquest and tyranny, and the persecuted sects fled to the happy land where they might profess what they thought, and practise what they professed. The religions of the Sabians and Magians, of the Jews and Christians, were disseminated from the Persian Gulf to the Red Sea. In a remote period of antiquity Sabianism was diffused over Asia by the science of the Chaldæans and the arms of the Assyrians. From the observations of two thousand years the priests and astronomers of Babylon[4] deduced the eternal laws of nature and providence. They adored the seven gods, or angels, who directed the course of the seven planets and shed their irresistible influence on the earth. The attributes of the seven planets, with the twelve signs of the zodiac, and the twenty-four constellations of the northern and southern hemisphere, were represented by images and talismans; the seven days of the week were dedicated to their respective deities; the Sabians prayed thrice each day; and the temple of the moon at Haran was the term of their pilgrimage. But the flexible genius of their faith

[4]The earliest date of the Chaldæan observations is the year 2234 before Christ. After the conquest of Babylon by Alexander, they were communicated, at the request of Aristotle, to the astronomer Hipparchus. What a moment in the annals of science!

was always ready either to teach or to learn: in the tradition of the creation, the deluge, and the patriarchs, they held a singular agreement with their Jewish captives; they appealed to the secret books of Adam, Seth, and Enoch; and a slight infusion of the Gospel has transformed the last remnant of the Polytheists into the Christians of St. John, in the territory of Bassora. The altars of Babylon were overturned by the Magians; but the injuries of the Sabians were revenged by the sword of Alexander; Persia groaned above five hundred years under a foreign yoke; and the purest disciples of Zoroaster escaped from the contagion of idolatry, and breathed with their adversaries the freedom of the desert. Seven hundred years before the death of Mohammed the Jews were settled in Arabia; and a far greater multitude was expelled from the Holy Land in the wars of Titus and Hadrian. The industrious exiles aspired to liberty and power: they erected synagogues in the cities, and castles in the wilderness; and their Gentile converts were confounded with the children of Israel, whom they resembled in the outward mark of circumcision. The Christian missionaries were still more active and successful: the Catholics asserted their universal reign; the sects whom they oppressed successively retired beyond the limits of the Roman empire; the Marcionites and Manichæans dispersed their *fantastic* opinions and apocryphal gospels; the churches of Yemen, and the princes of Hira and Gassan, were instructed in a purer creed by the Jacobite and Nestorian bishops. The liberty of choice was presented to the tribes: each Arab was free to elect or to compose his private religion; and the rude superstition of his house was mingled with the sublime theology of saints and philosophers. A fundamental article of faith was inculcated by the consent of the learned strangers; the existence of one supreme God, who is exalted above the powers of heaven and earth, but who has often revealed himself to mankind by the ministry of his angels and prophets, and whose grace or justice has interrupted, by seasonable miracles, the order of nature. The most rational of the Arabs acknowledged his power, though they neglected his worship; and it was habit rather than conviction that still attached them to the relics of idolatry. The Jews and Christians were the people of the *Book;* the Bible was already translated into the Arabic language, and the volume of the Old Testament was accepted by the concord of these implacable enemies. In the story of the Hebrew patriarchs the Arabs were pleased to discover the fathers of their nation. They applauded the birth and promises of Ismael; revered the faith and virtue of Abraham; traced his pedigree and their own to the creation of the first man, and imbibed with equal credulity the prodigies of the holy text, and the dreams and traditions of the Jewish rabbis.

The base and plebeian origin of Mohammed is an unskilful calumny of the Christians, who exalt instead of degrading the merit of their adversary. His descent from Ismael was a national privilege or fable; but if the first steps of the pedigree are dark and doubtful, he could produce many generations of pure and genuine nobility: he sprung from the tribe of Koreish and the family of Hashem, the most illustrious of the Arabs, the princes of Mecca, and the hereditary guardians of the Caaba. The grandfather of Mohammed was Abdol Motalleb, the son of Hashem, a wealthy and generous citizen, who relieved the distress of famine with the supplies of commerce. Mecca, which had been fed by the liberality of the father, was saved by the courage of the son. The kingdom of Yemen was subject to the Christian princes of Abyssinia: their vassal Abrahah was provoked by an insult to avenge the honour of the cross; and the holy city was invested by a train of elephants and an army of Africans. A treaty was proposed; and, in the first audience, the grandfather of Mohammed demanded the restitution of his cattle. "And why," said Abrahah, "do you not rather implore my clemency in favour of your temple, which I have threatened to destroy?" "Because," replied the intrepid chief, "the cattle is my own; the Caaba belongs to the gods, and *they* will defend their house from injury and sacrilege." The want of provisions, or the valour of the Koreish, compelled the Abyssinians to a disgraceful retreat: their discomfiture has been adorned with a miraculous flight of birds, who showered down stones on the heads of the infidels; and the deliverance was long commemorated by the era of the elephant. The glory of Abdol Motalleb was crowned with domestic happiness; his life was prolonged to the age of one hundred and ten years; and he became the father of six daughters and thirteen sons. His best beloved Abdallah was the most beautiful and modest of the Arabian youth; and in the first night, when he consummated his marriage with Amina, of the noble race of the Zahrites, two hundred virgins are said to have expired of jealousy and despair. Mohammed, the only son of Abdallah and Amina, was born at Mecca, four years after the death of Justinian, and two months after the defeat of the Abyssinians, whose victory would have introduced into the Caaba the religion of the Christians. In his early infancy he was deprived of his father, his mother, and his grandfather; his uncles were strong and numerous; and, in the division of the inheritance, the orphan's share was reduced to five camels and an Æthiopian maid-servant. At home and abroad, in peace and war, Abu Taleb, the most respectable of his uncles, was the guide and guardian of his youth; in his twenty-fifth year he entered into the service of Cadijah, a rich and noble widow of Mecca, who soon rewarded his fidelity with the gift of her hand and fortune. The marriage contract, in the simple style of antiquity, recites the mutual love of Mohammed and Cadijah; describes him as the most accomplished of the tribe of Koreish; and stipulates a dowry of twelve ounces of gold and twenty camels, which was supplied by the liberality of his uncle. By this alliance the son of Abdallah was restored to the station of his ancestors; and the judicious matron was content with his domestic virtues, till, in the fortieth year of his age, he assumed the title of a prophet, and proclaimed the religion of the Koran.

According to the tradition of his companions, Mohammed was distinguished by the beauty of his person, an outward gift which is seldom despised, except by those to whom it has been refused. Before he spoke, the orator engaged on his side the affections of a public or private audience. They applauded his commanding presence, his majestic aspect, his piercing eye, his gracious smile, his flowing beard, his countenance that painted every sensation of the soul and his gestures that enforced each expression of the tongue. In the familiar offices of life he scrupulously adhered to the grave and ceremonious politeness of his country: his respectful attention to the rich and powerful was dignified by his condescension and affability to the poorest citizens of Mecca: the frankness of his manner concealed the artifice of his views; and the habits of courtesy were imputed to personal friendship or universal benevolence. His memory was capacious and retentive; his wit easy and social; his imagination sublime; his judgment clear, rapid, and decisive. He possessed the courage both of thought and action; and, although his designs might gradually expand with his success, the first idea which he entertained of his divine mission bears the stamp of an original and superior genius. The son of Abdallah was educated in the bosom of the noblest race, in the use of the purest dialect of Arabia; and the fluency of his speech was corrected and enhanced by the practice of discreet and seasonable silence. With these powers of eloquence, Mohammed was an illiterate barbarian: his youth had never been instructed in the arts of reading and writing; the common ignorance exempted him from shame or reproach, but he was reduced to a narrow circle of existence, and deprived of those faithful mirrors which reflect to our mind the minds of sages and heroes. Yet the book of nature and of man was open to his view; and some fancy has been indulged in the political and philosophical observations which are ascribed to the Arabian *traveller*. He compares the nations and the religions of the earth; discovers the weakness of the Persian and Roman monarchies; beholds with pity and indignation the degeneracy of the times; and resolves to unite under one God and one king the invincible spirit and primitive virtues of the Arabs. Our more accurate inquiry will suggest, that, instead of visiting the courts, the camps, the temples of the East, the two journeys of Mohammed into Syria were confined to the fairs of Bostra and Damascus; that he was only thirteen years of age when he accompanied the caravan of his uncle; and that his duty compelled him to return as soon as he had disposed of the merchandise of Cadijah. In these hasty and superficial excursions the eye of genius might discern some objects invisible to his grosser companions; some seeds of knowledge might be cast upon a fruitful soil; but his ignorance of the Syriac language must have checked his curiosity; and I cannot perceive in the life or writings of Mohammed that his prospect was far extended beyond the limits of the Arabian world. From every region of that solitary world the pilgrims of Mecca were annually assembled by the calls of devotion and commerce: in the free concourse of multitudes, a simple citizen, in his native tongue, might study the political state and character of the tribes, the theory and practice of the Jews and Christians. Some useful strangers might be tempted, or forced, to implore the rights of hospitality; and the enemies of Mohammed have named the Jew, the Persian, and the Syrian monk, whom they accuse of lending their secret aid to the composition of the Koran. Conversation enriches the understanding, but solitude is the school of genius; and the uniformity of a work denotes the hand of a single artist. From his earliest youth Mohammed was addicted to religious contemplation; each year, during the month of Ramadan, he withdrew from the world and from the arms of Cadijah: in the cave of Hera, three miles from Mecca, he consulted the spirit of fraud or enthusiasm, whose abode is not in the heavens, but in the mind of the prophet. The faith which, under the name of *Islam*, he preached to his family and nation, is compounded of an eternal truth and a necessary fiction, THAT THERE IS ONLY ONE GOD, AND THAT MOHAMMED IS THE APOSTLE OF GOD.

Gibbon now shows how the corruptions of the other monotheist religions in Arabia—Judaism and Christianity—caused Mohammed to see himself as a reforming prophet in the tradition of the Hebrew prophets and Jesus; how he claimed to have received his message direct from God; and how that message was written down by himself, in the Koran, and elaborated by his disciples. He then returns to the personal history and mission of Mohammed.

The first and most arduous conquests of Mohammed were those of his wife, his servant, his pupil, and his friend; since he presented himself as a prophet to those who were most conversant with his infirmities as a man. Yet Cadijah believed the words, and cherished the glory, of her husband; the obsequious and affectionate Zeid was tempted by the prospect of freedom; the illustrious Ali, the son of Abu Taleb, embraced the sentiments of his cousin with the spirit of a youthful hero; and the wealth, the moderation, the veracity of Abubeker, confirmed the religion of the prophet whom he was destined to succeed. By his persuasion ten of the most respectable citizens of Mecca were introduced to the private lessons of Islam; they yielded to the voice of reason and enthusiasm; they repeated the fundamental creed, "There is but one God, and Mohammed is the apostle of God;" and their faith, even in this life, was rewarded with riches and honours, with the command of armies and the government of kingdoms. Three years were silently employed in the conversion of fourteen proselytes, the first-fruits of his mission; but in the fourth year he assumed the prophetic office, and, resolving to impart to his family the light of divine truth, he prepared a banquet, a lamb, as it is said, and a bowl of milk, for the entertainment of forty guests of the race of Hashem. "Friends and kinsmen," said

459

Mohammed to the assembly, "I offer you, and I alone can offer, the most precious gifts, the treasures of this world and of the world to come. God has commanded me to call you to his service. Who among you will support my burden? Who among you will be my companion and my vizir?" No answer was returned, till the silence of astonishment, and doubt, and contempt was at length broken by the impatient courage of Ali, a youth in the fourteenth year of his age. "O prophet, I am the man: whosoever rises against thee, I will dash out his teeth, tear out his eyes, break his legs, rip up his belly. O prophet, I will be thy vizir over them." Mohammed accepted his offer with transport, and Abu Taleb was ironically exhorted to respect the superior dignity of his son. In a more serious tone, the father of Ali advised his nephew to relinquish his impracticable design. "Spare your remonstrances," replied the intrepid fanatic to his uncle and benefactor; "if they should place the sun on my right hand, and the moon on my left, they should not divert me from my course." He persevered ten years in the exercise of his mission; and the religion which has overspread the East and the West advanced with a slow and painful progress within the walls of Mecca. Yet Mohammed enjoyed the satisfaction of beholding the increase of his infant congregation of Unitarians, who revered him as a prophet, and to whom he seasonably dispensed the spiritual nourishment of the Koran. The number of proselytes may be esteemed by the absence of eighty-three men and eighteen women, who retired to Æthiopia in the seventh year of his mission; and his party was fortified by the timely conversion of his uncle Hamza, and of the fierce and inflexible Omar, who signalised in the cause of Islam the same zeal which he had exerted for its destruction. Nor was the charity of Mohammed confined to the tribe of Koreish, or the precincts of Mecca: on solemn festivals, in the days of pilgrimage, he frequented the Caaba, accosted the strangers of every tribe, and urged, both in private converse and public discourse, the belief and worship of

460

a sole Deity. Conscious of his reason and of his weakness, he asserted the liberty of conscience, and disclaimed the use of religious violence;[5] but he called the Arabs to repentance, and conjured them to remember the ancient idolaters of Ad and Thamud, whom the divine justice had swept away from the face of the earth.

The people of Mecca were hardened in their unbelief by superstition and envy. The elders of the city, the uncles of the prophet, affected to despise the presumption of an orphan, the reformer of his country: the pious orations of Mohammed in the Caaba were answered by the clamours of Abu Taleb. "Citizens and pilgrims, listen not to the tempter, hearken not to his impious novelties. Stand fast in the worship of Al Lâta and Al Uzzah." Yet the son of Abdallah was ever dear to the aged chief: and he protected the fame and person of his nephew against the assaults of the Koreishites, who had long been jealous of the pre-eminence of the family of Hashem. Their malice was coloured with the pretence of religion: in the age of Job the crime of impiety was punished by the Arabian magistrate; and Mohammed was guilty of deserting and denying the national deities. But so loose was the policy of Mecca, that the leaders of the Koreish, instead of accusing a criminal, were compelled to employ the measures of persuasion or violence. They repeatedly addressed Abu Taleb in the style of reproach and menace. "Thy nephew reviles our religion; he accuses our wise forefathers of ignorance and folly; silence him quickly, lest he kindle tumult and discord in the city. If he persevere, we shall draw our swords against him and his adherents, and thou wilt be responsible for the blood of thy fellow-citizens." The weight and moderation of Abu Taleb eluded the violence of religious faction; the most helpless or timid of the disciples retired to Æthiopia, and the prophet withdrew himself to various places of

---

[5] The passages of the Koran in behalf of toleration are strong and numerous. This character alone may generally decide the doubts of the learned, whether a chapter was revealed at Mecca or Medina.

strength in the town and country. As he was still supported by his family, the rest of the tribe of Koreish
engaged themselves to renounce all intercourse with the
children of Hashem—neither to buy nor sell, neither to
marry nor to give in marriage, but to pursue them with
implacable enmity, till they should deliver the person of
Mohammed to the justice of the gods. The decree was
suspended in the Caaba before the eyes of the nation:
the messengers of the Koreish pursued the Musulman
exiles in the heart of Africa; they besieged the prophet
and his most faithful followers, intercepted their water,
and inflamed their mutual animosity by the retaliation
of injuries and insults. A doubtful truce restored the
appearance of concord, till the death of Abu Taleb
abandoned Mohammed to the power of his enemies, at
the moment when he was deprived of his domestic comforts by the loss of his faithful and generous Cadijah.
Abu Sophian, the chief of the branch of Ommiyah, succeeded to the principality of the republic of Mecca. A
zealous votary of the idols, a mortal foe of the line of
Hashem, he convened an assembly of the Koreishites and
their allies to decide the fate of the apostle. His imprisonment might provoke the despair of his enthusiasm; and
the exile of an eloquent and popular fanatic would
diffuse the mischief through the provinces of Arabia.
His death was resolved; and they agreed that a sword
from each tribe should be buried in his heart, to divide
the guilt of his blood, and baffle the vengeance of the
Hashemites. An angel or a spy revealed their conspiracy,
and flight was the only resource of Mohammed. At the
dead of night, accompanied by his friend Abubeker, he
silently escaped from his house; the assassins watched at
the door; but they were deceived by the figure of Ali, who
reposed on the bed, and was covered with the green
vestment, of the apostle. The Koreish respected the piety
of the heroic youth; but some verses of Ali, which are
still extant, exhibit an interesting picture of his anxiety,
his tenderness, and his religious confidence. Three days
Mohammed and his companion were concealed in the

cave of Thor, at the distance of a league from Mecca;
and in the close of each evening they received from the
son and daughter of Abubeker a secret supply of intelligence and food. The diligence of the Koreish explored
every haunt in the neighbourhood of the city: they
arrived at the entrance of the cavern; but the providential
deceit of a spider's web and a pigeon's nest is supposed
to convince them that the place was solitary and inviolate.
"We are only two," said the trembling Abubeker. "There
is a third," replied the prophet; "it is God himself." No
sooner was the pursuit abated than the two fugitives
issued from the rock and mounted their camels: on the
road to Medina they were overtaken by the emissaries of
the Koreish; they redeemed themselves with prayers and
promises from their hands. In this eventful moment the
lance of an Arab might have changed the history of the
world. The flight of the prophet from Mecca to Medina
has fixed the memorable era of the *Hegira*, which, at the
end of twelve centuries, still discriminates the lunar
years of the Mohammedan nations.

The religion of the Koran might have perished in its
cradle had not Medina embraced with faith and reverence the holy outcasts of Mecca. Medina, or the *city*,
known under the name of Yathreb before it was sanctified by the throne of the prophet, was divided between
the tribes of the Charegites and the Awsites, whose
hereditary feud was rekindled by the slightest provocations: two colonies of Jews, who boasted a sacerdotal
race, were their humble allies, and, without converting
the Arabs, they introduced the taste of science and
religion, which distinguished Medina as the city of the
Book. Some of her noblest citizens, in a pilgrimage to the
Caaba, were converted by the preaching of Mohammed;
on their return they diffused the belief of God and his
prophet, and the new alliance was ratified by their deputies in two secret and nocturnal interviews on a hill in
the suburbs of Mecca. In the first, ten Charegites and two
Awsites, united in faith and love, protested, in the name
of their wives, their children and their absent brethren,

that they would for ever profess the creed and observe the precepts of the Koran. The second was a political association, the first vital spark of the empire of the Saracens. Seventy-three men and two women of Medina held a solemn conference with Mohammed, his kinsmen, and his disciples, and pledged themselves to each other by a mutual oath of fidelity. They promised, in the name of the city, that if he should be banished they would receive him as a confederate, obey him as a leader, and defend him to the last extremity, like their wives and children. "But if you are recalled by your country," they asked with a flattering anxiety, "will you not abandon your new allies?" "All things," replied Mohammed, with a smile, "are now common between us; your blood is as my blood, your ruin as my ruin. We are bound to each other by the ties of honour and interest. I am your friend, and the enemy of your foes." "But if we are killed in your service, what," exclaimed the deputies of Medina, "will be our reward?" "PARADISE," replied the prophet. "Stretch forth thy hand." He stretched it forth, and they reiterated the oath of allegiance and fidelity. Their treaty was ratified by the people, who unanimously embraced the profession of Islam; they rejoiced in the exile of the apostle, but they trembled for his safety, and impatiently expected his arrival. After a perilous and rapid journey along the sea-coast, he halted at Koba, two miles from the city, and made his public entry into Medina, sixteen days after his flight from Mecca. Five hundred of the citizens advanced to meet him; he was hailed with acclamations of loyalty and devotion; Mohammed was mounted on a she-camel, an umbrella shaded his head, and a turban was unfurled before him to supply the deficiency of a standard. His bravest disciples, who had been scattered by the storm, assembled round his person; and the equal, though various, merit of the Moslems was distinguished by the names of *Mohagerians* and *Ansars*, the fugitives of Mecca, and the auxiliaries of Medina. To eradicate the seeds of jealousy, Mohammed judiciously coupled his principal followers with the rights and obligations of brethren; and when Ali found himself without a peer, the prophet tenderly declared that *he* would be the companion and brother of the noble youth. The expedient was crowned with success; the holy fraternity was respected in peace and war, and the two parties vied with each other in a generous emulation of courage and fidelity. Once only the concord was slightly ruffled by an accidental quarrel: a patriot of Medina arraigned the insolence of the strangers, but the hint of their expulsion was heard with abhorrence; and his own son most eagerly offered to lay at the apostle's feet the head of his father.

From his establishment at Medina, Mohammed assumed the exercise of the regal and sacerdotal office; and it was impious to appeal from a judge whose decrees were inspired by the divine wisdom. A small portion of ground, the patrimony of two orphans, was acquired by gift or purchase; on that chosen spot he built a house and a mosch, more venerable in their rude simplicity than the palaces and temples of the Assyrian caliphs. His seal of gold, or silver, was inscribed with the apostolic title; when he prayed and preached in the weekly assembly, he leaned against the trunk of a palm tree; and it was long before he indulged himself in the use of a chair or pulpit of rough timber. After a reign of six years fifteen hundred Moslems, in arms and in the field, renewed their oath of allegiance; and their chief repeated the assurance of protection till the death of the last member, or the final dissolution of the party. It was in the same camp that the deputy of Mecca was astonished by the attention of the faithful to the words and looks of the prophet, by the eagerness with which they collected his spittle, a hair that dropped on the ground, the refuse water of his lustrations, as if they participated in some degree of the prophetic virtue. "I have seen," said he, "the Chosroes of Persia and the Cæsar of Rome, but never did I behold a king among his subjects like Mohammed among his companions." The devout fervour of enthusiasm acts with more energy and truth than the cold and formal servility of courts.

In the state of nature every man has a right to defend, by force of arms, his person and his possessions; to repel, or even to prevent, the violence of his enemies, and to extend his hostilities to a reasonable measure of satisfaction and retaliation. In the free society of the Arabs, the duties of subject and citizen imposed a feeble restraint; and Mohammed, in the exercise of a peaceful and benevolent mission, had been despoiled and banished by the injustice of his countrymen. The choice of an independent people had exalted the fugitive of Mecca to the rank of a sovereign; and he was invested with the just prerogative of forming alliances, and of waging offensive or defensive war. The imperfection of human rights was supplied and armed by the plenitude of divine power: the prophet of Medina assumed, in his new revelation, a fiercer and more sanguinary tone, which proves that his former moderation was the effect of weakness: the means of persuasion had been tried, the season of forbearance was elapsed, and he was now commanded to propagate his religion by the sword, to destroy the monuments of idolatry, and, without regarding the sanctity of days or months, to pursue the unbelieving nations of the earth.

> *Mohammed's first military campaigns were against the rulers of Mecca, the Koreish, who were alarmed by the threat to their caravans from the new power in Medina. In three campaigns, called the wars of Bedr, Ohud and the Ditch, Mohammed defeated the Koreish. Then, before attempting the conquest of Mecca, he turned his arms against the accessible Jewish tribes, some of whom had imprudently supported the Koreish.*

The choice of Jerusalem for the first kebla of prayer discovers the early propensity of Mohammed in favour of the Jews; and happy would it have been for their temporal interest had they recognised in the Arabian prophet the hope of Israel and the promised Messiah. Their obstinacy converted his friendship into implacable hatred, with which he pursued that unfortunate people to the last moment of his life; and in the double character of an apostle and a conqueror, his persecution was extended to both worlds. The Kainoka dwelt at Medina under the protection of the city: he seized the occasion of an accidental tumult, and summoned them to embrace his religion or contend with him in battle. "Alas," replied the trembling Jews, "we are ignorant of the use of arms, but we persevere in the faith and worship of our fathers; why wilt thou reduce us to the necessity of a just defence?" The unequal conflict was terminated in fifteen days; and it was with extreme reluctance that Mohammed yielded to the importunity of his allies, and consented to spare the lives of the captives. But their riches were confiscated, their arms became more effectual in the hands of the Musulmans; and a wretched colony of seven hundred exiles was driven with their wives and children to implore a refuge on the confines of Syria. The Nadhirites were more guilty, since they conspired in friendly interview to assassinate the prophet. He besieged their castle, three miles from Medina; but their resolute defence obtained an honourable capitulation; and the garrison, sounding their trumpets and beating their drums, was permitted to depart with the honours of war. The Jews had excited and joined the war of the Koreish: no sooner had the *nations* retired from the *ditch*, than Mohammed, without laying aside his armour, marched on the same day to extirpate the hostile race of the children of Koraidha. After a resistance of twenty-five days they surrendered at discretion. They trusted to the intercession of their old allies of Medina: they could not be ignorant that fanaticism obliterates the feelings of humanity. A venerable elder, to whose judgment they appealed, pronounced the sentence of their death: seven hundred Jews were dragged in chains to the market-place of the city; they descended alive into the grave prepared

for their execution and burial; and the apostle beheld
with an inflexible eye the slaughter of his helpless
enemies. Their sheep and camels were inherited by the
Musulmans: three hundred cuirasses, five hundred pikes,
a thousand lances, composed the most useful portion of
the spoil. Six days' journey to the north-east of Medina,
the ancient and wealthy town of Chaibar was the seat of
the Jewish power in Arabia: the territory, a fertile spot
in the desert, was covered with plantations and cattle,
and protected by eight castles, some of which were
esteemed of impregnable strength. The forces of Mohammed consisted of two hundred horse and fourteen
hundred foot: in the succession of eight regular and
painful sieges they were exposed to danger, and fatigue,
and hunger; and the most undaunted chiefs despaired of
the event. The apostle revived their faith and courage by
the example of Ali, on whom he bestowed the surname
of the Lion of God: perhaps we may believe that a
Hebrew champion of gigantic stature was cloven to the
chest by his irresistible scimitar; but we cannot praise the
modesty of romance, which represents him as tearing
from its hinges the gate of a fortress and wielding the
ponderous buckler in his left hand. After the reduction
of the castles the town of Chaibar submitted to the yoke.
The chief of the tribe was tortured, in the presence of
Mohammed, to force a confession of his hidden treasure:
the industry of the shepherds and husbandmen was
rewarded with a precarious toleration: they were permitted, so long as it should please the conqueror, to
improve their patrimony, in equal shares, for *his*
emolument and their own. Under the reign of Omar, the
Jews of Chaibar were transplanted to Syria; and the
caliph alleged the injunction of his dying master, that
one and the true religion should be professed in his
native land of Arabia.

Five times each day the eyes of Mahammed were
turned towards Mecca, and he was urged by the most
sacred and powerful motives to revisit, as a conqueror,
the city and the temple from whence he had been driven

as an exile. The Caaba was present to his waking and sleeping fancy: an idle dream was translated into vision and prophecy; he unfurled the holy banner; and a rash promise of success too hastily dropped from the lips of the apostle. His march from Medina to Mecca displayed the peaceful and solemn pomp of a pilgrimage: seventy camels, chosen and bedecked for sacrifice, preceded the van; the sacred territory was respected; and the captives were dismissed without ransom to proclaim his clemency and devotion. But no sooner did Mohammed descend into the plain, within a day's journey of the city, than he exclaimed, "They have clothed themselves with the skins of tigers:" the numbers and resolution of the Koreish opposed his progress; and the roving Arabs of the desert might desert or betray a leader whom they had followed for the hopes of spoil. The intrepid fanatic sunk into a cool and cautious politician: he waved in the treaty his title of apostle of God; concluded with the Koreish and their allies a truce of ten years; engaged to restore the fugitives of Mecca who should embrace his religion; and stipulated only, for the ensuing year, the humble privilege of entering the city as a friend, and of remaining three days to accomplish the rites of the pilgrimage. A cloud of shame and sorrow hung on the retreat of the Musulmans, and their disappointment might justly accuse the failure of a prophet who had so often appealed to the evidence of success. The faith and hope of the pilgrims were rekindled by the prospect of Mecca: their swords were sheathed: seven times in the footsteps of the apostle they encompassed the Caaba: the Koreish had retired to the hills, and Mohammed, after the customary sacrifice, evacuated the city on the fourth day. The people was edified by his devotion; the hostile chiefs were awed, or divided, or seduced; and both Caled and Amrou, the future conquerors of Syria and Egypt, most seasonably deserted the sinking cause of idolatry. The power of Mohammed was increased by the submission of the Arabian tribes; ten thousand soldiers were assembled for the conquest of Mecca; and the idolators, the weaker

party, were easily convicted of violating the truce. Enthusiasm and discipline impelled the march, and preserved the secret, till the blaze of ten thousand fires
proclaimed to the astonished Koreish the design, the
approach, and the irresistible force of the enemy. The
haughty Abu Sophian presented the keys of the city;
admired the variety of arms and ensigns that passed before him in review; observed that the son of Abdallah had
acquired a mighty kingdom; and confessed, under the
scimitar of Omar, that he was the apostle of the true God.
The return of Marius and Sylla was stained with the
blood of the Romans: the revenge of Mohammed was
stimulated by religious zeal, and his injured followers
were eager to execute or to prevent the order of a massacre. Instead of indulging their passions and his own,
the victorious exile forgave the guilt, and united the
factions, of Mecca. His troops, in three divisions, marched
into the city: eight-and-twenty of the inhabitants were
slain by the sword of Caled; eleven men and six women
were proscribed by the sentence of Mohammed; but he
blamed the cruelty of his lieutenant; and several of the
most obnoxious victims were indebted for their lives to
his clemency or contempt. The chiefs of the Koreish were
prostrate at his feet. "What mercy can you expect from
the man whom you have wronged?" "We confide in the
generosity of our kinsman." "And you shall not confide in
vain: begone! you are safe, you are free." The people of
Mecca deserved their pardon by the profession of Islam;
and after an exile of seven years, the fugitive missionary
was enthroned as the prince and prophet of his native
country. But the three hundred and sixty idols of the
Caaba were ignominiously broken: the house of God was
purified and adorned: as an example to future times, the
apostle again fulfilled the duties of a pilgrim; and a perpetual law was enacted that no unbeliever should dare to
to set his foot on the territory of the holy city.

The conquest of Mecca determined the faith and
obedience of the Arabian tribes; who, according to the
vicissitudes of fortune, had obeyed, or disregarded, the

eloquence or the arms of the prophet. Indifference for rites and opinions still marks the character of the Bedoweens; and they might accept, as loosely as they hold, the doctrine of the Koran. Yet an obstinate remnant still adhered to the religion and liberty of their ancestors, and the war of Honain derived a proper appellation from the *idols*, whom Mohammed had vowed to destroy, and whom the confederates of Tayef had sworn to defend. Four thousand Pagans advanced with secrecy and speed to surprise the conqueror: they pitied and despised the supine negligence of the Koreish, but they depended on the wishes, and perhaps the aid, of a people who had so lately renounced their gods, and bowed beneath the yoke of their enemy. The banners of Medina and Mecca were displayed by the prophet; a crowd of Bedoweens increased the strength or numbers of the army, and twelve thousand Musulmans entertained a rash and sinful presumption of their invincible strength. They descended without precaution into the valley of Honain: the heights had been occupied by the archers and slingers of the confederates; their numbers were oppressed, their discipline was confounded, their courage was appalled, and the Koreish smiled at their impending destruction. The prophet, on his white mule, was encompassed by the enemies: he attempted to rush against their spears in search of a glorious death: ten of his faithful companions interposed their weapons and their breasts; three of these fell dead at his feet: "O my brethren," he repeatedly cried with sorrow and indignation, "I am the son of Abdallah, I am the apostle of truth! O man, stand fast in the faith! O God, send down thy succour!" His uncle Abbas, who, like the heroes of Homer, excelled in the loudness of his voice, made the valley resound with the recital of the gifts and promises of God: the flying Moslems returned from all sides to the holy standard; and Mohammed observed with pleasure that the furnace was again rekindled: his conduct and example restored the battle, and he animated his victorious troops to inflict a merciless revenge on the authors of their shame. From the field of Honain he marched without delay to the siege of Tayef, sixty miles to the south-east of Mecca, a fortress of strength, whose fertile lands produce the fruits of Syria in the midst of the Arabian desert. A friendly tribe, instructed (I know not how) in the art of sieges, supplied him with a train of battering-rams and military engines, with a body of five hundred artificers. But it was in vain that he offered freedom to the slaves of Tayef; that he violated his own laws by the extirpation of the fruit-trees; that the ground was opened by the miners; that the breach was assaulted by the troops. After a siege of twenty days the prophet sounded a retreat; but he retreated with a song of devout triumph, and affected to pray for the repentance and safety of the unbelieving city. The spoil of this fortunate expedition amounted to six thousand captives, twenty-four thousand camels, forty thousand sheep, and four thousand ounces of silver: a tribe who had fought at Honain redeemed their prisoners by the sacrifice of their idols: but Mohammed compensated the loss by resigning to the soldiers his fifth of the plunder, and wished, for their sake, that he possessed as many head of cattle as there were trees in the province of Tehama. Instead of chastising the disaffection of the Koreish, he endeavoured to cut out their tongues (his own expression), and to secure their attachment, by a superior measure of liberality: Abu Sophian alone was presented with three hundred camels and twenty ounces of silver; and Mecca was sincerely converted to the profitable religion of the Koran.

The *fugitives* and *auxiliaries* complained that they who had borne the burden were neglected in the season of victory. "Alas!" replied their artful leader, "suffer me to conciliate these recent enemies, these doubtful proselytes, by the gift of some perishable goods. To your guard I intrust my life and fortunes. You are the companions of my exile, of my kingdom, of my paradise." He was followed by the deputies of Tayef, who dreaded the repetition of a siege. "Grant us, O apostle of God! a truce of three years with the toleration of our ancient worship." "Not a month, not an hour." "Excuse us at least from the obligation of prayer." "Without prayer religion is of no avail." They submitted in silence: their temples were demolished, and the same sentence of destruction was executed on all the idols of Arabia. His lieutenants, on the shores of the Red Sea, the Ocean, and the Gulf of Persia, were saluted by the acclamations of a faithful people; and the ambassadors who knelt before the throne of Medina were as numerous (says the Arabian proverb) as the dates that fall from the maturity of a palm-tree. The nation submitted to the God and the sceptre of Mohammed: the opprobrious name of tribute was abolished: the spontaneous or reluctant oblations of alms and tithes were applied to the service of religion; and one hundred and fourteen thousand Moslems accompanied the last pilgrimage of the apostle.

When Heraclius returned in triumph from the Persian war, he entertained, at Emesa, one of the ambassadors of Mohammed, who invited the princes and nations of the earth to the profession of Islam. On this foundation the zeal of the Arabians has supposed the secret conversion of the Christian emperor: the vanity of the Greeks has feigned a personal visit of the prince of Medina, who accepted from the royal bounty a rich domain, and a secure retreat, in the province of Syria. But the friendship of Heraclius and Mohammed was of short continuance: the new religion had inflamed rather than assuaged the rapacious spirit of the Saracens; and the murder of an envoy afforded a decent pretence for invading, with three thousand soldiers, the territory of Palestine, that extends to the eastward of the Jordan. The holy banner was intrusted to Zeid; and such was the discipline or enthusiasm of the rising sect, that the noblest chiefs served without reluctance under the slave of the prophet. On the event of his decease, Jaafar and Abdallah were successively substituted to the command; and if the three should perish in the war, the troops were authorised to elect their general. The three leaders were slain in the battle of Muta, the first military action which tried the valour of the Moslems against a foreign enemy. Zeid fell, like a soldier, in the foremost ranks: the death of Jaafar was heroic and memorable: he lost his right hand: he shifted the standard to his left: the left was severed from his body: he embraced the standard with his bleeding stumps, till he was transfixed to the ground with fifty honourable wounds. "Advance," cried Abdallah, who stepped into the vacant place, "advance with confidence: either victory or paradise is our own." The lance of a Roman decided the alternative; but the falling standard was rescued by Caled, the proselyte of Mecca: nine swords were broken in his hand; and his valour withstood and repulsed the superior numbers of the Christians. In the nocturnal council of the camp he was chosen to command: his skilful evolutions of the ensuing day secured either the victory or the retreat of the Saracens; and Caled is renowned among his brethren and his enemies by the glorious appellation of the *Sword of God*. In the pulpit, Mohammed described, with prophetic rapture, the crowns of the blessed martyrs; but in private he betrayed the feelings of human nature: he was surprised as he wept over the daughter of Zeid: "What do I see?" said the astonished votary. "You see," replied the apostle, "a friend who is deploring the loss of his most faithful friend." After the conquest of Mecca the sovereign of Arabia affected to prevent the hostile preparations of Heraclius; and solemnly proclaimed war against the Romans, without attempting to disguise the hardships and dangers of the enterprise. The Moslems were discouraged: they alleged the want of money, or horses, or provisions; the season of harvest, and the intolerable heat of the summer: "Hell is much hotter," said the indignant prophet. He disdained to compel their service: but on his return he admonished the most guilty, by an excommunication of fifty days. Their desertion enhanced the merit of Abubeker, Othman, and the faithful companions who devoted their lives and fortunes; and Mohammed displayed his banner at the head of ten thousand horse and twenty thousand foot. Painful indeed was the distress of the march: lassitude and thirst were aggravated by the scorching and pestilential winds of the desert: ten men rode by turns on the same camel; and they were reduced to the shameful necessity of drinking the water from the belly of that useful animal. In the mid-way, ten days' journey from Medina and Damascus, they reposed near the grove and fountain of Tabuc. Beyond that place Mohammed declined the prosecution of the war: he declared himself satisfied with the peaceful intentions, he was more probably daunted by the martial array, of the emperor of the East. But the active and intrepid Caled spread around the terror of his name; and the prophet received the submission of the tribes and cities, from the Euphrates to Ailah, at the head of the Red Sea. To his Christian subjects Mohammed readily granted the security of their persons, the freedom of their trade, the property of their goods, and the toleration of their worship. The weakness of their Arabian brethren had restrained them from opposing his ambition; the disciples of Jesus were endeared to the enemy of the Jews; and it was the interest of a conqueror to propose a fair capitulation to the most powerful religion of the earth.

Till the age of sixty-three years the strength of Mohammed was equal to the temporal and spiritual fatigues of his mission. His epileptic fits, an absurd calumny of the Greeks, would be an object of pity rather than abhorrence; but he seriously believed that he was poisoned at Chaibar by the revenge of a Jewish female. During four years the health of the prophet declined; his infirmities increased; but his mortal disease was a fever of fourteen days, which deprived him by intervals of the use of reason. As soon as he was conscious of his danger, he edified his brethren by the humility of his virtue or penitence. "If there be any man," said the apostle from the pulpit, "whom I have unjustly scourged, I submit my own back to the lash of retaliation. Have I aspersed the reputation of a Musulman? let him proclaim *my* faults in the face of the congregation. Has any one been despoiled of his goods? the little that I possess shall compensate the principal and the interest of the debt." "Yes," replied a voice from the crowd, "I am entitled to three drachms of silver." Mohammed heard the complaint, satisfied the demand, and thanked his creditor for accusing him in this world rather than at the day of judgment. He beheld with temperate firmness the approach of death; enfranchised his slaves (seventeen men, as they are named, and eleven women); minutely directed the order of his funeral; and moderated the lamentations of his weeping friends, on whom he bestowed the benediction of peace. Till the third day before his death he regularly performed the function of public prayer: the choice of Abubeker to supply his place appeared to mark that ancient and faithful friend as his successor in the sacerdotal and regal office; but he prudently declined the risk and envy of a more explicit nomination. At a moment when his faculties were visibly impaired, he called for pen and ink to write, or, more properly, to dictate, a divine book, the sum and accomplishment of all his revelations: a dispute arose in the chamber whether he should be allowed to supersede the authority of the Koran; and the prophet was forced to reprove the indecent vehemence of his disciples. If the slightest credit may be afforded to the tradition of his wives and companions, he maintained, in the bosom of his family, and to the last moments of his life, the dignity of an apostle, and the faith of an enthusiast; described the visits of Gabriel, who bid an everlasting farewell to the earth; and expressed his lively confidence, not only of the mercy, but of the favour, of the Supreme Being. In a familiar discourse he had mentioned his special prerogative, that the angel of death was not allowed to take his soul till he had respectfully asked the permission of the prophet. The request was granted; and Mohammed immediately fell into the agony of his dissolution: his head was reclined on the lap of Ayesha, the best beloved of all his wives; he fainted with the violence of pain; recovering his spirits, he raised his eyes towards the roof of the house, and, with a steady look, though a faltering voice, uttered the last broken, though articulate words: "O God! . . . pardon my sins. . . . Yes

476

. . . I come . . . among my fellow citizens on high;" and thus peaceably expired on a carpet spread upon the floor. An expedition for the conquest of Syria was stopped by this mournful event: the army halted at the gates of Medina; the chiefs were assembled round their dying master. The city, more especially the house, of the prophet, was a scene of clamorous sorrow or silent despair: fanaticism alone could suggest a ray of hope and consolation. "How can he be dead, our witness, our intercessor, our mediator, with God? By God he is not dead: like Moses and Jesus, he is wrapt in a holy trance, and speedily will he return to his faithful people." The evidence of sense was disregarded; and Omar, unsheathing his scimitar, threatened to strike off the heads of the infidels who should dare to affirm that the prophet was no more. The tumult was appeased by the weight and moderation of Abubeker. "Is it Mohammed," said he to Omar and the multitude, "or the God of Mohammed, whom you worship? The God of Mohammed liveth for ever; but the apostle was a mortal like ourselves, and, according to his own prediction, he has experienced the common fate of mortality." He was piously interred by the hands of his nearest kinsman, on the same spot on which he expired: Medina has been sanctified by the death and burial of Mohammed; and the innumerable pilgrims of Mecca often turn aside from the way, to bow, in voluntary devotion, before the simple tomb of the prophet.

At the conclusion of the life of Mohammed it may perhaps be expected that I should balance his faults and virtues, that I should decide whether the title of enthusiast or impostor more properly belongs to that extraordinary man. Had I been intimately conversant with the son of Abdallah, the task would still be difficult, and the success uncertain: at the distance of twelve centuries I darkly contemplate his shade through a cloud of religious incense; and could I truly delineate the portrait of an hour, the fleeting resemblance would not equally apply to the solitary of Mount Hera, to the preacher of Mecca, and to the conqueror of Arabia. The author of a mighty revolution appears to have been endowed with a pious and contemplative disposition: so soon as marriage had raised him above the pressure of want, he avoided the paths of ambition and avarice; and till the age of forty he lived with innocence, and would have died without a name. The unity of God is an idea most congenial to nature and reason; and a slight conversation with the Jews and Christians would teach him to despise and detest the idolatry of Mecca. It was the duty of a man and a citizen to impart the doctrine of salvation, to rescue his country from the dominion of sin and error. The energy of a mind incessantly bent on the same object would convert a general obligation into a particular call; the warm suggestions of the understanding or the fancy would be felt as the inspirations of Heaven; the labour of thought would expire in rapture and vision; and the inward sensation, the invisible monitor, would be described with the form and attributes of an angel of God. From enthusiasm to imposture the step is perilous and slippery; the demon of Socrates affords a memorable instance how a wise man may deceive himself, how a good man may deceive others, how the conscience may slumber in a mixed and middle state between self-illusion and voluntary fraud. Charity may believe that the original motives of Mohammed were those of pure and genuine benevolence; but a human missionary is incapable of cherishing the obstinate unbelievers who reject his claims, despise his arguments, and persecute his life; he might forgive his personal adversaries, he may lawfully hate the enemies of God; the stern passions of pride and revenge were kindled in the bosom of Mohammed, and he sighed, like the prophet of Nineveh, for the destruction of the rebels whom he had condemned. The injustice of Mecca and the choice of Medina transformed the citizen into a prince, the humble preacher into the leader of armies; but his sword was consecrated by the example of the saints; and the same God who afflicts a sinful world with pestilence and earthquakes might inspire for their conversion or chastisement the valour of his servants. In the exercise of political government he was compelled to abate of the stern rigour of fanaticism, to comply in some measure with the prejudices and passions of his followers, and to employ even the vices of mankind as the instruments of their salvation. The use of fraud and perfidy, of cruelty and injustice, were often subservient to the propagation of the faith; and Mohammed commanded or approved the assassination of the Jews and idolaters who had escaped from the field of battle. By the repetition of such acts the character of Mohammed must have been gradually stained; and the influence of such pernicious habits would be poorly compensated by the practice of the personal and social virtues which are necessary to maintain the reputation of a prophet among his sectaries and friends. Of his last years ambition was the ruling passion; and a politician will suspect that he secretly smiled (the victorious impostor!) at the enthusiasm of his youth, and the credulity of his proselytes. A philosopher will observe that *their* credulity and *his* success would tend more strongly to fortify the assurance of his divine mission, that his interest and religion were inseparably connected, and that his conscience would be soothed by the persuasion that he alone was absolved by the Deity from the obligation of positive and moral laws. If he retained any vestige of his native innocence, the sins of Mohammed may be allowed as an evidence of his sincerity. In the support of truth, the arts of fraud and fiction may be deemed less criminal; and he would have started at the foulness of the means, had he not been satisfied of the importance and justice of the end. Even in a conqueror or a priest I can surprise a word or action of unaffected humanity; and the decree of Mohammed, that, in the sale of captives, the mothers should never be separated from their children, may suspend, or moderate, the censure of the historian.

The good sense of Mohammed despised the pomp of royalty; the apostle of God submitted to the menial offices of the family; he kindled the fire, swept the floor, milked the ewes, and mended with his own hands his shoes and his woollen garment. Disdaining the penance and merit of a hermit, he observed, without effort or vanity, the abstemious diet of an Arab and a soldier. On solemn occasions he feasted his companions with rustic and hospitable plenty; but in his domestic life many weeks would elapse without a fire being kindled on the hearth of the prophet. The interdiction of wine was confirmed by his example; his hunger was appeased with a sparing allowance of barley-bread: he delighted in the taste of milk and honey; but his ordinary food consisted of dates and water. Perfumes and women were the two sensual enjoyments which his nature required, and his religion did not forbid; and Mohammed affirmed that the fervour of his devotion was increased by these innocent pleasures. The heat of the climate inflames the blood of the Arabs, and their libidinous complexion has been noticed by the writers of antiquity. Their incontinence was regulated by the civil and religious laws of the Koran: their incestuous alliances were blamed: the boundless licence of polygamy was reduced to four legitimate wives or concubines; their rights both of bed and of dowry were equitably determined; the freedom of divorce was discouraged; adultery was condemned as a capital offence; and fornication, in either sex, was punished with a hundred stripes. Such were the calm and rational precepts of the legislator; but in his private conduct Mohammed indulged the appetites of a man, and abused the claims of a prophet. A special revelation dispensed him from the laws which he had imposed on his nation; the female sex, without reserve, was abandoned to his desires; and this singular prerogative excited the envy rather than the scandal, the veneration rather than the envy, of the devout Musulmans. If we remember the seven hundred wives and three hundred concubines of the wise Solomon, we shall applaud the modesty of the Arabian, who espoused no more than seventeen or fifteen wives; eleven are enumerated who occupied at Medina their separate apartments round the house of the apostle, and enjoyed in their turns the favour of his conjugal society. What is singular enough, they were all widows, excepting only Ayesha, the daughter of Abubeker. *She* was doubtless a virgin, since Mohammed consummated his nuptials (such is the premature ripeness of the climate) when she was only nine years of age. The youth, the beauty, the spirit of Ayesha gave her a superior ascendant: she was beloved and trusted by the prophet; and, after his death, the daughter of Abubeker was long revered as the mother of the faithful. Her behaviour had been ambiguous and indiscreet: in a nocturnal march she was accidentally left behind, and in the morning Ayesha returned to the camp with a man. The temper of Mohammed was inclined to jealousy; but a divine revelation assured him of her innocence: he chastised her accusers, and published a law of domestic peace, that no woman should be condemned unless four male witnesses had seen her in the act of adultery.[6] In his adventures with Zeineb, the wife of Zeid, and with Mary, an Egyptian captive, the amorous prophet forgot the interest of his reputation. At the house of Zeid, his freedman and adopted son, he beheld, in a loose undress, the beauty of Zeineb, and burst forth into an ejaculation of devotion and desire. The servile, or grateful, freedman understood the hint, and yielded without hesitation to the love of his benefactor. But as the filial relation had excited some doubt and scandal, the angel Gabriel descended from heaven to ratify the deed, to annul the adoption, and gently to reprove the apostle for distrusting the indulgence of his God. One of his wives, Hafna, the daughter of Omar, surprised him on her own bed in the embraces of his Egyptian captive: she promised secrecy and forgiveness: he swore that he would renounce the possession of Mary. Both parties forgot their engagements; and Gabriel again descended with a chapter of the Koran to absolve him from his oath, and to exhort him freely to enjoy his captives and concubines without listening to the clamour of his wives. In a solitary retreat of

---

[6] In a memorable case, the Caliph Omar decided that all presumptive evidence was of no avail; and that all the four witnesses must have actually seen *stylum in pyxide*.

thirty days he laboured alone with Mary to fulfil the commands of the angel. When his love and revenge were satiated, he summoned to his presence his eleven wives, reproached their disobedience and indiscretion, and threatened them with a sentence of divorce, both in this world and in the next—a dreadful sentence, since those who had ascended the bed of the prophet were for ever excluded from the hope of a second marriage. Perhaps the incontinence of Mohammed may be palliated by the tradition of his natural or preternatural gifts: he united the manly virtue of thirty of the children of Adam; and the apostle might rival the thirteenth labour of the Grecian Hercules.[7] A more serious and decent excuse may be drawn from his fidelity to Cadijah. During the twenty-four years of their marriage her youthful husband abstained from the right of polygamy, and the pride or tenderness of the venerable matron was never insulted by the society of a rival. After her death he placed her in the rank of the four perfect women, with the sister of Moses, the mother of Jesus, and Fatima, the best beloved of his daughters. "Was she not old?" said Ayesha, with the insolence of a blooming beauty; "has not God given you a better in her place?" "No, by God," said Mohammed, with an effusion of honest gratitude, "there never can be a better! She believed in me when men despised me; she relieved my wants when I was poor and persecuted by the world."

In the largest indulgence of polygamy, the founder of a religion and empire might aspire to multiply the chances of a numerous posterity and a lineal succession. The hopes of Mohammed were fatally disappointed. The virgin Ayesha, and his ten widows of mature age and approved fertility, were barren in his potent embraces. The four sons of Cadijah died in their infancy. Mary, his Egyptian concubine, was endeared to him by the birth of

---

[7] The common and most glorious legend includes, in a single night, the fifty victories of Hercules over the virgin daughters of Thestius. But Athenæus allows seven nights, and Apollodorus fifty, for this arduous achievement of Hercules, who was then no more than eighteen years of age.

Ibrahim. At the end of fifteen months the prophet wept over his grave; but he sustained with firmness the raillery of his enemies, and checked the adulation or credulity of the Moslems by the assurance that an eclipse of the sun was *not* occasioned by the death of the infant. Cadijah had likewise given him four daughters, who were married to the most faithful of his disciples: the three eldest died before their father; but Fatima, who possessed his confidence and love, became the wife of her cousin Ali, and the mother of an illustrious progeny. The merit and misfortunes of Ali and his descendants will lead me to anticipate, in this place, the series of the Saracen caliphs, a title which describes the commanders of the faithful as the vicars and successors of the apostle of God.

After a digression on the life of Ali, and the religious schism caused by the claims of his followers, the Shi'ites, Gibbon summarises the character and achievements of Mohammed.

The talents of Mohammed are entitled to our applause; but his success has, perhaps, too strongly attracted our admiration. Are we surprised that a multitude of proselytes should embrace the doctrine and the passions of an eloquent fanatic? In the heresies of the church the same seduction has been tried and repeated from the time of the apostles to that of the reformers. Does it seem incredible that a private citizen should grasp the sword and the sceptre, subdue his native country, and erect a monarchy by his victorious arms? In the moving picture of the dynasties of the East, a hundred fortunate usurpers have arisen from a baser origin, surmounted more formidable obstacles, and filled a larger scope of empire and conquest. Mohammed was alike instructed to preach and to fight; and the union of these opposite qualities, while it enhanced his merit, contributed to his success: the operation of force and persuasion, of enthusiasm and fear, continually acted on each other, till every barrier yielded to their irresistible power. His voice invited the

Arabs to freedom and victory, to arms and rapine, to the indulgence of their darling passions in this world and the other: the restraints which he imposed were requisite to establish the credit of the prophet, and to exercise the obedience of the people; and the only objection to his success was his rational creed of the unity and perfections of God. It is not the propagation, but the permanancy of his religion, that deserves our wonder: the same pure and perfect impression which he engraved at Mecca and Medina is preserved, after the revolutions of twelve centuries, by the Indian, the African, and the Turkish proselytes of the Koran. If the Christian apostles, St. Peter or St. Paul, could return to the Vatican, they might possibly inquire the name of the Deity who is worshipped with such mysterious rites in that magnificent temple: at Oxford or Geneva they would experience less surprise; but it might still be incumbent on them to peruse the catechism of the church, and to study the orthodox commentators on their own writings and the words of their Master. But the Turkish dome of St. Sophia, with an increase of splendour and size, represents the humble tabernacle erected at Medina by the hands of Mohammed. The Mohammedans have uniformly withstood the temptation of reducing the object of their faith and devotion to a level with the senses and imagination of man. "I believe in one God, and Mohammed the apostle of God," is the simple and invariable profession of Islam. The intellectual image of the Deity has never been degraded by any visible idol; the honours of the prophet have never transgressed the measure of human virtue; and his living precepts have restrained the gratitude of his disciples within the bounds of reason and religion. The votaries of Ali have, indeed, consecrated the memory of their hero, his wife, and his children; and some of the Persian doctors pretend that the divine essence was incarnate in the person of the Imams; but their superstition is universally condemned by the Sonnites; and their impiety has afforded a seasonable warning against the worship of saints and martyrs. The metaphysical questions on the attributes of God, and the liberty of man, have been agitated in the schools of the Mohammedans as well as in those of the Christians; but among the former they have never engaged the passions of the people, or disturbed the tranquillity of the state. The cause of this important difference may be found in the separation or union of the regal and sacerdotal characters. It was the interest of the caliphs, the successors of the prophet and commanders of the faithful, to repress and discourage all religious innovations: the order, the discipline, the temporal and spiritual ambition of the clergy, are unknown to the Moslems; and the sages of the law are the guides of their conscience and the oracles of their faith. From the Atlantic to the Ganges the Koran is acknowledged as the fundamental code, not only of theology but of civil and criminal jurisprudence; and the laws which regulate the actions and the property of mankind are guarded by the infallible and immutable sanction of the will of God. This religious servitude is attended with some practical disadvantage; the illiterate legislator had been often misled by his own prejudices and those of his country; and the institutions of the Arabian desert may be ill adapted to the wealth and numbers of Ispahan and Constantinople. On these occasions the Cadhi respectfully places on his head the holy volume, and substitutes a dexterous interpretation more apposite to the principles of equity and the manners and policy of the times.

His beneficial or pernicious influence on the public happiness is the last consideration in the character of Mohammed. The most bitter or most bigoted of his Christian or Jewish foes will surely allow that he assumed a false commission to inculcate a salutary doctrine, less perfect only than their own. He piously supposed, as the basis of his religion, the truth and sanctity of *their* prior revelations, the virtues and miracles of their founders. The idols of Arabia were broken before the throne of God; the blood of human victims was expiated by prayer, and fasting, and alms, the laudable or innocent arts of devotion; and his rewards and punishments of a future life were painted by the images most congenial to an ignorant and carnal generation. Mohammed was, perhaps, incapable of dictating a moral and political system for the use of his countrymen: but he breathed among the faithful a spirit of charity and friendship; recommended the practice of the social virtues; and checked, by his laws and precepts, the thirst of revenge, and the oppression of widows and orphans. The hostile tribes were united in faith and obedience, and the valour which had been idly spent in domestic quarrels was vigorously directed against a foreign enemy. Had the impulse been less powerful, Arabia, free at home, and formidable abroad, might have flourished under a succession of her native monarchs. Her sovereignty was lost by the extent and rapidity of conquest. The colonies of the nation were scattered over the East and West, and their blood was mingled with the blood of their converts and captives. After the reign of three caliphs, the throne was transported from Medina to the valley of Damascus and the banks of the Tigris; the holy cities were violated by impious war; Arabia was ruled by the rod of a subject, perhaps or a stranger; and the Bedoweens of the desert, awakening from their dream of dominion, resumed their old and solitary independence.

CHAPTER XIX

THE ARAB ATTACK ON EUROPE

Immediately after the death of Mohammed, his successors, the caliphs, or "commanders of the faithful", launched their revolutionary armies simultaneously against the empires of both Persia and Rome. The Persian empire was totally conquered, the Sassanian dynasty ended, the religion of Zoraster replaced by that of Mohammed (632–651). From Rome, the provinces of Syria and Egypt were detached: the emperor Heraclius, who had recovered Jerusalem from the "Great King" Chosroes II, now lost it again to the Caliph Omar. Then the Arabs conquered the whole length of North Africa and by 713 had overthrown the Visigothic monarchy of Spain and occupied the whole Peninsula up to the Pyrenees. They thus stood at the gates of Europe in both the East and the West.

In the East, they had first laid siege to Constantinople in 668–675; they now repeated the attempt (716–718). Both sieges ended in failure. In the West, the Moslems crossed the Pyrenees from 721, and in 732 penetrated France as far as Tours, where they were decisively defeated by Charles Martel, the "mayor of the palace" to the Merovingian king of France. In his fifty-second chapter, Gibbon describes these Arab attempts to break into Europe, and their frustration.

When the Arabs first issued from the desert they must have been surprised at the ease and rapidity of their own success. But when they advanced in the career of victory to the banks of the Indus and the summit of the Pyrenees, when they had repeatedly tried the edge of their scimitars and the energy of their faith, they might be equally astonished that any nation could resist their invincible arms, that any boundary should confine the dominion of the successor of the prophet. The confidence of soldiers and fanatics may indeed be excused, since the calm historian of the present hour, who strives to follow the rapid course of the Saracens, must study to explain by what means the church and state were saved from this impending, and, as it should seem, from this inevitable danger. The deserts of Scythia and Sarmatia might be guarded by their extent, their climate, their poverty, and the courage of the northern shepherds; China was remote and inaccessible; but the greatest part of the temperate zone was subject to the Mohammedan conquerors, the Greeks were exhausted by the calamities of war and the loss of their fairest provinces, and the barbarians of Europe might justly tremble at the precipitate fall of the Gothic monarchy. In this inquiry I shall unfold the events that rescued our ancestors of Britain, and our neighbours of Gaul, from the civil and religious yoke of the Koran; that protected the majesty of Rome, and delayed the servitude of Constantinople; that invigorated the defence of the Christians, and scattered among their enemies the seeds of division and decay.

Forty-six years after the flight of Mohammed from Mecca his disciples appeared in arms under the walls of Constantinople. They were animated by a genuine or fictitious saying of the prophet, that, to the first army which besieged the city of the Cæsars, their sins were forgiven: the long series of Roman triumphs would be meritoriously transferred to the conquerors of New Rome; and the wealth of nations was deposited in this well-chosen seat of royalty and commerce. No sooner had the caliph Moawiyah suppressed his rivals and established his throne, than he aspired to expiate the guilt of civil blood by the success and glory of this holy expedition; his preparations by sea and land were adequate to the importance of the object; his standard was intrusted to Sophian, a veteran warrior, but the troops were encouraged by the example and presence of Yezid, the son and presumptive heir of the commander of the faithful. The Greeks had little to hope, nor had their enemies any reasons of fear, from the courage and vigilance of the reigning emperor, who disgraced the name of Constantine, and imitated only the inglorious years of his grandfather Heraclius. Without delay or opposition, the naval forces of the Saracens passed through the unguarded channel of the Hellespont, which even now, under the feeble and disorderly government of the Turks, is maintained as the natural bulwark of the capital. The Arabian fleet cast anchor, and the troops were disembarked near the palace of Hebdomon, seven miles from the city. During many days, from the dawn of light to the evening, the line of assault was extended from the golden gate to the eastern promontory, and the foremost warriors were impelled by the weight and effort of the succeeding columns. But the besiegers had formed an insufficient estimate of the strength and resources of Constantinople. The solid and lofty walls were guarded by numbers and discipline: the spirit of the Romans was rekindled by the last danger of their religion and empire: the fugitives from the conquered provinces more successfully renewed the defence of Damascus and Alexandria; and the Saracens were dismayed by the strange and prodigious effects of artificial fire. This firm and effectual resistance diverted their arms to the more easy attempts of plundering the European and Asiatic coasts of the Propontis; and, after keeping the sea from the month of April to that of September, on the approach of winter they retreated fourscore miles from the capital, to the isle of Cyzicus, in which they had established their magazine of spoil and provisions. So patient was their perseverance, or so languid were their operations, that they repeated in

the six following summers the same attack and retreat,
with a gradual abatement of hope and vigour, till the
mischances off shipwreck and disease, of the sword and
of fire, compelled them to relinquish the fruitless enterprise. They might bewail the loss, or commemorate the
martyrdom, of thirty thousand Moslems who fell in the
siege of Constantinople; and the solemn funeral of Abu
Ayub, or Job, excited the curiosity of the Christians themselves. That venerable Arab, one of the last of the companions of Mohammed, was numbered among the *ansars*,
or auxiliaries, of Medina, who sheltered the head of the
flying prophet. In his youth he fought, at Beder and
Ohud, under the holy standard: in his mature age he was
the friend and follower of Ali; and the last remnant of his
strength and life was consumed in a distant and dangerous war against the enemies of the Koran. His memory
was revered; but the place of his burial was neglected
and unknown, during a period of seven hundred and
eighty years, till the conquest of Constantinople by
Mohammed the Second. A seasonable vision (for such are
the manufacture of every religion) revealed the holy spot
at the foot of the walls and the bottom of the harbour;
and the mosch of Ayub has been deservedly chosen for
the simple and martial inauguration of the Turkish
sultans.

The event of the siege revived, both in the East and
West, the reputation of the Roman arms, and cast a
momentary shade over the glories of the Saracens. The
Greek ambassador was favourably received at Damascus,
in a general council of the emirs or Koreish: a peace, or
truce, of thirty years was ratified between the two empires; and the stipulation of an annual tribute, fifty
horses of a noble breed, fifty slaves, and three thousand
pieces of gold, degraded the majesty of the command of
the faithful. The aged caliph was desirous of possessing
his dominions, and ending his days, in tranquillity and
repose: while the Moors and Indians trembled at his
name, his palace and city of Damascus was insulted by
the Mardaites, or Maronites, of Mount Libanus, the

firmest barrier of the empire, till they were disarmed and transplanted by the suspicious policy of the Greeks. After the revolt of Arabia and Persia, the house of Ommiyah was reduced to the kingdoms of Syria and Egypt: their distress and fear enforced their compliance with the pressing demands of the Christians; and the tribute was increased to a slave, a horse, and a thousand pieces of gold, for each of the three hundred and sixty-five days of the solar year. But as soon as the empire was again united by the arms and policy of Abdalmalek, he disclaimed a badge of servitude not less injurious to his conscience than to his pride; he discontinued the payment of the tribute; and the resentment of the Greeks was disabled from action by the mad tyranny of the second Justinian, the just rebellion of his subjects, and the frequent change of his antagonists and successors. Till the reign of Abdalmalek the Saracens had been content with the free possession of the Persian and Roman treasures in the coin of Chosroes and Cæsar. By the command of that caliph a national mint was established, both for silver and gold, and the inscription of the Dinar, though it might be censured by some timorous casuists, proclaimed the unity of the God of Mohammed. Under the reign of the caliph Walid, the Greek language and characters were excluded from the accounts of the public revenue. If this change was productive of the invention or familiar use of our present numerals, the Arabic or Indian ciphers, as they are commonly styled, a regulation of office has promoted the most important discoveries of arithmetic, algebra, and the mathematical sciences.

Whilst the caliph Walid sat idle on the throne of Damascus, while his lieutenants achieved the conquest of Transoxiana and Spain, a third army of Saracens overspread the provinces of Asia Minor, and approached the borders of the Byzantine capital. But the attempt and disgrace of the second siege was reserved for his brother Soliman, whose ambition appears to have been quickened by a more active and martial spirit. In the revolutions of the Greek empire, after the tyrant Justinian[1] had been punished and avenged, a humble secretary, Anastasius or Artemius, was promoted by chance or merit to the vacant purple. He was alarmed by the sound of war; and his ambassador returned from Damascus with the tremendous news that the Saracens were preparing an armament by sea and land, such as would transcend the experience of the past, or the belief of the present, age. The precautions of Anastasius were not unworthy of his station, or of the impending danger. He issued a peremptory mandate, that all persons who were not provided with the means of subsistence for a three years' siege should evacuate the city: the public granaries and arsenals were abundantly replenished; the walls were restored and strengthened; and the engines for casting stones, or darts, or fire, were stationed along the ramparts, or in the brigantines of war, of which an additional number was hastily constructed. To prevent is safer, as well as more honourable, than to repel an attack; and a design was meditated, above the usual spirit of the Greeks, of burning the naval stores of the enemy, the cypress timber that had been hewn in Mount Libanus, and was piled along the sea-shore of Phœnicia, for the service of the Egyptian fleet. This generous enterprise was defeated by the cowardice or treachery of the troops, who, in the new language of the empire, were styled of the *Obsequian Theme*.[2] They murdered their chief, deserted their standard in the isle of Rhodes, dispersed themselves over the adjacent continent, and deserved pardon or reward by investing with the purple a simple officer of the revenue. The name of Theodosius might recommend him to the senate and people; but after some months he sunk into a cloister, and resigned, to the firmer

---

[1] [Justinian II, the last emperor of the house of Heraclius, reigned from 685 to 695 and again from 705 to 711. During his reign 'he considered the axe, the cord and the rack as the only instruments of royalty'. *Ed.*]

[2] [The Byzantine army had been reorganised in *Themes* by Heraclius. *Ed.*]

hand of Leo the Isaurian, the urgent defence of the capital and empire. The most formidable of the Saracens, Moslemah the brother of the caliph, was advancing at the head of one hundred and twenty thousand Arabs and Persians, the greater part mounted on horses or camels; and the successful sieges of Tyana, Amorium, and Pergamus were of sufficient duration to exercise their skill and to elevate their hopes. At the well-known passage of Abydus, on the Hellespont, the Mohammedan arms were transported, for the first[3] time, from Asia to Europe. From thence, wheeling round the Thracian cities of the Propontis, Moslemah invested Constantinople on the land side, surrounded his camp with a ditch and rampart, prepared and planted his engines of assault, and declared, by words and actions, a patient resolution of expecting the return of seed-time and harvest, should the obstinacy of the besieged prove equal to his own. The Greeks would gladly have ransomed their religion and empire by a fine or assessment of a piece of gold on the head of each inhabitant of the city; but the liberal offer was rejected with disdain, and the presumption of Moslemah was exalted by the speedy approach and invincible force of the navies of Egypt and Syria. They are said to have amounted to eighteen hundred ships: the number betrays their inconsiderable size; and of the twenty stout and capacious vessels, whose magnitude impeded their progress, each was manned with no more than one hundred heavy-armed soldiers. This huge armada proceeded on a smooth sea, and with a gentle gale, towards the mouth of the Bosphorus; the surface of the strait was overshadowed, in the language of the Greeks, with a moving forest, and the same fatal night had been fixed by the Saracen chief for a general assault by sea and land. To allure the confidence of the enemy the emperor had thrown aside the chain that usually guarded the entrance of the harbour; but while they hesitated whether they should seize the opportunity or apprehend the snare, the

[3] In fact, the second: the first such attempt had been in 677. *Ed.*]

ministers of destruction were at hand. The fire-ships of
the Greeks were launched against them; the Arabs, their
arms, and vessels were involved in the same flames; the
disorderly fugitives were dashed against each other or
overwhelmed in the waves; and I no longer find a vestige
of the fleet that had threatened to extirpate the Roman
name. A still more fatal and irreparable loss was that of
the caliph Soliman, who died of an indigestion,[4] in his
camp near Kinnisrin or Chalcis in Syria, as he was preparing to lead against Constantinople the remaining
forces of the East. The brother of Moslemah was succeeded by a kinsman and an enemy; and the throne of an
active and able prince was degraded by the useless and
pernicious virtues of a bigot. While he started and satisfied the scruples of a blind conscience, the siege was
continued through the winter by the neglect, rather than
by the resolution of the caliph Omar. The winter proved
uncommonly rigorous: above a hundred days the ground
was covered with deep snow, and the natives of the sultry
climes of Egypt and Arabia lay torpid and almost lifeless
in their frozen camp. They revived on the return of
spring; a second effort had been made in their favour,
and their distress was relieved by the arrival of two
numerous fleets laden with corn, and arms, and soldiers;
the first from Alexandria, of four hundred transports and
galleys; the second, of three hundred and sixty vessels,
from the ports of Africa. But the Greek fires were again
kindled, and, if the destruction was less complete, it was
owing to the experience which had taught the Moslems
to remain at a safe distance, or to the perfidy of the
Egyptian mariners, who deserted with their ships to the
emperor of the Christians. The trade and navigation of
the capital were restored; and the produce of the fisheries
supplied the wants, and even the luxury, of the inhabi-

---

[4] The caliph had emptied two baskets of eggs and of figs, which he
swallowed alternately, and the repast was concluded with marrow and
sugar. In one of his pilgrimages to Mecca, Soliman ate, at a single meal,
seventy pomegranates, a kid, six fowls, and a huge quantity of the
grapes of Tayef. If the bill of fare be correct, we must admire the
appetite, rather than the luxury, of the sovereign of Asia.

tants. But the calamities of famine and disease were soon felt by the troops of Moslemah, and, as the former was miserably assuaged, so the latter was dreadfully propagated, by the pernicious nutriment which hunger compelled them to extract from the most unclean or unnatural food. The spirit of conquest, and even of enthusiasm, was extinct: the Saracens could no longer straggle beyond their lines, either single or in small parties, without exposing themselves to the merciless retaliation of the Thracian peasants. An army of Bulgarians was attracted from the Danube by the gifts and promises of Leo; and these savage auxiliaries made some atonement for the evils which they had inflicted on the empire by the defeat and slaughter of twenty-two thousand Asiatics. A report was dexterously scattered that the Franks, the unknown nations of the Latin world, were arming by sea and land in the defence of the Christian cause, and their formidable aid was expected with far different sensations in the camp and city. At length, after a siege of thirteen months, the hopeless Moslemah received from the caliph the welcome permission of retreat. The march of the Arabian cavalry over the Hellespont and through the provinces of Asia was executed without delay or molestation; but an army of their brethren had been cut in pieces on the side of Bithynia, and the remains of the fleet were so repeatedly damaged by tempest and fire, that only five galleys entered the port of Alexandria to relate the tale of their various and almost incredible disasters.

In the two sieges the deliverance of Constantinople may be chiefly ascribed to the novelty, the terrors, and the real efficacy of the *Greek fire*. The important secret of compounding and directing this artificial flame was imparted by Callinicus, a native of Heliopolis in Syria, who deserted from the service of the caliph to that of the emperor. The skill of a chemist and engineer was equivalent to the succour of fleets and armies; and this discovery or improvement of the military art was fortunately reserved for the distressful period when the degenerate Romans of the East were incapable of contending with

495

the warlike enthusiasm and youthful vigour of the Saracens. The historian who presumes to analyse this extraordinary composition should suspect his own ignorance and that of his Byzantine guides, so prone to the marvellous, so careless, and, in this instance, so jealous of the truth. From their obscure, and perhaps fallacious hints, it should seem that the principal ingredient of the Greek fire was the *naptha*, or liquid bitumen, a light, tenacious, and inflammable oil, which springs from the earth, and catches fire as soon as it comes in contact with the air. The naptha was mingled, I know not by what method or in what proportions; with sulphur and with the pitch that is extracted from evergreen firs. From this mixture, which produced a thick smoke and a loud explosion, proceeded a fierce and obstinate flame, which not only rose in perpendicular ascent, but likewise burnt with equal vehemence in descent or lateral progress; instead of being extinguished, it was nourished and quickened by the element of water; and sand, urine, or vinegar, were the only remedies that could damp the fury of this powerful agent, which was justly denominated by the Greeks the *liquid*, or the *maritime*, fire. For the annoyance of the enemy, it was employed with equal effect by sea and land, in battles or in sieges. It was either poured from the rampart in large boilers, or launched in red-hot balls of stone and iron, or darted in arrows and javelins, twisted round with flax and tow, which had deeply imbibed the inflammable oil; sometimes it was deposited in fireships, the victims and instruments of a more ample revenge, and was most commonly blown through long tubes of copper, which were planted on the prow of a galley, and fancifully shaped into the mouths of savage monsters, that seemed to vomit a stream of liquid and consuming fire. This important art was preserved at Constantinople, as the palladium of the state: the galleys and *artillery* might occasionally be lent to the allies of Rome; but the composition of the Greek fire was concealed with the most jealous scruple, and the terror of the enemies was increased and prolonged by their ignorance and surprise. In the treatise of the administration of the empire, the royal author[5] suggests the answers and excuses that might best elude the indiscreet curiosity and importunate demands of the barbarians. They should be told that the mystery of the Greek fire had been revealed by an angel to the first and greatest of the Constantines, with a sacred injunction that this gift of Heaven, this peculiar blessing of the Romans, should never be communicated to any foreign nation: that the prince and subject were alike bound to religious silence under the temporal and spiritual penalties of treason and sacrilege; and that the impious attempt would provoke the sudden and supernatural vengeance of the God of the Christians. By these precautions the secret was confined, above four hundred years, to the Romans of the East; and at the end of the eleventh century, the Pisans, to whom every sea and every art were familiar, suffered the effects, without understanding the composition, of the Greek fire. It was at length either discovered or stolen by the Mohammedans; and, in the holy wars of Syria and Egypt, they retorted an invention, contrived against themselves, on the heads of the Christians. A knight, who despised the swords and lances of the Saracens, relates with heartfelt sincerity his own fears, and those of his companions, at the sight and sound of the mischievous engine that discharged a torrent of the Greek fire, the *feu Gregeois*, as it is styled by the more early of the French writers. It came flying through the air, says Joinville, like a winged long-tailed dragon, about the thickness of a hogshead, with the report of thunder and the velocity of lightning; and the darkness of the night was dispelled by this deadly illumination. The use of the Greek, or, as it might now be called, of the Saracen fire, was continued to the middle of the fourteenth century, when the scientific or casual compound of nitre, sulphur,

[5]|i.e. Constantinus VII, Porphynogenitus, emperor 913–959, who wrote a work generally known by its Latin title, *de Administrando Imperio. Ed.*]

and charcoal effected a new revolution in the art of war and the history of mankind.

Constantinople and the Greek fire might exclude the Arabs from the eastern entrance of Europe; but in the West, on the side of the Pyrenees, the provinces of Gaul were threatened and invaded by the conquerors of Spain. The decline of the French monarchy invited the attack of these insatiate fanatics. The descendants of Clovis had lost the inheritance of his martial and ferocious spirit; and their misfortune or demerit has affixed the epithet of *lazy* to the last kings of the Merovingian race. They ascended the throne without power, and sunk into the grave without a name. A country palace, in the neighbourhood of Compiègne, was allotted for their residence or prison: but each year, in the month of March or May, they were conducted in a waggon drawn by oxen to the assembly of the Franks, to give audience to foreign ambassadors and to ratify the acts of the mayor of the palace. That domestic officer was become the minister of the nation and the master of the prince. A public employment was converted into the patrimony of a private family: the elder Pepin left a king of mature years under the guardianship of his own widow and her child; and these feeble regents were forcibly dispossessed by the most active of his bastards. A government half savage and half corrupt, was almost dissolved; and the tributary dukes, and provincial counts, and the territorial lords, were tempted to despise the weakness of the monarch, and to imitate the ambition of the mayor. Among these independent chiefs, one of the boldest and most successful was Eudes duke of Aquitain, who in the southern provinces of Gaul usurped the authority, and even the title, of king. The Goths, the Gascons, and the Franks assembled under the standard of this Christian hero: he repelled the first invasion of the Saracens; and Zama, lieutenant of the caliph, lost his army and his life under the walls of Toulouse. The ambition of his successors was stimulated by revenge; they repassed the Pyrenees with the means and the resolution of conquest. The advantageous situation which had recommended Narbonne as the first Roman colony was again chosen by the Moslems: they claimed the province of Septimania or Languedoc as a just dependence of the Spanish monarchy: the vineyards of Gascony and the city of Bordeaux were possessed by the sovereign of Damascus and Samarcand; and the south of France, from the mouth of the Garonne to that of the Rhône, assumed the manners and religion of Arabia.

But these narrow limits were scorned by the spirit of Abdalrahman, or Abderame, who had been restored by the caliph Hashem to the wishes of the soldiers and people of Spain. That veteran and daring commander adjudged to the obedience of the prophet whatever yet remained of France or of Europe; and prepared to execute the sentence, at the head of a formidable host in the full confidence of surmounting all opposition either of nature or of man. His first care was to suppress a domestic rebel, who commanded the most important passes of the Pyrenees: Munuza, a Moorish chief, had accepted the alliance of the duke of Aquitain; and Eudes, from a motive of private or public interest, devoted his beauteous daughter to the embraces of the African misbeliever. But the strongest fortresses of Cerdagne were invested by a superior force; the rebel was overtaken and slain in the mountains; and his widow was sent a captive to Damascus, to gratify the desires, or more probably the vanity, of the commander of the faithful. From the Pyrenees, Abderame proceeded without delay to the passage of the Rhône and the siege of Arles. An army of Christians attempted the relief of the city: the tombs of their leaders were yet visible in the thirteenth century; and many thousands of their dead bodies were carried down the rapid stream into the Mediterranean Sea. The army of Abderame were not less successful on the side of the ocean. He passed without opposition the Garonne and Dordogne, which unite their waters in the gulf of Bordeaux; but he found, beyond those rivers, the camp of the intrepid Eudes, who had formed a second army and sustained a second defeat, so fatal to the Christians, that, according to their sad confession, God alone could reckon the number of the slain. The victorious Saracen overran the provinces of Aquitain, whose Gallic names are disguised, rather than lost, in the modern appellations of Perigord, Saintonge, and Poitou: his standards were planted on the walls, or at least before the gates, of Tours and of Sens; and his detachments overspread the kingdom of Burgundy as far as the well-known cities of Lyons and Besançon. The memory of these devastations, for Abderame did not spare the country or the people, was long preserved by tradition; and the invasion of France by the Moors or Mohammedans affords the groundwork of those fables which have been so wildly disfigured in the romances of chivalry, and so elegantly adorned by the Italian muse. In the decline of society and art, the deserted cities could supply a slender booty to the Saracens; their richest spoil was found in the churches and monasteries, which they stripped of their ornaments and delivered to the flames: and the tutelar saints, both Hilary of Poitiers and Martin of Tours, forgot their miraculous powers in the defence of their own sepulchres. A victorious line of march had been prolonged above a thousand miles from the rock of Gibraltar to the banks of the Loire; the repetition of an equal space would have carried the Saracens to the confines of Poland and the Highlands of Scotland; the Rhine is not more impassable than the Nile or Euphrates, and the Arabian fleet might have sailed without a naval combat into the mouth of the Thames. Perhaps the interpretation of the Koran would now be taught in the schools of Oxford, and her pulpits might demonstrate to a circumcised people the sanctity and truth of the revelation of Mohammed.

From such calamities was Christendom delivered by the genius and fortune of one man. Charles, the illegitimate son of the elder Pepin, was content with the titles of mayor or duke of the Franks; but he deserved to become the father of a line of kings. In a laborious administration of twenty-four years he restored and supported the dignity of the throne, and the rebels of Germany and Gaul were successively crushed by the activity of a warrior who in the same campaign could display his banner on the Elbe, the Rhône, and the shores of the ocean. In the public danger he was summoned by the voice of his country; and his rival, the duke of Aquitain, was reduced to appear among the fugitives and suppliants. "Alas!" exclaimed the Franks, "what a misfortune! what an indignity! We have long heard of the name and conquests of the Arabs: we were apprehensive of their attack from the East; they have now conquered Spain, and invade our country on the side of the West. Yet their numbers and (since they have no buckler) their arms are inferior to our own." "If you follow my advice," replied the prudent mayor of the palace, "you will not interrupt their march, nor precipitate your attack. They are like a torrent, which it is dangerous to stem in its career. The thirst of riches, and the consciousness of success, redouble their valour, and valour is of more avail than arms or numbers. Be patient till they have loaded themselves with the incumbrance of wealth. The possession of wealth will divide their counsels and assure your victory." This subtle policy is perhaps a refinement of the Arabian writers; and the situation of Charles will suggest a more narrow and selfish motive of procrastination; the secret desire of humbling the pride and wasting the provinces of the rebel duke of Aquitain. It is yet more probable that the delays of Charles were inevitable and reluctant. A standing army was unknown under the first and second race; more than half the kingdom was now in the hands of the Saracens: according to their respective situation, the Franks of Neustria and Austrasia were too conscious or too careless of the impending danger; and the voluntary aids of the Gepidæ and Germans were separated by a long interval from the standard of the Christian general. No sooner had he collected his forces than he sought and found the enemy in the centre of France, between Tours and Poitiers. His well-conducted march was covered by a range of hills, and Abderame appears to have been surprised by his unexpected presence. The nations of Asia, Africa, and Europe advanced with equal ardour to an encounter which would change the history of the world. In the six first days of desultory combat the horsemen and archers of the East maintained their advantage; but in the closer onset of the seventh day the Orientals were oppressed by the strength and stature of the Germans, who, with stout hearts and *iron* hands, asserted the civil and religious freedom of their posterity. The epithet of *Martel*, the *hammer*, which has been added to the name of Charles, is expressive of his weighty and irresistible strokes: the valour of Eudes was excited by resentment and emulation; and their companions, in the eye of history, are the true Peers and Paladins of French chivalry. After a bloody field, in which Abderame was slain, the Saracens, in the close of the evening, retired to their camp. In the disorder and despair of the night the various tribes of Yemen and Damascus, of Africa and Spain, were provoked to turn their arms against each other: the remains of their host were suddenly dissolved, and each *emir* consulted his safety by a hasty and separate retreat. At the dawn of day the stillness of a hostile camp was suspected by the victorious Christians: on the report of their spies they ventured to explore the riches of the vacant tents; but if we except some celebrated relics, a small portion of the spoil was restored to the innocent and lawful owners. The joyful tidings were soon diffused over the Catholic world, and the monks of Italy could affirm and believe that three hundred and fifty, or three hundred and seventy-five, thousand of the Mohammedans had been crushed by the hammer of Charles, while no more than fifteen hundred Christians were slain in the field of Tours. But this incredible tale is sufficiently disproved by the caution of the French general, who apprehended the snares and accidents of a pursuit, and dismissed his German allies to their native forests. The inactivity of a conqueror betrays the loss of strength and blood, and the most cruel execution is inflicted, not in the ranks of battle, but on the backs of a flying enemy. Yet the victory of the Franks was complete and final; Aquitain was recovered by the arms of Eudes; the Arabs never resumed the conquest of Gaul, and they were soon driven beyond the Pyrenees by Charles Martel and his valiant race. It might have been expected that the saviour of Christendom would have been canonised, or at least applauded, by the gratitude of the clergy, who are indebted to his sword for their present existence. But in the public distress the mayor of the palace had been compelled to apply the riches, or at least the revenues, of the bishops and abbots to the relief of the state and the reward of the soldiers. His merits were forgotten, his sacrilege alone was remembered, and, in an epistle to a Carlovingian prince, a Gallic synod presumes to declare that his ancestor was damned; that on the opening of his tomb the spectators were affrighted by a smell of fire and the aspect of a horrid dragon; and that a saint of the times was indulged with a pleasant vision of the soul and body of Charles Martel burning, to all eternity, in the abyss of hell.

CHAPTER XX

THE ICONOCLASTIC MOVEMENT

*The emperor who successfully defended Con-
stantinople from the great Arab attack of 716–718
was Leo III, the Isaurian (717–741), the founder
of a new imperial dynasty. Leo III reorganised
the defences of the Empire, restored internal order
and revised the laws; but his reign also saw the
beginning of the "iconoclastic" movement: a
puritan attack on the outward splendour, and
particularly the images of the Church, which
convulsed the empire for over a century and
began that progressive alienation of Rome from
Byzantium which would ultimately lead to the
complete separation of the Churches. In his
chapter XLIX Gibbon describes the origins of the
iconoclastic movement, the iconoclastic measures
of Leo III, and the resistance to them of the
successive popes Gregory II (715–731) and
Gregory III (731–741).*

IN the connection of the church and state I have
considered the former as subservient only, and relative,
to the latter; a salutary maxim, if in fact as well as in
narrative it had ever been held sacred. The oriental
philosophy of the Gnostics, the dark abyss of predestination and grace, and the strange transformation of the
Eucharist from the sign to the substance of Christ's body,[1]

---

[1] The learned Selden has given the history of transubstantiation in a
comprehensive and pithy sentence: "This opinion is only rhetoric
turned into logic."

504

I have purposely abandoned to the curiosity of speculative divines. But I have reviewed with diligence and pleasure the objects of ecclesiastical history by which the decline and fall of the Roman empire were materially affected, the propagation of Christianity, the constitution of the Catholic church, the ruin of Paganism, and the sects that arose from the mysterious controversies concerning the Trinity and incarnation. At the head of this class we may justly rank the worship of images, so fiercely disputed in the eighth and ninth centuries; since a question of popular superstition produced the revolt of Italy, the temporal power of the popes, and the restoration of the Roman empire in the West.

The primitive Christians were possessed with an unconquerable repugnance to the use and abuse of images; and this aversion may be ascribed to their descent from the Jews, and their enmity to the Greeks. The Mosaic law had severely proscribed all representations of the Deity; and that precept was firmly established in the principles and practice of the chosen people. The wit of the Christian apologists was pointed against the foolish idolaters who bowed before the workmanship of their own hands; the images of brass and marble, which, had *they* been endowed with sense and motion, should have started rather from the pedestal to adore the creative powers of the artist. Perhaps some recent and imperfect converts of the Gnostic tribe might crown the statues of Christ and St. Paul with the profane honours which they paid to those of Aristotle and Pythagoras; but the public religion of the Catholics was uniformly simple and spiritual; and the first notice of the use of pictures is in the censure of the council of Illiberis, three hundred years after the Christian æra. Under the successors of Constantine, in the peace and luxury of the triumphant church, the more prudent bishops condescended to indulge a visible superstition for the benefit of the multitude; and after the ruin of Paganism they were no longer restrained by the apprehension of an odious parallel. The first introduction of a symbolic worship was in the veneration of the cross and of relics. The saints and martyrs, whose intercession was implored, were seated on the right hand of God; but the gracious and often supernatural favours which, in the popular belief, were showered round their tomb, conveyed an unquestionable sanction of the devout pilgrims who visited, and touched, and kissed these lifeless remains, the memorials of their merits and sufferings. But a memorial more interesting than the skull or the sandals of a departed worthy is the faithful copy of his person and features, delineated by the arts of painting or sculpture. In every age such copies, so congenial to human feelings, have been cherished by the zeal of private friendship or public esteem: the images of the Roman emperors were adored with civil and almost religious honours; a reverence less ostentatious, but more sincere, was applied to the statues of sages and patriots; and these profane virtues, these splendid sins, disappeared in the presence of the holy men who had died for their celestial and everlasting country. At first the experiment was made with caution and scruple; and the venerable pictures were discreetly allowed to instruct the ignorant, to awaken the cold, and to gratify the prejudices of the heathen proselytes. By a slow though inevitable progression the honours of the original were transferred to the copy: the devout Christian prayed before the image of a saint; and the Pagan rites of genuflexion, luminaries, and incense again stole into the Catholic church. The scruples of reason or piety were silenced by the strong evidence of visions and miracles; and the pictures which speak, and move, and bleed, must be endowed with a divine energy, and may be considered as the proper objects of religious adoration. The most audacious pencil might tremble in the rash attempt of defining by forms and colours the infinite Spirit, the eternal Father, who pervades and sustains the universe. But the superstitious mind was more easily reconciled to paint and to worship the angels, and, above all, the Son of God, under the human shape which on earth they have condescended to assume. The second person of the Trinity had been clothed with a real and mortal body; but that body had ascended into heaven: and had not some similitude been presented to the eyes of his disciples, the spiritual worship of Christ might have been obliterated by the visible relics and representations of the saints. A similar indulgence was requisite and propitious for the Virgin Mary: the place of her burial was unknown; and the assumption of her soul and body into heaven was adopted by the credulity of the Greeks and Latins. The use, and even the worship, of images was firmly established before the end of the sixth century: they were fondly cherished by the warm imagination of the Greeks and Asiatics: the Pantheon and Vatican were adorned with the emblems of a new superstition; but this semblance of idolatry was more coldly entertained by the rude barbarians and the Arian clergy of the West. The bolder forms of sculpture, in brass or marble, which peopled the temples of antiquity, were offensive to the fancy or conscience of the Christian Greeks; and a smooth surface of colours has ever been esteemed a more descent and harmless mode of imitation.

The merit and effect of a copy depends on its resemblance with the original; but the primitive Christians were ignorant of the genuine features of the Son of God, his mother, and his apostles: the statue of Christ at Paneas, in Palestine, was more probably that of some temporal saviour; the Gnostics and their profane monuments were reprobated, and the fancy of the Christian artists could only be guided by the clandestine imitation of some heathen model. In this distress a bold and dexterous invention assured at once the likeness of the image and the innocence of the worship. A new superstructure of fable was raised on the popular basis of a Syrian legend on the correspondence of Christ and Abgarus, so famous in the days of Eusebius, so reluctantly deserted by our modern advocates. The bishop of Cæsarea records the epistle, but he most strangely forgets the picture of Christ—the perfect impression of his face on a linen, with which he gratified the faith of the royal stranger who had invoked his healing power, and offered the strong city of Edessa to protect him against the malice of the Jews. The ignorance of the primitive church is explained by the long imprisonment of the image in a niche of the wall, from whence, after an oblivion of five hundred years, it was released by some prudent bishop, and seasonably presented to the devotion of the times. Its first and most glorious exploit was the deliverance of the city from the arms of Chosroes Nushirvan; and it was soon revered as a pledge of the divine promise that Edessa should never be taken by a foreign enemy. It is true, indeed, that the text of Procopius ascribes the double deliverance of Edessa to the wealth and valour of her citizens, who purchased the absence and repelled the assaults of the Persian monarch. He was ignorant, the profane historian, of the testimony which he is compelled to deliver in the ecclesiastical page of Evagrius, that the Palladium was exposed on the rampart, and that the water which had been sprinkled on the holy face, instead of quenching, added new fuel to the flames of the besieged. After this important service the image of Edessa was preserved with respect and gratitude; and if the Armenians rejected the legend, the more credulous Greeks adored the similitude, which was not the work of any mortal pencil, but the immediate creation of the divine original. The style and sentiments of a Byzantine hymn will declare how far their worship was removed from the grossest idolatry. "How can we with mortal eyes contemplate this image, whose celestial splendour the host of heaven presumes not to behold? HE who dwells in heaven condescends this day to visit us by his venerable image; HE who is seated on the cherubim visits us this day by a picture, which the Father has delineated with his immaculate hand, which he has formed in an ineffable manner, and which we sanctify by adoring it with fear and love." Before the end of the sixth century these images, *made without hands* (in Greek it is a single word), were propagated in the camps and cities of the Eastern empire; they were the objects of worship, and the instruments of miracles; and in the hour of danger or tumult their venerable presence could revive the hope, rekindle the courage, or repress the fury of the Roman legions. Of these pictures the far greater part, the transcripts of a human pencil, could only pretend to a secondary likeness and improper title; but there are some of higher descent, who derived their resemblance from an immediate contact with the original, endowed for that purpose with a miraculous and prolific virtue. The most ambitious aspired from a filial to a fraternal relation with the image of Edessa; and such is the *veronica* of Rome, or Spain, or Jerusalem, which Christ in his agony and bloody sweat applied to his face, and delivered to a holy matron. The fruitful precedent was speedily transferred to the Virgin Mary, and the saints and martyrs. In the church of Diospolis, in Palestine, the features of the Mother of God were deeply inscribed in a marble column: the East and West have been decorated by the pencil of St. Luke; and the Evangelist, who was perhaps a physician, has been forced to exercise the occupation of a painter, so profane and odious in the eyes of the primitive Christians. The Olympian Jove, created by the muse of Homer and the chisel of Phidias, might inspire a philosophic mind with momentary devotion; but these Catholic images were faintly and flatly delineated by monkish artists in the last degeneracy of taste and genius.[2]

The worship of images had stolen into the church by insensible degrees, and each petty step was pleasing to the superstitious mind, as productive of comfort and innocent of sin. But in the beginning of the eighth century, in the full magnitude of the abuse, the more timorous Greeks were awakened by an apprehension that, under the mask of Christianity, they had restored the religion of their fathers: they heard, with grief and

[2] "Your scandalous figures stand quite out from the canvas: they are as bad as a group of statues!" It was thus that the ignorance and bigotry of a Greek priest applauded the pictures of Titian, which he had ordered, and refused to accept.

impatience, the name of idolaters—the incessant charge
of the Jews and Mohammedans, who derived from the
Law and the Koran an immortal hatred to graven images
and all relative worship. The servitude of the Jews might
curb their zeal and depreciate their authority; but the
triumphant Musulmans, who reigned at Damascus, and
threatened Constantinople, cast into the scale of reproach
the accumulated weight of truth and victory. The cities
of Syria, Palestine, and Egypt had been fortified with the
images of Christ, his mother, and his saints; and each
city presumed on the hope or promise of miraculous
defence. In a rapid conquest of ten years the Arabs subdued those cities and these images; and, in their opinion,
the Lord of Hosts pronounced a decisive judgment
between the adoration and contempt of these mute and
inanimate idols. For a while Edessa had braved the
Persian assaults; but the chosen city, the spouse of
Christ, was involved in the common ruin; and his divine
resemblance became the slave and trophy of the infidels.
After a servitude of three hundred years, the Palladium
was yielded to the devotion of Constantinople, for a
ransom of twelve thousand pounds of silver, the redemption of two hundred Musulmans, and a perpetual truce
for the territory of Edessa. In this season of distress and
dismay the eloquence of the monks was exercised in the
defence of images; and they attempted to prove that the
sin and schism of the greatest part of the Orientals had
forfeited the favour and annihilated the virtue of these
precious symbols. But they were now opposed by the
murmurs of many simple or rational Christians, who
appealed to the evidence of texts, of facts, and of the
primitive times, and secretly desired the reformation of
the church. As the worship of images had never been
established by any general or positive law, its progress
in the Eastern empire had been retarded, or accelerated,
by the differences of men and manners, the local degrees
of refinement, and the personal characters of the bishops.
The splendid devotion was fondly cherished by the levity
of the capital and the inventive genius of the Byzantine

clergy; while the rude and remote districts of Asia were strangers to this innovation of sacred luxury. Many large congregations of Gnostics and Arians maintained, after their conversion, the simple worship which had preceded their separation; and the Armenians, the most warlike subjects of Rome, were not reconciled, in the twelfth century, to the sight of images. These various denominations of men afforded a fund of prejudice and aversion, of small account in the villages of Anatolia or Thrace, but which, in the fortune of a soldier, a prelate, or a eunuch, might be often connected with the powers of the church and state.

Of such adventures the most fortunate was the emperor Leo the Third, who, from the mountains of Isauria, ascended the throne of the East. He was ignorant of sacred and profane letters; but his education, his reason, perhaps his intercourse with the Jews and Arabs, had inspired the martial peasant with a hatred of images; and it was held to be the duty of a prince to impose on his subjects the dictates of his own conscience. But in the outset of an unsettled reign, during ten years of toil and danger, Leo submitted to the meanness of hypocrisy, bowed before the idols which he despised, and satisfied the Roman pontiff with the annual professions of his orthodoxy and zeal. In the reformation of religion his first steps were moderate and cautious: he assembled a great council of senators and bishops, and enacted, with their consent, that all the images should be removed from the sanctuary and altar to a proper height in the churches, where they might be visible to the eyes, and inaccessible to the superstition, of the people. But it was impossible on either side to check the rapid though adverse impulse of veneration and abhorrence: in their lofty position the sacred images still edified their votaries and reproached the tyrant. He was himself provoked by resistance and invective; and his own party accused him of an imperfect discharge of his duty, and urged for his imitation the example of the Jewish king, who had broken without scruple the brazen serpent of the temple.

By a second edict he proscribed the existence as well as the use of religious pictures; the churches of Constantinople and the provinces were cleansed from idolatry; the images of Christ, the Virgin, and the saints were demolished, or a smooth surface of plaster was spread over the walls of the edifice. The sect of the Iconoclasts was supported by the zeal and despotism of six emperors, and the East and West were involved in a noisy conflict of one hundred and twenty years. It was the design of Leo the Isaurian to pronounce the condemnation of images as an article of faith, and by the authority of a general council: but the convocation of such an assembly was reserved for his son Constantine; and though it is stigmatised by triumphant bigotry as a meeting of fools and atheists, their own partial and mutilated acts betray many symptoms of reason and piety. The debates and decrees of many provincial synods introduced the summons of the general council which met in the suburbs of Constantinople, and was composed of the respectable number of three hundred and thirty-eight bishops of Europe and Anatolia; for the patriarchs of Antioch and Alexandria were the slaves of the caliph, and the Roman pontiff had withdrawn the churches of Italy and the West from the communion of the Greeks. This Byzantine synod assumed the rank and powers of the seventh general council; yet even this title was a recognition of the six preceding assemblies, which had laboriously built the structure of the Catholic faith. After a serious deliberation of six months, the three hundred and thirty-eight bishops pronounced and subscribed a unanimous decree, that all visible symbols of Christ, except in the Eucharist, were either blasphemous or heretical; that image-worship was a corruption of Christianity and a renewal of Paganism; that all such monuments of idolatry should be broken or erased; and that those who should refuse to deliver the objects of their private superstition were guilty of disobedience to the authority of the church and of the emperor. In their loud and loyal acclamations they celebrated the merits of their temporal redeemer; and to his zeal and justice they intrusted the execution of their spiritual censures. At Constantinople, as in the former councils, the will of the prince was the rule of episcopal faith; but on this occasion I am inclined to suspect that a large majority of the prelates sacrificed their secret conscience to the temptations of hope and fear. In the long night of superstition the Christians had wandered far away from the simplicity of the Gospel: nor was it easy for them to discern the clue, and tread back the mazes of the labyrinth. The worship of images was inseparably blended, at least to a pious fancy, with the Cross, the Virgin, the saints and their relics; the holy ground was involved in a cloud of miracles and visions; and the nerves of the mind, curiosity and scepticism, were benumbed by the habits of obedience and belief. Constantine himself is accused of indulging a royal licence to doubt, or deny, or deride the mysteries of the Catholics, but they were deeply inscribed in the public and private creed of his bishops; and the boldest Iconoclast might assault with a secret horror the monuments of popular devotion, which were consecrated to the honour of his celestial patrons. In the reformation of the sixteenth century freedom and knowledge had expanded all the faculties of man: the thirst of innovation superseded the reverence of antiquity; and the vigour of Europe could disdain those phantoms which terrified the sickly and servile weakness of the Greeks.

The scandal of an abstract heresy can be only proclaimed to the people by the blast of the ecclesiastical trumpet; but the most ignorant can perceive, the most torpid must feel, the profanation and downfall of their visible deities. The first hostilities of Leo were directed against a lofty Christ on the vestibule, and above the gate, of the palace. A ladder had been planted for the assault; but it was furiously shaken by a crowd of zealots and women: they beheld, with pious transport, the ministers of sacrilege tumbling from on high and dashed against the pavement; and the honours of the ancient martyrs were prostituted to these criminals, who justly

513

suffered for murder and rebellion. The execution of the Imperial edicts was resisted by frequent tumults in Constantinople and the provinces; the person of Leo was endangered, his officers were massacred, and the popular enthusiasm was quelled by the strongest efforts of the civil and military power. Of the Archipelago, or Holy Sea, the numerous islands were filled with images and monks: their votaries abjured, without scruple, the enemy of Christ, his mother, and the saints; they armed a fleet of boats and galleys, displayed their consecrated banners, and boldly steered for the harbour of Constantinople, to place on the throne a new favourite of God and the people. They depended on the succour of a miracle: but their miracles were inefficient against the *Greek fire;* and, after the defeat and conflagration of their fleet, the naked islands were abandoned to the clemency or justice of the conqueror. The son of Leo, in the first year of his reign, had undertaken an expedition against the Saracens: during his absence the capital, the palace, and the purple were occupied by his kinsman Artavasdes, the ambitious champion of the orthodox faith. The worship of images was triumphantly restored: the patriarch renounced his dissimulation, or dissembled his sentiments; and the righteous claim of the usurper was acknowledged, both in the new and in ancient Rome. Constantine flew for refuge to his paternal mountains; but he descended at the head of the bold and affectionate Isaurians; and his final victory confounded the arms and predictions of the fanatics. His long reign was distracted with clamour, sedition, conspiracy, and mutual hatred and sanguinary revenge: the persecution of images was the motive or pretence of his adversaries; and, if they missed a temporal diadem, they were rewarded by the Greeks with the crown of martyrdom. In every act of open and clandestine treason the emperor felt the unforgiving enmity of the monks, the faithful slaves of the superstition to which they owed their riches and influence. They prayed, they preached, they absolved, they inflamed, they conspired; the solitude of Palestine poured forth a torrent of invective; and the pen of St. John Damascenus, the last of the Greek fathers, devoted the tyrant's head, both in this world and the next. I am not at leisure to examine how far the monks provoked, nor how much they have exaggerated their real and pretended sufferings, nor how many lost their lives or limbs, their eyes or their beards, by the cruelty of the emperor. From the chastisement of individuals he proceeded to the abolition of the order; and, as it was wealthy and useless, his resentment might be stimulated by avarice, and justified by patriotism. The formidable name and mission of the *Dragon*, his visitor-general, excited the terror and abhorrence of the *black* nation: the religious communities were dissolved, the buildings were converted into magazines or barracks; the lands, movables, and cattle were confiscated; and our modern precedents will support the charge, that much wanton or malicious havoc was exercised against the relics, and even the books, of the monasteries. With the habit and profession of monks, the public and private worship of images was rigorously proscribed; and it should seem that a solemn abjuration of idolatry was exacted from the subjects, or at least from the clergy, of the Eastern empire.

The patient East abjured with reluctance her sacred images; they were fondly cherished, and vigorously defended, by the independent zeal of the Italians. In ecclesiastical rank and jurisdiction the patriarch of Constantinople and the pope of Rome were nearly equal. But the Greek prelate was a domestic slave under the eye of his master, at whose nod he alternatively passed from the convent to the throne, and from the throne to the convent. A distant and dangerous station, amidst the barbarians of the West, excited the spirit and freedom of the Latin bishops. Their popular election endeared them to the Romans: the public and private indigence was relieved by their ample revenue; and the weakness or neglect of the emperors compelled them to consult, both in peace and war, the temporal safety of the city. In the school of adversity the priest insensibly imbibed the virtues and the ambition of a prince; the same character was assumed, the same policy was adopted, by the Italian, the Greek, or the Syrian, who ascended the chair of St. Peter; and, after the loss of her legions and provinces, the genius and fortune of the popes again restored the supremacy of Rome. It is agreed that in the eighth century their dominion was founded on rebellion, and that the rebellion was produced, and justified, by the heresy of the Iconoclasts; but the conduct of the second and third Gregory, in this memorable contest, is variously interpreted by the wishes of their friends and enemies. The Byzantine writers unanimously declare that, after a fruitless admonition, they pronounced the separation of the East and West, and deprived the sacrilegious tyrant of the revenue and sovereignty of Italy. Their excommunication is still more clearly expressed by the Greeks, who beheld the accomplishment of the papal triumphs; and as they are more strongly attached to their religion than to their country, they praise, instead of blaming, the zeal and orthodoxy of these apostolical men. The modern champions of Rome are eager to accept the praise and the precedent: this great and glorious example of the deposition of royal heretics is celebrated by the cardinals Baronius and Bellarmine; and if they are asked why the same thunders were not hurled against the Neros and Julians of antiquity? they reply, that the weakness of the primitive church was the sole cause of her patient loyalty. On this occasion the effects of love and hatred are the same; and the zealous Protestants, who seek to kindle the indignation and to alarm the fears of princes and magistrates, expatiate on the insolence and treason of the two Gregories against their lawful sovereign. They are defended only by the moderate Catholics, for the most part of the Gallican church, who respect the saint without approving the sin. These common advocates of the crown and the mitre circumscribe the truth of facts by the rule of equity, Scripture, and tradition, and appeal to the evidence of the Latins, and the lives and epistles of the popes themselves.

Two original epistles, from Gregory the Second to the emperor Leo, are still extant; and if they cannot be praised as the most perfect models of eloquence and logic, they exhibit the portrait, or at least the mask, of the founder of the papal monarchy. "During ten pure and fortunate years," says Gregory to the emperor, "we have tasted the annual comfort of your royal letters, subscribed in purple ink with your own hand, the sacred pledges of your attachment to the orthodox creed of our fathers. How deplorable is the change! how tremendous the scandal! You now accuse the Catholics of idolatry; and, by the accusation, you betray your own impiety and ignorance. To this ignorance we are compelled to adapt the grossness of our style and arguments: the first elements of holy letters are sufficient for your confusion; and were you to enter a grammar-school, and avow yourself the enemy of our worship, the simple and pious children would be provoked to cast their horn-books at your head." After this decent salutation the pope attempts the usual distinction between the idols of antiquity and the Christian images. The former were the fanciful representations of phantoms or demons, at a time when the true God had not manifested his person in any visible likeness. The latter are the genuine forms of Christ, his mother, and his saints, who had approved, by a crowd of miracles, the innocence and merit of this relative worship. He must indeed have trusted to the ignorance of Leo, since he could assert the perpetual use of images from the apostolic age, and their venerable presence in the six synods of the Catholic church. A more specious argument is drawn from present possession and recent practice: the harmony of the Christian world supersedes the demand of a general council; and Gregory frankly confesses that such assemblies can only be useful under the reign of an orthodox prince. To the impudent and inhuman Leo, more guilty than a heretic, he recommends peace, silence, and implicit obedience to his spiritual guides of Constantinople and Rome. The limits of civil and ecclesiastical powers are defined by the pontiff. To the former he

appropriates the body; to the latter the soul: the sword
of justice is in the hands of the magistrate: the more
formidable weapon of excommunication is intrusted to
the clergy; and in the exercise of their divine commission
a zealous son will not spare his offending father: the
successor of St. Peter may lawfully chastise the kings of
the earth. "You assault us, O tyrant! with a carnal and
military hand: unarmed and naked we can only implore
the Christ, the prince of the heavenly host, that he will
send unto you a devil for the destruction of your body
and the salvation of your soul. You declare, with foolish
arrogance, I will despatch my orders to Rome: I will
break in pieces the image of St. Peter; and Gregory, like
his predecessor Martin, shall be transported in chains
and in exile to the foot of the imperial throne. Would to
God that I might be permitted to tread in the footsteps of
the holy Martin! but may the fate of Constans serve as a
warning to the persecutors of the church! After his just
condemnation by the bishops of Sicily, the tyrant was cut
off in the fulness of his sins, by a domestic servant: the
saint is still adored by the nations of Scythia, among
whom he ended his banishment and his life. But it is our
duty to live for the edification and support of the faithful
people; nor are we reduced to risk our safety on the event
of a combat. Incapable as you are of defending your
Roman subjects, the maritime situation of the city may
perhaps expose it to your depredation; but we can remove
to the distance of four-and-twenty *stadia*, to the first
fortress of the Lombards, and then——you may pursue
the winds. Are you ignorant that the popes are the bond
of union, the mediators of peace between the East and
West? The eyes of the nations are fixed on our humility;
and they revere, as a God upon earth, the apostle St.
Peter, whose image you threaten to destroy. The remote
and interior kingdoms of the West present their homage
to Christ and his vicegerent; and we now prepare to visit
one of their most powerful monarchs who desires to
receive from our hands the sacrament of baptism. The
barbarians have submitted to the yoke of the Gospel,

15

The "image of Edessa," the perfect impression of Christ's face on linen, which became an important object of worship.

while you alone are deaf to the voice of the shepherd. These pious barbarians are kindled into rage: they thirst to avenge the persecution of the East. Abandon your rash and fatal enterprise; reflect, tremble, and repent. If you persist, we are innocent of the blood that will be spilt in the contest; may it fall on your own head!"

The first assault of Leo against the images of Constantinople had been witnessed by a crowd of strangers from Italy and the West, who related with grief and indignation the sacrilege of the emperor. But on the reception of his proscriptive edict they trembled for their domestic deities; the images of Christ and the Virgin, of the angels, martyrs, and saints, were abolished in all the churches of Italy; and a strong alternative was proposed to the Roman pontiff, the royal favour as the price of his compliance, degradation and exile as the penalty of his disobedience. Neither zeal nor policy allowed him to hesitate; and the haughty strain in which Gregory addressed the emperor displays his confidence in the truth of his doctrine or the powers of resistance. Without depending on prayers or miracles, he boldly armed against the public enemy, and his pastoral letters admonished the Italians of their danger and their duty. At this signal, Ravenna, Venice, and the cities of the Exarchate and Pentapolis adhered to the cause of religion; their military force by sea and land consisted, for the most part, of the natives; and the spirit of patriotism and zeal was transfused into the mercenary strangers. The Italians swore to live and die in the defence of the pope and the holy images; the Roman people was devoted to their father, and even the Lombards were ambitious to share the merit and advantage of this holy war. The most treasonable act, but the most obvious revenge, was the destruction of the statues of Leo himself: the most effectual and pleasing measure of rebellion was the withholding the tribute of Italy, and depriving him of a power which he had recently abused by the imposition of a new capitation. A form of administration was preserved by the election of magistrates and governors; and so high was the public indignation, that the

Italians were prepared to create an orthodox emperor, and to conduct him with a fleet and army to the palace of Constantinople. In that palace the Roman bishops, the second and third Gregory, were condemned as the authors of the revolt, and every attempt was made, either by fraud or force, to seize their persons and to strike at their lives. The city was repeatedly visited or assaulted by captains of the guards, and dukes and exarchs of high dignity or secret trust; they landed with foreign troops, they obtained some domestic aid, and the superstition of Naples may blush that her fathers were attached to the cause of heresy. But these clandestine or open attacks were repelled by the courage and vigilance of the Romans; the Greeks were overthrown and massacred, their leaders suffered an ignominious death, and the popes, however inclined to mercy, refused to intercede for these guilty victims. At Ravenna, the several quarters of the city had long exercised a bloody and hereditary feud; in religious controversy they found a new aliment of faction: but the votaries of images were superior in numbers or spirit, and the exarch, who attempted to stem the torrent, lost his life in a popular sedition. To punish this flagitious deed, and restore his dominion in Italy, the emperor sent a fleet and army into the Hadriatic gulf. After suffering from the winds and waves much loss and delay, the Greeks made their descent in the neighbourhood of Ravenna: they threatened to depopulate the guilty capital, and to imitate, perhaps to surpass, the example of Justinian the Second, who had chastised a former rebellion by the choice and execution of fifty of the principal inhabitants. The women and clergy, in sackcloth and ashes, lay prostrate in prayer; the men were in arms for the defence of their country; the common danger had united the factions, and the event of a battle was preferred to the slow miseries of a siege. In a hard-fought day, as the two armies alternately yielded and advanced, a phantom was seen, a voice was heard, and Ravenna was victorious by the assurance of victory. The strangers retreated to their ships, but the populous sea-coast poured forth a multitude of boats; the waters of the Po were so deeply infected with blood, that during six years the public prejudice abstained from the fish of the river; and the institution of an annual feast perpetuated the worship of images and the abhorrence of the Greek tyrant. Amidst the triumph of the Catholic arms, the Roman pontiff convened a synod of ninety-three bishops against the heresy of the Iconoclasts. With their consent, he pronounced a general excommunication against all who by word or deed should attack the tradition of the fathers and the images of the saints: in this sentence the emperor was tactily involved, but the vote of a last and hopeless remonstrance may seem to imply that the anathema was yet suspended over his guilty head. No sooner had they confirmed their own safety, the worship of images, and the freedom of Rome and Italy, than the popes appear to have relaxed of their severity, and to have spared the relics of the Byzantine dominion. Their moderate counsels delayed and prevented the election of a new emperor, and they exhorted the Italians not to separate from the body of the Roman monarchy. The exarch was permitted to reside within the walls of Ravenna, a captive rather than a master; and till the Imperial coronation of Charlemagne, the government of Rome and Italy was exercised in the name of the successors of Constantine.

The liberty of Rome, which had been oppressed by the arms and arts of Augustus, was rescued, after seven hundred and fifty years of servitude, from the persecution of Leo the Isaurian. By the Cæsars the triumphs of the consuls had been annihilated: in the decline and fall of the empire, the god Terminus, the sacred boundary, had insensibly receded from the ocean, the Rhine, the Danube, and the Euphrates; and Rome was reduced to her ancient territory from Viterbo to Terracina, and from Narni to the mouth of the Tiber. When the kings were banished, the republic reposed on the firm basis which had been founded by their wisdom and virtue. Their perpetual jurisdiction was divided between two annual magistrates: the senate continued to exercise the powers of administration and counsel; and the legislative authority was distributed in the assemblies of the people by a well-proportioned scale of property and service. Ignorant of the arts of luxury, the primitive Romans had improved the science of government and war: the will of the community was absolute: the rights of individuals were sacred: one hundred and thirty thousand citizens were armed for defence or conquest; and a band of robbers and outlaws was moulded into a nation, deserving of freedom and ambitious of glory. When the sovereignty of the Greek emperors was extinguished, the ruins of Rome presented the sad image of depopulation and decay: her slavery was a habit, her liberty an accident; the effect of superstition, and the object of her own amazement and terror. The last vestige of the substance, or even the forms, of the constitution, was obliterated from the practice and memory of the Romans; and they were devoid of knowledge, or virtue, again to build the fabric of a commonwealth. Their scanty remnant, the offspring of slaves and strangers, was despicable in the eyes of the victorious barbarians. As often as the Franks or Lombards expressed their most bitter contempt of a foe, they called him a Roman; "and in this name," says the bishop Liutprand, "we include whatever is base, whatever is cowardly, whatever is perfidious, the extremes of avarice and luxury, and every vice that can prostitute the dignity of human nature." By the necessity of their situation, the inhabitants of Rome were cast into the rough model of a republican government: they were compelled to elect some judges in peace and some leaders in war: the nobles assembled to deliberate, and their resolves could not be executed without the union and consent of the multitude. The style of the Roman senate and people was revived, but the spirit was fled; and their new independence was disgraced by the tumultuous conflict of licentiousness and oppression. The want of laws could only be supplied by the influence of religion, and their foreign and domestic counsels were moderated by the authority of the bishop. His alms, his sermons, his correspondence with the kings and prelates of the West, his recent services, their gratitude and oath, accustomed the Romans to consider him as the first magistrate or prince of the city. The Christian humility of the popes was not offended by the name of *Dominus*, or Lord; and their face and inscription are still apparent on the most ancient coins. Their temporal dominion is now confirmed by the reverence of a thousand years; and their noblest title is the free choice of a people whom they had redeemed from slavery.

CHAPTER XXI

BYZANTINE ENLIGHTENMENT, ROMAN DARKNESS

[*After the Arab conquests, which deprived Constantinople not only of the conquests of Justinian
but also of the ancient Roman provinces of Syria,
Egypt and North Africa, both Rome and Constantinople passed through years of crisis. Their relations with each other also deteriorated. After the
death of Charlemagne (814) the Byzantine emperors declined to recognise his successors as emperors of the West. As the bishops of Rome and
Constantinople were both at the mercy of the lay
rulers, spiritual relations naturally deteriorated
with secular. In 858, the Byzantine emperor appointed a learned layman, Photius, as Patriarch.
This was not relished at Rome and the schism of
the two churches began (or at least was thought
in retrospect to have begun) with the reign of "the
execrable Photius." After this "the darkness and
corruption of the tenth century suspended the intercourse, without reconciling the minds, of the
two nations." How difficult such reconciliation
was is shown by a comparison of the two societies.
In the ninth century Byzantium emerged from the
years of crisis and, under the "Macedonian" dynasty, which reigned from 867 to 1081, enjoyed a
prosperity and a culture whose extent and limita-
tions Gibbon describes in chapter LIII.*]

524

In the ninth century we trace the first dawnings of the restoration of science. After the fanaticism of the Arabs had subsided, the caliphs aspired to conquer the arts, rather than the provinces, of the empire: their liberal curiosity rekindled the emulation of the Greeks, brushed away the dust from their ancient libraries, and taught them to know and reward the philosophers, whose labours had been hitherto repaid by the pleasure of study and the pursuit of truth. The Cæsar Bardas, the uncle of Michael the Third, was the generous protector of letters, a title which alone has preserved his memory and excused his ambition. A particle of the treasures of his nephew was sometimes diverted from the indulgence of vice and folly; a school was opened in the palace of Magnaura, and the presence of Bardas excited the emulation of the masters and students. At their head was the philosopher Leo, archbishop of Thessalonica; his profound skill in astronomy and the mathematics was admired by the strangers of the East, and this occult science was magnified by vulgar credulity, which modestly supposes that all knowledge superior to its own must be the effect of inspiration or magic. At the pressing entreaty of the Cæsar, his friend, the celebrated Photius, renounced the freedom of a secular and studious life, ascended the patriarchal throne, and was alternately excommunicated and absolved by the synods of the East and West. By the confession even of priestly hatred, no art or science, except poetry, was foreign to this universal scholar, who was deep in thought, indefatigable in reading, and eloquent in diction. Whilst he exercised the office of protospathaire, or captain of the guards, Photius was sent ambassador to the caliph of Bagdad. The tedious hours of exile, perhaps of confinement, were beguiled by the hasty composition of his *Library*, a living monument of erudition and criticism. Two hundred and fourscore writers, historians, orators, philosophers, theologians, are reviewed without any regular method; he abridges their narrative or doctrine, appreciates their style and character, and judges even the fathers of the church with a discreet freedom which often breaks through the superstition of the times. The emperor Basil, who lamented the defects of his own education, intrusted to the care of Photius his son and successor Leo the Philosopher, and the reign of that prince and of his son Constantine Porphyrogenitus forms one of the most prosperous eras of the Byzantine literature. By their munificence the treasures of antiquity were deposited in the Imperial library; by their pens, or those of their associates, they were imparted in such extracts and abridgments as might amuse the curiosity, without oppressing the indolence, of the public. Besides the *Basilics*, or code of laws, the arts of husbandry and war, of feeding or destroying the human species, were propagated with equal diligence; and the history of Greece and Rome was digested into fifty-three heads or titles, of which two only (of embassies, and of virtues and vices) have escaped the injuries of time. In every station the reader might contemplate the image of the past world, apply the lesson or warning of each page, and learn to admire, perhaps to imitate, the examples of a brighter period. I shall not expatiate on the works of the Byzantine Greeks, who, by the assiduous study of the ancients, have deserved, in some measure, the remembrance and gratitude of the moderns. The scholars of the present age may still enjoy the benefit of the philosophical commonplace-book of Stobæus, the grammatical and historic lexicon of Suidas, the Chiliads of Tzetzes, which comprise six hundred narratives in twelve thousand verses, and the commentaries on Homer of Eustathius archbishop of Thessalonica, who, from his horn of plenty, has poured the names and authorities of four hundred writers. From these originals, and from the numerous tribe of scholiasts and critics, some estimate may be formed of the literary wealth of the twelfth century. Constantinople was enlightened by the genius of Homer and Demosthenes, of Aristotle and Plato; and in the enjoyment or neglect of our present

riches we must envy the generation that could still peruse the history of Theopompus, the orations of Hyperides,
the comedies of Menander, and the odes of Alcæus and
Sappho. The frequent labour of illustration attests not
only the existence but the popularity of the Grecian
classics; the general knowledge of the age may be deduced from the example of two learned females, the empress Eudocia and the princess Anna Comnena, who
cultivated, in the purple, the arts of rhetoric and philosophy. The vulgar dialect of the city was gross and barbarous: a more correct and elaborate style distinguished
the discourse, or at least the compositions, of the church
and palace, which sometimes affected to copy the purity
of the Attic models.

In our modern education, the painful though necessary
attainment of two languages which are no longer living
may consume the time and damp the ardour of the youthful student. The poets and orators were long imprisoned
in the barbarous dialects of our Western ancestors, devoid of harmony or grace; and their genius, without precept or example, was abandoned to the rude and native
powers of their judgment and fancy. But the Greeks of
Constantinople, after purging away the impurities of their
vulgar speech, acquired the free use of their ancient language, the most happy composition of human art, and a
familiar knowledge of the sublime masters who had
pleased or instructed the first of nations. But these advantages only tend to aggravate the reproach and shame
of a degenerate people. They held in their lifeless hands
the riches of their fathers, without inheriting the spirit
which had created and improved that sacred patrimony:
they read, they praised, they compiled, but their languid
souls seemed alike incapable of thought and action. In
the revolution of ten centuries, not a single discovery was
made to exalt the dignity or promote the happiness of
mankind. Not a single idea has been added to the speculative systems of antiquity, and a succession of patient
disciples became in their turn the dogmatic teachers of

the next servile generation. Not a single composition of history, philosophy, or literature, has been saved from oblivion by the intrinsic beauties of style or sentiment, of original fancy, or even of successful imitation. In prose, the least offensive of the Byzantine writers are absolved from censure by their naked and unpresuming simplicity: but the orators, most eloquent in their own conceit, are the farthest removed from the models whom they affect to emulate. In every page our taste and reason are wounded by the choice of gigantic and obsolete words, a stiff and intricate phraseology, the discord of images, the childish play of false or unseasonable ornament, and the painful attempt to elevate themselves, to astonish the reader, and to involve a trivial meaning in the smoke of obscurity and exaggeration. Their prose is soaring to the vicious affection of poetry: their poetry is sinking below the flatness and insipidity of prose. The tragic, epic, and lyric muses were silent and inglorious: the bards of Constantinople seldom rose above a riddle or epigram, a panegyric or tale; they forgot even the rules of prosody; and with the melody of Homer yet sounding in their ears, they confound all measure of feet and syllables in the impotent strains which have received the name of *political* or city verses. The minds of the Greeks were bound in the fetters of a base and imperious superstition, which extends her dominion round the circle of profane science. Their understandings were bewildered in metaphysical controversy: in the belief of visions and miracles they had lost all principles of moral evidence, and their taste was vitiated by the homilies of the monks, an absurd medley of declamation and Scripture. Even these contemptible studies were no longer dignified by the abuse of superior talents: the leaders of the Greek church were humbly content to admire and copy the oracles of antiquity, nor did the schools or pulpit produce any rivals of the fame of Athanasius and Chrysostom.

In all the pursuits of active and speculative life, the emulation of states and individuals is the most powerful spring of the efforts and improvements of mankind. The cities of ancient Greece were cast in the happy mixture of union and independence, which is repeated on a larger scale, but in a looser form, by the nations of modern Europe: the union of language, religion, and manners, which renders them the spectators and judges of each other's merit: the independence of government and interest, which asserts their separate freedom, and excites them to strive for pre-eminence in the career of glory. The situation of the Romans was less favourable; yet in the early ages of the republic, which fixed the national character, a similar emulation was kindled among the states of Latium and Italy; and in the arts and sciences they aspired to equal or surpass their Grecian masters. The empire of the Cæsars undoubtedly checked the activity and progress of the human mind: its magnitude might indeed allow some scope for domestic competition; but when it was gradually reduced, at first to the East, and at last to Greece and Constantinople, the Byzantine subjects were degraded to an abject and languid temper, the natural effect of their solitary and insulated state. From the North they were oppressed by nameless tribes of barbarians, to whom they scarcely imparted the appellation of men. The language and religion of the more polished Arabs were an insurmountable bar to all social intercourse. The conquerors of Europe were their brethren in the Christian faith; but the speech of the Franks or Latins was unknown, their manners were rude, and they were rarely connected, in peace or war, with the successors of Heraclius. Alone in the universe, the self-satisfied pride of the Greeks was not disturbed by the comparison of foreign merit; and it is no wonder if they fainted in the race, since they had neither competitors to urge their speed, nor judges to crown their victory. The nations of Europe and Asia were mingled by the expeditions to the Holy Land; and it is under the Comnenian dynasty that a faint emulation of knowledge and military virtue was rekindled in the Byzantine empire.

[*Such a society, so civilised, so insulated, so complacent, could afford to despise the barbarians of the West and their spiritual leaders. In chapter XLIX Gibbon gives a picture of the Popes whose learning and piety were outraged by the appointment of the accomplished and scholarly Photius.*]

These emperors, in the election of the popes, continued to exercise the powers which had been assumed by the Gothic and Grecian princes; and the importance of this prerogative increased with the temporal estate and spiritual jurisdiction of the Roman church. In the Christian aristocracy the principal members of the clergy still formed a senate to assist the administration, and to supply the vacancy, of the bishop. Rome was divided into twenty-eight parishes, and each parish was governed by a cardinal-priest, or presbyter—a title which, however common and modest in its origin, has aspired to emulate the purple of kings. Their number was enlarged by the association of the seven deacons of the most considerable hospitals, the seven palatine judges of the Lateran, and some dignitaries of the church. This ecclesiastical senate was directed by the seven cardinal-bishops of the Roman province, who were less occupied in the suburb dioceses of Ostia, Porto, Velitræ, Tusculum, Præneste, Tibur, and the Sabines, than by their weekly service in the Lateran, and their superior share in the honours and authority of the apostolic see. On the death of the pope these bishops recommended a successor to the suffrage of the college of cardinals, and their choice was ratified or rejected by the applause or clamour of the Roman people. But the election was imperfect; nor could the pontiff be legally consecrated till the emperor, the advocate of the church, had graciously signified his approbation and consent. The royal commissioner examined on the spot the form and freedom of the proceedings; nor was it till after a previous scrutiny into the qualifications of the candidates that he accepted an oath of fidelity, and confirmed the donations which had successively enriched the patrimony of St. Peter. In the frequent schisms the rival claims were submitted to the sentence of the emperor; and in a synod of bishops he presumed to judge, to condemn, and to punish the crimes of a guilty pontiff. Otho the First imposed a treaty on the senate and people, who engaged to prefer the candidate most acceptable to his majesty: his successors anticipated or prevented their choice: they bestowed the Roman benefice, like the bishoprics of Cologne or Bamberg, on their chancellors or preceptors; and whatever might be the merit of a Frank or Saxon, his name sufficiently attests the interposition of foreign power. These acts of prerogative were most speciously excused by the vices of a popular election. The competitor who had been excluded by the cardinals appealed to the passions or avarice of the multitude; the Vatican and the Lateran were stained with blood; and the most powerful senators, the marquises of Tuscany and the counts of Tusculum, held the apostolic see in a long and disgraceful servitude. The Roman pontiffs of the ninth and tenth centuries were insulted, imprisoned, and murdered by their tyrants; and such was their indigence, after the loss and usurpation of the ecclesiastical patrimonies, that they could neither support the state of a prince, nor exercise the charity of a priest. The influence of two sister prostitutes, Marozia and Theodora, was founded on their wealth and beauty, their political and amorous intrigues: the most strenuous of their lovers were rewarded with the Roman mitre, and their reign may have suggested to the darker ages[1] the fable of a female pope.[2]

---

[1] The advocates for Pope Joan produce one hundred and fifty witnesses, or rather echoes, of the fourteenth, fifteenth, and sixteenth centuries. They bear testimony against themselves and the legend, by multiplying the proof that so curious a story *must* have been repeated by writers of every description to whom it was known. On those of the ninth and tenth centuries the recent event would have flashed with a double force. Would Photius have spared such a reproach? Could Liutprand have missed such scandal? It is scarcely worth while to discuss the various read-

The bastard son, the grandson, and the great-grandson of Marozia, a rare genealogy, were seated in the chair of St. Peter; and it was at the age of nineteen years that the second of these became the head of the Latin church. His youth and manhood were of a suitable complexion; and the nations of pilgrims could bear testimony to the charges that were urged against him in a Roman synod, and in the presence of Otho the Great. As John XII had renounced the dress and decencies of his profession, the *soldier* may not perhaps be dishonoured by the wine which he drank, the blood that he spilt, the flames that he kindled, or the licentious pursuits of gaming and hunting. His open simony might be the consequence of distress; and his blasphemous invocation of Jupiter and Venus, if it be true, could not possibly be serious. But we read, with some surprise, that the worthy grandson of Marozia lived in public adultery with the matrons of Rome; that the Lateran palace was turned into a school for prostitution; and that his rapes of virgins and widows had deterred the female pilgrims from visiting the tomb of St. Peter, lest, in the devout act, they should be violated by his successor. The Protestants have dwelt with malicious pleasure on these characters of Antichrist; but to a philosophic eye the vices of the clergy are far less dangerous than their virtues. After a long series of scandal the apostolic see was reformed and exalted by the austerity and zeal of Gregory VII. That ambitious monk devoted his life to the execution of two projects. I. To fix

ings of Martinus Polonus, Sigebert of Gemblours, or even Marianus Scotus; but a most palpable forgery is the passage of Pope Joan which has been foisted into some MSS. and editions of the Roman Anastasius.

[2] Till the Reformation the tale was repeated and believed without offence: and Joan's female statue long occupied her place among the popes in the cathedral of Sienna. She has been annihilated by two learned Protestants, Blondel and Bayle: but their brethren were scandalised by this equitable and generous criticism. Spanheim and Lenfant attempt to save this poor engine of controversy; and even Mosheim condescends to cherish some doubt and suspicion.

in the college of cardinals the freedom and independence of election, and for ever to abolish the right of usurpation of the emperors and the Roman people. II. To bestow and resume the Western empire as a fief or benefice of the church, and to extend his temporal dominion over the kings and kingdoms of the earth. After a contest of fifty years the first of these designs was accomplished by the firm support of the ecclesiastical order, whose liberty was connected with that of their chief. But the second attempt, though it was crowned with some partial and apparent success, has been vigorously resisted by the secular power, and finally extinguished by the improvement of human reason.

CHAPTER XXII

THE CRUSADES

[*The distance between Rome and Byzantium was suddenly narrowed, at the end of the eleventh century, by the new conquests of the Seljuk Turks. In 1071 Byzantium, already threatened in the Balkans by barbarians from the North, lost the relics of Italy to the Normans. In the same year Alp Arslan, the Turkish leader, by the decisive victory of Manzikert, opened the way to Asia Minor, the source of the Byzantine armies; and his successors, from their new capital of Nice, only a hundred miles away, threatened Constantinople itself. At the same time the Turks overran Syria, and captured Jerusalem, where their intolerance of pilgrims (contrasting with the tolerance of their Arab predecessors) provoked the Christians of Western Europe. This double threat alarmed both East and West. The Byzantine emperor looked westward to the hitherto despised barbarians of Europe for allies to defend his capital; and he found an unexpectedly warm response. "A new spirit had arisen of religious chivalry and papal dominion; a nerve was touched of exquisite feeling; and the sensation vibrated to the heart of Europe." In chapter LVIII Gibbon describes the realisation of this new spirit in the first Crusade.*]

About twenty years after the conquest of Jerusalem by the Turks, the holy sepulchre was visited by a hermit of the name of Peter, a native of Amiens, in the province of Picardy in France. His resentment and sympathy were excited by his own injuries and the oppression of the Christian name; he mingled his tears with those of the patriarch, and earnestly inquired if no hopes of relief could be entertained from the Greek emperors of the East. The patriarch exposed the vices and weakness of the successors of Constantine. "I will rouse," exclaimed the hermit, "the martial nations of Europe in your cause;" and Europe was obedient to the call of the hermit. The astonished patriarch dismissed him with epistles of credit and complaint; and no sooner did he land at Bari than Peter hastened to kiss the feet of the Roman pontiff. His stature was small, his appearance contemptible; but his eye was keen and lively, and he possessed that vehemence of speech which seldom fails to impart the persuasion of the soul. He was born of a gentleman's family (for we must now adopt a modern idiom), and his military service was under the neighbouring counts of Boulogne, the heroes of the first crusade. But he soon relinquished the sword and the world; and if it be true that his wife, however noble, was aged and ugly, he might withdraw with the less reluctance from her bed to a convent, and at length to a hermitage. In this austere solitude his body was emaciated, his fancy was inflamed; whatever he wished, he believed; whatever he believed, he *saw* in dreams and revelations. From Jerusalem the pilgrim returned an accomplished fanatic; but as he excelled in the popular madness of the times, Pope Urban the Second received him as a prophet, applauded his glorious design, promised to support it in a general council, and encouraged him to proclaim the deliverance of the Holy Land. Invigorated by the approbation of the pontiff, his zealous missionary traversed, with speed and success, the provinces of Italy and France. His diet was abstemious, his prayers long and fervent, and the alms which he received with one hand, he distributed with the other: his head was bare, his feet naked, his meagre body was wrapped

535

in a coarse garment; he bore and displayed a weighty crucifix; and the ass on which he rode was sanctified, in the public eye, by the service of the man of God. He preached to innumerable crowds in the churches, the streets, and the highways: the hermit entered with equal confidence the palace and the cottage; and the people, for all was people, was impetuously moved by his call to repentance and arms. When he painted the sufferings of the natives and pilgrims of Palestine, every heart was melted to compassion; every breast glowed with indignation when he challenged the warriors of the age to defend their brethren, and rescue their Saviour: his ignorance of art and language was compensated by sighs, and tears, and ejaculations; and Peter supplied the deficiency of reason by loud and frequent appeals to Christ and his mother, to the saints and angels of paradise, with whom he had personally conversed. The most perfect orator of Athens might have envied the success of his eloquence: the rustic enthusiast inspired the passions which he felt, and Christendom expected with impatience the counsels and decrees of the supreme pontiff.

The magnanimous spirit of Gregory the Seventh had already embraced the design of arming Europe against Asia; the ardour of his zeal and ambition still breathes in his epistles; from either side of the Alps fifty thousand Catholics had enlisted under the banner of St. Peter; and his successor reveals *his* intention of marching at their head against the impious sectaries of Mohammed. But the glory or reproach of executing, though not in person, this holy enterprise, was reserved for Urban the Second, the most faithful of his disciples. He undertook the conquest of the East, whilst the larger portion of Rome was possessed and fortified by his rival Guibert of Ravenna, who contended with Urban for the name and honours of the pontificate. He attempted to unite the powers of the West, at a time when the princes were separated from the church, and the people from their princes, by the excommunication which himself and his predecessors had thundered against the emperor and the king of France. Philip the First of France supported with patience the censures which he had provoked by his scandalous life and adulterous marriage. Henry the Fourth of Germany asserted the right of investitures, the prerogative of confirming his bishops by the delivery of the ring and crosier. But the emperor's party was crushed in Italy by the arms of the Normans and the countess Mathilda; and the long quarrel had been recently envenomed by the revolt of his son Conrad and the shame of his wife, who, in the synods of Constance and Placentia, confessed the manifold prostitutions to which she had been exposed by a husband regardless of her honour and his own. So popular was the cause of Urban, so weighty was his influence, that the council which he summoned at Placentia was composed of two hundred bishops of Italy, France, Burgundy, Swabia, and Bavaria. Four thousand of the clergy and thirty thousand of the laity attended this important meeting; and, as the most spacious cathedral would have been inadequate to the multitude, the session of seven days was held in a plain adjacent to the city. The ambassadors of the Greek emperor, Alexius Comnenus, were introduced to plead the distress of their sovereign, and the danger of Constantinople, which was divided only by a narrow sea from the victorious Turks, the common enemies of the Christian name. In their suppliant address they flattered the pride of the Latin princes; and, appealing at once to their policy and religion, exhorted them to repel the barbarians on the confines of Asia, rather than to expect them in the heart of Europe. At the sad tale of the misery and perils of their Eastern brethren the assembly burst into tears: the most eager champions declared their readiness to march; and the Greek ambassadors were dismissed with the assurance of a speedy and powerful succour. The relief of Constantinople was included in the larger and most distant project of the deliverance of Jerusalem; but the prudent Urban adjourned the final decision to a second synod, which he proposed to celebrate in some city of France in the autumn of the same year. The short delay would propagate the flame of enthusiasm; and his firmest hope was in a nation of soldiers still proud of the pre-eminence of their name, and ambitious to emulate their hero Charlemagne, who, in the popular romance of Turpin, had achieved the conquest of the Holy Land. A latent motive of affection or vanity might influence the choice of Urban: he was himself a native of France, a monk of Clugny, and the first of his countrymen who ascended the throne of St. Peter. The pope had illustrated his family and province; nor is there perhaps a more exquisite gratification than to revisit, in a conspicuous dignity, the humble and laborious scenes of our youth.

It may occasion some surprise that the Roman pontiff should erect, in the heart of France, the tribunal from whence he hurled his anathemas against the king; but our surprise will vanish so soon as we form a just estimate of a king of France of the eleventh century. Philip the First was the great-grandson of Hugh Capet, the founder of the present race, who, in the decline of Charlemagne's posterity, added the regal title to his patrimonial estates of Paris and Orleans. In this narrow compass he was possessed of wealth and jurisdiction; but in the rest of France Hugh and his first descendants were no more than the feudal lords of about sixty dukes and counts, of independent and hereditary power, who disdained the control of laws and legal assemblies, and whose disregard of their sovereign was revenged by the disobedience of their inferior vassals. At Clermont, in the territories of the count of Auvergne, the pope might brave with impunity the resentment of Philip; and the council which he convened in that city was not less numerous or respectable than the synod of Placentia. Besides his court and council of Roman cardinals, he was supported by thirteen archbishops and two hundred and twenty-five bishops; the number of mitred prelates was computed at four hundred; and the fathers of the church were blessed by the saints and enlightened by the doctors of the age. From the adjacent kingdoms a martial train of lords and knights of power and renown attended the council, in high expectation of its resolves; and such was the ardour of zeal and curiosity, that the city was filled, and many thousands, in the month of November, erected their tents or huts in the open field. A session of eight days produced some useful or edifying canons for the reformation of manners; a severe censure was pronounced against the licence of private war; the Truce of God was confirmed, a suspension of hostilities during four days of the week; women and priests were placed under the safeguard of the church; and a protection of three years was extended to husbandmen and merchants, the defenceless victims of military rapine. But a law, however venerable be the sanction, cannot suddenly transform the temper of the times; and the benevolent efforts of Urban deserve the less praise, since he laboured to appease some domestic quarrels that he might spread the flames of war from the Atlantic to the Euphrates. From the synod of Placentia the rumour of his great design had gone forth among the nations: the clergy on their return had preached in every diocese the merit and glory of the deliverance of the Holy Land; and when the pope ascended a lofty scaffold in the market-place of Clermont, his eloquence was addressed to a well-prepared and impatient audience. His topics were obvious, his exhortation was vehement, his success inevitable. The orator was interrupted by the shout of thousands, who with one voice, and in their rustic idiom, exclaimed aloud, "God wills it, God wills it!" "It is indeed the will of God," replied the pope; "and let this memorable word, the inspiration surely of the Holy Spirit, be for ever adopted as your cry of battle, to animate the devotion and courage of the champions of Christ. His cross is the symbol of your salvation; wear it, a red, a bloody cross, as an external mark, on your breasts or shoulders, as a pledge of your sacred and irrevocable engagement." The proposal was joyfully accepted; great numbers, both of the clergy and laity, impressed on their garments the sign of the cross, and solicited the pope to march at their head. This dangerous honour was declined by the more prudent successor of Gregory, who alleged the schism of the church, and the duties of his pastoral office, recommending to the faithful, who were disqualified by sex or profession, by age or infirmity, to aid with their prayers and alms the personal service of their robust brethren. The name and powers of his legate he devolved on Adhemar, bishop of Puy, the first who had received the cross at his hands. The foremost of the temporal chiefs was Raymond, count of Toulouse, whose ambassadors in the council excused the absence, and pledged the honour, of their master. After the confession and absolution of their sins, the champions of the cross were dismissed with a superfluous admonition to invite their countrymen and friends; and their departure for the Holy Land was fixed to the festival of the Assumption, the fifteenth of August, of the ensuing year.

So familiar, and as it were so natural to man, is the practice of violence, that our indulgence allows the slightest provocation, the most disputable right, as a sufficient ground of national hostility. But the name and nature of a *holy* war demands a more rigorous scrutiny; nor can we hastily believe that the servants of the Prince of Peace would unsheathe the sword of destruction unless the motive were pure, the quarrel legitimate, and the necessity inevitable. The policy of an action may be determined from the tardy lessons of experience; but before we act, our conscience should be satisfied of the justice and propriety of our enterprise. In the age of the crusades, the Christians, both of the East and West, were persuaded of their lawfulness and merit; their arguments are clouded by the perpetual abuse of Scripture and rhetoric; but they seem to insist on the right of natural and religious defence, their peculiar title to the Holy Land,

and the impiety of their Pagan and Mohammedan foes.[1]
I. The right of a just defence may fairly include our civil
and spiritual allies: it depends on the existence of danger; and that danger must be estimated by the twofold
consideration of the malice and the power of our enemies. A pernicious tenet has been imputed to the Mohammedans, the duty of *extirpating* all other religions
by the sword. This charge of ignorance and bigotry is re-
futed by the Koran, by the history of the Musulman conquerors, and by their public and legal toleration of the
Christian worship. But it cannot be denied that the Oriental churches are depressed under their iron yoke; that, in
peace and war, they assert a divine and indefeasible
claim of universal empire; and that, in their orthodox
creed, the unbelieving nations are continually threatened
with the loss of religion or liberty. In the eleventh century the victorious arms of the Turks presented a real
and urgent apprehension of these losses. They had subdued in less than thirty years the kingdoms of Asia, as
far as Jerusalem and the Hellespont; and the Greek empire tottered on the verge of destruction. Besides an honest sympathy for their brethren, the Latins had a right
and interest in the support of Constantinople, the most
important barrier of the West; and the privilege of defence must reach to prevent, as well as to repel, an impending assault. But this salutary purpose might have
been accomplished by a moderate succour; and our
calmer reason must disclaim the innumerable hosts and
remote operations which overwhelmed Asia and depopulated Europe. II. Palestine could add nothing to the
strength or safety of the Latins; and fanaticism alone
could pretend to justify the conquest of that distant and
narrow province. The Christians affirmed that their in-

---

[1] If the reader will turn to the first scene of the First Part of
Henry the Fourth, he will see in the text of Shakespeare the
natural feelings of enthusiasm; and in the notes of Dr. Johnson
the workings of a bigoted, though vigorous, mind, greedy of every
pretence to hate and persecute those who dissent from his creed.

alienable title to the promised land had been sealed by the blood of their divine Saviour; it was their right and duty to rescue their inheritance from the unjust possessors, who profaned his sepulchre, and oppressed the pilgrimage of his disciples. Vainly would it be alleged that the pre-eminence of Jerusalem and the sanctity of Palestine have been abolished with the Mosaic law; that the God of the Christians is not a local deity, and that the recovery of Bethlehem or Calvary, his cradle or his tomb, will not atone for the violation of the moral precepts of the Gospel. Such arguments glance aside from the leaden shield of superstition; and the religious mind will not easily relinquish its hold on the sacred ground of mystery and miracle. III. But the holy wars which have been waged in every climate of the globe, from Egypt to Livonia, and from Peru to Hindostan, require the support of some more general and flexible tenet. It has been often supposed, and sometimes affirmed, that a difference of religion is a worthy cause of hostility; that obstinate unbelievers may be slain or subdued by the champions of the cross; and that grace is the sole fountain of dominion as well as of mercy. Above four hundred years before the first crusade, the eastern and western provinces of the Roman empire had been acquired about the same time, and in the same manner, by the barbarians of Germany and Arabia. Time and treaties had legitimated the conquests of the *Christian* Franks; but in the eyes of their subjects and neighbours the Mohammedan princes were still tyrants and usurpers, who, by the arms of war or rebellion, might be lawfully driven from their unlawful possession.

As the manners of the Christians were relaxed, their discipline of penance was enforced; and with the multiplication of sins the remedies were multiplied. In the primitive church a voluntary and open confession prepared the work of atonement. In the middle ages the bishops and priests interrogated the criminal, compelled him to account for his thoughts, words, and actions, and prescribed the terms of his reconciliation with God. But as this discretionary power might alternately be abused by indulgence and tyranny, a rule of discipline was framed to inform and regulate the spiritual judges. This mode of legislation was invented by the Greeks; their *penitentials* were translated, or imitated, in the Latin church; and in the time of Charlemagne the clergy of every diocese were provided with a code, which they prudently concealed from the knowledge of the vulgar. In this dangerous estimate of crimes and punishments each case was supposed, each difference was remarked, by the experience or penetration of the monks; some sins are enumerated which innocence could not have suspected, and others which reason cannot believe; and the more ordinary offences of fornication and adultery, of perjury and sacrilege, of rapine and murder, were expiated by a penance which, according to the various circumstances, was prolonged from forty days to seven years. During this term of mortification the patient was healed, the criminal was absolved, by a salutary regimen of fasts and prayers: the disorder of his dress was expressive of grief and remorse; and he humbly abstained from all the business and pleasure of social life. But the rigid execution of these laws would have depopulated the palace, the camp, and the city; the barbarians of the West believed and trembled; but nature often rebelled against principle; and the magistrate laboured without effect to enforce the jurisdiction of the priest. A literal accomplishment of penance was indeed impracticable: the guilt of adultery was multiplied by daily repetition; that of homicide might involve the massacre of a whole people; each act was separately numbered; and, in those times of anarchy and vice, a modest sinner might easily incur a debt of three hundred years. His insolvency was relieved by a commutation or *indulgence:* a year of penance was appreciated at twenty-six *solidi* of silver, about four pounds sterling, for the rich; at three solidi, or nine shillings, for the indigent: and these alms were soon

appropriated to the use of the church, which derived
from the redemption of sins an inexhaustible source of
opulence and dominion. A debt of three hundred years,
or twelve hundred pounds, was enough to impoverish a
plentiful fortune; the scarcity of gold and silver was supplied by the alienation of land; and the princely donations of Pepin and Charlemagne are expressly given for
the *remedy* of their soul. It is a maxim of the civil law,
that whosover cannot pay with his purse must pay with
his body; and the practice of flagellation was adopted by
the monks—a cheap though painful equivalent. By a
fantastic arithmetic, a year of penance was taxed at
three thousand lashes; and such was the skill and patience of a famous hermit, St. Dominic of the Iron Cuirass, that in six days he could discharge an entire century
by a whipping of three hundred thousand stripes. His
example was followed by many penitents of both sexes;
and as a vicarious sacrifice was accepted, a sturdy dis-
ciplinarian might expiate on his own back the sins of his
benefactors. These compensations of the purse and the
person introduced, in the eleventh century, a more honourable mode of satisfaction. The merit of military service against the Saracens of Africa and Spain had been
allowed by the predecessors of Urban the Second. In the
council of Clermont, that pope proclaimed a *plenary indulgence* to those who should enlist under the banner
of the cross; the absolution of *all* their sins, and a full
receipt for *all* that might be due of canonical penance.
The cold philosophy of modern times is incapable of feeling the impression that was made on a sinful and
fanatic world. At the voice of their pastor, the robber, the
incendiary, the homicide, arose by thousands to redeem
their souls by repeating on the infidels the same deeds
which they had exercised against their Christian brethren; and the terms of atonement were eagerly embraced
by offenders of every rank and denomination. None were
pure; none were exempt from the guilt and penalty of
sin; and those who were the least amenable to the jus-

tice of God and the church were the best entitled to the
temporal and eternal recompense of their pious courage.
If they fell, the spirit of the Latin clergy did not hesitate to adorn their tomb with the crown of martyrdom;
and should they survive, they could expect without impatience the delay and increase of their heavenly reward. They offered their blood to the Son of God, who
had laid down his life for their salvation: they took up
the cross, and entered with confidence into the way of
the Lord. His providence would watch over their safety;
perhaps his visible and miraculous power would smooth
the difficulties of their holy enterprise. The cloud and
pillar of Jehovah had marched before the Israelites into
the promised land. Might not the Christians more reason-
ably hope that the rivers would open for their passage;
that the walls of the strongest cities would fall at the
sound of their trumpets; and that the sun would be arrested in his mid-career to allow them time for the destruction of the infidels?

Of the chiefs and soldiers who marched to the holy
sepulchre, I will dare to affirm that *all* were prompted by
the spirit of enthusiasm, the belief of merit, the hope of
reward, and the assurance of divine aid. But I am equally
persuaded that in *many* it was not the sole, that in *some*
it was not the leading, principle of action. The use and
abuse of religion are feeble to stem, they are strong and
irresistible to impel, the stream of national manners.
Against the private wars of the barbarians, their bloody
tournaments, licentious loves, and judicial duels, the
popes and synods might ineffectually thunder. It is a
more easy task to provoke the metaphysical disputes of
the Greeks, to drive into the cloister the victims of anarchy or despotism, to sanctify the patience of slaves and
cowards, or to assume the merit of the humanity and
benevolence of modern Christians. War and exercise were
the reigning passions of the Franks or Latins; they were
enjoined, as a penance, to gratify those passions, to visit
distant lands, and to draw their swords against the na-

tions of the East. Their victory, or even their attempt, would immortalise the names of the intrepid heroes of the cross; and the purest piety could not be insensible to the most splendid prospect of military glory. In the petty quarrels of Europe they shed the blood of their friends and countrymen for the acquisition, perhaps, of a castle or a village. They could march with alacrity against the distant and hostile nations who were devoted to their arms; their fancy already grasped the golden sceptres of Asia; and the conquest of Apulia and Sicily by the Normans might exalt to royalty the hopes of the most private adventurer. Christendom, in her rudest state, must have yielded to the climate and cultivation of the Mohammedan countries; and their natural and artificial wealth had been magnified by the tales of pilgrims and the gifts of an imperfect commerce. The vulgar, both the great and small, were taught to believe every wonder, of lands flowing with milk and honey, of mines and treasures, of gold and diamonds, of palaces of marble and jasper, and of odoriferous groves of cinnamon and frankincense. In this earthly paradise each warrior depended on his sword to carve a plenteous and honourable establishment, which he measured only by the extent of his wishes. Their vassals and soldiers trusted their fortunes to God and their master: the spoils of a Turkish emir might enrich the meanest follower of the camp; and the flavour of the wines, the beauty of the Grecian women, were temptations more adapted to the nature, than to the profession, of the champions of the cross. The love of freedom was a powerful incitement to the multitudes who were oppressed by feudal or ecclesiastical tyranny. Under this holy sign, the peasants and burghers, who were attached to the servitude of the glebe, might escape from a haughty lord, and transplant themselves and their families to a land of liberty. The monk might release himself from the discipline of his convent, the debtor might suspend the accumulation of usury and the pursuit of his creditors, and outlaws and malefactors of every cast might continue to brave the laws and elude the punishment of their crimes.

These motives were potent and numerous: when we have singly computed their weight on the mind of each individual, we must add the infinite series, the multiplying powers of example and fashion. The first proselytes became the warmest and most effectual missionaries of the cross: among their friends and countrymen they preached the duty, the merit, and the recompense of their holy vow, and the most reluctant hearers were insensibly drawn within the whirlpool of persuasion and authority. The martial youth were fired by the reproach or suspicion of cowardice; the opportunity of visiting with an army the sepulchre of Christ was embraced by the old and infirm, by women and children, who consulted rather their zeal than their strength; and those who in the evening had derided the folly of their companions were the most eager, the ensuing day, to tread in their footsteps. The ignorance which magnified the hopes, diminished the perils, of the enterprise. Since the Turkish conquest, the paths of pilgrimage were obliterated; the chiefs themselves had an imperfect notion of the length of the way and the state of their enemies; and such was the stupidity of the people, that, at the sight of the first city or castle beyond the limits of their knowledge, they were ready to ask whether that was not the Jerusalem, the term and object of their labours. Yet the more prudent of the crusaders, who were not sure that they should be fed from heaven with a shower of quails or manna, provided themselves with those precious metals which, in every country, are the representatives of every commodity. To defray, according to their rank, the expenses of the road, princes alienated their provinces, nobles their lands and castles, peasants their cattle and the instruments of husbandry. The value of property was depreciated by the eager competition of multitudes; while the price of arms and horses was raised to an exorbitant height by the wants and impatience of the buyers. Those

547

who remained at home, with sense and money, were enriched by the epidemical disease: the sovereigns acquired at a cheap rate the domains of their vassals, and the ecclesiastical purchasers completed the payment by the assurance of their prayers. The cross, which was commonly sewed on the garment, in cloth or silk, was inscribed by some zealots on their skin: an hot iron, or indelible liquor, was applied to perpetuate the mark; and a crafty monk, who showed the miraculous impression on his breast, was repaid with the popular veneration and the richest benefices of Palestine.

The fifteenth of August had been fixed in the council of Clermont for the departure of the pilgrims; but the day was anticipated by the thoughtless and needy crowd of plebeians; and I shall briefly despatch the calamities which they inflicted and suffered before I enter on the more serious and successful enterprise of the chiefs. Early in the spring, from the confines of France and Lorraine, above sixty thousand of the populace of both sexes flocked round the first missionary of the crusade, and pressed him, with clamorous importunity, to lead them to the holy sepulchre. The hermit, assuming the character, without the talents or authority, of a general, impelled or obeyed the forward impulse of his votaries along the banks of the Rhine and Danube. Their wants and numbers soon compelled them to separate, and his lieutenant, Walter the Penniless, a valiant though needy soldier, conducted a vanguard of pilgrims, whose condition may be determined from the proportion of eight horsemen to fifteen thousand foot. The example and footsteps of Peter were closely pursued by another fanatic, the monk Godescal, whose sermons had swept away fifteen or twenty thousand peasants from the villages of Germany. Their rear was again pressed by a herd of two hundred thousand, the most stupid and savage refuse of the people, who mingled with their devotion a brutal licence of rapine, prostitution, and drunkenness. Some counts and gentlemen, at the head of

16
Peter the Hermit preaching the First Crusade to the French.

three thousand horse, attended the motions of the multitude to partake in the spoil: but their genuine leaders (may we credit such folly?) were a goose and a goat, who were carried in the front, and to whom these worthy Christians ascribed an infusion of the divine spirit. Of these, and of other bands of enthusiasts, the first and most easy warfare was against the Jews, the murderers of the Son of God. In the trading cities of the Moselle and the Rhine their colonies were numerous and rich, and they enjoyed, under the protection of the emperor and the bishops, the free exercise of their religion. At Verdun, Treves, Mentz, Spires, Worms, many thousands of that unhappy people were pillaged and massacred, nor had they felt a more bloody stroke since the persecution of Hadrian. A remnant was saved by the firmness of their bishops, who accepted a feigned and transient conversion; but the more obstinate Jews opposed their fanaticism to the fanaticism of the Christians, barricaded their houses, and, precipitating themselves, their families, and their wealth into the rivers or the flames, disappointed the malice, or at least the avarice, of their implacable foes.

Between the frontiers of Austria and the seat of the Byzantine monarchy the crusaders were compelled to traverse an interval of six hundred miles, the wild and desolate countries of Hungary and Bulgaria. The soil is fruitful, and intersected with rivers; but it was then covered with morasses and forests, which spread to a boundless extent whenever man has ceased to exercise his dominion over the earth. Both nations had imbibed the rudiments of Christianity: the Hungarians were ruled by their native princes, the Bulgarians by a lieutenant of the Greek emperor; but, on the slightest provocation, their ferocious nature was rekindled, and ample provocation was afforded by the disorders of the first pilgrims. Agriculture must have been unskilful and languid among a people whose cities were built of reeds and timber, which were deserted in the summer season for the tents of hunters and shepherds. A scanty supply of provisions was rudely demanded, forcibly seized, and greedily consumed, and on the first quarrel the crusaders gave a loose to indignation and revenge. But their ignorance of the country, of war, and of discipline exposed them to every snare. The Greek præfect of Bulgaria commanded a regular force; at the trumpet of the Hungarian king, the eighth or the tenth of his martial subjects bent their bows and mounted on horseback; their policy was insidious, and their retaliation on these pious robbers was unrelenting and bloody. About a third of the naked fugitives, and the hermit Peter was of the number, escaped to the Thracian mountains; and the emperor, who respected the pilgrimage and succour of the Latins, conducted them by secure and easy journeys to Constantinople, and advised them to await the arrival of their brethren. For a while they remembered their faults and losses, but no sooner were they revived by the hospitable entertainment, than their venom was again inflamed; they stung their benefactor, and neither gardens, nor palaces, nor churches, were safe from their depredations. For his own safety, Alexius allured them to pass over to the Asiatic side of the Bosphorus; but their blind impetuosity soon urged them to desert the station which he had assigned, and to rush headlong against the Turks, who occupied the road of Jerusalem. The hermit, conscious of his shame, had withdrawn from the camp to Constantinople; and his lieutenant, Walter the Penniless, who was worthy of a better command, attempted without success to introduce some order and prudence among the herd of savages. They separated in quest of prey, and themselves fell an easy prey to the arts of the sultan. By a rumour that their foremost companions were rioting in the spoils of his capital, Soliman tempted the main body to descend into the plain of Nice: they were overwhelmed by the Turkish arrows, and a pyramid of bones informed their companions of the place of their defeat. Of the first crusaders, three hundred thousand had already perished before a single city was rescued from the infidels, before their graver and more noble brethren had completed the preparations of their enterprise.

None of the great sovereigns of Europe embarked their persons in the first crusade. The emperor Henry the Fourth was not disposed to obey the summons of the pope; Philip the First of France was occupied by his pleasures; William Rufus of England by a recent conquest; the kings of Spain were engaged in a domestic war against the Moors; and the northern monarchs of Scotland, Denmark, Sweden, and Poland were yet strangers to the passions and interests of the South. The religious ardour was more strongly felt by the princes of the second order, who held an important place in the feudal system. Their situation will naturally cast under four distinct heads the review of their names and characters; but I may escape some needless repetition, by observing at once that courage and the exercise of arms are the common attribute of these Christian adventurers. I. The first rank both in war and council is justly due to Godfrey of Bouillon; and happy would it have been for the crusaders, if they had trusted themselves to the sole conduct of that accomplished hero, a worthy representative of Charlemagne, from whom he was descended in the female line. His father was of the noble race of the counts of Boulogne: Brabant, the lower province of Lorraine, was the inheritance of his mother; and by the emperor's bounty he was himself invested with that ducal title, which has been improperly transferred to his lordship of Bouillon in the Ardennes. In the service of Henry the Fourth he bore the great standard of the empire, and pierced with his lance the breast of Rodolph, the rebel king: Godfrey was the first who ascended the walls of Rome; and his sickness, his vow, perhaps his remorse for bearing arms against the pope, confirmed an early resolution of visiting the holy sepulchre, not as a pilgrim, but a deliverer. His valour was matured by prudence and moderation; his piety, though blind, was sincere;

and, in the tumult of a camp, he practised the real and
fictitious virtues of a convent. Superior to the private factions of the chiefs, he reserved his enmity for the enemies of Christ; and though he gained a kingdom by the
attempt, his pure and disinterested zeal was acknowledged by his rivals. Godfrey of Bouillon was accompanied
by his two brothers, by Eustace the elder, who had succeeded to the county of Boulogne, and by the younger,
Baldwin, a character of more ambiguous virtue. The
duke of Lorraine was alike celebrated on either side of
the Rhine: from his birth and education, he was equally
conversant with the French and Teutonic languages: the
barons of France, Germany, and Lorraine assembled
their vassals; and the confederate force that marched
under his banner was composed of fourscore thousand
foot and about ten thousand horse. II. In the parliament
that was held at Paris, in the king's presence, about two
months after the council of Clermont, Hugh, count of
Vermandois, was the most conspicuous of the princes
who assumed the cross. But the appellation of *the Great*
was applied, not so much to his merit or possessions
(though neither were contemptible), as to the royal
birth of the brother of the king of France. Robert, duke
of Normandy, was the eldest son of William the Conqueror; but on his father's death he was deprived of the
kingdom of England, by his own indolence and the activity of his brother Rufus. The worth of Robert was degraded by an excessive levity and easiness of temper: his
cheerfulness seduced him to the indulgence of pleasure;
his profuse liberality impoverished the prince and people; his indiscriminate clemency multiplied the number
of offenders; and the amiable qualities of a private man
became the essential defects of a sovereign. For the
trifling sum of ten thousand marks he mortgaged Normandy during his absence to the English usurper; but
his engagement and behaviour in the holy war announced in Robert a reformation of manners, and restored him in some degree to the public esteem. Another

Robert was count of Flanders, a royal province, which, in this century, gave three queens to the thrones of France, England, and Denmark: he was surnamed the Sword and Lance of the Christians; but in the exploits of a soldier he sometimes forgot the duties of a general. Stephen, count of Chartres, of Blois, and of Troyes, was one of the richest princes of the age; and the number of his castles has been compared to the three hundred and sixty-five days of the year. His mind was improved by literature; and, in the council of the chiefs, the eloquent Stephen was chosen to discharge the office of their president. These four were the principal leaders of the French, the Normans, and the pilgrims of the British isles: but the list of the barons who were possessed of three or four towns would exceed, says a contemporary, the catalogue of the Trojan war. III. In the south of France the command was assumed by Adhemar, bishop of Puy, the pope's legate, and by Raymond count of St. Giles and Toulouse, who added the prouder titles of duke of Narbonne and marquis of Provence. The former was a respectable prelate, alike qualified for this world and the next. The latter was a veteran warrior, who had fought against the Saracens of Spain, and who consecrated his declining age, not only to the deliverance, but to the perpetual service, of the holy sepulchre. His experience and riches gave him a strong ascendant in the Christian camp, whose distress he was often able, and sometimes willing, to relieve. But it was easier for him to extort the praise of the Infidels than to preserve the love of his subjects and associates. His eminent qualities were clouded by a temper, haughty, envious, and obstinate; and, though he resigned an ample patrimony for the cause of God, his piety, in the public opinion, was not exempt from avarice and ambition. A mercantile, rather than a martial, spirit prevailed among his *provincials*, a common name, which included the natives of Auvergne and Languedoc, the vassals of the kingdom of Burgundy or Arles. From the adjacent frontier of

Spain he drew a band of hardy adventurers; as he marched through Lombardy, a crowd of Italians flocked to his standard, and his united force consisted of one hundred thousand horse and foot. If Raymond was the first to enlist and the last to depart, the delay may be excused by the greatness of his preparation and the promise of an everlasting farewell. IV. The name of Bohemond, the son of Robert Guiscard, was already famous by his double victory over the Greek emperor: but his father's will had reduced him to the principality of Tarentum, and the remembrance of his Eastern trophies, till he was awakened by the rumour and passage of the French pilgrims. It is in the person of this Norman chief that we may seek for the coolest policy and ambition, with a small alloy of religious fanaticism. His conduct may justify a belief that he had secretly directed the design of the pope, which he affected to second with astonishment and zeal: at the siege of Amalphi his example and discourse inflamed the passions of a confederate army; he instantly tore his garment to supply crosses for the numerous candidates, and prepared to visit Constantinople and Asia at the head of ten thousand horse and twenty thousand foot. Several princes of the Norman race accompanied this veteran general; and his cousin Tancred was the partner, rather than the servant, of the war. In the accomplished character of Tancred we discover all the virtues of a perfect knight, the true spirit of chivalry, which inspired the generous sentiments and social offices of man far better than the base philosophy, or the baser religion, of the times. . . .

Such were the troops, and such the leaders, who assumed the cross for the deliverance of the holy sepulchre. As soon as they were relieved by the absence of the plebeian multitude, they encouraged each other, by interviews and messages, to accomplish their vow, and hasten their departure. Their wives and sisters were desirous of partaking the danger and merit of the pilgrimage: their portable treasures were conveyed in bars of silver and

gold; and the princes and barons were attended by their
equipage of hounds and hawks to amuse their leisure
and to supply their table. The difficulty of procuring subsistence for so many myriads of men and horses engaged them to separate their forces: their choice or
situation determined the road; and it was agreed to meet
in the neighbourhood of Constantinople, and from thence
to begin their operations against the Turks. From the
banks of the Meuse and the Moselle, Godfrey of Bouillon
followed the direct way of Germany, Hungary, and Bulgaria; and, as long as he exercised the sole command,
every step afforded some proof of his prudence and virtue. On the confines of Hungary he was stopped three
weeks by a Christian people, to whom the name, or at
least the abuse, of the cross was justly odious. The Hungarians still smarted with the wounds which they had
received from the first pilgrims: in their turn they had
abused the right of defence and retaliation; and they
had reason to apprehend a severe revenge from a hero
of the same nation, and who was engaged in the same
cause. But, after weighing the motives and the events,
the virtuous duke was content to pity the crimes and
misfortunes of his worthless brethren; and his twelve
deputies, the messengers of peace, requested in his name
a free passage and an equal market. To remove their
suspicions, Godfrey trusted himself, and afterwards his
brother, to the faith of Carloman, king of Hungary, who
treated them with a simple but hospitable entertainment:
the treaty was sanctified by their common Gospel; and a
proclamation, under pain of death, restrained the animosity and licence of the Latin soldiers. From Austria
to Belgrade, they traversed the plains of Hungary, without enduring or offering an injury; and the proximity of
Carloman, who hovered on their flanks with his numerous cavalry, was a precaution not less useful for their
safety than for his own. They reached the banks of the
Save; and no sooner had they passed the river than the
king of Hungary restored the hostages, and saluted their

departure with the fairest wishes for the success of their enterprise. With the same conduct and discipline Godfrey pervaded the woods of Bulgaria and the frontiers of Thrace; and might congratulate himself that he had almost reached the first term of his pilgrimage without drawing his sword against a Christian adversary. After an easy and pleasant journey through Lombardy, from Turin to Aquileia, Raymond and his provincials marched forty days through the savage country of Dalmatia and Sclavonia. The weather was a perpetual fog; the land was mountainous and desolate; the natives were either fugitive or hostile: loose in their religion and government, they refused to furnish provisions or guides; murdered the stragglers; and exercised by night and day the vigilance of the count, who derived more security from the punishment of some captive robbers than from his interview and treaty with the prince of Scodra. His march between Durazzo and Constantinople was harassed, without being stopped, by the peasants and soldiers of the Greek emperor; and the same faint and ambiguous hostility was prepared for the remaining chiefs, who passed the Adriatic from the coast of Italy. Bohemond had arms and vessels, and foresight and discipline; and his name was not forgotten in the provinces of Epirus and Thessaly. Whatever obstacles he encountered were surmounted by his military conduct and the valour of Tancred; and if the Norman prince affected to spare the Greeks, he gorged his soldiers with the full plunder of an heretical castle. The nobles of France pressed forwards with the vain and thoughtless ardour of which their nation has been sometimes accused. From the Alps to Apulia the march of Hugh the Great, of the two Roberts, and of Stephen of Chartres, through a wealthy country, and amidst the applauding Catholics, was a devout or triumphant progress: they kissed the feet of the Roman pontiff; and the golden standard of St. Peter was delivered to the brother of the French monarch. But in this visit of piety and pleasure they neglected to secure the season and the means of their embarkation: the winter was insensibly lost: their troops were scattered and corrupted in the towns of Italy. They separately accomplished their passage, regardless of safety or dignity; and within nine months from the feast of the Assumption, the day appointed by Urban, all the Latin princes had reached Constantinople. But the count of Vermandois was produced as a captive; his foremost vessels were scattered by a tempest; and his person, against the law of nations, was detained by the lieutenants of Alexius. Yet the arrival of Hugh had been announced by four-and-twenty knights in golden armour, who commanded the emperor to revere the general of the Latin Christians, the brother of the king of kings.

In some Oriental tale I have read the fable of a shepherd who was ruined by the accomplishment of his own wishes: he had prayed for water; the Ganges was turned into his grounds, and his flock and cottage were swept away by the inundation. Such was the fortune, or at least the apprehension, of the Greek emperor Alexius Comnenus, whose name has already appeared in this history, and whose conduct is so differently represented by his daughter Anna, and by the Latin writers.[2] In the council of Placentia his ambassadors had solicited a moderate succour, perhaps of ten thousand soldiers; but he was astonished by the approach of so many potent chiefs and fanatic nations. The emperor fluctuated between hope and fear, between timidity and courage; but in the crooked policy which he mistook for wisdom, I cannot believe, I cannot discern, that he maliciously conspired against the life or honour of the French heroes. The promiscuous multitudes of Peter the Hermit were savage beasts, alike destitute of humanity and reason: nor was it possible for Alexius to prevent or deplore their destruc-

[2] In their views of the character and conduct of Alexius, Maimbourg has favoured the *Catholic* Franks, and Voltaire has been partial to the *schismatic* Greeks. The prejudice of a philosopher is less excusable than that of a Jesuit.

tion. The troops of Godfrey and his peers were less contemptible, but not less suspicious, to the Greek emperor.
Their motives *might* be pure and pious; but he was
equally alarmed by his knowledge of the ambitious Bohemond, and his ignorance of the Transalpine chiefs: the
courage of the French was blind and headstrong; they
might be tempted by the luxury and wealth of Greece,
and elated by the view and opinion of their invincible
strength; and Jerusalem might be forgotten in the prospect of Constantinople. After a long march and painful
abstinence, the troops of Godfrey encamped in the plains
of Thrace; they heard with indignation that their brother,
the count of Vermandois, was imprisoned by the Greeks;
and their reluctant duke was compelled to indulge them
in some freedom of retaliation and rapine. They were
appeased by the submission of Alexius: he promised to
supply their camp; and as they refused, in the midst of
winter, to pass the Bosphorus, their quarters were assigned among the gardens and palaces on the shores of
that narrow sea. But an incurable jealousy still rankled
in the minds of the two nations, who despised each other
as slaves and barbarians. Ignorance is the ground of
suspicion, and suspicion was inflamed into daily provocations: prejudice is blind, hunger is deaf; and Alexius
is accused of a design to starve or assault the Latins in a
dangerous post, on all sides encompassed with the waters.
Godfrey sounded his trumpets, burst the net, overspread
the plain, and insulted the suburbs: but the gates of
Constantinople were strongly fortified; the ramparts were
lined with archers; and after a doubtful conflict, both
parties listened to the voice of peace and religion. The
gifts and promises of the emperor insensibly soothed the
fierce spirit of the Western strangers; as a Christian warrior, he rekindled their zeal for the prosecution of their
holy enterprise, which he engaged to second with his
troops and treasures. On the return of spring, Godfrey
was persuaded to occupy a pleasant and plentiful camp
in Asia; and no sooner had he passed the Bosphorus than

the Greek vessels were suddenly recalled to the opposite shore. The same policy was repeated with the succeeding chiefs, who were swayed by the example, and weakened by the departure, of their foremost companions. By his skill and diligence Alexius prevented the union of any two of the confederate armies at the same moment under the walls of Constantinople; and before the feast of the Pentecost not a Latin pilgrim was left on the coast of Europe.

The same arms which threatened Europe might deliver Asia, and repel the Turks from the neighbouring shores of the Bosphorus and Hellespont. The fair provinces from Nice to Antioch were the recent patrimony of the Roman emperor; and his ancient and perpetual claim still embraced the kingdoms of Syria and Egypt. In his enthusiasm, Alexius indulged, or affected, the ambitious hope of leading his new allies to subvert the thrones of the East; but the calmer dictates of reason and temper dissuaded him from exposing his royal person to the faith of unknown and lawless barbarians. His prudence, or his pride, was content with extorting from the French princes an oath of homage and fidelity, and a solemn promise that they would either restore, or hold, their Asiatic conquests, as the humble and loyal vassals of the Roman empire. Their independent spirit was fired at the mention of this foreign and voluntary servitude: they successively yielded to the dexterous application of gifts and flattery; and the first proselytes became the most eloquent and effectual missionaries to multiply the companions of their shame. The pride of Hugh of Vermandois was soothed by the honours of his captivity; and in the brother of the French king the example of submission was prevalent and weighty. In the mind of Godfrey of Bouillon every human consideration was subordinate to the glory of God and the success of the crusade. He had firmly resisted the temptations of Bohemond and Raymond, who urged the attack and conquest of Constantinople. Alexius esteemed his virtues, deservedly named him the champion of the empire, and dignified his homage with the filial name and the rights of adoption. The hateful Bohemond was received as a true and ancient ally; and if the emperor reminded him of former hostilities, it was only to praise the valour that he had displayed, and the glory that he had acquired, in the fields of Durazzo and Larissa. . . . The two Roberts, the son of the conqueror of England, and the kinsman of three queens, bowed in their turn before the Byzantine throne. A private letter of Stephen of Chartres attests his admiration of the emperor, the most excellent and liberal of men, who taught him to believe that he was a favourite, and promised to educate and establish his youngest son. In his southern province, the count of St. Giles and Toulouse faintly recognised the supremacy of the king of France, a prince of a foreign nation and language. At the head of a hundred thousand men, he declared that he was the soldier and servant of Christ alone, and that the Greek might be satisfied with an equal treaty of alliance and friendship. His obstinate resistance enhanced the value and the price of his submission; and he shone, says the princess Anna, among the barbarians, as the sun amidst the stars of heaven. His disgust of the noise and insolence of the French, his suspicions of the designs of Bohemond, the emperor imparted to his faithful Raymond; and that aged statesman might clearly discern, that, however false in friendship, he was sincere in his enmity. The spirit of chivalry was last subdued in the person of Tancred; and none could deem themselves dishonoured by the imitation of that gallant knight. He disdained the gold and flattery of the Greek monarch; assaulted in his presence an insolent patrician; escaped to Asia in the habit of a private soldier; and yielded with a sigh to the authority of Bohemond, and the interest of the Christian cause. The best and most ostensible reason was the impossibility of passing the sea and accomplishing their vow without the licence and the vessels of Alexius; but they cherished a secret hope, that, as soon as they trod the continent of Asia, their swords would obliterate their shame, and dissolve the engagement, which on his side might not be very faithfully performed. The ceremony of their homage was grateful to a people who had long since considered pride as the substitute of power. High on his throne the emperor sat mute and immovable: his majesty was adored by the Latin princes; and they submitted to kiss either his feet or his knees, an indignity which their own writers are ashamed to confess, and unable to deny. . . .

The conquest of Asia was undertaken and achieved by Alexander, with thirty-five thousand Macedonians and Greeks; and his best hope was in the strength and discipline of his phalanx of infantry. The principal force of the crusaders consisted in their cavalry; and when that force was mustered in the plains of Bithynia, the knights and their martial attendants on horseback amounted to one hundred thousand fighting men, completely armed with the helmet and coat of mail. The value of these soldiers deserved a strict and authentic account; and the flower of European chivalry might furnish, in a first effort, this formidable body of heavy horse. A part of the infantry might be enrolled for the service of scouts, pioneers, and archers; but the promiscuous crowd were lost in their own disorder; and we depend not on the eyes or knowledge, but on the belief and fancy, of a chaplain of Count Baldwin, in the estimate of six hundred thousand pilgrims able to bear arms, besides the priests and monks, the women and children, of the Latin camp. The reader starts; and before he is recovered from his surprise I shall add, on the same testimony, that, if all who took the cross had accomplished their vow, above SIX MILLIONS would have migrated from Europe to Asia. Under this oppression of faith I derive some relief from a more sagacious and thinking writer, who, after the same review of the cavalry, accuses the credulity of the priest of Chartres, and even doubts whether the *Cisalpine* regions (in the geography of a Frenchman) were sufficient to produce and pour forth such incredible multitudes. The coolest scepticism will remember that of these religious volunteers great numbers never beheld Constantinople and Nice. Of enthusiasm the influence is irregular and transient: many were detained at home by reason or cowardice, by poverty or weakness; and many were repulsed by the obstacles of the way, the more insuperable as they were unforeseen to these ignorant fanatics. The savage countries of Hungary and Bulgaria were whitened with their bones: their vanguard was cut in pieces by the Turkish sultan; and the loss of the first adventure, by the sword, or climate, or fatigue, has already been stated at three hundred thousand men. Yet the myriads that survived, that marched, that pressed forwards on the holy pilgrimage, were a subject of astonishment to themselves and to the Greeks. The copious energy of her language sinks under the efforts of the princess Anna: the images of locusts, of leaves and flowers, of the sands of the sea, or the stars of heaven, imperfectly represent what she had seen and heard; and the daughter of Alexius exclaims that Europe was loosened from its foundations, and hurled against Asia. The ancient hosts of Darius and Xerxes labour under the same doubt of a vague and indefinite magnitude; but I am inclined to believe that a larger number has never been contained within the lines of a single camp than at the siege of Nice, the first operation of the Latin princes. Their motives, their characters, and their arms, have been already displayed. Of their troops, the most numerous portion were natives of France: the Low Countries, the banks of the Rhine, and Apulia sent a powerful reinforcement: some bands of adventurers were drawn from Spain, Lombardy, and

England; and from the distant bogs and mountains of Ireland and Scotland issued some naked and savage fanatics, ferocious at home, but unwarlike abroad. Had not superstition condemned the sacrilegious prudence of depriving the poorest or weakest Christian of the merit of the pilgrimage, the useless crowd, with mouths but without hands, might have been stationed in the Greek empire till their companions had opened and secured the way of the Lord. A small remnant of the pilgrims, who passed the Bosphorus, was permitted to visit the holy sepulchre. Their northern constitution was scorched by the rays, and infected by the vapours, of a Syrian sun. They consumed, with heedless prodigality, their stores of water and provision: their numbers exhausted the in-land country: the sea was remote, the Greeks were un-friendly, and the Christians of every sect fled before the voracious and cruel rapine of their brethren. In the dire necessity of famine, they sometimes roasted and devoured the flesh of their infant or adult captives. Among the Turks and Saracens, the idolaters of Europe were ren-dered more odious by the name and reputation of can-nibals; the spies, who introduced themselves into the kitchen of Bohemond, were shown several human bodies turning on the spit: and the artful Norman encouraged a report which increased at the same time the abhor-rence and the terror of the infidels.

I have expatiated with pleasure on the first steps of the crusaders, as they paint the manners and character of Europe: but I shall abridge the tedious and uniform narrative of their blind achievements, which were per-formed by strength and are described by ignorance. From their first station in the neighbourhood of Nicomedia, they advanced in successive divisions; passed the con-tracted limit of the Greek empire; opened a road through the hills; and commenced, by the siege of his capital, their pious warfare against the Turkish sultan.

[The crusaders captured the Turkish capital, and so gave permanent relief to Byzantium; they then went on and established the Latin Kingdom of Jerusalem under Godfrey de Bouillon. At first the new Christian kingdom was cramped and precarious; but later . . .]

By the arms of Godfrey himself, and of the two Baldwins, his brother and cousin, who succeeded to the throne, the Latins breathed with more ease and safety; and at length they equalled, in the extent of their dominions, though not in the millions of their subjects, the ancient princes of Judah and Israel. After the reduction of the maritime cities of Laodicea, Tripoli, Tyre, and Ascalon, which were powerfully assisted by the fleets of Venice, Genoa, and Pisa, and even of Flanders and Norway, the range of sea-coast from Scanderoon to the borders of Egypt was possessed by the Christian pilgrims. If the prince of Antioch disclaimed his supremacy, the counts of Edessa and Tripoli owned themselves the vassals of the king of Jerusalem: the Latins reigned beyond the Euphrates; and the four cities of Hems, Hamah, Damascus, and Aleppo were the only relics of the Mohammedan conquests in Syria. The laws and language, the manners and titles, of the French nation and Latin church, were introduced into these transmarine colonies. According to the feudal jurisprudence, the principal states and subordinate baronies descended in the line of male and female succession: but the children of the first conquerors, a motley and degenerate race, were dissolved by the luxury of the climate; the arrival of new crusaders from Europe was a doubtful hope and a casual event. The service of the feudal tenures was performed by six hundred and sixty-six knights, who might expect the aid of two hundred more under the banner of the count of Tripoli; and each knight was attended to the field by four squires or archers on horseback. Five thousand and seventy-five *serjeants*, most probably foot-soldiers, were supplied by the churches and cities; and the whole legal militia of the kingdom could not exceed eleven thousand men, a slender defence against the surrounding myriads of Saracens and Turks. But the firmest bulwark of Jerusalem was founded on the knights of the Hospital of St. John, and of the temple of Solomon; on the strange association of a monastic and military life, which fanaticism might suggest, but which policy must approve. The flower of the nobility of Europe aspired to wear the cross, and to profess the vows, of these respectable orders; their spirit and discipline were immortal; and the speedy donation of twenty-eight thousand farms, or manors, enabled them to support a regular force of cavalry and infantry for the defence of Palestine. The austerity of the convent soon evaporated in the exercise of arms:- the world was scandalised by the pride, avarice, and corruption of these Christian soldiers; their claims of immunity and jurisdiction disturbed the harmony of the church and state; and the public peace was endangered by their jealous emulation. But in their most dissolute period the knights of the hospital and temple maintained their fearless and fanatic character: they neglected to live, but they were prepared to die, in the service of Christ; and the spirit of chivalry, the parent and offspring of the crusades, has been transplanted by this institution from the holy sepulchre to the isle of Malta.

[*The Crusades were more fatal to Constantinople than to the Moslems. They introduced the "Franks" of Western Europe to the East and sharpened their appetite not only against their enemies, the "infidel" Turks, but also against their allies, the Christian but "schismatic" Greeks. If the first Crusade established the Latin Kingdom of Jerusalem, it also increased the distrust between Franks and Greeks, and the fourth Crusade, diverted by the Venetians from Egypt to Constantinople, ended in 1204 with the sack of the city, the division of the Empire between Frankish feudatories and Venetian capitalists, and the conversion of its shrunken heart into the Latin Empire of the East.*

To all appearances, the historic Byzantine Empire ended with the conquest of 1204: the revenge of the West for the conquest and ruin of Rome by Justinian.

In fact it was not so. From their base in Nice or Nicæa, the seat of the first General Council of the Church and the temporary capital of the Seljuk Turks, the Greeks, led by the able "emperor of Nicæa" John Vatatzes, skilfully undermined the Latin empire of Constantinople just as the Mamelukes of Egypt undermined the Latin Kingdom of Jerusalem. In 1261 the last Latin Emperor was driven out and the capital recovered by Vatatzes' general and successor, John Palæologus. In 1291 the last relics of the Kingdom of Jerusalem fell to the Mamelukes. Thus by the end of the thirteenth century the Crusades had failed and, in Gibbon's words, "a mournful and solitary silence prevailed along the coast which had so long resounded with the WORLD'S DEBATE." In chapter LXI Gibbon summarises the results of the whole movement.]

After this narrative of the expeditions of the Latins to Palestine and Constantinople, I cannot dismiss the subject without revolving the general consequences on the countries that were the scene, and on the nations that were the actors, of these memorable crusades. As soon as the arms of the Franks were withdrawn, the impression, though not the memory, was erased in the Mohammedan realms of Egypt and Syria. The faithful disciples of the prophet were never tempted by a profane desire to study the laws or language of the idolaters; nor did the simplicity of their primitive manners receive the slightest alteration from their intercourse in peace and war with the unknown strangers of the West. The Greeks, who thought themselves proud, but who were only vain, showed a disposition somewhat less inflexible. In the efforts for the recovery of their empire they emulated the valour, discipline, and tactics of their antagonists. The modern literature of the West they might justly despise; but its free spirit would instruct them in the rights of man; and some institutions of public and private life were adopted from the French. The correspondence of Constantinople and Italy diffused the knowledge of the Latin tongue; and several of the fathers and classics were at length honoured with a Greek version. But the national and religious prejudices of the Orientals were inflamed by persecution; and the reign of the Latins confirmed the separation of the two churches.

If we compare, at the era of the crusades, the Latins of Europe with the Greeks and Arabians, their respective degrees of knowledge, industry, and art, our rude ancestors must be content with the third rank in the scale of nations. Their successive improvement and present superiority may be ascribed to a peculiar energy of character, to an active and imitative spirit, unknown to their more polished rivals, who at that time were in a stationary or retrograde state. With such a disposition the Latins should have derived the most early and essential benefits from a series of events which opened to their eyes the prospect of the world, and introduced them to a long and frequent intercourse with the more cultivated regions of the East. The first and most obvious progress was in trade and manufactures, in the arts which are strongly prompted by the thirst of wealth, the calls of necessity, and the gratification of the sense or vanity. Among the crowd of unthinking fanatics a captive or a pilgrim might sometimes observe the superior refinements of Cairo and Constantinople: the first importer of windmills[3] was the benefactor of nations; and if such blessings are enjoyed without any grateful remembrance, history has condescended to notice the more apparent luxuries of silk and sugar, which were transported into Italy from Greece and Egypt. But the intellectual wants of the Latins were more slowly felt and supplied; the ardour of studious curiosity was awakened in Europe by different causes and more

[3] Windmills, first invented in the dry country of Asia Minor, were used in Normandy as early as the year 1105.

recent events; and, in the age of the crusades, they viewed with careless indifference the literature of the Greeks and Arabians. Some rudiments of mathematical and medicinal knowledge might be imparted in practice and in figures; necessity might produce some interpreters for the grosser business of merchants and soldiers; but the commerce of the Orientals had not diffused the study and knowledge of their languages in the schools of Europe. If a similar principle of religion repulsed the idiom of the Koran, it should have excited their patience and curiosity to understand the original text of the Gospel; and the same grammar would have unfolded the sense of Plato and the beauties of Homer. Yet, in a reign of sixty years, the Latins of Constantinople disdained the speech and learning of their subjects; and the manuscripts were the only treasures which the natives might enjoy without rapine or envy. Aristotle was indeed the oracle of the Western universities, but it was a barbarous Aristotle; and, instead of ascending to the fountain head, his Latin votaries humbly accepted a corrupt and remote version from the Jews and Moors of Andalusia. The principle of the crusades was a savage fanaticism; and the most important effects were analogous to the cause. Each pilgrim was ambitious to return with his sacred spoils, the relics of Greece and Palestine;[4] and each relic was preceded and followed by a train of miracles and visions. The belief of the Catholics was corrupted by new legends, their practice by new superstitions; and the establishment of the inquisition, the mendicant orders of monks and friars, the last abuse of indulgences, and the final progress of idolatry, flowed from the baleful fountain of the holy war. The active spirit of the Latins preyed on the vitals of their reason and religion; and if the ninth and tenth centuries were

[4] Such was the opinion of the great Leibnitz, a master of the history of the middle ages. I shall only instance the pedigree of the Carmelites and the flight of the house of Loretto, which were both derived from Palestine.

the times of darkness, the thirteenth and fourteenth were the age of absurdity and fable.

In the profession of Christianity, in the cultivation of a fertile land, the northern conquerors of the Roman empire insensibly mingled with the provincials and rekindled the embers of the arts of antiquity. Their settlements about the age of Charlemagne had acquired some degree of order and stability, when they were overwhelmed by new swarms of invaders, the Normans, Saracens, and Hungarians, who replunged the western countries of Europe into their former state of anarchy and barbarism. About the eleventh century the second tempest had subsided by the expulsion or conversion of the enemies of Christendom: the tide of civilisation, which had so long ebbed, began to flow with a steady and accelerated course; and a fairer prospect was opened to the hopes and efforts of the rising generations. Great was the increase, and rapid the progress, during the two hundred years of the crusades; and some philosophers have applauded the propitious influence of these holy wars, which appear to me to have checked rather than forwarded the maturity of Europe.[5] The lives and labours of millions which were buried in the East would have been more profitably employed in the improvement of their native country: the accumulated stock of industry and wealth would have overflowed in navigation and trade; and the Latins would have been enriched and enlightened by a pure and friendly correspondence with the climates of the East. In one respect I can indeed perceive the accidental operation of the crusades, not so much in producing a benefit as in removing an evil. The larger portion of the inhabitants of Europe was chained to the soil, without freedom, or property, or knowledge; and the two orders of eccle-

[5] On this interesting subject, the progress of society in Europe, a strong ray of philosophic light has broke from Scotland in our own times; and it is with private, as well as public regard, that I repeat the names of Hume, Robertson, and Adam Smith.

siastics and nobles, whose numbers were comparatively small, alone deserved the name of citizens and men. This oppressive system was supported by the arts of the clergy and the swords of the barons. The authority of the priests operated in the darker ages as a salutary antidote: they prevented the total extinction of letters, mitigated the fierceness of the times, sheltered the poor and defenceless, and preserved or revived the peace and order of civil society. But the independence, rapine, and discord of the feudal lords were unmixed with any semblance of good; and every hope of industry and improvement was crushed by the iron weight of the martial aristocracy. Among the causes that undermined that Gothic edifice, a conspicuous place must be allowed to the crusades. The estates of the barons were dissipated, and their race was often extinguished in these costly and perilous expeditions. Their poverty extorted from their pride those charters of freedom which unlocked the fetters of the slave, secured the farm of the peasant and the shop of the artificer, and gradually restored a substance and a soul to the most numerous and useful part of the community. The conflagration which destroyed the tall and barren trees of the forest gave air and scope to the vegetation of the smaller and nutritive plants of the soil.

CHAPTER XXIII

THE MONGOL INVASIONS
AND THE RISE
OF THE OTTOMAN TURKS

With the failure of the crusades, Constantino-
ple resumed its old position as the capital of a
Greek empire. Indeed, under its last dynasty of
the Palæologi—the last and longest in its whole
history—it was more Greek than ever; for all the
non-Greek provinces were lost. But it was also
weaker than ever. It emerged from its troubles as
little more than a protectorate, first, of rival Italian
cities, then of successive Turkish sultans.

For meanwhile the last enemy was closing in.
Where the Franks of the West had failed, the
Ottoman Turks of the East, the conquerors and
successors of the Seljuks, would succeed. The
Ottoman Turks first appeared as a menace to
Byzantium at the end of the 13th century. But in
order to explain their rise, Gibbon turns from
Constantinople and hither Asia to the Far East
and in his chapter LXIV he describes their pre-
cursors, the Mongol (or Mogul, or Tartar) con-
querors of Asia and Eastern Europe. The first
Mongol conqueror was Genghis (or, as Gibbon
calls him, Zingis) Khan, who ruled from 1206 to
1227.

From the petty quarrels of a city and her suburbs, from
the cowardice and discord of the falling Greeks, I shall
now ascend to the victorious Turks; whose domestic
slavery was ennobled by martial discipline, religious en-

thusiasm, and the energy of the national character. The rise and progress of the Ottomans, the present sovereigns of Constantinople, are connected with the most important scenes of modern history; but they are founded on a previous knowledge of the great eruption of the Moguls and Tartars, whose rapid conquests may be compared with the primitive convulsions of nature, which have agitated and altered the surface of the globe. I have long since asserted my claim to introduce the nations, the immediate or remote authors of the fall of the Roman empire; nor can I refuse myself to those events which, from their uncommon magnitude, will interest a philosophic mind in the history of blood.

From the spacious highlands between China, Siberia, and the Caspian Sea the tide of emigration and war has repeatedly been poured. These ancient seats of the Huns and Turks were occupied in the twelfth century by many pastoral tribes, of the same descent and similar manners, which were united and led to conquest by the formidable Zingis. In his ascent to greatness that barbarian (whose private appellation was Temugin) had trampled on the necks of his equals. His birth was noble; but it was in the pride of victory that the prince or people deduced his seventh ancestor from the immaculate conception of a virgin. His father had reigned over thirteen hordes, which composed about thirty or forty thousand families: above two-thirds refused to pay tithes or obedience to his infant son; and at the age of thirteen Temugin fought a battle against his rebellious subjects. The future conqueror of Asia was reduced to fly and to obey; but he rose superior to his fortune, and in his fortieth year he had established his fame and dominion over the circumjacent tribes. In a state of society in which policy is rude and valour is universal, the ascendant of one man must be founded on his power and resolution to punish his enemies and recompense his friends. His first military league was ratified by the simple rites of sacrificing a horse and tasting of a running stream: Temugin pledged himself to divide with his followers the sweets and the bitters of life; and when he had shared among them his horses and apparel, he was rich in their gratitude and his own hopes. After his first victory he placed seventy caldrons on the fire, and seventy of the most guilty rebels were cast headlong into the boiling water. The sphere of his attraction was continually enlarged by the ruin of the proud and the submission of the prudent; and the boldest chieftains might tremble when they beheld, enchased in silver, the skull of the khan of the Keraites; who, under the name of Prester John, had corresponded with the Roman pontiff and the princes of Europe. The ambition of Temugin condescended to employ the arts of superstition; and it was from a naked prophet, who could ascend to heaven on a white horse, that he accepted the title of Zingis, the *most great*; and a divine right to the conquest and dominion of the earth. In a general *couroultai*, or diet, he was seated on a felt, which was long afterwards revered as a relic, and solemnly proclaimed great khan or emperor of the Moguls[1] and Tartars.[2] Of these kindred, though rival, names, the former had given birth to the imperial race, and the latter has been extended by accident or error over the spacious wilderness of the north.

The code of laws which Zingis dictated to his subjects was adapted to the preservation of domestic peace and the exercise of foreign hostility. The punishment of death was inflicted on the crimes of adultery, murder, perjury, and the capital thefts of a horse or ox; and the fiercest of men were mild and just in their intercourse with each other. The future election of the great khan was vested in the princes of his family and the heads of the tribes; and the regulations of the chase were essential to the pleasures and plenty of a Tartar camp. The victorious nation was held sacred from all servile labours, which

---

[1] The name of Moguls has prevailed among the Orientals, and still adheres to the titular sovereign, the Great Mogul of Hindostan.

[2] The Tartars (more properly Tatars) were descended from Tatar Khan, the brother of Mogul Khan (see Abulghazi, parts i. and ii.), and once formed a horde of 70,000 families on the borders of Kitay. In the great invasion of Europe (A.D. 1238) they seem to have led the vanguard; and the similitude of the name of *Tartarei* recommended that of Tarars to the Latins.

were abandoned to slaves and strangers; and every labour was servile except the profession of arms. The service and discipline of the troops, who were armed with bows, scimitars, and iron maces, and divided by hundreds, thousands, and ten thousands, were the institutions of a veteran commander. Each officer and soldier was made responsible, under pain of death, for the safety and honour of his companions; and the spirit of conquest breathed in the law that peace should never be granted unless to a vanquished and suppliant enemy. But it is the religion of Zingis that best deserves our wonder and applause. The Catholic inquisitors of Europe, who defended nonsense by cruelty, might have been confounded by the example of a barbarian, who anticipated the lessons of philosophy,[3] and established by his laws a system of pure theism and perfect toleration. His first and only article of faith was the existence of one God, the Author of all good, who fills by his presence the heavens and earth, which he has created by his power. The Tartars and Moguls were addicted to the idols of their peculiar tribes; and many of them had been converted by the foreign missionaries to the religions of Moses, of Mohammed, and of Christ. These various systems in freedom and concord were taught and practised within the precincts of the same camp; and the Bonze, the Imam, the Rabbi, the Nestorian, and the Latin priest, enjoyed the same honourable exemption from service and tribute: in the mosque of Bochara the insolent victor might trample the Koran under his horse's feet, but the calm legislator respected the prophets and pontiffs of the most hostile sects. The reason of Zingis was not informed by books; the khan could neither read nor write; and, except the tribe of the Igours, the greatest part of the Moguls and Tartars were as illiterate as their sovereign. The memory of their exploits was preserved by tradition: sixty-eight years after the death of Zingis these traditions

---

[3] A singular conformity may be found between the religious laws of Zingis Khan and of Mr. Locke (Constitutions of Carolina).

were collected and transcribed; the brevity of their domestic annals may be supplied by the Chinese, Persians, Armenians, Syrians, Arabians, Greeks, Russians, Poles, Hungarians, and Latins; and each nation will deserve credit in the relation of their own disasters and defeats.

The arms of Zingis and his lieutenants successively reduced the hordes of the desert, who pitched their tents between the wall of China and the Volga; and the Mogul emperor became the monarch of the pastoral world, the lord of many millions of shepherds and soldiers, who felt their united strength, and were impatient to rush on the mild and wealthy climates of the south. His ancestors had been the tributaries of the Chinese emperors; and Temugin himself had been disgraced by a title of honour and servitude. The court of Pekin was astonished by an embassy from its former vassal, who, in the tone of the king of nations, exacted the tribute and obedience which he had paid, and who affected to treat the *son of heaven* as the most contemptible of mankind. A haughty answer disguised their secret apprehensions; and their fears were soon justified by the march of innumerable squadrons, who pierced on all sides the feeble rampart of the great wall. Ninety cities were stormed, or starved, by the Moguls; ten only escaped; and Zingis, from a knowledge of the filial piety of the Chinese, covered his vanguard with their captive parents; an unworthy, and by degrees a fruitless, abuse of the virtue of his enemies. His invasion was supported by the revolt of a hundred thousand Khitans, who guarded the frontier: yet he listened to a treaty; and a princess of China, three thousand horses, five hundred youths and as many virgins, and a tribute of gold and silk, were the price of his retreat. In his second expedition he compelled the Chinese emperor to retire beyond the Yellow River to a more southern residence. The siege of Pekin was long and laborious: the inhabitants were reduced by famine to decimate and devour their fellow-citizens; when their ammunition was spent, they discharged ingots of gold and silver from their engines; but the Moguls introduced a mine to the centre of the capital; and the conflagration of the palace burnt above thirty days. China was desolated by Tartar war and domestic faction; and the five northern provinces were added to the empire of Zingis.

In the West he touched the dominions of Mohammed sultan of Carizme, who reigned from the Persian Gulf to the borders of India and Turkestan; and who, in the proud imitation of Alexander the Great, forgot the servitude and ingratitude of his fathers to the house of Seljuk. It was the wish of Zingis to establish a friendly and commercial intercourse with the most powerful of the Moslem princes; nor could he be tempted by the secret solicitations of the caliph of Bagdad, who sacrificed to his personal wrongs the safety of the church and state. A rash and inhuman deed provoked and justified the Tartar arms in the invasion of the southern Asia. A caravan of three ambassadors and one hundred and fifty merchants was arrested and murdered at Otrar, by the command of Mohammed; nor was it till after a demand and denial of justice, till he had prayed and fasted three nights on a mountain, that the Mogul emperor appealed to the judgment of God and his sword. Our European battles, says a philosophic writer,[4] are petty skirmishes, if compared to the numbers that have fought and fallen in the fields of Asia. Seven hundred thousand Moguls and Tartars are said to have marched under the standard of Zingis and his four sons. In the vast plains that extend to the north of the Sihon or Jaxartes they were encountered by four hundred thousand soldiers of the sultan; and in the first battle, which was suspended by the night, one hundred and sixty thousand Carizmians were slain. Mohammed was astonished by the multitude and valour of his enemies; he withdrew from the scene of danger, and distributed his troops in the frontier towns; trusting

---

[4] M. de Voltaire, Essai sur l'Histoire Générale, tom. iii. c. 60, p. 8. His account of Zingis and the Moguls contains, as usual, much general sense and truth, with some particular errors.

that the barbarians, invincible in the field, would be repulsed by the length and difficulty of so many regular sieges. But the prudence of Zingis had formed a body of Chinese engineers, skilled in the mechanic arts; informed perhaps of the secret of gunpowder, and capable, under his discipline, of attacking a foreign country with more vigour and success than they had defended their own. The Persian historians will relate the sieges and reduction of Otrar, Cogende, Bochara, Samarcand, Carizme, Herat, Merou, Nisabour, Balch, and Candahar; and the conquest of the rich and populous countries of Transoxiana, Carizme, and Chorazan. The destructive hostilities of Attila and the Huns have long since been elucidated by the example of Zingis and the Moguls; and in this more proper place I shall be content to observe, that, from the Caspian to the Indus, they ruined a tract of many hundred miles, which was adorned with the habitations and labours of mankind, and that five centuries have not been sufficient to repair the ravages of four years. The Mogul emperor encouraged or indulged the fury of his troops: the hope of future possession was lost in the ardour of rapine and slaughter; and the cause of the war exasperated their native fierceness by the pretence of justice and revenge. The downfall and death of the sultan Mohammed, who expired, unpitied and alone, in a desert island of the Caspian Sea, is a poor atonement for the calamities of which he was the author. Could the Carizmian empire have been saved by a single hero, it would have been saved by his son Gelaleddin, whose active valour repeatedly checked the Moguls in the career of victory. Retreating, as he fought, to the banks of the Indus, he was oppressed by their innumerable host, till, in the last moment of despair, Gelaleddin spurred his horse into the waves, swam one of the broadest and most rapid rivers of Asia, and extorted the admiration and applause of Zingis himself. It was in this camp that the Mogul conqueror yielded with reluctance to the murmurs of his weary and wealthy troops, who sighed for the enjoyment of their native land. Incumbered with the spoils of Asia, he slowly measured back his footsteps, betrayed some pity for the misery of the vanquished, and declared his intention of rebuilding the cities which had been swept away by the tempest of his arms. After he had repassed the Oxus and Jaxartes he was joined by two generals whom he had detached with thirty thousand horse to subdue the western provinces of Persia. They had trampled on the nations which opposed their passage, penetrated through the gates of Derbend, traversed the Volga and the desert, and accomplished the circuit of the Caspian Sea, by an expedition which had never been attempted, and has never been repeated. The return of Zingis was signalised by the overthrow of the rebellious or independent kingdoms of Tartary; and he died in the fulness of years and glory, with his last breath exhorting and instructing his sons to achieve the conquest of the Chinese empire.

The harem of Zingis was composed of five hundred wives and concubines; and of his numerous progeny, four sons, illustrious by their birth and merit, exercised under their father the principal offices of peace and war. Toushi was his great huntsman, Zagatai his judge, Octai his minister, and Tuli his general; and their names and actions are often conspicuous in the history of his conquests. Firmly united for their own and the public interest, the three brothers and their families were content with dependent sceptres; and Octai, by general consent, was proclaimed great khan, or emperor of the Moguls and Tartars. He was succeeded by his son Gayuk, after whose death the empire devolved to his cousins Mangou and Cublai, the sons of Tuli, and the grandsons of Zingis. In the sixty-eight years of his four first successors, the Mogul subdued almost all Asia and a large portion of Europe. Without confining myself to the order of time, without expatiating on the detail of events, I shall present a general picture of the progress of their arms; I. In the East; II. In the South; III. In the West; and IV. In the North.

I. Before the invasion of Zingis, China was divided

into two empires or dynasties of the North and South;
and the difference of origin and interest was smoothed by
a general conformity of laws, language, and national
manners. The Northern empire, which had been dismembered by Zingis, was finally subdued seven years after his
death. After the loss of Pekin, the emperor had fixed his
residence at Kaifong, a city many leagues in circumference, and which contained, according to the Chinese
annals, fourteen hundred thousand families of inhabitants and fugitives. He escaped from thence with only
seven horsemen, and made his last stand in a third
capital, till at length the hopeless monarch, protesting
his innocence and accusing his fortune, ascended a
funeral pile, and gave orders that, as soon as he had
stabbed himself, the fire should be kindled by his attendants. The dynasty of the *Song*, the native and ancient
sovereigns of the whole empire, survived about forty-five
years the fall of the Northern usurpers; and the perfect
conquest was reserved for the arms of Cublai. During
this interval the Moguls were often diverted by foreign
wars; and, if the Chinese seldom dared to meet their
victors in the field, their passive courage presented an
endless succession of cities to storm and of millions to
slaughter. In the attack and defence of places the engines
of antiquity and the Greek fire were alternately employed: the use of gunpowder in cannon and bombs
appears as a familiar practice; and the sieges were conducted by the Mohammedans and Franks, who had been
liberally invited into the service of Cublai. After passing
the great river the troops and artillery were conveyed
along a series of canals, till they invested the royal residence of Hamcheu, or Quinsay, in the country of silk,
the most delicious climate of China. The emperor, a
defenceless youth, surrendered his person and sceptre;
and before he was sent in exile into Tartary he struck
nine times the ground with his forehead, to adore in
prayer or thanksgiving the mercy of the great khan. Yet
the war (it was now styled a rebellion) was still maintained in the southern provinces from Hamcheu to

Canton; and the obstinate remnant of independence and hostility was transported from the land to the sea. But when the fleet of the *Song* was surrounded and oppressed by a superior armament, their last champion leaped into the waves with his infant emperor in his arms. "It is more glorious," he cried, "to die a prince than to live a slave." A hundred thousand Chinese imitated his example; and the whole empire, from Tonkin to the great wall, submitted to the dominion of Cublai. His boundless ambition aspired to the conquest of Japan: his fleet was twice shipwrecked; and the lives of a hundred thousand Moguls and Chinese were sacrificed in the fruitless expedition. But the circumjacent kingdoms, Corea, Tonkin, Cochin-china, Pegu, Bengal, and Thibet, were reduced in different degrees of tribute and obedience by the effort or terror of his arms. He explored the Indian Ocean with a fleet of a thousand ships: they sailed in sixty-eight days, most probably to the isle of Borneo, under the equinoctial line; and though they returned not without spoil or glory, the emperor was dissatisfied that the savage king had escaped from their hands.

II. The conquest of Hindostan by the Moguls was reserved in a later period for the house of Timour; but that of Iran, or Persia, was achieved by Holagou Khan, the grandson of Zingis, the brother and lieutenant of the two successive emperors, Mangou and Cublai. I shall not enumerate the crowd of sultans, emirs, and atabeks whom he trampled into dust; but the extirpation of the *Assassins*, or Ismaelians of Persia, may be considered as a service to mankind. Among the hills to the south of the Caspian these odious sectaries had reigned with impunity above a hundred and sixty years; and their prince, or imam, established his lieutenant to lead and govern the colony of Mount Libanus, so famous and formidable in the history of the crusades.[5] With the fanaticism of the Koran the Ismaelians had blended the Indian trans-

---

[5] The Ismaelians of Syria, 40,000 Assassins, had acquired or founded ten castles in the hills above Tortosa. About the year 1280 they were extirpated by the Mamalukes.

17
The capture of a Chinese town by Zingis (or Genghis) Khan
and his Mongol horde.

migration and the visions of their own prophets; and it was their first duty to devote their souls and bodies in blind obedience to the vicar of God. The daggers of his missionaries were felt both in the East and West: the Christians and the Moslems enumerate, and perhaps multiply, the illustrious victims that were sacrificed to the zeal, avarice, or resentment of *the old man* (as he was corruptly styled) *of the mountain*. But these daggers, his only arms, were broken by the sword of Holagou, and not a vestige is left of the enemies of mankind, except the word *assassin*, which, in the most odious sense, has been adopted in the languages of Europe. The extinction of the Abbassides cannot be indifferent to the spectators of their greatness and decline. Since the fall of their Seljukian tyrants the caliphs had recovered their lawful dominion of Bagdad and the Arabian Irak; but the city was distracted by theological factions, and the commander of the faithful was lost in a harem of seven hundred concubines. The invasion of the Moguls he encountered with feeble arms and haughty embassies. "On the divine decree," said the caliph Mostasem, "is founded the throne of the sons of Abbas: and their foes shall surely be destroyed in this world and in the next. Who is this Holagou that dares to rise against them? If he be desirous of peace, let him instantly depart from the sacred territory; and perhaps he may obtain from our clemency the pardon of his fault." This presumption was cherished by a perfidious vizir, who assured his master that, even if the barbarians had entered the city, the women and children from the terraces would be sufficient to overwhelm them with stones. But when Holagou touched the phantom, it instantly vanished into smoke. After a siege of two months Bagdad was stormed and sacked by the Moguls; and their savage commander pronounced the death of the caliph Mostasem, the last of the temporal successors of Mohammed; whose noble kinsmen, of the race of Abbas, had reigned in Asia above five hundred years. Whatever might be the designs of the conqueror, the holy cities of Mecca and Medina were protected by the

Arabian desert; but the Moguls spread beyond the Tigris and Euphrates, pillaged Aleppo and Damascus, and threatened to join the Franks in the deliverance of Jerusalem. Egypt was lost had she been defended only by her feeble offspring; but the Mamalukes had breathed in their infancy the keenness of a Scythian air: equal in valour, superior in discipline, they met the Moguls in many a well-fought field; and drove back the stream of hostility to the eastward of the Euphrates. But it overflowed with resistless violence the kingdoms of Armenia and Anatolia, of which the former was possessed by the Christians and the latter by the Turks. The sultans of Iconium opposed some resistance to the Mogul arms till Azzadin sought a refuge among the Greeks of Constantinople, and his feeble successors, the last of the Seljukian dynasty, were finally extirpated by the khans of Persia.

III. No sooner had Octai subverted the northern empire of China than he resolved to visit with his arms the most remote countries of the West. Fifteen hundred thousand Moguls and Tartars were inscribed on the military roll: of these the great khan selected a third, which he intrusted to the command of his nephew Batou, the son of Tuli; who reigned over his father's conquests to the north of the Caspian Sea. After a festival of forty days Batou set forwards on this great expedition; and such was the speed and ardour of his innumerable squadrons, that in less than six years they had measured a line of ninety degrees of longitude, a fourth part of the circumference of the globe. The great rivers of Asia and Europe, the Volga and Kama, the Don and Borysthenes, the Vistula and Danube, they either swam with their horses or passed on the ice, or traversed in leathern boats, which followed the camp and transported their waggons and artillery. By the first victories of Batou the remains of national freedom were eradicated in the immense plains of Turkestan and Kipzak.[6] In his rapid progress he overran the

[6] The *Dashté Kipzak*, or plain of Kipzak, extends on either side of the Volga, in a boundless space towards the Jaik and Borysthenes, and is supposed to contain the primitive name and nation of the Cossacks.

kingdoms, as they are now styled, of Astracan and
Cazan; and the troops which he detached towards Mount
Caucasus explored the most secret recesses of Georgia
and Circassia. The civil discord of the great dukes, or
princes, of Russia betrayed their country to the Tartars.
They spread from Livonia to the Black Sea, and both
Moscow and Kiow, the modern and the ancient capitals,
were reduced to ashes; a temporary ruin, less fatal than
the deep, and perhaps indelible, mark which a servitude
of two hundred years has imprinted on the character of
the Russians. The Tartars ravaged with equal fury the
countries which they hoped to possess and those which
they were hastening to leave. From the permanent conquest of Russia they made a deadly, though transient,
inroad into the heart of Poland, and as far as the borders
of Germany. The cities of Lublin and Cracow were
obliterated: they approached the shores of the Baltic; and
in the battle of Lignitz they defeated the dukes of Silesia,
the Polish palatines, and the great master of the Teutonic
order, and filled nine sacks with the right ears of the
slain. From Lignitz, the extreme point of their western
march, they turned aside to the invasion of Hungary; and
the presence or spirit of Batou inspired the host of five
hundred thousand men: the Carpathian hills could not
be long impervious to their divided columns; and their
approach had been fondly disbelieved till it was irre-
sistibly felt. The king, Bela the Fourth, assembled the
military force of his counts and bishops; but he had
alienated the nation by adopting a vagrant horde of forty
thousand families of Comans, and these savage guests
were provoked to revolt by the suspicion of treachery and
the murder of their prince. The whole country north of
the Danube was lost in a day and depopulated in a summer; and the ruins of cities and churches were overspread with the bones of the natives who expiated the
sins of their Turkish ancestors. An ecclesiastic who fled
from the sack of Waradin describes the calamities which
he had seen or suffered; and the sanguinary rage of sieges
and battles is far less atrocious than the treatment of

the fugitives, who had been allured from the woods under a promise of peace and pardon, and who were coolly slaughtered as soon as they had performed the labours of the harvest and vintage. In the winter the Tartars passed the Danube on the ice and advanced to Gran or Strigonium, a German colony, and the metropolis of the kingdom. Thirty engines were planted against the walls; the ditches were filled with sacks of earth and dead bodies; and after a promiscuous massacre, three hundred noble matrons were slain in the presence of the khan. Of all the cities and fortresses of Hungary three alone survived the Tartar invasion, and the unfortunate Bela hid his head among the islands of the Adriatic.

The Latin world was darkened by this cloud of savage hostility: a Russian fugitive carried the alarm to Sweden; and the remote nations of the Baltic and the ocean trembled at the approach of the Tartars,[7] whom their fear and ignorance were inclined to separate from the human species. Since the invasion of the Arabs in the eighth century Europe had never been exposed to a similar calamity; and if the disciples of Mohammed would have oppressed her religion and liberty, it might be apprehended that the shepherds of Scythia would extinguish her cities, her arts, and all the institutions of civil society. The Roman pontiff attempted to appease and convert these invincible pagans by a mission of Franciscan and Dominican friars; but he was astonished by the reply of the khan, that the sons of God and of Zingis were invested with a divine power to subdue or extirpate the nations; and that the pope would be involved in the universal destruction, unless he visited in person and as a suppliant the royal horde. The emperor Frederic the Second embraced a more generous mode of defence; and

---

[7] In the year 1238 the inhabitants of Gothia (*Sweden*) and Frise were prevented, by their fear of the Tartars from sending, as usual, their ships to the herring-fishery on the coast of England; and, as there was no exportation, forty or fifty of these fish were sold for a shilling (Matthew Paris, p. 396). It is whimsical enough that the orders of a Mogul khan, who reigned on the borders of China, should have lowered the price of herrings in the English market.

his letters to the kings of France and England and the princes of Germany represented the common danger, and urged them to arm their vassals in this just and rational crusade. The Tartars themselves were awed by the fame and valour of the Franks: the town of Neustadt in Austria was bravely defended against them by fifty knights and twenty cross-bows; and they raised the siege on the appearance of a German army. After wasting the adjacent kingdoms of Servia, Bosnia, and Bulgaria, Batou slowly retreated from the Danube to the Volga to enjoy the rewards of victory in the city and palace of Serai, which started at his command from the midst of the desert.

IV. Even the poor and frozen regions of the north attracted the arms of the Moguls: Sheibani khan, the brother of the great Batou, led a horde of fifteen thousand families into the wilds of Siberia; and his descendants reigned at Tobolskoi above three centuries till the Russian conquest. The spirit of enterprise which pursued the course of the Oby and Yenisei must have led to the discovery of the Icy Sea. After brushing away the monstrous fables of men with dogs' heads and cloven feet, we shall find that, fifteen years after the death of Zingis, the Moguls were informed of the name and manners of the Samoyedes in the neighbourhood of the polar circle, who dwelt in subterraneous huts and derived their furs and their food from the sole occupation of hunting.

While China, Syria, and Poland were invaded at the same time by the Moguls and Tartars, the authors of the mighty mischief were content with the knowledge and declaration that their word was the sword of death. Like the first caliphs, the first successors of Zingis seldom appeared in person at the head of their victorious armies. On the banks of the Onon and Selinga the royal or *golden horde* exhibited the contrast of simplicity and greatness; of the roasted sheep and mare's milk which composed their banquets; and of a distribution in one day of five hundred waggons of gold and silver. The ambassadors and princes of Europe and Asia were compelled to undertake this distant and laborious pilgrimage; and the life and reign of the great dukes of Russia, the kings of Georgia and Armenia, the sultans of Iconium, and the emirs of Persia, were decided by the frown or smile of the great khan. The sons and grandsons of Zingis had been accustomed to the pastoral life; but the village of Caracorum was gradually ennobled by their election and residence. A change of manners is implied in the removal of Octai and Mangou from a tent to a house; and their example was imitated by the princes of their family and the great officers of the empire. Instead of the boundless forest, the enclosure of a park afforded the more indolent pleasures of the chase; their new habitations were decorated with painting and sculpture; their superfluous treasures were cast in fountains, and basins, and statues of massy silver; and the artists of China and Paris vied with each other in the service of the great khan. Caracorum contained two streets, the one of Chinese mechanics, the other of Mohammedan traders; and the places of religious worship, one Nestorian church, two mosques, and twelve temples of various idols, may represent in some degree the number and division of inhabitants. Yet a French missionary declares that the town of St. Denys, near Paris, was more considerable than the Tartar capital; and that the whole palace of Mangou was scarcely equal to a tenth part of that Benedictine abbey. The conquests of Russia and Syria might amuse the vanity of the great khans; but they were seated on the borders of China; the acquisition of that empire was the nearest and most interesting object; and they might learn from their pastoral economy that it is for the advantage of the shepherd to protect and propagate his flock. I have already celebrated the wisdom and virtue of a mandarin who prevented the desolation of five populous and cultivated provinces. In a spotless administration of thirty years this friend of his country and of mankind continually laboured to mitigate, or suspend, the havoc of war; to save the monuments, and to rekindle the flame, of science; to restrain the military commander by the restoration of civil magistrates; and to instil the love of peace and justice into the minds of the Moguls. He struggled with the barbarism of the first conquerors; but his salutary lessons produced a rich harvest in the second generation. The northern, and by degrees the southern, empire acquiesced in the government of Cublai, the lieutenant, and afterwards the successor, of Mangou; and the nation was loyal to a prince who had been educated in the manners of China. He restored the forms of her venerable constitution; and the victors submitted to the laws, the fashions, and even the prejudices, of the vanquished people. This peaceful triumph, which has been more than once repeated, may be ascribed, in a great measure, to the numbers and servitude of the Chinese. The Mogul army was dissolved in a vast and populous country; and their emperors adopted with pleasure a political system which gives to the prince the solid substance of despotism, and leaves to the subject the empty names of philosophy, freedom, and filial obedience. Under the reign of Cublai, letters and commerce, peace and justice, were restored; the great canal of five hundred miles was opened from Nankin to the capital; he fixed his residence at Pekin; and displayed in his court the magnificence of the greatest monarch of Asia. Yet this learned prince declined from the pure and simple religion of his great ancestor: he sacrificed to the idol Fo; and his blind attachment to the lamas of Thibet and the bonzes of China provoked the censure of the disciples of Confucius. His successors polluted the palace with a crowd of eunuchs, physicians, and astrologers, while thirteen millions of their subjects were consumed in the provinces by famine. One hundred and forty years after the death of Zingis, his degenerate race, the dynasty of the Yuen, was expelled by a revolt of the native Chinese; and the Mogul emperors were lost in the oblivion of the desert. Before this revolution they had forfeited their supremacy over the dependent branches of their house, the khans of Kipzak and Russia, the khans of Zagatai or Transoxiana, and the khans of Iran or Persia. By their distance and power these royal lieutenants had soon been released from the duties of obedience; and after the death of Cublai they scorned to accept a sceptre or a title from his unworthy successors. According to their respective situation, they maintained the simplicity of the pastoral life, or assumed the luxury of the cities of Asia; but the princes and their hordes were alike disposed for the reception of a foreign worship. After some hesitation between the Gospel and the Koran, they conformed to the religion of Mohammed; and while they adopted for their brethren the Arabs and Persians, they renounced all intercourse with the ancient Moguls, the idolaters of China.

In this shipwreck of nations some surprise may be excited by the escape of the Roman empire, whose relics, at the time of the Mogul invasion, were dismembered by the Greeks and Latins. Less potent than Alexander, they were pressed, like the Macedonian, both in Europe and Asia, by the shepherds of Scythia; and had the Tartars undertaken the siege, Constantinople must have yielded to the fate of Pekin, Samarcand, and Bagdad. The glorious and voluntary retreat of Batou from the Danube was insulted by the vain triumph of the Franks and Greeks; and in a second expedition death surprised him in full march to attack the capital of the Cæsars. His brother Borga carried the Tartar arms into Bulgaria and Thrace; but he was diverted from the Byzantine war by a visit to Novogorod, in the fifty-seventh degree of latitude, where he numbered the inhabitants, and regulated the tributes, of Russia. The Mogul khan formed an alliance with the Mamalukes against his brethren of Persia: three hundred thousand horse penetrated through the gates of Derbend, and the Greeks might rejoice in the first example of domestic war. After the recovery of Constantinople, Michael Palæologus, at a distance from his court and army, was surprised and surrounded in a Thracian castle by twenty thousand Tartars. But the object of their march was a private interest: they came to the deliverance of Azzadin the Turkish sultan, and were content with his person and the treasure of the emperor. Their general

Noga, whose name is perpetuated in the hordes of Astracan, raised a formidable rebellion against Mengo Timour, the third of the khans of Kipzak, obtained in marriage Maria the natural daughter of Palæologus, and guarded the dominions of his friend and father. The subsequent invasions of a Scythian cast were those of outlaws and fugitives; and some thousands of Alani and Comans, who had been driven from their native seats, were reclaimed from a vagrant life and enlisted in the service of the empire. Such was the influence in Europe of the invasion of the Moguls. The first terror of their arms secured rather than disturbed the peace of the Roman Asia. The sultan of Iconium solicited a personal interview with John Vataces;[8] and his artful policy encouraged the Turks to defend their barrier against the common enemy. That barrier indeed was soon overthrown, and the servitude and ruin of the Seljukians exposed the nakedness of the Greeks. The formidable Holagou threatened to march to Constantinople at the head of four hundred thousand men; and the groundless panic of the citizens of Nice will present an image of the terror which he had inspired. The accident of a procession, and the sound of a doleful litany, "From the fury of the Tartars, good Lord, deliver us," had scattered the hasty report of an assault and massacre. In the blind credulity of fear the streets of Nice were crowded with thousands of both sexes, who knew not from what or to whom they fled; and some hours elapsed before the firmness of the military officers could relieve the city from this imaginary foe. But the ambition of Holagou and his successors was fortunately diverted by the conquest of Bagdad and a long vicissitude of Syrian wars; their hostility to the Moslems inclined them to unite with the Greeks and Franks; and their generosity or contempt had offered the kingdom of Anatolia as the reward of an Armenian vassal. The fragments of the Seljukian monarchy were disputed by the emirs

---

[8] John Ducas Vataces, Greek 'emperor' of Nicaea or Nice, (1222–1254) was the champion of the Byzantine cause while Constantinople itself was in the hands of its Frankish conquerors.

who had occupied the cities or the mountains; but they all confessed the supremacy of the khans of Persia; and he often interposed his authority, and sometimes his arms, to check their depredations, and to preserve the peace and balance of his Turkish frontier. The death of Cazan, one of the greatest and most accomplished princes of the house of Zingis, removed this salutary control; and the decline of the Moguls gave a free scope to the rise and progress of the OTTOMAN EMPIRE.

CHAPTER XXIV

THE FALL OF CONSTANTINOPLE

*The Ottoman Turks, dislodged from their orig-
inal home in Khorasan by the Mongol invasions,
were settled in the old Seljuk territory in Asia
Minor about 1280. Within twenty years they were
pressing on the Asiatic frontier of Byzantium, and
by the second half of the fourteenth century they
had effectively encircled it, being firmly established in Europe with their capital at Adrianople.
As Gibbon writes, Constantinople "had often, in
the lapse of a thousand years, been assaulted by
the barbarians of the East and West; but never till
this fatal hour had the Greeks been surrounded,
both in Asia and Europe, by the arms of the same
hostile monarchy".*

*Faced with this double threat, successive Byzan-
tine emperors sought to buy Western support,
even by submitting to the religion of Rome, and in
1439 the emperor John Palæologus would actually
subscribe an Act of Union at the Council of
Florence; but the support thus obtained was always illusory and the religious concessions were
invariably repudiated by the Greek people. Even
the meteoric conquests of the Mongols under
Timur (or Tamerlane) only gave a temporary
respite. Having conquered Persia, Georgia, Tartary, south Russia, North India, and Syria, Timur
turned his arms against the Ottoman Empire and
in 1402, at Ankara, totally defeated and captured
the Turkish sultan Bayezid. But after Timur's
death, Bayezid's successors reconstituted his state*

591

*and resumed its pressure on Europe. By 1451,
when Mohammed II became sultan, Constantinople was already surrounded and the end was
in sight. Mohammed resolved to hasten it. In
chapter LXVIII Gibbon describes the final conquest and the death of the last Christian emperor,
Constantine XI, Palæologus.*

The siege of Constantinople by the Turks attracts our
first attention to the person and character of the great
destroyer. Mohammed the Second was the son of the
second Amurath; and though his mother has been decorated with the titles of Christian and princess, she is more
probably confounded with the numerous concubines who
peopled from every climate the harem of the sultan. His
first education and sentiments were those of a devout
Musulman; and as often as he conversed with an infidel
he purified his hands and face by the legal rites of ablution. Age and empire appear to have relaxed this narrow
bigotry: his aspiring genius disdained to acknowledge
a power above his own; and in his looser hours he presumed (it is said) to brand the prophet of Mecca as a
robber and impostor. Yet the sultan persevered in a decent reverence for the doctrine and discipline of the
Koran: his private indiscretion must have been sacred
from the vulgar ear; and we should suspect the credulity
of strangers and sectaries, so prone to believe that a mind
which is hardened against truth must be armed with
superior contempt for absurdity and error. Under the tuition of the most skilful masters Mohammed advanced
with an early and rapid progress in the paths of knowledge; and besides his native tongue it is affirmed that he
spoke or understood five languages. . . .

The history and geography of the world were familiar
to his memory: the lives of the heroes of the East, perhaps of the West, excited his emulation: his skill in
astrology is excused by the folly of the times, and supposes some rudiments of mathematical science; and a

profane taste for the arts is betrayed in his liberal invitation and reward of the painters of Italy. But the influence of religion and learning were employed without effect on his savage and licentious nature. I will not transcribe, nor do I firmly believe, the stories of his fourteen pages whose bellies were ripped open in search of a stolen melon, or of the beauteous slave whose head he severed from her body to convince the Janizaries that their master was not the votary of love. His sobriety is attested by the silence of the Turkish annals, which accuse three, and three only, of the Ottoman line of the vice of drunkenness. But it cannot be denied that his passions were at once furious and inexorable; that in the palace, as in the field, a torrent of blood was spilt on the slightest provocation; and that the noblest of the captive youth were often dishonoured by his unnatural lust. In the Albanian war he studied the lessons, and soon surpassed the example, of his father; and the conquest of two empires, twelve kingdoms, and two hundred cities, a vain and flattering account, is ascribed to his invincible sword. He was doubtless a soldier, and possibly a general; Constantinople has sealed his glory; but if we compare the means, the obstacles, and the achievements, Mohammed the Second must blush to sustain a parallel with Alexander or Timur. Under his command the Ottoman forces were always more numerous than their enemies, yet their progress was bounded by the Euphrates and the Adriatic, and his arms were checked by Huniades and Scanderbeg, by the Rhodian knights, and by the Persian king.

In the reign of Amurath he twice tasted of royalty, and twice descended from the throne: his tender age was incapable of opposing his father's restoration, but never could he forgive the vizirs who had recommended that salutary measure. His nuptials were celebrated with the daughter of a Turkman emir; and, after a festival of two months, he departed from Adrianople with his bride to reside in the government of Magnesia. Before the end of six weeks he was recalled by a sudden message from the divan which announced the decease of Amurath and the mutinous spirit of the Janizaries. His speed and vigour commanded their obedience: he passed the Hellespont with a chosen guard: and at the distance of a mile from Adrianople the vizirs and emirs, the imams and cadhis, the soldiers and the people, fell prostrate before the new sultan. They affected to weep, they affected to rejoice: he ascended the throne at the age of twenty-one years, and removed the cause of sedition by the death, the inevitable death, of his infant brothers. The ambassadors of Europe and Asia soon appeared to congratulate his accession and solicit his friendship, and to all he spoke the language of moderation and peace. The confidence of the Greek emperor was revived by the solemn oaths and fair assurances with which he sealed the ratification of the treaty: and a rich domain on the banks of the Strymon was assigned for the annual payment of three hundred thousand aspers, the pension of an Ottoman prince who was detained at his request in the Byzantine court. Yet the neighbours of Mohammed might tremble at the severity with which a youthful monarch reformed the pomp of his father's household: the expenses of luxury were applied to those of ambition, and a useless train of seven thousand falconers was either dismissed from his service or enlisted in his troops. In the first summer of his reign he visited with an army the Asiatic provinces; but after humbling the pride Mohammed accepted the submission of the Caramanian, that he might not be diverted by the smallest obstacle from the execution of his great design.

The Mohammedan, and more especially the Turkish casuists, have pronounced that no promise can bind the faithful against the interest and duty of their religion, and that the sultan may abrogate his own treaties and those of his predecessors. The justice and magnanimity of Amurath had scorned this immoral privilege; but his son, though the proudest of men, could stoop from ambition to the basest arts of dissimulation and deceit. Peace was on his lips while war was in his heart: he incessantly sighed for the possession of Constantinople; and the Greeks, by their own indiscretion, afforded the first pretence of the fatal rupture. Instead of labouring to be forgotten, their ambassadors pursued his camp to demand the payment, and even the increase, of their annual stipend: the divan was importuned by their complaints; and the vizir, a secret friend of the Christians, was constrained to deliver the sense of his brethren. "Ye foolish and miserable Romans," said Calil, "we know your devices, and ye are ignorant of your own danger! the scrupulous Amurath is no more; his throne is occupied by a young conqueror whom no laws can bind, and no obstacles can resist: and if you escape from his hands, give praise to the divine clemency, which yet delays the chastisement of your sins. Why do ye seek to affright us by vain and indirect menaces? Release the fugitive Orchan, crown him sultan of Romania, call the Hungarians from beyond the Danube, arm against us the nations of the West, and be assured that you will only provoke and precipitate your ruin." But if the fears of the ambassadors were alarmed by the stern language of the vizir, they were soothed by the courteous audience and friendly speeches of the Ottoman prince; and Mohammed assured them that on his return to Adrianople he would redress the grievances, and consult the true interests of the Greeks. No sooner had he repassed the Hellespont than he issued a mandate to suppress their pension, and to expel their officers from the banks of the Strymon: in this measure he betrayed a hostile mind; and the second order announced, and in some degree commenced, the siege of Constantinople. In the narrow pass of the Bosphorus an Asiatic fortress had formerly been raised by his grandfather; in the opposite situation, on the European side, he resolved to erect a more formidable castle, and a thousand masons were commanded to assemble in the spring on a spot named Asomaton, about five miles from the Greek metropolis.[1] Persuasion is the resource of the feeble; and the feeble can seldom persuade: the ambassadors of the emperor attempted, without success, to divert Mohammed from the execution of his design. They represented that his grandfather had solicited the permission of Manuel to build a castle on his own territories; but that this double fortification, which would command the strait, could only tend to violate the alliance of the nations, to intercept the Latins who traded in the Black Sea, and perhaps to annihilate the subsistence of the city. "I form no enterprise," replied the perfidious sultan, "against the city; but the empire of Constantinople is measured by her walls. Have you forgot the distress to which my father was reduced when you formed a league with the Hungarians, when they invaded our country by land, and the Hellespont was occupied by the French galleys? Amurath was compelled to force the passage of the Bosphorus; and your strength was not equal to your malevolence. I was then a child at Adrianople; the Moslems trembled, and for a while the *Gabours* insulted our disgrace. But when my father had triumphed in the field of Varna, he vowed to erect a fort on the western shore, and that vow it is my duty to accomplish. Have ye the right, have ye the power, to control my actions on my own ground? For that ground *is* my own: as far as the shores of the Bosphorus Asia is inhabited by the Turks, and Europe is deserted by the Romans. Return, and inform your king that the present Ottoman is far different from his predecessors, that *his* resolutions surpass *their* wishes, and that *he* performs more than *they* could resolve. Return in safety; but the next who delivers a similar message may expect to be flayed alive." After this declaration, Constantine, the first of the Greeks in spirit as in rank, had determined to unsheathe the sword, and to resist the approach and establishment of the Turks on the Bosphorus. He was disarmed by the advice of his civil and ecclesiastical ministers, who recommended a

[1][This is the great fortress of Rumeli Hisar, still standing. *Ed.*]

system less generous, and even less prudent, than his
own, to approve their patience and long-suffering, to
brand the Ottoman with the name and guilt of an
aggressor, and to depend on chance and time for their
own safety, and the destruction of a fort which could not
long be maintained in the neighbourhood of a great and
populous city. Amidst hope and fear, the fears of the
wise and the hopes of the credulous, the winter rolled
away; the proper business of each man and each hour
was postponed; and the Greeks shut their eyes against
the impending danger, till the arrival of the spring and
the sultan decided the assurance of their ruin.

Of a master who never forgives, the orders are seldom
disobeyed. On the twenty-sixth of March the appointed
spot of Asomaton was covered with an active swarm of
Turkish artificers; and the materials by sea and land
were diligently transported from Europe and Asia. The
lime had been burnt in Cataphrygia, the timber was cut
down in the woods of Heraclea and Nicomedia, and the
stones were dug from the Anatolian quarries. Each of the
thousand masons was assisted by two workmen; and a
measure of two cubits was marked for their daily task.
The fortress was built in a triangular form; each angle
was flanked by a strong and massy tower, one on the
declivity of the hill, two along the sea-shore; a thickness
of twenty-two feet was assigned for the walls, thirty for
the towers; and the whole building was covered with a
solid platform of lead. Mohammed himself pressed and
directed the work with indefatigable ardour: his three
vizirs claimed the honour of finishing their respective
towers; the zeal of the cadhis emulated that of the Janizaries; the meanest labour was ennobled by the service
of God and the sultan; and the diligence of the multitude
was quickened by the eye of a despot whose smile was
the hope of fortune, and whose frown was the messenger
of death. The Greek emperor beheld with terror the irresistible progress of the work, and vainly strove by flattery and gifts to assuage an implacable foe, who sought,

and secretly fomented, the slightest occasion of a quarrel. Such occasions must soon and inevitably be found. The ruins of stately churches, and even the marble columns which had been consecrated to Saint Michael the archangel, were employed without scruple by the profane and rapacious Moslems; and some Christians, who presumed to oppose the removal, received from their hands the crown of martyrdom. Constantine had solicited a Turkish guard to protect the fields and harvests of his subjects: the guard was fixed; but their first order was to allow free pasture to the mules and horses of the camp, and to defend their brethren if they should be molested by the natives. The retinue of an Ottoman chief had left their horses to pass the night among the ripe corn; the damage was felt, the insult was resented, and several of both nations were slain in a tumultuous conflict. Mohammed listened with joy to the complaint; and a detachment was commanded to exterminate the guilty village: the guilty had fled; but forty innocent and unsuspecting reapers were massacred by the soldiers. Till this provocation Constantinople had been open to the visits of commerce and curiosity: on the first alarm the gates were shut; but the emperor, still anxious for peace, released on the third day his Turkish captives, and expressed, in a last message, the firm resignation of a Christian and a soldier. "Since neither oaths, nor treaty, nor submission can secure peace; pursue," said he to Mohammed, "your impious warfare. My trust is in God alone: if it should please him to mollify your heart, I shall rejoice in the happy change; if he delivers the city into your hands, I submit without a murmur to his holy will. But until the Judge of the earth shall pronounce between us, it is my duty to live and die in the defence of my people." The sultan's answer was hostile and decisive: his fortifications were completed; and before his departure for Adrianople he stationed a vigilant Aga and four hundred Janizaries to levy a tribute on the ships of every nation that should pass within the reach of their

cannon. A Venetian vessel, refusing obedience to the
new lords of the Bosphorus, was sunk with a single bullet. The master and thirty sailors escaped in the boat;
but they were dragged in chains to the *Porte:* the chief
was impaled, his companions were beheaded; and the
historian Ducas beheld, at Demotica, their bodies exposed
to the wild beasts. The siege of Constantinople was deferred till the ensuing spring; but an Ottoman army
marched into the Morea to divert the force of the brothers
of Constantine. At this era of calamity one of these
princes, the despot Thomas, was blessed or afflicted with
the birth of a son—"the last heir," says the plaintive
Phranza, "of the last spark of the Roman empire."

The Greeks and the Turks passed an anxious and
sleepless winter: the former were kept awake by their
fears, the latter by their hopes; both by the preparations
of defence and attack; and the two emperors, who
had the most to lose or to gain, were the most deeply
affected by the national sentiment. In Mohammed that
sentiment was inflamed by the ardour of his youth and
temper: he amused his leisure with building at Adrianople the lofty palace of Jehan Numa (the watch-tower
of the world); but his serious thoughts were irrevocably
bent on the conquest of the city of Cæsar.

[*Mohammed made a particular study of "the recent and
tremendous discovery of the Latins," gunpowder, and
found a renegade Christian gunfounder, Urban, who made
for him "a piece of brass ordnance of stupendous and
almost incredible magnitude," which was carried 150
miles on "a frame or carriage of thirty waggons linked
together and drawn along by a team of sixty oxen."*]

While Mohammed threatened the capital of the East,
the Greek emperor implored with fervent prayers the
assistance of earth and Heaven. But the invisible powers
were deaf to his supplications; and Christendom beheld

with indifference the fall of Constantinople, while she
derived at least some promise of supply from the jealous
and temporal policy of the sultan of Egypt. Some states
were too weak, and others too remote; by some the danger
was considered as imaginary, by others as inevitable: the
Western princes were involved in their endless and domestic quarrels; and the Roman pontiff was exasperated
by the falsehood or obstinacy of the Greeks. Instead of
employing in their favour the arms and treasures of Italy,
Nicholas the Fifth had foretold their approaching ruin;
and his honour was engaged in the accomplishment of
his prophecy. Perhaps he was softened by the last extremity of their distress; but his compassion was tardy;
his efforts were faint and unavailing; and Constantinople
had fallen before the squadrons of Genoa and Venice
could sail from their harbours. Even the princes of the
Morea and of the Greek islands affected a cold neutrality:
the Genoese colony of Galata negotiated a private treaty;
and the sultan indulged them in the delusive hope that
by his clemency they might survive the ruin of the empire. A plebeian crowd and some Byzantine nobles basely
withdrew from the danger of their country; and the
avarice of the rich denied the emperor, and reserved for
the Turks, the secret treasures which might have raised
in their defence whole armies of mercenaries. The indigent and solitary prince prepared however to sustain
his formidable adversary; but if his courage were equal
to the peril, his strength was inadequate to the contest.
In the beginning of the spring the Turkish vanguard
swept the towns and villages as far as the gates of
Constantinople: submission was spared and protected;
whatever presumed to resist was exterminated with fire
and sword. The Greek places on the Black Sea, Mesem-
bria, Acheloum, and Bizon, surrendered on the first summons; Selymbria alone deserved the honours of a siege
or blockade; and the bold inhabitants, while they were
invested by land, launched their boats, pillaged the opposite coast of Cyzicus, and sold their captives in the

public market. But on the approach of Mohammed himself all was silent and prostrate: he first halted at the
distance of five miles; and, from thence advancing in
battle array, planted before the gate of St. Romanus the
Imperial standard; and on the sixth day of April formed
the memorable siege of Constantinople.

The troops of Asia and Europe extended on the right
and left from the Propontis to the harbour; the Janizaries
in the front were stationed before the sultan's tent; the
Ottoman line was covered by a deep intrenchment; and a
subordinate army enclosed the suburb of Galata, and
watched the doubtful faith of the Genoese. . . . The whole
mass of the Turkish powers is magnified by Ducas,
Chalcocondyles, and Leonard of Chios, to the amount of
three or four hundred thousand men; but Phranza was
a less remote and more accurate judge; and his precise
definition of two hundred and fifty-eight thousand does
not exceed the measure of experience and probability.
The navy of the besiegers was less formidable: the Propontis was overspread with three hundred and twenty
sail; but of these no more than eighteen could be rated
as galleys of war; and the far greater part must be degraded to the condition of store-ships and transports,
which poured into the camp fresh supplies of men, ammunition, and provisions. In her last decay Constantinople was still peopled with more than a hundred
thousand inhabitants; but these numbers are found in
the accounts, not of war, but of captivity; and they mostly
consisted of mechanics, of priests, of women, and of
men devoid of that spirit which even women have sometimes exerted for the common safety. I can suppose, I
could almost excuse, the reluctance of subjects to serve
on a distant frontier, at the will of a tyrant; but the man
who dares not expose his life in the defence of his children and his property has lost in society the first and
most active energies of nature. By the emperor's command a particular inquiry had been made through the
streets and houses, how many of the citizens, or even

of the monks, were able and willing to bear arms for their country. The lists were intrusted to Phranza, and after a diligent addition he informed his master, with grief and surprise, that the national defence was reduced to four thousand nine hundred and seventy *Romans*. Between Constantine and his faithful minister this comfortless secret was preserved; and a sufficient proportion of shields, cross-bows, and muskets, was distributed from the arsenal to the city bands. They derived some accession from a body of two thousand strangers, under the command of John Justiniani, a noble Genoese; a liberal donative was advanced to these auxiliaries; and a princely recompense, the isle of Lemnos, was promised to the valour and victory of their chief. A strong chain was drawn across the mouth of the harbour: it was supported by some Greek and Italian vessels of war and merchandise; and the ships of every Christian nation, that successively arrived from Candia and the Black Sea, were detained for the public service. Against the powers of the Ottoman empire, a city of the extent of thirteen, perhaps of sixteen, miles was defended by a scanty garrison of seven or eight thousand soldiers. Europe and Asia were open to the besiegers; but the strength and provisions of the Greeks must sustain a daily decrease; nor could they indulge the expectation of any foreign succour or supply.

The primitive Romans would have drawn their swords in the resolution of death or conquest. The primitive Christians might have embraced each other, and awaited in patience and charity the stroke of martyrdom. But the Greeks of Constantinople were animated only by the spirit of religion, and that spirit was productive only of animosity and discord. Before his death the emperor John Palæologus had renounced the unpopular measure of a union with the Latins; nor was the idea revived till the distress of his brother Constantine imposed a last trial of flattery and dissimulation. With the demand of temporal aid his ambassadors were instructed to mingle the assurance of spiritual obedience: his neglect of the church was excused by the urgent cares of the state; and his orthodox wishes solicited the presence of a Roman legate. The Vatican had been too often deluded; yet the signs of repentance could not decently be overlooked; a legate was more easily granted than an army; and about six months before the final destruction, the cardinal Isidore of Russia appeared in that character with a retinue of priests and soldiers. The emperor saluted him as a friend and father; respectfully listened to his public and private sermons; and with the most obsequious of the clergy and laymen subscribed the act of union, as it had been ratified in the council of Florence. On the twelfth of December the two nations, in the church of St. Sophia, joined in the communion of sacrifice and prayer; and the names of the two pontiffs were solemnly commemorated; the names of Nicholas the Fifth, the vicar of Christ, and of the patriarch Gregory, who had been driven into exile by a rebellious people.

But the dress and language of the Latin priest who officiated at the altar were an object of scandal; and it was observed with horror that he consecrated a cake or wafer of *unleavened* bread, and poured cold water into the cup of the sacrament. A national historian acknowledges with a blush that none of his countrymen, not the emperor himself, were sincere in this occasional conformity. Their hasty and unconditional submission was palliated by a promise of future revisal; but the best, or the worst, of their excuses was the confession of their own perjury. When they were pressed by the reproaches of their honest brethren, "Have patience," they whispered, "have patience till God shall have delivered the city from the great dragon who seeks to devour us. You shall then perceive whether we are truly reconciled with the Azymites."[2] But patience is not the attribute of zeal; nor can the arts of a court be adapted to the freedom and violence of popular enthusiasm. From the dome of St.

[2] [Users of unleavened bread: a Greek term for the 'schismatic' Catholics. *Ed.*]

Sophia the inhabitants of either sex, and of every degree, rushed in crowds to the cell of the monk Gennadius, to consult the oracle of the church. The holy man was invisible; entranced as it should seem, in deep meditation, or divine rapture: but he had exposed on the door of his cell a speaking tablet; and they successively withdrew, after reading these tremendous words: "O miserable Romans, why will ye abandon the truth; and why, instead of confiding in God, will ye put your trust in the Italians? In losing your faith you will lose your city. Have mercy on me, O Lord! I protest in thy presence that I am innocent of the crime. O miserable Romans, consider, pause, and repent. At the same moment that you renounce the religion of your fathers, by embracing impiety, you submit to a foreign servitude." According to the advice of Gennadius, the religious virgins, as pure as angels, and as proud as demons, rejected the act of union, and abjured all communion with the present and future associates of the Latins; and their example was applauded and imitated by the greatest part of the clergy and people. From the monastery the devout Greeks dispersed themselves in the taverns; drank confusion to the slaves of the pope; emptied their glasses in honour of the image of the holy Virgin; and besought her to defend against Mohammed the city which she had formerly saved from Chosroes and the Chagan. In the double intoxication of zeal and wine, they valiantly exclaimed, "What occasion have we for succour, or union, or Latins? far from us be the worship of the Azymites!" During the winter that preceded the Turkish conquest the nation was distracted by this epidemical frenzy; and the season of Lent, the approach of Easter, instead of breathing charity and love, served only to fortify the obstinacy and influence of the zealots. The confessors scrutinised and alarmed the conscience of their votaries, and a rigorous penance was imposed on those who had received the communion from a priest who had given an express or tacit consent to the union. His service at the altar propagated the infection to the mute and simple spectators of the ceremony: they forfeited, by the impure spectacle, the virtue of the sacerdotal character; nor was it lawful, even in danger of sudden death, to invoke the assistance of their prayers or absolution. No sooner had the church of St. Sophia been polluted by the Latin sacrifice than it was deserted as a Jewish synagogue, or a heathen temple, by the clergy and people; and a vast and gloomy silence prevailed in that venerable dome, which had so often smoked with a cloud of incense, blazed with innumerable lights, and resounded with the voice of prayer and thanksgiving. The Latins were the most odious of heretics and infidels; and the first minister of the empire, the great duke, was heard to declare that he had rather behold in Constantinople the turban of Mohammed than the pope's tiara or a cardinal's hat. A sentiment so unworthy of Christians and patriots was familiar and fatal to the Greeks: the emperor was deprived of the affection and support of his subjects; and their native cowardice was sanctified by resignation to the divine decree or the visionary hope of a miraculous deliverance.

Of the triangle which composes the figure of Constantinople the two sides along the sea were made inaccessible to an enemy; the Propontis by nature, and the harbour by art. Between the two waters, the basis of the triangle, the land side was protected by a double wall and a deep ditch of the depth of one hundred feet. Against this line of fortification, which Phranza, an eye-witness, prolongs to the measure of six miles, the Ottomans directed their principal attack; and the emperor, after distributing the service and command of the most perilous stations, undertook the defence of the external wall. In the first days of the siege the Greek soldiers descended into the ditch, or sallied into the field; but they soon discovered that, in the proportion of their numbers, one Christian was of more value than twenty Turks; and, after these bold preludes, they were prudently content to maintain the rampart with their missile weapons. Nor

605

should this prudence be accused of pusillanimity. The nation was indeed pusillanimous and base; but the last Constantine deserves the name of a hero: his noble band of volunteers was inspired with Roman virtue; and the foreign auxiliaries supported the honour of the Western chivalry. The incessant volleys of lances and arrows were accompanied with the smoke, the sound, and the fire of their musketry and cannon. Their small arms discharged at the same time either five, or even ten, balls of lead, of the size of a walnut; and, according to the closeness of the ranks and the force of the powder, several breast-plates and bodies were transpierced by the same shot. But the Turkish approaches were soon sunk in trenches or covered with ruins. Each day added to the science of the Christians; but their inadequate stock of gunpowder was wasted in the operations of each day. Their ordnance was not powerful either in size or number; and if they pos-sessed some heavy cannon, they feared to plant them on the walls, lest the aged structure should be shaken and overthrown by the explosion. The same destructive secret had been revealed to the Moslems; by whom it was employed with the superior energy of zeal, riches, and despotism. The great cannon of Mohammed has been separately noticed: an important and visible object in the history of the times; but that enormous engine was flanked by two fellows almost of equal magnitude: the long order of the Turkish artillery was pointed against the walls; fourteen batteries thundered at once on the most accessible places; and of one of these it is am-biguously expressed that it was mounted with one hun-dred and thirty guns, or that it discharged one hundred and thirty bullets. Yet in the power and activity of the sultan we may discern the infancy of the new science. Under a master who counted the moments the great can-non could be loaded and fired no more than seven times in one day. The heated metal unfortunately burst; sev-eral workmen were destroyed, and the skill of an artist was admired who bethought himself of preventing the danger and the accident, by pouring oil, after each explosion, into the mouth of the cannon.

The first random shots were productive of more sound than effect; and it was by the advice of a Christian that the engineers were taught to level their aim against the two opposite sides of the salient angles of a bastion. However imperfect, the weight and repetition of the fire made some impression on the walls; and the Turks, pushing their approaches to the edge of the ditch, attempted to fill the enormous chasm and to build a road to the assault. Innumerable fascines, and hogsheads, and trunks of trees, were heaped on each other; and such was the impetuosity of the throng, that the foremost and the weakest were pushed headlong down the precipice and instantly buried under the accumulated mass. To fill the ditch was the toil of the besiegers; to clear away the rubbish was the safety of the besieged; and, after a long and bloody conflict, the web that had been woven in the day was still unravelled in the night. The next resource of Mohammed was the practice of mines; but the soil was rocky; in every attempt he was stopped and undermined by the Christian engineers; nor had the art been yet invented of replenishing those subterraneous passages with gunpowder and blowing whole towers and cities into the air. A circumstance that distinguishes the siege of Constantinople is the reunion of the ancient and modern artillery. The cannon were intermingled with the mechanical engines for casting stones and darts; the bullet and the battering-ram were directed against the same walls; nor had the discovery of gunpowder superseded the use of the liquid and unextinguishable fire. A wooden turret of the largest size was advanced on rollers: this portable magazine of ammunition and fascines was protected by a threefold covering of bulls' hides; incessant volleys were securely discharged from the loopholes; in the front three doors were contrived for the alternate sally and retreat of the soldiers and workmen. They ascended by a staircase to the upper platform, and, as high as the level of that platform, a scaling-ladder could be raised by pulleys to form a bridge and grapple with the adverse rampart. By these various arts of annoyance, some as new as they were pernicious to the Greeks, the tower of St. Romanus was at length overturned: after a severe struggle the Turks were repulsed from the breach and interrupted by darkness; but they trusted that with the return of light they should renew the attack with fresh vigour and decisive success. Of this pause of action, this interval of hope, each moment was improved by the activity of the emperor and Justiniani, who passed the night on the spot, and urged the labours which involved the safety of the church and city. At the dawn of day the impatient sultan perceived, with astonishment and grief, that his wooden turret had been reduced to ashes: the ditch was cleared and restored, and the tower of St. Romanus was again strong and entire. He deplored the failure of his design, and uttered a profane exclamation, that the word of the thirty-seven thousand prophets should not have compelled him to believe that such a work, in so short a time, could have been accomplished by the infidels.

The generosity of the Christian princes was cold and tardy; but in the first apprehension of a siege Constantine had negotiated, in the isles of the Archipelago, the Morea, and Sicily, the most indispensable supplies. As early as the beginning of April, five great ships, equipped for merchandise and war, would have sailed from the harbour of Chios, had not the wind blown obstinately from the north. One of these ships bore the Imperial flag; the remaining four belonged to the Genoese; and they were laden with wheat and barley, with wine, oil, and vegetables, and, above all, with soldiers and mariners, for the service of the capital. After a tedious delay a gentle breeze, and on the second day a strong gale from the south, carried them through the Hellespont and the Propontis; but the city was already invested by sea and land, and the Turkish fleet, at the entrance of the

18
The Turkish Sultan, Mohammed the Second, whose forces
captured Constantinople and brought about the collapse of the
Roman Empire in the East.

Bosphorus, was stretched from shore to shore, in the form of a crescent, to intercept, or at least to repel, these bold auxiliaries. The reader who has present to his mind the geographical picture of Constantinople will conceive and admire the greatness of the spectacle. The five Christian ships continued to advance with joyful shouts, and a full press both of sails and oars, against the hostile fleet of three hundred vessels; and the rampart, the camp, the coasts of Europe and Asia, were lined with innumerable spectators, who anxiously awaited the event of this momentous succour. At the first view that event could not appear doubtful; the superiority of the Moslems was beyond all measure or account, and, in a calm, their numbers and valour must inevitably have prevailed. But their hasty and imperfect navy had been created, not by the genius of the people, but by the will of the sultan: in the height of their prosperity the Turks have acknowledged that, if God had given them the earth, he had left the sea to the infidels; and a series of defeats, a rapid progress of decay, has established the truth of their modest confession. Except eighteen galleys of some force, the rest of their fleet consisted of open boats, rudely constructed and awkwardly managed, crowded with troops, and destitute of cannon; and since courage arises in a great measure from the consciousness of strength, the bravest of the Janizaries might tremble on a new element. In the Christian squadron five stout and lofty ships were guided by skilful pilots, and manned with the veterans of Italy and Greece, long practised in the arts and perils of the sea. Their weight was directed to sink or scatter the weak obstacles that impeded their passage: their artillery swept the waters; their liquid fire was poured on the heads of the adversaries, who, with the design of boarding, presumed to approach them; and the winds and waves are always on the side of the ablest navigators. In this conflict the Imperial vessel, which had been almost overpowered, was rescued by the Genoese; but the Turks, in a distant and a closer attack, were twice repulsed with considerable loss. Mohammed himself sat on horseback on the beach, to encourage their valour by his voice and presence, by the promise of reward, and by fear more potent than the fear of the enemy. The passions of his soul, and even the gestures of his body, seemed to imitate the actions of the combatants; and, as if he had been the lord of nature, he spurred his horse with a fearless and impotent effort into the sea. His loud reproaches, and the clamours of the camp, urged the Ottomans to a third attack, more fatal and bloody than the two former; and I must repeat, though I cannot credit, the evidence of Phranza, who affirms, from their own mouth, that they lost above twelve thousand men in the slaughter of the day. They fled in disorder to the shores of Europe and Asia, while the Christian squadron, triumphant and unhurt, steered along the Bosphorus, and securely anchored within the chain of the harbour. The introduction of this supply revived the hopes of the Greeks, and accused the supineness of their Western allies. Amidst the deserts of Anatolia and the rocks of Palestine, the millions of the crusades had buried themselves in a voluntary and inevitable grave; but the situation of the Imperial city was strong against her enemies, and accessible to her friends; and a rational and moderate armament of the maritime states might have saved the relics of the Roman name, and maintained a Christian fortress in the heart of the Ottoman empire. Yet this was the sole and feeble attempt for the deliverance of Constantinople: the more distant powers were insensible of its danger; and the ambassador of Hungary, or at least of Huniades,[3] resided in the Turkish camp, to remove the fears and to direct the operations of the sultan.

It was difficult for the Greeks to penetrate the secret of the divan; yet the Greeks are persuaded that a resistance so obstinate and surprising had fatigued the perseverance

[3][John Hunyadi, King of Hungary. *Ed.*]

of Mohammed. He began to meditate a retreat; and the siege would have been speedily raised, if the ambition and jealousy of the second vizir had not opposed the perfidious advice of Calil Bashaw, who still maintained a secret correspondence with the Byzantine court. The reduction of the city appeared to be hopeless, unless a double attack could be made from the harbour as well as from the land; but the harbour was inaccessible: an impenetrable chain was now defended by eight large ships, more than twenty of a smaller size, with several galleys and sloops; and, instead of forcing this barrier, the Turks might apprehend a naval sally and a second encounter in the open sea. In this perplexity the genius of Mohammed conceived and executed a plan of a bold and marvellous cast, of transporting by land his lighter vessels and military stores from the Bosphorus into the higher part of the harbour. The distance is about ten miles; the ground is uneven, and was overspread with thickets; and, as the road must be opened behind the suburb of Galata, their free passage or total destruction must depend on the option of the Genoese. But these selfish merchants were ambitious of the favour of being the last devoured, and the deficiency of art was supplied by the strength of obedient myriads. A level way was covered with a broad platform of strong and solid planks; and to render them more slippery and smooth, they were anointed with the fat of sheep and oxen. Fourscore light galleys and brigantines of fifty and thirty oars were disembarked on the Bosphorus shore, arranged successively on rollers, and drawn forwards by the power of men and pulleys. Two guides or pilots were stationed at the helm and the prow of each vessel: the sails were unfurled to the winds, and the labour was cheered by song and acclamation. In the course of a single night this Turkish fleet painfully climbed the hill, steered over the plain, and was launched from the declivity into the shallow waters of the harbour, far above the molestation of the deeper vessels of the Greeks. The real importance of this operation was magnified by the consternation and confidence which it inspired; but the notorious, unquestionable fact was displayed before the eyes, and is recorded by the pens, of the two nations. A similar stratagem had been repeatedly practised by the ancients; the Ottoman galleys (I must again repeat) should be considered as large boats; and, if we compare the magnitude and the distance, the obstacles and the means, the boasted miracle has perhaps been equalled by the industry of our times.[4] As soon as Mohammed had occupied the upper harbour with a fleet and army, he constructed in the narrowest part a bridge, or rather mole, of fifty cubits in breadth and one hundred in length: it was formed of casks and hogsheads, joined with rafters, linked with iron, and covered with a solid floor. On this floating battery he planted one of his largest cannon, while the fourscore galleys, with troops and scaling-ladders, approached the most accessible side, which had formerly been stormed by the Latin conquerors. The indolence of the Christians has been accused for not destroying these unfinished works; but their fire, by a superior fire, was controlled and silenced; nor were they wanting in a nocturnal attempt to burn the vessels as well as the bridge of the sultan. His vigilance prevented their approach: their foremost galliots were sunk or taken; forty youths, the bravest of Italy and Greece, were inhumanly massacred at his command; nor could the emperor's grief be assuaged by the just though cruel retaliation of exposing from the walls the heads of two hundred and sixty Musulman captives. After a siege of forty days the fate of Constantinople could no longer be averted. The diminutive garrison was exhausted by a double attack: the fortifications, which had stood for ages against hostile violence, were dismantled on all sides by the

[4] I particularly allude to our own embarkations on the lakes of Canada in the years 1776 and 1777, so great in the labour, so fruitless in the event.

Ottoman cannon; many breaches were opened, and near the gate of St. Romanus four towers had been levelled with the ground. For the payment of his feeble and mutinous troops, Constantine was compelled to despoil the churches with the promise of a fourfold restitution; and his sacrilege offered a new reproach to the enemies of the union. A spirit of discord impaired the remnant of the Christian strength: the Genoese and Venetian auxiliaries asserted the pre-eminence of their respective service; and Justiniani and the great duke, whose ambition was not extinguished by the common danger, accused each other of treachery and cowardice.

During the siege of Constantinople the words of peace and capitulation had been sometimes pronounced; and several embassies had passed between the camp and the city. The Greek emperor was humbled by adversity; and would have yielded to any terms compatible with religion and royalty. The Turkish sultan was desirious of sparing the blood of his soldiers; still more desirous of securing for his own use the Byzantine treasures; and he accomplished a sacred duty in presenting to the *Gabours* the choice of circumcision, of tribute, or of death. The avarice of Mohammed might have been satisfied with an annual sum of one hundred thousand ducats; but his ambition grasped the capital of the East: to the prince he offered a rich equivalent, to the people a free toleration, or a safe departure: but after some fruitless treaty, he declared his resolution of finding either a throne or a grave under the walls of Constantinople. A sense of honour, and the fear of universal reproach, forbade Palæologus to resign the city into the hands of the Ottomans; and he determined to abide the last extremities of war. Several days were employed by the sultan in the preparations of the assault; and a respite was granted by his favourite science of astrology, which had fixed on the twenty-ninth of May as the fortunate and fatal hour. On the evening of the twenty-seventh he issued his final orders; assembled in his presence the mili-

tary chiefs; and dispersed his heralds through the camp
to proclaim the duty and the motives of the perilous enterprise. Fear is the first principle of a despotic government; and his menaces were expressed in the Oriental
style, that the fugitives and deserters, had they the wings
of a bird, should not escape from his inexorable justice.
The greatest part of his bashaws and Janizaries were the
offspring of Christian parents: but the glories of the
Turkish name were perpetuated by successive adoption;
and in the gradual change of individuals, the spirit of
a legion, a regiment, or an *oda*, is kept alive by imitation
and discipline. In this holy warfare the Moslems were
exhorted to purify their minds with prayer, their bodies
with seven ablutions; and to abstain from food till the
close of the ensuing day. A crowd of dervishes visited
the tents, to instil the desire of martyrdom, and the assurance of spending an immortal youth amidst the rivers
and gardens of paradise, and in the embraces of the
black-eyed virgins. Yet Mohammed principally trusted to
the efficacy of temporal and visible rewards. A double
pay was promised to the victorious troops: "The city and
the buildings," said Mohammed, "are mine; but I resign to
your valour the captives and the spoil, the treasures of
gold and beauty; be rich and be happy. Many are the
provinces of my empire: the intrepid soldier who first
ascends the walls of Constantinople shall be rewarded
with the government of the fairest and most wealthy;
and my gratitude shall accumulate his honours and
fortunes above the measure of his own hopes." Such various and potent motives diffused among the Turks a general ardour, regardless of life and impatient for action:
the camp re-echoed with the Moslem shouts of "God is
God: there is but one God, and Mohammed is the apostle
of God;" and the sea and land, from Galata to the seven
towers, were illuminated by the blaze of their nocturnal
fires.

Far different was the state of the Christians; who, with
loud and impotent complaints, deplored the guilt, or the

punishment, of their sins. The celestial image of the Virgin had been exposed in solemn procession; but their divine patroness was deaf to their entreaties: they accused the obstinacy of the emperor for refusing a timely surrender; anticipated the horrors of their fate; and sighed for the repose and security of Turkish servitude. The noblest of the Greeks, and the bravest of the allies, were summoned to the palace, to prepare them, on the evening of the twenty-eighth, for the duties and dangers of the general assault. The last speech of Palæologus was the funeral oration of the Roman empire: he promised, he conjured, and he vainly attempted to infuse the hope which was extinguished in his own mind. In this world all was comfortless and gloomy; and neither the Gospel nor the church have proposed any conspicuous recompense to the heroes who fall in the service of their country. But the example of their prince, and the confinement of a siege, had armed these warriors with the courage of despair; and the pathetic scene is described by the feelings of the historian Phranza, who was himself present at this mournful assembly. They wept, they embraced: regardless of their families and fortunes, they devoted their lives; and each commander, departing to his station, maintained all night a vigilant and anxious watch on the rampart. The emperor, and some faithful companions, entered the dome of St. Sophia, which in a few hours was to be converted into a mosque; and devoutly received, with tears and prayers, the sacrament of the holy communion. He reposed some moments in the palace, which resounded with cries and lamentations; solicited the pardon of all whom he might have injured; and mounted on horseback to visit the guards, and explore the motions of the enemy. The distress and fall of the last Constantine are more glorious than the long prosperity of the Byzantine Cæsars.

In the confusion of darkness an assailant may sometimes succeed; but in this great and general attack, the military judgment and astrological knowledge of Mohammed advised him to expect the morning, the memorable twenty-ninth of May, in the fourteen hundred and fifty-third year of the Christian era. The preceding night had been strenuously employed: the troops, the cannon, and the fascines were advanced to the edge of the ditch, which in many parts presented a smooth and level passage to the breach; and his fourscore galleys almost touched, with the prows and their scaling ladders, the less defensible walls of the harbour. Under pain of death, silence was enjoined; but the physical laws of motion and sound are not obedient to discipline or fear: each individual might suppress his voice and measure his footsteps; but the march and labour of thousands must inevitably produce a strange confusion of dissonant clamours, which reached the ears of the watchmen of the towers. At daybreak, without the customary signal of the morning gun, the Turks assaulted the city by sea and land; and the similitude of a twined or twisted thread has been applied to the closeness and continuity of their line of attack. The foremost ranks consisted of the refuse of the host, a voluntary crowd who fought without order or command; of the feebleness of age or childhood, of peasants and vagrants, and of all who had joined the camp in the blind hope of plunder and martyrdom. The common impulse drove them onwards to the wall; the most audacious to climb were instantly precipitated; and not a dart, not a bullet, of the Christians, was idly wasted on the accumulated throng. But their strength and ammunition were exhausted in this laborious defence: the ditch was filled with the bodies of the slain; they supported the footsteps of their companions; and of this devoted vanguard the death was more serviceable than the life. Under their respective bashaws and sanjaks, the troops of Anatolia and Romania were successively led to the charge: their progress was various and doubtful; but, after a conflict of two hours, the Greeks still maintained and improved their advantage; and the voice of the emperor was heard, encouraging his soldiers to achieve, by a last effort, the deliverance of their country. In that fatal moment the Janizaries arose, fresh, vigorous, and invincible. The sultan himself on horseback, with an iron mace in his hand, was the spectator and judge of their valour; he was surrounded by ten thousand of his domestic troops, whom he reserved for the decisive occasion; and the tide of battle was directed and impelled by his voice and eye. His numerous ministers of justice were posted behind the line, to urge, to restrain, and to punish; and if danger was in the front, shame and inevitable death were in the rear, of the fugitives. The cries of fear and of pain were drowned in the martial music of drums, trumpets, and attaballs; and experience has proved that the mechanical operation of sounds, by quickening the circulation of the blood and spirits, will act on the human machine more forcibly than the eloquence of reason and honour. From the lines, the galleys, and the bridge, the Ottoman artillery thundered on all sides; and the camp and city, the Greeks and the Turks, were involved in a cloud of smoke, which could only be dispelled by the final deliverance or destruction of the Roman empire. The single combats of the heroes of history or fable amuse our fancy and engage our affections: the skilful evolutions of war may inform the mind, and improve a necessary, though pernicious, science. But in the uniform and odious pictures of a general assault, all is blood, and horror, and confusion; nor shall I strive, at the distance of three centuries and a thousand miles, to delineate a scene of which there could be no spectators, and of which the actors themselves were incapable of forming any just or adequate idea.

The immediate loss of Constantinople may be ascribed to the bullet, or arrow, which pierced the gauntlet of John Justiniani. The sight of his blood, and the exquisite pain, appalled the courage of the chief, whose arms and counsels were the firmest rampart of the city. As he withdrew from his station in quest of a surgeon, his flight was perceived and stopped by the indefatigable emperor. "Your wound," exclaimed Palæologus, "is slight; the danger is pressing: your presence is necessary; and whither will you retire?"—"I will retire," said the trembling Genoese, "by the same road which God has opened to the Turks," and at these words he hastily passed through one of the breaches of the inner wall. By this pusillanimous act he stained the honours of a military life; and the few days which he survived in Galata, or the isle of Chios, were embittered by his own and the public reproach. His example was imitated by the greatest part of the Latin auxiliaries, and the defence began to slacken when the attack was pressed with redoubled vigour. The number of the Ottomans was fifty, perhaps a hundred, times superior to that of the Christians; the double walls were reduced by the cannon to a heap of ruins: in a circuit of several miles some places must be found more easy of access, or more feebly guarded; and if the besiegers could penetrate in a single point, the whole city was irrecoverably lost. The first who deserved the sultan's reward was Hassan the Janizary, of gigantic stature and strength. With his scimitar in one hand and his buckler in the other, he ascended the outward fortification: of the thirty Janizaries who were emulous of his valour, eighteen perished in the bold adventure. Hassan and his twelve companions had reached the summit: the giant was precipitated from the rampart: he rose on one knee, and was again oppressed by a shower of darts and stones. But his success had proved that the achievement was possible: the walls and towers were instantly covered with a swarm of Turks; and the Greeks, now driven from the vantage ground, were overwhelmed by increasing multitudes. Amidst these multitudes, the emperor, who accomplished all the duties of a general and a soldier, was long seen and finally lost. The nobles, who fought round his person, sustained, till their last breath, the honourable names of Palæologus and Cantacuzene: his mournful exclamation was heard, "Cannot there be found a Christian to cut off my head?" and his last fear was that of falling alive into the hands of the infidels. The prudent despair of Constantine cast away the purple: amidst the tumult he fell by an unknown hand, and his body was buried under a mountain of the slain. After his death resistance and order were no more: the Greeks fled towards the city; and many were pressed and stifled in the narrow pass of the gate of St. Romanus. The victorious Turks rushed through the breaches of the inner wall; and as they advanced into the streets, they were soon joined by their brethren, who had forced the gate Phenar on the side of the harbour. In the first heat of the pursuit about two thousand Christians were put to the sword; but avarice soon prevailed over cruelty; and the victors acknowledged that they should immediately have given quarter, if the valour of the emperor and his chosen bands had not prepared them for a similar opposition in every part of the capital. It was thus, after a siege of fifty-three days, that Constantinople, which had defied the power of Chosroes, the Chagan, and the caliphs, was irretrievably subdued by the arms of Mohammed the Second. Her empire only had been subverted by the Latins: her religion was trampled in the dust by the Moslem conquerors.

The tidings of misfortune fly with a rapid wing; yet such was the extent of Constantinople, that the more distant quarters might prolong, some moments, the happy ignorance of their ruin. But in the general consternation, in the feelings of selfish or social anxiety, in the tumult and thunder of the assault, a *sleepless* night and morning must have elapsed; nor can I believe that many Grecian ladies were awakened by the Janizaries from a sound and tranquil slumber. On the assurance of the public calamity, the houses and convents were instantly deserted; and the trembling inhabitants flocked together in the streets, like a herd of timid animals, as if accumulated weakness could be productive of strength, or in the vain hope that amid the crowd each individual might be safe and invisible. From every part of the capital they flowed into the church of St. Sophia: in the space of an hour, the sanctuary, the choir, the nave, the upper and lower galleries, were filled with the multitudes of fathers and husbands, of women and children, of priests, monks, and religious virgins: the doors were barred on the inside, and they sought protection from the sacred dome which they had so lately abhorred as a profane and polluted edifice. Their confidence was founded on the prophecy of an enthusiast or impostor, that one day the Turks would enter Constantinople, and pursue the Romans as far as the column of Constantine in the square before St. Sophia: but that this would be the term of their calamities; that an angel would descend from heaven with a sword in his hand, and would deliver the empire, with that celestial weapon, to a poor man seated at the foot of the column. "Take this sword," would he say, "and avenge the people of the Lord." At these animating words the Turks would instantly fly, and the victorious Romans would drive them from the West, and from all Anatolia, as far as the frontiers of Persia. It is on this occasion that Ducas, with some fancy and much truth, upbraids the discord and obstinacy of the Greeks. "Had that angel appeared," exclaims the historian, "had he offered to exterminate your foes if you would consent to the union of the church, even then, in that fatal moment, you would have rejected your safety, or have deceived your God."

While they expected the descent of the tardy angel, the doors were broken with axes; and as the Turks encountered no resistance, their bloodless hands were employed in selecting and securing the multitude of their prisoners. Youth, beauty, and the appearance of wealth, attracted their choice; and the right of property was decided among themselves by a prior seizure, by personal strength, and by the authority of command. In the space of an hour the male captives were bound with cords, the

females with their veils and girdles. The senators were
linked with their slaves; the prelates with the porters
of the church; and young men of a plebeian class with
noble maids whose faces had been invisible to the sun
and their nearest kindred. In this common captivity the
ranks of society were confounded; the ties of nature were
cut asunder; and the inexorable soldier was careless of
the father's groans, the tears of the mother, and the
lamentations of the children. The loudest in their wail-
ings were the nuns, who were torn from the altar with
naked bosoms, outstretched hands, and dishevelled hair;
and we should piously believe that few could be tempted
to prefer the vigils of the harem to those of the monastery. Of these unfortunate Greeks, of these domestic
animals, whole strings were rudely driven through the
streets; and as the conquerors were eager to return for
more prey, their trembling pace was quickened with
menaces and blows. At the same hour a similar rapine
was exercised in all the churches and monasteries, in
all the palaces and habitations, of the capital; nor could
any place, however sacred or sequestered, protect the
persons or the property of the Greeks. Above sixty thousand of this devoted people were transported from the
city to the camp and fleet; exchanged or sold according
to the caprice or interest of their masters, and dispersed
in remote servitude through the provinces of the Ottoman
empire. Among these we may notice some remarkable
characters. The historian Phranza, first chamberlain and
principal secretary, was involved with his family in the
common lot. After suffering four months the hardships
of slavery, he recovered his freedom: in the ensuing winter he ventured to Adrianople, and ransomed his wife
from the *mir bashi,* or master of the horse; but his two
children, in the flower of youth and beauty, had been
seized for the use of Mohammed himself. The daughter
of Phranza died in the seraglio, perhaps a virgin: his
son, in the fifteenth year of his age, preferred death to
infamy, and was stabbed by the hand of the royal lover.

A deed thus inhuman cannot surely be expiated by the taste and liberality with which he released a Grecian matron and her two daughters, on receiving a Latin ode from Philelphus, who had chosen a wife in that noble family. The pride or cruelty of Mohammed would have been most sensibly gratified by the capture of a Roman legate; but the dexterity of Cardinal Isidore eluded the search, and he escaped from Galata in a plebeian habit. The chain and entrance of the outward harbour was still occupied by the Italian ships of merchandise and war. They had signalised their valour in the siege: they embraced the moment of retreat, while the Turkish mariners were dissipated in the pillage of the city. When they hoisted sail, the beach was covered with a suppliant and lamentable crowd; but the means of transportation were scanty; the Venetians and Genoese selected their countrymen; and, notwithstanding the fairest promises of the sultan, the inhabitants of Galata evacuated their houses, and embarked with their most precious effects.

In the fall and the sack of great cities an historian is condemned to repeat the tale of uniform calamity: the same effects must be produced by the same passions; and when those passions may be indulged without control, small, alas! is the difference between civilised and savage man. Amidst the vague exclamations of bigotry and hatred, the Turks are not accused of a wanton or immoderate effusion of Christian blood: but according to their maxims (the maxims of antiquity), the lives of the vanquished were forfeited; and the legitimate reward of the conqueror was derived from the service, the sale, or the ransom of his captives of both sexes. The wealth of Constantinople had been granted by the sultan to his victorious troops; and the rapine of an hour is more productive than the industry of years. But as no regular division was attempted of the spoil, the respective shares were not determined by merit; and the rewards of valour were stolen away by the followers of the camp, who had declined the toil and danger of the battle. The narrative of their depredations could not afford either amusement or instruction: the total amount, in the last poverty of the empire, has been valued at four millions of ducats; and of this sum a small part was the property of the Venetians, the Genoese, the Florentines, and the merchants of Ancona. Of these foreigners the stock was improved in quick and perpetual circulation: but the riches of the Greeks were displayed in the idle ostentation of palaces and wardrobes, or deeply buried in treasures of ingots and old coin, lest it should be demanded at their hands for the defence of their country. The profanation and plunder of the monasteries and churches excited the most tragic complaints. The dome of St. Sophia itself, the earthly heaven, the second firmament, the vehicle of the cherubim, the throne of the glory of God, was despoiled of the oblations of ages; and the gold and silver, the pearls and jewels, the vases and sacerdotal ornaments, were most wickedly converted to the service of mankind. After the divine images had been stripped of all that could be valuable to a profane eye, the canvas, or the wood, was torn, or broken, or burnt, or trod under foot, or applied, in the stables or the kitchen, to the vilest uses. The example of sacrilege was imitated, however, from the Latin conquerors of Constantinople; and the treatment which Christ, the Virgin, and the saints had sustained from the guilty Catholic, might be inflicted by the zealous Musulman on the monuments of idolatry. Perhaps, instead of joining the public clamour, a philosopher will observe that in the decline of the arts the workmanship could not be more valuable than the work, and that a fresh supply of visions and miracles would speedily be renewed by the craft of the priest and the credulity of the people. He will more seriously deplore the loss of the Byzantine libraries, which were destroyed or scattered in the general confusion: one hundred and twenty thousand manuscripts are said to have disappeared; ten volumes might be purchased for a single ducat; and the same ignominious price, too high perhaps for a shelf of theology, included the whole works of Aristotle and Homer, the noblest productions of the science and literature of ancient Greece. We may reflect with pleasure that an inestimable portion of our classic treasures was safely deposited in Italy; and that the mechanics of a German town had invented an art which derides the havoc of time and barbarism.

From the first hour of the memorable twenty-ninth of May, disorder and rapine prevailed in Constantinople till the eighth hour of the same day, when the sultan himself passed in triumph through the gate of St. Romanus. He was attended by his viziers, bashaws, and guards, each of whom (says a Byzantine historian) was robust as Hercules, dexterous as Apollo, and equal in battle to any ten of the race of ordinary mortals. The conqueror gazed with satisfaction and wonder on the strange though splendid appearance of the domes and palaces, so dissimilar from the style of Oriental architecture. In the hippodrome, or *atmeidan,* his eye was attracted by the twisted column of the three serpents; and, as a trial of his strength, he shattered with his iron mace or battle-axe the under jaw of one of these monsters, which in the eyes of the Turks were the idols or talismans of the city. At the principal door of St. Sophia he alighted from his horse and entered the dome; and such was his jealous regard for that monument of his glory, that, on observing a zealous Musulman in the act of breaking the marble pavement, he admonished him with his scimitar that, if the spoil and captives were granted to the soldiers, the public and private buildings had been reserved for the prince. By his command the metropolis of the Eastern church was transformed into a mosque: the rich and portable instruments of superstition had been removed; the crosses were thrown down; and the walls, which were covered with images and mosaics, were washed and purified, and restored to a state of naked simplicity. On the same day, or on the ensuing Friday, the *muezin,* or crier, ascended the most lofty turret, and proclaimed the *ezan,* or public invitation, in the name of God and his prophet; the imam preached; and Mohammed the Second performed the *namaz* of prayer and thanksgiving on the great altar, where the Christian mysteries had so lately been celebrated before the last of the Cæsars. From St. Sophia he proceeded to the august but desolate mansion of a hundred successors of the great Constantine, but which in a few hours had been stripped of the pomp of royalty. A melancholy reflection on the vicissitudes of human greatness forced itself on his mind, and he repeated an elegant distich of Persian poetry: "The spider has wove his web in the Imperial palace, and the owl hath sung her watch-song on the towers of Afrasiab."

Yet his mind was not satisfied, nor did the victory seem complete, till he was informed of the fate of Constantine—whether he had escaped, or been made prisoner, or had fallen in the battle. Two Janizaries claimed the honour and reward of his death: the body, under a heap of slain, was discovered by the golden eagles embroidered on his shoes; the Greeks acknowledged with tears the head of their late emperor; and, after exposing the bloody trophy, Mohammed bestowed on his rival the honours of a decent funeral. . . . On the eighteenth of June the victorious sultan returned to Adrianople, and smiled at the base and hollow embassies of the Christian princes, who viewed their approaching ruin in the fall of the Eastern empire.

CHAPTER XXV

MEDIEVAL ROME

[*While New Rome was being transformed into the capital of Islam, Old Rome was resuming its position as the capital of Christendom. It had to resume it because in the fourteenth century it was nearly lost. In 1309, the Popes, like the Emperors a thousand years before, had abandoned the turbulent city which, even at the height of their world-power, they had never been able to control, and established themselves under French protection at Avignon. But Rome did not accept its fallen status lightly, and in the abandoned and impoverished city the mood of resentment was dignified, in the middle of the century, by the classical revivalism of Petrarch (himself a Tuscan who lived at Avignon) and the political romanticism of his plebeian hero, the Roman Cola Rienzi. In 1347, Rienzi made himself popular dictator, or "tribune," of Rome; but his rule was short-lived, and thereafter Petrarch contented himself with urging the return to the city of its old masters, the Popes. Ultimately, in 1378, an Italian pope, Urban VI, was elected; but the French cardinals, who had been intimidated into electing him, were determined to keep the papacy in France. They were "attached to the language, manners and climate of Avignon; to their stately palaces; above all, to the wines of Burgundy"; and so they escaped from Rome and elected a French Pope, who remained at Avignon and was recognised by France, Spain and their client states. Thus the seventy years of "Babylonish captivity" in Avignon were merely followed by the forty years of "the Great Schism," which lasted until the Council of Constance (1414-1418) deposed all Popes (there were now three of them) and procured the election of Martin V. In chapter LXX Gibbon describes the Great Schism and its end.]*

From the banks of the Tiber and the Rhône the hostile pontiffs encountered each other with the pen and the sword: the civil and ecclesiastical order of society was disturbed; and the Romans had their full share of the mischiefs of which they may be arraigned as the primary authors. They had vainly flattered themselves with the hope of restoring the seat of the ecclesiastical monarchy, and of relieving their poverty with the tributes and offerings of the nations; but the separation of France and Spain diverted the stream of lucrative devotion; nor could the loss be compensated by the two jubilees which were crowded into the space of ten years. By the avocations of the schism, by foreign arms, and popular tumults, Urban the Sixth and his three successors were often compelled to interrupt their residence in the Vatican. The Colonna and Ursini still exercised their deadly feuds: the bannerets of Rome asserted and abused the privileges of a republic: the vicars of Christ, who had levied a military force, chastised their rebellion with the gibbet, the sword, and the dagger; and, in a friendly conference, eleven deputies of the people were perfidiously murdered and cast into the street. Since the invasion of Robert the Norman, the Romans had pursued their domestic quarrels without the dangerous interposition of a stranger. But in the disorders of the schism, an aspiring neighbour, Ladislaus king of Naples, alternately supported and betrayed the pope and the people; by the former he was declared *gonfalonier,* or general, of the church, while the latter submitted to his choice the nomination of their magistrates. Besieging Rome by land and water, he thrice entered the gates as a barbarian conqueror; profaned the altars, violated the virgins, pillaged the merchants, performed his devotions at St. Peter's, and left a garrison in the castle of St. Angelo. His arms were sometimes unfortunate, and to a delay of three days he was indebted for his life and crown: but Ladislaus triumphed in his turn; and it was only his premature death that could save the metropolis and the ecclesiastical state from the ambitious conqueror, who had assumed the title, or at least the powers, of King of Rome.

I have not undertaken the ecclesiastical history of the schism; but Rome, the object of these last chapters, is deeply interested in the disputed succession of her sovereigns. The first counsels for the peace and union of Christendom arose from the university of Paris, from the faculty of the Sorbonne, whose doctors were esteemed, at least in the Gallican church, as the most consummate masters of theological science. Prudently waiving all invidious inquiry into the origin and merits of the dispute, they proposed, as a healing measure, that the two pretenders of Rome and Avignon should abdicate at the same time, after qualifying the cardinals of the adverse factions to join in a legitimate election; and that the nations should *subtract* their obedience, if either of the competitors preferred his own interest to that of the public. At each vacancy these physicians of the church deprecated the mischiefs of a hasty choice; but the policy of the conclave and the ambition of its members were deaf to reason and entreaties; and whatsoever promises were made, the pope could never be bound by the oaths of the cardinal. During fifteen years the pacific designs of the university were eluded by the arts of the rival pontiffs, the scruples or passions of their adherents, and the vicissitudes of French factions, that ruled the insanity of Charles the Sixth. At length a vigorous resolution was embraced; and a solemn embassy, of the titular patriarch of Alexandria, two archbishops, five bishops, five abbots, three knights, and twenty doctors, was sent to the courts of Avignon and Rome, to require, in the name of the church and king, the abdication of the two pretenders, of Peter de Luna, who styled himself Benedict the Thirteenth, and of Angelo Corrario, who assumed the name of Gregory the Twelfth. For the ancient honour of Rome, and the success of their commission, the ambassadors solicited a conference with the magistrates of the city, whom they gratified by a positive declaration that the most Christian king did not entertain a wish of transporting the holy see from the Vatican, which he considered as the genuine and proper seat of the successor of St. Peter. In the name of the senate and people, an eloquent Roman asserted their desire to co-operate in the union of the church, deplored the temporal and spiritual calamities of the long schism, and requested the protection of France against the arms of the king of Naples. The answers of Benedict and Gregory were alike edifying and alike deceitful; and, in evading the demand of their abdication, the two rivals were animated by a common spirit. They agreed on the necessity of a previous interview; but the time, the place, and the manner, could never be ascertained by mutual consent. "If the one advances," says a servant of Gregory, "the other retreats; the one appears an animal fearful of the land, the other a creature apprehensive of the water. And thus, for a short remnant of life and power, will these aged priests endanger the peace and salvation of the Christian world."

The Christian world was at length provoked by their obstinacy and fraud: they were deserted by their cardinals, who embraced each other as friends and colleagues; and their revolt was supported by a numerous assembly of prelates and ambassadors. With equal justice, the council of Pisa deposed the popes of Rome and Avignon; the conclave was unanimous in the choice of Alexander the Fifth, and his vacant seat was soon filled by a similar election of John the Twenty-third, the most profligate of mankind. But instead of extinguishing the schism, the rashness of the French and Italians had given a third pretender to the chair of St. Peter. Such new claims of the synod and conclave were disputed; three kings, of Germany, Hungary, and Naples, adhered to the cause of Gregory the Twelfth: and Benedict the Thirteenth, himself a Spaniard, was acknowledged by the devotion and patriotism of that powerful nation. The rash proceedings of Pisa were corrected by the council of Constance; the emperor Sigismond acted a conspicuous part as the advocate or protector of the Catholic church; and the number and weight of civil and ecclesiastical members might seem to constitute the states-general of Europe. Of the three popes, John the Twenty-third was the first victim: he fled and was brought back a prisoner: the most scandalous charges were suppressed; the vicar of Christ was only accused of piracy, murder, rape, sodomy, and incest; and after subscribing his own condemnation, he expiated in prison the imprudence of trusting his person to a free city beyond the Alps. Gregory the Twelfth, whose obedience was reduced to the narrow precincts of Rimini, descended with more honour from the throne; and his ambassador convened the session in which he renounced the title and authority of lawful pope. To vanquish the obstinacy of Benedict the Thirteenth or his adherents, the emperor in person undertook a journey from Constance to Perpignan. The kings of Castile, Arragon, Navarre, and Scotland, obtained an equal and honourable treaty: with the concurrence of the Spaniards, Benedict was deposed by the council; but the harmless old man was left in a solitary castle to excommunicate twice each day the rebel kingdoms which had deserted his cause. After thus eradicating the remains of the schism, the synod of Constance proceeded with slow and cautious steps to elect the sovereign of Rome and the head of the church. On this momentous occasion the college of twenty-three cardinals was fortified with thirty deputies; six of whom were chosen in each of the five great nations of Christendom—the Italian, the German, the French, the Spanish, and the English; the interference of strangers was softened by their generous preference of an Italian and a Roman; and the hereditary, as well as personal, merit of Otho Colonna recommended him to the conclave. Rome accepted with joy and obedience the noblest of her sons; the ecclesiastical state was defended by his powerful family; and the elevation of Martin the Fifth is the era of the restoration and establishment of the popes in the Vatican.

The royal prerogative of coining money, which had been exercised near three hundred years by the senate, was *first* resumed by Martin the Fifth, and his image and superscription introduce the series of the papal medals. Of his two immediate successors, Eugenius the Fourth was the *last* pope expelled by the tumults of the Roman people, and Nicholas the Fifth, the *last* who was importuned by the presence of a Roman emperor.

[*Restored to unity and to Rome, the Popes soon recovered and increased their authority. With the aid of an impregnable citadel, a standing army and the novelty of gunpowder, they subdued, as never before, the turbulent populace and nobility, and the city gradually acquired a new character.*]

The long habits of obedience and education subdued the turbulent spirit of the nobles and commons of Rome. The barons forgot the arms and factions of their ancestors, and insensibly became the servants of luxury and government. Instead of maintaining a crowd of tenants and followers, the produce of their estates was consumed in the private expenses which multiply the pleasures and diminish the power of the lord. The Colonna and Ursini vied with each other in the decoration of their palaces and chapels; and their antique splendour was rivalled or surpassed by the sudden opulence of the papal families.

In Rome the voice of freedom and discord is no longer heard; and, instead of the foaming torrent, a smooth and stagnant lake reflects the image of idleness and servitude.

A Christian, a philosopher, and a patriot, will be equally scandalised by the temporal kingdom of the clergy; and the local majesty of Rome, the remembrance of her consuls and triumphs, may seem to embitter the sense and aggravate the shame of her slavery. If we calmly weigh the merits and defects of the ecclesiastical government, it may be praised in its present state as a mild, decent, and tranquil system, exempt from the dangers of a minority, the sallies of youth, the expenses of luxury, and the calamities of war. But these advantages are overbalanced by a frequent, perhaps a septennial, election of a sovereign, who is seldom a native of the country: the reign of a *young* statesman of threescore, in the decline of his life and abilities, without hope to accomplish, and without children to inherit, the labours of his transitory reign. The successful candidate is drawn from the church, and even the convent—from the mode of education and life the most adverse to reason, humanity, and freedom. In the trammels of servile faith he has learned to believe because it is absurd, to revere all that is contemptible, and to despise whatever might deserve the esteem of a rational being; to punish error as a crime, to reward mortification and celibacy as the first of virtues; to place the saints of the calendar above the heroes of Rome and the sages of Athens; and to consider the missal, or the crucifix, as more useful instruments than the plough or the loom. In the office of nuncio, or the rank of cardinal, he may acquire some knowledge of the world; but the primitive stain will adhere to his mind and manners: from study and experience he may suspect the mystery of his profession; but the sacerdotal artist will imbibe some portion of the bigotry which he inculcates. The genius of Sixtus the Fifth burst from the gloom of a Franciscan cloister. In a reign of five years he exterminated the outlaws and banditti, abolished the *profane* sanctuaries of Rome, formed a naval and military force, restored and emulated the monuments of antiquity, and, after a liberal use and large increase of the revenue, left five millions of crowns in the castle of St. Angelo. But his justice was sullied with cruelty, his activity was prompted by the ambition of conquest: after his decease the abuses revived; the treasury was dissipated; he entailed on posterity thirty-five new taxes and the venality of offices; and, after his death, his statue was demolished by an ungrateful or an injured people. The wild and original character of Sixtus the Fifth stands alone in the series of the pontiffs: the maxims and effects of their temporal government may be collected from the positive and comparative view of the arts and philosophy, the agriculture and trade, the wealth and population, of the ecclesiastical state. For myself, it is my wish to depart in charity with all mankind, nor am I willing, in these last moments, to offend even the pope and clergy of Rome.

[*In the new peace of the Popes and the classical revival which Petrarch had inaugurated, the Romans began to study the relics of ancient greatness around them. In his last chapter Gibbon describes the ruinous state of Rome at the close of the Middle Ages and analyses the causes of its decay in the 1300 years of his* History. *He ascribes it to four main causes:*]

I. The injuries of time and nature. II. The hostile attacks of the barbarians and Christians. III. The use and abuse of the materials. And, IV. The domestic quarrels of the Romans.

I. The art of man is able to construct monuments far more permanent than the narrow span of his own existence: yet these monuments, like himself, are perishable and frail; and in the boundless annals of time his life and his labours must equally be measured as a fleeting moment. Of a simple and solid edifice it is not easy how-

633

ever to circumscribe the duration. As the wonders of ancient days, the pyramids attracted the curiosity of the ancients: a hundred generations, the leaves of autumn, have dropped into the grave; and after the fall of the Pharaohs and Ptolemies, the Cæsars and caliphs, the same pyramids stand erect and unshaken above the floods of the Nile. A complex figure of various and minute parts is more accessible to injury and decay; and the silent lapse of time is often accelerated by hurricanes and earthquakes, by fires and inundations. The air and earth have doubtless been shaken; and the lofty turrets of Rome have tottered from their foundations; but the seven hills do not appear to be placed on the great cavities of the globe; nor has the city, in any age, been exposed to the convulsions of nature, which, in the climate of Antioch, Lisbon, or Lima, have crumbled in a few moments the works of ages into dust. Fire is the most powerful agent of life and death: the rapid mischief may be kindled and propagated by the industry or negligence of mankind; and every period of the Roman annals is marked by the repetition of similar calamities. A memorable conflagration, the guilt or misfortune of Nero's reign, continued, though with unequal fury, either six or nine days. Innumerable buildings, crowded in close and crooked streets, supplied perpetual fuel for the flames; and when they ceased, four only of the fourteen regions were left entire; three were totally destroyed, and seven were deformed by the relics of smoking and lacerated edifices. In the full meridian of empire the metropolis arose with fresh beauty from her ashes; yet the memory of the old deplored their irreparable losses, the arts of Greece, the trophies of victory, the monuments of primitive or fabulous antiquity. In the days of distress and anarchy every wound is mortal, every fall irretrievable; nor can the damage be restored either by the public care of government, or the activity of private interest. Yet two causes may be alleged which render the calamity of

fire more destructive to a flourishing than a decayed city.
1. The more combustible materials of brick, timber, and
metals, are first melted or consumed; but the flames may
play without injury or effect on the naked walls and
massy arches that have been despoiled of their ornaments. 2. It is among the common and plebeian habitations that a mischievous spark is most easily blown to a
conflagration; but as soon as they are devoured, the
greater edifices which have resisted or escaped are left
as so many islands in a state of solitude and safety.
From her situation, Rome is exposed to the danger of
frequent inundations. Without excepting the Tiber, the
rivers that descend from either side of the Apennine have
a short and irregular course; a shallow stream in the
summer heats; an impetuous torrent when it is swelled
in the spring or winter, by the fall of rain and the melt-
ing of the snows. When the current is repelled from the
sea by adverse winds, when the ordinary bed is inadequate to the weight of waters, they rise above the banks,
and overspread, without limits or control, the plains and
cities of the adjacent country. Soon after the triumph
of the first Punic war the Tiber was increased by unusual
rains; and the inundation, surpassing all former measure
of time and place, destroyed all the buildings that were
situate below the hills of Rome. According to the variety
of ground, the same mischief was produced by different
means: and the edifices were either swept away by the
sudden impulse, or dissolved and undermined by the long
continuance, of the flood. Under the reign of Augustus
the same calamity was renewed: the lawless river overturned the palaces and temples on its banks; and, after
the labours of the emperor in cleansing and widening
the bed that was encumbered with ruins, the vigilance
of his successors was exercised by similar dangers and
designs. The project of diverting into new channels the
Tiber itself, or some of the dependent streams, was long
opposed by superstition and local interests; nor did the
use compensate the toil and cost of the tardy and imper-

fect execution. The servitude of rivers is the noblest and most important victory which man has obtained over the licentiousness of nature;[1] and if such were the ravages of the Tiber under a firm and active government, what could oppose, or who can enumerate, the injuries of the city after the fall of the Western empire? A remedy was at length produced by the evil itself: the accumulation of rubbish and the earth that has been washed down from the hills is supposed to have elevated the plain of Rome fourteen or fifteen feet, perhaps, above the ancient level; and the modern city is less accessible to the attacks of the river.

II. The crowd of writers of every nation, who impute the destruction of the Roman monuments to the Goths and the Christians, have neglected to inquire how far they were animated by a hostile principle, and how far they possessed the means and the leisure to satiate their enmity. In the preceding volumes of this History I have described the triumph of barbarism and religion; and I can only resume, in a few words, their real or imaginary connection with the ruin of ancient Rome. Our fancy may create, or adopt, a pleasing romance, that the Goths and Vandals sallied from Scandinavia, ardent to avenge the flight of Odin; to break the chains, and to chastise the oppressors, of mankind; that they wished to burn the records of classic literature, and to found their national architecture on the broken members of the Tuscan and Corinthian orders. But in simple truth, the northern conquerors were neither sufficiently savage, nor sufficiently refined, to entertain such aspiring ideas of destruction and revenge. The shepherds of Scythia and Germany had been educated in the armies of the empire, whose discipline they acquired, and whose weakness they invaded: with the familiar use of the Latin tongue they

---

[1]See the *Epoques de la Nature* of the eloquent and philosophic Buffon. His picture of Guyana, in South America, is that of a new and savage land, in which the waters are abandoned to themselves, without being regulated by human industry.

19-20
The remains of the Roman Forum, and an eighteenth-century
engraving of the Coliseum in ruins.

had learned to reverence the name and titles of Rome; and, though incapable of emulating, they were more inclined to admire than to abolish the arts and studies of a brighter period. In the transient possession of a rich and unresisting capital, the soldiers of Alaric and Genseric were stimulated by the passions of a victorious army; amidst the wanton indulgence of lust or cruelty, portable wealth was the object of their search: nor could they derive either pride or pleasure from the unprofitable reflection that they had battered to the ground the works of the consuls and Cæsars. Their moments were indeed precious: the Goths evacuated Rome on the sixth, the Vandals on the fifteenth day; and, though it be far more difficult to build than to destroy, their hasty assault would have made a slight impression on the solid piles of antiquity. We may remember that both Alaric and Genseric affected to spare the buildings of the city; that they subsisted in strength and beauty under the auspicious government of Theodoric; and that the momentary resentment of Totila was disarmed by his own temper and the advice of his friends and enemies. From these innocent barbarians the reproach may be transferred to the Catholics of Rome. The statues, altars, and houses of the dæmons were an abomination in their eyes; and in the absolute command of the city, they might labour with zeal and perseverance to erase the idolatry of their ancestors. The demolition of the temples in the East affords to *them* an example of conduct, and to *us* an argument of belief; and it is probable that a portion of guilt or merit may be imputed with justice to the Roman proselytes. Yet their abhorrence was confined to the monuments of heathen superstition; and the civil structures that were dedicated to the business or pleasure of society might be preserved without injury or scandal. The change of religion was accomplished, not by a popular tumult, but by the decrees of the emperors, of the senate, and of time. Of the Christian hierarchy, the bishops of Rome were commonly the most prudent and least fanatic; nor can any positive charge be opposed to the meritorious act of saving and converting the majestic structure of the Pantheon.

III. The value of any object that supplies the wants or pleasures of mankind is compounded of its substance and its form, of the materials and the manufacture. Its price must depend on the number of persons by whom it may be acquired and used; on the extent of the market; and consequently on the ease or difficulty of remote exportation, according to the nature of the commodity, its local situation, and the temporary circumstances of the world. The barbarian conquerors of Rome usurped in a moment the toil and treasure of successive ages; but, except the luxuries of immediate consumption, they must view without desire all that could not be removed from the city in the Gothic waggons or the fleet of the Vandals. Gold and silver were the first objects of their avarice; as in every country, and in the smallest compass, they represent the most ample command of the industry and possessions of mankind. A vase or a statue of those precious metals might tempt the vanity of some barbarian chief; but the grosser multitude, regardless of the form, was tenacious only of the substance; and the melted ingots might be readily divided and stamped into the current coin of the empire. The less active or less fortunate robbers were reduced to the baser plunder of brass, lead, iron, and copper: whatever had escaped the Goths and Vandals was pillaged by the Greek tyrants; and the emperor Constans, in his rapacious visit, stripped the bronze tiles from the roof of the Pantheon. The edifices of Rome might be considered as a vast and various mine; the first labour of extracting the materials was already performed; the metals were purified and cast; the marbles were hewn and polished; and after foreign and domestic rapine had been satiated, the remains of the city, could a purchaser have been found, were still venal. The monuments of antiquity had been left naked of their precious ornaments; but the Romans would demolish with their own hands the arches and walls, if the hope of profit could surpass the cost of the labour and exportation. If Charlemagne had fixed in Italy the seat of the Western empire, his genius would have aspired to restore, rather than to violate, the works of the Cæsars; but policy confined the French monarch to the forests of Germany; his taste could be gratified only by destruction; and the new palace of Aix-la-Chapelle was decorated with the marbles of Ravenna and Rome. Five hundred years after Charlemagne, a king of Sicily, Robert, the wisest and most liberal sovereign of the age, was supplied with the same materials by the easy navigation of the Tiber and the sea; and Petrach sighs an indignant complaint, that the ancient capital of the world should adorn from her own bowels the slothful luxury of Naples. But these examples of plunder or purchase were rare in the darker ages; and the Romans, alone and unenvied, might have applied to their private or public use the remaining structures of antiquity, if in their present form and situation they had not been useless in a great measure to the city and its inhabitants. The walls still described the old circumference, but the city had descended from the seven hills into the Campus Martius; and some of the noblest monuments which had braved the injuries of time were left in a desert far remote from the habitations of mankind. The palaces of the senators were no longer adapted to the manners or fortunes of their indigent successors: the use of baths[2] and porticoes was forgotten: in the sixth century the games of the theatre, amphitheatre, and circus had been interrupted: some temples were devoted to the prevailing worship; but the Christian churches preferred the holy figure of the cross; and fashion, or reason, had distributed after a peculiar model the cells and offices of the cloister. Under the ecclesiastical reign the number of these pious foundations was enormously multiplied; and the city was crowded with forty monas-

---

[2] Yet Charlemagne washed and swam at Aix-la-Chapelle with a hundred of his courtiers; and Muratori describes, as late as the year 814, the public baths which were built at Spoleto in Italy.

teries of men, twenty of women, and sixty chapters and
colleges of canons and priests, who aggravated, instead
of relieving, the depopulation of the tenth century. But
if the forms of ancient architecture were disregarded by
a people insensible of their use and beauty, the plentiful
materials were applied to every call of necessity or superstition; till the fairest columns of the Ionic and Corinthian orders, the richest marbles of Paros and Numidia,
were degraded, perhaps to the support of a convent or a
stable. The daily havoc which is perpetrated by the Turks
in the cities of Greece and Asia may afford a melancholy
example; and in the gradual destruction of the monuments of Rome, Sixtus the Fifth may alone be excused
for employing the stones of the Septizonium in the glorious edifice of St. Peter's. A fragment, a ruin, howsoever
mangled or profaned, may be viewed with pleasure and
regret; but the greater part of the marble was deprived
of substance, as well as of place and proportion; it was
burnt to lime for the purpose of cement. Since the arrival
of Poggius the temple of Concord and many capital structures had vanished from his eyes; and an epigram of
the same age expresses a just and pious fear that the continuance of this practice would finally annihilate all the
monuments of antiquity. The smallness of their numbers
was the sole check on the demands and depredations of
the Romans. The imagination of Petrarch might create
the presence of a mighty people; and I hesitate to believe
that, even in the fourteenth century, they could be reduced to a contemptible list of thirty-three thousand inhabitants. From that period to the reign of Leo the Tenth,
if they multiplied to the amount of eighty-five thousand,
the increase of citizens was in some degree pernicious
to the ancient city.

IV. I have reserved for the last the most potent and
forcible cause of destruction, the domestic hostilities of
the Romans themselves. Under the dominion of the Greek
and French emperors the peace of the city was disturbed
by accidental, though frequent, seditions: it is from the

decline of the latter, from the beginning of the tenth century, that we may date the licentiousness of private war, which violated with impunity the laws of the Code and the Gospel, without respecting the majesty of the absent sovereign, or the presence and person of the vicar of Christ. In a dark period of five hundred years Rome was perpetually afflicted by the sanguinary quarrels of the nobles and the people, the Guelphs and Ghibelines, the Colonna and Ursini; and if much has escaped the knowledge, and much is unworthy of the notice, of history, I have exposed in the two preceding chapters the causes and effects of the public disorders. At such a time, when every quarrel was decided by the sword, and none could trust their lives or properties to the impotence of law, the powerful citizens were armed for safety, or offence, against the domestic enemies whom they feared or hated. Except Venice alone, the same dangers and designs were common to all the free republics of Italy; and the nobles usurped the prerogative of fortifying their houses, and erecting strong towers that were capable of resisting a sudden attack. The cities were filled with these hostile edifices; and the example of Lucca, which contained three hundred towers, her law, which confined their height to the measure of fourscore feet, may be extended with suitable latitude to the more opulent and populous states. The first step of the senator Brancaleone in the establishment of peace and justice was to demolish (as we have already seen) one hundred and forty of the towers of Rome; and, in the last days of anarchy and discord, as late as the reign of Martin the Fifth, forty-four still stood in one of the thirteen or fourteen regions of the city. To this mischievous purpose the remains of antiquity were most readily adapted: the temples and arches afforded a broad and solid basis for the new structures of brick and stone; and we can name the modern turrets that were raised on the triumphal monuments of Julius Cæsar, Titus, and the Antonines. With some slight alterations, a theatre, an amphitheatre, a mausoleum, was transformed into a strong and spacious citadel. I need not repeat that the mole of Hadrian has assumed the title and form of the castle of St. Angelo; the Septizonium of Severus was capable of standing against a royal army; the sepulchre of Metella has sunk under its outworks; the theatres of Pompey and Marcellus were occupied by the Savelli and Ursini families; and the rough fortress has been gradually softened to the splendour and elegance of an Italian palace. Even the churches were encompassed with arms and bulwarks, and the military engines on the roof of St. Peter's were the terror of the Vatican and the scandal of the Christian world. Whatever is fortified will be attacked; and whatever is attacked may be destroyed. Could the Romans have wrested from the popes the castle of St. Angelo, they had resolved by a public decree to annihilate that monument of servitude. Every building of defence was exposed to a siege; and in every siege the arts and engines of destruction were laboriously employed. After the death of Nicholas the Fourth, Rome, without a sovereign or a senate, was abandoned six months to the fury of civil war. "The houses," says a cardinal and poet of the times, "were crushed by the weight and velocity of enormous stones; the walls were perforated by the strokes of the battering-ram; the towers were involved in fire and smoke; and the assailants were stimulated by rapine and revenge." The work was consummated by the tyranny of the laws; and the factions of Italy alternately exercised a blind and thoughtless vengeance on their adversaries, whose houses and castles they razed to the ground. In comparing the *days* of foreign with the *ages* of domestic hostility, we must pronounce that the latter have been far more ruinous to the city; and our opinion is confirmed by the evidence of Petrarch. "Behold," says the laureate, "the relics of Rome, the image of her pristine greatness! neither time nor the barbarian can boast the merit of this stupendous destruction: it was perpetrated by her own citizens, by the most illustrious of her sons;

and your ancestors (he writes to a noble Annibaldi) have done with battering-ram what the Punic hero could not accomplish with the sword." The influence of the two last principles of decay must in some degree be multiplied by each other; since the houses and towers which were subverted by civil war required a new and perpetual supply from the monuments of antiquity.

[*As a particular example, Gibbon gives the history of the Coliseum, whose fabric survived the Dark and Middle Ages almost intact.*]

The inside was damaged; but in the middle of the sixteenth century, an era of taste and learning, the exterior circumference of one thousand six hundred and twelve feet was still entire and inviolate: a triple elevation of fourscore arches, which rose to the height of one hundred and eight feet. Of the present ruin the nephews of Paul the Third are the guilty agents; and every traveller who views the Farnese palace may curse the sacrilege and luxury of these upstart princes. A similar reproach is applied to the Barberini; and the repetition of injury might be dreaded from every reign, till the Coliseum was placed under the safeguard of religion by the most liberal of the pontiffs, Benedict the Fourteenth, who consecrated a spot which persecution and fable had stained with the blood of so many Christian martyrs.

When Petrarch first gratified his eyes with a view of those monuments whose scattered fragments so far surpass the most eloquent descriptions, he was astonished at the supine indifference of the Romans themselves; he was humbled rather than elated by the discovery that, except his friend Rienzi, and one of the Colonna, a stranger of the Rhône was more conversant with these antiquities than the nobles and natives of the metropolis. . . .

But the clouds of barbarism were gradually dispelled; and the peaceful authority of Martin the Fifth and his successors restored the ornaments of the city as well as the order of the ecclesiastical state. The improvements of Rome, since the fifteenth century, have not been the spontaneous produce of freedom and industry. The first and most natural root of a great city is the labour and populousness of the adjacent country, which supplies the materials of subsistence, of manufactures, and of foreign trade. But the greater part of the Campagna of Rome is reduced to a dreary and desolate wilderness: the overgrown estates of the princes and the clergy are cultivated by the lazy hands of indigent and hopeless vassals; and the scanty harvests are confined or exported for the benefit of a monopoly. A second and more artificial cause of the growth of a metropolis is the residence of a monarch, the expense of a luxurious court, and the tributes of dependent provinces. Those provinces and tributes had been lost in the fall of the empire; and if some streams of the silver of Peru and the gold of Brazil have been attracted by the Vatican, the revenues of the cardinals, the fees of office, the oblations of pilgrims and clients, and the remnant of ecclesiastical taxes, afford a poor and precarious supply, which maintains, however, the idleness of the court and city. The population of Rome, far below the measure of the great capitals of Europe, does not exceed one hundred and seventy thousand inhabitants; and within the spacious enclosure of the walls, the largest portion of the seven hills is overspread with vineyards and ruins. The beauty and splendour of the modern city may be ascribed to the abuses of the government, to the influence of superstition. Each reign (the exceptions are rare) has been marked by the rapid elevation of a new family, enriched by the childless pontiff at the expense of the church and country. The palaces of these fortunate nephews are the most costly monuments of elegance and servitude: the perfect arts of architecture, painting, and sculpture, have been prostituted in their service; and their galleries and gardens are decorated with the most precious works of antiquity, which taste or vanity has prompted them to collect. The ecclesiastical revenues were more decently employed by the popes themselves in the pomp of the Catholic worship; but it is superfluous to enumerate their pious foundations of altars, chapels, and churches, since these lesser stars are eclipsed by the sun of the Vatican, by the dome of St. Peter, the most glorious structure that ever has been applied to the use of religion. The fame of Julius the Second, Leo the Tenth, and Sixtus the Fifth, is accompanied by the superior merit of Bramante and Fontana, of Raphael and Michæl Angelo; and the same munificence which had been displayed in palaces and temples was directed with equal zeal to revive and emulate the labours of antiquity. Prostrate obelisks were raised from the ground, and erected in the most conspicuous places; of the eleven aqueducts of the Cæsars and consuls, three were restored; the artificial rivers were conducted over a long series of old or of new arches, to discharge into marble basins a flood of salubrious and refreshing waters: and the spectator, impatient to ascend the steps of St. Peter's, is detained by a column of Egyptian granite, which rises between two lofty and perpetual fountains to the height of one hundred and twenty feet. The map, the description, the monuments of ancient Rome, have been elucidated by the diligence of the antiquarian and the student; and the footsteps of heroes, the relics, not of superstition, but of empire, are devoutly visited by a new race of pilgrims from the remote and once savage countries of the North.

Of these pilgrims, and of every reader, the attention will be excited by a History of the Decline and Fall of the Roman Empire; the greatest, perhaps, and most awful scene in the history of mankind. The various causes and progressive effects are connected with many of the events most interesting in human annals: the artful policy of the Cæsars, who long maintained the name and image of a free republic; the disorders of military despotism; the rise, establishment, and sects of Christianity; the foundation of Constantinople; the division of the monarchy; the invasion and settlements of the barbarians of Germany and Scythia; the institutions of the civil law; the character and religion of Mohammed; the temporal sovereignty of the popes; the restoration and decay of the Western empire of Charlemagne; the crusades of the Latins in the East; the conquests of the Saracens and Turks; the ruin of the Greek empire; the state and revolutions of Rome in the middle age. The historian may applaud the importance and variety of his subject; but, while he is conscious of his own imperfections, he must often accuse the deficiency of his materials. It was among the ruins of the Capitol that I first conceived the idea of a work which has amused and exercised near twenty years of my life, and which, however inadequate to my own wishes, I finally deliver to the curiosity and candour of the public.

LAUSANNE, *June 27, 1787.*

APPRECIATION

by

HUGH TREVOR-ROPER

21
Edward Gibbon, a painting by Walton.

Gibbon's great work, of which less than a tenth is represented in this volume, filled, in the first edition, six quarto volumes; and yet, as I have observed in the introduction, in spite of its great length, and enormous range, both in time and space, it has a remarkable unity. That unity is supplied by what Gibbon and his contemporaries called its "philosophy." For Gibbon saw himself, above all, as a "philosophic historian." This term, in the eighteenth century, was a term of art, and had a clear and distinct meaning. In order to appreciate Gibbon's achievement, it is well to begin by defining the "philosophic history" which he so deliberately set out to write.

Gibbon himself often uses the term "philosophic history" and, from his use of it, its meaning is plain enough. He distinguished sharply between "history," as he understood it, and the mere establishment and description of fact, however authentic. The function of a historian, he once wrote, was as noble as that of mere chronicler or *faiseur de gazettes* was contemptible. Not all his contemporaries recognised this distinction. One of the greatest of them, Dr. Johnson, firmly denied it. He declared roundly that in history "there is but a shallow stream of thought"; and he once added, in Gibbon's hearing, that there was very little "real authentic history," since it could all be reduced to the bare statements "that certain kings reigned and certain battles were fought": all else, he said, "all the colouring, all the philosophy of history is conjecture." Boswell, who records the conversation, remarks that Gibbon, who was then at work on his first volume, was silent; but long afterwards, in a footnote in the last volume of his great work, he effectively replied. "Dr. Johnson," he wrote, "praises Knolles (*A General History of the Turks . . .* 1603) as the first of historians, unhappy only in his choice of subject. Yet I much doubt whether a partial and verbose compilation from Latin writers, 1300 folio pages of speeches and battles, can either instruct or amuse an enlightened age which requires from the historian some tincture of philosophy and criticism."

"Some tincture of philosophy and criticism . . ." What did that mean? To Gibbon it meant what it had meant to a few predecessors and a few contemporaries whom he always named with reverence: those "heretical" historians who had had the courage, in the last two centuries, to stand aside from the orthodoxy of their time and look, in history, not for mere pedestrian accuracy (necessary though that was), nor for the justification of parties in Church or State, but for objective evidence of the operation of natural laws. In one of those footnotes which reveal so much of his method, Gibbon traced the pedigree of this "philosophic history." Machiavelli and Guicciardini, he wrote, "with their worthy successors Fra Paolo [Sarpi] and Davila" are justly esteemed the founders of modern history "till in the present age, Scotland arose to dispute the prize with Italy herself." In his autobiography, and in other notes or footnotes, he added other names: "the grave Thuanus"—the Frenchman J. A. de Thou who wrote in the time of Henri IV; the enlightened historian of Naples, Pietro Giannone; the cool Hanoverian churchman J. L. Mosheim. Among the ancient historians, his favourite was "the philosophic historian whose writings will instruct the last generations of mankind," Tacitus. The modern Scottish writers to whom he referred were David Hume, William Robertson, Adam Ferguson and Adam Smith.

Such was the apostolic succession of "philosophic historians" in which Gibbon, who from his earliest youth had "aspired to the character of a historian," hoped to insert himself. Almost all of them were, in some way, heretics. Machiavelli and de Thou had been Catholics whose works had been condemned at Rome. Sarpi was nearly, Giannone actually, martyred for his views. Hume was widely denounced as an "infidel." Even Robertson, though Moderator of the Kirk of Scotland for twenty years, was suspect—at least to Old Believers like John Wesley. And the heresy that united them was their insistence on looking, in history, not for divine purpose but for general causes, or at least for some general significance. Machiavelli had seen events controlled, in spite of fortune, by human *virtù*. Davila and de Thou had looked past the religious professions of the French civil wars to the political reality. Sarpi had seen the authority of the Church firmly rooted, not in its truth, but in its social and economic power: "should Rome and her religion be annihilated," Gibbon wrote, the Servite friar's "golden volume" on Benefices would still survive, "a philosophical history and a salutary warning." Giannone showed—in his life as well as his writings—the almost spontaneous "progress and abuse of sacerdotal power" at the expense of lay institutions. As for Tacitus, in his earliest work Gibbon acknowledged his debt to him. The other great Roman historian, Livy, he wrote, was a good narrative historian; but he explained nothing. How was it, for instance, that the laws and institutions of ancient Rome, "made for a small, half-civilised republic," having carried that republic "to the highest pitch of grandeur," then suddenly overturned it? To this great question of the rise and fall of the Roman Republic, Livy offered no answer. He seemed unaware of the question. But the answer can be found in Tacitus. "I know of no one except Tacitus," wrote Gibbon, "who has quite come up to my ideas of a philosophic historian."

But if a philosophical historian were to explain the rise and fall of states and empires, it was not enough to be original or heretical: to doubt the explanations of orthodoxy, or the past. In the eighteenth century such scepticism came too easily to many. These were the "Pyrrhonists," the disciples of the Greek sceptical philosopher, Pyrrho of Elis. All through the past century the "Pyrrhonists" had been at work, undermining the great systems of belief, and by now they had reduced the greatest intellectual constructions to crumbling heaps. Many a critical historian, looking at the ruins of Catholic history, Protestant history, of the Universal History of Bishop Bossuet or the Providential history of the Puritans, might well despair of explanation.

Such was the attitude of the most encyclopaedic mind of the late seventeenth century, the greatest of all "Pyrrhonists," Pierre Bayle, whose "disorderly erudition" would be both pillaged and pilloried by Gibbon. Such, at times, was the attitude of Bayle's most famous disciple, the universal monarch of letters in Gibbon's time, Voltaire. Brilliant, unsystematic, destructive, Voltaire at times would illuminate history as it had never been illuminated before. But ultimately his philosophy of history was wavering and uncertain. It rested on a rickety base of vast, miscellaneous reading and ended in mere scepticism: the scepticism implied in one of his titles, *Le Pyrrhonisme de l'Histoire.*

What distinguishes Gibbon from the French historians and philosophers of his time is his ultimate rejection of pyrrhonism, his continuing belief in the possibility of positive, secular explanation. Like them, he rejected the old theological explanations of history; but unlike them he never scoffed at the erudition by which they had been constructed, never doubted that, with a more modern "philosophy," that erudition could still be useful. Therefore he was grateful to all those predecessors who, from whatever motive, had lightened the labour of the modern philosopher. The French philosophers affected to despise those whom they condescendingly described as *érudits.* Gibbon, for all his eighteenth century "philosophy" was an unashamed *érudit*—indeed it is the depth and exactitude of his erudition which has caused his work to last while theirs has perished.

This ambivalent attitude towards his non-philosophical predecessors is apparent throughout Gibbon's writings:

indeed, it is what makes his historical writing, compared with that of the French Encyclopaedists, seem so mature. As a "philosopher," he will exercise his wit on their ponderous, even bigoted use of learning; but he never conceals his respect for learning itself. The great French Jansenist scholar, Sebastien Le Nain de Tillemont, may appear, on one occasion, as "the sure-footed mule of the Alps," but in the end Gibbon takes an almost tender farewell from "that incomparable guide whose bigotry is overbalanced by the merits of erudition, diligence, veracity and scrupulous minuteness." No praise is ever spared by the "infidel" Gibbon for those greatest of monastic scholars, the seventeenth century Benedictines of St. Maur, whose splendid library and busy historical "workshop," the abbey of St-Germain-des-Prés in Paris, he would visit as a devout, admiring pilgrim.

On the other hand, for Bayle with his "pyrrhonism," and for the French Encyclopaedists, with their glib anti-clericalism, their immediate, journalistic answers to complex questions, Gibbon expressed increasing disdain. "The dictionary of Bayle," he remarks on one occasion, "has more merit for lively reflexion than original research"; and on another, "in his article on Mohammed, Bayle has shown how indifferently wit and philosophy supply the absence of genuine information." Voltaire, in particular, irritated him as a superficial historian who could not be fair to his adversaries. Gibbon's comments on Voltaire in the *Decline and Fall* are numerous; and they are almost always hostile, from the first, on the extent of the Roman Empire, ("M. de Voltaire, unsupported by either fact or probability, has generously bestowed the Canary Islands on the Roman Empire") to the last, on the religious fervour of the Turks ("the pious zeal of Voltaire is excessive, and even ridiculous"). Voltaire's misfortune was that, in his *Essai sur les Mœurs*, he had run over Gibbon's chosen ground, casting, in Gibbon's phrase, "a keen and lively glance over the surface of history." He had also allowed his "philosophy" to run away with him, always automatically taking the anti-

clerical and anti-Christian side. This Gibbon could not
forgive. "In his way," he once exploded, after quoting
one such excess, "Voltaire was a bigot, an intolerant
bigot."

But if Gibbon hoped to triumph over "pyrrhonism"
and extract positive "philosophical" lessons from the
erudition of the past, some new organising principle was
needed. Where was this principle to be found? By a
singular good fortune Gibbon discovered it as the result
of the biographical accident which banished him from
England at the age of sixteen and settled him, for five
formative years, in the country which was then the seed-
plot of the European Enlightenment, Switzerland. We
must therefore look back for a moment to Gibbon's
youth and, particularly, to his years in Lausanne.

The cause of Gibbon's early exile to Lausanne is well
known from his own incomparable autobiography. A
delicate only child, neglected by his parents, his education constantly interrupted by illness, at the age of fifteen
he had been sent by his widowed father, out of "perplexity rather than prudence," to Magdalen College,
Oxford. There he spent, as he tells us, "fourteen months
the most idle and unprofitable of my whole life." There
also, left without guidance, intellectual or moral, he
wandered into the tempting fold of Roman Catholicism.
Socially, this conversion was regarded as catastrophic.
He was removed in disgrace from Oxford and, to reclaim
him for Protestantism, his shocked father sent him to
Lausanne, to be under the care and tuition of a sound
Protestant pastor, M. Pavillard.

It is improbable that Gibbon's father, in sending him
to Lausanne, had any idea of the intellectual effects of
such a sojourn. In fact they were enormous. Lausanne,
at that time, with Geneva, was enjoying a revival of
letters which made them the centre of European "philosophy." Both the university of Lausanne and the academy of Geneva had recently been liberalised by the
defeat of the strict Calvinist party, and the heretical
thinkers of France and Italy converged on the hospitable

shores of the lake of Geneva. It was to Geneva that
Giannone had fled to escape from persecution in Italy,
in Lausanne that he was seeking to reprint his great work,
the cause of his persecution, *The Civil History of Naples*.
It was in Geneva, to avoid the French censorship, that
Montesquieu published, in 1748, his greatest work,
De l'Esprit des Lois. It was in Geneva, at his house of Les
Délices, that Voltaire himself took refuge, and at Ferney,
within reach of the same sanctuary, that he established
himself. And it was a liberal pastor of Lausanne, Jacob
Vernet, who provided a personal link between all
three.

Liberal themselves, and attracting by their liberalism
the leading thinkers of Europe, the two cities of the lake
were twin capitals of modern culture; and it was in one
of them, in Lausanne, that Gibbon absorbed that culture.
In a memorable passage of his *Memoirs* he had described
what Lausanne had done for him. "If my childish revolt
against the religion of my country had not stripped me
in time of my academic gown, the five important years,
so liberally improved in the studies and conversation of
Lausanne, would have been steeped in port and prejudice
among the monks of Oxford. Had the fatigue of idleness
compelled me to read, the path of learning would not
have been enlightened by a ray of philosophic freedom";
and again, "such as I am, in genius or learning or manners, I owe my creation to Lausanne: it was in that school
that the statue was discovered in the block of marble."
Twenty-five years later he showed his recognition by
returning to live and finish his great work in Lausanne.

It has sometimes been remarked that Gibbon's least
perceptive critics have come from the Anglo-Saxon
world, and it is certainly true that some of his best
commentators have been European: not Frenchmen,
blinded by the partisan brilliance of Voltaire, but Swiss
and Italian. The reason is not far to seek. Gibbon, in a
sense, was not English. At Lausanne he severed himself
from the English intellectual tradition and inserted
himself in the continental tradition—to which England

had, of course, richly contributed. It was through continental interpreters that he discovered Locke and other English writers. He himself confessed that, after five years in Lausanne, he had ceased to be an Englishman. Afterwards, though he served in the Hampshire militia and the English House of Commons, he was never at home in the English literary establishment; he nearly wrote his great work in French; and the style of his last volumes, he would confess, was affected by his use of French, not English, as his first language. In his "general observations on the fall of the Roman Empire in the West" Gibbon contrasted the narrow loyalties of a "patriot" with the more enlarged view of a philosoper who would "consider Europe as one great republic whose various inhabitants have attained almost the same level of politeness and cultivation." In Lausanne he became a life-citizen of that republic.

How he earned that citizenship by his reading, he has described in his autobiography. For our purpose, one book is essential. It was in Lausanne that Gibbon discovered the work which would provide the organising principle of his historical ideas. After describing the other works which influenced him, he adds, "but my delight was in the frequent perusal of Montesquieu, whose energy of style and boldness of hypothesis were powerful to awaken and stimulate the genius of the age." For Montesquieu, the founder of the social sciences, was the thinker who, by his novel ideas, recreated the study of history. That great mass of erudition which the scholars of the seventeenth century had built up and the "pyrrhonists" had undermined, and whose ruins were being mocked by the "lively philosophers" of the Encyclopaedia, could now, thanks to him, be reorganised. The dry bones could live. This possibility, unquestionably, is what inspired Gibbon, whose past historical reading, as he tells us, had been vast but undigested. To the end of his life, Gibbon always venerated Montesquieu, and his great work *De l'Esprit des Lois*. "In the forty years since its publication," he wrote in his last volume, "no work has

22-23
Westminster College, London, the school attended by Gibbon
when his poor health permitted; and Magdalen College, Oxford,
where Gibbon was sent in the early 1750's to spend "the most
idle and unprofitable" months of his life.

24
Lausanne in Switzerland, where Gibbon was sent by his father
in 1753. On this first trip Gibbon was deeply impressed by the
intellectual climate of French Switzerland, where he stayed for
five years.

25
In Lausanne Gibbon was entrusted by his father to the care and tuition of the Reverend Daniel Pavillard, who by December 1754 had gently persuaded him to return from Catholicism to the Protestant fold.

26
Voltaire, whose plays Gibbon saw on his first trip to Switzerland.
Voltaire himself was already firmly established in residence at
Ferney, near Geneva. Gibbon was later to criticise Voltaire as
being a superficial historian.

27
Montesquieu, whose *L'Esprit des Lois* of 1748, published in Geneva, greatly influenced Gibbon, who read it in Lausanne.

28
Gibbon would have sported a uniform similar to this, worn by
an eighteenth century infantryman, when he served with the
Hampshire Militia in the early 1760's after his return to
England.

been more read and criticised, and the spirit of enquiry which it has excited is not the least of our obligations to the author." Without Montesquieu, it is not too much to say, we would never have had *The Decline and Fall of the Roman Empire*.

What was the lesson which Gibbon learned from Montesquieu? Basically, it was that history is not a mere pageant of events, nor a storehouse of noble (or deterrent) examples (as the old "humanist" historians had supposed), nor a meaningless mass of uncertain facts (as the pyrrhonists seemed to suggest), but a process, and a process governed, in its detail, not by a divine plan, ascertainable only by revelation, but by a complex of social forces operating according to natural laws, which could be empirically deduced by direct observation. Geography, climate, economic resources—these lay at the base of history; institutions, laws, religion—these, conditioned by them but developing their own momentum, created in turn new and subtler forces to whose interwoven pattern human behaviour was subject. Men, Montesquieu argued, are not entirely free. "They are governed by many things: climate, religion, laws, maxims of government, examples of things past, customs, manners; from all which is derived a general spirit"—the spirit which he called "the spirit of the laws." If a historian, in describing political history, took care always to remember this social background, which conditioned it, he would be able not only to narrate but, within limits —for there was always the accidental and the incidental, the genius, the crime and the folly—to explain.

The immediate effect of Montesquieu on Gibbon was shown in his first work, his *Essai sur l'Etude de la Littérature*, which he wrote, in French, in Lausanne, and published after his return to England, in 1761. This brief early work is Gibbon's profession of faith: in it he declares his position in relation to his European contemporaries, detaching himself from the Encyclopaedists and declaring his loyalty to Montesquieu. In his *Memoirs* he has described its origin: how, in France, he had found classical learning "neglected by a philosophic age" and "the new language of *érudits* contemptuously applied to the successors of Lipsius and Casaubon." He was "particularly provoked," he tells us, by the suggestion of d'Alembert that, at the end of every century, a selection be made of such knowledge as was judged worth preserving by the self-styled philosophers of the time, and the rest destroyed.

Against such intellectual arrogance Gibbon resolved to defend the old standards of exact scholarship with which no philosopher, he believed, could afford to dispense. All facts, he insisted, deserved respect: "a Montesquieu, from the meanest of them, will deduce consequences undreamed by ordinary men." Admittedly, the exclusive cult of facts led to pedantry, but neglect of facts is fatal. Firm in this conviction Gibbon declared himself unafraid of "the withering name of *érudit*"; he was confident that history could use the labours, even the pedantry of the past without itself becoming pedantic; and he set out his ideal of the philosophic historian, the historical disciple of Montesquieu. Even in style Gibbon owned his master. The style of his *Essai* has none of the later Gibbonian balance, amplitude, wit. It was concentrated apophthegmatic, even obscure. Afterwards, Gibbon recognised its stylistic faults. He lamented its "sententious and oracular brevity." "Alas," he wrote, "how fatal has been the imitation of Montesquieu!"

Thus by 1761 Gibbon's mind was formed, his purpose clear. He would combine erudition and philosophy to write a great work of historical explanation, using the new social science of Montesquieu. Even as he reflected on the task, examples were before him. For if Montesquieu had made little impact in England, he had been received with enthusiasm in another country—a country to which, intellectually, Gibbon would be increasingly drawn: Scotland.

The reception of Montesquieu in Scotland is an interesting episode in the intellectual history of Europe. No doubt there is a social explanation of it. In the early eighteenth century Scotland was still a backward, in some respects a very backward country. For at least a century it had been isolated, frustrated, closed in on itself and torn by political faction. But after the Union with England, in 1707, and the end of Jacobitism in 1745, the country was opened up and a group of highly intelligent and public spirited men in Edinburgh rose to the challenge. Ashamed of the visible stagnation of their country, they set out to bring Scotland up to the level of England: in other words, to achieve, in one generation, the progress which, in England, had been spread over two centuries. Moreover, they believed that this could and should be done by social, not political methods. The politics of Scotland, in the last two centuries and more, had been suicidal; and anyway, since 1707, the Scots were no longer masters of their political destiny; for the political centre had moved to London. But social change, they thought, could be achieved by their own efforts, if only those efforts were guided by clear understanding of the mechanics of change.

It is easy to see how such men were excited by the work of Montesquieu. Montesquieu did not answer their questions, but he told them where to look for the answers. He encouraged them to seek, in history, the laws of social change which they could then apply to their own country; and they were quick to follow his advice. In 1749, within a year of its publication, *L'Esprit des Lois* fell into the hands of David Hume, who happened to be in Turin. Through Hume it came to Scotland and was soon published in Edinburgh, both in French and in English translation. Its effect was soon apparent. Hume's own *History of England* began to appear in 1754. In 1759 his friend William Robertson published his *History of Scotland*. Both these books were deeply influenced by Montesquieu. In the following decade Robertson would publish his *History of Charles V* (1769) with its long opening chapter, or rather book, on the development of European society between the end of the Roman Empire and the Renaissance.

Meanwhile another Scotsman, Adam Ferguson, a friend of both Hume and Robertson, published his *Essay on Civil Government* (1767): a book thoroughly impregnated with Montesquieu's ideas and written, like Gibbon's *Essai*, in a similarly aphoristic style. Finally, in 1776—the same year which saw the publication of the first volume of the *Decline and Fall*—came Adam Smith's *Wealth of Nations* which showed (in Bagehot's phrase) "how man, from a savage, rose to be a Scotsman." The whole Scottish school of social historians was, in fact, the school of Montesquieu. As Smith's disciple John Millar would afterwards write: "the great Montesquieu pointed out the road. He was the Lord Bacon of this branch of study. Dr. Smith is the Newton."

Intellectually isolated in England, Gibbon was a great admirer of his Scottish fellow-disciples of Montesquieu. He venerated Hume and Robertson—"the Tacitus and the Livy of Scotland." Their names occur again and again, both in his private correspondence and in his published works. In his *Memoirs*, he describes his sensations on reading their earliest works, after his return to England: "the perfect composition, the nervous language, the well-turned periods of Dr. Robertson inflamed me to the ambitious hope that I might one day tread in his footsteps: the calm philosophy, the careless inimitable beauties of his friend and rival often forced me to close the volume with a mixed sensation of delight and despair." When the first volume of the *Decline and Fall* was published, Gibbon would send presentation copies to both Hume and Robertson, and would be delighted by their approval: "the candour of Dr. Robertson embraced his disciple. A letter from Mr. Hume overpaid the labour of ten years; but I have never presumed to accept a place in the triumvirate of British historians."

Gibbon also admired Adam Ferguson. When Ferguson's *Essay* was published, he wrote a long and laudatory review of it in the French periodical, *Mémoires littéraires de la Grande-Bretagne*, which he and his friend Deyverdun were then editing in London. He shared many of Ferguson's ideas, and when he published the first volume of the *Decline and Fall*, he would send a copy to Ferguson too. "I shall not pretend to deny," he wrote, in reply to Ferguson's congratulations, "that your approbation, and that of your literary friends at Edinburgh, has given me very great pleasure. I am not proud enough to be above vanity, and I have always looked up with the most sincere respect towards the northern part of our island, whither taste and philosophy seemed to have retired from the smoke and hurry of this immense capital." Ferguson was himself, at that time, working on a history of the Decline and Fall of the Roman Republic.

In the same letter to Ferguson, Gibbon expressed his delight with the newly published work of "our common friend Mr. Adam Smith." The *Wealth of Nations*, he wrote, was "an extensive science in a single book, and the most profound ideas expressed in the most perspicuous language." In London, that year, Gibbon and Adam Smith became close personal friends, and in his later volumes Gibbon would often quote Smith. In his last volume he would pay a general tribute to Hume, Robertson and Adam Smith as the three contemporary writers who had shed the most profound light on the progress of society in history, and in his will he would leave £100 each to the two of them who survived him. No English historian or man of letters enjoyed such close relations with Gibbon as this compact group of Scotsmen in Edinburgh.

But if Gibbon was inspired by Montesquieu, and Montesquieu's Scotch disciples, to write a great work of "philosophic history," what would that work be? In the five years after his return to England, when he studied in his father's house in Hampshire, or served in those tedious "exercises of the field and bottle" with the Hampshire militia, he considered various subjects: the life of Sir Walter Ralegh, the English baronial wars, the French invasion of Italy in 1494, Mediciean Florence, the history of the liberty of the Swiss. Then, in 1763, with the end of the European war, he seized his opportunity. Leaving

England, to which the war had confined him for the last five years, he returned, via Paris, to Lausanne; and from Lausanne he set out, with a friend, on that famous journey to Rome which, as he tells us, finally decided him to write not on any of these subjects but on the decline and fall of the Eternal City.

So he tells us, and so we may believe; and yet is this the whole truth? We all tend to dramatise, in retrospect, our great moments, and although there is no need to doubt Gibbon's account of his enthusiasm—how "after a sleepless night, I trod, with a lofty step, the ruins of the Forum; each memorable spot where Romulus stood, or Tully spoke, or Caesar fell, was at once present to my eye; and several days of intoxication were lost or enjoyed before I could descend to a cool and minute investigation"—there are certain facts to be noted before we ascribe the whole idea of the *Decline and Fall* to that moment when "the bare-footed friars were singing vespers in the temple of Jupiter."

For first, when Gibbon set out for Rome, he carried with him a library of books, not on medieval Switzerland or Renaissance Florence, but on the Roman Empire, which suggests that he was already studying it in some detail. Secondly, the idea which "started to his mind" on that famous occasion was the idea of writing the decline and fall not of the Empire but of the city of Rome—that city which was visible before his excited eyes. Thirdly, two years after his return to England, he actually began to write, not on the decline and fall even of the city of Rome, but on his old subject "the liberty of the Swiss." All this suggests that too much must not be ascribed to that sudden illumination at the temple of Jupiter. That experience must be set in a wider context of Gibbon's general aims.

Here we must remember that the subject of the decline and fall of the Roman Empire was not peculiar to Gibbon. We naturally think of this as his subject because he made it his subject, as no other writer did. But in fact, in the eighteenth century, the problem of the decline of

Rome had perplexed many other minds before Gibbon took it up. It was indeed the great intellectual challenge of the time. It is our good fortune that it was also faced by the greatest historian of the time.

The preoccupation of the eighteenth century historians with the decline of the Roman Empire is easy to understand. Since 1700—since that famous journalistic episode, "the Battle of the Books," between Ancients and Moderns—the attitude towards Antiquity had changed. Hitherto men had always looked up with veneration to the heroic age from which civilisation, it seemed, had declined. To the clergy, the apostolic age was a pattern which fallen men might revere but hardly restore. To the humanists, Greek and Roman civilisation was equally venerable. Even historians urged their readers to preserve intact the ancient constitutions which linked them, however tenuously, with their heroic origins. The idea of progress, the idea that modern civilisation could rival or even surpass those ancient models was unthinkable in a world which, to the theologian, was already hastening to its end. But in the eighteenth century the tide turned. Then at last a new generation discovered a new confidence. The historical idea of decline, the theological idea of fall, went out of fashion. Men found the new concept of progress, and they found it warranted by their own history. During the last centuries, they discovered, they had in fact progressed, and now, in Basil Willey's words, "across the vast gulf of the monkish and deluded past" they could "salute the ancients from an eminence perhaps as lofty as their own."

But if the idea of progress had arrived, its very acceptance entailed new problems. For how, men asked, did it occur? Evidently it was not automatic, for there behind them lay the vast gulf from which they had emerged and which also had to be explained. How was it that the Roman Empire, the culmination (as it seemed) of classical civilisation, had foundered in a Dark Age? How was it that the modern nations of Europe, after long foundering in that darkness, had finally climbed out of it to "the full light and freedom of the eighteenth century"? As men asked themselves these questions, another, more sinister question also forced itself upon them, chilling their new-found confidence. Was it possible that modern civilisation, which at present seemed so prosperous, would also, like that of Antiquity, decline? If the new social sciences could explain the mechanics of progress, it must be possible to deduce from them also the mechanics of decline and fall; and that too demanded explanation.

All the philosophical historians of the eighteenth century were exercised by this question. The earliest of them, Giannone, in his autobiography, has described how he wrestled with it, seeking in the legal and institutional history of the Lower Empire an explanation for the emergence of the barbarian kingdoms of Europe. Lord Bolingbroke, in his *Letters on History*, called for a history of "the whole progress of that [Roman] government from liberty to servitude, the whole series of causes and effects, apparent and real, public and private." Montesquieu himself, before writing his greatest work, had published a book on the greatness and decline of Rome. All Montesquieu's disciples were haunted by the same problem. As Dugald Stewart wrote, in his biographical sketch of Robertson: "It was indeed a subject worthy of their genius; for in the whole history of human affairs no spectacle occurs so wonderful in itself, or so momentous in its effects, as the growth of that system which took its rise from the conquests of the Barbarians": conquests which led to "a thick night of superstition and ignorance which lasted nearly a thousand years" but which yet "laid the foundation of a state of society far more favourable to the general and permanent happiness of the human race than any which the world had hitherto seen."

When we see this problem as it presented itself to his contemporaries, it is clear that Gibbon must have considered it even before his visit to Rome. Indeed, the particular topics which he contemplated were all, in different ways, elements of that greater, more complex

29-30
William Robertson and David Hume, two of the Scottish historians whom Gibbon greatly admired.

31
Adam Smith, author of the *Wealth of Nations*, a writer revered
by Gibbon, with whom he was to become personally acquainted
in 1776.

subject: partial solutions such as had been attempted by his predecessors. What he saw in Rome, on that famous 24th of October, 1764, was the possibility of tackling the whole subject, of linking it physically to the city whose antique ruins and transformed character made so powerful an impression on his imagination. In fact, of course, the study of so huge a problem led Gibbon far away from Rome. He visited, in imagination, but always with firm documentary support, the forests of Northern Europe, the deserts of Africa and Central Asia as well as the smiling classical landscape of Greece. He followed the Roman Caesars to Byzantium, saw them transformed into Oriental despots, and compared their rule with that of Moslem Caliphs, Mongol Khans and Turkish Sultans. He entered the doctrinal labyrinth not only of the Christian Church but of Zoroastrian Persia and Moslem Arabia. And yet always he kept a firm eye on the history of the city of Rome: that "eternal city" which remained a historical constant while other capitals rose and fell or, like Alexandria and Antioch, Jerusalem and Baghdad, even, in the end, Constantinople itself, were enslaved to foreign rule and a new religion.

Gibbon's subject is the revolutions of society between Antiquity and Modernity; but its centre is still the city of Rome. We see it at first, under the great "Antonine" emperors, the capital of the world. We see it again, under the "Lower Empire," reduced to a provincial city. We see it, in the fifth century, as a Christian city, sacked by Goths and Vandals. In the trough of the sixth century we see it about to disappear in the tide of history "like Thebes or Babylon or Carthage," had it not been given a new character by the old Roman virtues of Pope Gregory the Great, and again in the eighth century by his successors, Gregory II and Gregory III. We see it as the capital of the world once again under an insolent theocracy in the Middle Ages, and sunk again into neglect in the "Babylonish Captivity" of the Papacy at Avignon, when the poet Petrarch and the tribune Cola di Rienzi sought to recreate its ancient republican virtue. Finally, in his last chapter, we see the city physically before us, as Gibbon saw it in 1764, and learn how, over the centuries, the triumphal arches and aqueducts and amphitheatres of Antiquity had been ruined not by "those innocent barbarians," the Goths and Vandals, but by the secular feuds of the Romans, the iconoclastic zeal of the clergy, and the cupidity and ostentation of upstart princes of the Church. Such were the destructive forces which Gibbon summarised in his famous phrase, so often misapplied, "the triumph of barbarism and religion."

The Decline and Fall of the Roman Empire must thus be seen as a great work of explanation, in which all the erudition of the past is directed by the new "philosophy" of the eighteenth century in order to answer incidentally, by means of narrative, the greatest historical question of the time. This being so, we naturally ask what Gibbon's explanation is: how did he in fact account for the decline of Rome? To this question Gibbon's answer is never explicitly given. He was far too subtle and sensitive a historian to look for crude, single causes. His philosophy emerges gradually as we read. To those who read him in full, it is clear enough. Unfortunately there are plenty of shallow critics who have, perhaps, only read him in part, and who have sought to ascribe to him answers which he never gave, and would have disowned. The egregious Lytton Strachey, for instance, thought that Gibbon's sole interest was in a classical style—"the style once fixed, everything else followed." Bertrand Russell, in a rare lapse, has qualified him as a "Catholic atheist." Others have seen him as a complacent imperialist—did he not admire, above all, the age of the Antonines?—a pagan, an infidel. All these views are, I believe, demonstrably wrong. Even the customary view that Gibbon was fundamentally anti-Christian seems to me incorrect. His views on religion, I believe, were logically implied in his "philosophical" views on the nature of history and society. But I shall not waste time in debate: I shall

666

simply seek to analyse, from his own evidence, Gibbon's answer to the great question of his time concerning the decline of the Roman Empire.

That answer is given most succinctly in the "general observations on the fall of the Roman Empire in the West" which Gibbon placed at the end of his 38th chapter. There he asked the crucial question, whether it was possible that the "great republic" of modern Europe, like the Roman Empire, might also succumb to a new barbarism? To this question he answers confidently, no. He does not deny that political crime or folly may have a disastrous effect; and history in general, he once remarks, in a famous passage, is little other than the register of such crime and folly. But such setbacks, he believes, are essentially temporary. For the real motor of history, he believes—with Montesquieu and his disciples—is not political. It consists in the useful arts and sciences. "The history of empires," he wrote in his *Essai*, "is the record of human misery; the history of the sciences is that of the greatness and happiness of mankind." And in his conclusions he expresses, in different words, the same thought. The arts, which Europe has discovered or invented, have been diffused over the globe: "they can never be lost. We may therefore acquiesce in the pleasing conclusion that every age of the world has increased and still increases the real wealth, the happiness, the knowledge, and perhaps the virtue of the human race."

But this "pleasing conclusion," this confidence in the force of progress, did not, for Gibbon, rest on any automatic theory. For why (for instance) did such progress only occur at certain times and in certain places? Why did "the arts" not advance equally in all times? Quite apart from the effect of human crime or folly there were, Gibbon thought, other forces at work. In particular, there was the structure of society and the mentality which (as he believed with Montesquieu) was conditioned by that structure. Put briefly, Gibbon believed, with Machiavelli and the great republicans of Florence and Venice, and with his Scottish contemporaries, in *virtù*: in the

667

spirit of freedom, of public spirit, of public service by the subjects or citizens of a state. Despotism, centralised power, monopoly might be a source of patronage, they might enable a good prince to display his virtues, but only the republican virtues of active, responsible citizenship, only free competition, free interchange of goods and ideas, could ensure continuity of progress against the opposite tendency of centralisation whereby human ingenuity and wealth tended to be invested in mere power, propaganda, war or display.

This general philosophy is shown by Gibbon at the very beginning of his great work, where he pays his famous tribute to the "age of the Antonines"—or rather of the whole period from 98 to 180 A.D. when the Roman Empire was ruled by the five emperors from Nerva to Marcus Aurelius. "If a man were called to fix the period in the history of the world during which the condition of the human race was most happy and prosperous, he would, without hesitation, name that which elapsed from the death of Domitian to the accession of Commodus." It is less often observed that, in saying this, Gibbon does not necessarily himself endorse a view which to him, was simply a truism from the past. For the felicity of the Antonine age was, in his time, a well-worn theme. Indeed, Gibbon, in this passage, is merely echoing, almost word for word, a passage from Francis Bacon's *Advancement of Learning*. In this passage Bacon described "the age which passed from the death of Domitianus the emperor until the reign of Commodus" as "for temporal respects, the most happy and flourishing that ever the Roman Empire (which then was a model of the world) enjoyed." And Gibbon, we should note, in quoting this popular verdict, does not explicitly endorse it.

Indeed, from the very beginning, his praise of the Antonine age is qualified: for he sees in it—in the very structure of the imperial system which excluded the idea of *virtù*, of public spirit— the seeds of its decay. "That public virtue," he writes, "which among the ancients was denominated patriotism, is derived from a strong sense

668

of our own interest in the preservation and prosperity of the *free* govt. of *which we are members*. Such a sentiment, which had rendered the legions of the republic almost invincible, could make but a very feeble impression on the mercenary servants of a despotic prince." And at the end of the three chapters in which he describes the Antonine age, he emphasises "two peculiar circumstances" which exposed the subjects of the Roman emperors to a condition "more completely wretched than the victims of tyranny in any other age or country." These two circumstances lay in the memory of past freedom and in the universality of imperial power. "The division of Europe into a number of independent states . . . is productive of the most beneficial consequences to the liberty of mankind." The heretic, the non-conformist, could always find a base, and so ideas and experiments could not be stifled. But the monopoly of the Roman emperors was absolute. There was no rival power, no means of escape from at worst, tyranny, at best, deadening conformity. " 'Wherever you are,' said Cicero to the exiled Marcellus, 'remember that you are equally within the power of the conqueror'."

Public spirit, public service, *virtù*—this, to Gibbon, was the human motive force of progress; and it was generated, in his view, by the kind of society which, in turn, it created. It had created the republics of the Middle Ages, the city communes of Italy, the free cantons of Switzerland, the record of whose liberty he had once thought of writing. It had inspired Machiavelli in Florence and Sarpi in Venice, both of whom sought to revive it when they saw it being suppressed—in Florence by the secular power of France and Spain, in Venice by the Counter-Reformation Church. In Gibbon's own time it inspired the men of the Scottish Enlightenment who sought to raise post-Union Scotland from the "slavery" inherited from pre-Union times.

Gibbon's implicit criticism of the Antonine age might have been taken from Ferguson's *Essay on Civil Society*. There Ferguson explicitly refutes the idea "that if a succession of good princes could be found, despotical government is best calculated for the happiness of mankind." To this he answers that the vices of despotism are not dependent on the person of the despot, but inherent in the sytem, and that "liberty is never in greater danger than it is when we measure national felicity by the blessings which a prince may bestow, or by the mere tranquillity which may attend on equitable administration." "The benefits arising from liberty ... are not the fruits of a virtue, or of a goodness, which operate in the breast of one man, but the communication of virtue itself to many; and such a distribution of functions in civil society as gives to numbers the exercises and occupations which pertain to their natures." To Ferguson, as to Gibbon after him, the age of the Antonines was an age of "tranquillity" indeed, of good princes, of "equitable administration"; but it was inherently corrupt because it had stifled that laudable ambition, that active participation by the citizen in the pursuit of social ends which is the only spring of progress.

Progress, then, to Gibbon, depended not only directly on economic and social improvement, but also, indirectly, on political virtue; and that political virtue entailed the possibility of active participation by private citizens in "the free government of which we are members." Such participation did not necessarily entail a republican form of government—indeed, in argument with the French historian Mably, Gibbon defended the cause of monarchy against republicanism—but it did exclude any form of government, whether monarchical, oligarchic or even "democratic," which positively denied to subjects the opportunity of public service or made policy dependent on the arbitrary will even of a virtuous governor. As for the English Hanoverian monarchy, Gibbon no doubt agreed with Montesquieu, who had described it as "une monarchie cachée sous les formes d'une république."

It is within the context of this general theory that Gibbon's interpretation of Church history is to be seen.

Gibbon might not be interested in religious doctrine, but he was interested in the machinery of human progress, in the public spirit which activated that machinery, and in humanity; and it was the position of the Church in relation to that machinery, that spirit, and that humanity which he attempted to examine. Where the Church, or the early Christians, sustained or expressed public spirit, he would applaud them—as in his tributes to the great Popes of the Dark Ages who animated their city with "a vital principle which again restored her to honour and dominion." Where the Church supported the cause of real learning—as in the monastery of St-Germain-des-Prés—or of humanity—as in opposing gladiatorial contests or in alleviating the lot of the poor in feudal Europe—he would commend it. In a memorable passage on the crusades he remarks that the clergy "prevented the total extinction of letters, mitigated the fierceness of the times, sheltered the poor and defenceless, and preserved or revived the peace and order of civil society."

But in general he believed that the Church, as an institution, had been historically opposed to progress, in several ways. First, politically, by its teaching, at least in its early days, it corroded the old republican *virtù*. Instead of public service it positively advocated non-participation in civic life. Secondly, socially, by its adaptation into the centralised, hierarchical system of the Roman Empire, it helped to destroy the social basis upon which that virtue must ultimately rest. Finally, economically, it created a monopoly. The superfluous wealth of society was drained away from charitable or public uses, denied that free circulation which is the motor of industry, and either immobilised in outward magnificence or dissipated in sterile theological disputes. Gibbon hated to see the immobilisation of resources—economic or intellectual—and he would record with pleasure those occasions on which the barren treasures of the Church were "restored to their true proprietors, the poor of every country and every denomination," or "sacrilegiously converted to the uses of mankind."

This hatred of social immobility made Gibbon particularly hostile to monasticism as the growing canker which, in the Middle Ages, gradually ate up the resources of the Church, and, thereby, of society. Medieval monasticism, he says, in one of his strongest phrases, "counterbalanced all the temporal advantages of Christianity." His meaning is clear enough: we should not forget that he was writing in the eighteenth century, when Catholic rulers throughout Europe were dissolving monasteries by thousands in order to modernise their countries; but he made it even clearer when he described, in his *Memoirs*, the radical emotions which he had felt in 1755, standing before the magnificent, newly rebuilt rococo abbey of Einsiedeln. "I was astonished," he writes, "by the profuse ostentation of riches in the poorest quarter of Europe; amidst a savage scene of woods and mountains, a palace appeared to have been erected by magic; and it was erected by the potent magic of religion. A crowd of palmers and votaries was prostrate before the altar. The title and worship of the Mother of God provoked my indignation; and the lively naked image of superstition suggested to me, as in the same place it had done to Zwinglius, the most pressing argument for the reformation of the Church." Another Swiss abbey elicited from him an even more summary expression of his view of social progress and its impediments. "Within the ancient walls of Vindonissa," he would write in a footnote to the *Decline and Fall*, "the castle of Habsburg, the abbey of Königsfeld and the town of Bruck have successively risen. The philosophic traveller may compare the monuments of Roman conquest, of feudal or Austrian tyranny, of monkish superstition, and of industrious freedom. If he be truly a philosopher, he will applaud the merit and happiness of his own time."

"Industrious freedom"—this, in two words, is Gibbon's formula for the progress of society, and he judges the Church, as an organ of society, exclusively by its service or disservice to that ideal. For to him it is the social character of the Church that is all important: towards its

Edward Gibbon Esqr
Taking Snuff

The pilgrimage of Italy, which
I now accomplished, had long been the object of my curious
devotion. The passage of Mount Cenis, the regular streets
of Turin, the Gothic cathedral of Milan, the scenery of the
Boromean islands, the marble palaces of Genoa the beauties
of Florence, the wonders of Rome, the curiosities of Naples, the
galleries of Bologna, the singular aspect of Venice the amphi-
= theatre of Verona, and the Palladian architecture, are still
present to my mind. I read the Tuscan writers on the banks
of the Arno: but my conversation was with the dead rather
than the living; and the whole college of Cardinals was of
less value in my eyes than the transfiguration of Raphael
the Apollo of the Vatican or the massy greatness of the

32-33
Silhouettes of Gibbon taking snuff; and a page from the manus-
cript of Gibbon's *Autobiography* in which he describes his decision
to write about the fall of Rome, on his visit to Italy of 1764.

34-35
The summerhouse in Lausanne (Gibbon had returned here to
live in 1783) where Gibbon sat in 1787 to finish his great work;
and Fletching Church in Sussex where Gibbon was buried
after his death on January 16th, 1794.

doctrine he shows a genial, even contemptuous indifference. However, since this very indifference caused him
to be attacked as an "infidel," we may pause to consider
what were in fact those personal religious views which he
refused to expose in his writings.

Gibbon deeply resented "the invidious name of unbeliever" when it was publicly attached to him by the
unitarian chemist of Birmingham, Joseph Priestley. His
own beliefs are described by himself, with his usual exactitude, in his *Memoirs*. He there tells us how, having sam-
pled Catholicism at Oxford and been reconverted to
Protestantism in Lausanne ("I am now a good Protestant
and extremely glad of it," he reported to his aunt at the
time), he afterwards "suspended" his religious enquiries,
"acquiescing with implicit belief in the tenets and mysteries which are adopted by the general consent of Catholics and Protestants." This careful phrase is, if carefully
read, perfectly clear. Gibbon conformed on principle
with the established Church. He regarded such establishment as "a salutary maxim," commended the ancient
philosophers for their conformity, reproved Voltaire for
insulting "the religion of nations," and looked back on
his own apostasy as a "childish revolt against the religion
of my country." But this conformity, however firmly
defended, was purely social. In his personal religion,
Gibbon, like Voltaire, was a deist. In other words, he
believed that a divine creator was presupposed by the
universal and harmonious laws of Nature and morality,
but he rejected any further definition of His attributes
based upon documented or private revelation.

A careful reader of his works will find numerous evidences of Gibbon's deism, his rejection of the materialist
atheism of d'Holbach and La Mettrie. In his *Essai* of 1761
he explicitly rejects the atheism of Lucretius by reference
to Lucretius' own proofs of the laws of Nature. "The
God of Nature," he remarks in the *Decline and Fall*, "has
written his existence on all his works and his law in the
heart of men"; and again, "the unity of God is an idea
most congenial to Nature and reason"; and he commends

673

the Mongol conqueror Ginghiz Khan for "anticipating the lessons of philosophy and establishing by his laws a system of pure theism and perfect toleration. His first and only article of faith was the existence of one God, the author of all good, who fills by his presence the heavens and earth, which he has created by his power." It seems clear that Gibbon approved—in this at least—of Ginghiz Khan.

Within this general deism Gibbon rejected all sectarian differences, except on grounds of social utility. He was a Protestant by conformity, and because established Protestantism, in the eighteenth century, was more liberal, more rational, more tolerant than established Catholicism. But these were not inherent distinctions, and if Gibbon recognised the social necessity of periodic reformation of the Church, and admitted that "the names of Zwinglius, Luther and Calvin are pronounced with gratitude as the deliverers of nations," he would also blame the Protestant reformers for enforcing "absolute and essential terms of salvation," and turn the tables against them by his candid avowal that "many a sober Christian would rather admit that a wafer is God than that God is a cruel and capricious tyrant."

Gibbon's personal religion is, strictly speaking, irrelevant to his historical writing; but the principles which determined his choice—his rationality, his tolerance, his humanity—are not irrelevant. They animate his work throughout, and if ever his judgment is harsh, it is when one or other of these principles is violated. He disliked any restraint on natural reason—hence his distaste for so much of theological speculation; he detested intolerance and cruelty. Between him and Johnson there was a mutual dislike, which was not solely based on the insularity of the one, the un-Englishness of the other, or on their different views of the study of history. Johnson saw Gibbon as an "infidel" and hated him as such; Gibbon disliked Johnson's intolerance: he saw in his writings "the workings of a bigoted though vigorous mind, greedy of every pretence to hate and persecute those who dissent from his creed." Gibbon's own view is expressed at the expense of the emperor Julian the Apostate, who, though an ostentatious Hellenist, sought, in an unhellenic manner, to suppress the rival doctrines of Christianity: "the exultation of Julian that these impious sects, and even their writings, are extinguished may be consistent enough with the sacerdotal character; but it is unworthy of a philosopher to wish that any opinions and arguments the most repugnant to his own should be concealed from the knowledge of mankind."

Above all there is Gibbon's humanity, his hatred not only of cruelty but of every affront to social justice or human dignity. On his famous journey to Rome he deeply resented (as Alexander Humboldt did in South America) the necessity of being carried over dangerous mountain roads by human porters, *"mes semblables"*; he was horrified by the *corvées* imposed on the peasants of Savoy; and at the court of Turin he was disgusted by the empty splendour which needed such fiscal oppression to sustain it. "The servility of the courtiers," he wrote in his diary, "revolts me, and I look with horror on the magnificence of palaces, cemented with the blood of the people. In every gilded moulding I think I see a village of Savoyards ready to perish of hunger, cold and poverty." He felt as strongly as Montesquieu about the slave-trade. In the *Decline and Fall* he describes the tenth-century trade in eunuchs as "the last abomination of the abominable slave-trade"; and when Lord Sheffield, as member of parliament for the slaving city of Bristol, published a pamphlet supporting the trade, Gibbon protested in the name of "justice and humanity." "Do you not expect," he asked, "to work at Beelzebub's sugar-plantations in the infernal regions under the tender government of a Negro driver?"

Profound erudition directed by a new, rational, comprehensive philosophy towards the solution of a great historical problem; a vast range of comparison; a delicate scholarship and ironic wit; strong sense, an unfailing good temper, and an invincible humanity—these are the virtues which have made Gibbon's book one of the greatest works of history. Not everyone has appreciated all of them. In the nineteenth century—that century, in England at least, of new insularity, new assertiveness, new religiosity, new prudery—Gibbon's urbane, sceptical cosmopolitanism was often disliked. Englishmen then lost sight of his social explanation and expressed their abhorrence of his style, as too formal for a post-romantic age, of his irreverence, or of what his contemporary Richard Porson had called his "rage for indecency." Coleridge declared his style "detestable," adding that his style was not the worst thing about him. Macaulay accused him of "rank affectation"—to read him, he said, was like "dining on nothing but anchovy sauce." He also complained of his "gross partiality"—a complaint which, we may think, comes oddly from him.

In the twentieth century we find these objections less impressive: Gibbon has outlasted the critics of his style and philosophy as he has outlasted the more foolhardy critics of his scholarship. But even in the nineteenth century, even his stoutest enemies had to admit the fascination which he exercised over their reluctant minds. It is tempting to end this essay with the comments of the Scottish historian who broke most completely with the Scottish tradition so admired by Gibbon, and whose whole cast of mind was, we would suppose, entirely unsympathetic to him: Thomas Carlyle.

When Carlyle began reading Gibbon at the age of twenty-two, he did not like him, and said so: "his style is flowery, his sarcasms wicked, his notes oppressive, often beastly." Hume, Robertson, Gibbon "the whole historical triumvirate, are abundantly destitute of virtuous feeling, or indeed of any feeling at all. I wonder what benefit is derived from reading all this stuff." And yet, insensibly, as he read, Carlyle found himself, as every reader soon does, captivated by the range and depth, the strength, suppleness and subtlety of that majestic work by "the most strong-minded of all historians." While still protesting his dislike, he urged his friends to read it, and to read it through:

APPRECIATION

There is no other tolerable history of those times and nations within the reach of such readers as we are; it is a kind of bridge that connects the antique with the modern ages. And how gorgeously does it swing across the gloomy and tumultuous chasm of those barbarous centuries! Gibbon is a man whom one never forgets—unless oneself deserving to be forgotten: the perusal of his work forms an epoch in the history of one's mind.

SOURCES OF THE ILLUSTRATIONS

Frontispiece : Edward Gibbon, by Joshua Reynolds. By kind permission of Lord Primrose. Photo: National Galleries of Scotland.

1 Marcus Aurelius. Mansell Collection, London.

2 Detail from Trajan's column. Mansell Collection, London.

3 Painting by Thomas Couture of Roman decadence. Mansell Collection, London.

4 Zenobia, Queen of Palmyra and the East. Mansell Collection, London.

5 The Emperor Diocletian. Mansell Collection, London.

6 The head of the Emperor Constantine. Mansell Collection, London.

7 Mosaic showing gladiators. Mansell Collection, London.

8 Mosaic of Roman dancing girls. Mansell Collection, London.

9 Painting by Bosch of the temptation of St. Antony. Mansell Collection, London.

10 A mosaic from Daphni, early Byzantine Empire. Mansell Collection, London.

11 Mosaic of Justinian and his ministers. Mansell Collection, London.

12 Mosaic of the Empress Theodora among her maidens. Mansell Collection, London.

13 Pope Gregory the Great. Mansell Collection, London.

14 The Angel Gabriel appearing before Mohammed. Mansell Collection, London.

15 The "image of Edessa." Mansell Collection, London.

16 Peter the Hermit preaching the Crusade. Mansell Collection, London.

17 The capture of a Chinese town by Genghis Khan and his Mongol forces. Mansell Collection, London.

18 Mohammed the Second. Mansell Collection, London.